# ~~Now that BAPCPA~~ ~~are you prepared for the Act's striking new changes?~~



## Order extra copies now of *2005 Bankruptcy Reform Legislation with Analysis 2d*

Now that the Bankruptcy Abuse Prevention and Consumer Protection Act of 2005 has taken effect, your practice has a whole new set of rules, and it is more important than ever to be aware of these changes. The professional responsibilities and risk of liabilities are very real under the new Code. Are you ready?

To ensure that you and everyone in your office has ready access to these changes—and to cutting-edge analysis of their impact—order extra copies today of 2005 **Bankruptcy Reform Legislation with Analysis 2d,** by the Hon. William Houston Brown and Lawrence R. Ahern III.

One softbound pamphlet, published February 2006. $75

Multiple-copy discounts available:

- 10-24 copies: save 10%
- 25-49 copies: save 15%
- 50 or more copies: save 20%

To order, contact your
local West sales representative
or call **1-800-344-5009**
or go to west.thomson.com and enter OFFER NUMBER **508552**

---

Yes! I need extra copies of *2005 Bankruptcy Reform Legislation with Analysis 2d*. Please send me ___ copies at $75 per copy.

❑ Payment, including applicable tax, enclosed. (Send card in envelope)

❑ Charge to our West Account #______________________

Signature (required) ______________________________

Name ______________________________

Firm ______________________________

Address______________________________

City ______________________State __________Zip _____

Business Phone (______)______________________________


FG# 40449332-BI/3-06
OFFER NUMBER **508552**

# 2005 Bankruptcy Reform Legislation with Analysis 2d

## Commentary and Highlighted Text of the United States Bankruptcy Code as Amended by the Bankruptcy Abuse Prevention and Consumer Protection Act of 2005

## Public Law 109-8


by

**Honorable William Houston Brown**

United States Bankruptcy Judge

Western District of Tennessee

and

**Lawrence R. Ahern III**

Greenebaum Doll & McDonald PLLC

Nashville, Tennessee



THOMSON

WEST

*For Customer Assistance Call 1-800-328-4880*

Mat #40449332

ISBN 0-314-96005-8

# DEDICATION

We dedicate this publication to the United States Bankruptcy Judges, who, with the assistance of experienced members of the bankruptcy bar, will make the changes found in these amendments work in the real world of debtors and creditors.

# About The Authors

## HONORABLE WILLIAM HOUSTON BROWN

Honorable William Houston Brown is a U.S. bankruptcy judge for the Western District of Tennessee, sitting primarily in Memphis. He also has been designated to sit in the Middle District of Tennessee, the Southern District of Florida, the Eastern District of Michigan and the Western District of Kentucky. Brown served a four-year term on the Bankruptcy Appellate Panel for the Sixth Circuit from 1999 through 2002. After graduating first in his class, he received his law degree and was elected to the Order of Coif at the University of Tennessee College of Law. Brown is also a member of the American Bankruptcy Institute and the American College of Bankruptcy. Judge Brown is also the author of several other Thomson West publications, including Bankruptcy Exemption Manual, Debtor and Creditor Relations (Vols 9-11, West's Legal Forms), Debtor-Creditor Law and Practice (Vol. 16, Tennessee Practice Series), Bankruptcy Courts (Vols 6-6B, West's Federal Forms). He also is editor for Norton Adviser and a contributing editor to Norton Bankruptcy Law and Practice 2d.

## LAWRENCE R. AHERN III

Lawrence R. Ahern III practices bankruptcy and commercial law, with a practice based in Nashville, and is Member-in-Charge of the Nashville and Atlanta offices of Greenebaum Doll & McDonald PLLC. He is a graduate of Vanderbilt University Law School, where he has served as Adjunct Professor of Law, teaching Secured Transactions, since 1998. Mr. Ahern serves on the Advisory Board of the St. John's Bankruptcy LL.M. program and was Visiting Professor at Cumberland School of Law, Fall, 2002, teaching Secured Transactions and Banking. He is a Fellow of the American College of Bankruptcy. Certified since 1994 as a business bankruptcy specialist by the American Board of Certification, he since has been named Director and Secretary of the ABC. Mr. Ahern's other affiliations include the American Bankruptcy Institute (Director). He is admitted to practice law in all Tennessee state courts, all federal courts in Tennessee and the Eastern District of Michigan, the Third and Sixth Circuit Courts of Appeals, and the U.S. Supreme Court. He is also the author of several other Thomson West publications, including Bankruptcy Procedure Manual, Bankruptcy Exemption Manual, Commercial Transactions (Vols 12-15, West's Legal Forms), Bankruptcy Courts (Vols 6-6B, West's Federal Forms), Debtor and Creditor Relations (Vols 9-11, West's Legal Forms) and Debtor-Creditor Law and Practice (Vol. 16, Tennessee Practice Series).

# ACKNOWLEDGMENT

When we undertook this project and committed ourselves to work under a very tight deadline for the first edition, we knew we were facing many hours of work, and we could not have completed the task without the benefit of having talked with and read the analyses of others with expertise concerning the Bankruptcy Abuse Prevention and Consumer Protection Act of 2005 and prior similar Bankruptcy Reform Acts. Both of us are active members of the American Bankruptcy Institute, which has maintained an excellent base of information about the legislation on its website, www.abiworld.org. Through our involvement in ABI, the first edition particularly benefited from the analyses prepared by ABI's Executive Director, Samuel J. Gerdano, and by its former Scholar in Residence, Jeffrey W. Morris, Professor of Law at the University of Dayton School of Law. An ABI director and Chief Bankruptcy Judge for the Northern District of Illinois, Honorable Eugene R. Wedoff, had prepared excellent analyses of the Reform Acts in this and prior congressional sessions. Thomas J. Yerbich of Anchorage, Alaska, and a co-chair of ABI's consumer bankruptcy committee, had prepared a synopsis of the 2005 Act, which is posted on ABI's website.

We were also fortunate to have read the commentary on the consumer parts of this legislation prepared by Henry E. Hildebrand, III, Chapter 13 trustee for the Middle District of Tennessee. We have learned from our conversations with many lawyers experienced in bankruptcy, including E. Bruce Leonard of Cassels Brock, in Toronto; Judith Greenstone Miller and Jay L. Welford of Jaffe, Raitt, Heuer & Weiss, P.C., in Detroit; and Richardo J. Kilpatrick of Kilpatrick & Associates, P.C., in Auburn Hills, Michigan. We also acknowledge the contribution of the Davis Polk & Wardwell law firm through its early web posting of a version of the Bankruptcy Code, with amendments marked. As we read the Act itself and tried to find where its changes go in the Code, and before we prepared our own highlighted Code for the first edition, having access to that firm's edited version was of assistance. Finally, although the scope of this work did not include a detailed analysis of prior versions of the legislation, we valued the commentary prepared in 2001 by Hon. Randolph J. Haines and William L. Norton III.

For the second edition of this book, we continued to benefit from reading the excellent articles published in symposia issues of the American Bankruptcy Law Journal, volume 79, issues 2 and 3, and the American Bankruptcy Institute Law Review, volume 13, issue 2, as well as other articles and seminar materials on the Act. We particularly appreciate the permission of the ABI Law Review to use portions of Mr. Ahern's article in that issue, Homestead and Other

Exemptions under the Bankruptcy Abuse Prevention and Consumer Protection Act: Observations on "Asset Protection" after 2005, as the basis for our revision of chapter 8 in this edition. We have both participated in numerous seminars since October 2005 and each experience contributed to this second edition. Of particular help was the seminar material prepared for the Arkansas Bar Association by Professor Steve H. Nickles, C.C. Hope Chair in Law and Management at Wake Forest University, for the ABI by Professor Jack F. Williams of Georgia State University and BDO Seidman and by the speakers and panelists at the Annual Meeting and Winter Leadership Conference in 2005 and for the Association of Insolvency and Restructuring Advisors by Professor Grant Newton and others who participated in the AIRA's early teleconferences on the legislation. Several readers also offered valuable comments on the first edition, including Martin P. Sheehan, whose detailed comments on the venue limitations for preference actions illustrated the impressive effort that the bench and bar are making to decipher this legislation.

In preparing both editions of this work, we would not have been successful without the help of David W. Houston, IV and Darlene T. Marsh, attorneys at Greenebaum Doll & McDonald, PLLC, in Nashville, and Judge Brown's law clerk Donna T. Snow and former law clerk Rhoda H. Smith, in Memphis. For assistance with the daunting word-processing required to generate the highlighted Code and our commentary, we thank Linda B. Hulsey and Athena J. Gosnell, staff members of the Greenebaum Doll Nashville office; and we thank Sandy Beck of the Bankruptcy Court in Memphis.

We continue to welcome our readers' comments about this publication, and while we know that there are surely errors in our commentary and in the highlighted Code, we hope that they are small ones and do not detract from what we hope will contribute to the readers' gaining early insights into the significant amendments made to the Bankruptcy Code. Comments and suggested corrections to this work may be addressed to LRA@GDM.com. We look forward to the time down the road when we can see how you helped make these amendments work.

Nashville and Memphis, Tennessee
January 2006

# STATUS OF NEW FEDERAL RULES OF BANKRUPTCY PROCEDURE AND OFFICIAL FORMS

Because promulgating rules under the Rules Enabling Act takes a significant amount of time (as much as 2 years), all bankruptcy courts have been strongly urged to adopt as local rules, the Interim Bankruptcy Rules, which were approved by the Advisory Committee on Bankruptcy Rules and the Committee on Rules of Practice and Procedure. These rules, cited herein as "Interim Rules," are expected to apply to all bankruptcy cases from October 17, 2005, until final rules are promulgated and effective under the normal Rules Enabling Act process. The Interim Rules are found in the Appendix to this publication.

The process of promulgating forms is not so cumbersome. Some are described in this work. The new BAPCPA-compliant official forms are now available on Westlaw at www.westlaw.com, database identifier FBKR-FORMS. The forms in this new database are in a user-friendly"fillable" format so that the blanks can be filled in, and the forms can then be saved, e-mailed, or printed out. The forms are also available at http://www.uscourts.gov/bkforms/bankruptcy_forms.html. Official Form B22A, the means test form for Chapter 7 cases, is found in the Appendix to this publication.

# SUMMARY OF CONTENTS

# Table of Contents

## COMMENTARY ON AMENDED CODE

### CHAPTER 1 INTRODUCTION AND EFFECTIVE DATES



### CHAPTER 2 CHECKLISTS FOR DEBTORS, ATTORNEYS, CREDITORS, AND TRUSTEES

## CHAPTER 3 "SENSE OF CONGRESS" STATEMENTS



## CHAPTER 4 NEW FILING REQUIREMENTS FOR INDIVIDUAL DEBTORS AND FILING FEES



## CHAPTER 5 NEW DEFINITIONS



## CHAPTER 6 CHANGES FOR CONSUMER AND INDIVIDUAL BANKRUPTCY CASES

### A. CHAPTER 7 CASES



### B. INDIVIDUAL CHAPTER 11 CASES

## C. CHAPTER 12 CASES



## D. CHAPTER 13 CASES



# CHAPTER 7 CHANGES IN CODE SECTIONS THAT APPLY TO ALL CHAPTERS

## CHAPTER 8 EXEMPTIONS, EXCLUSIONS, AND ASSET PROTECTION

## A. LIMITATION OF HOMESTEAD AND OTHER EXEMPTIONS UNDER BAPCPA



## B. EXCLUSIONS FROM THE ESTATE WITH EXECUTIVE SUMMARY



## C. SELF-SETTLED TRUSTS WITH EXECUTIVE SUMMARY



## D. CHANGES IN DISCHARGE EXCEPTIONS WITH EXECUTIVE SUMMARY



# CHAPTER 9 CHANGES OF PRIMARY INTEREST TO PARTIES IN BUSINESS CASES

## A. SMALL BUSINESS CASES



## B. HEALTH CARE CASES

## C. CROSS-BORDER CASES



## D. OTHER CASE ADMINISTRATION ISSUES

## E. OTHER CONSTITUENCIES IN COMMERCIAL CASES



# APPENDICES

# COMMENTARY ON AMENDED CODE

# Chapter 1

# Introduction and Effective Dates





## § 1:1 Introduction and scope of commentary

On April 20, 2005, the President signed the Bankruptcy Abuse Prevention and Consumer Protection Act of 2005 ("BAPCPA"), Public Law 109-8, 119 Stat. 23, which makes the most substantial changes to the Bankruptcy Code since its enactment in 1978. The principal purpose of the second edition of this publication is to highlight and briefly comment upon the significant changes to the former Bankruptcy Code. As to some sections of the amended Code, we will suggest how the amendments may be interpreted, while in discussing other sections we will pose some of the questions that will remain unanswered until court decisions provide more guidance. Of course, judicial opinions on various provisions of BAPCPA will be issued, and to the extent that such opinions have been published prior to this second edition, we will comment upon them. Not all of the amendments are consistent with other amended sections, leaving open for interpretation how they may be applied, and we attempt to point out those inconsistencies. It is not the purpose of this publication to explore in depth each change to the Code, and the focus will be upon the consumer and commercial changes in the Code that will be applicable to cases filed in the United States. Since the predominant changes made by BAPCPA are directed to consumer bankruptcies, the larger part of this commentary is so directed. The cross-border insolvency provisions found in Chapter 15 of the amended Code and the financial transaction and tax changes made in the Bankruptcy and other titles of the United States Code will be described generally but not commented upon in depth, since those are of more limited interest in the typical bankruptcy case. That is not to say that those new financial provisions are unimportant; rather, the focus of this analysis of the 2005 bankruptcy legislation is on the changes made in the consumer and domestic commercial sections of the Bankruptcy Code.

Throughout the commentary, references to the Bankruptcy Code prior to its 2005 amendments will be to the former Code ("former Code § "); references to the Bankruptcy Abuse Prevention and Consumer Protection Act of 2005 will be to BAPCPA ("BAPCPA § "); references to the Bankruptcy Code as amended by BAPCPA will be to the 2005 Code ("Code § or 11 U.S.C.A. § "); and references to other titles of the United States Code as amended by BAPCPA will be to that title and section (e.g., "18 U.S.C.A. § ").

We begin this commentary with a review of the effective dates of the various amendments, followed by various checklists of the new duties imposed by the 2005 Code and some "sense of Congress" sections evidencing congressional intent. The organization of the substantive commentary is by bankruptcy subject matter divided into four groups: the consumer and individual debtor changes, identifying the significant changes in each chapter of the 2005 Code; the changes in various Code topics that will apply to all or most bankruptcy cases, arranged in a basic topical order; the changes to exemptions and exclusions from the bankruptcy estate with commentary on asset protection under the 2005 Code; and the business bankruptcy changes. In each of these four groups, we have executive summaries that are intended to highlight the most significant BAPCPA changes and to briefly compare the former and amended Bankruptcy Code provisions. Use of this commentary in conjunction with the highlighted Code found in Part Two of this publication will provide a full view of the changes to the Code. As we discuss amendments to the Bankruptcy Code, we will reference the amended 2005 Code by pointing to the highlighted version of the 2005 Code, found in the second part of this publication. The highlighted 2005 Code shows the actual changes by BAPCPA as follows: new language is in italics and language deleted from the former Code is shown by strikethrough. The changes in Titles 11, 18, and 28 are included but the amendments made by BAPCPA to other titles are not included, since the focus of this publication is on bankruptcy amendments.

In the highlighted Code, we have included an abridged legislative history, showing the following: a citation to Public Law 109-8; the basic changes made by BAPCPA to a Code section; the effective date for each section's amendment; and, for some amended Code sections, selected portions of the House Report 109-31, which accompanied the enacted BAPCPA, with a specific citation to that portion of the House Report for each Code section as found at 2005 U.S.C.C.A.N. (available on Westlaw).

This highlighted Code hopefully will be useful to the bankruptcy bar and judiciary, since those amendments that are not effective immediately upon enactment leave the bench and bar with two Bankruptcy Codes to contend with for quite some time. The pre-2005 Code will continue to apply to many cases and proceedings that remain in the courts beyond October 17, 2005, the general effective date of BAPCPA as discussed below. Timing of filings and events within cases may determine which version of the Code controls. Notice should be taken that there are technical errors within some of BAPCPA's amendments. There will, no doubt, be a technical amendments bill that will be considered by Congress at some point; however, at the time of this publication no such correction bill is pending.

In this second edition, we have the advantage of the Interim Bankruptcy Rules and the amended Official Bankruptcy Forms. We do not print the revised forms in full, since other Thomson/West publications do that, including Federal Bankruptcy Courts, volumes 6 to 6B of West's Federal Forms, and Debtor and Creditor Relations, volumes 9 to 9A of West's Legal Forms. We will, however, comment upon some of the amended forms, especially the means testing forms as used in Chapter 7 and 13 bankruptcy cases. Appendix A contains Official Form B22A, the means testing form for Chapter 7, and Appendix B holds the median income tables needed for the means test calculation. All 35 of the Interim Bankruptcy Rules are blacklined in their own section immediately following the Code. References to web sites where other data needed for the means test can be found are incorporated into the commentary, including its discussion of the means test in Chapter 7.

## § 1:2 Enactment date

The United States Senate passed BAPCPA on March 10, 2005, and the House of Representatives passed the Act without amendment on April 14, 2005, sending it to the President. President Bush signed the Act into law on April 20, 2005; thus that is the enactment date that triggers the various effective dates.

## § 1:3 General effective date 180 days from enactment

Although several specific provisions of BAPCPA are effective immediately upon enactment or at other times specified, the bulk of BAPCPA's amendments and additions to the former Code were effective for cases filed 180 days after enactment. The 180 days from the President's signing was October 17, 2005. BAPCPA § 1501 provides:

> Except as otherwise provided in this Act, this Act and the amendments made by this Act shall take effect 180 days after the date of enactment of this Act.
>
> (1) Except as otherwise provided in this Act and paragraph (2), the amendments made by this Act shall not apply with respect to cases commenced under title 11, United States Code, before the effective date of this Act.

(2) the amendments made by sections 308, 322, and 330 shall apply with respect to cases commenced under title 11, United States Code, on or after the date of the enactment of this Act.

As paragraph (1) indicates, the bulk of the amendments do not apply in bankruptcy cases or pending proceedings within cases that were pending before October 17, 2005; rather, they apply in those cases initially filed on or after that date. There are other effective dates spread throughout BAPCPA that apply to government agencies, including the Executive Office of United States Trustees, but this publication will not address most of those dates since they are of limited immediate interest to practitioners. The exceptions to the 180-day effectiveness that are of most interest to those engaged in bankruptcy practice are noted below.

## § 1:4 Amendments effective immediately upon enactment

| Code Section | General Topic |
|---|---|
| § 104(b) | New sections added to adjustment of dollar amounts |
| § 303(b)(1) | Involuntary bankruptcy; retroactive effect |
| §§ 363, 541 & 1129 | Rules for nonprofit property sales, subject to court considering effect in a confirmation |
| § 507(a)(4) & (5) | Priority of employee claims |
| § 547(i) | Insider avoidance; retroactive to proceeding pending |
| § 548(a) & (e) | Insider transfers |
| § 522(o) | Reduces homestead |
| § 522(p) | $125,000 cap on homestead |
| § 522(q) | $125,000 cap on homestead |
| § 727(a)(12) | Delays discharge for § 522(q) determination |
| § 1104(e) | Chapter 11 trustee appointment |
| § 1114(l) | Modification of retiree insurance benefits |
| § 1141(d) | Delays discharge for § 522(q) determination |
| §§ 1222(a)(2) & 1231(b) | Governmental claims, effective but specifically not retroactive |
| § 1228(f) | Delays discharge for § 522(q) determination |
| § 1328(h) | Delays discharge for § 522(q) determination |
| 28 U.S.C.A. § 152 | New bankruptcy judgeships |
| 28 U.S.C.A. § 1334 | Jurisdiction over 11 U.S.C.A. § 327 |
| 28 U.S.C.A. § 589a(b) | Changes in U.S. trustee system fund |

The sections of the 2005 Code that apply immediately upon enactment, on or after April 20, 2005, are as follows:

2005 Code § 522(o), as provided by BAPCPA § 308, reduces the homestead exemption to the extent that value is attributable to any portion of nonexempt property that the debtor disposed of within 10 years of filing bankruptcy, if the disposition was made with intent to hinder, delay, or defraud creditors.

2005 Code § 522(p), as provided by BAPCPA § 322, generally places a $125,000 cap on the homestead acquired within 1,215 days (approximately 3.3 years) of filing bankruptcy.

2005 Code § 522(q) extends that $125,000 cap to situations involving a felony criminal conviction or other violations specified in the section. See discussion of the new § 522(o) and its related §§ 522(p) and (q) in chapter 8 of this publication. Some case authority is already developing on these new sections, and that authority will be discussed in chapter 8.

2005 Code § 727(a)(12), § 1141(d), § 1228(f), and § 1328(h), as provided by BAPCPA § 330, delay the granting of a discharge when it appears that Code § 522(q) may be applicable. See discussion of those amendments in the discharge and exemption discussions.

In addition to these provisions that are specifically identified in BAPCPA § 1501(2), there are others that are effective upon enactment, according to specific BAPCPA sections:

Code § 104(b) adds several sections to its list for which dollar amounts are adjusted in 3-year intervals.

Changes to §§ 363, 541, and 1129 concerning the rules for nonprofit property sales are effective immediately, subject to the court considering in a confirmation hearing the effect of those rules on a party whose rights in the property had previously been established.

Code § 1222(a)(2) and § 1231(b), as provided in BAPCPA § 1003, are effective in all chapter 12 cases on the date of enactment, but specifically would not apply retroactively to Title 11 cases commenced before the enactment. New § 1222(a)(2) generally requires the payment of priority claims, except for a claim owed to a governmental unit that arose from the disposition of a farm asset, and amended § 1231(b) replaces former language with "any governmental unit." See discussion of these provisions under the Chapter 12 discussion in chapter 7 of this book.

Code § 547(i), as specified in BAPCPA § 1213, provides that in the event that the trustee successfully avoids a preferential transfer made by the debtor between 90 days and one year prior to bankruptcy to a creditor that is not an insider, but the transfer is for the benefit of an insider, the transfer is avoided only as to the creditor that is an insider. This amendment "shall apply to any case that is pending or commenced on or after the date of enactment"; thus this retroactive amendment reaches to those cases in which avoidance proceedings are pending upon enactment. A court has applied this retroactive protection to a defendant where the proceeding had been tried prior to the enactment date but a decision had not been made. See *In re ABC-Naco, Inc.*, 331 B.R. 773, 45 Bankr. Ct. Dec. (CRR) 154, Bankr. L. Rep. (CCH) P 80379 (Bankr. N.D. Ill. 2005).

Code § 548(a) was amended to add reference to "insider" and § 548(e) adds a new avoidance power for transfers of the debtor's interest made within 10 years prior to bankruptcy to "a self-settled trust or similar device." These changes were effective upon enactment, according to BAPCPA § 1406(b)(1). See the discussion in chapters 8 and 9.

BAPCPA § 1223 adds 28 temporary bankruptcy judgeships in various districts, effective upon enactment, by amendment to 28 U.S.C.A. § 152.

Code § 303(b)(1), as specified in BAPCPA § 1234, provides that a creditor may not commence an involuntary Chapter 7 or Chapter 11 case if the debtor's liability on a claim or the amount of the claim is contingent or is the subject of a bona fide dispute. This amendment "shall take effect on the date of the enactment of this Act and shall apply with respect to cases commenced under title 11 of the United States Code before, on, and after such date," again, a retroactive amendment. See discussion of these amendments under involuntary bankruptcy in chapter 7.

Sections 507(a)(4) and (5) make changes in the amount of employee priority claims, increasing the amounts to $10,000.

Section § 1104(e) requires the U.S. trustee to move for a Chapter 11 trustee appointment if it appears that current corporate management participated in fraud, dishonesty, or criminal conduct in the management of the debtor.

Section § 1114(l) provides for reinstatement of retiree benefits that the Chapter 11 debtor may have modified in the 180 days preceding filing.

Section 1334(e) of Title 28 is amended to give the district court jurisdiction over all claims or causes of action that involve construction or rules governing 11 U.S.C.A. § 327.

28 U.S.C.A. § 589a(b) makes changes in the U.S. trustee system fund.

## § 1:5 Other effective dates of significance to practitioners

| | |
|---|---|
| July 1, 2005 | Chapter 12 permanent in Code |
| July 30, 2002, Sarbanes-Oxley Enactment | § 523(a)(19)(B), securities fraud |
| One year after enactment | § 548(a) & (b), reach-back changed from 1 to 2 years |
| 60 days after promulgation of reporting forms | Chapter 11 small business debtor reporting requirements |

Chapter 12, the family farmer and now also a family fisherman chapter, is made a permanent part of the Bankruptcy Code effective July 1, 2005. Pending the enactment of BAPCPA, Congress had temporarily extended Chapter 12 several times. This July 1 date was the expiration date for the most recent temporary extension of Chapter 12.

Section 523(a)(19)(B), concerning an exception from discharge for securities fraud, is effective retroactively to July 30, 2002, the date of enactment of the Sarbanes-Oxley Act.

The reach-back period for fraudulent transfer avoidance under § 548(a) and (b) is changed from one to two years, effective one year following enactment.

New reporting requirements for small business debtors will become effective 60 days following the promulgation of the new reporting forms.

There are other effective dates spread throughout BAPCPA that apply to government agencies, including the Executive Office of United States Trustees, but this publication will not address those dates since they are of limited immediate interest to practitioners.

# Chapter 2

# Checklists for Debtors, Attorneys, Creditors, and Trustees

## § 2:1 Checklist of new duties for debtor—Rule 9011 verification

BAPCPA § 319 expresses the "sense of Congress" that Federal Rule of Bankruptcy Procedure 9011 should be modified to include the requirement that all documents, including schedules, whether signed or unsigned, that are submitted to the court or to a trustee by a debtor who is acting pro se or who is represented by an attorney should not be submitted until the debtor and the debtor's attorney have made "reasonable inquiry to verify that the information contained in such document is—(1) well grounded in fact; and (2) warranted by existing law or a good faith argument for the extension, modification, or reversal of existing law." While Congress does not normally establish procedural rules, this expression of congressional intent will affect the manner in which Bankruptcy Rule 9011 is interpreted. Basically, this expression by Congress puts an emphasis upon the debtor's responsibility to verify the factual accuracy and legal basis for everything contained in bankruptcy schedules and other documents. This general "sense of Congress" expression is in addition to the specific amendments to 11 U.S.C.A. § 707 that impose the Rule 9011 standard for the certification by a debtor's attorney about the need for filing under Chapter 7 and that the filing is both accurate and not an abuse. See the discussion of those amendments under the discussion of Chapter 7.

## § 2:2 Checklist of new duties for debtor—Prebankruptcy credit briefing

Section 109(h) requires, with limited exceptions, all individual debtors to obtain within 180 days of filing bankruptcy an individual or group briefing from an approved nonprofit budget and credit counseling agency, and the briefing must, at a minimum, have "outlined the opportunities for available credit counseling and assisted such individual in performing a related budget analysis." Unless an exception applies, as a condition to filing bankruptcy, the debtor must file with the court a certificate from the agency describing the services offered, and, if a debt repayment plan was created, the debtor must file that plan. See the later discussion of this requirement and its exceptions, including case authority, in chapter 7 of this book.

## § 2:3 Checklist of new duties for debtor—Provide tax returns

Section 521(e) requires the Chapter 7 and 13 debtor to provide to the trustee, prior to the meeting of creditors, a copy of the most recent year's federal tax return and to give a copy to any creditor requesting it. A transcript may be provided instead of the return. Failure to provide the return requires dismissal of the case unless the debtor can show that failure is due to circumstances beyond the debtor's control. See discussion of tax return requirements under chapters 7 and 13 and under conversion or dismissal of cases in chapter 6. The Administrative Office of the United States Courts has promulgated guidelines related to these tax return requirements, and those guidelines are discussed at 6:14.

In addition, Chapter 13 debtors must file all required tax returns (state, federal, or local) with the appropriate taxing authority prior to the meeting of creditors, and the trustee may delay that meeting only for 120 days to permit the filings. See 11 U.S.C.A. § 1308 and discussion of Chapter 13. Section 521(j) provides that, during any case of an individual debtor, if the taxing authority so requests and upon the debtor's failure to file postpetition returns, the court shall dismiss or convert the case, whichever is in the best interests of the creditors and the estate.

In a Chapter 7, 11, or 13 case of an individual debtor, upon request by the court, the U.S. trustee (and presumably bankruptcy administrator), or a party in interest, the debtor shall file a copy of all federal tax returns due while the case is pending, and in Chapter 13 these returns must be filed annually. See 11 U.S.C.A. § 521(f).

## § 2:4 Checklist of new duties for debtor—Debtor education

Prior to receiving a discharge, the individual Chapter 7 or 13 debtor must complete a personal financial management course. See 11 U.S.C.A. §§ 111, 727(a)(11), 1328(g), and the later discussion of debtor education.

## § 2:5 Checklist of new duties for debtor—Schedules

In addition to the typical schedules accompanying a petition, "unless the court orders otherwise," the debtor must file a certificate by the debtor's attorney or a petition preparer that the debtor has been given the extensive notice required by § 342(b); a copy of all "payment advices or other evidence of payment received within 60 days before" the bankruptcy filing from the debtor's employer; a statement of net monthly income, itemized to show how it was calculated (note that while different terminology is used, this must be the same as the current monthly income, after allowable deductions, that is the basis for a means test analysis); and a statement of reasonably anticipated increases in income or expenditures over the next 12 months. Some bankruptcy courts have already established by standing order or local rule that some of these requirements are waived, unless specifically requested. For example, rather than filing payment advices with the clerk of court, some courts are requiring debtors to provide those to the case trustee upon the trustee's request.

Failure of a Chapter 7 or 13 debtor to complete and file all required schedules within 45 days of filing shall result in "automatic" dismissal of the case, effective on the 46th day, unless the debtor, trustee, or a party in interest successfully moves for an extension, which cannot exceed another 45 days. See 11 U.S.C.A. § 521(i).

### § 2:6 Checklist of new duties for debtor—Compliance with Chapter 7 statement of intention

Within 30 days of the meeting of creditors, the Chapter 7 debtor must perform the stated intention of surrender, redemption, or reaffirmation, and the failure to do so will result in stay relief. See §§ 362(h) and 521(a)(2), and the discussion of automatic stay. Also, § 521(a)(6) provides that a Chapter 7 debtor may not retain possession of purchase-money collateral beyond 45 days from the meeting of creditors without redeeming the collateral or reaffirming the debt. Failure here also results in stay relief and the property no longer being property of the bankruptcy estate. The difference in §§ 521(a)(2) and (6)'s 30 and 45 days will create confusion.

### § 2:7 Checklist of new duties for debtor—Education individual retirement account

If the debtor has an interest in an education individual retirement account or a qualified state tuition program, the debtor must disclose that interest at the time of filing the schedules. See § 521(c) and the discussion of these accounts in exemptions and exclusions from the estate in chapter 8.

### § 2:8 Checklist of new duties for debtor—Preserve automatic stay

If the debtor has filed previously, the filings may trigger termination of the automatic stay or prevent the stay from taking effect. See 11 U.S.C.A. § 362(c)(3) and (4). To preserve the stay, or to activate it, in a subsequent filing, the debtor will need to take quick steps and carry a burden of proof. In addition, the debtor must disclose and notice a landlord who has obtained a prebankruptcy judgment, and for property subject to bailment or lease, any prebankruptcy defaults are retained as effective. For these and other reasons, familiarity with the changes in the automatic stay, discussed later in chapter 7, is essential.

### § 2:9 Checklist of new duties for debtor—Identification document

If the U.S. trustee or case trustee (and presumably bankruptcy administrator) requests it, the debtor must provide a document establishing identity, such as a driver's license or passport. 11 U.S.C.A. § 521(h).

### § 2:10 Checklist of new duties for debtor's attorney—Rule 9011 verification

BAPCPA § 319 states the "sense of Congress" that Federal Rule of

Bankruptcy Procedure 9011 should be modified to include the requirement that all documents, including schedules, whether signed or unsigned, that are submitted to the court or to a trustee by a debtor represented by an attorney should not be submitted until the attorney has made "reasonable inquiry to verify that the information contained in such document is—(1) well grounded in fact; and (2) warranted by existing law or a good faith argument for the extension, modification, or reversal of existing law."

Basically, this expression by Congress puts an emphasis upon the responsibility of the debtor's attorney to take reasonable steps to verify the factual accuracy and legal basis for everything contained in bankruptcy schedules and other documents. This general "sense of Congress" expression is in addition to the specific amendments to 11 U.S.C.A.§ 707 that place the Rule 9011 standard on the certification by a debtor's attorney about the need for filing under Chapter 7 and that the filing is both accurate and not an abuse. See the discussion of those amendments under the discussion of Chapter 7. Sanctions may be awarded under § 707(b)(4). What remains to be seen in practice is the extent to which the attorney for the debtor is held liable, under a Rule 9011 application, for inaccuracies in the debtor's schedules. The congressional expression is that there must be a reasonable inquiry.

## § 2:11 Checklist of new duties for debtor's attorney—Debt relief agency

Under the definition of debt relief agency in § 101(12A) and assisted person under § 101(3), an attorney providing bankruptcy assistance to a consumer debtor may be a debt relief agency and, if so, must comply with the strict restrictions and disclosure requirements for such agencies found in §§ § 526, § 527, and § 528. See the discussion in § 7:29, below, of debt relief agency, including case authority questioning whether attorneys are included in the definition of debt relief agency.

## § 2:12 Checklist of new duties for debtor's attorney—Enforce new debtor requirements and notice to debtor

In order to effectively represent consumer debtors under the amended Code, the debtor's attorney must assure that the debtor carries out all of the new and former duties. A part of what the debtor must file is a certification from the debtor's attorney that the debtor has been provided with the specific notice required by § 342(b). See 11 U.S.C.A. § 521(a)(1)(B)(iii).

## § 2:13 Checklist of new duties for debtor's attorney—Means test calculation

As will be seen, the means test is complex, and most consumer debtors will require the assistance of an attorney in calculating whether that test applies. BAPCPA amends 18 U.S.C.A. § 2075 to state that the bankruptcy rules shall prescribe a form for the statement of monthly income required by § 707(b)(2)(C). The Judicial Conference's Rules Committee has issued Interim Bankruptcy Rules and Official Bankruptcy Forms B22A, B, and C for means testing calculations in Chapters 7, 11, and 13, and those forms will be discussed under each Chapter's explanation of means testing.

### § 2:14 Checklist of new duties for debtor's attorney—Awareness of Code changes

Obviously, in order to effectively represent consumer debtors, an attorney must be familiar with the many changes in consumer bankruptcy law.

### § 2:15 Checklist of new duties for Chapter 7 trustees—Domestic support creditors

The Chapter 7 trustee has an expanded duty under Code § 704(a)(10) and (c)(10) to advise a domestic support creditor in writing of the existence of and right to use support enforcement and collection agencies and to provide notice of such a claim to those agencies. Also, the trustee must provide notice to the domestic support creditor and the support collection agencies of the debtor's Chapter 7 discharge, any reaffirmations, any debts excepted from discharge under §§ 523(a)(2), (4), or (14A), and current address information about the debtor and the debtor's employer. Similar changes are made in the Chapter 11 trustee's duties found in § 1106, the Chapter 12 trustee's duties under § 1202, and the Chapter 13 trustee's duties under § 1302. For a detailed discussion of the Chapter 7 trustees' duties under BAPCPA, see Samuel K. Crocker and Robert H. Waldschmidt, Impact of the 2005 Bankruptcy Amendments on Chapter 7 Trustees, 79 American Bankruptcy Law Journal 333 (2005), which is available on Westlaw under Legal Periodicals/Law Reviews. For a list of the state support service agencies, see William Houston Brown, Bankruptcy and Domestic Relations Manual, § A.18 (2005), a Thomson/West publication.

### § 2:16 Checklist of new duties for Chapter 7 trustees—Employee benefit plans

Under § 704(a)(11), the Chapter 7 trustee must continue to perform the duties of an employee benefit plan administrator, if the debtor was serving at the time of filing bankruptcy as a plan administrator, as that term is defined under ERISA.

### § 2:17 Checklist of new duties for Chapter 7 trustees—Health care business

If the debtor is in the health care business, the Chapter 7 trustee must use "all reasonable and best efforts" to transfer any patients of such a business being closed to another such business in the physical vicinity that provides substantially similar services with a reasonable quality of care. 11 U.S.C.A. § 704(a)(12). Obviously, in those few such cases, the trustee is given a duty of investigating the availability of and quality of similar health care businesses and seeing that patients are properly transferred.

## § 2:18 Checklist of new duties for Chapter 7 trustees—Uniform final reports

By amendment to 28 U.S.C.A. § 589b, as a part of the emphasis on improving bankruptcy data, the final reports required of trustees must be uniform, and the Attorney General is required to issue rules for those reports.

## § 2:19 Checklist of new duties for debtor in possession

Since a Chapter 11 debtor in possession has most of the duties of a trustee, and there is no change to Code § 1107, a debtor in possession would have the following new duties as well. (Some will be problematic for individual Chapter 11 debtors. For example, the duties owed to domestic support creditors will require the debtor in possession to provide personal information.)

## § 2:20 Checklist of new duties for Chapter 11 trustees—Domestic support creditors

The Chapter 11 trustee has an expanded duty under amended Code § 1106(a)(8) and (c) to advise a domestic support creditor of support enforcement and collection agencies in the same manner as Chapter 7 trustees. See those duties above under the Chapter 7 trustee discussion, and see Code §§ 1106(a)(8) and (c). For a list of the state support service agencies, see William Houston Brown, Bankruptcy and Domestic Relations Manual, § A.18 (2005), a Thomson/West publication.

## § 2:21 Checklist of new duties for Chapter 11 trustees—Employee benefit plans

Under 2005 Code § 1106(a)(1), the Chapter 11 trustee's duties incorporate § 704(a)(11); thus, like the Chapter 7 trustee, a trustee in Chapter 11 must continue to perform the duties of an employee benefit plan administrator, if the debtor was serving as a plan administrator at the time of the bankruptcy filing, as that term is defined under ERISA.

## § 2:22 Checklist of new duties for Chapter 11 trustees—Health care business

Under 2005 Code § 1106(a)(1), the Chapter 11 trustee's duties incorporate § 704(a)(12); thus, if the debtor is in the health care business, the Chapter 11 trustee must use "all reasonable and best efforts" to transfer any patients of such a business being closed to another such business in the physical vicinity that provides substantially similar services with reasonable quality of care. Obviously, in those few such cases, the trustee is given a duty of investigating the availability of and quality of similar health care businesses and seeing that patients are properly transferred.

### § 2:23 Checklist of new duties for Chapter 11 trustees—Uniform final reports

By amendment to 28 U.S.C.A. § 589b, as a part of the emphasis on improving bankruptcy data, the final reports required of trustees must be uniform, and the Attorney General is required to issue rules for those forms.

### § 2:24 Checklist of new duties for Chapter 12 and 13 trustees—Domestic support creditors

The Chapter 12 and 13 trustees have the expanded duties under 2005 Code § 1202(b)(6) and (c) and § 1302(b)(6) and (d) to advise a domestic support creditor of support enforcement and collection agencies in the same manner as Chapter 7 trustees. See those duties above under the Chapter 7 trustee, and see Code §§ 1202 (b)(6) and (c); § 1302(b)(6) and (d). For a list of the state support service agencies, see William Houston Brown, Bankruptcy and Domestic Relations Manual, § A.18 (2005), a Thomson/West publication. For a discussion of the impact of BAPCPA on Chapter 13 trustees, see Henry E. Hildebrand, Jr., Impact of the Bankruptcy Abuse Prevention and Consumer Protection Act of 2005 on Chapter 13 Trustees, 79 American Bankruptcy Law Journal 373 (2005), which is available on Westlaw under Legal Periodicals/Law Reviews.

### § 2:25 Checklist of new duties for Chapter 12 and 13 trustees—Uniform final reports

By amendment to 28 U.S.C.A. § 589b, as a part of the emphasis on improving bankruptcy data, the final reports required of trustees must be uniform, and the Attorney General is required to issue rules for those forms.

### § 2:26 Checklist of potential new duties for Chapter 13 trustees—Administer adequate protection payments

Amended § 1326(a) requires the debtor to commence payments, not later than 30 days following filing, "directly to" a lessor or to a creditor secured by personal property, with the latter payment in an amount "that provides adequate protection." There appears to be a developing trend for such adequate protection payments to be made through the Chapter 13 trustee in order to obtain the benefits of the trustee's accounting. See, e.g., Richard J. Hayden, Adequate Protection in Chapter 13 Cases Under the New Code § 1326(a), http://abiworld.net/newsletter/consumerbank/vol3numb5/1326.html.

### § 2:27 Checklist of new duties for creditors—Domestic support creditors

Although the focus of BAPCPA and of the publicity surrounding it has been upon changes impacting consumer debtors, there are changes that impose new responsibilities on creditors. The principal new creditor duties include a duty to domestic support creditors. In cases under Chapters 7, 11, 12, or 13 that include creditors holding domestic support claims, any other creditors in the case that hold a claim that was excepted from discharge under § 523(a)(2), (4), or (14A), or that was reaffirmed, have a duty to provide the last known address of the debtor upon request from the domestic support creditor. Creditors fulfilling this duty have protection from liability for the disclosure. See 11 U.S.C.A. §§ 704(b)(2); 1106(c)(2); 1202(c)(2); and 1302(d)(2).

## § 2:28 Checklist of new duties for creditors—Filing abuse motions (Rule 9011)

New § 707(b)(5) gives the court discretion on its own initiative or on motion of a party in interest to award the debtor reasonable costs and attorney's fees in contesting a § 707(b) motion that is not granted by the court, but there are strict limitations on this possibility. The creditor filing a motion to dismiss for abuse has some duty to comply with Rule 9011 standards in filing the motion. See discussion of this Rule under the discussion of Chapter 7.

## § 2:29 Checklist of new duties for U.S. trustee and bankruptcy administrator—Statement of abuse

By an addition to Code § 704(b), which formerly addressed only the duties of the Chapter 7 trustee, the U.S. trustee or bankruptcy administrator must file a statement of whether a case would be presumed abusive within 10 days of the § 341 meeting. Within five days of receiving the statement, the clerk of the court "shall provide a copy of the statement to all creditors," and, within 30 days of filing its statement, the U.S. trustee or bankruptcy administrator must file a § 707(b) motion based upon abuse or file a statement of why the case is not presumed abusive even though the debtor's current monthly income:

> . . . is not less than
>
> (A) in the case of a debtor in a household of 1 person, the median family income of the applicable State for 1 earner; or
>
> (B) in the case of a debtor in a household of 2 or more individuals, the highest median family income of the applicable State for a family of the same number or fewer individuals.

11 U.S.C.A. § 704(b)(2).

## § 2:30 Checklist of new duties for Executive Office for U.S. trustee—Chapter 13 administrative expense

Section 107 of BAPCPA requires the Director of the Executive Office for the United States Trustees to issue within 180 days of enactment "schedules of reasonable and necessary administrative expenses of administering a chapter 13 plan for each judicial district of the United States." The stated purpose for this directive is the implementation of the newly amended Code § 707(b), that is the means test, to aid in the calculation of current income for that test by knowing what the administrative costs in Chapter 13 would be. These schedules for each judicial district have been posted at the U.S. trustee's website, http://www.usdoj.gov/ust/eo/bapcpa/mt/ch13_exp_mult.htm.

## § 2:31 Checklist of new duties for Executive Office for U.S. trustee—Debtor education

Section 105 of BAPCPA requires the Director of the Executive Office for United States Trustees "to consult with a wide range of individuals who are experts in the field of debtor education," including Chapter 13 trustees, to develop a financial management curriculum and materials to educate individual debtors. Six judicial districts would be chosen to test the effectiveness of that curriculum and the financial management training materials, to be tested over an 18-month period beginning no later than 270 days after enactment. The Director will report to Congress the results of the testing within three months of its conclusion. Notwithstanding this study, a Chapter 7 or 13 debtor's requirement to obtain financial education as a precondition to discharge was effective on October 17, 2005. The list of approved debtor education providers is posted on the U.S. trustee's website, http://www.usdoj.gov/ust/bapcpa/ccde/de_approved.htm.

## § 2:32 Checklist of new duties for Executive Office for U.S. trustee—Household goods definition

Section 313(b) of the Act states that the Director of the Executive Office of United States Trustees is to submit a report to the Judiciary Committees of the House and Senate within two years of enactment, with the report to contain findings concerning the utilization of the new definition for household goods under § 522(f), including findings of the impact on debtors. That report may contain recommendations for any changes in § 522(f).

# Chapter 3
# "Sense of Congress" Statements



> **KeyCite®:** Cases and other legal materials listed in KeyCite Scope can be researched through the KeyCite service on Westlaw®. Use KeyCite to check citations for form, parallel references, prior and later history, and comprehensive citator information, including citations to other decisions and secondary materials.

## § 3:1 In general

In some sections of BAPCPA, Congress expressed its "sense" about changes in the procedural rules and in other aspects of bankruptcy procedure. These "sense of Congress" statements are not a part of the enacted amendments to the Bankruptcy Code, but they have importance in the way that the amendments may be interpreted and applied since they supply a form of legislative history and rationale.

## § 3:2 Rule 9011

BAPCPA § 319 expresses the "sense of Congress" that Federal Rule of Bankruptcy Procedure 9011 should be modified to include the requirement that all documents, including schedules, whether signed or unsigned, that are submitted to the court or to a trustee by a debtor who is acting pro se or who is represented by an attorney should not be submitted until the debtor and the debtor's attorney, if any, have made "reasonable inquiry to verify that the information contained in such document is—(1) well grounded in fact; and (2) warranted by existing law or a good faith argument for the extension, modification, or reversal of existing law."

### Practice Alerts for BAPCPA § 319

### Attorney Responsibility

**Practitioners should monitor Rule 9011 for future amendments to address "this sense of Congress." However, the Advisory Committee ignored this recommendation in the 2005 Interim Rules and Interim Rule 9011 currently does not require this "reasonable inquiry."**

## § 3:3 IRS standards

BAPCPA § 103 expresses the "sense of Congress" that the Internal Revenue Service Standard guidelines for repayment plans may be adjusted "by the Secretary of the Treasury as needed to accommodate their use for § 707(b) means testing purposes." Within two years of enactment, the Executive Office for the United States Trustees is to report to Congress on its "findings regarding the utilization of Internal Revenue Service Standards for determining" the § 707(b) monthly expenses and the impact of those standards on debtors and the bankruptcy court.

## § 3:4 Debtor education

Congress expresses a sense that states should develop personal finance curricula for elementary and secondary schools.

## § 3:5 Creditworthiness

A "sense of Congress" is also expressed that the Board of Governors of the Federal Reserve System shall conduct a study of the consumer credit industry practices of soliciting and extending credit and report within 12 months on its findings.

## § 3:6 Data

In conjunction with the part of BAPCPA that addresses the improvement of bankruptcy data and statistics, Congress expressed its sense that national policy should provide that all bankruptcy data be maintained by the clerks in electronic form, subject to appropriate privacy concerns. A single set of data definitions and forms should be established, and this may require changes in the electronic filing methods currently being used by the bankruptcy courts.

# Chapter 4

# New Filing Requirements for Individual Debtors and Filing Fees





## § 4:1 New filing requirements for individuals

**• Creditor address for notice—Code § 521(a)(1)(A).**

Under an amended Code § 521(a)(1)(A), debtors must continue to file the list of creditors or matrix, and the debtor has a new duty, if a creditor has so notified the debtor, to use the address for creditors provided in a prebankrutpcy notice from the creditors. See Code § 342(c) and notice discussion under § 7:47 of this book.

**• Required items, unless court orders otherwise—Code § 521(a)(1)(B).**

Amended Code § 521(a)(1)(B) states that, "unless the court orders otherwise," the debtor shall file:

1. The schedules of assets and liabilities (Official Form 6, containing Schedules A–H, as revised to comply with BAPCPA). All of the Official Forms are available at the U.S. Court's website, www.uscourts.gov/bkforms/index.html.
2. A schedule of current income and expenses (Official Form 6, Schedules I & J). Note that this is not the means testing form required by BAPCPA (See Official Forms B22A-C).
3. A statement of the debtor's financial affairs (Official Form 7, as revised to comply with BAPCPA).
4. If the debtor has primarily consumer debts, § 342(b) and § 521(a)(1)(B)(iii) require that the debtor's attorney or bankruptcy petition preparer sign the petition indicating that the attorney or preparer provided the debtor the notice required by § 342(b). If the debtor is not represented by an attorney and did not receive preparer assistance, the debtor must sign the petition indicating that the § 342(b) notice was received and read. See Official Form 1, as revised to comply with BAPCPA.
5. Copies of "payment advices" (payroll information) received

by the debtor from an employer within 60 days of filing bankruptcy. Note that this is one of the requirements that may be subject to the court ordering otherwise, and some bankruptcy courts' local rules or standing orders may direct that such advices not be filed with the clerk unless specifically requested; instead, such rules or orders may direct that the debtor furnish the advices to the case trustee or requesting parties.

6. A "statement of the amount of monthly net income, itemized to show how the amount is calculated." 11 U.S.C.A. § 521(a)(1)(B)(v). Apparently, this is a reference to the means testing form, which for Chapter 7, 11, and 13 debtors makes this calculation. See Official Forms B22A-C.
7. A "statement disclosing any reasonably anticipated increase in income or expenditures over the 12-month period following the date of the filing of the petition." 11 U.S.C.A. § 521(a)(1)(B)(vi).

**Practice Alerts for Code § 521(a)(1)**

**Failure of the Chapter 7 or 13 debtor to file items required by § 521(a)(1) within 45 days after the filing of the petition "shall" result in "automatic dismissal" of the case, unless the debtor within that 45 days requests an extension, which can only be for another 45 days. 11 U.S.C.A. § 521(i). There is a possible "good faith effort" and "best interest of creditors" exception to dismissal, but only upon motion of the case trustee. § 521(i)(4).**

- **Other required filings—§ 521(a)(2), (b), (c)**
  1. **The Chapter 7 debtor's statement of intention as to surrender or retention of property must be filed within 30 days after filing the petition or before the meeting of creditors, whichever is earlier, unless the court fixes a later time. 11 U.S.C.A. § 521(a)(2)(A). Note: The debtor must perform that stated intention within 30 days after the first date set for the meeting of creditors, failure of which results in stay relief. Compare § 521(a)(6)'s 45 days to reaffirm or redeem purchase money collateral.**
  2. **A certificate of completion of the required prebankruptcy credit briefing. 11 U.S.C.A. § 521(b)(1).**

**Practice Alerts for Code § 521(b)(1)**

**See later discussion of credit briefing for required certification of exigent circumstances and motion to extend time if the debtor seeks a waiver/extension of the time to complete the briefing.**

3. **A copy of the debt repayment plan, if any, that was developed by the credit briefing agency. 11 U.S.C.A. § 521(b)(2).**

**4. A record of any interest that the debtor has in an education individual retirement account or state tuition program. 11 U.S.C.A. § 521(c).**

**5. If requested, the Chapter 7, 11, or 13 individual debtor must file with the court a copy of each federal income tax return filed in each tax year while the case is pending and a copy of any returns, or transcripts of the returns, that were due for the 3 years prior to filing bankruptcy if the return(s) was (were) not filed until after the petition. 11 U.S.C.A. § 521(f)(1) to (3).**

**6. In a Chapter 13 case, file annually copies of such tax returns, or transcripts of the returns, until the case is closed. 11 U.S.C.A. § 521(f)(4).**

**Practice Alerts for Code § 521(j)**

**Upon failure of the debtor to file required tax returns with the tax authority, that authority may "request" an order converting or dismissing the case. 11 U.S.C.A. § 521(j).**

- **Other required items to be "provided"**

  **1. Not later than 7 days before the first date set for the meeting of creditors, the Chapter 7 or 13 debtor must provide to the case trustee a copy of the federal income tax return, or transcript of return, that was due for the most recent tax year preceding the bankruptcy filing. 11 U.S.C.A. § 521(e)(2)(A)(i).**

  **2. Provide a copy of such return to any creditor timely requesting it. 11 U.S.C.A. § 521(e)(2)(A)(i).**

**Practice Alerts for Code § 521(e)(2)(B) and (C)**

**Failure of the Chapter 7 or 13 debtor to provide such returns "shall" result in dismissal of the case, unless the debtor shows failure was due to circumstances beyond debtor's control. 11 U.S.C.A. § 521(e)(2)(B) and (C).**

**3. If requested by U.S. trustee or case trustee, provide a document establishing the identity of the debtor.**

### § 4:2 Filing fees

• Case fees: BAPCPA changed some but not all filing fees. For bankruptcy cases, the required filing fees (subject to possible in forma pauperis waiver for certain individual debtors—see in forma pauperis discussion later), are:

| Chapter | Statutory Fee | Other Fees | Total Fee |
|---|---|---|---|
| 7 | $220 | $15 trustee<br>$39 Administrative | $274 |

| Chapter | Statutory Fee | Other Fees | Total Fee |
|---|---|---|---|
| 9 | $1,000 | $39 Administrative | $1,039 |
| 11 | $1,000 | $39 Administrative | $1,039 |
| 12 | $200 | $39 Administrative | $239 |
| 13 | $150 | $39 Administrative | $189 |
| 15 | $1,000 | $39 Administrative | $1,039 |

• **Conversion fees:** According to information from the Administrative Office of U.S. Courts, the fees for converting cases from one chapter to another are:

Converting a Chapter 7 case to a Chapter 11 case is $780, which is the difference between the statutory filing fee for the two cases.

Converting a Chapter 13 case to a Chapter 11 case is $850, again the difference between the two statutory filing fees.

Converting a case from another Chapter to Chapter 7, the conversion fee is $15.

There is no additional fee for converting a case from another Chapter to Chapter 13.

The $39 administrative fee is not charged again upon any conversion.

• **Reopening fees:** The fee for reopening a closed case is the same as the statutory fee for filing that case, but no administrative fee is charged again for a reopening.

• **Adversary Proceeding fee:** The fee for filing an adversary proceeding is $250, effective for proceedings filed after September 20, 2005.

• **Automatic stay motions:** The fee for filing relief from automatic stay motions is $150.

• **Additional Fee Legislation:** The Deficit Reduction Act of 2005, S. 1932, passed in Congress and was signed by the President on February 8, 2006, in which the filing fees for bankruptcy cases would be raised again, effective 60 days after that enactment. The Act raises the statutory fees as follows: Chapter 7 to $245 and Chapter 13 to $235. Congress intended to increase the Chapter 11 fees to $2,750 but a drafting error caused a reference to the wrong part of 28 U.S.C.A. § 1930(a), and it is expected that a technical amendment will be made to so increase those fees. Such an increase in Chapter 11 fees would have the effect of raising Chapter 9 and 15 fees to $2,750. The applicable trustee and administrative fees would not change. Conversion fees would increase accordingly, and the adversary proceeding fee may increase to $350.

# Chapter 5

# New Definitions





## § 5:1 New definitions—11 U.S.C.A. § 101

Code § 101 is amended to add several new definitions:

Section 101(3) defines "assisted person" in bankruptcy, a term that applies only to consumer debtors with nonexempt property below $150,000 in value.

Section 101(4A) defines "bankruptcy assistance" as the providing of goods or services related to a title 11 bankruptcy case to an "assisted person"; thus "bankruptcy assistance" only comes into play in regard to consumer debtors.

Section 101(7A) defines "commercial fishing operation" and § 101(7B) defines "commercial fishing vessel." See the discussion of Chapter 12.

Section 101(10A) defines "current monthly income." See examination of that definition in Chapter 7's discussion of the means test.

Section 101(12A) defines "debt relief agency" to mean "any person who provides any bankruptcy assistance to an assisted person" or "who is a bankruptcy petition preparer under section 110," but the definition excludes some specific persons or entities. The exclusions include creditors who are assisting the consumer debtor in a debt restructuring effort and depository institutions or credit unions as well as employees of "debt relief agencies" or tax-exempt nonprofit organizations. Since "debt relief agency" is linked to "bankruptcy assistance" and an "assisted person," the bankruptcy debtor being assisted must be a consumer debtor. If an attorney, for example, is giving bankruptcy assistance to a consumer debtor, that attorney may be a "debt relief agency," but if an attorney is giving bankruptcy assistance to a corporate or other nonconsumer debtor, that attorney is not a "debt relief agency." The definition of "debt relief agency" is linked to a new Code § 526 that provides restrictions on such agencies. See the discussion under debt relief agencies, including case authority that has emerged on whether attorneys are included in the definition and on the scope of debt relief agency.

Section 101(13A) is added to define "debtor's principal residence," as:

(A) a residential structure, including incidental property, without regard to whether that structure is attached to real property; and

(B) includes an individual condominium or cooperative unit, a mobile or manufactured home, or trailer.

Section 101(14) is amended to exclude investment banker from the definition of "disinterested person."

Section 101(14A) defines "domestic support obligation," a term that replaces, but includes, "alimony, maintenance, or support" in §§ 523(a)(5) and (15) and in other areas of the Code. See the discussion of domestic support obligation.

Section 101(18)'s definition of "family farmer" is changed by an increase in the debt limit for that chapter. See the discussion of Chapter 12.

Section 101(19A) and (B) define "family fisherman," a term that is discussed in Chapter 12.

Section 101(22), as amended, modifies the definition of "financial institution."

Section 101(22A) defines "financial participant." See the discussion of the new Chapter 15.

Section 101(23) and (24) modify the definitions of "foreign proceeding" and "foreign representative." See the discussion of the new Chapter 15.

Section 101(25) modifies the definition of "forward contract."

Section 101(27A) defines "health care business."

Section 101(27B) is added to define "incidental property with respect to a debtor's principal residence."

Section 101(38A) defines "master netting agreement," and § 101(38B) defines "master netting agreement participant."

Section 101(39A), defines "median family income," which:

> means for any year—
>
> (A) the median family income both calculated and reported by the Bureau of the Census in the then most recent year; and
>
> (B) if not so calculated and reported in the then current year, adjusted annually after such most recent year until the next year in which median family income is both calculated and reported by the Bureau of the Census, to reflect the percentage change in the Consumer Price Index for All Urban Consumers during the period of years occurring after such most recent year and before such current year.

Section 101(40A) and (40B) define "patient" and "patient records."

Section 101(41A) is added to define "personally identifiable information."

Section 101(47) modifies the definition of "repurchase agreement."

Section 101(48A) defines "securities self regulatory organization."

Section 101(51C) and (51D) modify the definitions of "small business case" and "small business debtor." See the discussion of small business Chapter 11 cases.

Section 101(53B) modifies the definition of "swap agreement."

Section 101(54) modifies the definition of "transfer."

# Chapter 6

# Changes for Consumer and Individual Bankruptcy Cases

## A. CHAPTER 7 CASES



## B. INDIVIDUAL CHAPTER 11 CASES



## C. CHAPTER 12 CASES



## D. CHAPTER 13 CASES

## A. CHAPTER 7 CASES

### § 6:1 Executive summary of changes to Chapter 7

| New Law | Old Law |
|---|---|
| Case dismissal or conversion for abuse, with a financial means test and Official Form B22A | Case dismissal for substantial abuse, with no means test or form |
| Time between discharges 8 years | Time between discharges 6 years |
| Prerequisite for discharge: completion of instructional course in personal financial management | No comparable provisions |
| Discharge delayed if § 522(q) applies | No comparable provisions |
| Discharge revoked for failure to cooperate with an audit | No comparable provisions |

### § 6:2 Conversion

Code § 706(c) is amended to permit conversion to Chapter 12 or 13 with the "consent" of the debtor. The former section required: "The court may not convert a case under this chapter to a case under chapter 12 or 13 of this title unless the debtor requests such conversion." This change to add "or consent" after "requests" is a part of the "Needs-Based Bankruptcy" referred to in Title I of BAPCPA. Apparently, this is intended to facilitate conversion to Chapter 12 or 13 when the Chapter 7 case is subject to dismissal under the means test or other general-abuse standard.

If the bankruptcy case is filed originally under Chapter 11 or 13, a reduced version of the means test may be applicable in those chapters, as will be discussed later, but a question may exist whether the § 707(b) means test will be applied if the case is then converted to Chapter 7. As pointed out by G. Eric Brunstad, Jr., The Applicability of "Means Testing" to Cases Converted to Chapter 7, American Bankruptcy Institute Journal, 58 (Nov. 2005), the language of § 707(b)(1) may limit the Chapter 7 means test to cases "filed by an individual debtor under this chapter."

## § 6:3 Abuse

Code § 707(b)(1) is amended to permit the case trustee, U.S. trustee, bankruptcy administrator, and any party in interest, with some standing restrictions, to move for dismissal of an individual's Chapter 7 case, and the amendment reduces the former "substantial abuse" to "an abuse," while imposing a financial means test to presume an abuse when a debtor's "current monthly income" (a term defined in new § 101(10A) and to be discussed later) exceeds a formula amount, as described in the addition to 2005 Code § 707(b)(2)(A). As an alternative to dismissal for abuse, with the debtor's consent, the case may be converted to Chapter 12 or 13, and the case may be converted to Chapter 11 with or without the debtor's consent. 11 U.S.C.A. § 706(b) and (c).

### Practice Alerts for Code § 707(b)(3)

**We discuss the means test next, but if the presumption of abuse that arises under that test does not apply in a particular Chapter 7 case, or if the presumption arises but is sufficiently rebutted, 11 U.S.C.A. § 707(b)(3) states that the court shall consider whether the petition was otherwise filed in bad faith or whether the totality of circumstances involving the debtor's financial situation demonstrates an abuse. In other words, even without the means test's presumption of abuse, the former bad-faith or totality-of-circumstances test continues to be viable. In a totality-of-circumstances examination, § 707(b)(3) directs that the court also consider "whether the debtor seeks to reject a personal services contract and the financial need for such rejection as sought by the debtor."**

## § 6:4 Standing

Standing to file abuse motions is found first in the language of

§ 707(b)(1), giving the case trustee, U.S. trustee, bankruptcy administrator, or any party in interest general standing to file a motion to dismiss a consumer debtor's Chapter 7 case. The court may initiate the dismissal on its own motion. Standing to bring an abuse motion is, however, restricted to the court, U.S. trustee, or bankruptcy administrator if the debtor's current monthly income, multiplied by 12, is equal to or less than the annual median family income of the debtor's domicile state for a similar size family. 11 U.S.C.A. § 707(b)(6). Here, the income of the debtor's spouse is used only if it is a joint case. If the debtor's annualized current monthly income exceeds the relevant median family income, all of the above-named parties in interest may file § 707(b) motions.

Standing under the means test is even more restricted if the combined current monthly income of the debtor and the spouse, when multiplied by 12, is equal to or less than the same median family income. In such a situation, the § 707(b)(2) presumption-of-abuse test does not apply at all. Only if the debtor and spouse are separated, and the debtor so certifies under penalty of perjury, is the spouse's income excluded for this part of the standing test, even if only one of them files bankruptcy. 11 U.S.C.A. § 707(b)(7)(B). The official means testing form for Chapter 7, Official Form B22A, first includes the income of both spouses, even when only one files for bankruptcy under Chapter 7, and then permits a "marital deduction," subtracting the nonfiling spouse's income to the extent that it "was NOT regularly contributed to the household expenses of the debtor or the debtor's dependents." See Part IV, Official Form B22A, which is found in Appendix A.

## § 6:5 The means test

Suggested Resource: Hon. Eugene R. Wedoff, Means Testing in the New § 707(b), 79 Am. Bankr. L.J. 231 (2005), available on Westlaw under Legal Periodicals/Law Reviews.

This test is the heart of what has been called "need-based" bankruptcy reform, the concept being that an individual with primarily consumer debts will be permitted to file for Chapter 7 relief only if that chapter's relief is warranted, based upon an analysis of whether the debtor can repay a predetermined amount or percentage to unsecured creditors. In its most basic expression, a presumption of abuse is created if the debtor's current monthly income, after reductions as described below, when multiplied by 60 (for the maximum number of months of a Chapter 13 plan) is not less than the lesser of either $10,000 or 25% of the debtor's nonpriority unsecured creditors (or $6,000, whichever of the 25% or $6,000 is greater). As a minimum expression, therefore, if the debtor can repay out of adjusted or net current monthly income $100 monthly to unsecured creditors over 60 months, then the debtor has presumptively failed the means test. Using the $10,000 standard, if that is less than 25% of total unsecured debt, if the debtor could pay $166.67 per month to nonpriority, unsecured creditors over 60 months, the presumption of abuse exists.

Judge Wedoff's article, at 79 Am. Bankr. L. J. 231, 242, speaks of these as "trigger points" for the means test. Official Form B22A, at its Part VI, describes the methodology adopted for determining the § 707(b)(2) presumption of abuse. See § 6:7 below. Once the presumption of abuse is created under this formula, until the debtor rebuts the presumption with documented special circumstances or expenses, the case is subject to dismissal, unless the debtor consents to a conversion (presumably to Chapter 13, although in an appropriate case it could be to Chapter 11 or 12). See Appendix A for Official Form B22A, at its Part VII, for additional expenses that might rebut the abuse presumption.

This, however, is not a complete explanation of the § 707(b)(2) means test. The complete test takes the following statutory track:

a. The court may not consider in its abuse analysis the debtor's past or continued contributions to charitable entities as defined in § 548(d)(4). 11 U.S.C.A. § 707(b)(1).

b. The presumption is triggered by the current monthly income times 60, less allowable deductions described below, being no less than the lesser of 25% of the nonpriority unsecured creditors (or $6,000 if greater than the 25%) or $10,000. 11 U.S.C.A. § 707(b)(2)(A)(i)(I) and (II).

c. "Current monthly income" (CMI) is a defined term in § 101(10A), meaning a six-month average of the monthly income from all sources, whether taxable or not, and including both spouses if it is a joint case. The six-month period ends on the last calendar day of the month immediately preceding the filing (or a later date determined by the court if the debtor does not file the § 521(a)(1)(B)(ii) statement of current monthly income), and the calculation of current monthly income includes any amounts regularly paid by others for the debtor's or debtor's dependents' household expenses. The definition excludes, however, some income, as discussed below.

As suggested in the standing discussion, a question that exists under this definition is whether the income of the debtor's spouse should be considered at all in an abuse analysis unless it is a joint case. Under former law, the income of the debtor's spouse was often a part of a substantial abuse analysis, even though only one debtor filed for bankruptcy relief. The fact that the CMI definition looks to the spouse's income only for joint cases will perhaps permit some individual consumer debtors to qualify for Chapter 7 relief if they do not file jointly with their spouse. But, as mentioned previously, the official means test form, B22A, is structured to require inclusion of a nonfiling spouse's income, unless the spouses are actually separated. See Official Form B22A, Part II. A nonfiling spouse's income may be deducted later on that form if it is not actually "regularly contributed to the household expenses of the debtor or the debtor's dependents." Official Form B22A, Part IV.

Another question posed by the definition of CMI is related to debtors who may not have income in each of the six months used to average income. For example, if the debtor had been unemployed for three months out of that period but had then obtained employment with substantial income, a less than actual current monthly income would result, permitting some debtors to pass the means test while having the actual ability to pay the minimum amount to unsecured creditors. This defined method for calculating current monthly income diminishes the court's discretionary authority, although the court may still find actual abuse under § 707(b)(1). It should be noted that debtors are still required to file Schedules I and J of their actual income and expenses, and those schedules may form a basis for a general abuse dismissal.

d. Current monthly income excludes any Social Security Act benefits, payments to victims of war crimes or victims of crimes against humanity, and payments to victims of international or domestic terrorism. 11 U.S.C.A. § 101(10A). The exclusion of these designated benefits, most commonly social security benefits, would automatically permit a debtor whose sole income was from those benefits to pass the means test. Many such debtors may be currently filing for Chapter 13 relief in an effort to save houses or other collateral, but those debtors remain viable candidates for Chapter 7 relief under the means test. The exclusion of benefits under the Social Security Act leaves open for argument the possible exclusion of unemployment compensation benefits, which are typically funded by the Social Security Act. Official Form B22A, at its Part II, line 9, permits the debtor to make this argument. Judicial determinations will be needed on this issue.

e. The definition of current monthly income does not specify if it means gross income or net income after tax and other withholding deductions. Official Form B22A is structured to begin with gross income, except that for a debtor engaged in business, the net business income is used. See Official Form B22A, Part II. That form then permits deduction, at its line 25, of "the total average monthly expense that you actually incur for all federal, state and local taxes." The form's approach may be justified, based on the congressional adoption of the Internal Revenue Service Standards for allowable expense deductions from current monthly income. If one examines the Internal Revenue Manual, which will be referred to later, and which is available on Westlaw in its Library FTX-IRM, the IRS's allowable expense overview explains that the Service examines whether a taxpayer's tax withholdings are correct and allows only the correct deductions for those expenses. This method is not specified in § 707(b)(2)'s lengthy explanation of use of the IRS Standards. There is no mention in the statute of tax, social security, or other required withholdings.

f. The Official Form B22A, at its Part III, permits the debtor to stop before calculating allowable expenses and to check a box that "The Presumption does not arise," on the top of the form, when the annualized CMI falls below the median family income for the debtor's state of residence and household size. Under the standing test found in § 707(b)(7), if the joint current monthly income of the debtor and spouse falls below that applicable median income, no one can file a motion to dismiss based on the means test, but the judge, U.S. trustee, or bankruptcy administrator could file a motion based upon actual abuse. Many consumer debtors with minimal income will continue to qualify for Chapter 7 relief without extensive financial analysis. Presumably, Official Form B22A satisfies the requirement of § 707(b)(2)(C) that the debtor's § 521 schedule of current income and expenses include a statement of the current monthly income and the debtor's calculation of whether a presumption of abuse exists, which must "show how each such amount is calculated."

g. The median income numbers are taken from U.S. Census Bureau tables for each state, based upon the number of persons in the household. The Census Bureau has updated its tables, with an adjustment for cost of living increase based on the Consumer Price Index, and those tables for 2004 are found in the Appendix to this pamphlet, as well as are available at www.usdoj.gov/ust/bapcpa. See the definition of median family income at 11 U.S.C.A. § 101(39A).

h. Assuming that the debtor remains subject to the means test, once the average current monthly income is calculated, § 707(b)(2)(A)(ii) provides a list of expenses that may be deducted in arriving at the net current monthly income for means testing purposes. The allowed expenses begin with those defined under both the National and Local Standards established by the Internal Revenue Service. BAPCPA § 103 expresses the "sense of Congress" that the Internal Revenue Service Standard guidelines for repayment plans may be adjusted "by the Secretary of the Treasury as needed to accommodate their use for § 707(b) means testing purposes." Within two years of enactment, the Executive Office for the United States Trustees is to report to Congress on its "findings regarding the utilization of Internal Revenue Service Standards for determining" the § 707(b) monthly expenses and the impact of those Standards on debtors and the bankruptcy court. This study/report is apparently a reaction to criticism by some that the IRS Standards are not appropriate for bankruptcy means testing purposes.

Pending such a study and any future amendments to the test or adjustments to the Standards by the Secretary of Treasury, the IRS National Standards will govern such items as food, clothing, personal items, housekeeping supplies, and entertainment, while the local standards govern housing, utility, and transportation costs. Those IRS standards are found at www.irs.gov/irm/part5 and are on Westlaw as a part of the Internal Revenue Manual at Westlaw's library FTX-IRM.

That Manual summarizes the Standards as follows:

**Internal Revenue Manual**

**Part 5 —Collecting Process**

**5.15.1.7 —Allowable Expense Overview (05-01-2004)**

(1) Allowable expenses include those expenses that meet the necessary expense test. The necessary expense test is defined as expen-

ses that are necessary to provide for a taxpayer's and his or her family's health and welfare and/or production of income. The expenses must be reasonable. The total necessary expenses establish the minimum a taxpayer and family needs to live.

(2) There are three types of necessary expenses:

- National Standards
- Local Standards
- Other Expenses

(3) National Standards: These establish standards for reasonable amounts for five necessary expenses. Four of them come from the Bureau of Labor Statistics (BLS) Consumer Expenditure Survey: food, housekeeping supplies, apparel and services, and personal care products and services. The fifth category, miscellaneous, is a discretionary amount established by the Service. It is $100 for one person and $25 for each additional person in the taxpayer's household.

All five standards are included in one total national standard expense.

(4) Local Standards: These establish standards for two necessary expenses: housing and transportation. Taxpayers will be allowed the local standard or the amount actually paid, whichever is less.

(a.) Housing—Standards are established for each county within a state. When deciding if a deviation is appropriate, consider the cost of moving to a new residence; the increased cost of transportation to work and school that will result from moving to lower-cost housing and the tax consequences. The tax consequence is the difference between the benefit the taxpayer currently derives from the interest and property tax deductions on Schedule A to the benefit the taxpayer would derive without the same or adjusted expense.

(b.) Transportation—The transportation standards consist of nationwide figures for loan or lease payments referred to as ownership cost, and additional amounts for operating costs broken down by Census Region and Metropolitan Statistical Area. Operating costs were derived from BLS data. If a taxpayer has a car payment, the allowable ownership cost added to the allowable operating cost equals the allowable transportation expense. If a taxpayer has no car payment only the operating cost portion of the transportation standard is used to figure the allowable transportation expense. Under ownership costs, separate caps are provided for the first car and second car. If the taxpayer does not own a car a standard public transportation amount is allowed.

(5) Other—Other expenses may be allowed if they meet the necessary expense test. The amount allowed must be reasonable considering the taxpayer's individual facts and circumstances.

(6) Conditional expenses. These expenses do not meet the necessary expenses test. However, they are allowable if the tax liability, including projected accruals, can be fully paid within five years.

(7) National local expense standards are guidelines. If it is determined a standard amount is inadequate to provide for a specific taxpayer's basic living expenses, allow a deviation. Require the taxpayer to provide reasonable substantiation and document the case file.

(8) Generally, the total number of persons allowed for national standard expenses should be the same as those allowed as dependents on the taxpayer's current year income tax return. Verify exemptions claimed on taxpayer's income tax return meet the dependency requirements of the IRC. There may be reasonable exceptions. Fully document the reasons for any exceptions. For example, foster children or children for whom adoption is pending.

(9) A deviation from the local standard is not allowed merely because it is inconvenient for the taxpayer to dispose of valued assets.

(10) Revenue officers should consider the length of the payments. Although it may be appropriate to allow for payments made on the secured debts that meet the necessary expense test, if the debt will be fully repaid in one year only allow those payments for one year.

**5.15.1.8 —National Standards (05-01-2004)**

(1) National standards include the following expenses:

(a.) Apparel and services. Includes shoes and clothing, laundry and dry cleaning, and shoe repair.

(b.) Food. Includes all meals, home and away.

(c.) Housekeeping supplies. Includes laundry and cleaning supplies; other household products such as cleaning and toilet tissue, paper towels and napkins; lawn and garden supplies; postage and stationary; and other miscellaneous household supplies.

(d.) Personal care products and services. Includes hair care products, haircuts and beautician services, oral hygiene products and articles, shaving needs, cosmetics, perfume, bath preparations, deodorants, feminine hygiene products, electric personal care appliances, personal care services, and repair of personal care appliances. (e.) Miscellaneous. A discretionary allowance of $100 for one person and $25 for each additional person in a taxpayer's family.

(2) Allow taxpayers the total national standard amount for their income level.

Example: The taxpayer's expenses are: housekeeping supplies—$150, clothing—$150, food—$600, miscellaneous—$400 (Total Expenses—$1,300). The taxpayer is allowed the national standard of $1,100.

(3) A taxpayer that claims more than the total allowed by the national standards must substantiate and justify each separate expense of the total national standard amounts.

Example: A taxpayer may claim a higher food expense than allowed. Justification would be based on prescribed or required dietary needs.

**5.15.1.9 —Local Standards (05-01-2004)**

(1) Local standards include the following expenses:

(a.) Housing and Utilities. The utilities include gas, electricity, water, fuel, oil, bottled gas, trash and garbage collection, wood and other fuels, septic cleaning, and telephone. Housing expenses include: mortgage or rent, property taxes, interest, parking, necessary maintenance and repair, homeowner's or renter's insurance, homeowner dues and condominium fees. Usually, this is considered necessary only for the place of residence. Any other housing expenses should be allowed only if, based on a taxpayer's individual facts and circumstances, disallowance will cause the taxpayer economic hardship.

(b.) Transportation. Vehicle insurance, vehicle payment (lease or purchase), maintenance, fuel, state and local registration, required inspection, parking fees, tolls, driver's license, public transportation. Transportation costs not required to produce income or ensure the health and welfare of the family are not considered necessary. Consider availability of public transportation if car payments (purchase or lease) will prevent the tax liability from being paid in part or full. Public transportation costs could be an option if it does not significantly increase commuting time and inconvenience the taxpayer.

If the taxpayer has no car payment, or no car, question how the taxpayer travels to and from work, grocer, medical care, etc. The taxpayer is only allowed the operating cost or the cost of transportation.

**5.15.1.10 —Other Expenses (05-01-2004)**

(1) Other expenses may be considered if they meet the necessary expense test—they must provide for the health and welfare of the taxpayer and/or his or her family or they must be for the production of income. This is determined based on the facts and circumstances of each case.

(2) If other expenses are determined to be necessary and, therefore allowable, document the reasons for the decision in your history.

(3) The amount allowed for necessary or conditional expenses depends on the taxpayer's ability to fully pay the liability within five years and on the taxpayer's individual facts and circumstances. If the liability can be paid within 5 years, it may be appropriate to allow the taxpayer the excessive necessary and conditional expenses. If the taxpayer cannot pay within 5 years, it may be appropriate to allow the taxpayer the excessive necessary and conditional expenses for up to one year in order to modify or eliminate the expense.

**Practice Alert for Discretion Under the IRS Standards**

**As these explanations indicate, there is quite a bit of discre-**

**tion permitted to IRS collection officers in applying these standards, and it remains to be seen how this discretion will carry over to the courts. The Official Form B22A is structured on the basis that the IRS National and Local Standard amounts for each category are allowed as deductions from CMI, even if those amounts are higher than the debtor's actual expenses. As Professor Steve H. Nickles, a Thomson/West author, has pointed out in seminar materials, the form takes an opposite approach than does the IRS in its collection manual, which limits deductions to the actual expenses of the debtor if they are less than the IRS Standard allowances. The drafters of the Official Form B22A based their approach on the language of § 707(b)(2)(A)(ii), which allows the "applicable monthly expense amounts specified under the National Standards and Local Standards." This, of course, is good for the debtor if actual expenses in these Standards are lower than the Standards, but it may certainly be argued by creditors that the Code's reference to the IRS Standards mandates the use of all the criteria and calculation methods used by the IRS. For the expense categories other than ones found in the IRS National and Local Standards, Official Form B22A assumes that actual expenses are used. See lines 25–41 of Form B22A, found in the Appendix.**

IRS has published National Standard tables based upon the number of persons in the household and upon gross monthly income. So now, the debtor and counsel must go back to gross income for the expense calculations. These Standards include food, housekeeping supplies, apparel and services, personal care products and services, and miscellaneous. When there are more than four persons in the household, the Standards permit an additional amount per person.

The published State Standards provide housing and utilities expenses that are allowable by each state, and the Regional Standards are for transportation ownership or public transportation costs, as well as for transportation operating expenses. These regional standards are based upon the following regions: Northwest, Midwest, South, and West, and within each region there are Metropolitan Statistical Areas to account for the larger urban areas where transportation expenses are expected to be higher.

All of the IRS Standards are found at www.irs.gov and on the Executive Office for U.S. trustee website, www.usdoj.gov/ust/bapcpa. Local bankruptcy courts may also have these Standards and the median income tables on their court websites. Links to each bankruptcy court website are available at www.uscourts.gov.

i. In addition to these IRS Standard expenses, the actual monthly expenses of the debtor and dependents for the "Other Necessary Expense" categories are allowable. See lines 25–40 of Official Form B22A, in the Appendix. These expenses specifically include reasonably necessary health and disability insurance as well as health saving account expenses for the debtor and dependents. The calculation of actual monthly expenses does not include the debtor's ongoing monthly secured debt payments since those payments are brought into the formula later. If the debtor or dependents have monthly expenses for protection from family violence, as identified in the Family Violence Prevention and Services Act or other federal law, those expenses, to the extent reasonably necessary, are deductible under § 707(b)(2)(A)(ii)(I). If there are such expenses, the court is required to keep those expenses confidential. This will be problematic since the court does not create the calculation; rather, the debtor and debtor's counsel supply those numbers. Does this mean that part of such debtor's expenses would be filed under seal? How would the trustee and other parties in interest know of this expense? How would the court test reasonableness of the amount without a hearing? How would the hearing be kept confidential?

If the debtor could establish that it is reasonable and necessary, an additional allowance of monthly expenses for food and clothing up to 5% of the IRS national standards is allowable. 11 U.S.C.A. § 707(b)(2)(A)(ii)(I), and see Official Form B22A, line 39, in the Appendix. Of course, if contested, it would be the debtor's burden to establish that the increased amount was reasonable and necessary, but since the debtor and debtor's counsel prepare the expense calculation to start the process, the choice is theirs to enhance this amount up to the 5% maximum.

j. After deducting the above Standards and actual expenses, § 707(b)(2)(A)(ii)(II) permits the debtor to deduct continuing actual expenses for the reasonable and necessary care and support of an elderly, chronically ill, or disabled household member or such a member of the debtor's immediate family. See Official Form B22A, line 35. Immediate family is defined to include parents, grandparents, siblings, children and grandchildren of the debtor, the debtor's spouse, or debtor's dependents. This allowance depends upon the debtor actually paying those expenses and the inability of the supported person to pay those expenses. In a contested scenario, the court would be called upon to make factual findings of reasonableness and necessity as well as the inability of the supported person to pay for the expenses, a hearing that may involve persons that would otherwise have no connection with the bankruptcy case or court. There are obvious privacy issues as to those persons that are not addressed in the Code's amendment.

k. In addition to the above expenses, assuming that the debtor is otherwise eligible to file under Chapter 13 by its debt limits under § 109(e), the debtor may deduct the actual administrative expenses of a Chapter 13 plan in the debtor's judicial district, up to a maximum of 10% of projected Chapter 13 plan payments. The website for the Executive Office for U.S. Trustee has the allowable expense for each judicial district. See www.usdoj.gov/ust/bapcpa. This deduction is intended to calculate the cost of the debtor being in Chapter 13 rather than Chapter 7, but the calculation does not specifically include any allowance for the attorney's fees of the debtor in Chapter 13. In many judicial districts, the fees charged by attorneys for Chapter 13 filings are higher than for Chapter 7, and those fees are often paid through the plan. Does this maximum 10% allowance permit the debtor to include attorney's fees in that percentage if the Chapter 13 trustee's administrative expenses are less than the 10%? Note also that this deduction is based upon the projected Chapter 13 payments that would require the debtor and counsel to make all of the assumptions of what would be required in arriving at plan payments for a plan that is not filed. This obviously will require Chapter 7 attorneys to be familiar with the Chapter 13 practice in their district.

l. The debtor may deduct actual expenses for each dependent's and minor child's private or public elementary or secondary education expense, up to a maximum of $1,500 per year per child. The debtor must provide documentation of these expenses and a detailed explanation of why the expenses are reasonable and necessary. In addition, the debtor must explain why these education expenses are not already accounted for in the IRS National, Local, or other Standards described above. See Official Form B22A, line 38.

m. If the debtor can establish the need for it, monthly expenses may include an allowance for housing and utilities in excess of the IRS local housing and utilities Standards. Here, the debtor must establish that the home energy costs are actual and that they are reasonable and necessary. See Official Form B22A, line 37.

n. After deduction of all expenses under the IRS Standards and actual expense tests, the debtor deducts an average monthly payment of each secured debt, calculated as follows: The total of all contractually due amounts for each of the 60 months following filing of the petition, plus any additional payments that would be required in a Chapter 13 plan (curing arrearages) to maintain the debtor's primary residence, motor vehicle, or other collateral necessary for the support of the debtor and dependents would be divided by 60, and this 1/60th amount would be deducted from current monthly income. See Part VC of Official Form B22A.

Many questions are unanswered in this secured debt calculation, including: If the debtor only has 12 payments remaining on a secured debt, such as for furniture, is the total of those payments divided by 60? Official Form B22A only says that you include the payments that are "contractually due during the 60 months." See Official Form B22A, line 42. Obviously, for a home mortgage that will continue beyond the 60 months, you only use the total payments due contractually within the 60 months, but many secured debts will have less than 60 months contractually remaining; thus dividing those total payments by 60 will not produce a number in accord with reality. For home mortgages that include escrows for insurance and taxes, Official Form B22A, at line 42, assumes that the calculation includes those escrows or the debtor's obligation to otherwise pay insurance and realty taxes, if "required by the mortgage." This calculation is not the same as the one that would be required to arrive at a Chapter 13 plan payment, so it is not a true indicator of what the debtor's actual net income would be in a Chapter 13. For example, a 1/60th payment to a car lender under this calculation may be much less than the adequate protection payment that would be required to that creditor in a Chapter 13, especially where the car is older and secures a relatively high balance. The point is that if this means test is intended to measure the debtor's ability to repay creditors in a Chapter 13, the 1/60 division of secured debt may falsely indicate an ability to pay unsecured creditors. Moreover, as will be seen in discussion of Chapter 13, the length of a Chapter 13 debtor's plan is dependent upon a median income test, so using a 1/60 division is not necessarily indicative of the period of time a particular debtor would pay on secured or unsecured debt in Chapter 13.

Line 43 of Official Form B22A provides for 1/60th payments of "past due" secured claims, in other words, arrearages that would need to be cured in a Chapter 13 plan. This 1/60th amount may not be a true indicator of what a Chapter 13 debtor would have to pay monthly to satisfy a particular secured creditor.

o. The debtor's expenses for all priority claims, including taxes, child support, and alimony claims, would be totaled and divided by 60, again arriving at a 1/60th expense deducted from current monthly income. See Official Form B22A, line 44. There are some of the same problems with the 1/60 division as seen in the prior discussion. In Chapter 13, a priority creditor might not be willing to accept payments over a 60-month period, nor may this term be required of a particular Chapter 13 debtor under the median income test for length of plans. See Official Form B22C for Chapter 13.

p. After all deductions, we are now finally at the debtor's net current monthly income, what is called "monthly disposable income" on Official Form B22A at lines 50–51. Abuse is presumptively established if the net when multiplied by 60 exceeds the lesser of 25% (or $6,000 if greater than the 25%) or $10,000 numbers described above. See Official Form B22A, lines 52–55 for the actual calculation method.

q. A debtor may attempt to demonstrate a special circumstance that would rebut the presumption, but that is permitted only by such circumstances as a serious medical condition or a call to active military duty, and then the debtor must document the increased expenses and provide a detailed explanation, under oath as to accuracy, of the special circumstances. A showing of such circumstances and increased expenses still must bring the net current monthly income below the lesser of 25% (or $6,000) or $10,000 numbers. See 11 U.S.C.A. § 707(b)(2)(B). Official Form B22A, line 56 may arguably be more liberal than the actual Code language, with that line permitting "other expenses" that the debtor may "contend should be an additional deduction from your current monthly income."

r. Code § 707(b)(2)(D) states that no form of means testing shall be applied to dismiss a Chapter 7 case filed by a disabled veteran, as defined in 38 U.S.C.A. § 3741(1), if that veteran's indebtedness occurred primarily during a period of active duty or while performing a homeland defense activity. If it is disputed whether a disabled veteran qualifies for this exemption from the means testing, the bankruptcy court would need to make factual findings about the time period for the origination of the indebtedness and whether the debtor's military or homeland defense activity occurred during the time period. A finding adverse to the veteran would then result in the application of the means test. Official Form B22A begins with a check-off box for such a disabled veteran, and if used, that veteran would immediately check a box that "the presumption [of abuse] does not arise." But see 11 U.S.C.A. § 521(a)(1)(B)(v)'s requirement that each debtor file a statement of monthly net income, "itemized to show how the amount is calculated." Section 727(b)(2)(C) requires that all Chapter 7 debtors include in this statement the calculation of whether a presumption of abuse arises. Such a presumption would not arise for qualified disabled veterans under § 727(b)(2)(D), but there appears to be an inconsistency with the duty required for debtors in their § 521 scheduling. It is unclear why the latter section refers to "monthly net income," rather than "current monthly income," but they surely must be the same thing.

There are as many factual scenarios as there are potential debtors, and how the means test plays out in actual practice can only be seen with some experience, but the test's results clearly do not equate to what may be required of the same debtor in a Chapter 13 plan. It is entirely possible that a debtor may be forced into a Chapter 13 due to "failing" the Chapter 7 means test and then be unable to obtain confirmation of a plan in Chapter 13.

## § 6:6 Census Bureau median income tables

In Appendix B, we have included the current Census Bureau Median Income tables, and the website of the Executive Office of United States Trustees has published the median income tables, along with relevant IRS Standard tables in an easily accessed format. See www.usdoj.gov/ust/bapcpa.

## § 6:7 Means test form and committee notes to Official Form B22A

BAPCPA § 1232 amends 28 U.S.C.A. § 2075 to provide that the Bankruptcy Rules shall prescribe a form to be used for the calculation that must be made by the debtor under § 707(b)(2)(C). Such a form has been adopted by the Judicial Conference of the U.S. Courts as Official Form B22A and is found in Appendix A. The Committee Notes to this Official Form are instructive as to the reasons that the drafters of the Form adopted certain approaches. Those Committee Notes to Official Form B22A follow:

A. Overview. Among the changes introduced by the Bankruptcy Abuse Prevention and Consumer Protection Act of 2005 are interlocking provisions defining "current monthly income" and establishing a means test to determine whether relief under Chapter 7 should be presumed abusive. Current monthly income ("CMI") is defined in § 101(10A) of the Code, and the means test is set out in § 707(b)(2). These provisions have a variety of applications. In Chapter 7, if the debtor's CMI exceeds a defined level the debtor is subject to the means test, and § 707(b)(2)(C) specifically requires debtors to file a statement of CMI and calculations to determine the applicability of the means test presumption. In Chapters 11 and 13, CMI provides the starting point for determining the disposable income that must be contributed to payment of unsecured creditors. Moreover, Chapter 13 debtors with CMI above defined levels are required by § 1325(b)(3) to complete the means test in order to determine the amount of their monthly disposable income, and pursuant to § 1325(b)(4), the level of CMI determines the "applicable commitment period" over which projected disposable income must be paid to unsecured creditors.

To provide for the reporting and calculation of CMI and for the completion of the means test where required, three separate official forms have been created-one for Chapter 7, one for Chapter 11, and one for Chapter 13. This note first describes the calculation of CMI that is common to all three of the forms, next describes the means test as set out in the Chapter 7 and 13 forms, and finally addresses particular issues that are unique to each of the separate forms.

B. Calculation of CMI. Although Chapters 7, 11, and 13 use CMI for different purposes, the basic computation is the same in each. As defined in § 101(10A), CMI is the monthly average of certain income that the debtor (and in a joint case, the debtor's spouse) received in the six calendar months before the bankruptcy filing. The definition includes in this average (1) income from all sources, whether or not taxable, and (2) any amount paid by an entity other than the debtor (or the debtor's spouse in a joint case) on a regular basis for the household expenses of the debtor, the debtor's dependents, and (in a joint case) the debtor's spouse if not otherwise a dependent. At the same time, the definition excludes from the averaged income "benefits received under the Social Security Act" and certain payments to victims of terrorism, war crimes, and crimes against humanity.

Each of the forms provides for reporting income items constituting CMI. The items are reported in a set of entry lines—Part II of the Chapter 7 form and Part I of the forms for Chapter 11 and Chapter 13—that include separate columns for reporting income of the debtor and of the debtor's spouse. The first of these entry lines includes a set of instructions and check boxes indicating when the "debtor's spouse" column must be completed. The instructions also direct the required averaging of reported income.

The subsequent entry lines specify several common types of income and are followed by a "catch-all" line for other income. The specific entry lines address (a) gross wages; (b) business income; (c) rental income; (d) interest, dividends, and royalties; (e) pension and retirement income; (f) regular contributions to the debtor's household expenses; and (g) unemployment compensation. Gross wages (before taxes) are required to be entered. Consistent with usage in the Internal Revenue Manual and the American Community Survey of the Census Bureau, business and rental income is defined as gross receipts less ordinary and necessary expenses. Unemployment compensation is given special treatment. Because the federal government provides funding for state unemployment compensation under the Social Security Act, there may be a dispute about whether unemployment compensation is a "benefit received under the Social Security Act." The forms take no position on the merits of this argument, but give debtors the option of reporting unemployment compensation separately from the CMI calculation. This separate reporting allows parties in interest to determine the materiality of an exclusion of unemployment compensation and to challenge it. The forms provide for totaling the income lines.

C. The means test: deductions from current monthly income (CMI). The means test operates by deducting from CMI defined allowances for living expenses and payment of secured and priority debt, leaving disposable income presumptively available to pay unsecured non-priority debt. These deductions from CMI are set out in the Code at § 707(b)(2)(A)(ii) to (iv). The forms for Chapter 7 and Chapter 13 have identical sections (Parts V and III, respectively) for calculating these deductions. The calculations are divided into subparts reflecting three different kinds of allowed deductions.

1. Deductions under IRS standards. Subpart A deals with deductions from CMI, set out in § 707(b)(2)(A)(ii), for "the debtor's applicable monthly expense amounts specified under the National Standards and Local Standards, and the debtor's actual monthly expenses for the categories specified as Other Necessary Expenses issued by the Internal Revenue Service for the area in which the debtor resides." The forms provide entry lines for each of the specified expense deductions under the IRS standards, and instructions on the entry lines identify the website of the U.S. Trustee Program, where the relevant IRS allowances can be found. As with all of the deductions in § 707(b)(2)(A)(ii), deductions under the IRS standards are subject to the proviso that they not include "any payments for debts."

The IRS National Standards provide a single allowance for food, clothing, household supplies, personal care, and miscellany, depending on income and household size. The forms contain an entry line for the applicable allowance.

The IRS Local Standards provide one set of deductions for housing and utilities and another set for transportation expenses, with different amounts for different areas of the country, depending on the size of the debtor's family and the number of the debtor's vehicles. Each of the amounts specified in the Local Standards are treated by the IRS as a cap on actual expenses, but because § 707(b)(2)(A)(ii) provides for deductions in the "amounts specified under the . . . Local Standards," the forms treat these amounts as allowed deductions. The forms again direct debtors to the website of the U.S. trustee Program to obtain the appropriate allowances.

The Local Standards for housing and utilities, as published by the IRS for its internal purposes, present single amounts covering all housing expenses; however, for bankruptcy purposes, the IRS has separated these amounts into a non-mortgage component and a mortgage/rent component. The non-mortgage component covers a variety of expenses involved in maintaining a residence, such as utilities, repairs and maintenance. The mortgage/rent component covers the cost of acquiring the residence. For homeowners with mortgages, the mortgage/rent component involves debt payment, since the cost of a mortgage is part of the allowance. Accordingly, the forms require debtors to deduct from the mortgage/rent component their average monthly mortgage payment (including required payments for taxes and insurance), up to the full amount of the IRS mortgage/rent component, and instruct debtors that this average monthly payment is the one reported on the separate line of the forms for deductions of secured debt under § 707(b)(2)(a)(iii). The forms allow debtors to challenge the appropriateness of this method of computing the Local Standards allowance for housing and utilities and to claim any additional housing allowance to which they contend they are entitled, but the forms require specification of the basis for such a contention.

The IRS issues Local Standards for transportation in two components for its internal purposes as well as for bankruptcy: one component covers vehicle operation/public transportation expense and the other ownership/lease expense. The amount of the vehicle operation/public transportation allowance depends on the number of vehicles the debtor operates, with debtors who do not operate vehicles being given a public transportation allowance. The instruction for this line item makes it clear that every debtor is thus entitled to some transportation expense allowance. No debt payment is involved in this allowance. The ownership/lease component, on the other hand, may involve debt payment. Accordingly, the forms require debtors to reduce the allowance for ownership/lease expense by the average monthly loan payment amount (principal and interest), up to the full amount of the IRS ownership/lease expense amount. This average payment is reported on the separate line of the forms for deductions of secured debt under § 707(b)(2)(a)(iii).

The IRS does not set out specific dollar allowances for "Other Necessary Expenses." Rather, it specifies a number of categories for such expenses, and describes the nature of the expenses that may be deducted in each of these categories. Section 707(b)(2)(a)(ii) allows a deduction for the debtor's actual expenses in these specified categories, subject to its requirement that payment of debt not be included. Several of the IRS categories deal with debt repayment and so are not included in the forms. Several other categories deal with expense items that are more expansively addressed by specific statutory allowances. Subpart A sets out the remaining categories of "Other Necessary Expenses" in individual entry lines. Instructions in these entry lines reflect limitations imposed by the IRS and the need to avoid inclusion of items deducted elsewhere on the forms.

Subpart A concludes with a subtotal of the deductions allowed under the IRS standards.

2. Additional statutory expense deductions. In addition to the expense deductions allowed under the IRS standards, the means test makes provision-in subclauses (I), (II), (IV), and (V) of § 707(b)(2)(A)(ii)-for six special expense deductions. Each of these additional expense items is set out on a separate entry line in Subpart B, introduced by an instruction that there should not be double counting of any expense already included in the IRS deductions. Contributions to tax-exempt charities provide another statutory expense deduction. Section 1325(b)(2)(A)(ii) expressly allows a deduction from CMI for such contributions (up to 15% of the debtor's gross income), and § 707(b)(1) provides that in considering whether a Chapter 7 filing is an abuse, the court may not take into consideration "whether a debtor . . . continues to make [tax-exempt] charitable contributions." Accordingly, Subpart B also includes an entry line for charitable contributions. The subpart concludes with a subtotal of the additional statutory expense deductions.

3. Deductions for payment of debt. Subpart C of the forms

deals with the means test's deductions from CMI for payment of secured and priority debt, as well as a deduction for administrative fees that would be incurred if the debtor paid debts through a Chapter 13 plan. In accord with § 707(b)(2)(A)(iii), the deduction for secured debt is divided into two entry lines-one for payments that are contractually due during the 60 months following the bankruptcy filing, the other for amounts needed to retain necessary collateral securing debts in default. In each situation, the instructions for the entry lines require dividing the total payment amount by 60, as the statute directs. Priority debt, deductible pursuant to § 707(b)(2)(A)(iv), is treated on a single entry line, also requiring division by 60. The defined deduction for the expenses of administering a Chapter 13 plan is allowed by § 707(b)(2)(A)(ii)(III) only for debtors eligible for Chapter 13. The forms treat this deduction in an entry line requiring the eligible debtor to state the amount of the prospective Chapter 13 plan payment and multiply that payment amount by the percentage fee established for the debtor's district by the Executive Office for United States Trustees. The forms refer debtors to the website of the U.S. Trustee Program to obtain this percentage fee. The subpart concludes with a subtotal of debt payment deductions.

4. Total deductions. Finally, the forms direct that the subtotals from Subparts A, B, and C be added together to arrive at the total of allowed deductions from CMI under the means test.

5. Additional claimed deductions. The forms do not provide for means test deductions from CMI for expenses in categories that are not specifically identified as "Other Necessary Expenses" in the Internal Revenue Manual. However, debtors may wish to claim expenses that do not fall within the categories listed as "Other Necessary Expenses" in the forms. Part VII of the Chapter 7 form and Part VI of the Chapter 13 form provide for such expenses to be identified and totaled. Although expenses listed in these sections are not deducted from CMI for purposes of the means test calculation, the listing provides a basis for debtors to assert that these expenses should be deducted from CMI under § 707(b)(2)(A)(ii)(I), and that the results of the forms' calculation, therefore, should be modified.

D. The Chapter-specific forms. The Chapter 7 form has several unique aspects. The form includes, in the upper right corner of the first page, a check box directing the debtor to state whether or not the calculations required by the form result in a presumption of abuse. The debtor is not bound by this statement and may argue, in response to a motion brought under § 707(b)(1), that there should be no presumption despite the calculations required by the form. The check box is intended to give clerks of court a conspicuous indication of the cases for which they are required to provide notice of a presumption of abuse pursuant to § 342(d).

Part I of the form implements the provision of § 707(b)(2)(D) that excludes certain disabled veterans from all means testing, making it unnecessary to compute the CMI of such veterans.

Debtors who declare under penalty of perjury that they are disabled veterans within the statutory definition are directed to verify their declaration in Part VII, to check the "no presumption" box at the beginning of the form, and to disregard the remaining parts of the form.

Part II of the form is the computation of CMI. Section 707(b)(7) eliminates standing to assert the means test's presumption of abuse if the debtor's annualized CMI does not exceed a defined median state income. For this purpose, the statute directs that CMI of the debtor's spouse be combined with the debtor's CMI even if the debtor's spouse is not a joint debtor, unless the debtor declares under penalty of perjury that the spouses are legally separated or living separately other than for purposes of evading the means test. Accordingly, the calculation of CMI in Part II directs a computation of the CMI of the debtor's spouse not only in joint cases, but also in cases of married debtors who do not make the specified declaration, and the CMI of both spouses in these cases is combined for purposes of determining standing under § 707(b)(7).

Part III of the form provides for the comparison of the debtor's CMI to the applicable state median income for purposes of § 707(b)(7). It then directs debtors whose income does not exceed the applicable median to verify the form, to check the "no presumption" box at the beginning of the form, and not to complete the remaining parts of the form. Debtors whose CMI does exceed the applicable state median are required to complete the remaining parts of the form.

Part IV of the form provides for an adjustment to the CMI of a married debtor, not filing jointly, whose spouse's CMI was combined with the debtor's for purposes of determining standing to assert the means test presumption. The means test itself does not charge a married debtor in a non-joint case with the income of the non-filing spouse, but rather only with contributions made by that spouse to the household expenses of the debtor or the debtor's dependents, as provided in the definition of CMI in § 101(10A). Accordingly, Part IV calls for the combined CMI of Part II to be reduced by the amount of the non-filing spouse's income that was not contributed to the household expenses of the debtor or the debtor's dependents.

Part V of the form provides for a calculation of the means test's deductions from the debtor's CMI, as described above.

Part VI provides for a determination of whether the debtor's CMI, less the allowed deductions, gives rise to a presumption of abuse under § 707(b)(2)(A). Depending on the outcome of this determination, the debtor is directed to check the appropriate box at the beginning of the form and to sign the verification in Part VIII. Part VII allows the debtor to claim additional deductions, as discussed above.

## § 6:8 Rule 9011 and abuse—For benefit of a trustee

If a Chapter 7 trustee files a motion for dismissal of a Chapter 7 case on the basis of abuse, under either the actual abuse or the means-testing presumptive abuse standard, and if the court finds abusive cause for dismissal of the case, 11 U.S.C.A. § 707(b)(4)(A) directs that a Rule 9011 standard be applied. The court then must determine whether the debtor's attorney violated the Rule. If so, the sanction of reimbursement of the trustee's reasonable costs in prosecuting the § 707(b) motion, including the trustee's reasonable attorney's fees, may be ordered against the debtor's attorney.

## § 6:9 Civil penalty

Separate from the trustee's potential recovery for a Rule 9011 violation, 11 U.S.C.A. § 707(b)(4)(B) provides that the court may award a "civil penalty" against the debtor's attorney under Rule 9011. The court, on its own initiative or on motion of a party in interest, may assess such a penalty to be payable to the case trustee, U.S. trustee, or bankruptcy administrator, if a Rule 9011 violation is found.

## § 6:10 Certification by debtor's attorney

The signature of the debtor's attorney on the petition or any pleading constitutes a certification that the attorney has "performed a reasonable investigation into the circumstances that gave rise to the petition, pleading, or written motion," and that the attorney determined that the petition or other pleading is "well grounded in fact" and warranted under the law, and that the petition or pleading is not an abuse under § 707(b)(1). See 11 U.S.C.A. § 707(b)(4)(C). This is a broad certification by the debtor's attorney, one seemingly requiring some level of inquiry into why the debtor needs to file for Chapter 7 relief. The certification that the petition is not an abuse is broadly worded to include that it is not an abuse under either the general bad-faith or the means-testing standard. A separate certification is called for by § 707(b)(4)(D): "The signature of an attorney on the petition shall constitute a certification that the attorney has no knowledge after an inquiry that the information in the schedules filed with such petition is incorrect." Thus the debtor's attorney is certifying both that the debtor has good cause to file for Chapter 7 relief and that the attorney has no knowledge of incorrect information in the schedules.

Many questions arise under these certification rules. How much inquiry must the attorney make into the reasons for the bankruptcy filing and to what extent must the attorney inquire into accuracy? An obvious question is how willing attorneys are going to be to make this certification and how rigidly the Rule 9011 implications will be applied. Other questions are how this requirement for attorneys will impact the fees that they will charge for Chapter 7 work and how the broad certification will impact their professional liability insurance coverage and rates.

For further discussion of attorney liability issues, see Catherine E. Vance & Corinne Cooper, Nine Traps and One Slap: Attorney Liability under the New Bankruptcy Law, 79 Am. Bankr. L. J. 283 (Spring, 2005), available on Westlaw at Legal Periodicals/Law Reviews.

## § 6:11 Fees to debtor

Section 707(b)(5) does permit the court to award reasonable costs, including reasonable attorney's fees to the debtor under a limited circumstance when a motion for abuse dismissal is filed and not granted. First, the court may on its own initiative or on motion of a party in interest (which likely would always be the debtor) apply a Rule 9011 standard to see if the party filing a § 707(b) motion violated that Rule. The possibility of an award to the debtor does not apply when the motion is filed by a case trustee, U.S. trustee, or bankruptcy administrator, but it does apply when the motion is filed by another party in interest, such as a creditor. If the court finds that the filing party's position violated Rule 9011 or that the attorney who filed the motion did so "solely for the purpose of coercing a debtor into waiving a right guaranteed to the debtor under this title," the court may make the award, but a small business with an aggregate claim of less than $1,000 is exempt from such a penalty. A small business for this purpose is defined as one that has fewer than 25 full-time employees and is engaged in a commercial or business activity. 11 U.S.C.A. § 707(b)(5)(B) and (C).

### Practice Alerts for Fees Under Code § 707(b)

**This possible award to the debtor for creditor abuse seems hollow in reality. First, the door is open for a small business creditor to abuse the process with no penalty, but the larger issue is how the debtor could ever prove the requirements for an award. Note that the statute requires the court to find that the party who filed the motion violated Rule 9011 based upon the "position" of that party. We are talking about a § 707(b) motion that would be filed by the creditor under a statute that exposes virtually all Chapter 7 debtors to an abuse and means testing analysis, so how could a creditor's legal position in filing the motion be in violation of Rule 9011? As to the second part of the statute concerning possible violation by the creditor's attorney, that requires a showing that the motion was filed "solely" for the purpose of coercing the debtor to forego some guaranteed Title 11 right. Again, the motion being addressed is only the § 707(b) motion, and all Chapter 7 debtors are potentially subject to such a motion. How could the creditor's filing of such a motion be construed as an effort to coerce the debtor to give up a right not to have a § 707(b) motion filed? It is unlikely that this possible remedy for creditor abuse will see success for debtors.**

## § 6:12 U.S. trustee and bankruptcy administrator responsibility

By an addition to 11 U.S.C.A. § 704(b), which currently addresses the duties of the Chapter 7 trustee, the U.S. trustee or bankruptcy administrator must file a statement of whether a case would be presumed abusive within 10 days of the date of the § 341 meeting of creditors. Within five days of receiving the statement, the clerk of the court "shall provide a copy of the statement to all creditors." Note that this notice is in addition to the clerk's independent responsibility to notice creditors if the debtor's filing reflects that a presumption of abuse arises. See 11 U.S.C.A. § 342(d), which is discussed below. Within 30 days of the filing of its statement, the U. S. trustee or bankruptcy administrator must file a § 707(b) motion based upon abuse or a statement of why the case is not presumed abusive even though the debtor's current monthly income is not less than the applicable median family income. 11 U.S.C.A. § 704(b)(2).

In addition to the notices described above, Code § 342's notice provisions are amended by adding subsection (d) to require further notice from the clerk to creditors in each Chapter 7 case where abuse is presumed under the means test:

> (d) In a case under chapter 7 of this title in which the debtor is an individual and in which the presumption of abuse arises under section 707(b), the clerk shall give written notice to all creditors not later than 10 days after the date of the filing of the petition that the presumption of abuse has arisen.

11 U.S.C.A. § 342(d). This clerk's notice will be based upon what the debtor's required calculation shows at the time of filing, since the clerk at this point would not have the benefit of the analysis by the U.S. trustee or bankruptcy administrator. See the notice discussion for additional comments about the clerk's notice.

## § 6:13 Crime victim dismissal

Section 707(c) is added to provide for dismissal upon motion of a victim of a crime of violence or drug-trafficking crime, when the debtor has been convicted of such a crime, unless it is shown by a preponderance of evidence that the Chapter 7 bankruptcy "is necessary to satisfy the claim of a domestic support obligation." See the discussion of domestic support obligations.

## § 6:14 Tax returns

Under § 521(e)(2)(A)(i), a Chapter 7 (and 13) debtor must provide to the trustee the most recent tax year's return or transcript no later than seven days before the first date set for the § 341 meeting of creditors, and a copy must be provided to creditors who request it. Failure of the debtor to provide the required tax returns "shall" result in dismissal of the case, "unless the debtor demonstrates that the failure to so comply is due to circumstances beyond the control of the debtor." 11 U.S.C.A. § 521(e)(2)(B). It is expected that such showings by debtors will often involve the debtor's inability to obtain copies of tax returns in time to meet the requirements.

At the request of the court or a party in interest, the debtor is required to file with the court tax returns or transcripts for tax periods ending while the case is pending. See 11 U.S.C.A. § 521(f). This requirement is insignificant in most Chapter 7 cases since most move through the system to discharge quickly within a few months.

The Administrative Office of U.S. Courts, complying with a directive found in BAPCPA § 315(c), has promulgated procedures for safeguarding the confidentiality of tax information that may be required to be provided under 11 U.S.C.A. § 521. Some of those guidelines may be in tension with what creditors may perceive to be their statutory right to obtain copies of returns. A summary of the guidelines follows:

1. No tax information (a term including tax returns, transcripts of returns, amendments of returns, and any other document containing tax information provided by a debtor under § 521) filed with the bankruptcy court or otherwise provided by the debtor will be available to the public via the Internet, PACER, or CM/ECF.
2. Debtors providing tax information under § 521 should redact personal information as set forth in the Judicial Conference's Policy on Privacy and Public Access to Electronic Case Files. Such redactions include social security numbers, except for the last four digits; names of minor children; dates of birth, except for the year; and financial account numbers, except for the last four digits.
3. Procedure for requesting and obtaining access to tax information filed with the bankruptcy court under § 521(f) requires a written request filed with the court, containing (a) a description of the movant's status in the case, (b) a description of the specific tax information sought, (c) a statement indicating that the information cannot be obtained by the movant from another source, (d) a statement showing a demonstrated need for the tax information, and (e) a statement that the tax information gained will be confidential. The court may impose conditions for providing the tax information and may sanction improper use, disclosure, or dissemination of the information.

## § 6:15 Discharge changes

As will be seen in §§ 7:30 to 7:42, discussing discharge and exceptions from discharge, BAPCPA made significant changes in discharge provisions for all bankruptcy chapters. For Chapter 7 cases, § 727(a)(8) was amended to require expiration of 8 years rather than the former 6 years between discharges. The actual language prohibits a Chapter 7 discharge when the debtor has received a Chapter 7 or 11 discharge "in a case commenced within 8 years before the date of the filing of the [current] petition." In §§ 7:31 to 7:42, the changes to the § 523(a) exceptions from discharge are discussed.

## B. INDIVIDUAL CHAPTER 11 CASES

### § 6:16 Executive summary of changes for individual Chapter 11 debtors

| New Law | Old Law |
|---|---|
| New specific "causes" for conversion or dismissal of case found in amended § 1112(b)(3), including failure to pay post-bankruptcy domestic support obligations | Court had more discretion to determine cause |
| Property of estate includes postpetition property and earnings under new § 1115 | Property of estate looked to prepetition assets |
| Confirmation prerequisites: payment of postpetition domestic support obligation and dedication of disposable income to plan for a minimum of 5 years, with Official Form B22B used for disposable income calculation | No disposable income test |
| Generally, no discharge until completion of plan and discharge delayed if § 522(q) applies | Discharge upon confirmation of plan |

Suggested Resource: Robert J. Keach, Dead Man Filing Redux: Is the New Individual Chapter 11 Unconstitutional?, 13 Am. Bankr. Inst. L. Rev. 483 (2005).

### § 6:17 New provisions for individual Chapter 11 cases

Individual Chapter 11 debtors must comply with the § 521 duties for all debtors in bankruptcy. See discussion of those duties under the checklists of debtor duties. Chapter 11 individual debtors have the same rights to exemptions as other debtors; therefore, the new exclusions from the bankruptcy estate and new exemptions affect these debtors. See those discussions under exclusions from the estate and exemptions in chapter 8. Changes in discharge exceptions and denial of discharge may affect individual Chapter 11 debtors, and those discussions will address the extent to which Chapter 11 is impacted.

As noted under the Checklist of New Duties for Chapter 11 Trustees, if the debtor remains in possession, that debtor in possession will have the new trustee duties, including complying with the domestic relations creditor noticing requirements found in 11 U.S.C.A. § 1106(c).

Among the new grounds for dismissal or conversion of a Chapter 11 case is § 1112(b)(4)(P), which provides that the debtor's failure to pay a domestic support obligation that arose postbankruptcy is cause.

Many individual Chapter 11 cases have been filed for a purpose of adjusting alimony or support obligations, and the changes in the Code concerning domestic support obligations and their nondischargeability will decrease the likelihood of success of such filings. See the discussions of domestic support obligations. Other changes in § 1112 will be discussed in the business bankruptcy sections of this commentary.

Property of the estate for an individual debtor will now include all property described in § 541 that the debtor acquires after filing the case, as well as the debtor's earnings until the case is closed, dismissed, or converted. 11 U.S.C.A. § 1115. Moreover, a Chapter 11 plan filed by an individual debtor must provide for payment of "all or such portion of earnings from personal services performed by the debtor" after the date of the bankruptcy filing "or other future income of the debtor as is necessary for the execution of the plan." 11 U.S.C.A. § 1123(a)(8).

Confirmation requirements for Chapter 11 plans are amended by a new § 1129(a)(14) providing that "if the debtor is required by a judicial or administrative order, or by statute, to pay a domestic support obligation, the debtor has paid all amounts payable under such order or such statute for such obligation that first become payable after the date of the filing of the petition." In other words, the individual debtor may not obtain confirmation unless postpetition domestic support obligations are paid in full.

An additional confirmation requirement found in 11 U.S.C.A. § 1129(a)(15) affects only individual Chapter 11 debtors. In those cases where the holder of an allowed unsecured claim objects to confirmation, either the value of property distributed in the plan to the objecting unsecured creditor must be no less than the value of that unsecured claim or else the value of all property distributed under the plan must be no less than the projected disposable income of the debtor for the longer of a five-year period or the period for which the plan provides for payments. This establishes a disposable income test for individual Chapter 11 debtors, specifically using the definition of disposable income found in 11 U.S.C.A. § 1325(b)(2), and a presumptive minimum five-year plan would be the standard.

Confirmation of an individual debtor's plan will not have the effect of discharging debts until the completion of all plan payments, under 11 U.S.C.A. § 1141(d)(5)(A), except that the court may grant a discharge prior to plan completion under subpart (B). Such an early discharge is conditioned upon a lack of practical ability to modify the confirmed plan and the distribution of all property under the plan to be no less than unsecured creditors would have received in a Chapter 7 liquidation.

Under 11 U.S.C.A. § 1141(d)(5)(C), the court must delay granting any discharge if there is "reasonable cause to believe" that the new exemption § 522(q) applies to this individual debtor. This is the exemption section that caps the homestead exemption at $125,000 under the circumstances described in that section. See the discussion of this section under exemptions in chapter 8.

## § 6:18 Chapter 11 means test form—Official Form B22B

The Judicial Conference of U.S. Courts has adopted a one-page Form B22B for use in Chapter 11 cases filed by individuals, which has as its purpose the calculation of current monthly income for use in the Chapter 11 plan. As the Committee Notes to the form indicate, it is the simplest of the three means testing forms. Those Notes state: "Section 1129(a)(15) requires payments of disposable income 'as defined in section 1325(b)(2),' and that paragraph allows calculation of disposable income under judicially-determined standards, rather than pursuant to the means test deductions, specified for higher income Chapter 13 debtors by § 1325(b)(3). However, § 1325(b)(2) does require that CMI be used as the starting point in the judicial determination of disposable income, and so the Chapter 11 form requires this calculation (in Part I of the form), together with a verification (in Part II)."

### Practice Alerts for Individual Chapter 11

**The usefulness of Chapter 11 for individuals has obviously been reduced considerably. However, some advantages over Chapter 13 remain:**

- **No anti-strip-down under § 506**
- **No charitable contribution limitation**
- **No subsequent discharge limitation**

## C. CHAPTER 12 CASES

## § 6:19 Executive summary of Chapter 12 changes

| New Law | Old Law |
|---|---|
| Permanent chapter of Code | Subject to lapse and temporary extension |
| Extended to family fishermen | Limited to family farmers |
| Debt limit for family farmers increased to $3,237,000 | Debt limit $1,500,000 |
| Case dismissal upon failure to pay postpetition domestic support obligations | No comparable provision |
| Plan may pay less than 100% of domestic support obligation assigned to government, if disposable income dedicated for 5 years | No comparable provision |
| Plan may pay interest to nondischargeable debt if other allowed claims paid 100% | No comparable provision |

| New Law | Old Law |
|---|---|
| Disposable income test expanded to distributions for at least 3 years but excludes postpetition domestic support obligations | No comparable provision |
| Confirmation requires payment of postpetition domestic obligations | No comparable provision |
| Discharge requires payment or plan provision for all domestic support obligations and discharge may be delayed if § 522(q) applies | No comparable provision |

Suggested resources: Katherine M. Porter, Phantom Farmers: Chapter 12 of the Bankruptcy Code, 79 Am. Bankr. L.J. 729 (Summer 2005), available on Westlaw at Legal Periodicals/Law Reviews; Neil E. Harl, Joseph A. Peiffer and Roger McEowen, Major Developments in Chapter 12 Bankruptcy Agricultural Law Digest, Vol. 16, No.8, Page 57–59, April 22, 2005 (also published in Cracking the Code, American Bankruptcy Institute, May 27, 2005). See generally 13 Harl, Agricultural Law Ch. 120 (2005); Harl, Agricultural Law Manual Sec. 13.03 (2005).

## § 6:20 Permanent chapter

Chapter 12 is made a permanent part of the Bankruptcy Code, effective July 1, 2005. Pending the enactment of BAPCPA, Congress had temporarily extended Chapter 12. This July 1 date was the expiration date for the most recent temporary extension of Chapter 12.

## § 6:21 Family fisherman

Chapter 12 relief is extended to include family fishermen, a new term defined in Code § 101(19A) to include individuals "engaged in a commercial fishing operation," or corporations and partnerships engaged in such fishing, provided they are more than 50% owned by a family conducting the business. The debt limit for family fishermen is $1.5 million and at least 80% of the noncontingent, liquidated debts (excluding the debt for the principal residence of the individuals) must arise out of commercial fishing operations. As with family farmers, § 109(f) requires the family fisherman to have "regular annual income," and new § 101(19B) defines a family fisherman with regular annual income to be one with annual income "sufficiently stable and regular to enable" that person to make Chapter 12 plan payments.

## § 6:22 Debt limit increase for family farmer

The debt limit for family farmer is increased, however, from $1.5

million to $3,237,000, and the percentage of debt that must be attributed to the farming operation drops from 80% to 50%; therefore, more family farmers than family fishermen will qualify for Chapter 12 relief under the debt restrictions. 11 U.S.C.A. § 101(18). The debt limits are subject to periodic adjustment by amendment to 11 U.S.C.A. § 104(b). Family farmers are also given a longer look-back for purposes of determining whether 50% of the debt arose from farming, now looking back to the second and third taxable year preceding the filing of bankruptcy.

## § 6:23 Dismissal of case

Section 1208(c)(10) is added as a cause for dismissal of a Chapter 12 case, "failure of the debtor to pay any domestic support obligation that first becomes payable after the date of the filing of the petition." In other words, domestic support obligations, as defined in § 101(14A), that become due and payable after the bankruptcy filing must be paid.

## § 6:24 Plan contents

Chapter 12 plan contents are changed by the addition of § 1222(a)(4):

> [N]otwithstanding any other provision of this section, a plan may provide for less than full payment of all amounts owed for a claim entitled to priority under section 507(a)(1)(B) only if the plan provides that all of the debtor's projected disposable income for a 5-year period beginning on the date that the first payment is due under the plan will be applied to make payments under the plan.

This latter reference to new § 507(a)(1)(B) would apply to domestic support obligations that are assigned to a governmental unit, meaning that a plan might propose to pay less than 100% of such assigned claims only if disposable income is committed to plan payments for a full five years.

Section 1222(b)(11) is added to the effect that Chapter 12 plans would be permitted to "provide for the payment of interest accruing after the date of the filing of the petition on unsecured claims that are nondischargeable under section 1228(a), except that such interest may be paid only to the extent that the debtor has disposable income available to pay such interest after making provision for full payment of all allowed claims." This means that a plan may provide for payment of interest on such nondischargeable debts as student loans, but only if there is excess disposable income for that purpose.

Code § 1222(a)(2) is amended to provide for full payment of § 507 priority claims, unless the claimant agrees to a different treatment of the claim. An exception to this provision would be created for claims owed to a governmental unit as a result of the sale, transfer, exchange, or other disposition of a farm asset used in the debtor's farming operation. Any such governmental claim would be treated as an unsecured claim, not entitled to priority, if and only if the debtor receives a discharge. The specific provision states that a plan may:

(2) provide for the full payment, in deferred cash payments, of all claims entitled to priority under section 507, unless—

(A) the claim is a claim owed to a governmental unit that arises as a result of the sale, transfer, exchange, or other disposition of any farm asset used in the debtor's farming operation, in which case the claim shall be treated as an unsecured claim that is not entitled to priority under section 507, but the debt shall be treated in such manner only if the debtor receives a discharge; or

(B) the holder of a particular claim agrees to a different treatment of that claim.

BAPCPA § 1003 makes this change effective in all cases filed after the enactment, but it specifically does not apply retroactively to Title 11 cases filed before the enactment. The effect of this provision is that § 1222(a)(2) will apply to new Chapter 12 cases filed after enactment, but it would not apply to cases begun under another chapter prior to enactment and then converted to Chapter 12.

## § 6:25 Disposable income

If the trustee or an unsecured creditor objects to confirmation, thus triggering a disposable income application, § 1225(b)(1)(C) is added to provide an alternative method of determining the minimal distributions to unsecured creditors under the plan by looking to the value of the property to be distributed for a three-year period or such longer period as the court approves. This three-year period begins with the first distribution date under the proposed plan rather than looking back in time, and the total property to be distributed must be no less than the debtor's disposable income for that same time period. Unlike Chapter 13, there is no application of a means test in Chapter 12 that would affect the disposable income calculation, and no means testing Official Form exists for Chapter 12 cases.

The exclusion from disposable income is expanded by adding to § 1225(b)(2)(A) "or for a domestic support obligation that first becomes payable after the date of the filing of the petition," meaning that ongoing postpetition domestic support obligations would be excluded from the Chapter 12 debtor's disposable income.

## § 6:26 Confirmation

Plan confirmation in Chapter 12 would have the additional requirement that "the debtor has paid all amounts that are required to be paid under a domestic support obligation and that first become payable after the date of the filing of the petition if the debtor is required by a judicial or administrative order, or by statute, to pay such domestic support obligation." This is found in a new § 1222(a)(7).

## § 6:27 Modification of plan

Section 1229 is amended to prohibit attempts to modify a confirmed plan to increase the amount of any payment that is due under the plan before the proposed modification becomes effective, and this prohibition is applicable even if the debtor had an increase in disposable income, unless the debtor requested an increase in payments. In the final plan year, no one but the debtor may seek an increase in plan payments if it would leave the debtor with insufficient funds to continue the farming operation after completion of the plan.

### § 6:28 Discharge

A precondition to discharge after confirmation of a Chapter 12 plan is found in an addition to § 1228(a) by adding "and in the case of a debtor who is required by a judicial or administrative order, or by statute, to pay a domestic support obligation, after such debtor certifies that all amounts payable under such order or such statute that are due on or before the date of the certification (including amounts due before the petition was filed, but only to the extent provided for by the plan) have been paid" after the former language " . . . completion by the debtor of all payments under the plan." The gist of this addition is that a Chapter 12 debtor must certify the payment in full of domestic support obligations or that the confirmed plan provides for payment of prebankruptcy domestic support obligations. As we have already seen, payment of post-bankruptcy domestic support obligations is required prior to confirmation.

Under 11 U.S.C.A. § 1228(f), the court must delay granting any discharge if there is "reasonable cause to believe" that the new exemption § 522(q) applies to this individual debtor. This is the exemption section that caps the homestead exemption at $125,000 under the circumstances described in that section. See the discussion of this section under exemptions in chapter 8.

## D. CHAPTER 13 CASES

### § 6:29 Executive summary of Chapter 13 changes

| New Law | Old Law |
|---|---|
| New causes for case conversion or dismissal include failure to pay postpetition domestic support obligations and failure to file tax returns | No comparable provision |
| Prerequisites to plan confirmation include filing of required tax returns, filing of petition in good faith, and payment of postpetition domestic support obligations | No comparable provision |

| New Law | Old Law |
|---|---|
| Plan may pay less than 100% of domestic support obligation assigned to government, if disposable income dedicated for five years | No comparable provision |
| Plan may pay interest to nondischargeable debt if other allowed claims paid 100% | No comparable provision |
| Plan may not alter repayment of loans from pension or tax-sheltered plans and such repayments excluded from disposable income | No comparable provision |
| Plan length and disposable income determined by median family income | No comparable provision |
| Confirmation hearing held between 20 and 45 days after meeting of creditors | Confirmation hearing date dependent on local practice-no fixed time by Code |
| Lien of allowed secured claim retained until paid in full or discharge | Lien may have been satisfied prior to discharge |
| Valuations in Chapter 13 do not apply upon conversion to Chapter 7 | Valuations in Chapter 13 applied in any converted case |
| Periodic distributions to allowed secured claims must be in equal monthly amount, sufficient to provide adequate protection, and adequate protection payments begin prior to confirmation | No comparable provisions |
| § 506 valuation does not apply to purchase-money automobile acquired within 910 days of bankruptcy or to other purchase-money collateral acquired within one year | No comparable provisions |
| Prerequisites to discharge include payment of or plan provision for domestic support obligations, waiting period between discharges, and completion of personal financial management course | No comparable provisions |
| Exceptions from discharge expanded and discharge may be delayed if § 522(q)(1) applies | Super discharge more liberal |

## § 6:30 Conversion or dismissal

Section 1307(c)(11) adds as another cause for dismissal or conversion of a Chapter 13 case the "failure of the debtor to pay any domestic support obligation that first becomes payable after the date of the filing of the petition." The same amendment is made in Chapter 12. See § 7:42 for the discussion of domestic support obligation, a term defined in new § 101(14A).

Section 1307(e) requires the court to either dismiss or convert the case upon the failure of the debtor to file a tax return as required under new § 1308, to be discussed below. A party in interest or the U.S. trustee (and presumably a bankruptcy administrator) may move for dismissal or conversion for such failure, and the court "shall" dismiss or convert the case, "whichever is in the best interest of the creditors and the estate." Note that this best-interest analysis does not include consideration of the debtor's personal interest.

## § 6:31 Filing tax returns

A new § 1308 requires the Chapter 13 debtor to file all necessary tax returns (federal, state, or local) that are required under nonbankruptcy law for the four years preceding the bankruptcy filing, and these must be filed "with the appropriate tax authorities" no later than the "day before the date on which the meeting of creditors is first scheduled to be held under section 341(a)." Note that the "filing" referred to here is with the tax authorities and not with the clerk of court nor with the Chapter 13 trustee. However, if the returns are not filed by that date, the Chapter 13 trustee may delay the meeting of creditors for a "reasonable time" to permit the debtor to file any unfiled returns, but this additional time is limited to either the last date that the return is due under nonbankruptcy extensions or 120 days after the first date set for the § 341 meeting. Several questions are raised by these provisions, including: How will the Chapter 13 trustee know that the debtor has not filed with tax authorities, without asking at the meeting of creditors? How does the possible continuation of the creditors' meeting up to 120 days comport with the strict requirement in § 1324(b) that a confirmation hearing be held "not later than 45 days after the date" of the § 341 meeting?

The debtor may move the court for time in addition to what the Chapter 13 trustee may grant by holding open the creditors' meeting, provided that the debtor can demonstrate by a preponderance of evidence that the untimely filing is beyond the debtor's control, but the court's discretion is limited by allowing only an additional 30 days or the nonbankruptcy extension period that is applicable. See 11 U.S.C.A. § 1308(b)(2). This provision may be in tension with new § 1307(e), which requires conversion or dismissal upon the debtor's failure to file tax returns as required by § 1308. For example, if a party in interest moves for dismissal under § 1307(e), the debtor's failure to timely move for an extension under § 1308(b)(2) may require conversion or dismissal of the case. Since the tax filings referred to in §§ 1307(e) and 1308 are filings with the various tax authorities, one may wonder how parties in interest other than the tax authorities will know that the debtor has failed to file required returns, in order to trigger the filing of motions for conversion or dismissal.

In addition to possible conversion or dismissal of the case, a Chapter 13 plan may not be confirmed until the debtor has filed all tax returns required by § 1308. See 11 U.S.C.A. § 1325(a)(9).

These requirements are in addition to § 521(e)'s requirement for Chapter 7 and 13 debtors to "provide" the most recent prebankruptcy tax returns to the trustee no later than seven days prior to the first date set for the meeting of creditors, and the specific Chapter 13 tax filings are in addition to § 521(f)'s requirement for all Chapter 7, 11, and 13 individual debtors, "at the request of the court, the United States trustee, or any party in interest," to "file with the court" all Federal income tax returns, or transcript of returns, that become due during the pendency of the case. See also § 521(f)(4) for Chapter 13 debtors' requirements to file annually "a statement, under penalty of perjury, of the income and expenditures of the debtor during the tax year . . . most recently concluded."

## § 6:32 Plan contents

Chapter 13 plans contents are changed by the following new § 1322(a)(4):

> [N]otwithstanding any other provision of this section, a plan may provide for less than full payment of all amounts owed for a claim entitled to priority under section 507(a)(1)(B) only if the plan provides that all of the debtor's projected disposable income for a 5-year period beginning on the date that the first payment is due under the plan will be applied to make payments under the plan.

This reference to new § 507(a)(1)(B) applies to domestic support obligations that are assigned to a governmental unit, meaning that such claims may be paid less than 100% if disposable income is dedicated to the plan for a full five years. Note that while the language of new § 1322(a)(4) contains the permissive "may," the section itself is added to § 1322(a) which otherwise is preceded by "shall."

Former § 1322(b)(10) is redesignated as (11), and a new § 1322(b)(10) is added to the effect that Chapter 13 plans would be permitted to "provide for the payment of interest accruing after the date of the filing of the petition on unsecured claims that are nondischargeable under section 1328(a), except that such interest may be paid only to the extent that the debtor has disposable income available to pay such interest after making provision for full payment of all allowed claims." An example of this would be that a debtor could propose to pay interest on a nondischargeable student loan and that would be permissible if the debtor had remaining disposable income for that purpose and so long as the debtor's plan otherwise proposed to pay other allowed claims in full. Since the requirement is to pay other allowed claims in full, it is doubtful that many Chapter 13 debtors will have excess disposable income for payment of such interest. If such plan proposals are made, they may present new Chapter 13 plan classification issues, and unfair discrimination issues will arise under this provision. See 11 U.S.C.A. § 1322(b)(1), which was not amended by BAPCPA.

Under § 1322(f), a Chapter 13 plan may not propose any material alteration in a loan by the debtor from a pension, profit-sharing, stock bonus, or other tax-sheltered employee plans. New § 362(b)(19) excludes repayment of these types of loans from the automatic stay, and new § 1322(f) refers to this automatic stay exception for a description of the loans that may not be materially altered. In other words, the debtor's Chapter 13 plan must propose continuation of the terms of such a loan, and the amount needed to repay those loans is specifically excluded from disposable income.

## § 6:33 Length of plan

Code § 1322(d) is amended to substitute the following, which establishes the duration of Chapter 13 plans based upon whether the debtor's current monthly income (the term defined in § 101(10A)) is above or below the applicable median income for the debtor's state:

> (d)(1) If the current monthly income of the debtor and the debtor's spouse combined, when multiplied by 12, is not less than—
>
> (A) in the case of a debtor in a household of 1 person, the median family income of the applicable State for 1 earner;
>
> (B) in the case of a debtor in a household of 2, 3, or 4 individuals, the highest median family income of the applicable State for a family of the same number or fewer individuals; or
>
> (C) in the case of a debtor in a household exceeding 4 individuals, the highest median family income of the applicable State for a family of 4 or fewer individuals, plus $525 per month for each individual in excess of 4,
>
> the plan may not provide for payments over a period that is longer than 5 years.
>
> (2) If the current monthly income of the debtor and the debtor's spouse combined, when multiplied by 12, is less than—
>
> (A) in the case of a debtor in a household of 1 person, the median family income of the applicable State for 1 earner;
>
> (B) in the case of a debtor in a household of 2, 3, or 4 individuals, the highest median family income of the applicable State for a family of the same number or fewer individuals; or
>
> (C) in the case of a debtor in a household exceeding 4 individuals, the highest median family income of the applicable State for a family of 4 or fewer individuals, plus $525 per month for each individual in excess of 4,
>
> the plan may not provide for payments over a period that is longer than 3 years, unless the court, for cause, approves a longer period, but the court may not approve a period that is longer than 5 years.

In this reduced form of means testing, therefore, whether a Chapter 13 debtor's plan must last for three or five years is determined by current monthly income measured against the median income for a family of like size. The statute requires use of both spouses' current monthly income, even if only one spouse is a debtor in bankruptcy, and Official Form B22C is structured accordingly, but permits a "marital adjustment," as seen in the Chapter 7 means testing form, to deduct the nonfiling spouse's CMI to the extent "NOT regularly contributed to the household expenses" of the debtor or debtor's dependents. See Official Form B22C, line 13.

Concurrent with the addition of § 1322(d), § 1325(b)(1)(B) is amended to substitute "applicable commitment period" for the "three-year period" in the former Code, and the term "applicable commitment period" is defined in a new § 1325(b)(4), again measuring the debtor's current monthly income against median income and using the same language as seen in § 1322(d).

Section 1329(c) is also amended to substitute "the applicable commitment period under section 1325(b)(1)(B)" for the former "three years."

## § 6:34 Confirmation hearing date

Code § 1324 is amended to add a subpart (b):

> (b) The hearing on confirmation of the plan may be held not earlier than 20 days and not later than 45 days after the date of the meeting of creditors under section 341(a), unless the court determines that it would be in the best interests of the creditors and the estate to hold such hearing at an earlier date and there is no objection to such earlier date.

Note that the court's discretion to permit an earlier confirmation hearing is dependent on the lack of any objection to the earlier date. Some bankruptcy courts may by local order or rule set the confirmation hearings earlier than the 20 days, or they may conduct preliminary confirmations prior to that time, in order to expedite payments to creditors by the Chapter 13 trustee. Under a strict reading of the statute, if any objection to an earlier confirmation is filed, the court would appear to lose its discretion to expedite the hearing.

## § 6:35 Plan confirmation

Code § 1325(a) is amended to add subsection (7) providing that confirmation of a plan is dependent upon whether "the action of the debtor in filing the petition was in good faith." Whether this addition of a good-faith requirement in the commencement of the case will present conflicts with the reality that the debtor may have been forced into Chapter 13 by dismissal of a Chapter 7 case, based upon abuse under the means test, remains to be seen. "Good faith" is not defined in the Code.

Code § 1325(a)(5)(B)(i) is amended to provide that the holder of an "allowed secured claim" retains its lien until the earlier of payment in full of the contractual obligation under nonbankruptcy law or the granting of a discharge under § 1328. Moreover, if the Chapter 13 case is dismissed or converted to another chapter prior to completion of the plan, the creditor's lien is retained to the extent recognized by the applicable nonbankruptcy law. The effect of these amendments is to prevent the Chapter 13 debtor from paying the secured claim as provided in the plan and obtaining a release of the creditor's lien prior to obtaining a Chapter 13 discharge. These provisions are consistent with the changes made to § 348(f)(1)(C).

Code § 348(f)(1) is amended by changing subpart (B) to provide that valuations in Chapter 13 shall apply in converted cases only if the case is converted to Chapter 11 or 12, but Chapter 13 valuations shall not apply when the case is converted to Chapter 7. Subpart 348(f)(1)(C) is added to control the claims of secured creditors when the Chapter 13 case is converted. The effect of these changes to § 348(f) is to require the secured creditor's claim, as determined under nonbankruptcy law, to be paid in full if the case is converted to Chapter 7 from Chapter 13. Therefore, regardless of any valuation placed on the collateral, assuming it is possible in view of the amendments to § 1325(a), the claim and lien are retained in full upon such a conversion. The debtor could not, for example, take advantage of redeeming the collateral in the case converted to Chapter 7 based upon a reduced value. Also, the effects of a prebankruptcy default are restored upon conversion unless that default has been cured in full while the case was in Chapter 13.

Section 1325(a)(5)(B) is also amended to add subsection (iii):

(iii) if—

(I) property to be distributed pursuant to this subsection is in the form of periodic payments, such payments shall be in equal monthly amounts; and

(II) the holder of the claim is secured by personal property, the amount of such payments shall not be less than an amount sufficient to provide to the holder of such claim adequate protection during the period of the plan.

These additions require that Chapter 13 plans must provide for payment to secured claims in equal monthly periodic payments that equal at least an amount sufficient to provide the secured creditor with adequate protection. Will these provisions disrupt the practical administration of Chapter 13 plans under current law? They will if they are interpreted to mean that all secured creditors must be paid in equal monthly payments, beginning promptly after filing. For example, current practice in many districts is to permit payment of the arrearages on home mortgages prior to beginning payment of automobile debts. If the automobile creditor must be paid in equal monthly payments and those payments must provide adequate protection throughout the plan, doesn't that mean that such creditors cannot be delayed in receiving payment? If the debtor's monthly income is not sufficient to cure the home mortgage arrearage while making ongoing mortgage payments and making monthly payments to all other secured creditors, either the plan will not be feasible or the debtor must make an election on which collateral will be retained.

Section 1325(a) is further amended to add at the end a provision that § 506 does not apply in determining a secured claim, for purposes of § 1325(a)(5), if the creditor has a purchase-money security interest in a motor vehicle purchased by the debtor for the debtor's personal use within 910 days before the filing of the bankruptcy or if the debtor has purchased other purchase-money collateral within one year of the filing. The Code uses the definition of "motor vehicle" found in 49 U.S.C.A. § 30102. The 910 days is approximately two and one-half years. Of course, there will be factual scenarios where the Chapter 13 debtor will have purchased a motor vehicle not for the debtor's personal use, in which event the prohibition against using § 506 would not control. The effect of this amendment is to prohibit the strip-down of purchase-money secured claims that are covered by the amendment, thus requiring their full payment under the contract terms. It is interesting that the same "personal use" restriction is not found in the reference to nonvehicle purchase-money collateral; therefore, it appears that any nonvehicle collateral purchased within one year of the bankruptcy and secured by a purchase-money security interest would be subject to full payment of the contract price in Chapter 13, even if it were not for purely personal use. Does this mean, for example, that if a business Chapter 13 debtor purchased nonvehicle collateral for business use, it would not be subject to strip-down in value? It would appear so.

Suggested Resource: Jean Braucher, *Rash* and the Ride-Through Redux: The Terms for Holding on to Cars, Homes, and Other Collateral Under the 2005 Act, 13 Am. Bankr. Inst. L. Rev. 457 (2005).

There are claims-allowance issues related to this addition to § 1325 since it refers to § 506 not applying to a claim described in § 1325(a)(5). Section 1325(a)(5) depends upon a claim being "allowed," and § 506 is the statute governing allowance of secured claims; thus questions will arise as to how a creditor can obtain a secured claim.

Plan confirmation in Chapter 13 will have the additional requirement that "the debtor has paid all amounts that are required to be paid under a domestic support obligation and that first become payable after the date of the filing of the petition if the debtor is required by a judicial or administrative order, or by statute, to pay such domestic support obligation." This is a new § 1325(a)(8). Also, under § 1325(a)(9), confirmation depends upon the debtor having filed those tax returns required by new § 1308.

## § 6:36 Disposable income

Code § 1325(b)(1)(A) is amended to require that the disposable income dedicated to the plan must be paid to unsecured creditors, but there is no change to the requirement that a disposable income test is only triggered if "the trustee or the holder of an allowed unsecured claim objects to the confirmation." Nevertheless, Official Form B22C is structured to require the debtor to analyze how disposable income will be calculated. See Official Form B22C, Part III.

The former § 1325(b)(2) defining disposable income is struck and in its place inserted:

> (2) For purposes of this subsection, the term "disposable income" means current monthly income received by the debtor (other than child support

payments, foster care payments, or disability payments for a dependent child made in accordance with applicable nonbankruptcy law to the extent reasonably necessary to be expended for such child) less amounts reasonably necessary to be expended—

(A)

(i) for the maintenance or support of the debtor or a dependent of the debtor, or for a domestic support obligation, that first becomes payable after the date the petition is filed; and

(ii) for charitable contributions (that meet the definition of 'charitable contribution' under section 548(d)(3) to a qualified religious or charitable entity or organization (as defined in section 548(d)(4)) in an amount not to exceed 15 percent of gross income of the debtor for the year in which the contributions are made; and

(B) if the debtor is engaged in business, for the payment of expenditures necessary for the continuation, preservation, and operation of such business.

(3) Amounts reasonably necessary to be expended under paragraph (2) shall be determined in accordance with subparagraphs (A) and (B) of section 707(b)(2), if the debtor has current monthly income, when multiplied by 12, greater than—

(A) in the case of a debtor in a household of 1 person, the median family income of the applicable State for 1 earner;

(B) in the case of a debtor in a household of 2, 3, or 4 individuals, the highest median family income of the applicable State for a family of the same number or fewer individuals; or

(C) in the case of a debtor in a household exceeding 4 individuals, the highest median family income of the applicable State for a family of 4 or fewer individuals, plus $525 per month for each individual in excess of 4.

As BAPCPA refers to these additions to § 1325(b), they represent a form of the means test applicable in Chapter 13. The monetary cap is subject to the periodic adjustment provided by amended 11 U.S.C.A. § 104(b). Official Form B22C, Part III compares the debtor's annualized current monthly income (as that term is defined in § 101(10A)) with median income for the debtor's family size and state of residence. If the CMI is more than the applicable median income, disposable income is determined under new § 1325(b)(3), which then takes into account the expense deductions found in the § 707(b)(2) Chapter 7 means test. If the CMI is not more than the applicable median income, disposable income is determined under the former "reasonably necessary" expense test, but disposable income still starts with CMI, which under § 101(10A) looks back to the debtor's prebankruptcy income rather than looking forward to projected income. As a result, serious issues include whether the trustee or unsecured creditors can effectively raise disposable income arguments based upon projected increases in the Chapter 13 debtor's income. The disposable income tests, under either median income approach, will not be an accurate measure of future ability to pay in a plan; rather, the tests look back to the CMI, a result that is not favorable to unsecured creditors.

Withholdings for deferred compensation and tax qualified retirement plans, as well as for repayment of loans from such plans, are not disposable income for purposes of § 1325(b)(2), but that provision is found in new § 1322(f). See also the discussion of the exclusion from the bankruptcy estate of such withholdings under the amendment to § 541(b)(7) and the amendment of § 362(b)(19), as well as the exception from discharge found in § 523(a)(18).

Section 1325(b)(2) is amended to exclude from disposable income in a Chapter 13 any amounts needed for the maintenance or support of the debtor or debtor's dependents or for a domestic support obligation that first becomes payable after the filing of the bankruptcy petition. Also excluded are any child support, foster care payments, or disability payments received by the debtor for a dependent child if those payments are made under nonbankruptcy law.

The charitable contribution exception from disposable income, up to 15% of the debtor's gross income, continues to exist in the amended Code. See 11 U.S.C.A. § 1325(b)(2)(A)(ii).

## § 6:37 Plan payments

Section 1326(a) is amended to replace the current section completely with the requirement that, unless the court orders otherwise, the debtor must begin plan payments no later than 30 days after the earlier of filing the plan or the order for relief. The plan payments must be paid to the trustee in the amount as proposed in the plan, but the debtor must pay directly to the lessor of personal property the amount of the lease that becomes due after the bankruptcy filing pending plan confirmation, and the amount payable to the trustee can be reduced by the lease payments, provided proof is given to the trustee.

Pending confirmation, the debtor must pay adequate protection payments to the holders of purchase-money claims that are secured by personal property, at least to the extent of that portion of the obligation that comes due after the bankruptcy filing, again reducing the payments to the trustee in that amount paid to such creditors, provided that proof of payment is given to the trustee.

The court may, after notice and hearing, increase or reduce the amount of the payments required to lessors and secured creditors, pending confirmation. 11 U.S.C.A. § 1326(a)(3).

Unless a practical solution is found, the payments directly to lessors and secured creditors will create administrative problems. How would such payments be accounted for and would those creditors be required to amend their claims to reflect the payments received from the debtor? How will the debtor deal with disputes about the amount of the claim when the trustee does not have records of payments made and is not the disburser of those payments? Courts may, by local rule or order, establish a procedure for preconfirmation adequate protection payments to be funneled through the Chapter 13 trustee, a result that all parties would likely favor in order to obtain the benefits of the trustee's accounting. See Richard J. Hayden, Adequate Protection in Chapter 13 Cases under the New Code § 1326(a), available at http://abiworld.net/newsletter/consumerbankr/vol13num5/1326.html.

## § 6:38 Insurance

By amendment to § 1326(a)(4):

> Not later than 60 days after the date of filing of a case under this chapter, a debtor retaining possession of personal property subject to a lease or securing a claim attributable in whole or in part to the purchase price of such property shall provide the lessor or secured creditor reasonable evidence of the maintenance of any required insurance coverage with respect to the use or ownership of such property and continue to do so for so long as the debtor retains possession of such property.

The current practice in some districts of requiring proof of insurance or otherwise forced placing of insurance in the plan for the benefit of the vehicle creditor is adopted and expanded to other secured creditors.

## § 6:39 Prior case trustee's claim

If a Chapter 7 trustee has been allowed compensation due to conversion or dismissal of a Chapter 7 case under § 707(b), the abuse test, any unpaid portion will be paid in the subsequent Chapter 13 case. The payment shall be monthly, with a cap depending upon the amount of other unsecured claims in the case. 11 U.S.C.A. § 1326(b)(3) and (d).

## § 6:40 Discharge

A precondition to discharge is found in an addition to § 1328(a), adding the following:

> [I]in the case of a debtor who is required by a judicial or administrative order, or by statute, to pay a domestic support obligation, after such debtor certifies that all amounts payable under such order or such statute that are due on or before the date of the certification (including amounts due before the petition was filed, but only to the extent provided for by the plan) have been paid.

The gist of this addition is that a Chapter 13 debtor must certify the payment in full of domestic support obligations or that the confirmed plan provides for payment of prebankruptcy domestic support obligations.

For Chapter 13 debtors, § 1328(f) is added to provide that the court may not grant a discharge under that chapter if the debtor has received a Chapter 7, 11, or 12 discharge in a prior case filed within four years preceding the filing of the current Chapter 13 case or, if the debtor has received a Chapter 13 discharge in a case filed within two years of the filing of the current case.

The Chapter 13 discharge that may be granted upon completion of plan payments is changed and more restricted by the substitution of a new § 1328(a), excepting from the discharge those debts:

(1) provided for under section 1322(b)(5);

(2) of the kind specified in section 507(a)(8)(C) or in paragraph (1)(B), (1)(C), (2), (3), (4), (5), (8), or (9) of section 523(a);

(3) for restitution, or a criminal fine, included in a sentence on the debtor's conviction of a crime; or

(4) for restitution, or damages, awarded in a civil action against the debtor as a result of willful or malicious injury by the debtor that caused personal injury to an individual or the death of an individual.

As a result of this amendment to § 1328(a), all debts that are excepted from discharge under § 523(a)(1)(B) and (C), (2), (3), (4), (5), (8), and (9) are now excepted from the Chapter 13 discharge. The reference to § 507(a)(8)(C) brings within the exception those taxes that the debtor was responsible for collecting or withholding. Also, any judgment for damages or restitution resulting from a willful or malicious injury that caused personal injury or death would be excepted from discharge. Note that this subsection uses "willful or malicious," rather than § 523(a)(6)'s requirement of "willful and malicious." Does this mean that the Chapter 13 discharge is even more limited than a possible discharge under Chapter 7? That would seem to be likely, since "or" is broader than "and."

The court may not grant a Chapter 13 debtor a discharge until the debtor has completed an "instructional course concerning personal financial management" as those courses are defined in § 111. See 11 U.S.C.A. § 1328(g) and the discussion of debtor education at 7:28.

In addition, the court must delay granting a discharge if it appears that the new § 522(q)(1) applies to the debtor or if any action is pending where the debtor may be found guilty of a felony as described in § 522(q)(1)(A) or liable for a debt as described in § 522(q)(1)(B). This and the other changes to discharge in Chapter 13 are discussed in William Houston Brown, Taking Exception to a Debtor's Discharge: The 2005 Bankruptcy Amendments Make It Easier, 79 Am. Bankr. L. J. 419 (Spring 2005), available on Westlaw at Legal Periodicals/Law Reviews.

## § 6:41 Modification of plan after confirmation

Code § 1329(a) is amended by adding subsection (4), providing that a Chapter 13 debtor's plan may be modified to reduce payments that might otherwise be required in order to permit the purchase of health insurance for the debtor and dependents without such insurance coverage, provided that the expenses are reasonable and necessary and that the amount of insurance and the cost of the premium are in line with coverage previously held or with coverage for similarly situated persons. Moreover, the debtor cannot double up this expense: If disposable income has already been reduced for health insurance, the new purchase cannot increase that prior deduction. Proof that the debtor purchased the health insurance can be demanded.

It is odd that permitting purchase of health insurance is found in the postconfirmation modification section. Surely a debtor would be permitted to purchase such insurance and deduct it from disposable income rather than waiting until after confirmation to do so. Note that Official Form B22C, which is used to determine the length of a Chapter 13 plan and possibly the disposable income, at line 39, allows a deduction for the expense of health and other insurance. The form assumes, therefore, that the debtor can obtain health insurance prior to confirmation.

## § 6:42 Chapter 13 means test form—Official Form B22C

As mentioned in prior discussion, new Official Form B22C has been issued for use in Chapter 13 to determine two things: the "applicable period," whether 3 or 5 years, for a Chapter 13 plan and the debtor's disposable income if the debtor's current monthly income exceeds the applicable median income. While that form is not replicated here, the Committee Notes to the form are instructive on the purposes and uses of the form, and those Notes provide:

> Like the Chapter 7 form, the form for Chapter 13 debtors contains a number of special provisions. The upper right corner of the first page includes check boxes requiring the debtor to state whether, under the calculations required by the statement, the applicable commitment period under § 1325(b)(4) is three years or five years and whether the means test deductions are required by § 1325(b)(3) to be used in determining the debtor's disposable income. The check box is intended to inform standing trustees and other interested parties about these items, but does not prevent the debtor from arguing that the calculations required by the form do not accurately reflect the debtor's disposable income.
>
> Part I of the form is a report of income to be used for determining CMI. Section 1325(b)(4) imposes a five-year applicable commitment period—rather than a three-year period—if the debtor's annualized CMI is not less than a defined median state income. For this purpose, as under § 707(b)(4), the CMI of the debtor's spouse is required by the statute to be combined with the debtor's CMI, and there is no exception for spouses who are legally separated or living separately. Accordingly, the report of income in Part I directs a combined reporting of the income of both spouses in all cases of married debtors.
>
> Part II of the form computes the applicable commitment period by annualizing the income calculated in Part I and comparing it to the applicable state median. The form allows debtors to contend that the income of a nonfiling spouse should not be treated as CMI and permits debtors to claim a deduction for any income of a nonfiling spouse to the extent that this income was not contributed to the household expenses of the debtor or the debtor's dependents. The debtor is directed to check the appropriate box at the beginning of the form, stating the applicable commitment period.
>
> Part III of the form compares the debtor's CMI to the applicable state median, allowing a determination of whether the means-test deductions must be used, pursuant to § 1325(b)(3), in calculating disposable income. For this purpose, since § 1325(b)(3) does not provide for including the income of the debtor's spouse, the form directs a deduction of the income of a nonfiling spouse that is not contributed to the household expenses of the debtor or the debtor's dependents. Again, the debtor is directed to check the appropriate box at the beginning of the form, indicating whether the means test deductions are applicable. If so, the debtor is directed to complete the remainder of the form. If not, the debtor is directed to complete the verification in Part VII but not complete the other parts of the form.
>
> Part IV provides for calculation of the means-test deductions provided

in § 707(b)(2), described above, as incorporated by § 1325(b)(3) for debtors with CMI above the applicable state median.

Part V provides for three adjustments required by special provisions affecting disposable income in Chapter 13. First, § 1325(b)(2) itself excludes from the CMI used in determining disposable income certain "child support payments, foster care payments, [and] disability payments for a dependent child." Because payments of this kind are included in the definition of CMI in § 101(10A), a line entry for deduction of these payments is provided. Second, a line entry is provided for deduction of contributions by the debtor to certain retirement plans, listed in § 541(b)(7)(B), since that provision states that such contributions "shall not constitute disposable income, as defined in section 1325(b)." Third, the same line entry also allows a deduction from disposable income for payments on loans from retirement accounts that are excepted from the automatic stay by § 362(b)(19), since § 1322(f) provides that for a "loan described in section 362(b)(19) . . . any amounts required to repay such loan shall not constitute 'disposable income' under section 1325."

The Chapter 13 form does not provide a deduction from disposable income for the Chapter 13 debtor's anticipated attorney fees. There is no specific statutory allowance for such a deduction, and none appears necessary. Section 1325(b)(1)(B) requires that disposable income contributed to a Chapter 13 plan be used to pay "unsecured creditors." A debtor's attorney who has not taken a security interest in the debtor's property is an unsecured creditor who may be paid from disposable income.

Part VI of the form allows the debtor to claim additional deductions, as described above, and Part VII is the verification.

# Chapter 7

# Changes in Code Sections That Apply to All Chapters

## § 7:1 Administrative expenses

Section 503(b)(1)(A) is amended to add a new subsection (A)(ii) allowing administrative expenses for the wages and benefits awarded by a judicial proceeding or an NLRB proceeding. Subsection 503(b)(1)(D) is added to make it clear that a governmental unit does not need to file a request for payment of expenses related to taxes in order to be allowed an administrative expense for those taxes and related fines or penalties.

Section 503(b)(7) is added concerning nonresidential real property leases previously assumed but then rejected. See the discussion of lease assumptions in chapter 9 of this book. Essentially, § 503(b)(7) sets a two-year cap on an administrative priority claim for damages resulting from rejection of a nonresidential lease that had been previously assumed. The two years is measured from the later of the rejection or the actual turnover of the property. All other such lease-rejection damages may be allowable as unsecured claims under § 502(b)(6).

Section 503(b)(8) is added to permit administrative expenses for the actual and necessary costs related to closing a health care business. See discussion of health care businesses in chapter 9.

Section 503(b)(9) adds an administrative expense claim for the value of goods received by the debtor within 20 days of the filing of the case where the goods were sold to the debtor in the ordinary course of the debtor's business. This new category works in hand with the expanded reclamation rights given the sellers of goods under the amendment to § 546(c), which are discussed in chapter 9. If such sellers fail to comply with those reclamation requirements, they may still have an administrative claim under § 503(b)(9).

Section 503(c) is added to restrict the allowance of administrative claims and severance payments for insiders of the debtor. This section is a part of the limitations imposed on Key Employee Retention Plans (KERPs), which are discussed further in chapter 9. This section sets out criteria and limitations on transfers to or for the benefit of insiders made "for the purpose of inducing such person to remain with the debtor's business," and a court finding that the criteria has been satisfied is required.

## § 7:2 Appeals

28 U.S.C.A. § 158(d) is amended to provide that the court of appeals has jurisdiction for all final orders of a bankruptcy court and may take an appeal directly if the bankruptcy court, district court, or bankruptcy appellate panel, on the lower court's own motion or on the motion of a party to the judgment, certifies that the bankruptcy court's final order involves a question of law on which there is no controlling decision in that circuit or that the issue involves one of public importance, or that an immediate appeal is otherwise necessary. See *In re Virissimo*, 332 B.R. 208, Bankr. L. Rep. (CCH) P 80385 (Bankr. D. Nev. 2005), certifying an appeal to the Ninth Circuit Court of Appeals.

## § 7:3 Attorneys and other professionals

28 U.S.C.A. § 1334 is amended to substitute a new subsection (e) giving the district court exclusive jurisdiction over not only all property of the debtor and of the bankruptcy estate but also over "all claims or causes of action that involve construction of section 327" of the Bankruptcy Code, as well as "rules relating to disclosure requirements under section 327." This amendment took effect upon enactment as to all cases filed after that date.

Section 504 of Title 11 dealing with sharing of compensation is amended by adding a new subsection (c) to remove from § 504's restrictions of any sharing of compensation "with a bona fide public service attorney referral program."

In compensating professional persons, the court may consider whether that person is board certified "or otherwise has demonstrated skill and experience in the bankruptcy field." 11 U.S.C.A. § 330(a)(3)(E).

By amendment to § 330(a)(7), a trustee's compensation must be calculated on a commission basis as described in § 326, while other professionals may be paid on an hourly, fixed fee, or percentage fee basis when they are employed under § 328. See 11 U.S.C.A. § 328(a).

A significant provision of BAPCPA that affects attorneys relates to the debt relief agency designation, and court decisions are emerging on whether that designation applies to attorneys practicing in bankruptcy court. See the discussion of debt relief agency in this chapter, as well as other discussions concerning professionals in chapter 9.

## § 7:4 Audits

The U.S. trustee or bankruptcy administrator will be responsible for conducting random audits of 0.4% of Chapter 7 and 13 cases with the purpose of determining the accuracy, veracity, and completeness of petitions and schedules. The debtor's failure to cooperate in such an audit is grounds for revocation of discharge under § 727(d)(4), and the debtor generally has a duty to cooperate. 11 U.S.C.A. § 521(a)(2)(C).

## § 7:5 Automatic stay—Executive summary of expanded exceptions

| New Law | Old Law |
|---|---|
| 28 exceptions from stay | 18 exceptions from stay |
| In rem relief as to real estate | No comparable provision |
| Domestic relations exception expanded | More limited exception under § 362(b)(2) |
| Retirement loan repayment exception | No comparable provision |
| Ineligible debtor exception | No comparable provision |
| Residential landlord exceptions | No comparable provision |
| Setoff of taxes | Setoff governed exclusively by § 553 |
| Effects of prior filings limit or prevent stay | No comparable provision |
| Failure to timely carry out § 522(a)(2) duty | No comparable provision |
| Termination of stay when court fails to decide within 60 days | 30 days, unless extended by court |
| Damages for stay violations more restricted under new § 362(k) | Damages formerly under § 362(h) |

Resource suggestion: Lisa A. Napoli, The Not-So-Automatic Stay: Legislative Changes to the Automatic Stay in a Case Filed by or Against an Individual Debtor, 79 Am. Bankr. L. J. 749 (2005), available on Westlaw at Legal Periodicals/Law Reviews.

## § 7:6 Automatic stay—Domestic relations exception

A new § 362(b)(2) replaces the former subsection (2), expanding the exception from the stay, and incorporating the term "domestic support obligation," which is defined in § 101(14A). The amended exception provides that the commencement of a bankruptcy case does not prevent:

(A) . . . the commencement or continuation of a civil action or proceeding—

(i) for the establishment of paternity;

(ii) for the establishment or modification of an order for domestic support obligations;

(iii) concerning child custody or visitation;

(iv) for the dissolution of a marriage, except to the extent that such proceeding seeks to determine the division of property that is property of the estate; or

(v) regarding domestic violence;

(B) . . . the collection of a domestic support obligation from property that is not property of the estate;

(C) with respect to the withholding of income that is property of the estate or property of the debtor for payment of a domestic support obligation under a judicial or administrative order or a statute;

(D) . . . the withholding, suspension, or restriction of a driver's license, a professional or occupational license, or a recreational license, under State law, as specified in section 466(a)(16) of the Social Security Act;

(E) . . . the reporting of overdue support owed by a parent to any consumer reporting agency as specified in section 466(a)(7) of the Social Security Act;

(F) . . . the interception of a tax refund, as specified in sections 464 and 466(a)(3) of the Social Security Act or under an analogous State law; or

(G) . . . the enforcement of a medical obligation, as specified under title IV of the Social Security Act.

11 U.S.C.A. § 362(b)(2). The expanded exception may conflict with a reorganizing debtor's ability to fund a plan; for example, permitting the collection of a domestic support obligation by allowing the suspension of a license will impact a debtor's ability to work. As a result, there will be an increased need for some debtors to attempt to obtain injunctive relief that would impose a stay against some creditor action.

Resource suggestion: William Houston Brown, Bankruptcy and Domestic Relations Manual (2005), a Thomson/West publication.

## § 7:7 Automatic stay—Tax impacts

A new proceeding stay is found in § 362(a)(8), staying tax court proceedings concerning a corporate debtor's liability for a taxable period that the bankruptcy court may determine or concerning the tax liability of an individual debtor for a taxable period ending before the date of the order for relief. This is the only change made by BAPCPA to § 362(a).

Section 362(b)(18) expands the exception for the creation or perfection of statutory liens for ad valorem property taxes, to add an exception for special taxes and assessments on real property whether or not they fall within the ad valorem category.

An exception from the stay is added in § 362(b)(26) to permit setoff under applicable nonbankruptcy law of an income tax refund by a governmental unit as to a taxable period ending before the order for relief against a tax liability for a period ending before the order for relief, unless nonbankruptcy law does not permit the setoff.

## § 7:8 Automatic stay—Pension loan repayment exception

Section 362(b)(19) excepts from the stay the continuing withholding from the debtor's wages and the collection of loan amounts due as a result of the debtor's borrowing from employer-sponsored pension, profit-sharing, stock bonus, or other plans recognized by the IRS as tax exempt. This exception goes hand-in-hand with the exclusion of such withholdings from property of the estate, Code § 541(b)(7); the exception from discharge of such repayment obligations, Code § 523(a)(18); and the recognition in Chapter 13 that such loan repayment withholdings are not disposable income, and with the prohibition against a Chapter 13 debtor materially modifying such loan terms, Code § 1322(f). These changes may be of benefit to some debtors, since some prior case law required debtors to stop such repayments or treated them as disposable income, which may have caused withdrawal penalties and other tax consequences.

## § 7:9 Automatic stay—In rem enforcement exception

A new subsection 362(b)(20) excludes from the automatic stay actions to enforce liens or security interests following entry of an in rem order described in the new § 362(d)(4), unless the debtor in the subsequent bankruptcy case successfully reinstates the automatic stay under the provisions of (d)(4), which would require the debtor in the subsequent case to show changed circumstances or other "good cause." Code § 362(d)(4) provides that, as to real property, if the court finds that the bankruptcy case was filed as part of a "scheme to delay, hinder, and defraud creditors" [note that the language is "and" rather than "or"], either by the transfer of all or part of an interest in the realty without the secured creditor's consent or by multiple bankruptcy filings that affect the realty (presumably stopping foreclosure actions, for example), the court may grant in rem relief from the automatic stay. That is, the relief from the stay would have a binding effect in any other bankruptcy case that might be filed within two years of the entry of the order, provided that the order was also recorded in compliance with state real estate noticing laws. A debtor in a subsequent case who may be affected by this in rem order could move for relief from the order to reinstate a stay, provided that the debtor must show a change of circumstances since entry of the order or other good cause. The subsection specifically provides that federal, state, or local governmental units must accept a certified copy of the in rem order for "indexing and recording."

Some bankruptcy courts had entered in rem orders prior to BAPCPA, even without specific statutory authority, and an issue arising from the addition of § 362(d)(4), which is restricted to realty, is whether courts implicitly now have no authority to give in rem relief as to personal property.

### § 7:10 Automatic stay—Ineligible debtor exception

A new § 362(b)(21) excludes from the automatic stay any action taken to enforce a lien or security interest if the debtor is ineligible to file bankruptcy under § 109(g) or if the case was filed in violation of a bankruptcy court order prohibiting the debtor from being a debtor under Title 11. Presumably, these provisions would mean that the stay does not come into effect, even though the court only later determined that the debtor was not eligible to file, but this creates a problem if the court finds that the debtor was in fact eligible to file.

### § 7:11 Automatic stay—Eviction exceptions

A new subsection (b)(22) excludes from the stay, but subject to a new § 362(l), the "continuation of any eviction, unlawful detainer action, or similar proceeding by a lessor" of residential property where a prebankruptcy judgment for possession has been obtained against the tenant/debtor. New subsection (b)(23) excludes from the stay, subject to new § 362(m), an "eviction action that seeks possession of the residential property in which the debtor resides as a tenant," if the eviction is based on "endangerment of such property or the illegal use of controlled substances on such property," but to take advantage of § 362(b)(23) the landlord must file with the court a "certification under penalty of perjury." The landlord's certification must assert that an eviction proceeding has begun or that the necessary endangerment or illegal use has occurred within 30 days of the bankruptcy filing.

The new subsection § 362(l) provides that the exception for the landlord in § 362(b)(22) shall be delayed for 30 days, that is, the stay would be in effect for that time, if the debtor files with the bankruptcy petition a certification under penalty of perjury that there are circumstances recognized by applicable nonbankruptcy law that would permit the debtor to cure "the entire monetary default that gave rise to the judgment for possession," and the debtor must deposit with the clerk of the court sufficient money to pay any rent becoming due during the 30-day period following bankruptcy filing. Assuming the debtor does all of this, the stay would be in effect until the court ordered otherwise, but if the landlord objected to the certification, a hearing must be held within 10 days of the objection. The revised Official Form 1, the petition, has boxes for the debtor to check, indicating that such a prebankrutpcy judgment has been taken and that the debtor is filing the necessary certification. The possible remedy offered to a debtor by § 362(l) may be hollow if nonbankrupcty law does not permit the curing of a defaulted lease after a judgment for possession has been entered.

Subsection 362(m) is similar to § 362(l) but requires the debtor to object within 15 days of the landlord's certification that the tenancy is endangering the property or that the tenant is conducting the described illegal activity. A hearing must be held within 10 days of the debtor's objection, and the debtor has the burden of satisfying the court that the conditions complained of by the landlord have been remedied in order to keep the stay in effect.

## § 7:12 Automatic stay—Transfer exception

A new subsection 362(b)(24) excludes from the stay "any transfer that is not avoidable under section 544 and that is not avoidable under section 549." While at first reading one wonders how a transfer could be both a prebankruptcy one covered by § 544 and a postbankrutpcy one covered by § 549, Judge Randy Haines in an article, Does BAPCPA Validate Some Postpetition Foreclosure Sales That Would Otherwise Violate the Automatic Stay?, in the Norton Bankruptcy Law Adviser (September 2005), points out that § 362(b)(24) could permit the foreclosure of property that began prebankruptcy and concluded postbankruptcy with a transfer to a good faith purchaser without knowledge of the bankruptcy filing. Judge Haines suggests that debtors' counsel need to consider whether recordation of a bankruptcy petition is wise in order to give notice through recording to such a potential good faith purchaser.

## § 7:13 Automatic stay—Securities regulation exception

Section 362(b)(25) excepts from the stay the commencement or continuation of an investigation or action by a securities regulatory agency.

## § 7:14 Automatic stay—Netting agreement setoff

Section 362(b)(27) recognizes an exception for a setoff by a master netting agreement participant.

## § 7:15 Automatic stay—Social Security Act exception

The stay does not apply to the Secretary of Health and Human Services for the purpose of excluding the debtor's participation in Medicare or other federal health care programs. 11 U.S.C.A. § 362(b)(28).

## § 7:16 Automatic stay—Effect of prior filings

Section 362(c) is amended to add subsections (3) and (4), which broadly restrict application of the stay when the debtor has previously been in bankruptcy within one year of the current case. If the individual debtor has been in a single or joint Chapter 7, 11, or 13 case, whether filed or merely pending, within one year of filing the current case and that prior case was dismissed (unless it was dismissed and the current case filed as a result of § 707(b)), § 362(c)(3) applies, providing that the automatic stay with respect to any action taken against the debtor as well as the debtor's property or lease "shall terminate with *respect to the debtor* on the 30th day" after filing the current case (emphasis added). Note that the statute says that the stay terminates "with respect to the debtor" but does not mention property of the bankruptcy estate. Obviously, an issue exists as to whether this § 362(c)(3) would permit the stay to remain in effect as to any property that had come into the bankruptcy estate upon the bankruptcy filing, even though the stay terminated as to the debtor personally. A party in interest, which would include the debtor and case trustee as well as other parties, may move to keep the stay in effect but only if a motion is filed within the first 30 days of the case and then the moving party must show that the current case was filed in good faith.

Good faith is not defined in the statute, and case law will interpret what is required to show the required good faith. See, for example, *In re Havner*, 2006 WL 51214 (Bankr. M.D. N.C. 2006), holding that good faith under § 362(c)(3) may be found under a totality-of-circumstances examination and applying the same guidelines for such an examination as existed under pre-BAPCPA law.

Section 362(c)(3) applies only when the debtor has been in one prior bankruptcy case within the preceding year. In those instances, there is a presumption that the current case was filed in bad faith if the prior case was dismissed due to the debtor's failure to file required documents or otherwise comply with a court order or if the debtor failed in the first case to pay adequate protection ordered by the court or otherwise perform plan terms. To defeat the presumption, the debtor must show that there has been a substantial change in circumstances and good reason to believe the debtor will carry the current case through to discharge. 11 U.S.C.A. § 362(c)(3)(C).

If the debtor was in two or more cases within the one-year period before the current bankruptcy filing and those cases were dismissed in that year, § 362(c)(4) provides that the automatic stay does not go into effect with the third or more filing. Here, the automatic stay is not triggered, therefore, unlike § 362(c)(3), there is not an question of whether it applies to property of the bankruptcy estate-it never comes into effect, unless the debtor or another party moves successfully to impose the automatic stay. On request of a party in interest, the court "shall promptly enter an order confirming that no stay is in effect." Presumably such an order would require the court to verify without the benefit of a hearing that the request for such an order was based upon correct facts; therefore, practice under § 362(c)(4) will determine whether courts require a hearing before entering such "comfort" orders. The debtor or another party in interest may still try to put the stay into effect by filing a motion within 30 days of the bankruptcy filing, again with the burden of showing that the latest filing was in good faith and again having to overcome any presumption of bad faith. Under § 362(c)(4), the presumption of lack of good faith exists more broadly than under § 362(c)(3), and the presumption must be overcome with "clear and convincing evidence to the contrary." 11 U.S.C.A. § 362(c)(4)(D).

**Practice Alerts for Code § 362(c)**

- **Debtors have an affirmative requirement to move to extend the automatic stay beyond the first 30 days of the case or to impose the automatic stay. Code § 362(c)(3) and (4).**
- **Such motions must be filed within the first 30 days of the**

**case and an expedited hearing should be requested, since the hearing must be completed within that 30 days; otherwise, the stay will terminate or never come into effect. Code § 362(c)(3)(B).**

**• If the court orders an imposition of the automatic stay under Code § 362(c)(4), the stay is only effective from entry of the order. Code § 362(c)(4)(C).**

**• Debtors and their counsel should consider whether injunctive relief, such as a temporary restraining order, is advisable, in addition to a motion to extend or impose the stay, especially where creditor action such as foreclosure is pending. Since the stay may not be effective until the court so orders, the creditor could be taking adverse actions, especially under Code § 362(c)(4), where no stay is in effect until the court order.**

**• Debtors and their counsel should determine their court's standards of proof required, and whether an actual hearing is required, to overcome the presumption of lack of good faith. Code § 362(c)(3)(C) and (c)(4)(D). An issue exists whether the presumption is triggered only by a creditor's objection to the motion or whether the statutory presumption requires the debtor to put on proof without an objection having been filed.**

**• Upon filing a motion for extension or imposition of the automatic stay, care should be taken to assure the proper notice is given to any creditor against which the stay is sought. See *In re Collins*, 334 B.R. 655, Bankr. L. Rep. (CCH) P 80413 (Bankr. D. Minn. 2005), holding that a debtor's motion for extension of the automatic stay beyond the first 30 days must be denied where no creditors were given notice of the motion.**

**• Be aware of the notice requirements of Code § 342 and § 342(g)(2)'s prohibition against damages for automatic stay violations when the creditor did not receive "notice effective" under § 342.**

**• Since § 362(c)(3) and (4) refer to cases pending within a prior year, there is a retroactive effect of these provisions to cases pending and dismissed prior to the effective date of BAPCPA; that is, those pre-BAPCPA cases will count for purposes of application of § 362(c).**

### § 7:17 Automatic stay—Effect of debtor's statement of intent

Former § 362(h) is redesignated as (k) and a new subsection (h) is added to provide that, consistent with the amendment to § 521(a)(2), if the individual Chapter 7 debtor does not timely file the statement of intention as to leased personal property or secured personal property or does not redeem or reaffirm as to that personalty within the 30 days from the first date set for the meeting of creditors, or does not timely assume an unexpired lease, the automatic stay terminates as to that property. Note that new subsection (h) refers to § 521(a)(2) for the time within which the debtor must carry out the statement of intent. Section 521(a)(2) reduced the time for the debtor to carry out those choices to 30 days. However, a new subsection 521(a)(6) retains 45 days as the trigger for automatic termination of the stay when the debtor fails to act on the statement of intent as to purchase-money collateral. This difference will no doubt cause confusion and litigation.

There is a savings clause in § 362(h)(1)(B): If the secured creditor does not agree to the reaffirmation proposed by the debtor, the stay does not automatically terminate; presumably, the creditor would then have to move for stay relief. Section 362(h)(2) provides that subparagraph (1)'s termination of the stay does not apply if the court finds on the trustee's motion that the personal property has "consequential value or benefit to the bankruptcy estate." If the court makes such a finding, the court must order adequate protection to the secured creditor and surrender of the collateral to the trustee, and, if the court does not grant the trustee's motion, which must be filed before the expiration of the § 521(a)(2) time for the debtor to file a statement of intent and to carry out that statement, the automatic stay terminates upon conclusion of the hearing on the trustee's motion. This would seem to say that termination is automatic, not requiring an order, but orders likely will be requested.

**Practice Alerts for Code § 362(h) and § 521(a)(2)**

**• Code § 362(h) is tied to § 521(a)(2)'s 30–day limits; thus the Chapter 7 debtor has an affirmative duty to timely file and comply with the statement of intention to redeem personal property or to reaffirm secured debts or assume personal property leases. Under this combination of statutes, the debtor must file the statement of intention within 30 days of filing the petition and must carry out the stated intention within 30 days from the first date set for the meeting of creditors. Note that the latter time is measured from the first setting and NOT from the date the meeting is held.**

**• This 30–day limit conflicts with § 521(a)(6), which provides that the Chapter 7 debtor may not "retain possession of personal property" subject to a purchase-money security interest unless the debtor reaffirms the debt or redeems the property within "45 days after the first meeting of creditors." Note that not only is the number of days different, the time is measured from a different point in time. To avoid potential litigation over whether the stay has automatically terminated, the debtor should consider complying with the 30-day time period rather than relying on a 45-day allowance.**

**• The case trustee must be alert to a need to move within the 30-day period set out in § 521(a)(2) to show that the personal property is of consequential value or benefit to the estate.**

## § 7:18 Automatic stay—Termination in 60 days

Section 362(e) is amended and renumbered to add a new subsection (2):

(2) Notwithstanding paragraph (1), in a case under Chapter 7, 11, or 13 in which the debtor is an individual, the stay under subsection (a) shall terminate on the date that is 60 days after a request is made by a party in interest under subsection (d), unless—

(A) a final decision is rendered by the court during the 60-day period beginning on the date of the request; or

(B) such 60-day period is extended—

(i) by agreement of all parties in interest; or

(ii) by the court for such specific period of time as the court finds is required for good cause, as described in findings made by the court.

This provision places a 60-day limitation from the filing of a motion for relief from the stay on the court's entry of an order deciding the motion. In the absence of a timely order or an appropriate judicial extension of that time, the stay would terminate automatically.

## § 7:19 Automatic stay—Effect of debt repayment plan

If a prior Chapter 7, 11, or 13 case was dismissed due to the debtor entering into a debt repayment plan, then no presumption of lack of good faith is created by the prior dismissal. This specifically relates to § 362(c)(3)'s presumption of lack of good faith when the debtor has been in one prior bankruptcy case that was dismissed within one year of the current case. 11 U.S.C.A. § 362(i). Note that § 362(i) does not mention § 362(c)(4). See the discussion of § 362(c)(3) and (4) above.

## § 7:20 Automatic stay—Willful violations

By amendment to § 362(k)(2), if a violation of the automatic stay, even though willful, was made by a creditor who in good faith believed that the debtor's prior case was dismissed due to the conditions specified in § 362(h), any recovery by the debtor is limited to actual damages. Section 362(h) is discussed above and relates to the termination of the automatic stay when the debtor has not timely complied with § 521(a)(2)'s statement of intention duties.

A significant change to potential damages for stay violations is found in § 342(g)(2), which provides that no monetary penalty may be imposed against a creditor, including under § 362(k), unless the alleged conduct occurred "after such creditor receives notice effective under" § 342. See the discussion of effective notice to creditors under § 7:47.

## § 7:21 Conversion or dismissal of case

See the discussions of each chapter for relief in chapter 6 of this book for new causes for conversion or dismissal of cases, with the principal one being abuse under amended § 707(b). In addition to these chapter-specific causes, 11 U.S.C.A. § 521 provides cause in all cases based upon the debtor's failure to file information or documents required by § 521(a)(1).

### Practice Alert for Code § 521 Automatic Dismissal

**Trustees faced with the risk of automatic dismissal under**

**Code § 521 may consider filing a motion under 11 U.S.C.A. § 521(i)(4) to relieve a debtor of the obligation to file information or documents. This device might be useful for a trustee to prevent a debtor from manipulating the system and seeking to trigger automatic dismissal by deliberately ignoring his or her duties to file information and documents.**

Moreover, as to tax returns, § 521(e)(2) requires the Chapter 7 or 13 debtor to provide the trustee a copy of the most recent year's federal income tax return (or a transcript of that return) at least seven days before the first date set for the meeting of creditors. If a creditor requests a copy, it must be provided to that creditor as well, and if the debtor fails to comply, the "court shall dismiss the case unless the debtor demonstrates that the failure . . . is due to circumstances beyond the control of the debtor." Moreover, in a duplicative statement, § 521(e)(2)(C) states that if the debtor fails to provide a copy to a requesting creditor at the same time as provided to the trustee, the court shall dismiss the case, again unless the debtor shows that the failure is beyond the debtor's control. Neither of these dismissal clauses mentions notice and hearing, but since the debtor is to be given an opportunity to show that circumstances were beyond the debtor's control, a hearing opportunity must exist.

As a second tax-related provision, § 521(j)(1) states that, in addition to any other provision in the Code, "if the debtor fails to file a tax return that becomes due after the commencement of the case or to properly obtain an extension of the due date of such return, the taxing authority may request that the court enter an order converting or dismissing the case." The filing referred to here is a filing not with the court but with the tax authority. Subparagraph (2) then provides that if the debtor does not file the required return or obtain an extension from the taxing authority within 90 days after the authority's request, the court "shall convert or dismiss the case, whichever is in the best interests of creditors and the estate." This must mean that the debtor has an automatic 90-day window to comply with the taxing authority's request for filing postpetition returns, but note that the ultimate decision to convert or dismiss does not mention that the court should consider the debtor's interests.

BAPCPA § 315 requires the Administrative Office of the United States Court to establish, within 180 days of enactment, procedures to safeguard the confidentiality of any tax information that is required to be provided under these increases in the debtor's duties. Within 540 days of enactment, the Administrative Office is to submit a report to Congress of the effectiveness of these procedures as well as any proposals for changes in legislation necessary to protect the confidentiality of tax information. The Administrative Office has issued guidelines for protection of tax information, and those guidelines are discussed in § 6:14.

Another cause for dismissal of a case that is common to all chapters for individual debtors is the debtor's failure to pay postpetition domestic support obligations. See the discussion of domestic support obligations in § 7:42.

## § 7:22 Credit briefing

Code § 109 is amended by adding subsection (h) to generally preclude an individual debtor from filing for bankruptcy before a briefing has been obtained from an approved nonprofit budget and credit counseling service within 180 days prior to filing. A list of service providers that have been approved by the U.S. trustee or bankruptcy administrator must be maintained by the clerk, and an exception exists for debtors in districts where the U.S. trustee or bankruptcy administrator has determined that nonprofit counseling services cannot provide adequate services. A debtor also could seek a court determination that this briefing was not possible due to exigent circumstances and that it was unavailable within five days of the debtor's request for the service. In the event of the waiver of the prefiling briefing, that debtor would be required to obtain the services within 30 days of filing for bankruptcy, and the court could extend that time for cause but for no more than an additional 15 days. See 11 U.S.C.A. § 109(h)(3).

The briefing requirements could be waived by the court after notice and hearing for a debtor who "is unable to complete those requirements because of an incapacity, disability, or active military duty in a military combat zone." "Incapacity" and "disability" are specifically defined for the purposes of such a waiver. 11 U.S.C.A. § 109(h)(4).

The debtor's filing duties under new Code § 521(b) include filing a certificate of receipt of the credit counseling agency services and any debt repayment plan developed by the service.

The statute uses the term "briefing" in § 109(h)(1), describing the required prebankruptcy task as "an individual or group briefing (including a briefing conducted by telephone or the Internet) that outlined the opportunities for available credit counseling and assisted such individual in performing a related budget analysis." This seems to require less than full-blown "counseling," since the briefing must advise the debtor about "available credit counseling," but the briefing must "assist" the debtor in "performing" a budget analysis. To add to possible confusion, in § 109(h)(3)(A), the Code uses the term "credit counseling services" concerning possible waiver of the requirement. Is there a difference between credit briefing and counseling? There would appear to be, but the extent to which the required briefing must reach true counseling will be fleshed out in judicial decisions.

See the article by David Lander, A Quick Update on Implementation of BAPCPA's Pre-Filing Briefing Requirement, Norton Bankruptcy Law Adviser (January 2006), discussing the briefing requirements, certification of the providers and some existing concerns about the briefing and providers. See also Karen Gross & Susan Block-Lieb, Empty Mandate or Opportunity for Innovation? Prepetition Credit Counseling and Postpetition Financial Management Education, 13 Am. Bankr. Inst. L. Rev. 549 (2005).

The Executive Office of U.S. Trustee has posted on its website a list of approved credit briefing providers: http://www.usdoj.gov/ust/bapcpa/ccde/cc_approved.htm.

**Practice Alerts for Code § 109 Credit Briefing Waivers**

- **Section 109(g) may be viewed as an eligibility requirement that individual debtors must satisfy prior to filing a bankruptcy petition. Debtors and counsel should be aware that any failure to obtain the briefing prior to filing bankruptcy incurs a risk that a motion for waiver will be denied.**
- **Judicial authority is emerging concerning a debtor's request for waivers of the prebankruptcy credit briefing. *In re Hubbard*, 332 B.R. 285, Bankr. L. Rep. (CCH) P 80384 (Bankr. S.D. Tex. 2005), and *In re Watson*, 332 B.R. 740, Bankr. L. Rep. (CCH) P 80395 (Bankr. E.D. Va. 2005), point out that § 109(h)(3) is written in the conjunctive, meaning that a debtor requesting an extension of the time to obtain the credit briefing after the filing of the case must show exigent circumstances that merit a waiver of the prebankruptcy requirement, that the motion must state that the debtor requested the prebankruptcy briefing but was unable to obtain it from a provider within five days of the request, and that these showings are "satisfactory to the court." The mere allegation that a debtor didn't obtain the briefing before filing bankruptcy because of a pending foreclosure does not appear to be sufficient cause to grant a waiver or extension of time.**
- **Official Form 1 contains a box for the debtor to check if the debtor is claiming "exigent circumstances," but the Code and form further require the debtor to file a "certification" describing the exigent circumstances and other grounds for a waiver or extension. For some courts, this certification may require a sworn pleading. See *In re Hubbard*, 332 B.R. 285, Bankr. L. Rep. (CCH) P 80384 (Bankr. S.D. Tex. 2005), so holding.**
- **Assuming the debtor's motion merits an extension, the debtor must obtain the briefing within 30 days of filing for bankruptcy relief, but the court may extend that for an additional 15 days "for cause." The practical effect is that a debtor who did not obtain the briefing prior to filing and seeks an extension should obtain the briefing promptly and should not wait for the court to grant an extension before obtaining it.**

## § 7:23 Claims

Code § 502 is amended to add subsection (k) at the end, providing for the potential reduction of a creditor's claim by no more than 20%. The conditions precedent to such a reduction are restrictive, however, suggesting that there will be few opportunities to actually make such a reduction. First, the reduction only applies to claims "based in whole on an unsecured consumer debt," thus ruling out partially secured claims from reduction. Second, the claim to be reduced would be one filed by a creditor who "unreasonably refused to negotiate a reasonable alternative repayment schedule" that was presented on behalf of the debtor by a budget and credit counseling agency. This is the type of agency that the debtor is generally required to consult with prior to filing bankruptcy. Note that the critical words are "unreasonably refused." Third, this section would only apply to unsecured debts that would be dischargeable; if any part of the debt would be nondischargeable, no reduction would be required. Finally, the debtor has the burden of proving "by clear and convincing evidence" that the creditor unreasonably refused to even "consider the debtor's proposal." This burden of proof requiring a showing of the creditor's lack of consideration is extremely heavy.

See the later discussion, at § 7:57, of the effect of the amendment to § 506(a)(2), which provides that, for Chapter 7 and 13 cases, the value of personal property securing an allowed claim shall be determined based on replacement value as of the date of filing bankruptcy without deducting for the costs of sale or marketing. For consumer personal property, the replacement value is retail, based on the age and condition of the property.

Section 503(b)(9) is amended to provide that, in a Chapter 13 case, the claim of a governmental unit for taxes related to a return described in § 1308 will be timely claims if filed within 60 days after such a return is filed with the tax authority.

## § 7:24 Creditor's meeting representative

By an amendment to § 341(c), a corporate partnership or limited liability company creditor holding a consumer debt may appear by a representative who is not an attorney at the meeting of creditors for a Chapter 7 or 13 debtor.

## § 7:25 Crimes related to bankruptcy

BAPCPA § 203 includes an amendment to 18 U.S.C.A. § 158(d) that requires the bankruptcy courts' development of "procedures for referring any case that may contain a materially fraudulent statement in a bankruptcy schedule to" the United States attorneys and agents of the FBI.

By amendment to 18 U.S.C.A. § 157, filing a fraudulent involuntary petition may be bankruptcy fraud. See the discussion of involuntary bankruptcy in § 7:45.

## § 7:26 Data

Amendments to 28 U.S.C.A. §§ 159 and 589b place emphasis upon the improvement of bankruptcy statistics and data. As a part of this, uniform forms for final reports of the trustees in all cases must be developed.

## § 7:27 Debtor's choices under § 521

Code § 521(a) is amended to add subsection (6) providing that the individual debtor's choices as to collateral do not include retention of personal property that is secured by an allowed purchase money claim, either entirely or partially. When such a claim exists, if the debtor wishes to retain the collateral, the debtor must either redeem the personal property or enter into a reaffirmation agreement within 45 days after the first meeting of creditors; otherwise, the automatic stay terminates with respect to that collateral, and the property is no longer property of the bankruptcy estate, unless the court, upon motion of the case trustee filed within the 45-day time, finds that the property has value for the estate. If the trustee's motion is granted, the order may provide for adequate protection to the secured creditor and for surrender of the property by the debtor to the trustee. This 45 days is longer than the 30 days from the first date set for the meeting of creditors that the debtor has under § 521(a)(2)(B) to carry out the statement of intent by redeeming, surrendering, or reaffirming. Section 521(a)(2)(C) is amended to specify that the debtor's or trustee's rights to the collateral are affected by new subsection 362(h), which provides that the automatic stay terminates when the debtor does not timely carry out one of the three choices.

Note that § 521(a)(2) is amended to delete "consumer," meaning that the debtor's duties concerning filing and complying with a statement of intent for collateral apply to all individual Chapter 7 debtors, not merely those who have consumer debts.

Section 521(d) is added to provide that if the debtor fails to timely take the action concerning a statement of intent with respect to property that is leased or subject to a bailment or property that is subject to a security interest that is not voidable under §§ 522(f), 544, 545, 547, 548, or 549, then nothing in the Bankruptcy Code prevents the operation of a default provision in the lease, bailment, or security instrument. Such a default provision may include insolvency or a Title 11 bankruptcy filing.

## § 7:28 Debtor education requirement

By an addition to Code § 727(a)(11) and to § 1328(g), a debtor would be unable to obtain a discharge in Chapter 7 or 13 until completing a newly required personal financial management course, unless such a course is unavailable as described in new § 109(h). The personal financial management course is in addition to the prebankruptcy budget and credit briefing discussed above. The education requirement is described in new Code § 111, which also describes the nonprofit budget and credit counseling agencies.

The Executive Office of U.S. Trustee has posted on its website a list of approved debtor education providers: http://www.usdoj.gov/ust/bapcpa/ccde/de_approved.htm.

Since obtaining this education is a prerequisite to a Chapter 7 or 13 discharge, the debtor will have a duty to file proof that the course has been completed. If the debtor fails to do that, the court may close the case at some point without granting a discharge, which would require the debtor to move to reopen the case if the education is later obtained.

Resource Suggestion: Karen Gross & Susan Block-Lieb, Empty Mandate or Opportunity for Innovation? Prepetition Credit Counseling and Postpetition Financial Management Education, 13 Am. Bankr. Inst. L. Rev 549 (2005).

## § 7:29 Debt relief agency

A new definition for "debt relief agency" is found in § 101(12A), as are related definitions for "assisted person" and "bankruptcy assistance" found in § 101(3) and § 101(4A). Essentially, these terms all become relevant in the consumer bankruptcy filings since an "assisted person" is defined as a consumer debtor with less than $150,000 in nonexempt assets. Persons who provide bankruptcy assistance to such debtors fall within the definition of a "debt relief agency" and will be subject to the restrictions and disclosure requirements placed upon those agencies by new Code §§ 526, 527, and 528. Judicial opinions are appearing on the issue of whether the term "debt relief agent" includes attorneys who practice bankruptcy. A bankruptcy court has held that attorneys who are members of the bar in that court are not "debt relief agencies" within the meaning of BAPCPA, provided that their actions fall within the practice of law. Although the definition of "debt relief agency" is broad enough to include attorneys, that court noted that the definition did not specifically include "attorney." Moreover, attorneys admitted in that court were regulated by state law and disciplinary rules, and there was no clear indication that Congress intended to start regulating attorneys. *In re Attorneys at Law and Debt Relief Agencies*, 332 B.R. 66, Bankr. L. Rep. (CCH) P 80374 (Bankr. S.D. Ga. 2005). Actions are pending in other courts on this issue, with some suits having been filed in district courts attacking the constitutionality of including attorneys within the definition of and restrictions imposed by "debt relief agencies." See, for example, *Geisenberger v. Gonzales*, Civil Action No. 05-CV-5460, U.S District Court, (Eastern Dist. Penn. 2005). Obviously, as more judicial opinions result from such litigation, it will be more clear the extent to which bankruptcy attorneys are included within these restrictions. For purposes of the following overview of debt relief agents, it will be assumed that attorneys representing consumer debtors fall within that term's requirements.

The restrictions in § 526(c) include potential voiding of any contract for services that do not comply fully with §§ 526 to 528 requirements; the potential liability in the amount of fees paid, actual damages, plus reasonable attorney's fees, if the debt relief agency intentionally or negligently fails to comply with those sections' requirements or with the Federal Rules of Bankruptcy Procedure; the enforcement of the new requirements by some designated state official; and injunctive relief and civil penalties for violations of these new requirements.

The new disclosures mandated by § 527 include providing the assisted consumer debtor with the information set out in the prebankruptcy notice requirement of § 342(b)(1), and, in addition to this notice, § 527(a)(2) requires specific, clear, and conspicuous written notice to the consumer debtor within three business days of the first date of services that all information provided in a bankruptcy petition must be complete, accurate, and truthful; that all assets and liabilities, with the replacement value of assets, must be stated; that current monthly income and disposable income in a Chapter 13 must be stated; and that failure to provide such information can result in dismissal of a case and other sanctions, including a criminal sanction. In a clear and conspicuous single document that is separate from any other documents, the consumer debtor must be provided with the information as specified in § 527(b). A debt relief agency must maintain for two years a copy of all notices given to the debtor as required by § 527(a).

Underlying the responsibility for accuracy by the consumer debtor and anyone assisting the debtor, § 527(c) requires that the debtor be given information to assist in valuing assets, completing the list of creditors and what they are owed, and how to determine exempt assets and their value under a replacement value approach. Note, however, that § 522(a)'s definition of "value" for exemption purposes was not amended.

New Code § 528 provides specific requirements for debt relief agencies. Under these requirements, the consumer debtor's attorney or other person providing bankruptcy assistance must execute a written contract with the debtor within five days of providing the first assistance and prior to the bankruptcy filing. All advertisements by such attorneys or assistance providers must disclose that the services are bankruptcy services, an attempt to reduce the advertisements that refer only to such things as debt restructuring or foreclosure prevention. The advertisement must contain a clear statement that this is a bankruptcy debt relief agency.

Assuming that these debt relief agency requirements do apply to consumer debtor's attorneys, they raise issues of how the requirements relate to the Code's other references to Rule 9011 and the attorney certifications implicit in signing the petition and other pleadings. If an attorney represents both consumer debtors and creditors in different cases, there is an obvious question of the impact that will result from that attorney being required to disclose or advertise that he or she assists debtors in obtaining bankruptcy relief.

**Practice Alerts for Code §§ 526, 527, and 528 Debt Relief Agents**

- **Until it is clear whether consumer debtor attorneys fall within the term and restrictions imposed on debt relief agencies, such attorneys should be aware of the duties and restrictions found in §§ 526, 527, and 528.**
- **Attorneys should review their consultation practices,**

**including telephonic and internet consultation, to see that they comply with debt relief agency requirements.**

- **It should be determined whether and when the notices specified by § 527(a) and the contract for services required by § 528(a) are required.**
- **Assure that the notices to the debtor comply with § 528(a).**
- **Assure that all advertisements comply with § 528(b).**
- **Attorneys who do not regularly practice consumer bankruptcy law may nevertheless fall within the "debt relief agency" term and restrictions if they provide advice or assistance to persons who are within the definition of "assisted person" and if that advice or assistance is related to bankruptcy. An example is a domestic relations attorney representing the spouse of a debtor in bankruptcy.**

Resource suggestion: Catherine E. Vance & Corinne Cooper, Nine Traps and One Slap: Attorney Liability under the New Bankruptcy Law, 79 Am. Bankr. L. J. 283 (2005), available on Westlaw at database Legal Periodicals/Law Reviews.

## § 7:30 Discharge and exceptions from discharge—Time between discharges

Section 727(a)(8) is changed to make the time between Chapter 7 discharges or discharges granted under § 1141 eight years rather than the current six years. The prohibition is that a debtor may not receive a discharge if one has been received under § 727(a) or § 1141 "in a case commenced within 8 years before the date of the filing of the [current] petition."

For Chapter 13 debtors, § 1328(f) is added to provide that the court may not grant a discharge under that chapter if the debtor has received a Chapter 7, 11, or 12 discharge in a prior case filed within four years preceding the filing of the current Chapter 13 case or if the debtor has received a Chapter 13 discharge in a case filed within two years of the current case.

Resource suggestion of discharge changes: William Houston Brown, Taking Exception to a Debtor's Discharge: The 2005 Bankruptcy Amendments Make it Easier, 79 Am. Bankr. L. J. 419 (2005), available on Westlaw at database Legal Periodicals/Law Reviews.

## § 7:31 Discharge—Delay in granting

Section 727(a) is amended to add a new subsection (11), providing that the court should not grant a discharge when the debtor has failed to complete the instructional course in personal financial management as described in § 109(h)(4). See the discussion of debtor education. A similar prerequisite for a Chapter 13 discharge is found in § 1328(g).

Section 727(a) is also amended to add a new subsection (12) providing that the court should not grant a discharge when it finds that there is "reasonable cause to believe" either that the new § 522(q)(1) applies or that there is a pending proceeding in which the debtor may be found guilty of a felony or liable for damages under the new § 522(q)(1)(A) or (B). A similar change is made to Chapter 11 by adding § 1141(d)(C); to Chapter 12 by adding § 1228(f); and to Chapter 13 by adding § 1328(h). See the discussion of § 522(q)(1) in chapter 8. It is not expected that this issue will arise in many consumer bankruptcies, and Interim Rule 4003 takes the position that these discharge provisions may have the effect of delaying rather than denying entry of discharge, with a potential delay being required in those cases where the provisions of § 522(q) may apply to a particular debtor. See the Interim Rules later in this book.

## § 7:32 Discharge—Revocation

Section 727(d)(4) adds as a cause to revoke a discharge the debtor's failure to satisfactorily explain a material misstatement made in reference to an audit that is randomly required in 28 U.S.C.A. § 586(f) or the debtor's failure to make available for inspection any of the debtor's accounts, papers, or financial records that are requested for audit purposes.

## § 7:33 Discharge—Luxury goods and advances exception

Section 523(a)(2)(C) is amended to change the amount of luxury goods from the former $1,225 to $500 and change the 60-day measuring period for their acquisition to 90 days, and other changes are made in the replaced subsection to eliminate possible exceptions for goods acquired for the support and maintenance of dependents of the debtor and the current "open end credit" provision. Cash advances under an open end credit plan are changed from the former $1,225 to $750 and the 60-day measuring period is expanded to 70 days.

## § 7:34 Discharge—Student loan exception

The exception from discharge for education benefits is expanded, with § 523(a)(8) amended to except from discharge, absent an undue hardship showing, any educational benefit debt or loan without regard to whether it was a debt to a profit-making entity, government entity, or to a government guaranteed creditor. In addition, any qualified educational loan, as broadly defined by Internal Revenue Code § 221(d)(1), is included in the exception.

## § 7:35 Discharge—Tax loan exception

A new exception from discharge is added for debts "incurred to pay a tax to a governmental unit, other than the United States, that would be nondischargeable under paragraph (1)." 11 U.S.C.A. § 523(a)(14A). Thus, if the debtor borrows money for the purpose of paying a state or local tax, that debt would be nondischargeable provided that the underlying tax is also nondischargeable under § 523(a)(1). The new exception does not include debts incurred for the payment of taxes owing to the United States.

### § 7:36 Discharge—Election law penalty exception

New § 523(a)(14B) excepts from discharge fines or penalties imposed under federal election laws.

### § 7:37 Discharge—Prisoner exception

Section § 523(a)(17) is amended to clarify that it applies only to fees imposed on prisoners by a court.

### § 7:38 Discharge—Membership association fee exception

Section § 523(a)(16) is expanded to except from discharge fees or assessments by home membership associations so long as the trustee or debtor "has a legal, equitable, or possessory ownership interest" in the living unit contained within the association.

### § 7:39 Discharge—Pension loan exception

Section § 523(a)(18) is added to except from discharge all debts for loans from pension, profit-sharing, stock bonus, or other tax-sheltered plans, but the fact that the loan is excepted from discharge is not to be construed to mean the obligation owed is a claim or a debt in the bankruptcy case. This latter provision is peculiar since it runs counter to the general concept of the definitions of a debt and claim; moreover, § 523(a) begins with the precept that only debts are excepted from discharge.

### § 7:40 Discharge—Chapter 13 exceptions

Significant increases in the types of debts excepted from discharge are made in the amendments to § 1328(a). See the discussion under Chapter 13 in chapter 6.

### § 7:41 Discharge injunction

Code § 524 is amended by adding subsections (i) and (j) at the end, with (i) making it a violation of the discharge injunction for a creditor to "willfully fail" to "credit payments received under" a confirmed plan under any chapter of the Code, with exceptions from that rule when plan confirmation is revoked, the plan is in default, or plan payments have not been received in accordance with the confirmed plan's provisions. Such a violation is only triggered "if the act of the creditor . . . to credit payments . . . caused material injury to the debtor." It may be difficult in most cases, especially Chapter 13 cases, for a debtor to show a "material injury." What such an injury must be is not defined by this amendment.

New subsection (j) provides a specific exception from the discharge injunction found in § 524(a)(2), which "operates as an injunction against the commencement or continuation of" collection from the debtor personally. This exception would permit a creditor secured by the debtor's principal residence to seek and obtain from the debtor "periodic payments associated with a valid security interest in lieu of pursuit of in rem relief to enforce the lien." In other words, the home mortgage creditor could pursue with the debtor continued payments rather than foreclose. There is no cross-reference here to the amended reaffirmation provisions found in § 524(c). It is uncertain whether subsection (j) is intended to permit retention of a home without reaffirming the secured debt, but that result could occur, notwithstanding the amendment of § 521 to give a Chapter 7 debtor only the choices of surrender, redemption, or reaffirmation. See the discussion of that amendment under the debtor's § 521 choices and redemption. Note also that subsection (j)(2) says that the creditor's actions must be in the ordinary course of business between the debtor and creditor. It is difficult to imagine that consumer debtors have an ordinary course of business that would include negotiating with their mortgage lender about continued payments in lieu of foreclosure.

Section 524(c)'s requirements for a valid reaffirmation agreement are expanded by the addition of very specific disclosures found in new § 524(k). See the discussion of reaffirmation agreements at § 7:53.

## § 7:42 Discharge—Domestic support and related exceptions

Resource suggestion: William Houston Brown, Bankruptcy and Domestic Relations Manual (2005), a Thomson/West publication, which analyzes § 523(a)(5) and (15), contrasting the differences in pre-BAPCPA and post-BAPCPA law.

In the place of former Code § 523(a)(5), the amended section simply provides that "a domestic support obligation" is excepted from discharge. Since that new term is not defined in the exception itself, reference to the definition of that obligation must be found in the new § 101(14A):

> "[D]omestic support obligation" means a debt that accrues before, on, or after the date of the order for relief in a case under this title, including interest that accrues on that debt as provided under applicable nonbankruptcy law notwithstanding any other provision of this title, that is—
>
> (A) owed to or recoverable by—
>
> (i) a spouse, former spouse, or child of the debtor or such child's parent, legal guardian, or responsible relative; or
>
> (ii) a governmental unit;
>
> (B) in the nature of alimony, maintenance, or support (including assistance provided by a governmental unit) of such spouse, former spouse, or child of the debtor or such child's parent, without regard to whether such debt is expressly so designated;
>
> (C) established or subject to establishment before, on, or after the date of the order for relief in a case under this title, by reason of applicable provisions of—
>
> (i) a separation agreement, divorce decree, or property settlement agreement;

(ii) an order of a court of record; or

(iii) a determination made in accordance with applicable nonbankruptcy law by a governmental unit; and

(D) not assigned to a nongovernmental entity, unless that obligation is assigned voluntarily by the spouse, former spouse, child of the debtor, or such child's parent, legal guardian, or responsible relative for the purpose of collecting the debt.

As will be seen in other amendments, this term "domestic support obligation" appears throughout the Code and replaces former references to "support, maintenance, and alimony." The definition of "domestic support obligation" gives § 523(a)(5) a broader scope because the definition of "domestic support obligation" includes postbankruptcy accruals and because the new definition changes the treatment of assigned debts.

First, the definition includes debts that accrue before or after the commencement of the case. This on its face should not expand the exception from discharge of these debts since § 523 generally covers only prebankruptcy debts. For example, a Chapter 7 discharge only discharges "debts that arose before the date of the order for relief." 11 U.S.C.A. § 727(b). It is likely that the reference to postbankruptcy accruals of these debts, "including interest that accrues," is intended to address the changes made in the confirmation of plans and obtaining of discharges that are preconditioned upon payment of postpetition domestic support obligations. Those changes are discussed under Chapters 11, 12, and 13.

The definition continues to refer to debts "in the nature of alimony, maintenance, or support" but that reference now specifically includes "assistance provided by a governmental unit," which, of course, can be either local, state, or federal. Tied to this expansion is the alternative requirement that the debt either be "owed to or recoverable by a spouse, former spouse, or child of the debtor" or "a governmental unit." Any doubt that might exist under the former statute that a debt held by a governmental unit but one never owing to or recoverable by the spouse or child might be nondischargeable is erased. Debts owing to or recoverable by the governmental unit that provided support assistance would be excepted from discharge even if the spouse or child who received that assistance could not recover the debt individually.

Another significant change is that the order, agreement, or determination creating the obligation could be one in existence prior to or coming into existence after the filing of the bankruptcy case. Again, this is not so much an expansion of the actual exception from discharge as a complement to the changes made to the automatic stay that will more broadly permit continuations of domestic relations actions in nonbankruptcy courts. Those automatic stay changes are discussed under that topic.

Former § 523(a)(15) is changed completely by deletion of its subpart (A) and (B) "defenses" to nondischargeability. The new § 523(a)(15) simply reads:

> (15) to a spouse, former spouse, or child of the debtor and not of the kind described in paragraph (5) that is incurred by the debtor in the course of a divorce or separation or in connection with a separation agreement, divorce decree or other order of a court of record or a determination made in accordance with State or territorial law by a governmental unit.

Thus the reach of subsection (15) may be to all marital-related obligations that are not alimony, maintenance, or support in nature and without the benefit to the debtor of the former ability-to-pay or balancing tests. Essentially, the combination of amended § 523(a)(5) and (15) would be to exclude from discharge all marital and domestic relations obligations, whether support in nature, property division, or hold-harmless, provided that they were incurred in the course of a divorce or separation or established in connection with a separation agreement, divorce decree, or other order of a court of record or a determination made in accordance with state or territorial law by a governmental unit. The only window in this broad reach of the exceptions may be that the amendment of § 523(a)(15) seems to limit it to debts to a spouse, former spouse, or a child of the debtor, but it would appear that only those parties would ever have a domestic relations-type claim under this section. Governmental support assistance agencies are covered by § 523(a)(5) and would not appear to be within the reach of § 523(a)(15). The only chapter of bankruptcy relief in which a discharge of § 523(a)(15)-type debts might be accomplished is Chapter 13, since the amended exceptions from that chapter's discharge do not include § 523(a)(15).

The former § 523(a)(5) permits the discharge of support-type debts that have been assigned to nongovernmental entities. See former 11 U.S.C.A. § 523(a)(5)(A). The new definition of domestic support obligations that is incorporated by reference into the amended § 523(a)(5) recognizes the nondischargeability of those debts that had been voluntarily assigned to a nongovernmental entity by the spouse, former spouse, a child, or other person responsible for the child, if assigned for the purposes of collection of the debt.

An extremely significant change is made to the timing requirements for filing complaints under § 523(a)(5) and (15). Formerly, complaints under § 523(a)(5) could be filed "at any time" while complaints under § 523(a)(15) had to be filed within 60 days of the first date set for the meeting of creditors. This requirement for § 523(a)(15) rested upon § 523(c), which included § (a)(15) in its list of subsections for which the debtor automatically received a discharge in the absence of a timely complaint. Subsection (c) is amended to delete subsection (15) from this list, meaning that complaints under § (a)(15) could be filed at any time, just like those for § (a)(5), and the debtor's discharge would automatically exclude both § (a)(5) and (a)(15) debts from the discharge unless a complaint for determination is filed and results in a dischargeable determination. With the expansion of both § 523(a)(5) and (15), the question may be asked when the filing of a complaint could result in a discharge of these debts.

Another change that impacts these types of debts is found in the amendment to § 522(c) concerning the continued liability of exempt property after discharge for debts covered by amended § 523(a)(5). See discussion of that change under exemptions in chapter 8.

The priority of domestic support obligations goes to the top of the list in an amendment to § 507(a)(7). See that discussion under priority at § 7:51.

An amendment to the preference section is made to protect domestic support transfers from avoidance. See the discussion under preferences at § 7:50 and chapter 9.

An amendment to § 522(f)(1)(A) incorporates the new § 523(a)(5) into the type of judicial lien that is not avoidable by the debtor. See lien avoidance at § 7:46.

Within 270 days following enactment, the Comptroller General must conduct a study of the feasibility, costs, and effectiveness of requiring all bankruptcy trustees to provide to offices of child support enforcement information about debtors in bankruptcy who may be obligated for child support. See the trustees' duties to such offices and to support creditors under new trustees' duties in chapter 2.

## § 7:43 Fees

BAPCPA § 325 increases the filing fee for Chapter 7 cases to $220 and reduces the fee for Chapter 13 cases to $150. Chapters 9 and 11 filing fees are increased to $1,000, and the Judicial Conference of the United States has approved a filing fee for cases under Chapter 15 of $1,000. Chapter 12 filing fees remain at $200. A $39 administrative fee is added to the filing fee required for each Chapter. See § 4:2 for a further increase in fees. The percentage upon which U.S. trustee fees are calculated is increased, and increased filing fees are dedicated to payment of the salaries and benefits for the additional bankruptcy judges provided for in BAPCPA § 1223, with any remainder going into the Treasury.

## § 7:44 In forma pauperis filings

In forma pauperis is recognized in an amendment to 28 U.S.C.A. § 1930(f), thus permitting the bankruptcy court to waive filing fees in appropriate cases. Guidelines and interim procedures for courts to follow in considering filing fee waivers have been approved by the Judicial Conference of the United States, found at http://www.uscourts.gov/bankruptcycourts/jcusguidelines.html.

## § 7:45 Involuntary bankruptcy

Code § 303(b)(1) is amended to provide that a creditor may not commence an involuntary Chapter 7 or Chapter 11 case if the debtor's liability on a claim or the amount of the claim is contingent or is the subject of a bona fide dispute. This amendment "shall take effect on the date of the enactment of this Act and shall apply with respect to cases commenced under title 11 of the United States Code before, on, and after such date." Former provisions of the Code made a creditor ineligible to seek involuntary relief if the claim is contingent as to liability or the subject of a bona fide dispute. The amendment would extend this to include bona fide disputes as to the amount of the claim. Section 303(h)(1) of the Code is amended accordingly to provide that relief shall be granted against an objecting debtor only if the debtor is not paying debts as they become due, unless the debts are subject to a bona fide dispute as to liability or amount.

A new § 303(l) is added to provide that if the involuntary petition is against an individual and the petition contains a "false, fictitious or fraudulent statement," and if the court dismisses the petition, the court shall seal all records of the case upon motion of the debtor. The court may prohibit consumer-reporting agencies from reporting anything concerning such a dismissed involuntary case. Finally, the court may expunge the record under this section. In line with this change, 18 U.S.C.A. § 157 is amended to include fraudulent involuntary bankruptcy in the bankruptcy fraud described under § 157(3).

## § 7:46 Lien avoidance

The debtor's ability to avoid judicial liens found in § 522(f)(1)(A) is reduced by the deletion of most of that former section. It now reads instead that a judicial lien could be avoided, "other than a judicial lien that secures a debt of a kind specified in section 523(a)(5)." Therefore, any judicial lien securing a domestic support obligation would be protected from avoidance.

Such obligations would also be fully protected from a trustee's avoidance under the preference statute. Section 547(c)(7)'s former exception from preference avoidance is changed to read: "to the extent such transfer was a bona fide payment of a debt for a domestic support obligation."

Section 522(f)(4)(A) is added to adopt a definition of "household goods" for purposes of nonpossesssory, nonpurchase-money lien avoidance under § 522(f)(1)(B). Section 313(b) of the Act states that the Director of the Executive Office of the U.S. Trustee is to submit a report to the Judiciary Committees of the House and Senate within two years of enactment, with the report to contain findings concerning the utilization of this definition under § 522(f), including findings of the impact on debtors. That report may contain recommendations for any changes in § 522(f).

## § 7:47 Notices to creditors

Section 342 is amended by the addition of subsections (c)(2), (e), (f), and (g), which concern the address and noticing that must be given to creditors based upon the address that may have been supplied to the debtor by the creditor prior to bankruptcy. Section 342(c) is directed to the address for creditors that the debtor should use on the creditor matrix and schedules. If within 90 days of the filing the debtor had received two or more communications from a creditor that requested a specific address for bankruptcy purposes, then the debtor is to use that address, including in the notice the account number for that creditor. Of course, the clerk will use the address that is listed by the debtor on the matrix.

However, creditors may provide an address to a bankruptcy court clerk indicating the address to be used for bankruptcy noticing by the clerk in a particular case. 11 U.S.C.A. § 342(e). If that differs from the address furnished by the debtor in a case, the clerk will use the address in the request from the creditor. Section 342(f) permits creditors to notice any bankruptcy court clerk of an address to be used for that creditor in all bankruptcy cases, including nationwide. Upon receipt of such a notice, a clerk would forward that to the bankruptcy noticing center that provides noticing services for bankruptcy courts, and that center would amend its database of addresses accordingly.

As was discussed under automatic stay changes, the debtor will need to assure that correct notices are used for creditors, since § 342(g) provides that the notice to a creditor by either the debtor or clerk is "not effective" if the requested address is not used, or at least until the actual notice "is brought to the attention of such creditor."

Within 10 days of the filing of an individual's Chapter 7 petition in which a presumption of abuse arises under § 707(b), the clerk is required to notice creditors that the presumption exists. This is problematic, since this 10 days is before the time that the U.S. trustee or bankruptcy administrator will have completed its abuse analysis; therefore, the clerk will only act upon the debtor's own calculation admitting that a presumption of abuse does or does not exist. See Official Form B22A in Appendix A.

Resource Suggestion: Henry E. Hildebrand, III, Getting Noticed: The New Notice Requirements of § 342, 13 Am. Bankr. Inst. L. Rev. 533 (2005).

## § 7:48 Notice to debtor

Code § 342(b) is amended to more specifically describe the prebankruptcy notice that the clerk of court is to give to individual debtors under any chapter of Title 11. Among other things, this notice alerts the debtor to possible bankruptcy crimes.

## § 7:49 Petition preparers

Code § 110 is substantially amended to specify the notices that must be given by nonattorney bankruptcy petition preparers and to more tightly regulate the fees that may be charged by them. The Supreme Court is given specific authority to promulgate rules "setting a maximum allowable fee chargeable by a bankruptcy petition preparer," and the preparer must notify the debtor of that maximum fee as well as of the fact that the preparer is not an attorney. Such a preparer may not give legal advice. The bankruptcy court may order the turnover of excess fees over the value of services provided, and a debtor may exempt any excess fees recovered. Specific injunctive authority is modified, and treble damages are authorized.

### § 7:50 Preferences and fraudulent transfers

Section 547 is amended in several important ways. First, § 547(c)(2) is amended to reduce the requirements for a transfer to be in the ordinary course of business. Now, that exception will be satisfied by the transfer being a payment made in the ordinary course of both the debtor and transferee (the subjective test) *or* being a payment made according to ordinary business terms (the objective test). The transfer still must be one for a debt incurred in the ordinary course of both the debtor and transferee.

Section 547(c)(3)(B) changes the time for perfection to 30 days from 20 days.

Code § 547(c)(7) is amended to simply exclude from the trustee's avoidance power a transfer "to the extent such transfer was a bona fide payment of a debt for a domestic support obligation."

Section 547(c)(9) sets $5,000 as the threshold for the trustee to initiate preference avoidance for the transfer of nonconsumer debts, and this is an aggregate amount. The consumer threshold remains at $600 under § 547(c)(8).

Code § 547(h) is also added to prohibit the trustee's avoidance of a transfer that was "made as a part of an alternative repayment schedule between the debtor and any creditor of the debtor created by an approved nonprofit budget and credit counseling agency." This is related to the credit briefing that the debtor is generally required to seek prior to filing bankruptcy.

An addition of § 547(c)(i) provides that, in the event that the trustee successfully avoids a transfer made by the debtor between 90 days and one year prior to bankruptcy to a creditor who is not an insider, but the transfer is for the benefit of a creditor who is an insider, the transfer is avoided only as to the creditor that is an insider. This amendment "shall apply to any case that is pending or commenced on or after the date of enactment," including those in which avoidance proceedings are pending. This is a further legislative limitation on the effect of the *DePrizio* decision, see *Levit v. Ingersoll Rand Financial Corp.*, 874 F.2d 1186, 19 Bankr. Ct. Dec. (CRR) 574, 22 Collier Bankr. Cas. 2d (MB) 36, 11 Employee Benefits Cas. (BNA) 1323, Bankr. L. Rep. (CCH) P 72910 (7th Cir. 1989) (disapproved of by, In re Arundel Housing Components, Inc., 126 B.R. 216, 21 Bankr. Ct. Dec. (CRR) 959, Bankr. L. Rep. (CCH) P 73922 (Bankr. D. Md. 1991)), and the majority of decisions from courts that have followed it. See further discussion of this change in chapter 9.

For fraudulent transfers, the trustee's reach-back period is extended to insiders, and the period is extended from one to two years. 11 U.S.C.A. § 548(a) and (b). The change to two years is not effective until April 20, 2006, one year after the enactment.

Section 548(e) is added concerning avoidable transfers to self-settled trusts. See the discussion under exclusions and exemptions in chapter 8.

## § 7:51 Priority

Section 507(a) is amended to move domestic support obligations to the first priority of § 507(a)(1), with subsection (C) giving the trustee a superpriority for payment of administrative expenses but only to the extent that the trustee administers assets that benefit domestic support claimants. This first priority includes domestic support claims that have been assigned to a governmental unit, unless the assignment was done voluntarily for the purpose of collection. See William Houston Brown, Bankruptcy and Domestic Relations Manual (2005), a Thomson/West publication, for discussion of this priority shift.

The priority for wage claims is increased to $10,000, as are the claims for contributions to employee benefit plans, but the priority amount for grain producers and fishermen remains at $4,000. Under § 507(a)(7), the priority amount for deposits is reduced to $1,800.

Under § 507(a)(8), the tax priority now formally recognizes what the Supreme Court had held, in *Young v. U.S.*, 2002-1 C.B. 954, 535 U.S. 43, 122 S. Ct. 1036, 152 L. Ed. 2d 79, 39 Bankr. Ct. Dec. (CRR) 45, 47 Collier Bankr. Cas. 2d (MB) 211, Bankr. L. Rep. (CCH) P 78601, 2002-1 U.S. Tax Cas. (CCH) P 50257, 89 A.F.T.R.2d 2002-1258 (2002), that the 240-day tax assessment period is tolled for any period of time that the automatic stay was in effect under Title 11, plus an additional 90 days. This priority has an effect on the nondischargeability of taxes that depend upon § 507(a)(8). See 11 U.S.C.A. § 523(a)(1).

A new tenth priority is added to § 507(a)(10) for personal injury and death claims "resulting from the operation of a motor vehicle or vessel if such operation was unlawful because the debtor was intoxicated from using alcohol, a drug, or another substance."

## § 7:52 Privacy of information and identity

Section 101(41A) is added to define "personally identifiable information," a term that will broadly include names, addresses, telephone numbers, birth dates, and social security numbers.

Several additions to the Code attempt to protect personally identifiable information about debtors and their minor children. Section 363(b)(1) is amended to add a restriction on the trustee's ability to sell property of the estate if it might include personally identifiable information about individuals who are not debtors but were connected to the debtor in some business transaction or otherwise. In line with this, and notwithstanding a sale of property of the estate by a trustee or debtor in possession, § 363 is amended by inserting a new subsection (o) to preserve claims and defenses in a consumer credit transaction or contract if it is one subject to the Truth in Lending Act or other defined consumer credit transaction. Note that this insertion of (o) does not replace the prior subsection (o), which deals with the trustee's burden of proof, and it is renumbered as subsection (p).

A new § 332 provides for a consumer privacy ombudsman to be appointed by the U.S. trustee or bankruptcy administrator upon a court order, when required for a hearing under the amended § 363(b)(1)(B). That ombudsman would assist the court by providing information concerning any personally identifiable information that might be involved in a sale of property of the bankruptcy estate. The ombudsman may be compensated from the estate as a professional by amendment to § 330(a)(1).

A new § 112 provides that if a debtor is required to furnish information about a minor child, for example in the schedules of expenses, the debtor may only be required to disclose the name of such a child in a nonpublic record, and the court and court officers shall not disclose the child's name. It is not clear how the debtor would protect a child's name without that document being filed under seal.

Code § 107(c) is added to authorize the court to protect an individual from disclosure of information that might expose that individual to identity theft or other unlawful injury. How this authority will fit with the debtor's requirements to file tax returns that are available to creditors upon request is not clear, and the Administrative Office of U.S. Courts is directed to prepare regulations for protection of the debtor concerning tax returns. Those guidelines are summarized under the tax discussion at § 6:14.

Code § 342(c) is amended to specify that notices to creditors give only the last four digits of the debtor's social security number, except where a creditor is being added to schedules, in which event that creditor shall be provided with the full social security number.

## § 7:53 Reaffirmation

Resource suggestion: David B. Wheeler & Douglas E. Wedge, A Fully-informed Decision: Reaffirmation, Disclosure and the Bankruptcy Abuse Prevention and Consumer Protection Act of 2005, 79 Am. Bankr. L. J. 789 (2005), available on Westlaw at database Legal Periodicals/Law Reviews; Jean Braucher, *Rash* and the Ride-Through Redux: The Terms for Holding on to Cars, Homes, and Other Collateral Under the 2005 Act, 13 Am. Bankr. Inst. L. Rev 457 (2005).

Code § 524 is amended to add a new subsection (k) at the end specifically setting out disclosures that must be in the reaffirmation agreements referred to in § 524(c). The written disclosures include an explanation about rescinding the agreement and the obligations incurred by a reaffirmation, and specific contents for such agreements are established. Since the statutory disclosures are so specific, it is not expected that the Judicial Conference of the United States will adopt an official reaffirmation form; however, a recommended form has been issued by the Administrative Office of the courts. See Procedural Form B240, revised October 2005 and available at the website of the courts, www.uscourts.gov/bankruptcy/forms, as well as in West's Federal Forms, volume 6A § 10131.

Subsection (m)(1) provides for a 60-day window after the filing of a reaffirmation agreement in which a presumption exists that the agreement "is an undue hardship on the debtor" if the debtor's net monthly income "is less than the scheduled payments on the reaffirmed debt." This presumption "shall be reviewed by the court," and it may be rebutted by a written explanation filed by the debtor. If the presumption is not rebutted, the court "may disapprove" the reaffirmation, but no such disapproval is permitted without "notice and a hearing," and the hearing "shall be concluded before the entry of the debtor's discharge." This subsection (m)(1) is specifically not applicable to reaffirmations with a credit union as defined by the Federal Reserve Act. See 11 U.S.C.A. § 524(m)(2).

BAPCPA also amends Title 18 of the Code to designate the U.S. attorneys and the FBI as responsible for investigating and addressing abusive reaffirmation practices as well as materially fraudulent statements made in bankruptcy schedules.

The Comptroller General is directed by BAPCPA § 205 to conduct a study of reaffirmation practices and report to Congress within 18 months of enactment any recommendations for legislation needed to address abusive or coercive tactics.

## § 7:54 Redemption

Section 722 is amended to specify that redemption of personal property in Chapter 7 requires payment of the allowed secured claim in full at the time of the redemption. This is intended to preclude redemptions by installment payments. See the discussion of valuation below at § 7:58 for Chapter 7 and 13 debtors. See Jean Braucher, *Rash* and the Ride-Through Redux: The Terms for Holding on to Cars, Homes, and Other Collateral Under the 2005 Act, 13 Am. Bankr. Inst. L. Rev. 457 (2005).

## § 7:55 Repeat filings

By several amendments, discouragement of repeat filings by debtors is seen. See the discussion under automatic stay at § 7:16 for changes in the effect of the stay, termination of the stay, or failure of the stay to be triggered, specifically § 362(c)(3) and (4).

## § 7:56 Utilities

Section 366(c) is added to specify what the term "assurance of payment" means and what forms of assurance are required. In what will make a significant difference in negotiations between the debtor and utility providers, including in Chapter 11 cases, § 366(c)(1)(B) specifically states that "an administrative priority shall not constitute an assurance of payment."

## § 7:57 Valuations

A significant change in the valuation standard is made for Chapter 7 and 13 cases, with § 506(a) amended to add a subsection (2):

(2) If the debtor is an individual in a case under Chapter 7 or 13, such value with respect to personal property securing an allowed claim shall be determined based on the replacement value of such property as of the date of the filing of the petition without deduction for costs of sale or marketing. With respect to property acquired for personal, family, or household purposes, replacement value shall mean the price a retail merchant would charge for property of that kind considering the age and condition of the property at the time value is determined.

This amendment overturns those opinions that had permitted valuations based upon wholesale valuations, including the Supreme Court's *Rash* decision, by requiring retail values to be used in Chapters 7 and 13, at least as to property acquired by the debtor for personal, family, or household use. *Associates Commercial Corp. v. Rash*, 520 U.S. 953, 117 S. Ct. 1879, 138 L. Ed. 2d 148, 30 Bankr. Ct. Dec. (CRR) 1254, 37 Collier Bankr. Cas. 2d (MB) 744, Bankr. L. Rep. (CCH) P 77409 (1997). However, the retail value is to take into account the age and condition of the property at the time of the value determination.

Valuation is not completely changed for all bankruptcy purposes, however. Section 522(a)'s definition of value for exemption purposes is not amended, nor is § 1325(a)(4)'s liquidation value test for confirmation purposes. However, for cramdown of a Chapter 13 plan, § 1325(a)(5) is modified by a new paragraph, discussed under Chapter 13, that prohibits use of § 506(a) valuation for certain motor vehicles purchased within 910 days of bankruptcy or other purchase-money collateral purchased within one year of bankruptcy. Section 361's adequate protection was not amended in its reference to a "decrease in the value" of the secured creditor's interest.

## § 7:58 Venue

Venue for recovery by a trustee of a consumer debt is changed to require that if the amount is less than $15,000 the suit must be in the district where the defendant resides. If the suit is against a noninsider and on a nonconsumer debt and for less than $10,000, again it must be filed in the district where the defendant resides. See 28 U.S.C.A. § 1409(b), but it is not clear that these venue restrictions apply to avoidance actions which arise under Title 11 since the statutory language of that section refers only to proceedings "arising in or related to such case." Venue for bankruptcy case filing is unchanged by BAPCPA. 28 U.S.C.A. § 1408.

# Chapter 8

# Exemptions, Exclusions, and Asset Protection





## § 8:1 Introduction

A major emphasis of BAPCPA's consumer provisions is the restriction of state-by-state shopping for favorable exemptions and other tools for asset protection. This chapter will review the new rules governing a variety of exemptions and exclusions, as well as new restrictions on "self-settled" asset protection trusts (APTs) and pertinent revisions to the discharge exceptions. BAPCPA made it very hard to establish domicile for the purpose of prebankruptcy exemption planning, absent very long-range planning; this difficulty increases with regard to homestead exemptions. Circumventing these new rules will prove difficult for most debtors.

The new retirement plan exemptions may provide a safety net for some debtors, but for asset protection purposes may not be very desirable or effective vehicles. The amendment of the rules limiting self-settled APTs does not change the effectiveness of domestic APT planning, as long as intentional fraud cannot be proven. This might be a good thing for debtors who would like to explore the self-settled trust vehicle for asset protection purposes. Consistent with the apparent intent of Congress, however, it leaves a cloud of uncertainty over the device because, by definition, asset protection generally means adversely affecting creditors, if not intentionally hindering, delaying, or defrauding them.

Asset protection planning has evolved in recent years into a veritable industry with many and varied domestic and offshore/foreign alternatives. In 2005, Congress heard continued criticism of the homestead and other aspects of the exemption system and sought to reduce, if not eliminate, a number of perceived abuses by implementing BAPCPA. This evidenced some hope that the loopholes would close and the bankruptcy process would be used appropriately by those who need it, not by those who seek only to exploit it.

This chapter is based in large part on a recent article in the American Bankruptcy Institute Law Review, which is suggested for additional information: Lawrence R. Ahern, III, Homestead and Other Exemptions Under the Bankruptcy Abuse Prevention and Consumer Protection Act: Observations on "Asset Protection" After 2005, 13 Am. Bankr. Inst. L. Rev. 585 (2005).

## A. LIMITATION OF HOMESTEAD AND OTHER EXEMPTIONS UNDER BAPCPA

### § 8:2 Executive summary of changes to homestead and other exemptions under BAPCPA

| New Law | Old Law |
|---|---|
| 730 days continuous domicile prior to filing required to choose law of state where the case is pending. | Exemption rules governed by state in which debtor domiciled greater of 180 days prior to filing. |

| New Law | Old Law |
|---|---|
| If rule above inapplicable, look to state in which debtor domiciled greater of preceding 180 days. | Exemption rules governed by state in which debtor domiciled greater of 180 days prior to filing. |
| If neither rule above provides debtor with exemptions, default to federal scheme. | Exemption rules governed by state in which debtor domiciled greater of 180 days prior to filing. |
| Homestead and similar exemption claims limited by amount attributable to fraudulent disposition of nonexempt property within 10 years prior to filing | No similar, objective limits. Some case law avoided exemption claims on account of fraud. |
| Generally limited to amount acquired within 1,215 days. | No similar, objective limits. Some case law avoided exemption claims on account of fraud. |
| Certain felons' and others' homesteads limited to $125,000. | No similar, objective limits. Some case law avoided exemption claims on account of fraud. |
| New federal preemptive exemptions for almost all qualified retirement and similar funds except IRAs. | State-by-state and federal exemption schemes varied in treatment of retirement funds. |
| IRAs exempt only up to $1 million plus amounts "rolled" in from other exempt retirement funds. | Federal exemption scheme allowed claim to entire IRA. State rules varied. |

## § 8:3 Limitation of homestead and other exemptions under BAPCPA—Domiciliary limits

The BAPCPA domiciliary tests utilize a formula similar to prior law, with several important exceptions specific to homestead exemptions, reflecting the political concern with exploitation of lenient state laws. See David A. Samole & David L. Rosendorf, Homestead Exemption No Longer "Debtors' Paradise," 24 Am. Bankr. Inst. J. No. 10, at 6 (December/January 2006). Under the previous test, the state of which the exemption laws applied was the state of domicile of the debtor for 180 days immediately preceding the date of the filing of the petition or the state where the debtor was domiciled for the greater portion of such 180-day period. The new rules enlarge that window to at least 730 days. 11 U.S.C.A. § 522(b)(3)(A). If the domicile for that period is not continuous, then applicable law is determined by the place where the debtor's domicile was located for the 180-day period preceding the 730-day period or where the debtor's domicile was located for a longer portion of that 180-day period than any other place.

These rules may not always produce a state's exemption laws that will apply. If, for example, the debtor filing in state A has been domiciled in state B for the requisite 730- or 180-day period and if state B's rules refer explicitly to property in state B and preclude use of its exemptions elsewhere, the effect may be to deprive the debtor of any exemption. Indeed, it may be the majority rule that homestead statutes have "no extraterritorial effect." *In re Owings*, 140 F. 739, 741(E.D. N.C. 1905); see also Hon. William Houston Brown, Lawrence R. Ahern III & Nancy Fraas MacLean, West's Bankruptcy Exemption Manual, App. F (2005 supp.) (discussing extraterritorial effect of exemption laws); William Houston Brown, Lawrence R. Ahern, III & Donna T. Snow, The Extraterritorial Effect of Homestead Exemption Statutes: An Emerging Issue, Norton Bankr. L. Adviser (Thomson/West) Jan. 2006. Congress therefore provided a default under section 522(b)(3). If the effect of the domiciliary requirement under section 522(b)(3)(A) is to render the debtor ineligible for any exemption, the debtor may elect to exempt the property specified under section 522(d)—the federal exemptions.

## § 8:4 Limitation of homestead and other exemptions under BAPCPA—Dollar limits

Under BAPCPA, homestead exemptions are not only subject to more stringent domiciliary tests but also to additional restrictions on dollar amounts that may be exempted, which are codified in new Bankruptcy Code subsections 522(o), (p) and (q). These new subsections all were effective immediately upon enactment, that is, the date the President signed the legislation, April 20, 2005. See BAPCPA § 1501(b)(2).

New section 522(o) reduces the homestead and similar exemptions to the extent that any portion of it is attributable to the debtor's disposal of nonexempt property during the 10-year period preceding the date the bankruptcy petition is filed when such disposal was made with the intent to hinder, delay, or otherwise defraud a creditor.

Section 522(o) applies only with respect to transfers of property that could not have been exempted (or a portion thereof that could not have been exempted) under section 522(b) if the debtor still held such property. The limitation applies to real or personal property that the debtor, or a dependent of the debtor, uses as a residence. It also applies to cooperatives used as residences by the debtor or a dependent of the debtor, burial plots for the debtor or a dependent of the debtor or real or personal property that the debtor or a dependent of the debtor claims as a homestead.

### Practice Alerts for Code § 522(p) and (q)

- **Subsections 522(p) and (q), but not (o), apply by their terms to override state or local law that is applied as a result of "electing under subsection (b)(2)(A) to exempt property under State or local law." One court has held that, because a debtor cannot make such an "election" in a state that has opted out of the federal exemption scheme, subsections 522(p) and (q) apply only in non-opt-**

**out states. *In re McNabb*, 326 B.R. 785, Bankr. L. Rep. (CCH) P 80333 (Bankr. D. Ariz. 2005); contra *In re Kaplan*, 331 B.R. 483 (Bankr. S.D. Fla. 2005); *In re Virissimo*, 332 B.R. 201 (Bankr. D. Nev. 2005).**

- **Practitioners in opt-out states should be aware of McNabb and its potential limitation on the effect of subsections 522(p) and (q).**

While new section § 522(o) reduces the amount that may be converted from nonexempt assets during the 10-year period preceding filing, new section 522(p) puts limits on the entire homestead or similar exemption allowed.

Under former law, once domicile was established a debtor could immediately take full advantage of whatever homestead exemption that state allowed. Understandably, states with generous homestead exemptions were reputed to have received new citizens, purchasing exempt homes on the eve of filing bankruptcy. Congress sought to limit, if not eliminate, this practice by enacting section 522(p). See Samuel K. Crocker & Robert H. Waldschmidt, Impact of the 2005 Bankruptcy Amendments on Chapter 7 Trustees, 79 Am. Bankr. L.J. 333, 349–54 (2005). Under this new provision, if the debtor chooses to exempt property under state or local law pursuant to the rules in new section 522(b)(3)(A), or has to use the state and local rules because the state in question has opted out of the federal exemptions, then the debtor may not exempt any amount of homestead interest acquired by the debtor during the 1,215-day period (approximately 40 months) preceding the date of the filing of the petition, which exceeds, in the aggregate, $125,000. Like subsection (o), the limitation under subsection (p) applies to real or personal property that the debtor or a dependent of the debtor uses as a residence and also applies to a cooperative used as a residence by a debtor or a dependent of the debtor, burial plots for the debtor or a dependent of the debtor, and real or personal property that the debtor or a dependent of the debtor claims as a homestead.

The limitation in new section § 522(p) is subject to two exceptions. First, it does not apply to an exemption claimed under new section 522(b)(3)(A) by a family farmer for the principal residence of such farmer. 11 U.S.C.A. § 522(p)(2)(A). Second, the value of home equity that is "rolled" into a new residence from a previous principal residence may be excluded from the 1,215-day holding period. 11 U.S.C.A. § 522(p)(2)(B). To qualify for this second exception, however, both the current and the previous residences must be located in the same state and the previous principal residence must have been acquired before the 1,215-day holding period.

In addition to the restrictions put in place by new sections 522(o) and (p), new subsection 522(q) limits the homestead further. Under this provision, if the court determines that the debtor has any felony conviction or any debt that is attributable to securities laws violations, regardless of when the debt arose, or crimes, torts or other misconduct causing serious physical injury or death within the past five (5) years, then the homestead that might otherwise be elected under state or federal law is capped at $125,000, regardless of when the property was acquired. This limitation applies even if the homestead was acquired before the 1,215-day holding period under subsection (o) and also applies if the homestead was acquired during the 1,215 days preceding the case under subsection (p). Congress seems to have viewed these circumstances as demonstrating that the bankruptcy filing was akin to an abusive filing. However, if the property is necessary for the support of the "debtor and any dependent," then the $125,000 limitation does not apply. It would seem that this relief was designed for married couples and the head of a household. See 11 U.S.C.A. § 522(a)(1) (defining dependent to include spouse, whether or not actually dependent).

## § 8:5 Retirement plans and similar funds under BAPCPA—New federal exemptions

Congress created a new class of exemptions in new paragraphs § 522(b)(3)(C) (applicable in opt-out states) and § 522(d)(12) (in the federal exemption scheme) for retirement plans, most of which can now be completely exempted from the bankruptcy estate by the debtor. New subsection 522(b)(3)(C) provides the following exemption:

> (3) Property listed in this paragraph is . . .
>
> (C) retirement funds to the extent that those funds are in a fund or account that is exempt from taxation under section 401, 403, 408, 408A, 414, 457, or 501(a) of the Internal Revenue Code of 1986.

Amended subsection 522(d)(12) creates a new federalized exemption scheme that exempts the following retirement funds, regardless of whether the state of domicile has opted out of the federal scheme for other property:

- qualified employer-sponsored and defined-contribution plans (e.g., 401(k) plans); 11 U.S.C.A. § 522(b)(2)(c) (referring to 26 U.S.C.A. § 401 (including Keogh Plans, under 26 U.S.C.A. § 401(c), which are not subject to the general rule that contributions reduce what may be placed in another qualified retirement vehicle));
- 403(b) plans; qualified annuity plans that are established by an employer for an employee under IRC §§ 404(a)(2) or 501(c)(3), which may be thought of as "401(k)s" for the nonprofit sector; 11 U.S.C.A. § 522(b)(2)(c) (referring to 26 U.S.C.A. § 403);
- individual retirement accounts (IRAs), simplified employee pensions (SEPs) and savings incentive match plans for employees (SIMPLEs), which are not eligible for rollovers because they are excluded from the definition of eligible retirement plan; 11 U.S.C.A. § 522(b)(2)(c) (referring to 26 U.S.C.A. § 408); see 26 U.S.C.A. § 408(d)(3)(A) (specifying what constitutes a rollover contribution); RIA Federal Tax Handbook ¶ 4363, at 710 (2005) (citing 26 U.S.C.A. § 402(c)(8)(B) ("An 'eligible retirement plan'

is: (1) an individual retirement account (not a Roth IRA), (2) an individual retirement annuity (other than an endowment contract), (3) a qualified trust, (4) an annuity plan, (5) a Code Sec. 403(b) annuity, and (6) a governmental section 457 plan."));

- Roth IRAs; 11 U.S.C.A. § 522(b)(2)(c) (referring to 26 U.S.C.A. § 408A) (showing that Roth IRAs are not eligible for rollovers because they are excluded from definition of "eligible retirement plans");
- other retirement plans for controlled groups of employees (predecessor employers, partnerships, proprietorships, governments, churches); 11 U.S.C.A. § 522(b)(2)(c) (referring to 26 U.S.C.A. § 414) (providing application of amendments and certain limitations applicable to debtors); and
- eligible deferred compensation plans established and maintained by eligible employers; 11 U.S.C.A. § 522(b)(2)(c) (referring to 26 U.S.C.A. § 457).

In addition to the plans specifically enumerated in new paragraphs 522(b)(3) and (d)(12), there is another provision in new section 522(b)(4)(A), providing that funds in a retirement vehicle that has received a favorable determination of its tax-exempt status from the Internal Revenue Service shall be presumed to be exempt from the estate. Even plans that have not received this favorable determination are exempt from the estate, so long as the IRS has not found them to be otherwise and there is either substantial compliance with the Internal Revenue Code or the debtor is not materially responsible for such noncompliance.

Now, even if some states may not allow retirement plans to be exempted from the reach of creditors, Congress has made this exemption available to all debtors by placing the language in section 522(b)(3)(C) to eliminate the opt-out. Thus either in an opt-out state or under the federal exemptions, the listed retirement funds are exempt from the bankruptcy estate. In addition, the qualified retirement plans are added to the list of federal exemptions. These provisions thus "ensure [ ] that the specified retirement funds are exempt under state as well as Federal law." H.R. Rep. No. 109-31, pt. 1, at 64 (2005), available at 2005 U.S.C.C.A.N. 88, 133.

Both direct and indirect transfers are allowed by new section 522(b)(4)(C). An example of a direct transfer would be when a debtor transfers, or "rolls," from trustee to trustee, a 401(k) into an IRA and the money never touches the debtor/taxpayer's hands. See 26 U.S.C.A. § 401(a)(31)(2000) (specifying that "such [eligible rollover distribution] shall be made in the form of a direct trustee-to-trustee transfer to the eligible retirement plan.").

Indirect rollovers are allowed as well, under section 522(b)(4)(D) (exempting "any distribution that qualifies as an eligible rollover distribution within the meaning of section 402(c) of the Internal Revenue Code of 1986"). Analogous to the "rollover" provisions accorded new residences and discussed in § 8:4 above, it appears that qualified plan rollovers will be accorded favorable and consistent treatment under BAPCPA because only a qualified plan balance may be rolled over into a continuing plan. Here, potential for abuse is not as keen and rollover treatment is necessary to meet the mandates of qualified plan portability, essential to the United States' mobile and transient workforce. An example of such an indirect transfer is when one IRA is cashed out, the funds are delivered to the debtor/taxpayer and a new IRA account is opened within 60 days of receipt of the funds; the funds must be placed in the trust within 60 days, and the key is for these funds to be held first in an "eligible retirement plan." See 26 U.S.C.A. § 402(c)(1)&(3)(2000) (listing rules applicable to rollovers from exempt trusts).

## § 8:6 Retirement plans and similar funds under BAPCPA—$1 million IRA cap

Having established a broad base of exemptions for a variety of retirement plans, BAPCPA then set a monetary limit on the use of only one of these vehicles for asset protection. New § 522(n) imposes a $1 million cap on any individual retirement account (IRA) or Roth IRA. This part of the legislation effectively limits a decision of the United States Supreme Court, rendered after passage of BAPCPA by the Senate, which suggested that the federal exemption under the terms of former section 522(d)(10)(E) would be unlimited. In *Rousey v. Jacoway*, 544 U.S. 320, 125 S. Ct. 1561, 1566, 161 L. Ed. 2d 563, 44 Bankr. Ct. Dec. (CRR) 144, 53 Collier Bankr. Cas. 2d (MB) 181, 34 Employee Benefits Cas. (BNA) 1929, Bankr. L. Rep. (CCH) P 80263, 2005-1 U.S. Tax Cas. (CCH) P 50258, 95 A.F.T.R.2d 2005-1716 (2005), the Supreme Court held that Chapter 7 debtors with access to the federal exemption scheme (i.e., whose states had not "opted out" under former section 522(b)(1)) could exempt their entire IRAs from the bankruptcy estate under section 522(d)(10)(E), which was not amended by BAPCPA (except for the $1 million cap on IRAs in subsection (n)).

The $1 million limit on the debtor's exemption for IRAs is in addition to rollovers from other kinds of more favored retirement plans. Thus the $1 million is calculated:

> . . . without regard to amounts attributable to rollover contributions under section 402(c), 402(e)(6), 403(a)(4), 403(a)(5), and 403(b)(8) of the Internal Revenue Code of 1986, and earnings thereon . . . .

See Margaret Howard, Exemptions Under the 2005 Bankruptcy Amendments: A Tale of Opportunity Lost, 79 Am. Bankr. L.J. 397, 417 (2005) (explaining operation of cap on exemptions despite its source from codified plans); John Hennigan, *Rousey* and the New Retirement Funds Exemption, 13 Am. Bankr. Inst. L. Rev. 777 (2005). While there is very little legislative history explaining most of the provisions of BAPCPA, Congress made this broad policy in favor of retirement plans clear:

> The intent of section 224 [of BAPCPA] is to expand the protection for

tax-favored retirement plans or arrangements that may not be already protected under Bankruptcy Code section 541(c)(2) pursuant to *Patterson v. Shumate*, 504 U.S. 753, 112 S. Ct. 2242, 119 L. Ed. 2d 519, 23 Bankr. Ct. Dec. (CRR) 89, 26 Collier Bankr. Cas. 2d (MB) 1119, 15 Employee Benefits Cas. (BNA) 1481, Bankr. L. Rep. (CCH) P 74621A (1992) or other state or Federal law.

H. Report No. 109-31 to accompany S. 256, 109th Cong., 1st Sess. (2005) pp. 63 to 64; available at 2005 U.S.C.C.A.N. 88 at 132 to 33.

## § 8:7 Retirement plans and similar funds under BAPCPA—Related changes in retirement plan loan rules

Finally, under new section 362(b)(19), the automatic stay does not apply to income withheld and used to pay down loans from retirement plans. See Hon. William Houston Brown, Taking Exception to a Debtor's Discharge: The 2005 Bankruptcy Amendments Make It Easier, 79 Am. Bankr. L.J. 419, 442 n. 108 (2005) (explaining that 362(b)(19) excludes from automatic stay withholding of income and collections of amounts withheld from a debtor's wages for funds listed in section 523(a)(18)); Melissa B. Jacoby, Ripple or Revolution? The Indeterminacy of Statutory Bankruptcy Reform, 79 Am. Bankr. L.J. 169, 174, 174 n. 31 (2005) (noting that § 362(b)(19) creates "exception to automatic stay for withholding of wages for pension loan repayment" and section 523(a)(18) creates an "exception to discharge for debt to pension plan[s]"); Lisa A. Napoli, The Not-So-Automatic Stay: Legislative Changes to the Automatic Stay in a Case Filed by or Against an Individual Debtor, 79 Am. Bankr. L.J. 749, 752 (2005) (stating that, in conjunction with new Code § 523(a)(18) which excepts from discharge debt owed to retirement plans, new paragraph 362(b)(19) "provides that the automatic stay does not apply to withholding of income from a debtor's wages if the withheld funds are used to repay loans from retirement plans").

Congress thus has again shown approval of maintenance of such funds, but this could have broader consequences, as debtors may borrow against their 401(k)s, etc. and could pay the loan back ahead of other creditors. The language in section 362(b)(19), however, makes it clear that exempting income used to pay down retirement plan loans does not mean the debtor has a claim against the estate for the balance due on such loans. Compare this with section 523(a)(18) excepting such loans from discharge, where no such clarifying language appears. Although it would appear that Congress intended that such loans "pass through" untouched by the bankruptcy process, one might anticipate continued litigation on this issue.

## B. EXCLUSIONS FROM THE ESTATE WITH EXECUTIVE SUMMARY

| Executive Summary | |
|---|---|
| **New Law** | **Old Law** |
| Education IRAs, tuition credits, certificates, and accounts for certain beneficiaries excluded from property of estate if funded more than 365 days before filing. Subject to $5,000 limit if funded within 720 days. | No comparable exclusions. |
| Employer funding of certain ERISA- and tax-qualified funds entirely excluded. | No comparable exclusions. |
| Pawned property generally excluded. | No comparable exclusions. |

### § 8:8 Exclusions from the estate—Education accounts

In addition to the exemptions provided and enhanced in BAPCPA, Congress also made significant changes in exclusions from the bankruptcy estate by amendments to section § 541(b), designed to protect certain education IRAs and similar funds. These new exclusions became effective 180 days following enactment: that is, on October 17, 2005. They were added to the Code by renumbering former subsection (5) to (9) and adding the following subsections:

(5) funds placed in an education individual retirement account (as defined in section 530(b)(1) of the Internal Revenue Code of 1986) not later than 365 days before the date of the filing of the petition in a case under this title, but—

(A) only if the designated beneficiary of such account was a child, stepchild, grandchild, or stepgrandchild of the debtor for the taxable year for which funds were placed in such account;

(B) only to the extent that such funds—

(i) are not pledged or promised to any entity in connection with any extension of credit; and

(ii) are not excess contributions (as described in section 4973(e) of the Internal Revenue Code of 1986); and

(C) in the case of funds placed in all such accounts having the same designated beneficiary not earlier than 720 days nor later than 365 days before such date, only so much of such funds as does not exceed $5,000;

(6) funds used to purchase a tuition credit or certificate or contributed to an account in accordance with section 529(b)(1)(A) of the Internal Revenue Code of 1986 under a qualified State tuition program (as defined in section 529(b)(1) of such Code) not later than 365 days before the date of the filing of the petition in a case under this title, but—

(A) only if the designated beneficiary of the amounts paid or contributed to such tuition program was a child, stepchild, grandchild, or stepgrandchild of the debtor for the taxable year for which funds were paid or contributed;

(B) with respect to the aggregate amount paid or contributed to such program having the same designated beneficiary, only so much of such amount as does not exceed the total contributions permitted under section 529(b)(7) of such Code with respect to such beneficiary, as adjusted beginning on the date of the filing of the petition in a case under this title by the annual increase or decrease (rounded to the nearest tenth of 1 percent) in the education expenditure category of the Consumer Price Index prepared by the Department of Labor; and

(C) in the case of funds paid or contributed to such program having the same designated beneficiary not earlier than 720 days nor later than 365 days before such date, only so much of such funds as does not exceed $5,000.

Moreover, a new subsection (e) appears at the end of section 541:

(e) In determining whether any of the relationships specified in paragraph (5)(A) or (6)(A) of subsection (b) exists, a legally adopted child of an individual (and a child who is a member of an individual's household, if placed with such individual by an authorized placement agency for legal adoption by such individual), or a foster child of an individual (if such child has as the child's principal place of abode the home of the debtor and is a member of the debtor's household) shall be treated as a child of such individual by blood.

The debtor has a new duty under new subsection 521(c), related to these education individual retirement accounts:

(c) In addition to meeting the requirements under subsection (a), a debtor shall file with the court a record of any interest that a debtor has in an education individual retirement account (as defined in section 530(b)(1) of the Internal Revenue Code of 1986) or under a qualified State tuition program (as defined in section 529(b)(1) of such Code).

## § 8:9 Exclusions from the estate—Employer funding

Section 541(b) is further expanded to exclude from the bankruptcy estate:

(7) any amount—

(A) withheld by an employer from the wages of employees for payment as contributions—

(i) to—

(I) an employee benefit plan that is subject to title I of the Employee Retirement Income Security Act of 1974 or under an employee benefit plan which is a governmental plan under section 414(d) of the Internal Revenue Code of 1986;

(II) a deferred compensation plan under section 457 of the Internal Revenue Code of 1986; or

(III) a tax-deferred annuity under section 403(b) of the Internal Revenue Code of 1986;

except that such amount under this subparagraph shall not constitute disposable income as defined in section 1325(b)(2); or

(ii) to a health insurance plan regulated by State law whether or not subject to such title; or

(B) received by an employer from employees for payment as contributions—

(i) to—

(I) an employee benefit plan that is subject to title I of the Employee Retirement Income Security Act of 1974 or under an employee benefit plan which is a governmental plan under section 414(d) of the Internal Revenue Code of 1986;

(II) a deferred compensation plan under section 457 of the Internal Revenue Code of 1986; or

(III) a tax-deferred annuity under section 403(b) of the Internal Revenue Code of 1986; except that such amount under this subparagraph shall not constitute disposable income, as defined in section 1325(b)(2); or

(ii) to a health insurance plan regulated by State law whether or not subject to such title . . . .

These provisions exclude ERISA employee benefit plans and other types of benefit plans or tax-sheltered trusts or plans referred to in several Internal Revenue Code sections:

- "Coverdell" education savings accounts, "meaning a trust created or organized in the United States exclusively for the purpose of paying the qualified education expenses of an individual who is the designated beneficiary of the trust";
- a "qualified tuition program," meaning "a program established and maintained by a State or agency or instrumentality thereof or by 1 or more eligible educational institutions," under which tuition credits may be purchased for a beneficiary; 11 U.S.C.A. § 541(b)(6) (referring to 26 U.S.C.A. § 529(b)(1);
- a "governmental plan" for retirement established and maintained by the United States, any state, or political subdivision of a state; 11 U.S.C.A. § 541(b)(7)(A)(i)(I) (referring to 26 U.S.C.A. § 414(d);
- an "eligible deferred compensation plan" established and maintained by an eligible employer; 11 U.S.C.A. § 541(b)(7)(A)(i)(II) (referring to 26 U.S.C.A. § 457); and
- a "qualified annuity plan" purchased for an employee by certain employers that generally include religious, charitable, scientific, public safety, literary, or educational corporations and organizations; 11 U.S.C.A. § 541(b)(7)(A)(i)(III) (referring to 26 U.S.C.A. § 403(b)).

### § 8:10 Exclusions from the estate—Pawned property

Section 541(b)(8) is another new exclusion from the estate for certain pawned property, excluding:

> any interest of the debtor in property where the debtor pledged or sold tangible personal property (other than securities or written or printed evidences of indebtedness or title) as collateral for a loan or advance of money given by a person licensed under law to make such loans or advances, where—
>
> (A) the tangible personal property is in the possession of the pledgee or transferee;
>
> (B) the debtor has no obligation to repay the money, redeem the collateral, or buy back the property at a stipulated price; and
>
> (C) neither the debtor nor the trustee have exercised any right to redeem provided under the contract or State law, in a timely manner as provided under State law and section 108(b) . . . .

## C. SELF-SETTLED TRUSTS WITH EXECUTIVE SUMMARY

### § 8:11 Executive summary

| New Law | Old Law |
|---|---|
| 10-year reach-back to set aside intentionally fraudulent transfers to self-settled trusts | Avoidance of transfers to such trusts left to general fraudulent transfer rules with one-year reach-back under federal law. |

Having thus established the broadly exempt status of qualified retirement funds and IRAs, at least up to the monetary cap on IRAs, BAPCPA makes another attempt to limit the use of fiduciary accounts for asset protection. Under this new provision of the trustee's independent powers under section 548 to avoid fraudulent transfers, the trustee in bankruptcy may avoid any transfer by the debtor, within 10 years before the filing of the petition, to a self-settled trust or "similar device," if the debtor is a beneficiary of the trust/device and the transfer was made with "actual intent to hinder, delay, or defraud any entity to which the debtor was or became, on or after the date that such transfer was made, indebted." 11 U.S.C.A. § 548(e)(1)(D); see David G. Shaftel and David H. Bundy, Impact of New Bankruptcy Provision on Domestic Asset Protection Trusts, 32 Est. Plan. 28, 28 (July 2005) (describing public and floor debates on Senate Bill 256, which became BAPCPA, and Sen. Charles Schumer's amendment that would have protected only $125,000 in a self-settled trust).

A self-settled trust may be defined as a trust in which the settlor is also the person who is to receive the benefits from the trust, often established in an attempt to protect the trust assets from creditors. See Black's Law Dictionary 1552 (8th ed. 2004); Restatement (Second) of Trusts § 156 (1959); Randall J. Gingiss, Putting a Stop to "Asset Protection" Trusts, 51 Baylor L. Rev. 987, 1007 (1999) ("[T]he definition of a self-settled trust is one in which the grantor is or may become a beneficiary.").

In order to show the requisite fraudulent intent that new § 548(e) requires, the trustee must relate the debtor's intent to actual (contemporaneous or subsequent) creditors rather than merely showing that the debtor created the device and transferred an asset to it. This "actual intent" language in new section 548(e) is substantially identical to the existing fraudulent transfer language of section 548(a)(1)(A). That general fraudulent transfer avoidance power was also expanded in 2005 by extending its reachback period from one year to two years under BAPCPA. 11 U.S.C.A. § 548(1)(a) and (b) (extending reach-back to two years); BAPCPA § 1406(b)(2) (making § 1402(1) effective only in cases commenced on and after April 20, 2006). The language is also substantially identical to the language used in the Uniform Fraudulent Transfers Act ("UFTA"), which has been enacted in 42 states. See, e.g., N.J. Ann. tit. § 25:2-25 (2005). Thus the new provision in section 548(e) is largely duplicative of existing law. It does not dramatically change the ground rules for asset protection planning, although it does enlarge the window through which a trustee may reach to set aside transfers without being required to find an actual unsecured creditor as to whom a particular transfer was voidable under UFTA and section 544(b) of the Bankruptcy Code. See 11 U.S.C.A. § 544(b) (allowing trustee to avoid transfer of interest of debtor or an obligation incurred by debtor "that is voidable under applicable law by a creditor holding an unsecured claim allowable under section 502 of this title or not allowable only under section 502(e) of this title").

## D. CHANGES IN DISCHARGE EXCEPTIONS WITH EXECUTIVE SUMMARY

| Executive Summary | |
|---|---|
| **New Law** | **Old Law** |
| Pending § 522(q) action delays granting of discharge. | No comparable provisions. |
| Exception to discharge for loans from certain retirement funds. | No comparable provisions. |
| Discharge may be revoked for audit-related misstatement or withholding of documents. | No comparable provisions. |
| Nondischargeability of "luxury" goods-related debts expanded. | Obligations for "luxuries" nondischargeable only with larger dollar amounts and smaller time frame. |

Several revisions to the discharge rules in § 727(a) may also have an adverse effect on asset protection efforts. New subsection (12) provides that the court should not grant a discharge when there is "reasonable cause to believe" that the new $125,000 cap on exemptions, contained in § 522(q), applies or when there is a pending proceeding that may result in the application of section 522(q) to limit the debtor's exemption to $125,000. See 11 U.S.C.A. § 727(a). Recall that new section 522(q), discussed in § 8:4 above, applies this limitation when the debtor has any felony conviction or any debt which is attributable to securities laws violations, regardless of when the conviction occurred, or crimes, torts, or other misconduct causing serious physical injury or death within the past five years. See Samuel K. Crocker & Robert H. Waldschmidt, Impact of the 2005 Bankruptcy Amendments on Chapter 7 Trustees, 79 Am. Bankr. L.J. 333, 352 (2005) ("The homestead exemption may . . . be limited to $125,000 if the debtor has committed certain criminal or tortious acts defined within the section, under a new § 522(q).").

Thus the felonious or tortious debtor is penalized twice. First, section 522(q) may reduce the debtor's homestead to $125,000, regardless of when acquired. Then § 727(a)(12) may be applied to delay a discharge until the section 522(q) proceeding is concluded, and the court may determine the applicability of the $125,000 cap, the process of which may produce grounds for one or more exceptions to discharge.

Another revision of the dischargeability rules appears in new § 523(a)(18), which excepts from discharge loans from pension, profit-sharing, stock bonus, or other tax-sheltered plans. See Hon. William Houston Brown, Taking Exception to a Debtor's Discharge: The 2005 Bankruptcy Amendments Make It Easier, 79 Am. Bankr. L.J. 419, 441 (2005) (noting that debts covered by former subsection (18) are "now covered by the new definition of domestic support obligation[,] and stating new subsection (18) relates to exemptions related to a bankruptcy debtor); Melissa B. Jacoby, Ripple or Revolution? The Indeterminacy of Statutory Bankruptcy Reform, 79 Am. Bankr. L.J. 169, 174, 174 n. 31 (2005); Lisa A. Napoli, The Not-So-Automatic Stay: Legislative Changes to the Automatic Stay in a Case Filed by or Against an Individual Debtor, 79 Am. Bankr. L.J. 749, 752 (2005) (explaining that section 523(a)(18), debt owed to retirement plans "will be excepted from a debtor's discharge"). This exception parallels the new exception to the automatic stay, extended to collection of such loans and discussed in § § 7:8 and 8:7 above.

Language was also added by BAPCPA to Code § 727(d)(4), providing new grounds for revocation of a discharge. If the debtor fails to explain satisfactorily a material misstatement made in reference to an audit that is randomly required under new 28 U.S.C.A. § 586(f) or fails to make required information available for such an audit, then the discharge is subject to revocation at the request of the trustee, a creditor, or the U.S. trustee. See Jack Seward, Empowerment of Creditor Rights: Section 727 Denial of Discharge and the BAPCPA of 2005, Am. Bankr. Instit. J. 18 (June 2005). Section 586(f) of Title 28 provides for random audits of the petitions, schedules, or other information that the debtor is required to provide in Chapter 7 and 13 cases. Audits are also required when the debtor's schedules of income and expenses reflect greater than average variances from the statistical norm for the district in which the case is filed. See generally Susan

Jensen, A Legislative History of the Bankruptcy Abuse Prevention and Consumer Protection Act of 2005, 79 Am. Bankr. L.J. 485, 486, 489–90 (2005). The audits are conducted under generally accepted auditing standards and, upon the discovery of a material misstatement, the U.S. trustee is authorized to commence an adversary proceeding to revoke the debtor's discharge. See 11 U.S.C.A. § 586.

In the spirit of the asset-protection changes, several changes have also been made to section 523(a)(2)(C), the presumption that certain debts for luxury goods or services are nondischargeable under section 523(a)(2)(A) if they are incurred on the eve of bankruptcy. Under former law, the exception applied to debts incurred in an aggregate amount of more than $1,225 to a single creditor within 60 days before commencement of the case. The amount is now reduced to $500 and the time period extended to 90 days, thereby enlarging the basket of nondischargeable "luxury" debts in two dimensions. Similarly, under former law, cash advances aggregating more than $1,225 to a single creditor, and incurred during the 60 days preceding the filing of the bankruptcy case, were presumed nondischargeable. Now, the amount has been reduced to $750 and the time period lengthened to 70 days, again casting a much larger net.

Similar to both § 522(q) (which limits exemptions on otherwise qualified property to $125,000 if the debtor has any felony conviction or any debt arising from securities laws violations, regardless of when they occurred, or crimes, torts or other misconduct causing serious physical injury or death within the past five years) and section 522(d)(10)(E) (exempting payments under certain IRC-qualified plans), section 523(a)(2)(C) also carves out amounts required for the support and maintenance of the debtor *or* any dependent. "[T]he term 'luxury goods or services' does not include goods or services reasonably necessary for the support or maintenance of the debtor or a dependent of the debtor." 11 U.S.C.A. § 523(a)(2)(C). However, § 522(q) and § 522(d)(10)(E) are phrased in the conjunctive, "debtor and any dependent," rather than the alternative "or." Why would Congress use "debtor and any dependent" in section 522(d)(10)(E) and section 522(q), but use "debtor or any dependent" in section 523(a)(2)(C)? Although dependent does include a spouse in section 522 (and only in section 522, for some reason), what about single debtors without dependents? Apparently, Congress intentionally limited this exemption to $125,000 under subsection 522(q) where the single, childless debtor is also the wrongdoer who has a felony conviction or debt attributable to securities laws violations that occurred any time prior to filing or any other debt arising from wrongdoing that caused serious physical injury or death within the past five years.

## § 8:12 New homestead/exemption timing examples

To illustrate the approach to the new rules for exemption choices, two hypothetical illustrations are presented below, from which we may draw some conclusions. The potential fact variations are virtually endless. We conclude this discussion of the new "consumer" provisions of the Bankruptcy Code in the hope that this will illustrate a road map to these difficult new exemption provisions.

◆ **Example 1:** A Tennessee businessman left his business partnership after a conflict with his former partners. This conflict resulted in extensive litigation and the risk of a judgment in the amount of $5 million. The businessman liquidated his real estate and other liquid assets in Tennessee where his homestead exemption would be $5,000 (or $7,500 in a joint filing).

The assets were liquidated after first transferring them to his wife's name.

They moved on January 1, 2005, to the state of Florida where they acquired a home with $500,000 equity.

◆ **Discussion:** Assuming that the former business partners succeed in obtaining an overwhelming judgment, the debtor has several difficult choices:

- If he files within two years (730 days) after moving his domicile to Florida, his homestead exemption will be capped at the amount of the Tennessee limit, ($5,000/$7,500). If Tennessee prohibits nonresidents from using its rules, he may be governed by the federal exemption scheme, with its $18,450 homestead exemption. 11 U.S.C.A. § 522(b).
- If he files more than two years but less than three years and four months (1,215 days) after acquiring the Florida home, the (otherwise unlimited) Florida exemption will be capped at $125,000. 11 U.S.C.A. § 522(p).
- If he files more than 1,215 days after acquiring the house but within 10 years and if the value in the house can be found to be attributable to the disposition of property with intent to hinder, delay, or defraud a creditor, all or such attributable part of the homestead exemption may be set aside. 11 U.S.C.A. § 522(o).

◆ **Example 2:** An attorney retired from a successful legal career and went into the business of selling proprietary legal software. In his practice, he had accumulated some assets of substance, including a $2 million tax-qualified individual retirement account and a house with $250,000 worth of equity, all of which was covered by his state's homestead exemption. In his new career, however, he incurred substantial contingent liabilities as a guarantor of the debts of his new company, which was not well capitalized.

◆ **Discussion:** If this debtor is forced into bankruptcy, a claim to exempt the IRA will be capped at $1 million, and the balance may be subject to administration in the bankruptcy estate, unless some portion of the IRA has been "rolled over" from a 401k or other qualified fund. 11 U.S.C.A. § 522(n). Whether this debtor's creditors could reach the IRA outside bankruptcy depends in part upon the protections built into an IRA by its creating statute and documentation and in part upon whether the debtor's domiciliary state law grants any exemption to such funds. If the latter should be true, the Supreme Court's *Rousey* decision could have some influence on how the particular state courts would interpret the reach of that state's nonbankruptcy exemption.

# Chapter 9

# Changes of Primary Interest to Parties in Business Cases

## A. SMALL BUSINESS CASES



## B. HEALTH CARE CASES



## C. CROSS-BORDER CASES



## D. OTHER CASE ADMINISTRATION ISSUES

## E. OTHER CONSTITUENCIES IN COMMERCIAL CASES

The remainder of Part One of this work deals with the BAPCPA "business" rules, which are surprisingly numerous in what many think of as a "consumer" statute. See Richard Levin & Alesia Ranney-Marinelli, The Creeping Repeal of Chapter 11: The Significant Business Provisions of the Bankruptcy Abuse Prevention and Consumer Protection Act of 2005, 79 Am. Bankr. L.J. 603 (Summer 2005). We start with three types of commercial cases that have received some broader focus in the 2005 amendments: small business cases, health care cases, and cross-border cases. We then turn to a group of general administrative issues, starting with several rules of general application that were actually enacted as a part of the "small business" provisions in BAPCPA. Finally, we conclude with several areas in which Congress has responded in some detail to the interests of various constituencies in commercial cases: secured creditors, parties to executory contracts and unexpired leases, unsecured creditors and committees, employees, attorneys, and other officers and professionals.

## A. SMALL BUSINESS CASES

### § 9:1 Executive Summary of Changes to Small Business Cases

| New Law | Old Law |
|---|---|
| Definition still not more than $2 million in debt but excludes debt to insiders and affiliates. | "Small business" defined as up to $2 million, not excluding debt to insiders of affiliates. |
| New component of definition: no active creditors' committee | Definition limited to debt cap. |

| New Law | Old Law |
|---|---|
| Mandatory classification if meet definition | Treatment based on voluntary election of debtor. |
| Numerous affirmative duties placed on trustee or debtor-in-possession in small business case. | No separate list of duties for debtor-in-possession or trustee |
| Initial meeting with U.S. trustee, prior to meeting of creditors | No initial meeting required by statute. |
| U.S. trustee must move for conversion or dismissal when grounds for such are discovered. | No comparable provision |
| Petition (or supplemental filing within seven days after filing) must attach debtor's most recent balance sheet, cash-flow statements and Federal income tax return; or statement under penalty of perjury that no such documents exist. | Same initial filing requirements for "small business" as other debtors |
| Requires periodic reports on profitability, projected receipts and disbursements, compliance with other filing requirements and payment of taxes, with failure a ground for conversion/ dismissal. | No special reporting requirements |
| If plan contains sufficient information, no disclosure statement required | Disclosure Statement always required |
| Standard forms allowed for disclosure statements | No such statutory procedure |
| Court to confirm plan not later than 45 days from its filing | No such deadline |
| 180-day exclusivity period; for an extension, debtor must show by preponderance that more likely than not a plan will be confirmed in reasonable time and order must be entered setting new deadline prior to expiration of 180–day period | 100-day exclusivity period, may be extended for cause for which debtor should not be held accountable |
| 300-day maximum for plan to be filed by any party, same requirements for extension | 160-day maximum for plan to be filed by any party; no specific mechanism for extensions |

## § 9:2 Small business cases—Introduction

BAPCPA builds on the 1994 attempt to provide a statutory framework for easier reorganization of smaller businesses in Chapter 11. While this goal has been attempted from place to place in various local jurisdictions, a real, comprehensive statutory framework for such a procedure has been lacking. It may be debated whether 2005 sees the perfection of such a procedure. Taking these requirements as a whole most charitably, however, it appears that Congress had at least two objectives. First, the rules seem designed to force the identification of "bad" cases early in the reorganization process. On the other hand, small businesses that can appropriately be reorganized are allowed to do so in a somewhat expedited confirmation process. See generally Thomas E. Carlson & Jennifer Frasier-Hayes, The Small Business Provisions of the 2005 Bankruptcy Amendment, 79 Am. Bankr. L.J. 645 (Summer 2005).

Many of the amendments impose new deadlines and reporting requirements that may be viewed as burdensome by debtors. These rules do, however, contain some provisions that will facilitate smaller companies' obtaining the benefits of Chapter 11 reorganization. Thus some of these provisions seem designed to facilitate a more economical and efficient reorganization of a smaller debtor in a nonconsumer case while others seem to be a product of skepticism about these debtors' prospects for reorganization. The latter sense arises from the heavy burden of reporting, with strict deadlines imposed by these rules under the threat of dismissal or conversion.

## § 9:3 Executive Summary of Differences between Small Business and regular Chapter 11 Cases

| Small Case | Large Case |
|---|---|
| More paperwork required with petition. | No change. |
| More reporting requirements. | No change. |
| 180-day "exclusivity period" within which only the debtor may file a plan. | 120-day exclusivity period. |
| 300-day absolute deadline to file the plan and disclosure statement. | No such ultimate deadline. |
| Plan must be confirmed within 45 days after filing. | No such time limit for confirmation. |
| Deadlines may be extended only by demonstrating confirmable plan. | Exclusivity may be extended for cause but not beyond 18 months. |

## § 9:4 Small business cases—"Small business" defined

BAPCPA § 432 provides a definition of a "small business" in Code § 101 in two parts—one based on the debtor's activities and the other based on the amount of its debt.

- A small business is a person (including the debtor's affiliates that are also in Chapter 11) engaged in commercial or business activities other than owning or operating real estate or activities incidental to owning real estate. Thus real estate ventures cannot be small businesses, although some real estate cases are given special treatment separately in BAPCPA, see §§ 9:23 below;
- It may not have more than $2 million in debt (excluding debt to insiders or affiliates). Thus the owner financing that is common in such businesses is no longer counted to exclude a small business from special treatment; and
- The $2 million debt standard applies "as of the date of the petition or the date of the order for relief." Thus incurring debt during the "gap" period (between the filing of an involuntary petition and entry of the order for relief) should not enable the debtor to escape small business treatment.

The *election* to be treated as a small business under former Code § 1121(e) has been eliminated. Anecdotal evidence suggests that this single change may dramatically affect the treatment of the majority of debtors in Chapter 11 cases in the United States in the future. If a person is a small business and files a Chapter 11 case, the case is a small business case and the panoply of new rules described here apply to all such cases.

This definition may be problematic at times, however. For the debtor to be a "small business debtor," the U.S. trustee must not have appointed a creditors' committee. Further, if a committee has been appointed, it is necessary that the committee be "sufficiently active and representative to provide effective oversight of the debtor." A case can be filed with the debtor otherwise meeting the definition of a small business debtor but then lose the status of a small business case if and when a committee is appointed. Might it reacquire the status of a small business debtor if and when the committee becomes insufficiently active and representative?

### Practice Alerts for Code § 101(51D) and Interim Rule 1020 Small Business Debtor

**On the face of the statute, it seems awkward to imagine how to apply this test, but Interim Rule 1020 provides useful guidance to assist with this problem. The debtor declares whether or not it is a small business on its petition.**

- **The debtor makes initial designation in petition (or within 15 days if an involuntary petition).**
- **The debtor's designation governs unless objected to.**

- **The deadline for objection is 30 days after the later of the 341 meeting or any amended designation.**
- **Any party in interest can object to the designation.**
- **The objection must be served on the debtor, debtor's counsel, any trustee, U.S. trustee, and either the committee or (if no committee) the top 20 unsecured creditors and others as the court directs.**
- **If a creditors' committee is appointed, however, the status changes and the court must determine that the committee is not sufficiently active and representative to provide effective oversight before the debtor is remanded to the small business rules.**
- **Any party can request that the court find that the committee is not sufficiently active and representative to provide effective oversight of the debtor.**
- **The U.S. trustee or another party in interest must file motion "within a reasonable time after the failure of the committee to be sufficiently active and representative."**
- **The debtor may also file such a motion.**

## § 9:5 Small business cases—New duties in small business cases

A new 11 U.S.C.A. § 1116 is added to the Code by BAPCPA § 4369, which consolidates many of the rules and practices that were previously scattered throughout the Code and the guidelines of the United States trustee. That section sets out a list of duties for the trustee or debtor in possession in small business cases:

(1) Append to the voluntary petition or, in an involuntary case, filed not later than seven days after the date of the order for relief—

(A) its most recent balance sheet, statement of operations, cash-flow statement, and Federal income tax return; or

(B) a statement made under penalty of perjury that no balance sheet, statement of operations, or cash-flow statement has been prepared and no Federal tax return has been filed;

(2) attend, through its senior management personnel and counsel, meetings scheduled by the Court or the United States trustee, including initial debtor interviews, scheduling conferences, and meetings of creditors convened under section 341 unless the court, after notice and a hearing, waives that requirement upon a finding of extraordinary and compelling circumstances;

(3) timely file all schedules and statements of financial affairs, unless the court, after notice and a hearing, grants an extension, which shall not extend such time period to a date later than thirty days after the date of the order for relief, absent extraordinary and compelling circumstances;

(4) file all postpetition financial and other reports required by the Federal Rules of Bankruptcy Procedure or by local rule of the district court;

(5) subject to section 363(c)(2), maintain insurance customary and appropriate to the industry;

(6) (A) timely file tax returns and other required government filings; and (B) subject to § 363(c)(2), timely pay all taxes entitled to administrative expense priority except those being contested by appropriate proceedings being diligently prosecuted; and

(7) allow the United States trustee, or a designated representative of the United States trustee, to inspect the debtor's business premises, books, and records at reasonable times, after reasonable prior written notice, unless notice is waived by the debtor.

Remember, it may be difficult at a given moment in some cases to determine whether the debtor is a small business debtor. See the discussion, above, of the new definition of a "small business" debtor added to Code § 101(51D) by BAPCPA § 432. So, the application of these duties may vary from time to time, depending on the determination described in the preceding section.

## § 9:6 Small business cases—Initial interview

BAPCPA § 439 adds a new section 586(a)(7) to Title 28, under which the U.S. trustee has a new statutory obligation to conduct initial interviews with small business debtors prior to the meeting of creditors under 11 U.S.C.A. § 341. To some extent, this codifies existing practices of the United States trustee. The interview is to evaluate the debtor's financial viability and business plan and to reach an agreement on scheduling. The U.S. trustee is also given an opportunity at this meeting to advise the debtor of its reporting and filing obligations, which, as described above, are significant. The U.S. trustee must also move promptly for conversion or dismissal whenever he or she discovers that there are grounds for such a motion.

28 U.S.C.A. § 586 (a)(7)(B) also requires that the United States trustee, "if determined to be appropriate and advisable, visit the appropriate business premises of the debtor, ascertaining the state of the debtor's books and records, and verify that the debtor has filed its tax returns . . . ." Given the possibility that a corporate debtor may still file in the venue of its incorporation, 28 U.S.C.A. § 1408, it is not difficult to imagine circumstances under which a site visit will be inappropriate or inadvisable. It is also possible, perhaps, that this will accelerate the practice of filing in a venue different from the one in which the debtor has a physical presence.

## § 9:7 Small business cases—Filing and reporting requirements

The debtor has a duty under new Code § 1116(1) to file financial and tax information along with its petition. The form is expected to call for the debtor to check a box indicating whether or not it is a "small business." This designation by the debtor is determinative unless and until the court reverses it. Interim Rule 1020.

New Code § 308 was added by BAPCPA § 434, imposing new reporting requirements on small business debtors as the case proceeds. These obligations do not become effective, however, until 60 days after rules are promulgated to establish the forms for use in reporting the data. BAPCPA § 435 required the Judicial Conference to prescribe the forms.

> Section 435(b) [of BAPCPA] requires the [small business] rules and forms to achieve a practical balance between the need for reasonably complete information by the bankruptcy court, United States trustee, creditors and other parties in interest, and the small business debtor's interest in having such forms be easy and inexpensive to complete. The forms should also be designed to help the small business debtor better understand its financial condition and plan its future.

H. Report No. 109-31 to accompany S. 256, 109th Cong., 1st Sess. (2005) p. 91; available at 2005 U.S.C.C.A.N. 88 at 157.

Periodic reports must be filed by these debtors describing their "profitability," defined as "the amount of money that the debtor has earned or lost during current and recent fiscal periods." The report must also provide reasonable approximations of projected cash receipts and disbursements and comparisons of actual receipts and disbursements to earlier projections and it must confirm compliance with the Bankruptcy Rules, tax and other governmental filing obligations, and payment of taxes.

**Practice Alerts for Code § 1116**

**Filing and Reporting Requirements**

- **The official form of petition will require that the debtor designate whether it has "small business" status.**
- **Within seven days of a "small business" bankruptcy filing, the debtor must file its most recent balance sheets, statement of operations, cash-flow statement, and federal income tax return, or certify that it has not prepared any of these financial records.**
- **Interim Rule 2015(a)(6) requires that the debtor file the section 308 reports on a monthly basis on the appropriate official form no later than 15 days after the last day of the calendar month.**

The serious nature of these reporting requirements is underscored by the fact that the unexcused failure to meet them is grounds for conversion or dismissal of the case. 11 U.S.C.A. § 1112 (b)(4)(F). If a debtor misses a reporting deadline and cannot prove a "reasonable justification" for such error, 11 U.S.C.A. § 1112 (b)(2)(B)(i), BAPCPA mandates dismissal or conversion upon motion of any party in interest, even if confirmation of a plan could be obtained within a reasonable time. Apart from the possibility that the court might consider the interests of other creditors or constituencies that would be harmed by conversion or dismissal as a part of its assessing the "reasonableness" of a justification for missing the deadline, there is no provision in the amended Code for considering those interests or balancing the gravity of the error and the consequences.

Moreover, these deadlines are established by the Code rather than by the Rules of Bankruptcy Procedure. Therefore, it is debatable whether any such deadlines can be extended by application of Rule 9006. Missed deadlines under Rule 9006 can sometimes be excused by its "excusable neglect" provision. See *Pioneer Inv. Services Co. v. Brunswick Associates Ltd. Partnership*, 507 U.S. 380, 113 S. Ct. 1489, 123 L. Ed. 2d 74, 24 Bankr. Ct. Dec. (CRR) 63, 28 Collier Bankr. Cas. 2d (MB) 267, Bankr. L. Rep. (CCH) P 75157A, 25 Fed. R. Serv. 3d 401 (1993). However, a statutory deadline may not be so excused. See *In re Butcher*, 829 F.2d 596, 16 Bankr. Ct. Dec. (CRR) 821, 17 Collier Bankr. Cas. 2d (MB) 1204, Bankr. L. Rep. (CCH) P 71989, 9 Fed. R. Serv. 3d 68 (6th Cir. 1987) (abrogated by, Bartlik v. U.S. Dept. of Labor, 62 F.3d 163, 10 I.E.R. Cas. (BNA) 1571, 130 Lab. Cas. (CCH) P 11407, 32 Fed. R. Serv. 3d 1032, 1995 FED App. 0247P (6th Cir. 1995)) (holding statutory preference deadline "jurisdictional" and therefore not subject to Rule 9006).

**Practice Alerts for Code § 1116**

**Sanctions and Consequences of Failure to Comply**

- **The motion must be heard within 30 days and decided on within 15 days of hearing.**
- **Dismissal, conversion, or appointment of a trustee moves from discretionary to mandatory ("shall" vs. "may").**
- **This requirement may be overcome, however, if the estate is not diminishing or may be rehabilitated and the best interests test cannot be met, i.e.:**
  - **an objection is filed;**
  - **there is a reasonable likelihood that a plan can be confirmed within a reasonable time;**
  - **the act that led to the creation of cause was "justifiable" and will be cured within a reasonable time fixed by the court.**

## § 9:8 Small business cases—Exclusivity, disclosure, confirmation, and modification

11 U.S.C.A. § 1125 is altered by BAPCPA § 431 and establishes the basis for a more flexible confirmation process in small business cases. The court may now determine that the plan contains sufficient information, and, in that event, no disclosure statement is required. Interim Rule 2002(b) requires 25 days' notice prior to a determination that the plan has adequate information and a disclosure statement is unnecessary. Interim Rule 3016 excepts the filing of a disclosure statement with the plan if the plan is intended to provide adequate information. If the plan is so intended, it is to be designated as such and Interim Rule 3017.1 applies as if the plan is a disclosure statement. Interim Rule 3016(b).

Disclosure statements can also be submitted on standard forms. The court may approve the filing of a disclosure statement based on a standard form. BAPCPA § 433 directs the Bankruptcy Rules Advisory Committee to propose standard form disclosure statements and plans of reorganization for small business debtors. Conditional approval is allowed and the court may then authorize solicitation based upon that approval, with final approval to be given at the confirmation hearing.

Even without a pre-approved form, it is also possible now to combine the hearing on approval of the disclosure statement and the confirmation hearing itself. A conditionally approved disclosure statement must be mailed at least 25 days before the confirmation hearing. Interim Rule 3017.1(c)(1); Interim Rule 2002.

These may prove to be real improvements that may allow the case confirmation process to operate at reduced cost to all participants. The tradeoff for those improvements, however, is a set of new deadlines for plan exclusivity and the filing and confirmation of a plan in a small business case, which are added by BAPCPA §§ 437 and 438.

The exclusive period in 11 U.S.C.A. § 1121 within which the small business debtor may file a plan is cut off by BAPCPA § 437 at 180 days after the order for relief. A plan and disclosure statement (if any), by whomever filed, must be filed no later than 300 days after the order for relief. Both of these deadlines may be extended but only by an order entered before the deadline expires and setting a new date, and only upon the debtor's showing "by a preponderance of the evidence that it is more likely than not that the court will confirm a plan within a reasonable period of time." 11 U.S.C.A. § 1121(e)(3)(A). A motion for an extension must therefore be made in time to allow the court to hear and determine whether an extension is warranted.

Under new 11 U.S.C.A. § 1129(e), as amended by BAPCPA § 438, the bankruptcy court is to confirm a plan in a small business case not later than 45 days after the plan is filed if it complies with the applicable provisions of the Bankruptcy Code. Like the deadlines for the exclusivity period and the time for filing plans, this time for confirmation of a filed plan can only be extended upon a showing by the debtor that confirmation of a plan will result at the end of the time. 11 U.S.C.A. § 1121(e)(3). Remember that an order extending this deadline must be signed before the deadline has expired. 11 U.S.C.A. § 1121(e)(3).

**Practice Alert for Code § 1129(e)**

**If a debtor files a plan that complies with the applicable provisions of the title within the period specified in § 1121(e), the court must confirm the plan no later than 45 days after the plan is filed, unless that date is extended in accordance with the provisions of § 1121(e)(3). Practitioners should contrast the 45-day deadline for confirmation of the small business plan with the notice requirements of Rule 2002, under which a disclosure statement and plan cannot in practice be approved in fewer than 50 days. Section 1129(e) and Rule 2002 are unworkable without careful action.**

- **The first confirmation hearing will be at least 28 days af-**

**ter the approval or conditional approval of the disclosure statement-more commonly 45 days (and confirmation hearings are often continued). Thus insufficient time will remain to give notice and obtain entry of an order modifying the time requirements.**

1. **One possible solution to this problem would be to accompany the plan with a motion to extend the 45-day period, so an order can be obtained prior to the expiration of the deadline, or to seek to shorten the time required by Rule 2002.**
   - **The deadline may be extended on notice and a hearing, if (a) the debtor demonstrates by a preponderance of the evidence that it is more likely than not that the court will confirm a plan within a reasonable period of time; (b) the new deadline is imposed at the time the extension is granted; and (c) the order extending time is signed before the existing deadline has expired. The court may also extend deadlines for cause.**
2. **An alternative approach would be to submit the disclosure statement in a standard, pre-approved form, if available. Interim Rule 3016(d) provides that the court may approve a small business' disclosure statement and may confirm a plan that conforms substantially to the appropriate Official Form or other standard form approved by the court.**
3. **A third would be to combine the plan and disclosure statement. Interim Rule 3016(b) excepts from the requirement of filing a disclosure statement where the plan is intended to provide adequate information under section 1125(f)(1).**
4. **Finally, counsel might seek conditional approval of the disclosure statement. See Interim Rule 3017.1. Rule 3017(a), (b), (c), and (e) do not apply to a conditionally approved disclosure statement. Interim Rule 3017(d) applies to such a disclosure statement, except that conditional approval is considered approval of the disclosure statement for the purpose of applying Rule 3017(d).**

- **The problem with alternatives three and four, above, appears if the disclosure statement is not finally approved and if creditors end up voting on the basis of an inadequate disclosure statement.**
- **In no event should the small business debtor's counsel file a plan without addressing this conflict between the statute and the rules.**
- **Again, the consequence of this may be harsh. The debtor would not have a confirmed plan, providing a basis for**

**conversion or dismissal of the case. 11 U.S.C.A. § 1112(b)(4)(J). The confirmation deadline can be extended only if the debtor demonstrates that it is more likely than not that confirmation of a plan would occur within a reasonable time (as well as again showing "reasonable justification" for the missed deadline), a new deadline is imposed when the extension is granted, and the extension order is entered before the deadline has expired.**

A final, related modification is found in 11 U.S.C.A. § 1127(e), which allows an individual debtor to modify a plan under certain circumstances even if the plan has been substantially consummated. Such post-consummation changes may be very important in light of all the new, shorter deadlines. These possible modifications have three important limitations, however. First, the nonindividual debtor may not seek such modifications; thus many small businesses will be unable to avail themselves of this procedure. Second, the modification must occur "before the completion of payments under the plan." Finally, the modifications are limited to three types:

(1) increase or reduce the amount of payments on claims of a particular class provided for by the plan;

(2) extend or reduce the time period for such payments; or

(3) alter the amount of the distribution to a creditor whose claim is provided for by the plan to the extent necessary to take account of any payment of such claim made other than through the plan.

11 U.S.C.A. § 1127(e).

**Practice Alert Regarding Code § 101(51D)**

**Small Business Definition**

**Perhaps the ultimate hazard of the definition of a small business under Code § 101(51D) is found in a consideration of the interplay of that definition with the confirmation rules.**

- **Example: a debtor, operating in a case with a creditors' committee, files a plan more than 10 months (300 days) after the commencement of the case. Thereafter, an interested party complains that the committee is not sufficiently active or representative. Is it now impossible for the debtor to proceed? Must the case be dismissed?**
- **Practitioners representing the debtor in such a case might consider arguing that the deadline to file a plan was passed while the debtor was not a small business and that the court cannot impose such an impossible condition.**
- **At the same time, the debtor may argue that circumstances exist under 11 U.S.C.A. § 1112(b), discussed below at § 9:29, for denying conversion or dismissal.**

## B. HEALTH CARE CASES

### § 9:9 Executive summary: health care cases

| New Law | Old Law |
|---|---|
| Trustee to publish notice providing patients and insurers one year to claim patient records | No comparable provisions |
| Trustee required to transfer patients from closing healthcare business to substantially similar facility | No comparable provisions |
| Patient care ombudsman appointed 30 days after case commencement; ombudsman represents interests of patients; ombudsman receives treatment as professional. | No comparable provisions |

### § 9:10 Health care cases—Introduction

The Bankruptcy Code as amended in 2005 contains several provisions designed to address concerns that are particularly applicable to bankruptcies involving health care providers. "Health care business," "patient," and "patient records" are all new definitions added to Code § 101 and are clearly designed to cover a broad range of health care institutions. See 11 U.S.C.A. § 101(27A) (defining "health care business" to include a variety of hospitals, treatment facilities, hospices, home health agencies, and "similar" institutions as well as long-term care facilities).

**Practice Alerts for Code §§ 333, 351, 503, 704**
**Health Care Cases**

**Taken together, the provisions discussed below impose burdens on health care cases that may be overwhelming, particularly for trustees appointed in Chapter 7 cases. See Harold L. Kaplan, BAPCPA: Healthcare Lenders Beware?, 24 Am. Bankr. Inst. J. No. 10, at 32 (December/January 2006).**

### § 9:11 Health care cases—Patient records

We will see elsewhere, in § 9:27, that the "dot com" collapse of the early 21st Century prompted concern in the 2005 amendments to Code § 362 over the handling of "personally identifiable information" collected in Internet businesses. Similarly, the occurrence of a financial crisis in the health care industry during the drafting that produced the 2005 legislation also led to a new Code § 351, in which the amended statute addresses preservation of patient records.

Anticipating that troubled health care businesses may not have resources available to pay for proper handling of patient records under applicable law, the trustee is obligated to publish a notice that provides patients and insurance providers a year within which to assert a claim to such information, after which the trustee may destroy the records. 11 U.S.C.A. § 351(1)(A). Thereafter, the trustee still must ask any appropriate federal agency for permission to deposit the patient records with that agency, although no duty is imposed on any such agency. 11 U.S.C.A. § 351(2). During the first 180 days of the one-year notice period, the trustee is also "promptly" to attempt to make direct contact with patients and insurance companies. 11 U.S.C.A. § 351(1)(B).

## § 9:12 Health care cases—Patient transfer

The concern for patients in financially troubled health care institutions goes beyond their records. New patient care duties are imposed on the debtor or trustee by amendment of Code § 704(a). The trustee is to "use all reasonable and best efforts to transfer patients from a health care business that is in the process of being closed to an appropriate health care business," according to 11 U.S.C.A. § 704(a)(12), which also specifies that the transferee institution should be in the vicinity of the closing facility, should provide the patient with substantially similar services, and should maintain a reasonable quality of care.

## § 9:13 Health care cases—New administrative expense claim

Recognizing that the obligations described in the preceding paragraphs may create a burden on the estate and the government, BAPCPA amends Code § 503(b) to allow an administrative expense claim for "actual necessary costs and expenses of closing a health care business incurred by a trustee or by a Federal agency," including those costs of disposing of records as well as the transfer of patients.

## § 9:14 Health care cases—Patient care ombudsman

In another similarity to the rules related to personally identifiable information, we have after 2005 a new third-party professional, the patient care "ombudsman." The debtor, trustee, and ombudsman all have special duties under these new provisions of Chapter 11. An entirely new Code § 333 was added by the 2005 amendments to establish the role of ombudsman in health care business bankruptcies in Chapter 7, 9, or 11 cases. BAPCPA § 1104. This new ombudsman is a "professional person" covered by Code § 330(a)(1). The ombudsman is to be appointed within 30 days after the commencement of the case and is to "monitor the quality of patient care and to represent the interests of the patients of the health care business unless the court finds that the appointment of such ombudsman is not necessary for the protection of patients under the specific facts of the case." 11 U.S.C.A. § 333(a)(1).

The ombudsman is required to report to the court regarding the quality of patient care within 60 days after appointment and every 60 days thereafter. 11 U.S.C.A. § 333(b)(2). The ombudsman is also required to file a special, immediate report upon determining "that the quality of patient care provided to patients of the debtor is declining significantly or is otherwise being materially compromised." 11 U.S.C.A. § 333(b)(3).

### § 9:15 Health care cases—Restriction on transfer of assets by nonprofit entities

The amended Bankruptcy Code also restricts the use, sale, or lease of property by other than moneyed, business or commercial entities, discussed below at § 9:27. These new rules will be of particular concern in nonprofit health care cases.

### § 9:16 Health care cases—Relief from stay for Department of Health and Human Services

As a final expression of the focus of Congress on these cases, BAPCPA § 1106 adds a new exception to the automatic stay. 11 U.S.C.A. § 362(b)(28). Under this provision, the Secretary of Heath and Human Services is allowed to exclude the debtor from participation in Medicare or any other federal health care program, as defined in and pursuant to the Social Security Act.

## C. CROSS-BORDER CASES

### § 9:17 Cross-border cases—Introduction

BAPCPA adds a new Chapter 15 to the Bankruptcy Code, which is almost identical to a model law proposed by the United Nations Commission on International Trade Law (UNCITRAL). The legislation is based on UNCITRAL's extensive work in numerous areas of international commercial law, which have resulted in several international conventions and model laws that have been widely adopted around the world and, most recently, the Model Law on Cross-Border Insolvency, which is the basis for Chapter 15 of the revised Bankruptcy Code. Chapter 15 replaces former Code § 304 and provides much more breadth and detail than that earlier attempt to address these issues. See generally Jay Lawrence Westbrook, Chapter 15 At Last, 79 Am. Bankr. L.J. 713 (Summer 2005).

A detailed analysis of Chapter 15 is somewhat beyond the scope of this publication. Its primary goals, however, are to increase international cooperation in cross-border cases, largely by enabling bankruptcy courts in the United States to recognize foreign insolvency proceedings. Such insolvency proceedings are divided into two categories, as defined in 11 U.S.C.A. § 1502(4) and (5). An insolvency proceeding that is pending in a country in which the debtor has "the center of its main interests" is defined as a "foreign main proceeding," while other insolvency proceedings in countries in which the debtor is carrying on "nontransitory economic activity" are defined as "foreign nonmain proceedings."

### § 9:18 Cross-border cases—Commencement of Chapter 15 case

A Chapter 15 case is commenced by the filing of a petition for "recognition" of a foreign proceeding (either main or nonmain) under Code § 1515. Upon recognition of a foreign proceeding, sections 361, 362, 365, 549, and 552 automatically apply with respect to the debtor, the property of the debtor, and transfers of interests of the debtor in property within the territorial jurisdiction of the United States and a foreign representative may operate the debtor's business and exercise the rights and powers of a trustee under Code §§ 363 and 552. 11 U.S.C.A. § 1520. The court may also grant additional stays against individual actions and proceedings to protect the debtor's assets, obligations, and liabilities in the United States beyond the scope of those basic provisions of the Bankruptcy Code. 11 U.S.C.A. § 1521. Such protection may even be granted on an expedited basis upon the filing of the petition under proper circumstances. 11 U.S.C.A. § 1519.

### § 9:19 Cross-border cases—Administrative issues

Additional actions may be undertaken by the foreign representative under sections 522, 544, 545, 547, 548, 550, 553, and 724(a). 11 U.S.C.A. § 1523. However, the power to commence such actions (to avoid acts detrimental to creditors) is limited where the foreign proceeding is "nonmain" in nature. 11 U.S.C.A. § 1523.

Chapter 15 contains several provisions to facilitate cooperation and communication between the United States bankruptcy courts and trustees with the foreign courts and representatives. 11 U.S.C.A. §§ 1525 to 30. For example, the courts may communicate directly with each other, under Code § 1525(b), "by any means considered appropriate by the court." 11 U.S.C.A. § 1527(2).

## D. OTHER CASE ADMINISTRATION ISSUES

### § 9:20 Other case administration issues—Introduction

BAPCPA, which purports to deal with small businesses, also has a number of provisions that seem to be more generally applicable in Chapter 11. Those and other rules of general interest in nonconsumer cases are addressed next.

## § 9:21 Other case administration issues—Status conferences with executive summary

| Executive Summary | |
|---|---|
| **New Law** | **Old Law** |
| The court is required to hold status conferences to further the expeditious and economical resolution of the case. | A status conference was authorized by the 1994 amendment of the Bankruptcy Code, but was optional. |

11 U.S.C.A. § 105(d), as amended by BAPCPA § 440, now affirmatively requires the bankruptcy court to hold "such status conferences as are necessary to further the expeditious and economical resolution of the case." This is an expansion of the effort begun in 1994 to empower the bankruptcy judge to influence the general administration of a bankruptcy case, without requiring the court to await the commencement of a contested matter or adversary proceeding.

## § 9:22 Other case administration issues—Automatic stay—In rem permanent relief after small business filing with executive summary

| Executive Summary | |
|---|---|
| **New Law** | **Old Law** |
| Automatic stay not applicable in a second case when debtor is currently a small business debtor or was in a case confirmed or dismissed within two years before the current order for relief. | No exemption for application of automatic stay in successive case filings |
| Stay denied to successor companies under similar circumstances. | No exemption for application of automatic stay in successive case filings |

The stay imposed by 11 U.S.C.A. § 362 is significantly limited by new subsection (n) when the small business debtor has filed a previous bankruptcy case. Under the amendment, the automatic stay does not apply in a small business case if the debtor has another case pending simultaneously (although perhaps the stay in that case would still be in effect) and the stay does not operate if the debtor was in a small business case that was dismissed within two years prior to the order for relief in the second case or if the debtor had a plan confirmed in a small business case within two years of the new case.

**Practice Alert for Code § 362(n)(1)(D)**
**Acquisition of Small Businesses**

**Here is the broader application: This limitation of the stay is also triggered in the case of an entity that acquired all or substantially all of the assets of a small business under the circumstances described above. 11 U.S.C.A. § 362(n)(1)(D). This successor debtor can overcome the denial of stay protection under Code § 362(n)(1)(D) if it can show by a preponderance of the evidence:**

- **that the subsequent bankruptcy filing resulted from circumstances beyond the debtor's control; and**
- **that it is more likely than not that the court will confirm a plan, other than a liquidating plan, in a reasonable time.**

## § 9:23 Other case administration issues—Automatic stay—Single-asset real estate cases with executive summary

**Executive Summary**

| New Law | Old Law |
|---|---|
| No debt limitation; excludes family farmer | Debt limitation of $4 million did not exclude family farmer |
| Must file confirmable plan or commence payments to secured creditor at nondefault contract rate of interest | File confirmable plan or commence payments to secured creditor at current fair market rate of interest |
| Requirements begin the later of 90 days after entry of order for relief or 30 days after court determines that debtor has "single asset real estate" | Requirements begin 90 days after entry of order for relief |
| Payments to secured creditor can be made from income generated by the property | Payments to secured creditor not specifically allowed to be made from income generated by the property |
| Payments to secured creditor may be made regardless of consent under a cash collateral order | No comparable provision |

BAPCPA § 444 deals with the oft-criticized "single asset real estate case." The underlying definition still requires that a single property or project, other than residential property of fewer than four units, generate substantially all the gross income of the debtor, while no substantial business is conducted other than operating the property and activities incidental thereto. 11 U.S.C.A. § 101(51B). However, the scope of such cases has been significantly increased by amendment of the definition of that phrase, which eliminates the debt limitation. 11 U.S.C.A. § 101(51B). Thus larger real estate developments may now be subject to these provisions. However, the new definition now excludes a family farmer. 11 U.S.C.A. § 101(51B).

Section 362 still imposes a requirement in such a case that the debtor must have either (1) filed a confirmable plan or (2) commenced monthly payments to the secured creditor in order to keep the automatic stay in effect. Under the former Code, the payment obligation arose 90 days after the entry of the order for relief. Former Code § 362(d)(3). However, because there was sometimes difficulty determining whether a particular case was a single-asset real estate case, section 362(d)(3) now provides that the date on which the requirement commences is the end of the 90-day period or 30 days after the court determines that the debtor has "single-asset real estate," whichever occurs later.

**Practice Alerts for Code § 362(d)(3)**
**Single-Asset Real Estate**

**Presumably, if there is some doubt, some interested party will wish to raise the issue before the running of the 90-day period.**

- **A lender seeking to assure the lapse of the automatic stay under 11 U.S.C.A. § 362(d)(3) should move promptly either to obtain an agreed order or to seek a court determination of single-asset real estate status.**
- **If an order is obtained at most 60 days into the case and if neither a confirmable plan is submitted nor payments commenced (as described below), the stay will lapse after the 90th day.**
- **If an order is obtained later than 60 days into the case and if neither a confirmable plan is submitted nor payments commenced, the stay will lapse 30 days after the court determines single-asset real estate status.**

Code § 362 also changes the amount of the payment necessary to continue the stay in effect. Under the former Code, the debtor was required to pay an amount "equal to interest at a current fair market rate on the value of the creditor's interest in the real estate." Now, in cases governed by BAPCPA § 444, the payment must be in the amount of the "nondefault contract rate of interest on the value of the creditor's interest in the real estate." Of course, prescribing rates in legislation is risky business. In a rising interest rate environment, this provision may actually benefit single-asset real estate debtors.

The monthly payments required in a single-asset real estate case under section 362 may be made notwithstanding the failure of the debtor to obtain consent for use of a lender's cash collateral under 11 U.S.C.A. § 363(c)(2). Thus the payments "may, in the debtor's sole discretion, notwithstanding section 363(c)(2), be made from rents or other income generated before, on, or after the date of the commencement of the case by or from the property to each creditor whose claim is secured by such real estate."

11 U.S.C.A. § 362(d)(3)(B)(i). This language is not perfectly clear, but it appears to require a correspondence between the collateral and the creditor to be paid. In other words, creditor A may be paid from its rents or other income generated by its collateral. Creditor B may not be paid from the collateral of creditor A, at least not without permission obtained under section 363.

### § 9:24 Other case administration issues—Automatic stay—Netting agreements

The amended Bankruptcy Code contains a series of complex rules championed by the federal securities and banking regulators and designed to reduce the risk of a systemic financial and economic failure in the United States. These provisions relate to securities contracts, commodity contracts, forward contracts, repurchase agreements, swap agreements, and master netting agreements.

A detailed discussion of these provisions is beyond the scope of this publication. Several commentators have addressed the issue in different contexts. See, e.g., Edward R. Morrison & Joerg Riegel, Financial Contracts and the New Bankruptcy Code: Insulating Markets from Bankrupt Debtors and Bankruptcy Judges, 13 Am. Bankr. Inst. L. Rev. 641 (2005); Federal Deposit Insurance Corporation, Adjusting the Rules: What Bankruptcy Reform Will Mean for Financial Market Contracts, http://www.fdic.gov/bank/analytical/fyi/2005/101105fyi.html (last visited December 18, 2005).

The pre-BAPCPA rules that had addressed this concern have been expanded to include a wide range of "financial participants," defined in 11 U.S.C.A. § 101 (22A). Their netting actions are removed from the coverage of the automatic stay. 11 U.S.C.A. § 362(b)(27). Their interests are not subject to avoidance as statutory liens or otherwise under sections 544, 545, 547, or 548. 11 U.S.C.A. § 546(e) to (h) & (j). Thus, for example, under Code § 546(j), a trustee may not avoid a transfer made by or to a master netting agreement participant in connection with any master netting agreement or any individual contract under such a master agreement prior to the commencement of the case unless it was actually a fraudulent conveyance and could have otherwise been avoided under an individual contract.

Similarly, the definitions of transactions benefiting from these new rules have been updated. For example:

> Section 901(f) of [BAPCPA] amends the definition of "swap agreement" to include an "interest rate swap, option, future, or forward agreement, including a rate floor, rate cap, rate collar, cross-currency rate swap, and basis swap; a spot, same day-tomorrow, tomorrow-next, forward, or other foreign exchange or precious metals agreement; a currency swap, option, future, or forward agreement; an equity index or equity swap, option, future, or forward agreement; a debt index or debt swap, option, future, or forward agreement; a total return, credit spread or credit swap, option, future, or forward agreement; a commodity index or commodity swap, option, future, or forward agreement; or a weather swap, weather derivative, or weather option." As amended, the definition of "swap agree-

ment" will update the statutory definition and achieve contractual netting across economically similar transactions that are the subject of recurring dealings in the swap agreements.

H. Report No. 109-31 to accompany S. 256, 109th Cong., 1st Sess. (2005) p. 121; available at 2005 U.S.C.C.A.N. 88 at 183.

## § 9:25 Other case administration issues—Automatic stay—Investor protection

11 U.S.C.A. § 362 is amended by BAPCPA to facilitate governmental protection for investors. This is accomplished by excepting "securities self-regulatory organizations" from the automatic stay. Such an organization is defined as a securities association registered with the Securities and Exchange Commission. 11 U.S.C.A. § 101(48A). Protected activity includes commencement or continuation of such organizations' investigations and actions, including enforcement and such other action as delisting, that are related to the regulatory power of such an organization or the failure to meet applicable regulatory requirements. 11 U.S.C.A. § 362(b)(25).

## § 9:26 Other case administration issues—Use, sale and lease of property—Transfers made by nonprofits with executive summary

**Executive Summary**

| New Law | Old Law |
|---|---|
| Trustee may use, sell, or lease property of a nonmoneyed business only in accordance with applicable nonbankruptcy law | No deference to nonbankruptcy law in use, sale or lease of property of a nonmoneyed business |
| Transfers of property of a nonmoneyed business under a plan, subject to applicable nonbankruptcy law | No deference to nonbankruptcy law in transfers of property of a nonmoneyed business under a plan |
| Attorney general from state where nonmoneyed debtor formed, does business, or is incorporated has standing to appear on all issues involving the use, lease, sale, or transfer of property | No comparable provision |

As suggested in our discussion of health care cases, § 9:9 et seq. above, Congress has shifted the balance of power substantially in cases involving nonprofit hospitals and other corporations or trusts that are not moneyed, business, or commercial in nature. Prior to enactment of BAPCPA, sales of such debtors' assets could be made to moneyed, commercial entities unless the sale was met with an objection that was upheld by the court. Now, Bankruptcy Code §§ 363, 541, and 1129 have been amended to reverse the order of such proceedings.

Note that these changes were effective as of the date of enactment and applied to cases pending on that date, except that the court is not to confirm a plan under Chapter 11 without consideration of the possibility that the changes would substantially affect the rights of a party in interest who first acquired rights with respect to the debtor after the commencement of such a pre-enactment case. BAPCPA § 1221(d). This and several other rules on this subject are found in extended rules of construction that apparently will not be codified.

Code § 363(d) has been amended to add a new proviso that the trustee may use, sell, or lease such property only "in accordance with applicable nonbankruptcy law that governs the transfer of property by a corporation or trust that is not a moneyed, business, or commercial corporation or trust." 11 U.S.C.A. § 363(d)(1). Thus Congress has deferred to nonbankruptcy law governing such debtors.

Similarly, a new clause has been added to Code § 1129(a), providing a new confirmation requirement that the court find that all transfers of property under the plan were made in accordance with applicable provisions in nonbankruptcy law that govern the transfer of property by a corporation or trust that is not a moneyed, business, or commercial corporation or trust. 11 U.S.C.A. § 1129(a)(16). Again, this is a significant deference to nonbankruptcy law.

Finally, BAPCPA adds a new subsection (f) to Code § 541 (as an apparent limitation on property of the estate) as follows:

> (f) Notwithstanding any other provision of this title, property that is held by a debtor that is a corporation described in § 501(c)(3) of the Internal Revenue Code of 1986 and exempt from tax under § 501(a) of such Code may be transferred to an entity that is not such a corporation, but only after the same conditions as would apply if the debtor had not filed a case under this title.

11 U.S.C.A. § 541(f).

With these substantive changes, BAPCPA makes two additional procedural changes. The attorney general of a state in which the debtor is incorporated, was formed, or does business is given standing to appear in a proceeding with respect to these issues. Again, the attorney general no longer must object to a sale in violation of one of the substantive provisions; however, nothing in these amendments is to be construed to require the bankruptcy court to remand or refer any proceeding or controversy to any other court or to require the approval of any other court for the transfer of property. BAPCPA § 1221(e) (establishing a Rule of Construction).

## § 9:27 Other case administration issues—Use, sale and lease of property—Transfer of personally identifiable information with executive summary

| Executive Summary | |
|---|---|
| **New Law** | **Old Law** |
| "Personally identifiable information" can only be transferred in accordance with policy of debtor or after court approval with finding of no violation of applicable nonbankruptcy law. | No comparable provisions |
| If transfer with court approval, "consumer privacy ombudsman" must be appointed. | No comparable provisions |

Code § 363 is amended in several ways to deal with narrow but significant issues of public interest, prompted in part by the notoriety of a few "dot com" cases in which the courts were asked to authorize the liquidation of contact information related to customers and other visitors to commercial websites. Under the amendment, if a debtor was in the business of offering products or services to individuals and had a policy of prohibiting the transfer of "personally identifiable information" about those individuals, then the trustee may not transfer such information unless (1) the proposed sale or lease is consistent with the policy or (2) the court approves the transaction after giving it due consideration and finding that no showing has been made that the transaction would violate applicable nonbankruptcy law. 11 U.S.C.A. § 362(b)(1)(B).

Before the second route described above (i.e., a sale or lease not consistent with a privacy policy but not violating nonbankruptcy law) may be taken, the court must order the U.S. trustee to appoint a "consumer privacy ombudsman" not later than five days before the commencement of the hearing. This ombudsman is a creature of new Code § 332, which suggests several issues for consideration at the hearing and prohibits the ombudsman from disclosing any personally identifiable information that he or she may obtain in the process.

## § 9:28 Other case administration issues—Appointment of a trustee or examiner in a Chapter 11 case with executive summary

| Executive Summary | |
|---|---|
| **New Law** | **Old Law** |
| Court may appoint trustee or examiner as an option in lieu of converting or dismissing a case. | No comparable provisions |
| United States trustee directed to move for appointment of trustee in circumstances indicating misfeasance or dishonesty in corporate governance. | No comparable provisions |
| Motion to convert or dismiss based on "substantial or continuing loss or diminution of the estate and absence of a reasonable likelihood of rehabilitation" must be granted. | No comparable provisions |

Related to the increased emphasis on potential conversion or dismissal of a Chapter 11 case, discussed next in § 9:29, the grounds for appointment of a trustee are expanded under the amended Bankruptcy Code. New 11 U.S.C.A. § 1104(a)(3), added by BAPCPA § 442, allows the court to appoint a trustee or examiner as an option instead of converting or dismissing the case. The court may appoint a trustee or examiner if grounds exist to convert or dismiss and if the court determines that such appointment is in the best interest of creditors and the estate. 11 U.S.C.A. § 1104(a)(3). At the same time, the United States trustee must move for appointment of a trustee in more circumstances, reflecting an increasing and more specific concern about corporate governance:

> The United States trustee shall move for the appointment of a trustee under subsection (a) if there are reasonable grounds to suspect that current members of the governing body of the debtor, the debtor's chief executive or chief financial officer, or members of the governing body who selected the debtor's chief executive or chief financial officer, participated in actual fraud, dishonesty, or criminal conduct in the management of the debtor or the debtor's public financial reporting.

11 U.S.C.A. § 1104(e). The "reasonable grounds to suspect" standard is very broad; it largely eliminates the U.S. trustee's prosecutorial discretion.

This provision, requiring the U.S. trustee to move for the appointment of a trustee in cases of fraud, is applicable to cases filed on or after April 20, 2005.

The court may appoint a trustee or examiner in lieu of converting or dismissing the case if it is in the best interests of creditors and the estate. 11 U.S.C.A. § 1104(a). Before a case is dismissed or converted, a debtor or other party in interest may move the court to deny the dismissal/conversion by establishing that there is a reasonable likelihood that a plan will be timely confirmed. However, if the "cause" for dismissal or conversion is "substantial or continuing loss or diminution of the estate and an absence of a reasonable likelihood of rehabilitation," the court is not to deny dismissal or conversion. 11 U.S.C.A. § 1112(b)(1). This is true even if the debtor attempts to show a reasonable likelihood of timely confirmation of a plan. Otherwise, again, the court may deny a motion for conversion or dismissal if it can be established that there is a reasonable likelihood of plan confirmation and that, as to the grounds for granting the motion, there is a reasonable justification for the act or omission and such failings will be cured within a reasonable time. 11 U.S.C.A. § 1112(b)(2).

### § 9:29 Other case administration issues—Conversion and dismissal with executive summary

| Executive Summary | |
|---|---|
| **New Law** | **Old Law** |
| 16 items of "cause" to dismiss or convert a Chapter 11 case | 10 items of "cause" to dismiss or convert a Chapter 11 case |
| "Parties in interest" may move for conversion or dismissal. | Parties in interest, U.S. trustee or bankruptcy administrator may move for conversion or dismissal. |
| Motion to convert or dismiss must be heard within 30 days of its filing and must be decided within 15 days of commencement of hearing absent movant's consent or "compelling circumstances." | No specific timeline for hearing motions to dismiss or convert |
| Court must grant conversion or dismissal unless it identifies specific circumstances such that relief is not in best interest of creditors and the estate. | No comparable provision |

The amendment of the Bankruptcy Code in 2005 has expanded the grounds for conversion or dismissal of a Chapter 11 case. Simultaneously, it makes it more difficult to defeat such a request and accelerates the procedures applicable to a conversion/dismissal motion. 11 U.S.C.A. § 1112 has been amended by BAPCPA § 442 to add to the list of examples of cause for conversion or dismissal of Chapter 11 cases. Note that section 442 is among the amendments categorized for "small business" but it actually applies to all cases.

First, the "cause" for dismissal or conversion under 11 U.S.C.A. § 1112(b)(4) has been expanded to include 16 items:

(A) substantial or continuing loss to or diminution of the estate and the absence of a reasonable likelihood of rehabilitation;

(B) gross mismanagement of the estate;

(C) failure to maintain appropriate insurance that poses a risk to the estate or to the public;

(D) unauthorized use of cash collateral substantially harmful to one or more creditors;

(E) failure to comply with an order of the court;

(F) unexcused failure to satisfy timely any filing or reporting requirement established by this title or by any rule applicable to a case under this chapter;

(G) failure to attend the meeting of creditors convened under § 341(a) or an examination ordered under Rule 2004 of the Federal Rules of Bankruptcy Procedure without good cause shown by the debtor;

(H) failure timely to provide information or attend meetings reasonably requested by the United States trustee (or the bankruptcy administrator, if any);

(I) failure timely to pay taxes owed after the date of the order for relief or to file tax returns due after the date of the order for relief;

(J) failure to file a disclosure statement, or to file or confirm a plan, within the time fixed by this title or by order of the court;

(K) failure to pay any fees or charges required under chapter 123 of Title 28;

(L) revocation of an order of confirmation under § 1144;

(M) inability to effectuate substantial consummation of a confirmed plan;

(N) material default by the debtor with respect to a confirmed plan;

(O) termination of confirmed plan by reason of the occurrence of a condition specified in the plan; and

(P) failure of the debtor to pay any domestic support obligation that first becomes payable after the date of the filing of the petition.

Thus former Code § 1112(b) has been embellished to add examples of grounds for dismissal or conversion, including such things as failure to maintain insurance under some circumstances and improper use of cash collateral. The old list was not exclusive, however, and the same is true of the new one.

In an unexplained semantic difference from former Code § 1112(b)(1), the parties eligible to move for conversion or dismissal have been reduced from "a party in interest or the United States trustee or bankruptcy administrator" in the former law to only "a party in interest." The U.S. trustee and bankruptcy administrator have been deleted as parties who may raise this issue. The Supreme Court has recently construed a similar deletion (in the 1994 amendments) very strictly. *Lamie v. U.S. Trustee*, 540 U.S. 526, 124 S. Ct. 1023, 157 L. Ed. 2d 1024, 42 Bankr. Ct. Dec. (CRR) 122, 50 Collier Bankr. Cas. 2d (MB) 1299, Bankr. L. Rep. (CCH) P 80038 (2004) (holding removal of debtor's attorney from list of persons entitled to payment from estate prevented payment of fees to debtor's attorney).

The legislative history offers no explanation for the deletion of the U.S. trustee and the bankruptcy administrator from pre-BAPCPA § 1112(b). However, this may be less likely to be construed as a congressional determination that those parties cannot raise the issue of conversion or dismissal of Chapter 11 cases, because 11 U.S.C.A. § 307 separately gives the U.S. trustee standing to appear and be heard on any issue. If this at least creates an ambiguity so that the courts may look behind the narrow language of Code § 1112(b)(1), the U.S. trustee may argue that Congress could not have intended to exclude this standing from the panoply of other powers so that the U.S. trustee could not move to dismiss or convert in appropriate circumstances. It may be more difficult to get around the omission of the bankruptcy administrators in Alabama and North Carolina cases, because administrators are not granted blanket standing by Code § 307.

In the context of considering the motion, the court is required to grant conversion or dismissal, whichever is in the best interest of the creditors and the estate, if the movant establishes one of the many grounds for conversion or dismissal, unless the court specifically identifies unusual circumstances such that the relief is not in the best interest of the creditors and the estate. In particular, subsection (b) contains two provisions. The first (paragraph (b)(1)) provides:

> Except as provided in paragraph (2) of this subsection, subsection (c) of this section, and section 1104(a)(3), on request of a party in interest, and after notice and a hearing, absent unusual circumstances specifically identified by the court that established that the requested conversion or dismissal is not in the best interests of creditors and the estate, the court shall convert a case under this chapter to a case under Chapter 7 or dismiss a case under this chapter, whichever is in the best interests of creditors and the estate, if the movant establishes cause.

11 U.S.C.A. § 1112(b)(1).

The next paragraph ((b)(2)) awkwardly adds another negative by providing that conversion/dismissal "shall not be granted absent unusual circumstances specifically identified by the court that establish that such relief is not in the best interests of creditors and the estate." This is further qualified by requiring that the debtor or other party in interest objecting to the motion must establish that:

> (A) there is a reasonable likelihood that a plan will be confirmed within the time frames established in §§ 1121(e) and 1129(e) of this title, or if such sections did not apply, within a reasonable period of time; and
>
> (B) the grounds for granting such relief includes an act or omission of the debtor other than under paragraph (4)(A)—
>
> (i) for which there exists a reasonable justification for the act or omission; and
>
> (ii) that will be cured within a reasonable period of time fixed by the court.

11 U.S.C.A. § 1112(b)(2). It remains to be seen how the courts will apply this language.

Like a motion for relief from the stay, filing a motion for conversion or dismissal is now given accelerated docketing by the statute. Under 11 U.S.C.A. § 1112(b)(3), the court must commence the hearing not later than 30 days after the filing of the motion and must decide the motion no later than 15 days after commencement of the hearing unless the movant agrees to a delay or unless there are "compelling circumstances" that "prevent the court from meeting the time limits established."

**Practice Alert for Code § 1112(b)(3)**
**Mandatory Time for Hearing and Deciding Motion for Conversion or Dismissal**

**The language of paragraph 1112(b)(3) is not self-effectuating. Failure of the court to commence the hearing or to decide the motion within the requisite time periods does not result in automatic conversion or dismissal. Is the only remedy to seek a writ of mandamus?**

## § 9:30 Other case administration issues—"Prepackaged" Chapter 11 plans with executive summary

| Executive Summary | |
|---|---|
| **New Law** | **Old Law** |
| Solicitation of votes on a "prepackaged" Chapter 11 plan can continue after commencement of case. | Solicitations for votes on "prepackaged" Chapter 11 plans must cease after commencement of case, pending approval of a disclosure statement. |
| Prepackaged plans can be confirmed prior to first meeting of creditors | First meeting of creditors must be held before prepackaged Chapter 11 plan can be confirmed? |

## § 9:31 Other case administration issues—"Prepackaged" Chapter 11 plans—Solicitation

The amendments that deal with "prepackaged" plans slightly alter the language in 11 U.S.C.A. § 1125. If a creditor received a solicitation prior to bankruptcy to vote in favor of a plan in a prepackaged Chapter 11, other lawful solicitations can now be made during the pendency of the case. Section 1125, as amended by BAPCPA § 408, now authorizes the solicitation of acceptances or rejections of a plan if the entity "was solicited before the commencement of the case in a manner complying with applicable nonbankruptcy law." Under prior law, solicitation could not continue after the commencement of the case until the disclosure statement had been approved by the court. Now, provided that a prepetition solicitation was commenced in compliance with applicable law, it may continue after filing.

## § 9:32 Other case administration issues—"Prepackaged" Chapter 11 plans—First meeting of creditors

The amendments also facilitate the approval of a prepackaged plan even before conducting the meeting of creditors under section 341.

This is accomplished by a new 11 U.S.C.A. § 341(e), which allows the court to cancel ("order that the United States trustee not convene") the meeting of creditors in the event that a plan has been filed with prepetition acceptances. This overrides some pre-amendment suggestion that a prepackaged plan could not be confirmed prior to the "first meeting." Thus if the debtor has filed a plan and solicited acceptances of the plan prior to the commencement of the case, new Code § 341(e) now allows the court, after notice and a hearing, to waive the requirement of a meeting of creditors.

## § 9:33 Other case administration issues—Confirmation and related issues—Exclusivity with executive summary

| Executive Summary | |
|---|---|
| **New Law** | **Old Law** |
| No extension of 120-day exclusive period for debtor to file plan beyond 18 months from date of order for relief. | 120-day exclusivity period could be extended for "good cause." |

The expeditious filing and confirmation of the plan in Chapter 11 has been a frequent theme of creditor concern and congressional action in the past. The amendments of 2005 are no exception. Again Congress has responded to the comments of a variety of creditors who wish to expedite the administration of Chapter 11 cases by focusing on the debtors' exclusive right to file a plan under 11 U.S.C.A. § 1121, and the Bankruptcy Code now substantially limits a debtor's ability to obtain extensions of its time to file and confirm its plan.

Under BAPCPA § 411, the long-standing 120-day exclusivity period may not be extended beyond 18 months from the date of the order for relief. The former Code allowed the court to extend or reduce the 120-day period for "cause" and the only limit on the extent to which the court could reduce or extend the period was a mandatory interlocutory appeal allowed by the 1994 legislation and later embodied in Rule 8001(a) of the Federal Rules of Bankruptcy Procedure. Now there is also an unconditional limit on the exclusivity period at 18 months from the date of the order for relief. 11 U.S.C.A. § 1121(d)(2)(A). Good cause is still required for an extension of the period, but no extension can be granted beyond the 18-month period. 11 U.S.C.A. § 1121(d)(2)(B).

The time within which a debtor must obtain acceptances of its plan filed within the exclusivity period continues to be 60 days longer than the exclusivity period itself. 11 U.S.C.A. § 1121 (d)(1). This deadline for obtaining acceptances "may not be extended beyond a date that is 20 months after the date of the order for relief." 11 U.S.C.A. § 1121(d)(2)(B).

**Practice Alert For Code § 1121**
**New Exclusivity Periods**

**The practical effect of these changes should be to force earlier negotiation of the terms of a plan.**

- **The lapse of exclusivity is always a serious problem for the debtor. Therefore, debtor's counsel should be proactive in this process.**
- **Will the effect of an ultimate deadline enable creditors to sit back for 18 months? This seems to be a glacial remedy.**
- **While a creditor's behavior of this nature seems unlikely to trigger "lender liability," it may be appropriate for a court to consider a motion to require good-faith negotiation.**

## § 9:34 Other case administration issues—Postpetition disclosure statements

The Bankruptcy Code now imposes additional requirements upon the disclosure statement as a part of the plan confirmation process. First, 11 U.S.C.A. § 1125(a) now requires the debtor to include (in the disclosure statement) a discussion of the "potential material Federal tax consequences of the plan to the debtor, any successor to the debtor, and a hypothetical investor typical of the holders of claims or interests in the case," thus confirming by statute what has been the practice in many cases.

The Code's disclosure requirements, however, are moderated by new language (also in 11 U.S.C.A. § 1125(a)) allowing the court to consider the complexity of the case, the benefit of additional information to creditors and other parties in interest, and the cost of providing such additional information in determining whether a disclosure statement provides adequate information. In an extremely complex case, this may be a greater burden on the debtor, but this would seem to allow the court to consider the disclosure statement more leniently in a smaller and less complex case.

## § 9:35 Other case administration issues—Modification of Chapter 11 plan

In addition to the new requirements for modification of an individual's Chapter 11 plan, discussed above at § 9:8, a new Code § 1127(f) makes it clear that all of the confirmation requirements of sections 1121 through 1129 apply to any modification. The court is to direct the level of disclosure for such a modification and is to approve it after notice and a hearing. The definition of "notice and a hearing" has not changed. 11 U.S.C.A. § 102(1).

## § 9:36 Other case administration issues—Tax issues

In §§ 701 et seq., BAPCPA deals at length with a number of issues regarding tax-related obligations of the bankruptcy estate and tax claims in bankruptcy cases. While many of these changes are beyond the scope of this publication, a few will be of interest to bankruptcy practitioners more generally.

### § 9:37 Other case administration issues—Tax issues—Notice to taxing authorities

Under Code § 505(b), the clerk is required to maintain a list of addresses designated by taxing authorities for requesting determination of a tax. In the absence of such a designation, the estate's request may be made to the address for filing a return or a protest.

### § 9:38 Other case administration issues—Tax issues—Interest on tax claims

The applicable interest rate on a tax claim, including the rate to be used in determining the present value of a tax claim, is the rate that would be applicable under nonbankruptcy law. 11 U.S.C.A. § 511. The rate is to be determined in the context of confirmation as of the month of confirmation. 11 U.S.C.A. § 511.

### § 9:39 Other case administration issues—Tax issues—Priority claims

Code § 507(a) has been amended to clarify the date and extent of priority tax claims. The priority now extends to taxes assessed during the 240-day period prior to the commencement of the case, plus any time that a stay was in effect, plus 90 days. 11 U.S.C.A. § 507(a)(8). The time is also extended by a pending request for a hearing or appeal. 11 U.S.C.A. § 507(a)(8). The one-year time for computing property taxes is to be determined as of the date the debt was incurred rather than the date on which it was assessed. 11 U.S.C.A. § 507(a)(8)(B).

### § 9:40 Other case administration issues—Tax issues—Confirmation standards with executive summary

| Executive Summary | |
|---|---|
| **New Law** | **Old Law** |
| Priority tax claims under a Chapter 11 plan must be paid in regular cash installments to be paid within five years of date from order for relief. | Priority tax claims to be paid in no specific fashion over a period of time not to exceed six years from date of assessment. |

| Executive Summary | |
|---|---|
| **New Law** | **Old Law** |
| Priority tax claims must be paid in a manner at least equal to most favorable treatment of nonpriority unsecured claims (except administrative convenience class) under the plan. | Priority tax claims to be paid in no specific fashion over a period of time not to exceed six years from date of assessment. |

Confirmation standards for treatment of tax payments have been changed significantly in Chapter 11. Tax payments were formerly to be paid in an indeterminate fashion over a period of six years measured from the date of assessment. Former Code § 1129(a)(9). Paragraph (9) has now been amended to require "regular installment payments in cash" that equal the allowed amount of the claim and may not extend beyond five years from the date of the order for relief. 11 U.S.C.A. § 1129(a)(9). In addition, they must be paid in a fashion that is at least as favorable as the most favorable treatment of nonpriority unsecured claims under the plan, other than claims in an "administrative convenience" class. 11 U.S.C.A. § 1129(a)(9)(C). The same rules apply to secured claims that otherwise qualify as priority tax claims. 11 U.S.C.A. § 1129(a)(9)(D).

## § 9:41 Other case administration issues—Tax issues—Tax returns with executive summary

| Executive Summary | |
|---|---|
| **New Law** | **Old Law** |
| Taxing authority may move for conversion or dismissal if debtor fails to file tax return or properly request extension. | No comparable provisions |
| After request filed by taxing authority, debtor has 90 days to file return or request for extension. | No comparable provisions |

The 2005 amendments also give some special attention to issues related to tax returns. A tax return includes a return that satisfies the requirements of applicable nonbankruptcy law. 11 U.S.C.A. § 523(a)(1)(B)(ii). It also includes a return prepared by taxing authorities or a written stipulation to a judgment or final order outside bankruptcy. BAPCPA § 714. It does not include, however, a return made pursuant to Internal Revenue Code § 6020(b) (by the IRS in case of the taxpayer's failure to make a return or submission of a false or fraudulent return) or similar state or local law. Code § 521 has been amended to allow a taxing authority to seek conversion or dismissal of the case based on a debtor's failure either to file a tax return that is due after commencement or to properly request an extension. Upon such a request by the taxing authority, the debtor has 90 days within which to file the return or request, after which the case is required to be converted or dismissed, whichever is in the best interest of creditors and the estate. 11 U.S.C.A. § 521(j)(2).

## § 9:42 Other case administration issues—Utility service with executive summary

| Executive Summary | |
|---|---|
| **New Law** | **Old Law** |
| Utility may alter, refuse, or discontinue service if assurance of payment is not received in a form satisfactory to the utility within 30 days from the filing of the petition or 20 days from the order for relief. | Adequate assurance of future payment of utility not ultimately up to satisfaction of utility. |
| Timely past payment and priority claim cannot be used as adequate assurance of future payment. | Timely payment history often served as adequate assurance of future payment. |
| Upon request of a party in interest, court may order modification of the amount of assurance of payment. | No comparable provision |
| Utility may recover or offset against a prepetition security deposit without notice or court order. | No such automatic exception to the stay. |

The amendments improve the protection given to utilities in bankruptcy. 11 U.S.C.A. § 366 now includes a detailed definition of "assurance of payment" for the purpose of maintaining utility service. The rights of the utility in cases in which the debtor fails to furnish adequate assurance under 11 U.S.C.A. § 366, however, can be very problematic for a debtor seeking to operate under the new amendments. Code § 366(b) allows a utility to alter, refuse, or discontinue service if such assurance is not furnished within 20 days after the order for relief. Subsection (c)(2) further allows the utility to alter, refuse, or discontinue if assurance is not received, satisfactory to the utility, within 30 days from the filing of the petition.

There are several express options now for assuring payment, including prepayment or surety bonds. 11 U.S.C.A. § 366(c)(1)(A). However, the amendment specifically precludes evidence of the timely past payment of utility charges as assurance of payment in the future. Similarly, it is not enough to rely on the availability of an administrative expense priority as "assurance." Ultimately, however, the adequate assurance of payment must be "satisfactory to the utility." 11 U.S.C.A. § 366(c)(2).

A new provision in Code § 366(c)(3) specifically allows the court to order modification of the amount of assurance of payment upon the request of a party in interest and after notice and a hearing.

Finally, new Code § 366(c)(4) explicitly allows a utility to recover or offset against a prepetition security deposit with neither notice nor any order of the court.

**Practice Alerts for Code § 366**

**Utilities**

**Taken together, these changes represent a significant shift in the balance of power toward utilities and may make it much more difficult in many cases for a debtor to satisfy utilities' adequate protection demands. These factors will need to be considered in budgeting for operations in Chapter 11 as well as in the tactics to be pursued by debtor's counsel.**

- **"Utility" is not defined, particularly as it relates to business with telecom companies, therefore, this may give rise to disputes over entitlement to the protections in section 366.**
- **It is also unclear for what period the debtor must furnish adequate assurance—one day, one week, one month?**
- **For debtors with high utility costs (e.g., manufacturers), a cash deposit requirement could mean the difference between reorganization and immediate liquidation. In bargaining, however, utilities may realize that they stand to recover less on pre-petition claims if the inability to provide postpetition assurance causes the debtor to liquidate.**
- **Because prepetition payment history no longer provides adequate assurance, the utility industry may find that some debtors will allow a larger obligation to accrue to a utility before filing and then use the cash saved to provide the postpetition assurance that they require.**

**An opinion decided shortly after the effective date of this provision, *In re Lucre, Inc.*, 333 B.R. 151, 45 Bankr. Ct. Dec. (CRR) 172, Bankr. L. Rep. (CCH) P 80412 (Bankr. W.D. Mich. 2005), holds that the bankruptcy court has no discretion under this provision to continue the automatic stay against the utility for more than thirty days after the petition date simply because the utility had failed to respond to the debtor's offers of adequate assurance. An offer of adequate assurance binds the utility to continue service only for the 21st through the 30th day following the petition.**

- **Counsel for the debtor should carefully consider the language of 11 U.S.C.A. § 366(c)(3)(A), comparing that language with former subsection 366(b).**

- **The debtor must react early in the case to obtain an order by the 30th day in order to maintain the stay in place. A "first day" request on this issue should become a routine part of Chapter 11 practice after BAPCPA.**
- **The *Lucre* case, however, suggests that the court may have no way to modify the requirements that the utility be "satisfied" by the offer of adequate assurance.**
- **In advance of filing the case, debtor's counsel should consider obtaining cash collateral usage sufficient to provide for the utilities of the debtor and, if possible, should discuss the issues with the utilities in advance of filing.**
- **Aside from the restrictive rule in the *Lucre* case, debtor's counsel might consider asking the court to determine that the proper amount of assurance is $0. Again, however, this may require first that the debtor and the utility come to terms on some adequate protection.**

## § 9:43 Other case administration issues—Preferential and fraudulent transfers with executive summary

**Executive Summary**

| New Law | Old Law |
|---|---|
| Ordinary course of business defense proved by showing *either* that transfer was made in ordinary course of business of the parties *or* made according to ordinary business terms (industry standard). | Ordinary course of business defense proved by showing *both* ordinary course of business of parties *and* made according to ordinary business terms (industry standard). |
| $5,000 minimum for preference actions in non consumer cases | No minimum dollar amount for preference actions in nonconsumer cases |
| Noninsider avoidance actions seeking less than $10,000 in nonconsumer case must be brought in district of defendant's residence | Avoidance actions seeking less than $1,000 must be brought in district of defendant's residence |
| Insider avoidance actions of less than $1,000 must be brought in district of defendant's residence | No comparable provision |
| New provision makes clear that transfers made more than 90 days prior to bankruptcy, from debtor to noninsider entity for benefit of insider-creditor, may be avoided only against insider. | 1994 amendment precluded *recovery* but not *avoidance* against noninsider |

| Executive Summary | |
|---|---|
| **New Law** | **Old Law** |
| Two-year look-back period for fraudulent transfers | One-year look-back period for fraudulent transfers |
| New provision allowing avoidance of transfers to insiders under employment contracts and not in the ordinary course of business | No comparable provision |

### § 9:44 Other case administration issues—Preferential and fraudulent transfers-introduction

Congress has given special attention to two groups of creditors who, as practitioners may attest, are often very aggrieved by the bankruptcy process. Perhaps no bankruptcy-related client is more deeply offended by the process than vendors who are sued for preferences. They perceive that they have delivered value to the debtor, they have been paid something to which they are entitled, they often have a claim on which they expect little or no distribution and, adding insult to injury, they are being asked to pay back something that they lawfully received. In 2005, Congress responded to these complaints about preferences in several ways but also added to the trustee's power to recover fraudulent transfers.

### § 9:45 Other case administration issues—Preferential and fraudulent transfers—The "ordinary course" defense

First, BAPCPA § 409 amended Code § 547(c)(2). This provision of section 547 is one of the affirmative defenses to a preference action, the "ordinary course defense." There has been some confusion over the meaning of paragraphs (B) and (C) of section 547(c)(2). Somewhat confusing was the meaning of the language of paragraph (C), which appeared to some courts to require that the preference defendant must qualify a transfer two ways: (1) as being in the ordinary course of the business or financial affairs of the parties, and (2) also as conforming to some broader industry standard. See, e.g., *In re A.W. & Associates, Inc.*, 136 F.3d 1439, 32 Bankr. Ct. Dec. (CRR) 422, 39 Collier Bankr. Cas. 2d (MB) 1078, Bankr. L. Rep. (CCH) P 77668 (11th Cir. 1998) (holding bankruptcy court was required to consider industry standards to sustain ordinary course defense).

Congress now has attempted to eliminate this problem by restructuring and tweaking the language slightly to change its meaning dramatically. Former phrase (A) has been moved up into the preamble of § 547(c)(2). The remaining phrases, previously found in (B) and (C), have now been relettered as (A) and (B). The smallest but most significant change, however, is that the "and," between former subparagraphs (B) and (C), becomes an "or" in the new section. The effect of this is to wipe out the difficulty formerly created by the conjunctively linked elements under § 547(c)(2). Now, in case of a transfer on account of a debt that was incurred in the ordinary course of the parties' business or financial affairs, as long as the defendant can show *either* that the transfer was "made in the ordinary course of business or financial affairs of the debtor and the transferee" *or* that it was "made according to ordinary business terms," then the defendant has a valid affirmative defense to an otherwise voidable preference action.

**Practice Alerts for Code § 547(c)(2)**
**"Ordinary Course" Defenses**

**The amendment should reduce the cost of defending a preference action because the defendant will no longer be required to produce expert testimony regarding industry standards. Moreover, the debate over whether expert testimony is even required to prove industry standards will no longer materialize if the defendant can show that the transfer was made in the ordinary course of business or financial affairs of the debtor and the transferee.**

**Both of these defenses may still be useful, as illustrated by the following examples:**

**1. Assume that a debtor has paid a creditor in the ordinary course of their business or financial affairs. It is no longer necessary for a defense under § 547(c)(2) for the creditor/defendant to put on proof of industry custom with respect to the terms of their relationship.**

**2. Assume alternatively that applicable "industry practice" is to have 15-day terms. If the debtor was an important customer of the creditor/defendants, however, then payment outside those industry terms may still be within the ordinary course of the affairs of the debtor and the creditor.**

**3. Suppose, on the other hand, that an attorney's client starts to delay its payments as the client's financial affairs deteriorate. This is not in keeping with the parties' practice. It may be possible, however, for the attorney to prove that this is not outside "ordinary business terms." The attorney's argument: It is common for clients experiencing financial difficulty to make payments outside the terms of the contract. Attorneys recognize and accept this; it is the "industry standard." Thus such payments are still within the scope of the new "ordinary course" defense.**

## § 9:46 Other case administration issues—Preferential and fraudulent transfers—Preference caps in nonconsumer cases

In addition to the other "affirmative defenses" to avoidance of preferences in Code § 547(c), a new item has been added as (c)(9). In nonconsumer cases, the recovery of preferences is precluded unless the aggregate property at issue is equal to or greater than $5,000. Although subsection (c)(8) has heretofore capped recoveries in consumer cases at $600, this is the first time that nonconsumer preferences have been so limited.

### § 9:47 Other case administration issues—Preferential and fraudulent transfers—Venue for nonconsumer actions to collect money or property

The next change favoring defendants in these avoidance actions is found in BAPCPA § 410. This is an amendment to 28 U.S.C.A. § 1409(b), the venue provision governing actions to collect money or property. By this amendment to Title 28, BAPCPA restricts actions on nonconsumer debts against noninsiders. Such actions seeking less than $10,000 must be filed in the district court in the district in which the defendant resides, even if the bankruptcy is pending in another district. 28 U.S.C.A. § 1409(b). Note that these limits on such actions are not limited to preference actions, although that seems likely to be the area of greatest impact of this change. Also note that the $10,000 debt limit does not protect a defendant that is an insider, in which case the $1,000 venue limit continues.

**Practice Alert for Code § 547(c)(9) and 28 U.S.C.A § 1409(b) Preference Caps**

**In the wake of the mass prosecution of preference actions in large commercial cases across the country, these new caps will provide relief to at least some defendants who otherwise could not justify the expense of defending the preference action, particularly where the lawsuit filed would have been in a foreign jurisdiction.**

- **Defense counsel should remember, however, that these are issues that must be raised affirmatively. This may be particularly important until the effect of BAPCPA becomes part of routine practice.**
- **In considering the venue cap, trustees and other practitioners should carefully analyze the possible residence of a corporate defendant. Such entities are "deemed to reside in any judicial district in which it is subject to personal jurisdiction." 28 U.S.C.A. § 1391(c). If the corporate defendant has been doing business with the debtor, it may have established sufficient contacts to be subject to jurisdiction under the forum state's long-arm statute. See Martin P. Sheehan, Dealing with Changes to Venue in Adversary Proceedings, NABTalk (Natl. Assn. Bankr. Trustees) Fall 2005 (analyzing this issue, suggesting that section 1409 venue rule may be largely insignificant and discussing actions against other entities).**
- **Note that 28 U.S.C.A. § 1409(b) refers to "proceedings arising in or related to" a bankruptcy case. It does not men-**

**tion proceeding "arising under" the Bankruptcy Code. Can the argument be made that it does not include avoidance actions on the basis that such actions "arise under" Title 11? See *Matter of Van Huffel Tube Corp.*, 71 B.R. 155, 15 Bankr. Ct. Dec. (CRR) 1038 (Bankr. N.D. Ohio 1987); (holding preference action is one "arising under" Code); contra, *In re Greiner*, 45 B.R. 715, 12 Bankr. Ct. Dec. (CRR) 820, 12 Collier Bankr. Cas. 2d (MB) 363 (Bankr. D. N.D. 1985); *In re Little Lake Industries, Inc.*, 146 B.R. 463, 27 Collier Bankr. Cas. 2d (MB) 1609, Bankr. L. Rep. (CCH) P 74978 (Bankr. N.D. Cal. 1992), aff'd and remanded, 158 B.R. 478, 24 Bankr. Ct. Dec. (CRR) 1132, Bankr. L. Rep. (CCH) P 75464 (B.A.P. 9th Cir. 1993) (holding former section 1409(b) applicable to preference action but suggesting action was not "arising in or related to" the case.)**

## § 9:48 Other case administration issues—Preferential and fraudulent transfers—Another attempt to fix the *Deprizio* problem

In *Levit v. Ingersoll Rand Financial Corp.*, 874 F.2d 1186, 19 Bankr. Ct. Dec. (CRR) 574, 22 Collier Bankr. Cas. 2d (MB) 36, 11 Employee Benefits Cas. (BNA) 1323, Bankr. L. Rep. (CCH) P 72910 (7th Cir. 1989) (disapproved of by, In re Arundel Housing Components, Inc., 126 B.R. 216, 21 Bankr. Ct. Dec. (CRR) 959, Bankr. L. Rep. (CCH) P 73922 (Bankr. D. Md. 1991)), the Seventh Circuit caused distress in the lending community by deciding that a noninsider creditor was subject to the one-year preference period when the transfer simply benefited an insider-guarantor. Thus a bank with no insider relationship with its borrower might be exposed to preference actions for up to a year after a payment to the bank simply because it had a guaranty from an insider who was indirectly benefited by the payment.

In 1994, Congress attempted to address this problem by an amendment to add Code § 550(c), which precluded *recovery* from a noninsider outside the basic 90-day preference period. This did not resolve the issue addressed in *In re Williams*, 234 B.R. 801, 34 Bankr. Ct. Dec. (CRR) 600 (Bankr. D. Or. 1999) (holding that the 1994 amendments did not preclude action against noninsider to *avoid* preferential security interest granted more than 90 days before bankruptcy).

Now, in an amendment to Code § 547, a new subparagraph (i) has been added to make it clear that not only may such transfers not be recovered, but also they may not be avoided if such a transfer was made more than 90 days prior to bankruptcy except with respect to an insider creditor. This is a change that became effective retroactively upon enactment of BAPCPA (for cases "pending" or commenced on or after April 20, 2005). BAPCPA § 1213(b); *In re ABC-Naco, Inc.*, 331 B.R. 773, 45 Bankr. Ct. Dec. (CRR) 154, Bankr. L. Rep. (CCH) P 80379 (Bankr. N.D. Ill. 2005) (holding that retroactive application of BAPCPA did not unconstitutionally deprive debtor of any contract right it possessed under its mortgage agreement with lender and BAPCPA could be applied retroactively without violating committee's substantive due process rights).

### § 9:49 Other case administration issues—Preferential and fraudulent transfers—Fraudulent transfer look-back period

11 U.S.C.A. § 548(a)(1) has been changed to double the size of the window through which the trustee may reach back to recover or avoid fraudulent transfers. The transfers subject to scrutiny are expanded from those made within one year to those made within two years. 11 U.S.C.A. § 548(a)(1). This is a provision that applies, however, only to cases commenced one year or more after enactment of BAPCPA (i.e., on or after April 20, 2006). BAPCPA § 1406(b)(2).

### § 9:50 Other case administration issues—Preferential and fraudulent transfers—Key employee retention plans as fraudulent transfers

The scrutiny of key employee retention plans and similar restrictions is discussed at length below at § 9:68 and 9:69, in the context of employer-employee relations in Chapter 11 more generally. Congress' addressing of these issues in BAPCPA included an amendment to the fraudulent transfer rules in the Bankruptcy Code. A benefit paid or obligation incurred to an insider under an employment contract may be avoided as a fraudulent transfer unless it was made in the ordinary course of business. 11 U.S.C.A. § 548(a)(1)(B)(ii)(IV) (effective in cases filed on or after April 20, 2005). Subsection (a)(1)(B) requires a showing that less than reasonably equivalent value was received in exchange for such transfer or obligation, but the new employee avoidance provision does not require a showing of insolvency of the debtor at the time of the transfer or obligation.

### § 9:51 Other case administration issues—Collection of data on other entities

BAPCPA § 419 continues the effort to measure progress in the reorganization process by ordering the Judicial Conference of the United States to promulgate forms by which Chapter 11 debtors are to disclose the "value, operations, and profitability" of entities in which the debtor holds a controlling or substantial interest. This is a curious provision, as practitioners will quickly realize, because the subject of the report is an entity that is not in bankruptcy and may not be controlled by the debtor but may simply be one in which the debtor's interest is "substantial." This entity is not a debtor, and the debtor may not be in a position either to obtain the information or to force the entity to complete the form. Nevertheless, failure to make such a report may be cause for conversion or dismissal, 11 U.S.C.A. § 1112(b)(4)(F), triggering the harsh procedures for dismissal previously discussed. See § 9:29 above.

## § 9:52 Other case administration issues—Postconfirmation discharge

The amended Code imposes two new kinds of limitations on discharges in Chapter 11. See Ralph Brubaker, Taking Exception to the New Corporate Discharge Exceptions, 13 Am. Bankr. Inst. L. Rev. 757 (2005). In addition to the new limitation in individual cases contained in 11 U.S.C.A. § 1141(d)(5) and discussed above at 6:17, corporations are also now precluded by 11 U.S.C.A. § 1141(d)(6) from obtaining a discharge by confirmation from certain categories of debt:

(1) debts owed to a domestic governmental unit arising from obtaining money, credit, etc., by false pretenses, false representations, actual fraud, or a false financial statement (as described in Code § 523(a)(2)(A)(B));

(2) debts arising from a qui tam claim or similar action under 31 U.S.C.A. §§ 3721 et seq.; and

(3) (3) debts for a tax or customs duty with respect to which the debtor made a fraudulent return or "willfully attempted in any manner to evade or defeat such tax or such customs duty."

### Practice Alerts for Code § 1141(d)(6) Nondischargeable Obligations in Corporate Chapter 11

**Except for qui tam and similar liability, the language of this provision leaves somewhat unclear whether the nondischargeable debts to governmental units must arise from the debtor's own fraudulent dealings with the government, or whether this extends to claims or fines the government could impose on account of the debtor's defrauding of investors or creditors.**

## E. OTHER CONSTITUENCIES IN COMMERCIAL CASES

## § 9:53 Other constituencies in commercial cases—Secured creditors—Perfection and the preference rules with executive summary

| Executive Summary | |
|---|---|
| **New Law** | **Old Law** |
| For preference purposes, 30-day grace period for secured creditors to perfect their security interests. | 10–day grace period |

BAPCPA § 403 amends 11 U.S.C.A. § 547(e)(2) to provide additional protection for secured creditors in the context of the preference rules. Subsection (e)(2) generally provides a grace period to a transferee within which to file its documents and "perfect" the transfer. Under the new law, that grace period has been extended from 10 days to 30 days. Thus, for example, a secured party taking a security interest in the equipment of a debtor should have 30 days within which to file its financing statement under Article 9. If the filing occurs within this time, the transfer is deemed to have taken effect at the time of the granting of a security interest.

### § 9:54 Other constituencies in commercial cases—Secured creditors—Perfection of the purchase-money security interest with executive summary

| Executive Summary | |
|---|---|
| **New Law** | **Old Law** |
| 30 days to perfect a PMSI | 20 days to perfect a PMSI |

A similar attempt to assist secured creditors is found in the expansion of the grace period allowed by Code § 547(c)(3). This is the affirmative defense to preference actions that protects purchase money security interests (enabling loans). Until the amendment of the Bankruptcy Code in 2005, both the Bankruptcy Code and Article 9 (section 9-324(a)) allowed 20 days within which to perfect after the debtor received possession of goods other than inventory or livestock. Now the Bankruptcy Code has been amended to increase the grace period to 30 days.

**Practice Alert for Code § 547(c)(3) Purchase-Money Security Interests**

**Commercial practitioners should not be misled by new subsection 547(c)(3), however, and should remember that purchase-money priority over other secured creditors, being governed by nonbankruptcy law, is dependent on filing within the 20 days or otherwise as allowed by the Uniform Commercial Code. See UCC § 9-324.**

### § 9:55 Other constituencies in commercial cases—Secured creditors—Warehouseman's lien with executive summary

| Executive Summary | |
|---|---|
| **New Law** | **Old Law** |
| New provision preventing trustee from avoiding warehouseman's lien | No comparable provision |

Congress has also addressed the interests of warehousemen who may have statutory liens for storage, transportation, and other charges. BAPCPA § 406 adds protections for such liens by protecting them from avoidance actions under Code § 545, although they are otherwise statutory liens subject to attack under that section. Now, under Code § 546(i), the trustee may not avoid such liens. The provision is to "be applied in a manner consistent with any State statute applicable to such lien that is similar to section 7-209 of the Uniform Commercial Code. [Lien of Warehouseman]." 11 U.S.C.A. § 546(i)(2).

### § 9:56 Other constituencies in commercial cases—Parties to executory contracts and unexpired leases with executive summary

| Executive Summary | |
|---|---|
| **New Law** | **Old Law** |
| Unexpired lease of nonresidential real estate deemed rejected at earlier of 120 days after case commencement or confirmation of plan. | Unexpired lease of nonresidential real property deemed rejected 60 days after order for relief. |
| Court may extend 120-day grace period for an additional 90 days, for cause. | Court may extend 60-day grace period, for cause. |
| Subsequent extensions only if landlord consents | Subsequent extensions not subject to landlord consent |

### § 9:57 Other constituencies in commercial cases—Parties to executory contracts and unexpired leases—-new (and improved?) deadline to assume or reject nonresidential real estate leases

Practitioners who represent real estate developers and others who own commercial space may confirm anecdotal evidence that their clients have been frustrated by their experiences as landlords in Chapter 11. A reorganization in bankruptcy is, by its nature, designed to give a business some time to reorganize. Thus, for example, retail businesses often wish to wait through a business cycle before assuming all of their obligations to their landlords. The Bankruptcy Code already required that leases be assumed or rejected within 60 days after the filing of a petition. Former Code § 365(d) (applying the 60-day standard with varying degrees of severity in cases under all of the chapters of the Code). The courts were allowed to extend this deadline, however, and the reality has been that the deadline was often extended. These extensions often lasted for many months and, especially in large cases, might delay the landlords' ability to exercise their rights for years. The 2005 amendment of the Bankruptcy Code tilts the playing field considerably. Landlords may feel that the effect of this is simply to level the field. Debtors and even other creditors may be less happy with the outcome.

BAPCPA § 404 amends former Code § 365(d)(4) to provide that unexpired leases of nonresidential real estate in which the debtor is the lessee are deemed rejected and must be immediately surrendered to the lessor by the earlier of 120 days after the commencement of the case or the date of the confirmation of a plan. The court, for cause, may extend the 120-day period for an additional 90 days, but any extension subsequent to the additional 90 days is available only with the consent of the lessor.

Thus the new law provides for automatic rejection of a nonresidential real estate lease if the reorganizing tenant does not assume the lease, and it imposes a strict timeline on this process. 11 U.S.C.A. § 365(d)(4). At the end of those scheduled events, the landlord is given a veto over the tenant's ability to extend the deadline further. This new timeline is designed to focus the judge's attention on the interests of landlords and, over the course of the bankruptcy process, to increase the pressure on the tenant.

It works this way: The timeline starts, in a voluntary Chapter 11 filed on or after October 17, 2005, with the filing of the petition itself. 11 U.S.C.A. § 365(d)(4) (counting the deadline from the order for relief). Measuring from that starting date, the tenant has 120 days within which to make a decision about the wisdom of assuming the lease. If, in the meantime, the tenant proposes a plan, then the 120 days is cut short at the date of confirmation. In other words, there is automatic rejection if the lease is not assumed by the earlier of (1) 120 days after the commencement of the voluntary case, or (2) the entry of a confirmation order. After that initial four-month grace period, the court may only extend the deadline (1) for cause, and (2) for a time not to exceed 90 days.

*Lease Rejection Timeline*

```
(1)---------------------->(2)-------------->(3) - - - - - >
     (first 120 days)      (90 more days)
(1)                       (2)               (3)
   Timeline                  Extension         Additional
   Starts with               After First       Extensions
   Filing of                 120 Days          Only With
   Petition                  Only For          Landlord's
   ("Order for               "Cause" and       Consent
   Relief")                  90-day
                             Maximum
```

So, the tenant reorganizing in bankruptcy has a possible maximum seven-month grace period within which to assume the lease. After four of those months (more precisely, 120 days), it must show "cause" for the extension, perhaps because it must wait to see whether its business turns up. At the end of another three months (90 days), however, the lease may only be assumed with "the prior written consent of the lessor" who may thus stop the process. It may be that granting additional time makes sense, but at that point it is the landlord's prerogative to make that decision.

### Practice Alerts for Code § 365

**Note that the deadlines for assumption/rejection of leases can be reduced by confirmation but may not be so extended. Thus, while pre-BAPCPA plans have typically set a postconfirmation deadline for such actions, this will no longer be possible.**

- **Debtor's counsel should analyze leases earlier.**
- **It may be possible to put leases into a special purpose vehicle, but such action may be subject to attack, either under the terms of the leases or on good-faith or fraudulent transfer grounds.**
- **Ultimately, leases need to be analyzed and prioritized between those that are clearly necessary for the continued operation and reorganization of the debtor versus those that are clearly not. Others will need to be the focus of analysis during the first few weeks of the case.**
- **Note that the extension of time to assume or reject must be granted by an order prior to the expiration of the 120-day initial deadline. Counsel for the debtor should therefore hesitate to negotiate for an extension shorter than the maximum 90 days. Extending only 30 days, for example, may prevent the court from being able to extend further at the end of the resulting 150 days.**

## § 9:58 Other constituencies in commercial cases—Parties to executory contracts and unexpired leases—Postassumption, postrejection lease claims with executive summary

| Executive Summary | |
|---|---|
| **New Law** | **Old Law** |
| New provision limits administrative claim of landlord whose lease was previously assumed and later rejected to two years rent and other monetary damages less sums received from third parties. | Rejection may result in administrative claim for full damages under the contract and under applicable nonbankruptcy law. |
| Claim measured from later of ultimate rejection or turnover of leased property. | Rejection may result in administrative claim for full damages under the contract and under applicable nonbankruptcy law. |
| Balance of claim treated as nonpriority under § 502(b)(6). | § 506(b)(6) limited unsecured claim resulting from rejection. |

These rules may have some unpleasant (and perhaps unintended) consequences. Trade creditors (and even other landlords whose leases are not assumed) may find themselves distressed by this development because the landlords who are able to force the tenant to assume their leases will put themselves in a priority position that may eviscerate the value of the estate in an ultimate liquidation. These side effects of the new law should not be ignored as trade creditors and landlords consider the dynamics of dealing with a tenant under the new Chapter 11 regime.

The amendments attempt to deal with this reality that the debtor may be forced into a premature assumption of a lease that is ultimately defaulted. The result may be an administrative claim for the full measure of damages under the lease and applicable nonbankruptcy law. See, e.g., *In re Baldwin Rental Centers, Inc.*, 228 B.R. 504, 511–12, 33 Bankr. Ct. Dec. (CRR) 875, 41 Collier Bankr. Cas. 2d (MB) 292, 38 U.C.C. Rep. Serv. 2d 123 (Bankr. S.D. Ga. 1998) (listing cases so holding). To ameliorate the effect on unsecured creditors that would be caused by such a premature assumption followed by later rejection, the amended Code limits the administrative claim resulting from that circumstance. The landlord may have a priority claim of up to two years' rent and other monetary damages after the ultimate rejection or turnover of the leased property, whichever occurs later. This amount is to be reduced by "sums actually received or to be received" from third parties (guarantors, etc.). The statute expresses this as follows:

> (b) after notice and a hearing, there shall be allowed administrative expenses, other than claims allowed under § 502 (f) of this title, including—

. . .

(7) with respect to a nonresidential real property lease previously assumed under § 365, and subsequently rejected, a settlement equal to all monetary obligations due, excluding those arising from or relating to a failure to operate or a penalty provision, for the period of two years following the later of the rejection date or the date of actual turnover of the premises, without reduction or setoff for any reason whatsoever except for sums actually received or to be received from an entity other than the debtor, and the claim for remaining sums due for the balance of the term of the lease shall be a claim under § 502(b)(6).

11 U.S.C.A. § 503(b)(7). The balance of the landlord's claim would be relegated to nonpriority unsecured status, subject to the cap imposed by 11 U.S.C.A. § 502(b)(6).

## § 9:59 Other constituencies in commercial cases—Parties to executory contracts and unexpired leases—Cure of nonmonetary defaults with executive summary

| Executive Summary | |
|---|---|
| **New Law** | **Old Law** |
| Nonmonetary defaults not resulting in a penalty payment must be cured prior to assumption subject to specific carve-outs for unexpired real estate leases. | Question in cases as to whether nonmonetary defaults not resulting in a penalty payment must be cured prior to assumption |
| Nonmonetary defaults of residential real estate leases not requiring a penalty payment, need not be cured prior to assumption if cure is "impossible." | No comparable provisions |
| Nonmonetary defaults of nonresidential real estate relating to operational issues must only be cured at and after the time of assumption. | No comparable provisions |

One of the recent and more contentious battles between landlords, tenants, and other parties to executory contracts has been fought over the need to cure defaults in the assumption process. See David G. Epstein & Lisa Normand, Real-World and Academic Questions About Nonmonetary Obligations Under the 2005 Version of 365(b), 13 Am. Bankr. Inst. L. Rev. 617 (2005). Before 2005, paragraph (1) of former Code § 365(b) required an assuming trustee/DIP to cure or provide for cure of defaults before assumption but subsection (b) went on to provide:

(2) paragraph (1) of this subsection does not apply to a default that is a breach of a provision relating to—

. . .

(D) the satisfaction of any penalty rate or provision relating to a default arising from any failure by the debtor to perform non-monetary obligations under the executory contract or unexpired lease.

Former Code § 365(b)(2)(D). This language produced a split in its interpretation by the circuits, which Congress has now attempted to resolve.

The circuit split is found in *In re Claremont Acquisition Corp., Inc.*, 113 F.3d 1029, 30 Bankr. Ct. Dec. (CRR) 1045, Bankr. L. Rep. (CCH) P 77469 (9th Cir. 1997) and *In re BankVest Capital Corp.*, 360 F.3d 291, 42 Bankr. Ct. Dec. (CRR) 210, Bankr. L. Rep. (CCH) P 80062 (1st Cir. 2004), cert. denied, 542 U.S. 919, 124 S. Ct. 2874, 159 L. Ed. 2d 776 (2004). In *BankVest* and *Claremont*, the two circuits analyzed former Code § 365(b)(2)(D) and came to different conclusions as to whether that language required that debtors cure nonmonetary defaults prior to assuming executory contracts and unexpired leases.

The *Claremont* decision arose from the attempted assumption of a franchise agreement for a car dealership. Prior to the debtor's bankruptcy, the debtor had ceased operations for a period of 14 days. The franchise agreement required that the operations at the dealership be continuous, and thus the shutdown breached the franchise agreement. When the debtor attempted to assume the franchise agreement, the franchisor objected and argued that the debtor's failure to abide by the continuous operation requirement constituted an "historical" default that the debtor could not cure. See *Claremont*, 113 F.3d 1029, 1033. The debtor argued that the continuous operation requirement is a nonmonetary obligation and, under former Code § 365(b)(2)(D), the debtor is not required to cure nonmonetary defaults. *Claremont*, 113 F.3d 1029, 1033.

Siding with the franchisor, the court determined that former Code § 365(b)(2)(D) only exempted from the debtor's cure requirements the payment of monetary penalties resulting from the failure to perform nonmonetary obligations. *Claremont*, 113 F.3d 1029, 1034. Thus the Ninth Circuit read the word "penalty" (meaning penalty payment) in former paragraph (2)(D) to modify both nouns following that modifier, "rate" and "provision," determining this to be the only proper grammatical reading of the former language. So, if either a penalty rate or other penalty payment was tied to a nonmonetary obligation, it need not be cured, but other nonmonetary defaults had to be cured, regardless of whether it was possible to do so. The court's decision was based in part on its review of the limited legislative history of the former Code section which suggested that debtors will be able to assume a lease by curing any default at the nondefault interest rate. The Claremont court took this to mean that Congress only intended to protect debtors from being required to pay monetary penalties resulting from nonmonetary defaults. The Ninth Circuit reasoned that the debtor's proposed reading of former Code § 365(b)(2)(D) would render the other three subsections useless or superfluous in that they would be covered by subsection (D). *Claremont*, 113 F.3d 1029. Thus all nonmonetary defaults were to be cured unless such default requires a payment by the debtor of a monetary penalty.

In *BankVest*, the First Circuit took the opposite approach. The court observed that the *Claremont* ruling produced a harsh result for debtors by creating situations in which the debtor's ability to cure a default under an expired lease or executory contract is impossible. See *BankVest*, 360 F.3d 291, 299. The *BankVest* court found the result reached in *Claremont* to be at odds with the underlying principles of the Bankruptcy Code, namely the rehabilitation of debtors. *BankVest*, 360 F.3d 291, 300. The First Circuit concluded that debtors may assume executory contracts and unexpired leases without first curing any nonmonetary defaults.

In BAPCPA, Congress has addressed this split in the circuits by taking pages from both the *Claremont* and *BankVest* opinions. First, in construing the language of former Code § 365(b)(2)(D), Congress sided with the *Claremont* court. Subsection (b)(2)(D) now reads as follows:

> (2) Paragraph (1) of this subsection does not apply to a default that is a breach of a provision relating to—
>
> . . .
>
> (D) The satisfaction of any penalty rate or *penalty* provision relating to a default arising from any failure by the debtor to perform nonmonetary obligations under the executory contract or unexpired lease.

11 U.S.C.A. § 365(b)(2)(D) (new text in italics). This change results in the same phrasing inferred by the *Claremont* court with the word "penalty" modifying both nouns, "rate" and "provision." Congress therefore has agreed with the view that Code § 365(b)(2)(D) should only except from debtors' cure obligations the payment of penalty rates or penalty provisions but that the escape clause (b)(2)(D) does not provide a catch-all exception for nonmonetary defaults. Unless the nonmonetary default requires some type of penalty payment, the debtor must cure the nonmonetary default prior to assumption.

However, in order to reduce somewhat the harsh effects illuminated in *BankVest*, Congress added the following language to Code § 365(b)(1)(A):

> (b)(1) if there has been a default in an executory contract or unexpired lease of the debtor, the trustee may not assume such contract or lease unless, at the time of assumption of such contract or lease, the trustee—
>
> (A) cures, or provides adequate assurance that the trustee will promptly cure, such default *other than a default that is a breach of a provision relating to the satisfaction of any provision (other than a penalty rate or penalty provision) relating to a default arising from any failure to perform non-monetary obligations under any unexpired lease of real property, if it is impossible for the trustee to cure such default by performing non-monetary acts at and after the time of assumption, except that if such default arises from a failure to operate in accordance with a non-residential real property lease, then such default shall be cured by performance at and after the time of assumption in accordance with such lease, and pecuniary losses resulting from such default shall be compensated in accordance with the provisions of this paragraph.*

11 U.S.C.A. § 365(b)(1)(A) (new text in italics).

The additional language of BAPCPA specifically exempts certain nonmonetary cure obligations of the debtor. These exceptions, however, only apply to unexpired leases of real property. Thus the result reached in *Claremont* would be the same today under the 2005 Code § 365(b)(1) and (2) because *Claremont* dealt with a franchise agreement and not a real property lease.

Note that 2005 changes do not except from the debtor's cure requirements every nonmonetary obligation under leases of nonresidential real property. This is true in two respects. First, the 2005 Code only excepts those nonmonetary acts which are "impossible" for the debtor to cure at or after the time of assumption. A new debate will certainly arise over what cure obligations are impossible. Further, the language under new paragraph 365(b)(1)(A) specifically requires that, at and after the time of assumption, the debtor perform any breach related to the failure to operate in accordance with a nonresidential real property lease. Debtors are therefore compelled to comply prospectively with all operational terms in nonresidential real property leases. The distinction between "operating" and nonoperating obligations may also be a source of debate.

Congress' modifications to former Code § 365 should add some clarity to the proper interpretation of 11 U.S.C.A. § 365(b)(2)(D). In the case of real property leases, the new language will prevent the harsh result enunciated in *BankVest*. However, in all other situations including franchise agreements, leases of personal property, and any other executory contracts or unexpired leases that are not leases of real property, the existence of a nonmonetary default that triggers a nonmonetary obligation of the debtor seems to provide the nondebtor party a means to block the assumption of otherwise valuable contracts. In many situations, these counterparties will thus continue to hold a trump card that may affect the debtor's ability to successfully reorganize. This is true because the *Claremont* rule continues to apply for all executory contracts and unexpired leases except "impossible" cure obligations in residential real estate leases and impossible cure of nonoperational obligations in nonresidential real estate leases.

The outcome of the particular facts in *Claremont* apparently would be the same under the 2005 Code, while the *BankVest* decision would be reversed as illustrated by the following matrix of facts and results.

*Analysis of Possible Circumstances and Outcomes Under New Code § 365*

| | Default and Penalty Circumstances | | |
|---|---|---|---|
| | Monetary Default | Non-Monetary Default | |
| | | Penalty Payment | No Penalty Payment |
| Personal Property Lease | Cure required | Cure not required | Cure required (Note: These are the *Bankvest* facts and cure would be required.) |
| Executory Contract (e.g, Franchise Agreement) | Cure required | Cure not required | Cure required (Note: These are the *Claremont* facts and cure would still be required.) |
| Non-Residential Real Estate Lease | Cure required | Cure not required | Cure not required if "impossible" *except* cure for failure to operate in accordance with the lease *prospectively* |
| Residential Real Estate Lease | Cure required | Cure not required | Cure not required if "impossible" |
| Note: It continues to be necessary to provide compensation to the lessor or counterparty for pecuniary losses resulting from any such default. | | | |

**Practice Alert for Code § 365**
**Executory Contracts**

**It is apparent from the chart above that executory contracts are treated in a manner that is much less favorable to debtors than nonresidential real estate leases. Counsel for parties to such contracts and leases should be mindful of this risk.**

- **Consider negotiating for contract terms that provide for defaults to be waived by the passage of time.**

### § 9:60 Other constituencies in commercial cases—Parties to executory contracts and unexpired leases—Personal property leases

A Chapter 7 debtor is specifically permitted to assume an unexpired lease of personalty. In Chapter 11 or 13 cases, however, if an individual debtor does not assume the lease in a plan, the lease will be rejected and not subject to the automatic stay.

**Practice Alert for Code § 365**
**Residential and Personal Property Leases**

**There is the same 60-day deadline to assume/reject residential and personal property leases. If rejected (including failure to assume), the automatic stay is automatically terminated**

### § 9:61 Other constituencies in commercial cases—Aircraft gates

11 U.S.C.A. § 365 as amended also deletes extensive language dealing with leases of aircraft gates and similar issues of interest in airline bankruptcies. These appear simply to be [long overdue] housekeeping changes. The provisions expired in 1993 but, like many other issues, were trapped in the Congressional deadlock on bankruptcy issues in the interim and had not been removed from the Code even though they are no longer applicable.

### § 9:62 Other constituencies in commercial cases—Unsecured creditors and committees with executive summary

| Executive Summary | |
|---|---|
| **New Law** | **Old Law** |
| Court may order U.S. trustee to adjust the number and make-up of creditors' committees. | U.S. trustee had broad discretion to adjust the number and make-up of creditors' committees. |

| Executive Summary | |
|---|---|
| **New Law** | **Old Law** |
| Court may order U.S. trustee to appoint a "small" business creditor to a committee if the creditor's claim is disproportionately large in comparison to its annual gross revenues. | No comparable provisions |
| New provision requiring committees to provide information to and solicit comments from its noncommittee member constituents. | No comparable provisions |
| Court may compel additional disclosure or reporting by the committee. | No comparable provisions |
| Members of creditors' committees excluded from seeking reimbursement of attorney's fees of individual members as an administrative priority expense. | Members of creditors' committees might seek reimbursement of their individual attorney's fees as an administrative priority expense. |

## § 9:63 Other constituencies in commercial cases—Unsecured creditors and committees—Committee composition

The 2005 amendments specifically address some of the concerns of smaller and trade creditors. The first of these changes involves the desire of trade creditors sometimes to serve on creditors' committees and the likelihood that they are excluded in favor of those listed as the debtor's largest creditors. This concern is addressed by confirmation of the authority of a bankruptcy court to order adjustment (by the U.S. trustee) of the number and makeup of committee members under 11 U.S.C.A. § 1102.

The provision also adds specific authority to order the U.S. trustee to include "small" businesses, as defined in Section 3(a)(1) of the Small Business Act, on a creditors' committee, if the claim held by the small business concern is disproportionately large in comparison with its annual gross revenue. Thus a small business with a disproportionately large claim may be given a role in the case by allowing it to serve on a committee (with expenses paid by the estate). The power of the court to order a change in the membership of a committee is a change from prior law, under which the power to change membership rested with the U.S. trustee.

## § 9:64 Other constituencies in commercial cases—Unsecured creditors and committees—Committee disclosure requirements

11 U.S.C.A. § 1102 is further amended in subsection (b) to require

that a committee provide its constituency with access to information and solicit and obtain comments from such creditors who are not appointed to the committee. The court may also compel additional reporting or disclosure.

**Practice Alerts for § 1102**

**Committee Responsibilities**

**These rules do not clearly state the kinds of information that the committee is to disclose. Presumably, a hearing on a request for such an order would provide some opportunity to raise questions because creditors who are not members of a committee may not have the same fiduciary or contractual duty to third parties and the estate:**

- **When and how must information be provided?**
- **What about privileged information?**
- **What about confidential information?**

**However, again, the amendment does not clearly address the consequences of refusal to release such information. There is likely to be some debate over whether the committee's constituency is entitled to its private analysis and strategic information or whether this simply requires the disclosure of information that is generally available from the records in the case.**

### § 9:65 Other constituencies in commercial cases—Unsecured creditors and committees—Pro se representation

The interests of creditors and equity security holders in participating in the process without excessive cost have been further enhanced by an amendment to Code § 541(c), allowing appearances and participation at the "first meeting" without an attorney. The new rule is, by its terms, applicable only to creditors holding consumer debts, but Congress expressly provided that this should not be "construed to require any creditor to be represented by an attorney at any meeting of creditors." 11 U.S.C.A. § 341(c). Whether this will be effective to override state ethics rules governing the unauthorized practice of law, especially outside the consumer setting, remains to be seen.

### § 9:66 Other constituencies in commercial cases—Unsecured creditors and committees—Committee members' professional fees

The amendments drew the line at one point, however. 11 U.S.C.A. § 503(b)(4) has been amended to reverse the result in the *First Merchants* case (*First Merchants Acceptance Corp. v. J.C. Bradford & Co.*, 198 F.3d 394, 35 Bankr. Ct. Dec. (CRR) 96, 43 Collier Bankr. Cas. 2d (MB) 442, Bankr. L. Rep. (CCH) P 78072 (3d Cir. 1999)). In that case, the Third Circuit concluded that the language of the 1994 amendments, strictly construed, allowed individual committee members to apply for reimbursement of their attorney's fees. By excluding persons listed in subsection (b)(3)(F) from those who are entitled to ask for reimbursement of attorney's fees under 11 U.S.C.A. § 503(b)(4), Congress has limited the professional fees related to creditors' committees to only those professionals who are retained by the committee under 11 U.S.C.A. § 1103.

### § 9:67 Other constituencies in commercial cases—Unsecured creditors and committees—Reclamation claims with executive summary

| Executive Summary | |
|---|---|
| **New Law** | **Old Law** |
| Reclamation demand must be made in writing not later than 45 days after the date of receipt of such goods by the debtor. | Reclamation demand must be made in writing 10 days after receipt of such goods by debtor. |
| If 45-day period expires after the commencement of the case, demand must be made not later than 20 days after commencement of case. | If 10-day period expires after the commencement of case, demand must be made before 20 days after receipt of such goods by debtor. |
| Sellers have administrative priority claim for value of goods provided to debtor within 20 days before commencement of case. | No comparable provision for administrative claim |
| Clarifies that reclamation rights are subject to holder of a security interest in the goods provided. | No explicit provision in Bankruptcy Code |

On the other hand, Congress was more considerate of trade creditors with reclamation claims. The amended Bankruptcy Code contains a complex series of changes designed to enhance the reclamation rights of trade creditors who deliver goods on the eve of bankruptcy. First, that "eve" of bankruptcy is now extended from 10 days to 45 days before the date of commencement of the case. The trustee's avoidance rights are subject to the right of an ordinary course seller who delivered goods to the debtor within 45 days prior to the filing of the petition and while the debtor was insolvent. 11 U.S.C.A. § 546(c)(1). The seller's right to reclaim, however, is contingent on making a demand in writing either (1) within 45 days after the debtor's receipt of the goods or (2) if the 45 days expires after the commencement of the case, the demand must be made not later than 20 days after the date of commencement. 11 U.S.C.A. § 546(c)(1).

Reclaiming sellers should be sensitive to a dangerous interpretation of this rule. Congress may have intended to allow reclamation within 20 days or the remainder of a 45-day reclamation window, whichever deadline occurs last. The language does not clearly say "whichever occurs later," however; therefore, courts may conclude that the smaller window applies. For example, suppose the seller delivers to debtor 10 days prior to the filing of debtor's petition. The 45-day window would not run until 35 days after the petition. Because "the 45-day period expires after the commencement of the case," however, the notice might have to be given in writing "not later than 20 days after the date of commencement." 11 U.S.C.A. § 546(c)(1)(B).

**Practice Alert for Code § 546(c)**
**Postbankruptcy Reclamation**

**Thus the time to reclaim is either (1) not later than 45 days after receipt or (2) not later than 20 days after the date of commencement of the case. The second deadline seems to apply by its terms only if the 45-day window expires postpetition. It is unclear, however, which deadline would apply. Unlike pre-BAPCPA reclamation, the 45-day reclamation period would, as a practical matter, always expire "after the commencement of the case." Thus it is prudent at least to assume that the language analyzed above means that one must exercise reclamation rights within 45 days after receipt of the goods but in no event later than the 20th day after the date of commencement of the case.**

- **Assume the seller has the earlier of 45 days after receipt of goods or 20 days after the petition date to assert its reclamation claim.**
- **In no event wait to make a demand more than 20 days after the date of bankruptcy.**

On the other hand, Code § 546 now also confirms the proposition that a security interest in goods subject to reclamation is prior to the rights of the reclaiming creditor. 11 U.S.C.A. § 546(c)(1).

As illustrated by the change to clarify the rights of secured creditors with valid security interests in inventory, reclamation claims are fragile rights. Such a security interest may prime the reclamation right. The debtor may simply consume the goods on hand. The debtor may have already sold the goods or may simply ignore the notice. These circumstances can be the source of considerable frustration to the reclaiming creditor. Congress attempted to ease this frustration by further amendments to Code § 503 that provide administrative expense treatment to a creditor with reclamation rights even if the seller fails to make a demand. 11 U.S.C.A. § 503(b)(9). This claim is limited, however, to the value of goods received by the debtor in the ordinary course of business within 20 days prior to the commencement of the case. The goods must be of a type sold in the ordinary course of the debtor's business. No written notice is required. There is no requirement that the seller show that the goods are still in the possession of the debtor. 11 U.S.C.A. § 503(b)(9).

**Practice Alerts for Code § 503(b)(9)**

**Vendor Administrative Claims**

**A seller is granted an administrative expense claim for goods delivered within 20 days of the petition date. This may dramatically change the debate over the "critical vendor" issue.**

- **The seller must show that the goods were delivered within 20 days of petition date and may then seek immediate payment of its administrative expense.**
- **The debtor must pay or prove that the case is administratively insolvent.**
- **If the case is administratively insolvent, then seller may seek assurance of payment and, if not provided, may seek to convert the case.**

## § 9:68 Other constituencies in commercial cases—Employers and employees—Key employee retention plans with executive summary

| Executive Summary | |
|---|---|
| **New Law** | **Old Law** |
| New provision disallows retention payments to insiders unless essential to retain an employee with a bona fide job offer from another business at the same or greater compensation. | No such express restrictions |
| No such retention payment to an insider may exceed 10 times the amount of a similar payment to a nonmanagement employee during the same calendar year. | No such express restrictions |
| If no such payment, the payment may not exceed 25 times the amount of any similar payment to an insider during the calendar year prior to the commencement of the case. | No such express restrictions |

A recurring complaint, both from organized labor and from media and regulatory observers, is the payment of what may be perceived as excessive amounts to management of troubled companies under the category of "key employee retention plans" (KERPs) or other devices such as those referred to in the pejorative as "golden parachutes." See *In re Georgetown Steel Co., LLC*, 306 B.R. 549, 42 Bankr. Ct. Dec. (CRR) 217 (Bankr. D. S.C. 2004) (approving implementation of key employee retention program over objections of union employees). An amendment of 11 U.S.C.A. § 503 late in the legislative process reflects Congress' desire to respond to these concerns. BAPCPA § 331. These and other provisions benefiting employees were made effective in all cases commenced on and after April 20, 2005. BAPCPA § 1406(a).

Code § 503 now sets forth limitations on the payment or allowance of claims for retention bonuses or severance pay to the debtor's insiders, "key" or otherwise. It disallows payments to induce persons who are insiders to remain in the debtor's employ unless the payment is essential to retain a person who is "essential to the survival of the business" and has "a bona fide job offer from another business at the same or a greater rate of compensation," with the reference rate being the amount to be paid under the KERP. 11 U.S.C.A. § 503(c)(1).

In addition, the amount of the payment may not exceed 10 times the amount of a similar transfer to a nonmanagement employee during the calendar year during which the transfer is made or obligation incurred. 11 U.S.C.A. § 503(c)(1)(C)(i). If no such transfer has been made to nonmanagement personnel during the calendar year, then it may not exceed 25 times the amount of any similar transfer to an insider in the calendar year prior to the year in which the transfer is made or the obligation incurred. 11 U.S.C.A. § 503(c)(1)(C)(ii).

## § 9:69 Other constituencies in commercial cases—Employers and employees—Severance compensation

In the same theme, severance pay to insiders is now limited to an amount not to exceed 10 times the amount of the mean severance pay given to nonmanagement employees during the calendar year in which the payment is made, unless the severance pay is a part of a program generally applicable to all employees. 11 U.S.C.A. § 503(c)(2).

### Practice Alerts for Code § 503(c)(1) KERP and Severance Payments

**Notice that the maximum amounts imposed on both of these types of payments are linked to payments made to other employees during different calendar years.**

- **This may include both pre- and postbankruptcy payments.**
- **More planning will be required to evaluate limitations (e.g. calculation of mean retention and severance payments within defined timeframes).**

**Taken together, a restructuring lender, debtor's counsel or other party interested in reorganizing the company may no longer take dramatic steps to keep management on board. This will now be the case even without an organized workforce.**

- **Debtor's counsel may be able to avoid these restrictions if the debtor has essential management employees who are not insiders.**
- **Debtor's counsel should also consider alternatives to**

**plans that are tied to the employees' staying with the debtor (e.g., performance incentive plans).**

### § 9:70 Other constituencies in commercial cases—Employers and employees—Retiree benefits

Another change reflecting concern over employer-employee relations in Chapter 11 is found in an amendment to Code § 1114 that restricts even prepetition modification of retiree health plans by debtors. Under the amendment, the court is to issue an order of reinstatement of retiree benefits as of the date that the modification was made if (1) the debtor modified the benefits during the 180 days preceding the commencement of the case, and (2) the debtor was insolvent at the time the benefits were modified. 11 U.S.C.A. § 1114(l). This requirement is qualified by allowing the court to find "that the balance of the equities clearly favors such modification." 11 U.S.C.A. § 1114(l)(2).

**Practice Alerts for Code § 1114**

**Retiree Benefits**

- **Bankruptcy planning will require examination of the effect and timing of modifications to retiree benefits.**
- **An estate may incur substantial expense in reinstating benefits.**

### § 9:71 Other constituencies in commercial cases—Employers and employees—Administrative and priority claims

As noted, in the broader context of expanded administrative claims above, § 7:1 and 7:51, protection for certain employee claims has been broadened under Code § 507(a)(4). The "look-back" period for accrual of priority wage and benefit claims has been increased from 90 to 180 days. The cap for wage and benefit claims has been raised from $4,925 to $10,000. Wages, salaries and commissions encompassed by this improved claim include individuals' vacation and similar obligations as well as sales commissions owed to a sole proprietorship or one-employee corporation doing 75% of its business with the debtor in the year before bankruptcy.

In addition, administrative expenses have been expanded to include certain postpetition back-pay awards regardless of the time of the underlying conduct. 11 U.S.C.A. § 503(b)(1)(A)(ii).

BAPCPA also more generally proscribed the payment or allowance of any other obligations outside of the ordinary course of business as priority administrative expenses unless they are "justified by the facts and circumstances of the case." 11 U.S.C.A. § 503(c)(3). This provision applies to an incentive-based compensation package for a new executive or consultant but is worded broadly.

**Practice Alerts for Code §§ 503 & 507**

**Employee Expense and Benefit Claims**

- **As with many of the changes in this area, the increase in these priority claims may reduce recoveries to general unsecured claimants.**
- **The back-pay amendment could have a significant impact if the Debtor is defending labor-related class action suits. See Robert J. Keach, BAPCPA and WARN Act "Back Pay:" Now Timing Isn't Everything, 24 Am. Bankr. Inst. J. No. 10, at 26 (December/January 2006).**

## § 9:72 Other constituencies in commercial cases—Attorneys and other officers and professionals—Disinterestedness with executive summary

| Executive Summary | |
|---|---|
| **New Law** | **Old Law** |
| Investment bankers for outstanding securities of the debtor are no longer automatically disqualified from being retained as professionals in a bankruptcy case for not being a disinterested person. | Investment bankers for outstanding securities of the debtor by definition were not disinterested persons and were disqualified. |

The "disinterestedness" definition in 11 U.S.C.A. § 101(14) has been made more permissive in a narrow but important situation by deleting language that automatically rendered investment bankers for a security of the debtor (without regard to the timing of the issuance of the securities) and their attorneys not disinterested. Section 101(14) was amended as follows (deleted material in strikethrough; new material in italics):

(14) ~~"disinterested person" means person that—~~

~~(A) is not a creditor, an equity security holder, or an insider;~~

~~(B) is not and was not an investment banker for any outstanding security of the debtor;~~

~~(C) has not been, within three years before the date of the filing of the petition, an investment banker for a security of the debtor, or an attorney for such an investment banker in connection with the offer, sale, or issuance of a security of the debtor;~~ *The term 'disinterested person' means a person that—*

*(A) is not a creditor, an equity security holder, or an insider;*

*(B) is not and was not, within 2 years before the date of the filing of the petition, a director, officer, or employee of the debtor; and*

*(C) does not have an interest materially adverse to the interest of the estate or of any class of creditors or equity security holders, by reason of any direct or indirect relationship to, connection with, or interest in, the debtor, or for any other reason;*

~~(D) is not and was not, within two years before the date of the filing of the petition, a director, officer, or employee of the debtor or of an investment banker specified in subparagraph (B) or (C) of this paragraph; and~~

~~(E) does not have an interest materially adverse to the interest of the estate or of any class of creditors or equity security holders, by reason of any direct or indirect relationship to, connection with, or interest in, the debtor or an investment banker specified in subparagraph (B) or (C) of this paragraph, or for any other reason;~~.

Now, the only circumstance that would render investment bankers not disinterested is found in the general provision that they may not have an interest materially adverse to the estate or any class of creditors or equity security holders.

This loosening of the disinterestedness standard prevailed in an arcane legislative and lobbying debate. The Securities and Exchange Commission resisted the change. In the course of debate, however, it was noted that a tiny group of banking houses would benefit from retention of the former restriction. In the end, more investment bankers were allowed into the coveted business of representing debtors in possession, although at the expense of customary disinterestedness. See Nancy B. Rapoport, Enron and the New Disinterestedness—The Foxes are Guarding the Hen House, 13 Am. Bankr. Inst. L. Rev. 521 (2005).

## § 9:73 Other constituencies in commercial cases—Attorneys and other officers and professionals—Certification and other enhancement of compensation

Section 415 of the bill adds a new subparagraph (E) to § 330(a)(3) of the Code, directing the court to consider whether a professional person is board certified or has otherwise demonstrated skill and experience in the bankruptcy field. The amendment makes board certification a specific factor in the award of compensation to professionals.

A final change affecting compensation is an amendment to Code § 328. Professionals may now be compensated "on a fixed or percentage fee basis."

# APPENDICES

# APPENDIX A

# Official Form B22A

**Form B22A (Chapter 7) (10/05)**
In re ____________________
Debtor(s)

Case Number: ____________________
(If known)

According to the calculations required by this statement:
☐ **The presumption arises.**
☐ **The presumption does not arise.**
(Check the box as directed in Parts I, III, and VI of this statement.)

## STATEMENT OF CURRENT MONTHLY INCOME AND MEANS TEST CALCULATION

FOR USE IN CHAPTER 7 ONLY

In addition to Schedule I and J, this statement must be completed by every individual Chapter 7 debtor, whether or not filing jointly, whose debts are primarily consumer debts. Joint debtors may complete one statement only.

| Part I. EXCLUSION FOR DISABLED VETERANS | |
|---|---|
| 1 | If you are a disabled veteran described in the Veteran's Declaration in this Part I, (1) check the box at the beginning of the Veteran's Declaration, (2) check the box for "The presumption does not arise" at the top of this statement, and (3) complete the verification in Part VIII. Do not complete any of the remaining parts of this statement.<br>☐ **Veteran's Declaration.** By checking this box, I declare under penalty of perjury that I am a disabled veteran (as defined in 38 U.S.C. § 3741(1)) whose indebtedness occurred primarily during a period in which I was on active duty (as defined in 10 U.S.C. § 101(d)(1)) or while I was performing a homeland defense activity (as defined in 32 U.S.C. §901(1)). |

| Part II. CALCULATION OF MONTHLY INCOME FOR § 707(b)(7) EXCLUSION | | | |
|---|---|---|---|
| 2 | **Marital/filing status.** Check the box that applies and complete the balance of this part of this statement as directed.<br>a. ☐ Unmarried. **Complete only Column A ("Debtor's Income") for Lines 3-11.**<br>b. ☐ Married, not filing jointly, with declaration of separate households. By checking this box, debtor declares under penalty of perjury: "My spouse and I are legally separated under applicable non-bankruptcy law or my spouse and I are living apart other than for the purpose of evading the requirements of § 707(b)(2)(A) of the Bankruptcy Code." **Complete only Column A ("Debtor's Income") for Lines 3-11.**<br>c. ☐ Married, not filing jointly, without the declaration of separate households set out in Line 2.b above. **Complete both Column A ("Debtor's Income") and Column B (Spouse's Income) for Lines 3-11.**<br>d. ☐ Married, filing jointly. **Complete both Column A ("Debtor's Income") and Column B ("Spouse's Income") for Lines 3-11.** | | |
| | All figures must reflect average monthly income for the six calendar months prior to filing the bankruptcy case, ending on the last day of the month before the filing. If you received different amounts of income during these six months, you must total the amounts received during the six months, divide this total by six, and enter the result on the appropriate line. | **Column A Debtor's Income** | **Column B Spouse's Income** |
| 3 | Gross wages, salary, tips, bonuses, overtime, commissions. | $ | $ |
| 4 | Income from the operation of a business, profession or farm. Subtract Line b from Line a and enter the difference on Line 4. Do not enter a number less than zero. **Do not include any part of the business expenses entered on Line b as a deduction in Part V.**<br>a. Gross receipts — $<br>b. Ordinary and necessary business expenses — $<br>c. Business income — Subtract Line b from Line a | $ | $ |
| 5 | Rent and other real property income. Subtract Line b from Line a and enter the difference on Line 5. Do not enter a number less than zero. **Do not include any part of the operating expenses entered on Line b as a deduction in Part V.**<br>a. Gross receipts — $<br>b. Ordinary and necessary operating expenses — $<br>c. Rental income — Subtract Line b from Line a | $ | $ |
| 6 | Interest, dividends and royalties. | $ | $ |
| 7 | Pension and retirement income. | $ | $ |
| 8 | Regular contributions to the household expenses of the debtor or the debtor's dependents, including child or spousal support. Do not include contributions from the debtor's spouse if Column B is completed. | $ | $ |

Form B 22A (Chapter 7) (10/05) 2

| | | | |
|---|---|---|---|
| 9 | Unemployment compensation. Enter the amount in Column A and, if applicable, Column B. However, if you contend that unemployment compensation received by you or your spouse was a benefit under the Social Security Act, do not list the amount of such compensation in Column A or B, but instead state the amount in the space below:<br>Unemployment compensation claimed to be a benefit under the Social Security Act \| Debtor $ ______ \| Spouse $ ______ | $ | $ |
| 10 | Income from all other sources. If necessary, list additional sources on a separate page. **Do not include** any benefits received under the Social Security Act or payments received as a victim of a war crime, crime against humanity, or as a victim of international or domestic terrorism. Specify source and amount.<br>a. ______ $<br>b. ______ $<br>Total and enter on Line 10 | $ | $ |
| 11 | **Subtotal of Current Monthly Income for § 707(b)(7).** Add Lines 3 thru 10 in Column A, and, if Column B is completed, add Lines 3 through 10 in Column B. Enter the total(s). | $ | $ |
| 12 | **Total Current Monthly Income for § 707(b)(7).** If Column B has been completed, add Line 11, Column A to Line 11, Column B, and enter the total. If Column B has not been completed, enter the amount from Line 11, Column A. | $ | |

| | | |
|---|---|---|
| | **Part III. APPLICATION OF § 707(b)(7) EXCLUSION** | |
| 13 | **Annualized Current Monthly Income for § 707(b)(7).** Multiply the amount from Line 12 by the number 12 and enter the result. | $ |
| 14 | **Applicable median family income.** Enter the median family income for the applicable state and household size. (This information is available by family size at www.usdoj.gov/ust/ or from the clerk of the bankruptcy court.)<br>a. Enter debtor's state of residence: ______ b. Enter debtor's household size: ______ | $ |
| 15 | **Application of Section 707(b)(7).** Check the applicable box and proceed as directed.<br>☐ **The amount on Line 13 is less than or equal to the amount on Line 14.** Check the box for "The presumption does not arise" at the top of page 1 of this statement, and complete Part VIII; do not complete Parts IV, V, VI or VII.<br>☐ **The amount on Line 13 is more than the amount on Line 14.** Complete the remaining parts of this statement. | |

**Complete Parts IV, V, VI, and VII of this statement only if required. (See Line 15.)**

| | | |
|---|---|---|
| | **Part IV. CALCULATION OF CURRENT MONTHLY INCOME FOR § 707(b)(2)** | |
| 16 | **Enter the amount from Line 12.** | $ |
| 17 | **Marital adjustment.** If you checked the box at Line 2.c, enter the amount of the income listed in Line 11, Column B that was NOT regularly contributed to the household expenses of the debtor or the debtor's dependents. If you did not check box at Line 2.c, enter zero. | $ |
| 18 | **Current monthly income for § 707(b)(2).** Subtract Line 17 from Line 16 and enter the result. | $ |

| | | |
|---|---|---|
| | **Part V. CALCULATION OF DEDUCTIONS ALLOWED UNDER § 707(b)(2)** | |
| | **Subpart A: Deductions under Standards of the Internal Revenue Service (IRS)** | |
| 19 | **National Standards: food, clothing, household supplies, personal care, and miscellaneous.** Enter "Total" amount from IRS National Standards for Allowable Living Expenses for the applicable family size and income level. (This information is available at www.usdoj.gov/ust/ or from the clerk of the bankruptcy court.) | $ |
| 20A | **Local Standards: housing and utilities; non-mortgage expenses.** Enter the amount of the IRS Housing and Utilities Standards; non-mortgage expenses for the applicable county and family size. | $ |

**Form B 22A (Chapter 7) (10/05)** 3

| | | |
|---|---|---|
| | (This information is available at www.usdoj.gov/ust/ or from the clerk of the bankruptcy court). | |
| 20B | **Local Standards: housing and utilities; mortgage/rent expense.** Enter, in Line a below, the amount of the IRS Housing and Utilities Standards; mortgage/rent expense for your county and family size (this information is available at www.usdoj.gov/ust/ or from the clerk of the bankruptcy court); enter on Line b the total of the Average Monthly Payments for any debts secured by your home, as stated in Line 42; subtract Line b from Line a and enter the result in Line 20B. **Do not enter an amount less than zero.**<br>a. IRS Housing and Utilities Standards; mortgage/rental expense — $<br>b. Average Monthly Payment for any debts secured by your home, if any, as stated in Line 42 — $<br>c. Net mortgage/rental expense — Subtract Line b from Line a. | $ |
| 21 | **Local Standards: housing and utilities; adjustment.** If you contend that the process set out in Lines 20A and 20B does not accurately compute the allowance to which you are entitled under the IRS Housing and Utilities Standards, enter any additional amount to which you contend you are entitled, and state the basis for your contention in the space below:<br>__________<br>__________<br>__________ | $ |
| 22 | **Local Standards: transportation; vehicle operation/public transportation expense.** You are entitled to an expense allowance in this category regardless of whether you pay the expenses of operating a vehicle and regardless of whether you use public transportation.<br>Check the number of vehicles for which you pay the operating expenses or for which the operating expenses are included as a contribution to your household expenses in Line 8.<br>☐ 0 ☐ 1 ☐ 2 or more.<br>Enter the amount from IRS Transportation Standards, Operating Costs & Public Transportation Costs for the applicable number of vehicles in the applicable Metropolitan Statistical Area or Census Region. (This information is available at www.usdoj.gov/ust/ or from the clerk of the bankruptcy court.) | $ |
| 23 | **Local Standards: transportation ownership/lease expense; Vehicle 1.** Check the number of vehicles for which you claim an ownership/lease expense. (You may not claim an ownership/lease expense for more than two vehicles.)<br>☐ 1 ☐ 2 or more.<br>Enter, in Line a below, the amount of the IRS Transportation Standards, Ownership Costs, First Car (available at www.usdoj.gov/ust/ or from the clerk of the bankruptcy court); enter in Line b the total of the Average Monthly Payments for any debts secured by Vehicle 1, as stated in Line 42; subtract Line b from Line a and enter the result in Line 23. **Do not enter an amount less than zero.**<br>a. IRS Transportation Standards, Ownership Costs, First Car — $<br>b. Average Monthly Payment for any debts secured by Vehicle 1, as stated in Line 42 — $<br>c. Net ownership/lease expense for Vehicle 1 — Subtract Line b from Line a. | $ |
| 24 | **Local Standards: transportation ownership/lease expense; Vehicle 2.** Complete this Line only if you checked the "2 or more" Box in Line 23.<br>Enter, in Line a below, the amount of the IRS Transportation Standards, Ownership Costs, Second Car (available at www.usdoj.gov/ust/ or from the clerk of the bankruptcy court); enter in Line b the total of the Average Monthly Payments for any debts secured by Vehicle 2, as stated in Line 42; subtract Line b from Line a and enter the result in Line 24. **Do not enter an amount less than zero.**<br>a. IRS Transportation Standards, Ownership Costs, Second Car — $<br>b. Average Monthly Payment for any debts secured by Vehicle 2, as stated in Line 42 — $<br>c. Net ownership/lease expense for Vehicle 2 — Subtract Line b from Line a. | $ |
| 25 | **Other Necessary Expenses: taxes.** Enter the total average monthly expense that you actually incur for all federal, state and local taxes, other than real estate and sales taxes, such as income taxes, self employment taxes, social security taxes, and Medicare taxes. **Do not include real estate or sales taxes.** | |
| 26 | **Other Necessary Expenses: mandatory payroll deductions.** Enter the total average monthly payroll deductions that are required for your employment, such as mandatory retirement contributions, union dues, and uniform costs. **Do not include discretionary amounts, such as non-mandatory 401(k) contributions.** | $ |

Form B 22A (Chapter 7) (10/05) 4

| | | |
|---|---|---|
| 27 | **Other Necessary Expenses: life insurance.** Enter average monthly premiums that you actually pay for term life insurance for yourself. **Do not include premiums for insurance on your dependents, for whole life or for any other form of insurance.** | $ |
| 28 | **Other Necessary Expenses: court-ordered payments.** Enter the total monthly amount that you are required to pay pursuant to court order, such as spousal or child support payments. **Do not include payments on past due support obligations included in Line 44.** | $ |
| 29 | **Other Necessary Expenses: education for employment or for a physically or mentally challenged child.** Enter the total monthly amount that you actually expend for education that is a condition of employment and for education that is required for a physically or mentally challenged dependent child for whom no public education providing similar services is available. | $ |
| 30 | **Other Necessary Expenses: childcare.** Enter the average monthly amount that you actually expend on childcare. **Do not include payments made for children's education.** | $ |
| 31 | **Other Necessary Expenses: health care.** Enter the average monthly amount that you actually expend on health care expenses that are not reimbursed by insurance or paid by a health savings account. **Do not include payments for health insurance listed in Line 34.** | $ |
| 32 | **Other Necessary Expenses: telecommunication services.** Enter the average monthly expenses that you actually pay for cell phones, pagers, call waiting, caller identification, special long distance or internet services necessary for the health and welfare of you or your dependents. **Do not include any amount previously deducted.** | $ |
| 33 | **Total Expenses Allowed under IRS Standards.** Enter the total of Lines 19 through 32. | $ |
| | **Subpart B: Additional Expense Deductions under § 707(b)**<br>**Note: Do not include any expenses that you have listed in Lines 19-32** | |
| 34 | **Health Insurance, Disability Insurance and Health Savings Account Expenses.** List the average monthly amounts that you actually expend in each of the following categories and enter the total.<br>a. Health Insurance $<br>b. Disability Insurance $<br>c. Health Savings Account $<br>Total: Add Lines a, b and c | $ |
| 35 | **Continued contributions to the care of household or family members.** Enter the actual monthly expenses that you will continue to pay for the reasonable and necessary care and support of an elderly, chronically ill, or disabled member of your household or member of your immediate family who is unable to pay for such expenses. | $ |
| 36 | **Protection against family violence.** Enter any average monthly expenses that you actually incurred to maintain the safety of your family under the Family Violence Prevention and Services Act or other applicable federal law. | $ |
| 37 | **Home energy costs in excess of the allowance specified by the IRS Local Standards.** Enter the average monthly amount by which your home energy costs exceed the allowance in the IRS Local Standards for Housing and Utilities. **You must provide your case trustee with documentation demonstrating that the additional amount claimed is reasonable and necessary.** | $ |
| 38 | **Education expenses for dependent children less than 18.** Enter the average monthly expenses that you actually incur, not to exceed $125 per child, in providing elementary and secondary education for your dependent children less than 18 years of age. **You must provide your case trustee with documentation demonstrating that the amount claimed is reasonable and necessary and not already accounted for in the IRS Standards.** | $ |
| 39 | **Additional food and clothing expense.** Enter the average monthly amount by which your food and clothing expenses exceed the combined allowances for food and apparel in the IRS National Standards, not to exceed five percent of those combined allowances. (This information is available at www.usdoj.gov/ust/ or from the clerk of the bankruptcy court.) **You must provide your case trustee with documentation demonstrating that the additional amount claimed is reasonable and necessary.** | $ |
| 40 | **Continued charitable contributions.** Enter the amount that you will continue to contribute in the form of cash or financial instruments to a charitable organization as defined in 26 U.S.C. § 170(c)(1)-(2). | $ |
| 41 | **Total Additional Expense Deductions under § 707(b).** Enter the total of Lines 34 through 40 | $ |

Form B 22A (Chapter 7) (10/05) 5

| | | |
|---|---|---|
| | **Subpart C: Deductions for Debt Payment** | |
| 42 | **Future payments on secured claims.** For each of your debts that is secured by an interest in property that you own, list the name of the creditor, identify the property securing the debt, and state the Average Monthly Payment. The Average Monthly Payment is the total of all amounts contractually due to each Secured Creditor in the 60 months following the filing of the bankruptcy case, divided by 60. Mortgage debts should include payments of taxes and insurance required by the mortgage. If necessary, list additional entries on a separate page.<br><br>\| \| Name of Creditor \| Property Securing the Debt \| 60-month Average Payment \|<br>\| a. \| \| \| $ \|<br>\| b. \| \| \| $ \|<br>\| c. \| \| \| $ \|<br>\| \| \| \| Total: Add Lines a, b and c. \| | $ |
| 43 | **Past due payments on secured claims.** If any of the debts listed in Line 42 are in default, and the property securing the debt is necessary for your support or the support of your dependents, you may include in your deductions 1/60th of the amount that you must pay the creditor as a result of the default (the "cure amount") in order to maintain possession of the property. List any such amounts in the following chart and enter the total. If necessary, list additional entries on a separate page.<br><br>\| \| Name of Creditor \| Property Securing the Debt in Default \| 1/60th of the Cure Amount \|<br>\| a. \| \| \| $ \|<br>\| b. \| \| \| $ \|<br>\| c. \| \| \| $ \|<br>\| \| \| \| Total: Add Lines a, b and c \| | $ |
| 44 | **Payments on priority claims.** Enter the total amount of all priority claims (including priority child support and alimony claims), divided by 60. | $ |
| 45 | **Chapter 13 administrative expenses.** If you are eligible to file a case under Chapter 13, complete the following chart, multiply the amount in line a by the amount in line b, and enter the resulting administrative expense.<br><br>\| a. \| Projected average monthly Chapter 13 plan payment. \| $ \|<br>\| b. \| Current multiplier for your district as determined under schedules issued by the Executive Office for United States Trustees. (This information is available at www.usdoj.gov/ust/ or from the clerk of the bankruptcy court.) \| x \|<br>\| c. \| Average monthly administrative expense of Chapter 13 case \| Total: Multiply Lines a and b \| | $ |
| 46 | **Total Deductions for Debt Payment.** Enter the total of Lines 42 through 45. | $ |
| | **Subpart D: Total Deductions Allowed under § 707(b)(2)** | |
| 47 | **Total of all deductions allowed under § 707(b)(2).** Enter the total of Lines 33, 41, and 46. | $ |

| | | |
|---|---|---|
| | **Part VI. DETERMINATION OF § 707(b)(2) PRESUMPTION** | |
| 48 | **Enter the amount from Line 18 (Current monthly income for § 707(b)(2))** | $ |
| 49 | **Enter the amount from Line 47 (Total of all deductions allowed under § 707(b)(2))** | $ |
| 50 | **Monthly disposable income under § 707(b)(2).** Subtract Line 49 from Line 48 and enter the result | $ |
| 51 | **60-month disposable income under § 707(b)(2).** Multiply the amount in Line 50 by the number 60 and enter the result. | $ |

Form B 22A (Chapter 7) (10/05) 6

| | |
|---|---|
| 52 | **Initial presumption determination.** Check the applicable box and proceed as directed.<br>☐ **The amount on Line 51 is less than $6,000** Check the box for "The presumption does not arise" at the top of page 1 of this statement, and complete the verification in Part VIII. Do not complete the remainder of Part VI.<br>☐ **The amount set forth on Line 51 is more than $10,000.** Check the box for "The presumption arises" at the top of page 1 of this statement, and complete the verification in Part VIII. You may also complete Part VII. Do not complete the remainder of Part VI.<br>☐ **The amount on Line 51 is at least $6,000, but not more than $10,000.** Complete the remainder of Part VI (Lines 53 through 55). |
| 53 | **Enter the amount of your total non-priority unsecured debt** $ |
| 54 | **Threshold debt payment amount.** Multiply the amount in Line 53 by the number 0.25 and enter the result. $ |
| 55 | **Secondary presumption determination.** Check the applicable box and proceed as directed.<br>☐ **The amount on Line 51 is less than the amount on Line 54.** Check the box for "The presumption does not arise" at the top of page 1 of this statement, and complete the verification in Part VIII.<br>☐ **The amount on Line 51 is equal to or greater than the amount on Line 54.** Check the box for "The presumption arises" at the top of page 1 of this statement, and complete the verification in Part VIII. You may also complete Part VII. |

## Part VII: ADDITIONAL EXPENSE CLAIMS

56 **Other Expenses.** List and describe any monthly expenses, not otherwise stated in this form, that are required for the health and welfare of you and your family and that you contend should be an additional deduction from your current monthly income under § 707(b)(2)(A)(ii)(I). If necessary, list additional sources on a separate page. All figures should reflect your average monthly expense for each item. Total the expenses.

| | Expense Description | Monthly Amount |
|---|---|---|
| a. | | $ |
| b. | | $ |
| c. | | $ |
| | Total: Add Lines a, b and c | $ |

## Part VIII: VERIFICATION

57 I declare under penalty of perjury that the information provided in this statement is true and correct. *(If this a joint case, both debtors must sign.)*

Date: ________________ Signature: ________________ (Debtor)

Date: ________________ Signature: ________________ (Joint Debtor, if any)

# APPENDIX B

# Census Bureau Median Family Income By Family Size

### Census Bureau Median Family Income By Family Size (in 2004 inflation-adjusted dollars) For Cases Filed from October 17, 2005 through February 12, 2006.

This table provides median family income data for completing Bankruptcy Forms B22A and B22C. (The U.S. Trustee Program will apply this income data to all cases filed between October 17, 2005, and February 12, 2006.)

| STATE | | FAMILY SIZE | | |
|---|---|---|---|---|
| | 1 EARNER | 2 PEOPLE | 3 PEOPLE | 4 PEOPLE * |
| ALABAMA | $32,762 | $39,755 | $48,957 | $54,338 |
| ALASKA | $43,709 | $59,980 | $68,140 | $76,369 |
| ARIZONA | $35,648 | $46,429 | $51,348 | $58,187 |
| ARKANSAS | $28,949 | $37,178 | $41,231 | $49,790 |
| CALIFORNIA | $42,012 | $53,506 | $59,633 | $68,310 |
| COLORADO | $40,044 | $54,187 | $58,565 | $66,664 |
| CONNECTICUT | $52,530 | $61,374 | $76,506 | $88,276 |
| DELAWARE | $38,944 | $51,955 | $61,508 | $72,003 |
| DISTRICT OF COLUMBIA | $38,349 | $62,167 | $62,167 | $62,167 |
| FLORIDA | $35,883 | $44,831 | $49,612 | $59,798 |
| GEORGIA | $34,396 | $45,775 | $49,855 | $58,060 |
| HAWAII | $45,513 | $54,534 | $64,554 | $75,785 |
| IDAHO | $32,531 | $42,990 | $47,288 | $55,914 |
| ILLINOIS | $41,602 | $51,572 | $62,178 | $70,357 |
| INDIANA | $35,373 | $46,603 | $50,804 | $63,276 |
| IOWA | $35,321 | $46,518 | $54,099 | $61,951 |
| KANSAS | $36,556 | $48,610 | $54,537 | $59,498 |
| KENTUCKY | $32,172 | $37,932 | $46,383 | $55,001 |
| LOUISIANA | $30,646 | $38,017 | $45,732 | $51,402 |
| MAINE | $36,527 | $46,340 | $52,432 | $64,083 |
| MARYLAND | $46,624 | $58,556 | $70,043 | $85,554 |
| MASSACHUSETTS | $47,176 | $55,291 | $71,416 | $85,157 |
| MICHIGAN | $40,504 | $47,444 | $60,431 | $68,563 |
| MINNESOTA | $40,650 | $54,598 | $64,851 | $73,498 |
| MISSISSIPPI | $28,288 | $35,729 | $37,794 | $49,893 |
| MISSOURI | $35,493 | $44,631 | $49,925 | $62,265 |

| | | | | |
|---|---|---|---|---|
| MONTANA | $30,603 | $41,984 | $44,732 | $50,666 |
| NEBRASKA | $35,868 | $45,541 | $54,248 | $59,979 |
| NEVADA | $37,243 | $50,387 | $51,645 | $52,750 |
| NEW HAMPSHIRE | $50,411 | $57,784 | $68,360 | $82,134 |
| NEW JERSEY | $52,493 | $58,547 | $75,470 | $88,401 |
| NEW MEXICO | $30,614 | $39,876 | $41,420 | $47,256 |
| NEW YORK | $39,463 | $48,492 | $57,430 | $67,564 |
| NORTH CAROLINA | $32,411 | $42,105 | $49,206 | $55,117 |
| NORTH DAKOTA | $32,769 | $45,821 | $53,580 | $58,298 |
| OHIO | $36,109 | $44,734 | $55,390 | $62,991 |
| OKLAHOMA | $31,375 | $41,058 | $47,703 | $49,881 |
| OREGON | $36,299 | $47,080 | $52,842 | $59,202 |
| PENNSYLVANIA | $38,931 | $44,361 | $58,986 | $66,569 |
| RHODE ISLAND | $40,463 | $51,334 | $57,967 | $69,029 |
| SOUTH CAROLINA | $32,378 | $43,263 | $48,557 | $59,694 |
| SOUTH DAKOTA | $32,083 | $42,014 | $51,678 | $59,479 |
| TENNESSEE | $33,031 | $41,468 | $49,017 | $55,907 |
| TEXAS | $33,280 | $46,454 | $48,755 | $56,246 |
| UTAH | $41,103 | $45,374 | $51,219 | $57,916 |
| VERMONT | $37,298 | $49,503 | $59,259 | $65,833 |
| VIRGINIA | $41,779 | $54,604 | $61,106 | $71,948 |
| WASHINGTON | $42,452 | $52,272 | $57,773 | $70,857 |
| WEST VIRGINIA | $32,599 | $35,183 | $45,629 | $51,795 |
| WISCONSIN | $37,873 | $48,281 | $58,135 | $67,869 |
| WYOMING | $38,518 | $50,957 | $52,181 | $62,014 |

* *Add $6,300 for each individual in excess of 4.*

| COMMON-WEALTH OR U.S. TERRITORY | | FAMILY SIZE | | |
|---|---|---|---|---|
| | 1 EARNER | 2 PEOPLE | 3 PEOPLE | 4 PEOPLE * |
| GUAM | $31,514 | $37,679 | $42,938 | $51,961 |
| NORTHERN MARIANA ISLANDS | $21,162 | $21,162 | $24,621 | $36,213 |
| PUERTO RICO | $17,513 | $17,513 | $19,263 | $22,738 |
| VIRGIN ISLANDS | $25,003 | $30,052 | $32,041 | $35,105 |

* *Add $6,300 for each individual in excess of 4.*

**Census Bureau Median Family Income By Family Size (in 2005 inflation-adjusted dollars) For Cases Filed from on or After February 13, 2006.**

The following table provides median family income data reproduced in a format designed for ease of use in completing Bankruptcy Forms B22A and B22C. (The U.S. Trustee Program will apply this median family income data to all cases filed on or after February 13, 2006. This median family income data is expected to be adjusted again in August/September 2006, shortly after the Census Bureau updates the data.)

| | FAMILY SIZE | | | |
|---|---|---|---|---|
| **STATE** | **1 EARNER** | **2 PEOPLE** | **3 PEOPLE** | **4 PEOPLE *** |
| ALABAMA | $33,873 | $41,103 | $50,617 | $56,180 |
| ALASKA | $45,191 | $62,013 | $70,450 | $78,958 |
| ARIZONA | $36,856 | $48,003 | $53,089 | $60,160 |
| ARKANSAS | $29,930 | $38,438 | $42,629 | $51,478 |
| CALIFORNIA | $43,436 | $55,320 | $61,655 | $70,626 |
| COLORADO | $41,401 | $56,024 | $60,550 | $68,924 |
| CONNECTICUT | $54,311 | $63,455 | $79,100 | $91,269 |
| DELAWARE | $40,264 | $53,716 | $63,593 | $74,444 |
| DISTRICT OF COLUMBIA | $39,649 | $64,274 | $64,274 | $64,274 |
| FLORIDA | $37,099 | $46,351 | $51,294 | $61,825 |
| GEORGIA | $35,562 | $47,327 | $51,545 | $60,028 |
| HAWAII | $47,056 | $56,383 | $66,742 | $78,354 |
| IDAHO | $33,634 | $44,447 | $48,891 | $57,809 |
| ILLINOIS | $43,012 | $53,320 | $64,286 | $72,742 |
| INDIANA | $36,572 | $48,183 | $52,526 | $65,421 |
| IOWA | $36,518 | $48,095 | $55,933 | $64,051 |
| KANSAS | $37,795 | $50,258 | $56,386 | $61,515 |
| KENTUCKY | $33,263 | $39,218 | $47,955 | $56,866 |
| LOUISIANA | $31,685 | $39,306 | $47,282 | $53,145 |
| MAINE | $37,765 | $47,911 | $54,209 | $66,255 |
| MARYLAND | $48,205 | $60,541 | $72,417 | $88,454 |
| MASSACHUSETTS | $48,775 | $57,165 | $73,837 | $88,044 |
| MICHIGAN | $41,877 | $49,052 | $62,480 | $70,887 |
| MINNESOTA | $42,028 | $56,449 | $67,049 | $75,990 |
| MISSISSIPPI | $29,247 | $36,940 | $39,075 | $51,584 |
| MISSOURI | $36,696 | $46,144 | $51,617 | $64,376 |
| MONTANA | $31,640 | $43,407 | $46,248 | $52,384 |
| NEBRASKA | $37,084 | $47,085 | $56,087 | $62,012 |
| NEVADA | $38,506 | $52,095 | $53,396 | $54,538 |
| NEW HAMPSHIRE | $52,120 | $59,743 | $70,677 | $84,918 |
| NEW JERSEY | $54,273 | $60,532 | $78,028 | $91,398 |
| NEW MEXICO | $31,652 | $41,228 | $42,824 | $48,858 |
| NEW YORK | $40,801 | $50,136 | $59,377 | $69,854 |
| NORTH CAROLINA | $33,510 | $43,532 | $50,874 | $56,985 |
| NORTH DAKOTA | $33,880 | $47,374 | $55,396 | $60,274 |
| OHIO | $37,333 | $46,250 | $57,268 | $65,126 |

| | | | | |
|---|---|---|---|---|
| OKLAHOMA | $32,439 | $42,450 | $49,320 | $51,572 |
| OREGON | $37,530 | $48,676 | $54,633 | $61,209 |
| PENNSYLVANIA | $40,251 | $45,865 | $60,986 | $68,826 |
| RHODE ISLAND | $41,835 | $53,074 | $59,932 | $71,369 |
| SOUTH CAROLINA | $33,476 | $44,730 | $50,203 | $61,718 |
| SOUTH DAKOTA | $33,171 | $43,438 | $53,430 | $61,495 |
| TENNESSEE | $34,151 | $42,874 | $50,679 | $57,802 |
| TEXAS | $34,408 | $48,029 | $50,408 | $58,153 |
| UTAH | $42,496 | $46,912 | $52,955 | $59,879 |
| VERMONT | $38,562 | $51,181 | $61,268 | $68,065 |
| VIRGINIA | $43,195 | $56,455 | $63,177 | $74,387 |
| WASHINGTON | $43,891 | $54,044 | $59,732 | $73,259 |
| WEST VIRGINIA | $33,704 | $36,376 | $47,176 | $53,551 |
| WISCONSIN | $39,157 | $49,918 | $60,106 | $70,170 |
| WYOMING | $39,824 | $52,684 | $53,950 | $64,116 |

* *Add $6,300 for each individual in excess of 4.*

| COMMON-WEALTH OR U.S. TERRITORY | | FAMILY SIZE | | |
|---|---|---|---|---|
| | 1 EARNER | 2 PEOPLE | 3 PEOPLE | 4 PEOPLE * |
| | | | | |
| GUAM | $32,582 | $38,956 | $44,394 | $53,722 |
| NORTHERN MARIANA ISLANDS | $21,879 | $21,879 | $25,456 | $37,441 |
| PUERTO RICO | $18,107 | $18,107 | $19,916 | $23,509 |
| VIRGIN ISLANDS | $25,851 | $31,071 | $33,127 | $36,295 |

* *Add $6,300 for each individual in excess of 4.*

# BANKRUPTCY CODE

# TITLE 11 UNITED STATES CODE

## Chapter 1 —General Provisions

§ 101. Definitions
§ 102. Rules of construction
§ 103. Applicability of chapters
§ 104. Adjustment of dollar amounts
§ 105. Power of court
§ 106. Waiver of sovereign immunity
§ 107. Public access to papers
§ 108. Extension of time
§ 109. Who may be a debtor
§ 110. Penalty for persons who negligently or fraudulently prepare bankruptcy petitions
§ 111. *Nonprofit budget and credit counseling agencies; financial management instructional courses*
***§ 112. Prohibition on disclosure of name of minor children***

## Chapter 3 —Case Administration

### Subchapter I——Commencement of a Case

§ 301. Voluntary cases
§ 302. Joint cases
§ 303. Involuntary cases
~~**§ 304. Cases ancillary to foreign proceedings**~~
§ 305. Abstention
§ 306. Limited appearance
§ 307. United States trustee
§ 308. *Debtor Reporting Requirements*
§ 321. Eligibility to serve as trustee
§ 322. Qualification of trustee
§ 323. Role and capacity of trustee
§ 324. Removal of trustee or examiner
§ 325. Effect of vacancy
§ 326. Limitation on compensation of trustee
§ 327. Employment of professional persons
§ 328. Limitation on compensation of professional persons
§ 329. Debtor's transactions with attorneys
§ 330. Compensation of officers
§ 331. Interim compensation
***§ 332. Consumer privacy ombudsman***
***§ 333. Appointment of patient care ombudsman***
§ 341. Meetings of creditors and equity security holders

§ 342. Notice
§ 343. Examination of the debtor
§ 344. Self-incrimination; immunity
§ 345. Money of estates
~~§ 346. Special tax provisions~~
***§ 346. Special provisions related to the treatment of State and local taxes***
§ 347. Unclaimed property
§ 348. Effect of conversion
§ 349. Effect of dismissal
§ 350. Closing and reopening cases
***§ 351. Disposal of patient records***
§ 361. Adequate protection
§ 362. Automatic stay
§ 363. Use, sale, or lease of property
§ 364. Obtaining credit
§ 365. Executory contracts and unexpired leases
§ 366. Utility service

# Chapter 5 —Creditors, the Debtor, and the Estate

## Subchapter I——Creditors and Claims

§ 501. Filing of proofs of claims or interests
§ 502. Allowance of claims or interests
§ 503. Allowance of administrative expenses
§ 504. Sharing of compensation
§ 505. Determination of tax liability
§ 506. Determination of secured status
§ 507. Priorities
§ 508. Effect of distribution other than under this title
§ 509. Claims of codebtors
§ 510. Subordination
***§ 511. Rate of interest on tax claims***

## Subchapter II——Debtor's Duties and Benefits

§ 521. Debtor's duties
§ 522. Exemptions
§ 523. Exceptions to discharge
§ 524. Effect of discharge
§ 525. Protection against discriminatory treatment
***§ 526. Restrictions on debt relief agencies***
***§ 527. Disclosures***
***§ 528. Requirements for debt relief agencies***

## Subchapter III——The Estate

§ 541. Property of the estate

§ 542. Turnover of property to the estate
§ 543. Turnover of property by a custodian
§ 544. Trustee as lien creditor and as successor to certain creditors and purchasers
§ 545. Statutory liens
§ 546. Limitations on avoiding powers
§ 547. Preferences
§ 548. Fraudulent transfers and obligations
§ 549. Postpetition transactions
§ 550. Liability of transferee of avoided transfer
§ 551. Automatic preservation of avoided transfer
§ 552. Postpetition effect of security interest
§ 553. Setoff
§ 554. Abandonment of property of the estate
§ 555. ~~**Contractual right to liquidate a securities contract**~~***Contractual right to liquidate, terminate, or accelerate a securities contract***
§ 556. ~~**Contractual right to liquidate a commodities contract or forward contract**~~ ***Contractual right to liquidate, terminate, or accelerate a commodities contract or forward contract***
§ 557. Expedited determination of interests in, and abandonment or other disposition of grain assets
§ 558. Defenses of the estate
§ 559. ~~**Contractual right to liquidate a repurchase agreement**~~ ***Contractual right to liquidate, terminate, or accelerate a repurchase agreement***
§ 560. ***Contractual right to liquidate, terminate, or accelerate a swap agreement*** ~~**Contractual right to terminate a swap agreement**~~
***§ 561. Contractual right to terminate, liquidate, accelerate, or offset under a master netting agreement and across contracts; proceedings under chapter 15***
***§ 562. Timing of damage measurement in connection with swap agreements, securities contracts, forward contracts, commodity contracts, repurchase agreements, and master netting agreements***

# Chapter 7 —Liquidation

## Subchapter I——Officers and Administration

§ 701. Interim trustee
§ 702. Election of trustee
§ 703. Successor trustee
§ 704. Duties of trustee
§ 705. Creditor's committee
§ 706. Conversion
§ 707. Dismissal ***of a case or conversion to a case under Chapter 11 or 13***

## Subchapter II——Collection, Liquidation, and

## Distribution of the Estate



## Subchapter III——Stockbroker Liquidation



## Subchapter IV——Commodity Broker Liquidation



SUBCHAPTER V CLEARING BANK LIQUIDATION



## Chapter 9 —Adjustment of Debts of a

# Municipality

## Subchapter I—General Provisions



## Subchapter II—Administration



## Subchapter III—The Plan



# Chapter 11 —Reorganization



## Subchapter II—The Plan

§ 1123. Contents of plan
§ 1124. Impairment of claims or interests
§ 1125. Postpetition disclosure and solicitation
§ 1126. Acceptance of plan
§ 1127. Modification of plan
§ 1128. Confirmation hearing
§ 1129. Confirmation of plan

## Subchapter III——Postconfirmation Matters

§ 1141. Effect of confirmation
§ 1142. Implementation of plan
§ 1143. Distribution
§ 1144. Revocation of an order of confirmation
§ 1145. Exemption from securities laws
§ 1146. Special tax provisions

## Subchapter IV——Railroad Reorganization

§ 1161. Inapplicability of other sections
§ 1162. Definition
§ 1163. Appointment of trustee
§ 1164. Right to be heard
§ 1165. Protection of the public interest
§ 1166. Effect of subtitle IV of title 49 and of Federal, State, or local regulations
§ 1167. Collective bargaining agreements
§ 1168. Rolling stock equipment
§ 1169. Effect of rejection of lease of railroad line
§ 1170. Abandonment of railroad line
§ 1171. Priority claims
§ 1172. Contents of plan
§ 1173. Confirmation of plan
§ 1174. Liquidation

# Chapter 12 —Adjustment of Debts of a Family Farmer *or Fisherman* with Regular Annual Income

## Subchapter I——Officers, Administration, and the Estate

§ 1201. Stay of action against codebtor
§ 1202. Trustee
§ 1203. Rights and powers of debtor
§ 1204. Removal of debtor as debtor in possession
§ 1205. Adequate protection
§ 1206. Sales free of interests
§ 1207. Property of the estate

§ 1208. Conversion or dismissal

### Subchapter II—The Plan

§ 1221. Filing of plan
§ 1222. Contents of plan
§ 1223. Modification of plan before confirmation
§ 1224. Confirmation hearing
§ 1225. Confirmation of plan
§ 1226. Payments
§ 1227. Effect of confirmation
§ 1228. Discharge
§ 1229. Modification of plan after confirmation
§ 1230. Revocation of an order of confirmation
§ 1231. Special tax provisions

## Chapter 13 —Adjustment of Debts of an Individual with Regular Income

### Subchapter I—Officers, Administration, and the Estate

§ 1301. Stay of action against codebtor
§ 1302. Trustee
§ 1303. Rights and powers of debtor
§ 1304. Debtor engaged in business
§ 1305. Filing and allowance of postpetition claims
§ 1306. Property of the estate
§ 1307. Conversion or dismissal
***§ 1308. Filing of prepetition tax returns***

### Subchapter II—The Plan

§ 1321. Filing of plan
§ 1322. Contents of plan
§ 1323. Modification of plan before confirmation
§ 1324. Confirmation hearing
§ 1325. Confirmation of plan
§ 1326. Payments
§ 1327. Effect of confirmation
§ 1328. Discharge
§ 1329. Modification of plan after confirmation
§ 1330. Revocation of an order of confirmation

## Chapter 15 —~~Repealed~~ *Ancillary and Other Cross-Border Cases*

***§ 1501. Purpose and scope of application***
***§ 1502. Definitions***
***§ 1503. International obligations of the United States***

*§ 1504. Commencement of ancillary case*
*§ 1505. Authorization to act in a foreign country*
*§ 1506. Public policy exception*
*§ 1507. Additional assistance*
*§ 1508. Interpretation*
*§ 1509. Right of direct access*
*§ 1510. Limited jurisdiction*
*§ 1511. Commencement of case under section 301 or 303*
*§ 1512. Participation of a foreign representative in a case under this title*
*§ 1513. Access of foreign creditors to a case under this title*
*§ 1514. Notification to foreign creditors concerning a case under this title*
*§ 1515. Application for recognition*
*§ 1516. Presumptions concerning recognition*
*§ 1517. Order granting recognition*
*§ 1518. Subsequent information*
*§ 1519. Relief that may be granted upon filing petition for recognition*
*§ 1520. Effects of recognition of a foreign main proceeding*
*§ 1521. Relief that may be granted upon recognition*
*§ 1522. Protection of creditors and other interested persons*
*§ 1523. Actions to avoid acts detrimental to creditors*
*§ 1524. Intervention by a foreign representative*
*§ 1525. Cooperation and direct communication between the court and foreign courts or foreign representatives*
*§ 1526. Cooperation and direct communication between the trustee and foreign courts or foreign representatives*
*§ 1527. Forms of cooperation*
*§ 1528. Commencement of a case under this title after recognition of a foreign main proceeding*
*§ 1529. Coordination of a case under this title and a foreign proceeding*
*§ 1530. Coordination of more than 1 foreign proceeding*
*§ 1531. Presumption of insolvency based on recognition of a foreign main proceeding*
*§ 1532. Rule of payment in concurrent proceedings*

# Chapter 1
# —General Provisions



## § 101. Definitions

~~In this title—~~*In this title the following definitions shall apply:*

(1) *The term* "accountant" means accountant authorized under applicable law to practice public accounting, and includes professional accounting association, corporation, or partnership, if so authorized.;

(2) *The term* "affiliate" means—

(A) entity that directly or indirectly owns, controls, or holds with power to vote, 20 percent or more of the outstanding voting securities of the debtor, other than an entity that holds such securities—

(i) in a fiduciary or agency capacity without sole discretionary power to vote such securities; or

(ii) solely to secure a debt, if such entity has not in fact exercised such power to vote;

(B) corporation 20 percent or more of whose outstanding voting securities are directly or indirectly owned, controlled, or held with power to vote, by the debtor, or by an entity that directly or indirectly owns, controls, or holds with power to vote, 20 percent or more of the outstanding voting securities of the debtor, other than an entity that holds such securities—

(i) in a fiduciary or agency capacity without sole discretionary power to vote such securities; or

(ii) solely to secure a debt, if such entity has not in fact exercised such power to vote;

(C) person whose business is operated under a lease or operating agreement by a debtor, or person substantially all of whose property is operated under an operating agreement with the debtor; or

(D) entity that operates the business or substantially all of the property of the debtor under a lease or operating agreement.;

*(3) The term "assisted person" means any person whose debts consist primarily of consumer debts and the value of whose nonexempt property is less than $150,000.*

[(3) Redesignated (21B)]

(4) *The term* "attorney" means attorney, professional law association, corporation, or partnership, authorized under applicable law to practice law.;

*(4A) The term "bankruptcy assistance" means any goods or services sold or otherwise provided to an assisted person with the express or implied purpose of providing information, advice, counsel, document preparation, or filing, or attendance at a creditors' meeting or appearing in a case or proceeding on behalf of another or providing legal representation with respect to a case or proceeding under this title.*

(5) *The term* "claim" means—

(A) right to payment, whether or not such right is reduced to judgment, liquidated, unliquidated, fixed, contingent, matured, unmatured, disputed, undisputed, legal, equitable, secured, or unsecured; or

(B) right to an equitable remedy for breach of performance if such breach gives rise to a right to payment, whether or not such right to an equitable remedy is reduced to judgment, fixed, contingent, matured, unmatured, disputed, undisputed, secured, or unsecured;.

(6) *The term* "commodity broker" means futures commission merchant, foreign futures commission merchant, clearing organization, leverage transaction merchant, or commodity options dealer, as defined in section 761 of this title, with respect to which there is a customer, as defined in section 761 of this title;.

(7) *The term* "community claim" means claim that arose before the commencement of the case concerning the debtor for which property of the kind specified in section 541(a)(2) of this title is liable, whether or not there is any such property at the time of the commencement of the case;.

*(7A) The term "commercial fishing operation" means—*

*(A) the catching or harvesting of fish, shrimp, lobsters, urchins, seaweed, shellfish, or other aquatic species or products of such species; or*

*(B) for purposes of section 109 and chapter 12, aquaculture activities consisting of raising for market any species or product described in subparagraph (A).*

*(7B) The term "commercial fishing vessel" means a vessel used by a family fisherman to carry out a commercial fishing operation.;*

(8) *The term* "consumer debt" means debt incurred by an individual primarily for a personal, family, or household purpose~~;~~.

(9) *The term* "corporation"—

(A) includes—

(i) association having a power or privilege that a private corporation, but not an individual or a partnership, possesses;

(ii) partnership association organized under a law that makes only the capital subscribed responsible for the debts of such association;

(iii) joint-stock company;

(iv) unincorporated company or association; or

(v) business trust; but

(B) does not include limited partnership~~;~~.

(10) *The term* "creditor" means—

(A) entity that has a claim against the debtor that arose at the time of or before the order for relief concerning the debtor;

(B) entity that has a claim against the estate of a kind specified in section 348(d), 502(f), 502(g), 502(h) or 502(i) of this title; or

(C) entity that has a community claim~~;~~.

*(10A) The term "current monthly income"—*

*(A) means the average monthly income from all sources that the debtor receives (or in a joint case the debtor and the debtor's spouse receive) without regard to whether such income is taxable income, derived during the 6-month period ending on—*

*(i) the last day of the calendar month immediately preceding the date of the commencement of the case if the debtor files the schedule of current income required by section 521(a)(1)(B)(ii); or*

*(ii) the date on which current income is determined by the court for purposes of this title if the debtor does not file the schedule of current income required by section 521(a)(1)(B)(ii); and*

*(B) includes any amount paid by any entity other than the debtor (or in a joint case the debtor and the debtor's spouse), on a regular basis for the household expenses of the debtor or the debtor's dependents (and in a joint case the debtor's spouse if not otherwise a dependent), but excludes benefits received under the Social Security Act, payments to victims of war crimes or crimes against humanity on account of their status as victims of such crimes, and payments to victims of international terrorism (as defined in section 2331 of title 18) or domestic terrorism (as defined in section 2331 of title 18) on account of their status as victims of such terrorism.*

(11) *The term* "custodian" means—

(A) receiver or trustee of any of the property of the debtor, appointed in a case or proceeding not under this title;

(B) assignee under a general assignment for the benefit of the debtor's creditors; or

(C) trustee, receiver, or agent under applicable law, or under a contract, that is appointed or authorized to take charge of property of the debtor for the purpose of enforcing a lien against such property, or for the purpose of general administration of such property for the benefit of the debtor's creditors.~~;~~

(12) *The term* "debt" means liability on a claim.~~;~~

*(12A) The term "debt relief agency" means any person who provides any bankruptcy assistance to an assisted person in return for the payment of money or other valuable consideration, or who is a bankruptcy petition preparer under section 110, but does not include—*

*(A) any person who is an officer, director, employee, or agent of a person who provides such assistance or of the bankruptcy petition preparer;*

*(B) a nonprofit organization that is exempt from taxation under section 501(c)(3) of the Internal Revenue Code of 1986;*

*(C) a creditor of such assisted person, to the extent that the creditor is assisting such assisted person to restructure any debt owed by such assisted person to the creditor;*

*(D) a depository institution (as defined in section 3 of the Federal Deposit Insurance Act) or any Federal credit union or State credit union (as those terms are defined in section 101 of the Federal Credit Union Act), or any affiliate or subsidiary of such depository institution or credit union; or*

*(E) an author, publisher, distributor, or seller of works subject to copyright protection under title 17, when acting in such capacity.*

~~(12A) "debt for child support" means a debt of a kind specified in section 523(a)(5) of this title for maintenance or support of a child of the debtor;~~

(13) *The term* "debtor" means person or municipality concerning which a case under this title has been commenced~~;~~.

*(13A) The term "debtor's principal residence"—*

*(A) means a residential structure, including incidental property, without regard to whether that structure is attached to real property; and*

*(B) includes an individual condominium or cooperative unit, a mobile or manufactured home, or trailer.*

(14) *The term* "disinterested person" means *a* person that—

~~(A) is not a creditor, an equity security holder, or an insider;~~

~~(B) is not and was not an investment banker for any outstanding security of the debtor;~~

~~(C) has not been, within three years before the date of the filing of the petition, an investment banker for a security of the debtor, or an attorney for such an investment banker in connection with the offer, sale, or issuance of a security of the debtor;~~

*(A) is not a creditor, an equity security holder, or an insider;*

*(B) is not and was not, within 2 years before the date of the filing of the petition, a director, officer, or employee of the debtor; and*

*(C) does not have an interest materially adverse to the interest of the estate or of any class of creditors or equity security holders, by reason of any direct or indirect relationship to, connection with, or interest in, the debtor, or for any other reason;*

~~**(D) is not and was not, within two years before the date of the filing of the petition, a director, officer, or employee of the debtor or of an investment banker specified in subparagraph (B) or (C) of this paragraph; and**~~

~~**(E) does not have an interest materially adverse to the interest of the estate or of any class of creditors or equity security holders, by reason of any direct or indirect relationship to, connection with, or interest in, the debtor or an investment banker specified in subparagraph (B) or (C) of this paragraph, or for any other reason;**~~.

*(14A) The term "domestic support obligation" means a debt that accrues before, on, or after the date of the order for relief in a case under this title, including interest that accrues on that debt as provided under applicable nonbankruptcy law notwithstanding any other provision of this title, that is—*

*(A) owed to or recoverable by—*

*(i) a spouse, former spouse, or child of the debtor or such child's parent, legal guardian, or responsible relative; or*

*(ii) a governmental unit;*

*(B) in the nature of alimony, maintenance, or support (including assistance provided by a governmental unit) of such spouse, former spouse, or child of the debtor or such child's parent, without regard to whether such debt is expressly so designated;*

*(C) established or subject to establishment before, on, or after the date of the order for relief in a case under this title, by reason of applicable provisions of—*

*(i) a separation agreement, divorce decree, or property settlement agreement;*

*(ii) an order of a court of record; or*

*(iii) a determination made in accordance with applicable nonbankruptcy law by a governmental unit; and*

*(D) not assigned to a nongovernmental entity, unless that obligation is assigned voluntarily by the spouse, former spouse, child of the debtor, or such child's parent, legal guardian, or responsible relative for the purpose of collecting the debt.*

(15) *The term* "entity" includes person, estate, trust, governmental unit, and United States trustee.~~;~~

(16) *The term* "equity security" means—

(A) share in a corporation, whether or not transferable or denominated "stock", or similar security;

(B) interest of a limited partner in a limited partnership; or

(C) warrant or right, other than a right to convert, to purchase, sell, or subscribe to a share, security, or interest of a kind specified in subparagraph (A) or (B) of this paragraph.~~;~~

(17) *The term* "equity security holder" means holder of an equity security of the debtor.~~;~~

(18) *The term* "family farmer" means—

(A) individual or individual and spouse engaged in a farming operation whose aggregate debts do not exceed $~~1,500,000~~ *3,237,000* and not less than ~~80~~ *50* percent of whose aggregate noncontingent, liquidated debts (excluding a debt for the principal residence of such individual or such individual and spouse unless such debt arises out of a farming operation), on the date the case is filed, arise out of a farming operation owned or operated by such individual or such individual and spouse, and such individual or such individual and spouse receive from such farming operation more than 50 percent of such individual's or such individual and spouse's gross income ~~for the taxable year preceding the taxable year~~ *for*—

*(i) the taxable year preceding; or*

*(ii) each of the 2d and 3d taxable years preceding the taxable year* in which the case concerning such individual or such individual and spouse was filed; or

(B) corporation or partnership in which more than 50 percent of the outstanding stock or equity is held by one family, or by one family and the relatives of the members of such family, and such family or such relatives conduct the farming operation, and

(i) more than 80 percent of the value of its assets consists of assets related to the farming operation;

(ii) its aggregate debts do not exceed $~~1,500,000~~ *3,237,000* and not less than ~~80~~ *50* percent of its aggregate noncontingent, liquidated debts (excluding a debt for one dwelling which is owned by such corporation or partnership and which a shareholder or partner maintains as a principal residence, unless such debt arises out of a farming operation), on the date the case is filed, arise out of the farming operation owned or operated by such corporation or such partnership; and

(iii) if such corporation issues stock, such stock is not publicly traded.~~;~~

(19) *The term* "family farmer with regular annual income" means family farmer whose annual income is sufficiently stable and regular to enable such family farmer to make payments under a plan under chapter 12 of this title~~;~~.

*(19A) The term "family fisherman" means—*

*(A) an individual or individual and spouse engaged in a commercial fishing operation—*

*(i) whose aggregate debts do not exceed $1,500,000 and not less than 80 percent of whose aggregate noncontingent, liquidated debts (excluding a debt for the principal residence of such individual or such individual and spouse, unless such debt arises out of a commercial fishing operation), on the date the case is filed, arise out of a commercial fishing operation owned or operated by such individual or such individual and spouse; and*

*(ii) who receive from such commercial fishing operation more than 50 percent of such individual's or such individual's and spouse's gross income for the taxable year preceding the taxable year in which the case concerning such individual or such individual and spouse was filed; or*

*(B) a corporation or partnership—*

*(i) in which more than 50 percent of the outstanding stock or equity is held by—*

*(I) 1 family that conducts the commercial fishing operation; or*

*(II) 1 family and the relatives of the members of such family, and such family or such relatives conduct the commercial fishing operation; and*

*(ii) (I) more than 80 percent of the value of its assets consists of assets related to the commercial fishing operation;*

*(II) its aggregate debts do not exceed $1,500,000 and not less than 80 percent of its aggregate noncontingent, liquidated debts (excluding a debt for 1 dwelling which is owned by such corporation or partnership and which a shareholder or partner maintains as a principal residence, unless such debt arises out of a commercial fishing operation), on the date the case is filed, arise out of a commercial fishing operation owned or operated by such corporation or such partnership; and*

*(III) if such corporation issues stock, such stock is not publicly traded.*

*(19B) The term "family fisherman with regular annual income" means a family fisherman whose annual income is sufficiently stable and regular to enable such family fisherman to make payments under a plan under chapter 12 of this title.*

(20) *The term* "farmer" means (except when such term appears in the term "family farmer") person that received more than 80 percent of such person's gross income during the taxable year of such person immediately preceding the taxable year of such person during which the case under this title concerning such person was commenced from a farming operation owned or operated by such person;.

(21) *The term* "farming operation" includes farming, tillage of the soil, dairy farming, ranching, production or raising of crops, poultry, or livestock, and production of poultry or livestock products in an unmanufactured state;.

(21A) *The term* "farmout agreement" means a written agreement in which—

(A) the owner of a right to drill, produce, or operate liquid or gaseous hydrocarbons on property agrees or has agreed to transfer or assign all or a part of such right to another entity; and

(B) such other entity (either directly or through its agents or its assigns), as consideration, agrees to perform drilling, reworking, recompleting, testing, or similar or related operations, to develop or produce liquid or gaseous hydrocarbons on the property~~;~~.

(21B) *The term* "Federal depository institutions regulatory agency" means—

(A) with respect to an insured depository institution (as defined in section 3(c)(2) of the Federal Deposit Insurance Act) for which no conservator or receiver has been appointed, the appropriate Federal banking agency (as defined in section 3(q) of such Act);

(B) with respect to an insured credit union (including an insured credit union for which the National Credit Union Administration has been appointed conservator or liquidating agent), the National Credit Union Administration;

(C) with respect to any insured depository institution for which the Resolution Trust Corporation has been appointed conservator or receiver, the Resolution Trust Corporation; and

(D) with respect to any insured depository institution for which the Federal Deposit Insurance Corporation has been appointed conservator or receiver, the Federal Deposit Insurance Corporation.~~;~~

(22) *The*~~the~~ term "financial institution" *means—*

~~(A) means—~~

~~(i) a Federal reserve bank or an entity (domestic or foreign) that is a commercial or savings bank, industrial savings bank, savings and loan association, trust company, or receiver or conservator for such entity and, when any such Federal reserve bank, receiver, conservator, or entity is acting as agent or custodian for a customer in connection with a securities contract, as defined in section 741 of this title, the customer; or~~

~~(ii) in connection with a securities contract, as defined in section 741 of this title, an investment company registered under the Investment Company Act of 1940; and~~

~~(B) includes any person described in subparagraph (A) which operates, or operates as, a multilateral clearing organization pursuant to section 409 of the Federal Deposit Insurance Corporation Improvement Act of 1991;~~

*(A) a Federal reserve bank, or an entity (domestic or foreign) that is a commercial or savings bank, industrial savings bank, savings and loan association, trust company, federally-insured credit union, or receiver, liquidating agent, or conservator for such entity and, when any such Federal reserve bank, receiver, liquidat-*

*ing agent, conservator or entity is acting as agent or custodian for a customer in connection with a securities contract (as defined in section 741) such customer; or*

*(B) in connection with a securities contract (as defined in section 741) an investment company registered under the Investment Company Act of 1940.*

*(22A) The term "financial participant" means—*

*(A) an entity that, at the time it enters into a securities contract, commodity contract, swap agreement, repurchase agreement, or forward contract, or at the time of the date of the filing of the petition, has one or more agreements or transactions described in paragraph (1), (2), (3), (4), (5), or (6) of section 561(a) with the debtor or any other entity (other than an affiliate) of a total gross dollar value of not less than $1,000,000,000 in notional or actual principal amount outstanding on any day during the previous 15-month period, or has gross mark-to-market positions of not less than $100,000,000 (aggregated across counterparties) in one or more such agreements or transactions with the debtor or any other entity (other than an affiliate) on any day during the previous 15-month period; or*

*(B) a clearing organization (as defined in section 402 of the Federal Deposit Insurance Corporation Improvement Act of 1991).*

(23) ~~"foreign proceeding" means proceeding, whether judicial or administrative and whether or not under bankruptcy law, in a foreign country in which the debtor's domicile, residence, principal place of business, or principal assets were located at the commencement of such proceeding, for the purpose of liquidating an estate, adjusting debts by composition, extension, or discharge, or effecting a reorganization;~~*The term "foreign proceeding" means a collective judicial or administrative proceeding in a foreign country, including an interim proceeding, under a law relating to insolvency or adjustment of debt in which proceeding the assets and affairs of the debtor are subject to control or supervision by a foreign court, for the purpose of reorganization or liquidation.*

(24) ~~"foreign representative" means duly selected trustee, administrator, or other representative of an estate in a foreign proceeding;~~*The term "foreign representative" means a person or body, including a person or body appointed on an interim basis, authorized in a foreign proceeding to administer the reorganization or the liquidation of the debtor's assets or affairs or to act as a representative of such foreign proceeding.*

(25) *The term* "forward contract" ~~means a contract~~ *means—*

*(A) a contract* (other than a commodity contract) for the purchase, sale, or transfer of a commodity, as defined in section 761(8) of this title, or any similar good, article, service, right, or interest which is presently or in the future becomes the subject of dealing in the forward contract trade, or product or byproduct thereof, with a maturity date more than two days after the date

the contract is entered into, including, but not limited to, a repurchase transaction, reverse repurchase transaction, consignment, lease, swap, hedge transaction, deposit, loan, option, allocated transaction, unallocated transaction, ~~or any combination thereof or option thereon~~ *or any other similar agreement;*

*(B) any combination of agreements or transactions referred to in subparagraphs (A) and (C);*

*(C) any option to enter into an agreement or transaction referred to in subparagraph (A) or (B);*

*(D) a master agreement that provides for an agreement or transaction referred to in subparagraph (A), (B), or (C), together with all supplements to any such master agreement, without regard to whether such master agreement provides for an agreement or transaction that is not a forward contract under this paragraph, except that such master agreement shall be considered to be a forward contract under this paragraph only with respect to each agreement or transaction under such master agreement that is referred to in subparagraph (A), (B), or (C); or*

*(E) any security agreement or arrangement, or other credit enhancement related to any agreement or transaction referred to in subparagraph (A), (B), (C), or (D), including any guarantee or reimbursement obligation by or to a forward contract merchant or financial participant in connection with any agreement or transaction referred to in any such subparagraph, but not to exceed the damages in connection with any such agreement or transaction, measured in accordance with section 562.*

(26) ~~"forward contract merchant" means a person whose business consists in whole or in part of entering into forward contracts as or with merchants in a commodity, as defined in section 761(8) of this title, or any similar good, article, service, right, or interest which is presently or in the future becomes the subject of dealing in the forward contract trade;~~*The term "forward contract merchant" means a Federal reserve bank, or an entity the business of which consists in whole or in part of entering into forward contracts as or with merchants in a commodity (as defined in section 761) or any similar good, article, service, right, or interest which is presently or in the future becomes the subject of dealing in the forward contract trade.*

(27) *The term* "governmental unit" means United States; State; Commonwealth; District; Territory; municipality; foreign state; department, agency, or instrumentality of the United States (but not a United States trustee while serving as a trustee in a case under this title), a State, a Commonwealth, a District, a Territory, a municipality, or a foreign state; or other foreign or domestic government.~~;~~

*(27A) The term "health care business"—*

*(A) means any public or private entity (without regard to whether that entity is organized for profit or not for profit) that is primarily engaged in offering to the general public facilities and services for—*

*(i) the diagnosis or treatment of injury, deformity, or disease; and*

*(ii) surgical, drug treatment, psychiatric, or obstetric care; and*

*(B) includes—*

*(i) any—*

*(I) general or specialized hospital;*

*(II) ancillary ambulatory, emergency, or surgical treatment facility;*

*(III) hospice;*

*(IV) home health agency; and*

*(V) other health care institution that is similar to an entity referred to in subclause (I), (II), (III), or (IV); and*

*(ii) any long-term care facility, including any—*

*(I) skilled nursing facility;*

*(II) intermediate care facility;*

*(III) assisted living facility;*

*(IV) home for the aged;*

*(V) domiciliary care facility; and*

*(VI) health care institution that is related to a facility referred to in subclause (I), (II), (III), (IV), or (V), if that institution is primarily engaged in offering room, board, laundry, or personal assistance with activities of daily living and incidentals to activities of daily living.*

*(27B) The term "incidental property" means, with respect to a debtor's principal residence—*

*(A) property commonly conveyed with a principal residence in the area where the real property is located;*

*(B) all easements, rights, appurtenances, fixtures, rents, royalties, mineral rights, oil or gas rights or profits, water rights, escrow funds, or insurance proceeds; and*

*(C) all replacements or additions.*

(28) *The term* "indenture" means mortgage, deed of trust, or indenture, under which there is outstanding a security, other than a voting-trust certificate, constituting a claim against the debtor, a claim secured by a lien on any of the debtor's property, or an equity security of the debtor.;

(29) *The term* "indenture trustee" means trustee under an indenture.;

(30) *The term* "individual with regular income" means individual whose income is sufficiently stable and regular to enable such individual to make payments under a plan under chapter 13 of this title, other than a stockbroker or a commodity broker;.

(31) *The term* "insider" includes—

(A) if the debtor is an individual—

(i) relative of the debtor or of a general partner of the debtor;

(ii) partnership in which the debtor is a general partner;

(iii) general partner of the debtor; or

(iv) corporation of which the debtor is a director, officer, or person in control;

(B) if the debtor is a corporation—

(i) director of the debtor;

(ii) officer of the debtor;

(iii) person in control of the debtor;

(iv) partnership in which the debtor is a general partner;

(v) general partner of the debtor; or

(vi) relative of a general partner, director, officer, or person in control of the debtor;

(C) if the debtor is a partnership—

(i) general partner in the debtor;

(ii) relative of a general partner in, general partner of, or person in control of the debtor;

(iii) partnership in which the debtor is a general partner;

(iv) general partner of the debtor; or

(v) person in control of the debtor;

(D) if the debtor is a municipality, elected official of the debtor or relative of an elected official of the debtor;

(E) affiliate, or insider of an affiliate as if such affiliate were the debtor; and

(F) managing agent of the debtor.~~;~~

(32) *The term* "insolvent" means—

(A) with reference to an entity other than a partnership and a municipality, financial condition such that the sum of such entity's debts is greater than all of such entity's property, at a fair valuation, exclusive of—

(i) property transferred, concealed, or removed with intent to hinder, delay, or defraud such entity's creditors; and

(ii) property that may be exempted from property of the estate under section 522 of this title;

(B) with reference to a partnership, financial condition such that the sum of such partnership's debts is greater than the aggregate of, at a fair valuation—

(i) all of such partnership's property, exclusive of property of the kind specified in subparagraph (A)(i) of this paragraph; and

(ii) the sum of the excess of the value of each general partner's nonpartnership property, exclusive of property of the kind specified in subparagraph (A) of this paragraph, over such partner's nonpartnership debts; and

(C) with reference to a municipality, financial condition such that the municipality is—

(i) generally not paying its debts as they become due unless such debts are the subject of a bona fide dispute; or

(ii) unable to pay its debts as they become due.~~;~~

(33) *The term* "institution-affiliated party"—

(A) with respect to an insured depository institution (as defined in section 3(c)(2) of the Federal Deposit Insurance Act), has the meaning given it in section 3(u) of the Federal Deposit Insurance Act; and

(B) with respect to an insured credit union, has the meaning given it in section 206(r) of the Federal Credit Union Act.~~;~~

(34) *The term* "insured credit union" has the meaning given it in section 101(7) of the Federal Credit Union Act.~~;~~

(35) *The term* "insured depository institution"—

(A) has the meaning given it in section 3(c)(2) of the Federal Deposit Insurance Act; and

(B) includes an insured credit union (except in the case of paragraphs ~~(21B) and (33)(A)~~ *(23) and (35)* of this subsection).~~;~~

(35A) *The term* "intellectual property" means—

(A) trade secret;

(B) invention, process, design, or plant protected under title 35;

(C) patent application;

(D) plant variety;

(E) work of authorship protected under title 17; or

(F) mask work protected under chapter 9 of title 17;

to the extent protected by applicable nonbankruptcy law.~~; and~~

(36) *The term* "judicial lien" means lien obtained by judgment, levy, sequestration, or other legal or equitable process or proceeding.~~;~~

(37) *The term* "lien" means charge against or interest in property to secure payment of a debt or performance of an obligation.~~;~~

(38) *The term* "margin payment" means, for purposes of the forward contract provisions of this title, payment or deposit of cash, a security or other property, that is commonly known in the forward contract trade as original margin, initial margin, maintenance margin, or variation margin, including mark-to-market payments, or variation payments.~~; and~~

*(38A) The term "master netting agreement"—*

*(A) means an agreement providing for the exercise of rights, including rights of netting, setoff, liquidation, termination, acceleration, or close out, under or in connection with one or more contracts that are described in any one or more of paragraphs (1) through (5) of section 561(a), or any security agreement or arrangement or other credit enhancement related to one or more of the foregoing, including any guarantee or reimbursement obligation related to 1 or more of the foregoing; and*

*(B) if the agreement contains provisions relating to agreements*

*or transactions that are not contracts described in paragraphs (1) through (5) of section 561(a), shall be deemed to be a master netting agreement only with respect to those agreements or transactions that are described in any one or more of paragraphs (1) through (5) of section 561(a).*

*(38B) The term "master netting agreement participant" means an entity that, at any time before the date of the filing of the petition, is a party to an outstanding master netting agreement with the debtor.*

(39) *The term* "mask work" has the meaning given it in section 901(a)(2) of title 17.

*(39A) The term "median family income" means for any year—*

*(A) the median family income both calculated and reported by the Bureau of the Census in the then most recent year; and*

*(B) if not so calculated and reported in the then current year, adjusted annually after such most recent year until the next year in which median family income is both calculated and reported by the Bureau of the Census, to reflect the percentage change in the Consumer Price Index for All Urban Consumers during the period of years occurring after such most recent year and before such current year.*

(40) *The term* "municipality" means political subdivision or public agency or instrumentality of a State.;

*(40A) The term "patient" means any individual who obtains or receives services from a health care business.*

*(40B) The term "patient records" means any written document relating to a patient or a record recorded in a magnetic, optical, or other form of electronic medium.*

(41) *The term* "person" includes individual, partnership, and corporation, but does not include governmental unit, except that a governmental unit that—

(A) acquires an asset from a person—

(i) as a result of the operation of a loan guarantee agreement; or

(ii) as receiver or liquidating agent of a person;

(B) is a guarantor of a pension benefit payable by or on behalf of the debtor or an affiliate of the debtor; or

(C) is the legal or beneficial owner of an asset of—

(i) an employee pension benefit plan that is a governmental plan, as defined in section 414(d) of the Internal Revenue Code of 1986; or

(ii) an eligible deferred compensation plan, as defined in section 457(b) of the Internal Revenue Code of 1986;

shall be considered, for purposes of section 1102 of this title, to be a person with respect to such asset or such benefit.;

*(41A) The term "personally identifiable information" means—*

*(A) if provided by an individual to the debtor in connection with*

*obtaining a product or a service from the debtor primarily for personal, family, or household purposes—*

*(i) the first name (or initial) and last name of such individual, whether given at birth or time of adoption, or resulting from a lawful change of name;*

*(ii) the geographical address of a physical place of residence of such individual;*

*(iii) an electronic address (including an e-mail address) of such individual;*

*(iv) a telephone number dedicated to contacting such individual at such physical place of residence;*

*(v) a social security account number issued to such individual; or*

*(vi) the account number of a credit card issued to such individual; or*

*(B) if identified in connection with 1 or more of the items of information specified in subparagraph (A)—*

*(i) a birth date, the number of a certificate of birth or adoption, or a place of birth; or*

*(ii) any other information concerning an identified individual that, if disclosed, will result in contacting or identifying such individual physically or electronically.*

*(42) The term* "petition" means petition filed under section 301, 302, 303, or 304 of this title, as the case may be, commencing a case under this title.~~;~~

(42A) *The term* "production payment" means a term overriding royalty satisfiable in cash or in kind—

(A) contingent on the production of a liquid or gaseous hydrocarbon from particular real property; and

(B) from a specified volume, or a specified value, from the liquid or gaseous hydrocarbon produced from such property, and determined without regard to production costs.~~;~~

(43) *The term* "purchaser" means transferee of a voluntary transfer, and includes immediate or mediate transferee of such a transferee.~~;~~

(44) *The term* "railroad" means common carrier by railroad engaged in the transportation of individuals or property or owner of trackage facilities leased by such a common carrier.~~;~~

(45) *The term* "relative" means individual related by affinity or consanguinity within the third degree as determined by the common law, or individual in a step or adoptive relationship within such third degree.~~;~~

(46) *The term* "repo participant" means an entity that, ~~on any day during the period beginning 90 days before the date of~~ *at any time before* the filing of the petition, has an outstanding repurchase agreement with the debtor.~~;~~

(47) *The term* "repurchase agreement" ~~(which definition also applies to a reverse repurchase agreement) means an agreement, including related terms, which provides for the transfer of certificates of deposit, eligible bankers' acceptances, or securities that are direct obligations of, or that are fully guaranteed as to principal and interest by, the United States or any agency of the United States against the transfer of funds by the transferee of such certificates of deposit, eligible bankers' acceptances, or securities with a simultaneous agreement by such transferee to transfer to the transferor thereof certificates of deposit, eligible bankers' acceptances, or securities as described above, at a date certain not later than one year after such transfers or on demand, against the transfer of funds;~~ *(which definition also applies to a reverse repurchase agreement)—*

*(A) means—*

*(i) an agreement, including related terms, which provides for the transfer of one or more certificates of deposit, mortgage related securities (as defined in section 3 of the Securities Exchange Act of 1934), mortgage loans, interests in mortgage related securities or mortgage loans, eligible bankers' acceptances, qualified foreign government securities (defined as a security that is a direct obligation of, or that is fully guaranteed by, the central government of a member of the Organization for Economic Cooperation and Development), or securities that are direct obligations of, or that are fully guaranteed by, the United States or any agency of the United States against the transfer of funds by the transferee of such certificates of deposit, eligible bankers' acceptances, securities, mortgage loans, or interests, with a simultaneous agreement by such transferee to transfer to the transferor thereof certificates of deposit, eligible bankers' acceptance, securities, mortgage loans, or interests of the kind described in this clause, at a date certain not later than 1 year after such transfer or on demand, against the transfer of funds;*

*(ii) any combination of agreements or transactions referred to in clauses (i) and (iii);*

*(iii) an option to enter into an agreement or transaction referred to in clause (i) or (ii);*

*(iv) a master agreement that provides for an agreement or transaction referred to in clause (i), (ii), or (iii), together with all supplements to any such master agreement, without regard to whether such master agreement provides for an agreement or transaction that is not a repurchase agreement under this paragraph, except that such master agreement shall be considered to be a repurchase agreement under this paragraph only with respect to each agreement or transaction under the master agreement that is referred to in clause (i), (ii), or (iii); or*

*(v) any security agreement or arrangement or other credit enhancement related to any agreement or transaction referred to in clause (i), (ii), (iii), or (iv), including any guarantee or*

*reimbursement obligation by or to a repo participant or financial participant in connection with any agreement or transaction referred to in any such clause, but not to exceed the damages in connection with any such agreement or transaction, measured in accordance with section 562 of this title; and*

*(B) does not include a repurchase obligation under a participation in a commercial mortgage loan.*

(48) *The term* "securities clearing agency" means person that is registered as a clearing agency under section 17A of the Securities Exchange Act of 1934, *or exempt from such registration under such section pursuant to an order of the Securities and Exchange Commission,* or whose business is confined to the performance of functions of a clearing agency with respect to exempted securities, as defined in section 3(a)(12) of such Act for the purposes of such section 17A.;

*(48A) The term "securities self regulatory organization" means either a securities association registered with the Securities and Exchange Commission under section 15A of the Securities Exchange Act of 1934 or a national securities exchange registered with the Securities and Exchange Commission under section 6 of the Securities Exchange Act of 1934.*

(49) *The term* "security"—

(A) includes—

(i) note;

(ii) stock;

(iii) treasury stock;

(iv) bond;

(v) debenture;

(vi) collateral trust certificate;

(vii) pre-organization certificate or subscription;

(viii) transferable share;

(ix) voting-trust certificate;

(x) certificate of deposit;

(xi) certificate of deposit for security;

(xii) investment contract or certificate of interest or participation in a profit-sharing agreement or in an oil, gas, or mineral royalty or lease, if such contract or interest is required to be the subject of a registration statement filed with the Securities and Exchange Commission under the provisions of the Securities Act of 1933, or is exempt under section 3(b) of such Act from the requirement to file such a statement;

(xiii) interest of a limited partner in a limited partnership;

(xiv) other claim or interest commonly known as "security"; and

(xv) certificate of interest or participation in, temporary or interim certificate for, receipt for, or warrant or right to subscribe to or purchase or sell, a security; but

(B) does not include—

(i) currency, check, draft, bill of exchange, or bank letter of credit;

(ii) leverage transaction, as defined in section 761 of this title;

(iii) commodity futures contract or forward contract;

(iv) option, warrant, or right to subscribe to or purchase or sell a commodity futures contract;

(v) option to purchase or sell a commodity;

(vi) contract or certificate of a kind specified in subparagraph (A)(xii) of this paragraph that is not required to be the subject of a registration statement filed with the Securities and Exchange Commission and is not exempt under section 3(b) of the Securities Act of 1933 from the requirement to file such a statement; or

(vii) debt or evidence of indebtedness for goods sold and delivered or services rendered.~~;~~

(50) *The term* "security agreement" means agreement that creates or provides for a security interest.~~;~~

(51) *The term* "security interest" means lien created by an agreement.~~;~~

(51A) *The term* "settlement payment" means, for purposes of the forward contract provisions of this title, a preliminary settlement payment, a partial settlement payment, an interim settlement payment, a settlement payment on account, a final settlement payment, a net settlement payment, or any other similar payment commonly used in the forward contract trade.~~;~~

(51B) *The term* "single asset real estate" means real property constituting a single property or project, other than residential real property with fewer than 4 residential units, which generates substantially all of the gross income of a debtor *who is not a family farmer* and on which no substantial business is being conducted by a debtor other than the business of operating the real property and activities incidental ~~thereto having aggregate noncontingent, liquidated secured debts in an amount no more than $4,000,000~~.~~;~~

(51C) ~~"small business" means a person engaged in commercial or business activities (but does not include a person whose primary activity is the business of owning or operating real property and activities incidental thereto) whose aggregate noncontingent liquidated secured and unsecured debts as of the date of the petition do not exceed $2,000,000;~~*The term 'small business case' means a case filed under chapter 11 of this title in which the debtor is a small business debtor.*

(51D) *The term "small business debtor"—*

*(A) subject to subparagraph (B), means a person engaged in commercial or business activities (including any affiliate of such person that is also a debtor under this title and excluding a person whose primary activity is the business of owning or operating real*

*property or activities incidental thereto) that has aggregate noncontingent liquidated secured and unsecured debts as of the date of the petition or the date of the order for relief in an amount not more than $2,000,000 (excluding debts owed to 1 or more affiliates or insiders) for a case in which the United States trustee has not appointed under section 1102(a)(1) a committee of unsecured creditors or where the court has determined that the committee of unsecured creditors is not sufficiently active and representative to provide effective oversight of the debtor; and*

*(B) does not include any member of a group of affiliated debtors that has aggregate noncontingent liquidated secured and unsecured debts in an amount greater than $2,000,000 (excluding debt owed to 1 or more affiliates or insiders).*

(52) *The term* "State" includes the District of Columbia and Puerto Rico, except for the purpose of defining who may be a debtor under chapter 9 of this title.~~;~~

(53) *The term* "statutory lien" means lien arising solely by force of a statute on specified circumstances or conditions, or lien of distress for rent, whether or not statutory, but does not include security interest or judicial lien, whether or not such interest or lien is provided by or is dependent on a statute and whether or not such interest or lien is made fully effective by statute.~~;~~

(53A) *The term* "stockbroker" means person—

(A) with respect to which there is a customer, as defined in section 741 of this title; and

(B) that is engaged in the business of effecting transactions in securities—

(i) for the account of others; or

(ii) with members of the general public, from or for such person's own account.~~;~~

(53B) *The term* "swap agreement" ~~means—~~

~~(A) an agreement (including terms and conditions incorporated by reference therein) which is a rate swap agreement, basis swap, forward rate agreement, commodity swap, interest rate option, forward foreign exchange agreement, spot foreign exchange agreement, rate cap agreement, rate floor agreement, rate collar agreement, currency swap agreement, cross-currency rate swap agreement, currency option, any other similar agreement (including any option to enter into any of the foregoing);~~

~~(B) any combination of the foregoing; or~~

~~(C) a master agreement for any of the foregoing together with all supplements;~~

*(A) means—*

*(i) any agreement, including the terms and conditions incorporated by reference in such agreement, which is—*

*(I) an interest rate swap, option, future, or forward agreement, including a rate floor, rate cap, rate collar, cross-currency rate swap, and basis swap;*

*(II) a spot, same day-tomorrow, tomorrow-next, forward, or other foreign exchange or precious metals agreement;*

*(III) a currency swap, option, future, or forward agreement;*

*(IV) an equity index or equity swap, option, future, or forward agreement;*

*(V) a debt index or debt swap, option, future, or forward agreement;*

*(VI) a total return, credit spread or credit swap, option, future, or forward agreement;*

*(VII) a commodity index or a commodity swap, option, future, or forward agreement; or*

*(VIII) a weather swap, weather derivative, or weather option;*

*(ii) any agreement or transaction that is similar to any other agreement or transaction referred to in this paragraph and that—*

*(I) is of a type that has been, is presently, or in the future becomes, the subject of recurrent dealings in the swap markets (including terms and conditions incorporated by reference therein); and*

*(II) is a forward, swap, future, or option on one or more rates, currencies, commodities, equity securities, or other equity instruments, debt securities or other debt instruments, quantitative measures associated with an occurrence, extent of an occurrence, or contingency associated with a financial, commercial, or economic consequence, or economic or financial indices or measures of economic or financial risk or value;*

*(iii) any combination of agreements or transactions referred to in this subparagraph;*

*(iv) any option to enter into an agreement or transaction referred to in this subparagraph;*

*(v) a master agreement that provides for an agreement or transaction referred to in clause (i), (ii), (iii), or (iv), together with all supplements to any such master agreement, and without regard to whether the master agreement contains an agreement or transaction that is not a swap agreement under this paragraph, except that the master agreement shall be considered to be a swap agreement under this paragraph only with respect to each agreement or transaction under the master agreement that is referred to in clause (i), (ii), (iii), or (iv); or*

*(vi) any security agreement or arrangement or other credit enhancement related to any agreements or transactions referred to in clause (i) through (v), including any guarantee or reimbursement obligation by or to a swap participant or financial participant in connection with any agreement or transaction referred to in any such clause, but not to exceed the damages in connection with any such agreement or transaction, measured in accordance with section 562; and*

*(B) is applicable for purposes of this title only, and shall not be construed or applied so as to challenge or affect the characterization, definition, or treatment of any swap agreement under any other statute, regulation, or rule, including the Securities Act of 1933, the Securities Exchange Act of 1934, the Public Utility Holding Company Act of 1935, the Trust Indenture Act of 1939, the Investment Company Act of 1940, the Investment Advisers Act of 1940, the Securities Investor Protection Act of 1970, the Commodity Exchange Act, the Gramm-Leach-Bliley Act, and the Legal Certainty for Bank Products Act of 2000.*

(53C) *The term* "swap participant" means an entity that, at any time before the filing of the petition, has an outstanding swap agreement with the debtor.~~;~~

(56A) [(53D)] *The term* "overriding royalty" means an interest in liquid or gaseous hydrocarbons in place or to be produced from particular real property that entitles the owner thereof to a share of production, or the value thereof, for a term limited by time, quantity, or value realized.

(53D) [(53E)] *The term* "timeshare plan" means and shall include that interest purchased in any arrangement, plan, scheme, or similar device, but not including exchange programs, whether by membership, agreement, tenancy in common, sale, lease, deed, rental agreement, license, right to use agreement, or by any other means, whereby a purchaser, in exchange for consideration, receives a right to use accommodations, facilities, or recreational sites, whether improved or unimproved, for a specific period of time less than a full year during any given year, but not necessarily for consecutive years, and which extends for a period of more than three years. A "timeshare interest" is that interest purchased in a timeshare plan which grants the purchaser the right to use and occupy accommodations, facilities, or recreational sites, whether improved or unimproved, pursuant to a timeshare plan.~~;~~

(54) *The term* 'transfer' means ~~every mode, direct or indirect, absolute or conditional, voluntary or involuntary, of disposing of or parting with property or with an interest in property, including retention of title as a security interest and foreclosure of the debtor's equity of redemption;~~—

*(A) the creation of a lien;*

*(B) the retention of title as a security interest;*

*(C) the foreclosure of a debtor's equity of redemption; or*

*(D) each mode, direct or indirect, absolute or conditional, voluntary or involuntary, of disposing of or parting with—*

*(i) property; or*

*(ii) an interest in property.*

(54A) *T*~~t~~he term "uninsured State member bank" means a State member bank (as defined in section 3 of the Federal Deposit Insurance Act) the deposits of which are not insured by the Federal Deposit Insurance Corporation. ~~; and~~

(55) *The term* "United States", when used in a geographical sense, includes all locations where the judicial jurisdiction of the United States extends, including territories and possessions of the United States;.

**Section 101**

(April 20, 2005, P. L. 109-8, 119 Stat. 23)

# HISTORY: ANCILLARY LAWS AND DIRECTIVES

**Amendments:**

**2005.** Act April 20, 2005, inserted "The term" at beginning of each subsection; added new definitions: in para. 3 for "assisted person," in para. 4A for "bankruptcy assistance, in para. 7A for "commercial fishing operation," in para. 7B for "commercial fishing vessel," in para. 10A for "current monthly income," in para. 12A for "debt relief agency," in para. 13A for "debtor's principal residence," in para. 14A for "domestic support obligation," in para. 19A for "family fisherman," in para. 19B for "family fisherman with regular income," in para. 22A for "financial participant," in para. 27A for "health care business," in para. 27B for "incidental property," in para. 38A for "master netting agreement," in para. 39A for "median family income," in para. 40A for "patient," in para. 40B for "patient records," in para. 41A for "personally identifiable information," in para. 48A for "securities self-regulatory organization," in para. 51C for "small business case," and in para. 51D for "small business debtor." The Act also deleted or amended the following existing definitions: in para. 12A deleted "debt for child support," in para. 14 amended "disinterested person," in para. 18 amended the amounts related to "family farmer," in para. 22 amended "financial institution," in para. 23 amended "foreign proceeding," in para. 24 amended "foreign representative," in para. 25 amended "forward contract," in para. 26 amended "forward contract merchant," in para. 35 amended internal references related to "insured depository institution," in para. 47 amended "repurchase agreement," in para. 48 amended "securities clearing agency," in para. 51B amended "single asset real estate," in para. 51C deleted "small business," in para. 53B amended "swap agreement," in para. 54 amended "transfer."

**Short Titles:**

Act April 20, 2005, P. L. 109-8, Section 1(a), 119 Stat. 23 [amending substantial sections of Title 11, Chapters 1, 3, 5, 7, 11, 12 and 13, and adding Chapter 15], generally effective 180 days following enactment, as provided by § 1501(a) of such Act, provides: "This Act may be cited as the 'Bankruptcy Abuse Prevention and Consumer Protection Act of 2005'."

**Other provisions:**

**Effective date and application of Act April 20, 2005.**

Act April 20, 2005, Pub.L. 109-8, Title XV, § 1501, 119 Stat. 23, is generally effective 180 days after enactment [October 17, 2005]. Section 1501 provides:

EFFECTIVE DATE; APPLICATION OF AMENDMENTS.

(a) EFFECTIVE DATE— Except as otherwise provided in this Act, this Act and the amendments made by this Act shall take effect 180 days after the date of enactment of this Act.

(b) APPLICATION OF AMENDMENTS-

(1) IN GENERAL- Except as otherwise provided in this Act and paragraph (2), the amendments made by this Act shall not apply with respect to cases commenced under title 11, United States Code, before the effective date of this Act.

(2) CERTAIN LIMITATIONS APPLICABLE TO DEBTORS- The amendments made by sections 308, 322, and 330 shall apply with respect to cases commenced under title 11, United States Code, on or after the date of the enactment of this Act.

**Abridged Legislative History**

**2005 Act.**

**Section 101** (April 20, 2005, P. L. 109-8, Title XII, § 1201, 119 Stat. 23)

(H. Report No. 109-31 to accompany S. 256, 109th Cong., 1st Sess. (2005) p.140; avail-

able at 2005 U.S.C.C.A.N. 88, at 199.)
**Section 101(3)** (April 20, 2005, P. L. 109-8, Title IIC, § 226(a)(1), 119 Stat. 23)
(H. Report No. 109-31 to accompany S. 256, 109th Cong., 1st Sess. (2005) p. 65; available at 2005 U.S.C.C.A.N. 88, at 134.)
**Section 101(4A)** (April 20, 2005, P. L. 109-8, Title IIC, § 226(a)(2), 119 Stat. 23)
(H. Report No. 109-31 to accompany S. 256, 109th Cong., 1st Sess. (2005) p. 65; available at 2005 U.S.C.C.A.N. 88, at 134.)
**Section 101(7A), 7(B), (19A), (19B)** (H. Report No. 109-31 to accompany S. 256, 109th Cong., 1st Sess. (2005) pp. 137–138; available at 2005 U.S.C.C.A.N. 88, at 197.)
**Section 101(10A)** (April 20, 2005, P. L. 109-8, Title I, § 102(b), 119 Stat. 23)
(H. Report No. 109-31 to accompany S. 256, 109th Cong., 1st Sess. (2005) pp. 51–52; available at 2005 U.S.C.C.A.N. 88, at 122.)
**Section 101(12A)** (April 20, 2005, P. L. 109-8, Title IIC, § 226(a)(3), 119 Stat. 23)
(H. Report No. 109-31 to accompany S. 256, 109th Cong., 1st Sess. (2005) pp. 65–66; available at 2005 U.S.C.C.A.N. 88, at 134.)
**Section 101(13A)** (April 20, 2005, P. L. 109-8, Title III, § 306(c)(1), 119 Stat. 23)
(H. Report No. 109-31 to accompany S. 256, 109th Cong., 1st Sess. (2005) p.72; available at 2005 U.S.C.C.A.N. 88, at 140.)
**Section 101(14)** (April 20, 2005, P. L. 109-8, Title IVA, § 414, 119 Stat. 23)
(H. Report No. 109-31 to accompany S. 256, 109th Cong., 1st Sess. (2005) p.89; available at 2005 U.S.C.C.A.N. 88, at 155.)
**Section 101(14A)** (April 20, 2005, P. L. 109-8, Title IIB, § 211, 119 Stat. 23)
(H. Report No. 109-31 to accompany S. 256, 109th Cong., 1st Sess. (2005) p. 59; available at 2005 U.S.C.C.A.N. 88, at 129.)
**Section 101(18)** (April 20, 2005, P. L. 109-8, Title X, §§ 1004 and 1005, 119 Stat. 23; chapter 12 becomes a permanent chapter of the Bankruptcy Code, effective July 1, 2005, see section 1001(a)(2) of P. L. No. 109-8)
(H. Report No. 109-31 to accompany S. 256, 109th Cong., 1st Sess. (2005) p.136–37; available at 2005 U.S.C.C.A.N. 88, at 196–97.)
**Section 101(22 and 22A)** (April 20, 2005, P. L. 109-8, Title IX, § 907(b)(1 and 2), 119 Stat. 23)
(H. Report No. 109-31 to accompany S. 256, 109th Cong., 1st Sess. (2005) pp. 130–131; available at 2005 U.S.C.C.A.N. 88, at 191–92.)
**Section 101(23 and 24)** (April 20, 2005, P. L. 109-8, Title VIII, § 802(b), 119 Stat. 23)
(H. Report No. 109-31 to accompany S. 256, 109th Cong., 1st Sess. (2005) p.118; available at 2005 U.S.C.C.A.N. 88, at 180–81.)
**Section 101(25 and 26)** (April 20, 2005, P. L. 109-8, Title IX, § 907(a)(1) and (b)(3), 119 Stat. 23)
(H. Report No. 109-31 to accompany S. 256, 109th Cong., 1st Sess. (2005) p.127–28; available at 2005 U.S.C.C.A.N. 88, at 188–189.)
**Section 101(27A)** (April 20, 2005, P. L. 109-8, Title XI, § 1101(a), 119 Stat. 23)
(H. Report No. 109-31 to accompany S. 256, 109th Cong., 1st Sess. (2005) p.138; available at 2005 U.S.C.C.A.N. 88, at 197–98.)
**Section 101(27B)** (April 20, 2005, P. L. 109-8, Title III, § 306(c)(2), 119 Stat. 23)
(H. Report No. 109-31 to accompany S. 256, 109th Cong., 1st Sess. (2005) p.72; available at 2005 U.S.C.C.A.N. 88, at 140.)
**Section 101(38A and 38B)** (April 20, 2005, P. L. 109-8, Title IX, § 907(c), 119 Stat. 23)
(H. Report No. 109-31 to accompany S. 256, 109th Cong., 1st Sess. (2005) pp. 131–132; available at 2005 U.S.C.C.A.N. 88, at 192.)
**Section 101(39A)** (April 20, 2005, P. L. 109-8, Title I, § 102(k), 119 Stat. 23)
(H. Report No. 109-31 to accompany S. 256, 109th Cong., 1st Sess. (2005) p.53; available at 2005 U.S.C.C.A.N. 88, at 124.)
**Section 101(40A) and (40B)** (April 20, 2005, P. L. 109-8, Title XI, § 1101(b), 119 Stat. 23)

(H. Report No. 109-31 to accompany S. 256, 109th Cong., 1st Sess. (2005) p.138; available at 2005 U.S.C.C.A.N. 88, at 198.)

**Section 101(41A)** (April 20, 2005, P. L. 109-8, Title IIC, § 231(b), 119 Stat. 23)
(H. Report No. 109-31 to accompany S. 256, 109th Cong., 1st Sess. (2005) p. 68; available at 2005 U.S.C.C.A.N. 88, at 136.)

**Section 101(46), (47), and (48)** (April 20, 2005, P. L. 109-8, Title IX, § 907(a)(1), 119 Stat. 23)
(H. Report No. 109-31 to accompany S. 256, 109th Cong., 1st Sess. (2005) pp. 127–28; available at 2005 U.S.C.C.A.N. 88, at 188–89.)

**Section 101(48A)** (April 20, 2005, P. L. 109-8, Title IVA, § 401(a), 119 Stat. 23)
(H. Report No. 109-31 to accompany S. 256, 109th Cong., 1st Sess. (2005) p. 86; available at 2005 U.S.C.C.A.N. 88, at 152.)

**Section 101(51B)** (April 20, 2005, P. L. 109-8, Title XII, § 1201(5), 119 Stat. 23)
(H. Report No. 109-31 to accompany S. 256, 109th Cong., 1st Sess. (2005) pp. 140–141; available at 2005 U.S.C.C.A.N. 88, at 199–200.)

**Section 101(51C and D)** (April 20, 2005, P. L. 109-8, Title IVB, § 432(a), 119 Stat. 23)
(H. Report No. 109-31 to accompany S. 256, 109th Cong., 1st Sess. (2005) p. 90; available at 2005 U.S.C.C.A.N. 88, at 156.)

**Section 101(53B)** (April 20, 2005, P. L. 109-8, Title IX, § 907(a)(1), 119 Stat. 23)
(H. Report No. 109-31 to accompany S. 256, 109th Cong., 1st Sess. (2005) pp. 127–129; available at 2005 U.S.C.C.A.N. 88, at 188–90.)

**Section 101(54)** (April 20, 2005, P. L. 109-8, Title XII, § 1201(6), 119 Stat. 23)
(H. Report No. 109-31 to accompany S. 256, 109th Cong., 1st Sess. (2005) p.141; available at 2005 U.S.C.C.A.N. 88, at 200.)

## § 102. Rules of construction

In this title—

(1) "after notice and a hearing", or a similar phrase—

(A) means after such notice as is appropriate in the particular circumstances, and such opportunity for a hearing as is appropriate in the particular circumstances; but

(B) authorizes an act without an actual hearing if such notice is given properly and if—

(i) such a hearing is not requested timely by a party in interest; or

(ii) there is insufficient time for a hearing to be commenced before such act must be done, and the court authorizes such act;

(2) "claim against the debtor" includes claim against property of the debtor;

(3) "includes" and "including" are not limiting;

(4) "may not" is prohibitive, and not permissive;

(5) "or" is not exclusive;

(6) "order for relief" means entry of an order for relief;

(7) the singular includes the plural;

(8) a definition, contained in a section of this title that refers to another section of this title, does not, for the purpose of such reference, affect the meaning of a term used in such other section; and

(9) "United States trustee" includes a designee of the United States trustee.

## § 103. Applicability of chapters

(a) Except as provided in section 1161 of this title, chapters 1, 3, and 5 of this title apply in a case under chapter 7, 11, 12, or 13 of this title, *and this chapter, sections 307, 362(n), 555 through 557, and 559 through 562 apply in a case under chapter 15*.

(b) Subchapters I and II of chapter 7 of this title apply only in a case under such chapter.

(c) Subchapter III of chapter 7 of this title applies only in a case under such chapter concerning a stockbroker.

(d) Subchapter IV of chapter 7 of this title applies only in a case under such chapter concerning a commodity broker.

(e) Scope of application.—Subchapter V of chapter 7 of this title shall apply only in a case under such chapter concerning the liquidation of an uninsured State member bank, or a corporation organized under section 25A of the Federal Reserve Act, which operates, or operates as, a multilateral clearing organization pursuant to section 409 of the Federal Deposit Insurance Corporation Improvement Act of 1991.

(f) Except as provided in section 901 of this title, only chapters 1 and 9 of this title apply in a case under such chapter 9.

(g) Except as provided in section 901 of this title, subchapters I, II, and III of chapter 11 of this title apply only in a case under such chapter.

(h) Subchapter IV of chapter 11 of this title applies only in a case under such chapter concerning a railroad.

(i) Chapter 13 of this title applies only in a case under such chapter.

(j) Chapter 12 of this title applies only in a case under such chapter.

*(k) Chapter 15 applies only in a case under such chapter, except that—*

*(1) sections 1505, 1513, and 1514 apply in all cases under this title; and*

*(2) section 1509 applies whether or not a case under this title is pending.*

**Section 103**

(April 20, 2005, P. L. 109-8, Title VIII, § 802(a), 119 Stat. 23)

### HISTORY: ANCILLARY LAWS AND DIRECTIVES

**Amendments:**

**2005.** Act April 20, 2005 (effective 180 days after enactment of April 20, 2005, as provided by § 1501(a) of P. L. 109-8) amends 11 USC § 103 to clarify the provisions of the Code that apply to chapter 15 and to specify which portions of chapter 15 apply in cases under other chapters of title 11. Section 802(b) of such Act amends the Bankruptcy Code's definitions of foreign proceeding and foreign representative in section 101.

**Other provisions:**

**Effective date and application of amendments made by Act April 20, 2005.** Act April 20, 2005, P.L. 109-8, Title XV, § 1501(a), 119 Stat. 23, provided that the amendments made to this section would be effective 180 days after enactment of

April 20, 2005.

**Abridged Legislative History**

(H. Report No. 109-31 to accompany S. 256, 109th Cong., 1st Sess. (2005) p.118; available at 2005 U.S.C.C.A.N. 88, at 180.)

## § 104. Adjustment of dollar amounts

(a) The Judicial Conference of the United States shall transmit to the Congress and to the President before May 1, 1985, and before May 1 of every sixth year after May 1, 1985, a recommendation for the uniform percentage adjustment of each dollar amount in this title and in section 1930 of title 28.

(b) (1) On April 1, 1998, and at each 3-year interval ending on April 1 thereafter, each dollar amount in effect under sections *101(3), 101(18), 101(19A), 101(51D),* 109(e), 303(b), 507(a), 522(d), *522(f)(3) and 522(f)(4), 522(n), 522(p), 522(q),* ~~and~~ 523(a)(2)(C), *541(b), 547(c)(9), 707(b), 1322(d), 1325(b)(3) and 1326(b)(3) of this title and section 1409(b) of title 28* immediately before such April 1 shall be adjusted—

(A) to reflect the change in the Consumer Price Index for All Urban Consumers, published by the Department of Labor, for the most recent 3-year period ending immediately before January 1 preceding such April 1, and

(B) to round to the nearest $25 the dollar amount that represents such change.

(2) Not later than March 1, 1998, and at each 3-year interval ending on March 1 thereafter, the Judicial Conference of the United States shall publish in the Federal Register the dollar amounts that will become effective on such April 1 under sections *101(3), 101(18), 101(19A), 101(51D),* 109(e), 303(b), 507(a), 522(d), *522(f)(3) and 522(f)(4), 522(n), 522(p), 522(q),* ~~and~~ 523(a)(2)(C), *541(b), 547(c)(9), 707(b), and 1322(d), 1325(b), and 1326(b)(3) of this title and section 1409(b) of title 28* ~~of this title~~.

(3) Adjustments made in accordance with paragraph (1) shall not apply with respect to cases commenced before the date of such adjustments.

**Section 104**

(April 20, 2005, P. L. 109-8, Title I § 102(j); Title IIC §§ 224(e)(2)(a), 226(b); Title III § 322(b); Title IVB § 432(c); Title X § 1002; Title XII § 1202, 119 Stat. 23)

### HISTORY: ANCILLARY LAWS AND DIRECTIVES

**Amendments:**

**2005.** Act April 20, 2005 (effective 180 days after enactment of April 20, 2005, as provided by § 1501(a) of P. L. 109-8), amends 11 USC § 104 to provide for periodic adjustment of monetary amounts affected by other amendments made by such Act.

**Other provisions:**

**Effective date and application of amendments made by Act April 20, 2005.** Act April 20, 2005, P.L. 109-8, Title XV, § 1501(a), 119 Stat. 23, provided that the amendments made to this section would be effective 180 days after enactment of April 20, 2005.

**Abridged Legislative History**
(H. Report No. 109-31 to accompany S. 256, 109th Cong., 1st Sess. (2005) pp. 53, 65–66, 82, 90, 136, 141; available at 2005 U.S.C.C.A.N. 88, at 124, 133–34, 135, 148, 156, 196, 200–01.)

## § 105. Power of court

(a) The court may issue any order, process, or judgment that is necessary or appropriate to carry out the provisions of this title. No provision of this title providing for the raising of an issue by a party in interest shall be construed to preclude the court from, sua sponte, taking any action or making any determination necessary or appropriate to enforce or implement court orders or rules, or to prevent an abuse of process.

(b) Notwithstanding subsection (a) of this section, a court may not appoint a receiver in a case under this title.

(c) The ability of any district judge or other officer or employee of a district court to exercise any of the authority or responsibilities conferred upon the court under this title shall be determined by reference to the provisions relating to such judge, officer, or employee set forth in title 28. This subsection shall not be interpreted to exclude bankruptcy judges and other officers or employees appointed pursuant to chapter 6 of title 28 from its operation.

(d) The court, on its own motion or on the request of a party in interest~~, may—~~

(1) ~~hold a status conference regarding any case or proceeding under this title after notice to the parties in interest; and~~ *shall hold such status conferences as are necessary to further the expeditious and economical resolution of the case; and*

(2) unless inconsistent with another provision of this title or with applicable Federal Rules of Bankruptcy Procedure, issue an order at any such conference prescribing such limitations and conditions as the court deems appropriate to ensure that the case is handled expeditiously and economically, including an order that—

(A) sets the date by which the trustee must assume or reject an executory contract or unexpired lease; or

(B) in a case under chapter 11 of this title—

(i) sets a date by which the debtor, or trustee if one has been appointed, shall file a disclosure statement and plan;

(ii) sets a date by which the debtor, or trustee if one has been appointed, shall solicit acceptances of a plan;

(iii) sets the date by which a party in interest other than a debtor may file a plan;

(iv) sets a date by which a proponent of a plan, other than the debtor, shall solicit acceptances of such plan;

(v) fixes the scope and format of the notice to be provided regarding the hearing on approval of the disclosure statement; or

(vi) provides that the hearing on approval of the disclosure statement may be combined with the hearing on confirmation of the plan.

**Section 105**

(April 20, 2005, P. L. 109-8, Title IVB, § 440, 119 Stat. 23)

## HISTORY: ANCILLARY LAWS AND DIRECTIVES

**Amendments:**

**2005.** Act April 20, 2005 (effective 180 days after enactment of April 20, 2005, as provided by § 1501(a) of P. L. 109-8), amends 11 USC § 105 to require status conferences when necessary.

**Other provisions:**

**Effective date and application of amendments made by Act April 20, 2005.** Act April 20, 2005, P.L. 109-8, Title XV, § 1501(a), 119 Stat. 23, provided that the amendments made to this section would be effective 180 days after enactment of April 20, 2005.

**Abridged Legislative History**

(H. Report No. 109-31 to accompany S. 256, 109th Cong., 1st Sess. (2005) p. 93; available at 2005 U.S.C.C.A.N. 88, at 158.)

# § 106. Waiver of sovereign immunity

(a) Notwithstanding an assertion of sovereign immunity, sovereign immunity is abrogated as to a governmental unit to the extent set forth in this section with respect to the following:

(1) Sections 105, 106, 107, 108, 303, 346, 362, 363, 364, 365, 366, 502, 503, 505, 506, 510, 522, 523, 524, 525, 542, 543, 544, 545, 546, 547, 548, 549, 550, 551, 552, 553, 722, 724, 726, 728, 744, 749, 764, 901, 922, 926, 928, 929, 944, 1107, 1141, 1142, 1143, 1146, 1201, 1203, 1205, 1206, 1227, 1231, 1301, 1303, 1305, and 1327 of this title.

(2) The court may hear and determine any issue arising with respect to the application of such sections to governmental units.

(3) The court may issue against a governmental unit an order, process, or judgment under such sections or the Federal Rules of Bankruptcy Procedure, including an order or judgment awarding a money recovery, but not including an award of punitive damages. Such order or judgment for costs or fees under this title or the Federal Rules of Bankruptcy Procedure against any governmental unit shall be consistent with the provisions and limitations of section 2412(d)(2)(A) of title 28.

(4) The enforcement of any such order, process, or judgment against any governmental unit shall be consistent with appropriate nonbankruptcy law applicable to such governmental unit and, in the case of a money judgment against the United States, shall be paid as if it is a judgment rendered by a district court of the United States.

(5) Nothing in this section shall create any substantive claim for relief or cause of action not otherwise existing under this title, the Federal Rules of Bankruptcy Procedure, or nonbankruptcy law.

(b) A governmental unit that has filed a proof of claim in the case is deemed to have waived sovereign immunity with respect to a claim against such governmental unit that is property of the estate and that arose out of the same transaction or occurrence out of which the claim of such governmental unit arose.

(c) Notwithstanding any assertion of sovereign immunity by a governmental unit, there shall be offset against a claim or interest of a governmental unit any claim against such governmental unit that is property of the estate.

## § 107. Public access to papers

(a) Except as provided in ~~subsection (b)~~ *subsections (b) and (c)* of this section *and subject to section 112*, a paper filed in a case under this title and the dockets of a bankruptcy court are public records and open to examination by an entity at reasonable times without charge.

(b) On request of a party in interest, the bankruptcy court shall, and on the bankruptcy court's own motion, the bankruptcy court may—

(1) protect an entity with respect to a trade secret or confidential research, development, or commercial information; or

(2) protect a person with respect to scandalous or defamatory matter contained in a paper filed in a case under this title.

*(c) (1) The bankruptcy court, for cause, may protect an individual, with respect to the following types of information to the extent the court finds that disclosure of such information would create undue risk of identity theft or other unlawful injury to the individual or the individual's property:*

*(A) Any means of identification (as defined in section 1028(d) of title 18) contained in a paper filed, or to be filed, in a case under this title.*

*(B) Other information contained in a paper described in subparagraph (A).*

*(2) Upon ex parte application demonstrating cause, the court shall provide access to information protected pursuant to paragraph (1) to an entity acting pursuant to the police or regulatory power of a domestic governmental unit.*

*(3) The United States trustee, bankruptcy administrator, trustee, and any auditor serving under section 586(f) of title 28—*

*(A) shall have full access to all information contained in any paper filed or submitted in a case under this title; and*

*(B) shall not disclose information specifically protected by the court under this title.*

**Section 107**

(April 20, 2005, P. L. 109-8, Title IIC, §§ 233(c); 234(a), (e), 119 Stat. 23)

### HISTORY: ANCILLARY LAWS AND DIRECTIVES

**Amendments:**

**2005.** Act April 20, 2005 (effective 180 days after enactment of April 20, 2005, as provided by § 1501(a) of P. L. 109-8), amends 11 USC § 107 to add privacy protections and other provisions concerning access to information.

**Other provisions:**

**Effective date and application of amendments made by Act April 20, 2005.** Act April 20, 2005, P.L. 109-8, Title XV, § 1501(a), 119 Stat. 23, provided that the amendments made to this section would be effective 180 days after enactment of April 20, 2005.

**Abridged Legislative History**

(H. Report No. 109-31 to accompany S. 256, 109th Cong., 1st Sess. (2005) pp. 68–69; available at 2005 U.S.C.C.A.N. 88, at 137.)

## § 108. Extension of time

(a) If applicable nonbankruptcy law, an order entered in a nonbankruptcy proceeding, or an agreement fixes a period within which the debtor may commence an action, and such period has not expired before the date of the filing of the petition, the trustee may commence such action only before the later of—

(1) the end of such period, including any suspension of such period occurring on or after the commencement of the case; or

(2) two years after the order for relief.

(b) Except as provided in subsection (a) of this section, if applicable nonbankruptcy law, an order entered in a nonbankruptcy proceeding, or an agreement fixes a period within which the debtor or an individual protected under section 1201 or 1301 of this title may file any pleading, demand, notice, or proof of claim or loss, cure a default, or perform any other similar act, and such period has not expired before the date of the filing of the petition, the trustee may only file, cure, or perform, as the case may be, before the later of—

(1) the end of such period, including any suspension of such period occurring on or after the commencement of the case; or

(2) 60 days after the order for relief.

(c) Except as provided in section 524 of this title, if applicable nonbankruptcy law, an order entered in a nonbankruptcy proceeding, or an agreement fixes a period for commencing or continuing a civil action in a court other than a bankruptcy court on a claim against the debtor, or against an individual with respect to which such individual is protected under section 1201 or 1301 of this title, and such period has not expired before the date of the filing of the petition, then such period does not expire until the later of—

(1) the end of such period, including any suspension of such period occurring on or after the commencement of the case; or

(2) 30 days after notice of the termination or expiration of the stay under section 362, 922, 1201, or 1301 of this title, as the case may be, with respect to such claim.

**Section 108**

(April 20, 2005, P. L. 109-8, Title XII, § 1203, 119 Stat. 23)

## HISTORY: ANCILLARY LAWS AND DIRECTIVES

**Amendments:**

2005. Act April 20, 2005 (effective 180 days after enactment of April 20, 2005, as provided by § 1501(a) of P. L. 109-8), makes a technical amendment to reference notes to 11 USC § 108 [the amendment purports to add "or 1301" to § 109(c)(2), but that correction has been made to the actual text previously].

**Other provisions:**

Effective date and application of amendments made by Act April 20, 2005. Act April 20, 2005, P.L. 109-8, Title XV, § 1501(a), 119 Stat. 23 provided that the amendments made to this section would be effective 180 days after enactment of April 20, 2005.

**Abridged Legislative History**

(H. Report No. 109-31 to accompany S. 256, 109th Cong., 1st Sess. (2005) p. 142; available at 2005 U.S.C.C.A.N. 88, at 201.)

## § 109. Who may be a debtor

(a) Notwithstanding any other provision of this section, only a person that resides or has a domicile, a place of business, or property in the United States, or a municipality, may be a debtor under this title.

(b) A person may be a debtor under chapter 7 of this title only if such person is not—

(1) a railroad;

(2) a domestic insurance company, bank, savings bank, cooperative bank, savings and loan association, building and loan association, homestead association, a New Markets Venture Capital company as defined in section 351 of the Small Business Investment Act of 1958, a small business investment company licensed by the Small Business Administration under ~~subsection (c) or (d) of~~ section 301 of the Small Business Investment Act of 1958, credit union, or industrial bank or similar institution which is an insured bank as defined in section 3(h) of the Federal Deposit Insurance Act, except that an uninsured State member bank, or a corporation organized under section 25A of the Federal Reserve Act, which operates, or operates as, a multilateral clearing organization pursuant to section 409 of the Federal Deposit Insurance Corporation Improvement Act of 1991 may be a debtor if a petition is filed at the direction of the Board of Governors of the Federal Reserve System; or

(3) ~~a foreign insurance company, bank, savings bank, cooperative bank, savings and loan association, building and loan association, homestead association, or credit union, engaged in such business in the United States.~~*(A) a foreign insurance company, engaged in such business in the United States; or*

*(B) a foreign bank, savings bank, cooperative bank, savings and loan association, building and loan association, or credit union, that has a branch or agency (as defined in section 1(b) of the International Banking Act of 1978 in the United States.*

(c) An entity may be a debtor under chapter 9 of this title if and only if such entity—

(1) is a municipality;

(2) is specifically authorized, in its capacity as a municipality or by name, to be a debtor under such chapter by State law, or by a

governmental officer or orga nization empowered by State law to authorize such entity to be a debtor under such chapter;

(3) is insolvent;

(4) desires to effect a plan to adjust such debts; and

(5) (A) has obtained the agreement of creditors holding at least a majority in amount of the claims of each class that such entity intends to impair under a plan in a case under such chapter;

(B) has negotiated in good faith with creditors and has failed to obtain the agreement of creditors holding at least a majority in amount of the claims of each class that such entity intends to impair under a plan in a case under such chapter;

(C) is unable to negotiate with creditors because such negotiation is impracticable; or

(D) reasonably believes that a creditor may attempt to obtain a transfer that is avoidable under section 547 of this title.

(d) Only a railroad, a person that may be a debtor under chapter 7 of this title (except a stockbroker or a commodity broker), and an uninsured State member bank, or a corporation organized under section 25A of the Federal Reserve Act, which operates, or operates as, a multilateral clearing organization pursuant to section 409 of the Federal Deposit Insurance Corporation Improvement Act of 1991 may be a debtor under chapter 11 of this title.

(e) Only an individual with regular income that owes, on the date of the filing of the petition, noncontingent, liquidated, unsecured debts of less than $307,675 and noncontingent, liquidated, secured debts of less than $922,975, or an individual with regular income and such individual's spouse, except a stockbroker or a commodity broker, that owe, on the date of the filing of the petition, noncontingent, liquidated, unsecured debts that aggregate less than $307,675 and noncontingent, liquidated, secured debts of less than $922,975 may be a debtor under chapter 13 of this title.

(f) Only a family farmer *or family fisherman* with regular annual income may be a debtor under chapter 12 of this title.

(g) Notwithstanding any other provision of this section, no individual or family farmer may be a debtor under this title who has been a debtor in a case pending under this title at any time in the preceding 180 days if—

(1) the case was dismissed by the court for willful failure of the debtor to abide by orders of the court, or to appear before the court in proper prosecution of the case; or

(2) the debtor requested and obtained the voluntary dismissal of the case following the filing of a request for relief from the automatic stay provided by section 362 of this title.

*(h) (1) Subject to paragraphs (2) and (3), and notwithstanding any other provision of this section, an individual may not be a debtor under this title unless such individual has, during the 180-day period preceding the date of filing of the petition by such individual,*

*received from an approved nonprofit budget and credit counseling agency described in section 111(a) an individual or group briefing (including a briefing conducted by telephone or on the Internet) that outlined the opportunities for available credit counseling and assisted such individual in performing a related budget analysis.*

*(2) (A) Paragraph (1) shall not apply with respect to a debtor who resides in a district for which the United States trustee (or the bankruptcy administrator, if any) determines that the approved nonprofit budget and credit counseling agencies for such district are not reasonably able to provide adequate services to the additional individuals who would otherwise seek credit counseling from such agencies by reason of the requirements of paragraph (1).*

*(B) The United States trustee (or the bankruptcy administrator, if any) who makes a determination described in subparagraph (A) shall review such determination not later than 1 year after the date of such determination, and not less frequently than annually thereafter. Notwithstanding the preceding sentence, a nonprofit budget and credit counseling agency may be disapproved by the United States trustee (or the bankruptcy administrator, if any) at any time.*

*(3) (A) Subject to subparagraph (B), the requirements of paragraph (1) shall not apply with respect to a debtor who submits to the court a certification that—*

*(i) describes exigent circumstances that merit a waiver of the requirements of paragraph (1);*

*(ii) states that the debtor requested credit counseling services from an approved nonprofit budget and credit counseling agency, but was unable to obtain the services referred to in paragraph (1) during the 5-day period beginning on the date on which the debtor made that request; and*

*(iii) is satisfactory to the court.*

*(B) With respect to a debtor, an exemption under subparagraph (A) shall cease to apply to that debtor on the date on which the debtor meets the requirements of paragraph (1), but in no case may the exemption apply to that debtor after the date that is 30 days after the debtor files a petition, except that the court, for cause, may order an additional 15 days.*

*(4) The requirements of paragraph (1) shall not apply with respect to a debtor whom the court determines, after notice and hearing, is unable to complete those requirements because of incapacity, disability, or active military duty in a military combat zone. For the purposes of this paragraph, incapacity means that the debtor is impaired by reason of mental illness or mental deficiency so that he is incapable of realizing and making rational decisions with respect to his financial responsibilities; and 'disability' means that the debtor is so physically impaired as to be unable, after reasonable effort, to participate in an in person, telephone, or Internet briefing required under paragraph (1).*

**Section 109**

(April 20, 2005, P. L. 109-8, Title I, § 106(a); Title VIII, § 802(d)(1); Title X, § 1007(b); Title XII, § 1204(1), 119 Stat. 23)

# HISTORY: ANCILLARY LAWS AND DIRECTIVES

**Amendments:**

**2005.** Act April 20, 2005 (effective 180 days after enactment of April 20, 2005, as provided by § 1501(a) of P. L. 109-8), amends 11 USC § 109(b)(3)'s requirements for recognition of a foreign insurance company's bankruptcy and adds § 109(h) to generally require individuals to obtain a prebankruptcy credit briefing. "Family fisherman" is added to § 109(f).

**Other provisions:**

**Effective date and application of amendments made by Act April 20, 2005.** Act April 20, 2005, P.L. 109-8, Title XV, § 1501(a), 119 Stat. 23, provided that the amendments made to this section would be effective 180 days after enactment of April 20, 2005.

**Abridged Legislative History**

Debtor Financial Management Training Test Program. Section 105 of the Act requires the Director of the Executive Office for United States Trustees to: (1) consult with a wide range of debtor education experts who operate financial management education programs; and (2) develop a financial management training curriculum and materials that can be used to teach individual debtors how to manage their finances better. The Director must select six judicial districts to test the effectiveness of the financial management training curriculum and materials for an 18-month period beginning not later than 270 days after the Act's enactment date. For these six districts, the curricula and materials must be used as the instructional personal financial management course required under Bankruptcy Code section 111. Over the period of the study, the Director must evaluate the effectiveness of the curriculum and materials as well as consider a sample of existing consumer education programs (such as those described in the Report of the National Bankruptcy Review Commission) that are representative of consumer education programs sponsored by the credit industry, chapter 13 trustees, and consumer counseling groups. Not later than three months after concluding such evaluation, the Director must submit to Congress a report with findings regarding the effectiveness and cost of the curricula, materials, and programs.

Section 106(a) of the Act amends section 109 of the Bankruptcy Code to require an individual—as a condition of eligibility for bankruptcy relief—to receive credit counseling within the 180-day period preceding the filing of a bankruptcy case by such individual. The credit counseling must be provided by an approved, nonprofit budget and credit counseling agency consisting of either an individual or group briefing (which may be conducted telephonically or via the Internet) that outlines opportunities for available credit counseling and assists the individual in performing a budget analysis. This requirement does not apply to a debtor who resides in a district where the United States trustee or bankruptcy administrator has determined that approved, nonprofit budget and credit counseling agencies in that district are not reasonably able to provide adequate services to such individuals. Although such determination must be reviewed annually, the United States trustee or bankruptcy administrator may disapprove a nonprofit budget and credit counseling agency at any time.

Section 802(d) amends section 109 of the Bankruptcy Code to permit recognition of foreign proceedings involving foreign insurance companies and involving foreign banks which do not have a branch or agency in the United States (as defined in 12 U.S.C. 3101). While a foreign bank not subject to United States regulation will be eligible for chapter 15 as a consequence of the amendment to section 109, section 303 prohibits the commencement of a full involuntary case against such a foreign bank unless the bank is a debtor in a foreign proceeding.

(H. Report No. 109-31 to accompany S. 256, 109th Cong., 1st Sess. (2005) pp. 54–55, 118–119, 137–138, 142; available at 2005 U.S.C.C.A.N. 88, at 124–25, 180–81, 197,

201.)

## § 110. Penalty for persons who negligently or fraudulently prepare bankruptcy petitions

(a) In this section—

(1) "bankruptcy petition preparer" means a person, other than an attorney ~~or an employee of an attorney~~ *for the debtor or an employee of such attorney under the direct supervision of such attorney*, who prepares for compensation a document for filing; and

(2) "document for filing" means a petition or any other document prepared for filing by a debtor in a United States bankruptcy court or a United States district court in connection with a case under this title.

(b) (1) A bankruptcy petition preparer who prepares a document for filing shall sign the document and print on the document the preparer's name and address. *If a bankruptcy petition preparer is not an individual, then an officer, principal, responsible person, or partner of the bankruptcy petition preparer shall be required to—*

*(A) sign the document for filing; and*

*(B) print on the document the name and address of that officer, principal, responsible person, or partner.*

(2) ~~A bankruptcy petition preparer who fails to comply with paragraph (1) may be fined not more than $500 for each such failure unless the failure is due to reasonable cause.~~*(A) Before preparing any document for filing or accepting any fees from a debtor, the bankruptcy petition preparer shall provide to the debtor a written notice which shall be on an official form prescribed by the Judicial Conference of the United States in accordance with rule 9009 of the Federal Rules of Bankruptcy Procedure.*

*(B) The notice under subparagraph (A)—*

*(i) shall inform the debtor in simple language that a bankruptcy petition preparer is not an attorney and may not practice law or give legal advice;*

*(ii) may contain a description of examples of legal advice that a bankruptcy petition preparer is not authorized to give, in addition to any advice that the preparer may not give by reason of subsection (e)(2); and*

*(iii) shall—*

*(I) be signed by the debtor and, under penalty of perjury, by the bankruptcy petition preparer; and*

*(II) be filed with any document for filing.*

(c) (1) A bankruptcy petition preparer who prepares a document for filing shall place on the document, after the preparer's signature, an identifying number that identifies individuals who prepared the document.

(2) *(A) Subject to subparagraph (B), for* ~~For~~ purposes of this section, the identifying number of a bankruptcy petition preparer

shall be the Social Security account number of each individual who prepared the document or assisted in its preparation.

*(B) If a bankruptcy petition preparer is not an individual, the identifying number of the bankruptcy petition preparer shall be the Social Security account number of the officer, principal, responsible person, or partner of the bankruptcy petition preparer.*

~~(3) A bankruptcy petition preparer who fails to comply with paragraph (1) may be fined not more than $500 for each such failure unless the failure is due to reasonable cause.~~

(d) ~~(1)~~ A bankruptcy petition preparer shall, not later than the time at which a document for filing is presented for the debtor's signature, furnish to the debtor a copy of the document.

~~(2) A bankruptcy petition preparer who fails to comply with paragraph (1) may be fined not more than $500 for each such failure unless the failure is due to reasonable cause.~~

(e) (1) A bankruptcy petition preparer shall not execute any document on behalf of a debtor.

(2) ~~A bankruptcy petition preparer may be fined not more than $500 for each document executed in violation of paragraph (1).~~ *(A) A bankruptcy petition preparer may not offer a potential bankruptcy debtor any legal advice, including any legal advice described in subparagraph (B).*

*(B) The legal advice referred to in subparagraph (A) includes advising the debtor—*

*(i) whether—*

*(I) to file a petition under this title; or*

*(II) commencing a case under chapter 7, 11, 12, or 13 is appropriate;*

*(ii) whether the debtor's debts will be discharged in a case under this title;*

*(iii) whether the debtor will be able to retain the debtor's home, car, or other property after commencing a case under this title;*

*(iv) concerning—*

*(I) the tax consequences of a case brought under this title; or*

*(II) the dischargeability of tax claims;*

*(v) whether the debtor may or should promise to repay debts to a creditor or enter into a reaffirmation agreement with a creditor to reaffirm a debt;*

*(vi) concerning how to characterize the nature of the debtor's interests in property or the debtor's debts; or*

*(vii) concerning bankruptcy procedures and rights.*

(f) ~~(1)~~ A bankruptcy petition preparer shall not use the word "legal" or any similar term in any advertisements, or advertise under any category that includes the word "legal" or any similar term.

~~(2) A bankruptcy petition preparer shall be fined not more than $500 for each violation of paragraph (1).~~

(g) ~~(1)~~ A bankruptcy petition preparer shall not collect or receive any payment from the debtor or on behalf of the debtor for the court fees in connection with filing the petition.

~~(2) A bankruptcy petition preparer shall be fined not more than $500 for each violation of paragraph (1).~~

(h) *(1) The Supreme Court may promulgate rules under section 2075 of title 28, or the Judicial Conference of the United States may prescribe guidelines, for setting a maximum allowable fee chargeable by a bankruptcy petition preparer. A bankruptcy petition preparer shall notify the debtor of any such maximum amount before preparing any document for filing for a debtor or accepting any fee from the debtor.*

(~~1~~*2*) ~~Within 10 days after the date of the filing of a petition, a bankruptcy petition preparer shall file a~~ *A* declaration under penalty of perjury *by the bankruptcy petition preparer shall be filed together with the petition,* disclosing any fee received from or on behalf of the debtor within 12 months immediately prior to the filing of the case, and any unpaid fee charged to the debtor. *If rules or guidelines setting a maximum fee for services have been promulgated or prescribed under paragraph (1), the declaration under this paragraph shall include a certification that the bankruptcy petition preparer complied with the notification requirement under paragraph (1).*

~~(2) The court shall disallow and order the immediate turnover to the bankruptcy trustee of any fee referred to in paragraph (1) found to be in excess of the value of services rendered for the documents prepared. An individual debtor may exempt any funds so recovered under section 522(b).~~

*(3) (A) The court shall disallow and order the immediate turnover to the bankruptcy trustee any fee referred to in paragraph (2) found to be in excess of the value of any services—*

*(i) rendered by the bankruptcy petition preparer during the 12-month period immediately preceding the date of the filing of the petition; or*

*(ii) found to be in violation of any rule or guideline promulgated or prescribed under paragraph (1).*

*(B) All fees charged by a bankruptcy petition preparer may be forfeited in any case in which the bankruptcy petition preparer fails to comply with this subsection or subsection (b), (c), (d), (e), (f), or (g).*

*(C) An individual may exempt any funds recovered under this paragraph under section 522(b).*

(~~3~~*4*) The debtor, the trustee, a creditor, ~~or~~ the United States trustee *(or the bankruptcy administrator, if any) or the court, on the initiative of the court,* may file a motion for an order under paragraph (2).

(~~4~~*5*) A bankruptcy petition preparer shall be fined not more than $500 for each failure to comply with a court order to turn over funds within 30 days of service of such order.

(i) (1) ~~If a bankruptcy case or related proceeding is dismissed because of the failure to file bankruptcy papers, including papers specified in section 521(1) of this title, the negligence or intentional disregard of this title or the Federal Rules of Bankruptcy Procedure by a bankruptcy petition preparer, or if a bankruptcy petition preparer violates this section or commits any fraudulent, unfair, or deceptive act, the bankruptcy court shall certify that fact to the district court, and the district court, on motion of the debtor, the trustee, or a creditor and after a hearing, shall order the bankruptcy petition preparer to pay to the debtor~~*If a bankruptcy petition preparer violates this section or commits any act that the court finds to be fraudulent, unfair, or deceptive, on the motion of the debtor, trustee, United States trustee (or the bankruptcy administrator, if any), and after notice and a hearing, the court shall order the bankruptcy petition preparer to pay to the debtor—*

(A) the debtor's actual damages;

(B) the greater of—

(i) $2,000; or

(ii) twice the amount paid by the debtor to the bankruptcy petition preparer for the preparer's services; and

(C) reasonable attorneys' fees and costs in moving for damages under this subsection.

(2) If the trustee or creditor moves for damages on behalf of the debtor under this subsection, the bankruptcy petition preparer shall be ordered to pay the movant the additional amount of $1,000 plus reasonable attorneys' fees and costs incurred.

(j) (1) A debtor for whom a bankruptcy petition preparer has prepared a document for filing, the trustee, a creditor, or the United States trustee in the district in which the bankruptcy petition preparer resides, has conducted business, or the United States trustee in any other district in which the debtor resides may bring a civil action to enjoin a bankruptcy petition preparer from engaging in any conduct in violation of this section or from further acting as a bankruptcy petition preparer.

(2) (A) In an action under paragraph (1), if the court finds that—

(i) a bankruptcy petition preparer has—

(I) engaged in conduct in violation of this section or of any provision of this title ~~a violation of which subjects a person to criminal penalty~~;

(II) misrepresented the preparer's experience or education as a bankruptcy petition preparer; or

(III) engaged in any other fraudulent, unfair, or deceptive conduct; and

(ii) injunctive relief is appropriate to prevent the recurrence of such conduct,

the court may enjoin the bankruptcy petition preparer from engaging in such conduct.

(B) If the court finds that a bankruptcy petition preparer has continually engaged in conduct described in subclause (I), (II), or (III) of clause (i) and that an injunction prohibiting such conduct would not be sufficient to prevent such person's interference with the proper administration of this title, ~~or has not paid a penalty~~ *has not paid a penalty* imposed under this section, *or failed to disgorge all fees ordered by the court* the court may enjoin the person from acting as a bankruptcy petition preparer.

*(3) The court, as part of its contempt power, may enjoin a bankruptcy petition preparer that has failed to comply with a previous order issued under this section. The injunction under this paragraph may be issued on the motion of the court, the trustee, or the United States trustee (or the bankruptcy administrator, if any).*

(~~3~~*4*) The court shall award to a debtor, trustee, or creditor that brings a successful action under this subsection reasonable attorneys'~~s~~ fees and costs of the action, to be paid by the bankruptcy petition preparer.

(k) Nothing in this section shall be construed to permit activities that are otherwise prohibited by law, including rules and laws that prohibit the unauthorized practice of law.

*(l) (1) A bankruptcy petition preparer who fails to comply with any provision of subsection (b), (c), (d), (e), (f), (g), or (h) may be fined not more than $500 for each such failure.*

*(2) The court shall triple the amount of a fine assessed under paragraph (1) in any case in which the court finds that a bankruptcy petition preparer—*

*(A) advised the debtor to exclude assets or income that should have been included on applicable schedules;*

*(B) advised the debtor to use a false Social Security account number;*

*(C) failed to inform the debtor that the debtor was filing for relief under this title; or*

*(D) prepared a document for filing in a manner that failed to disclose the identity of the bankruptcy petition preparer.*

*(3) A debtor, trustee, creditor, or United States trustee (or the bankruptcy administrator, if any) may file a motion for an order imposing a fine on the bankruptcy petition preparer for any violation of this section.*

*(4) (A) Fines imposed under this subsection in judicial districts served by United States trustees shall be paid to the United States trustee, who shall deposit an amount equal to such fines in a special account of the United States Trustee System Fund referred to in section 586(e)(2) of title 28. Amounts deposited under this subparagraph shall be available to fund the enforcement of this section on a national basis.*

*(B) Fines imposed under this subsection in judicial districts served by bankruptcy administrators shall be deposited as offset-*

*ting receipts to the fund established under section 1931 of title 28, and shall remain available until expended to reimburse any appropriation for the amount paid out of such appropriation for expenses of the operation and maintenance of the courts of the United States.*

**Section 110**

(April 20, 2005, P. L. 109-8, Title IIC, § 221; Title XII, § 1205, 119 Stat. 23)

## HISTORY: ANCILLARY LAWS AND DIRECTIVES

**Amendments:**

**2005.** Act April 20, 2005 (effective 180 days after enactment of April 20, 2005, as provided by § 1501(a) of P. L. 109-8), amends 11 USC § 110's requirements for bankruptcy petition preparers.

**Other provisions:**

**Effective date and application of amendments made by Act April 20, 2005.** Act April 20, 2005, P.L. 109-8, Title XV, § 1501(a), 119 Stat. 23, provided that the amendments made to this section would be effective 180 days after enactment of April 20, 2005.

**Abridged Legislative History**

(H. Report No. 109-31 to accompany S. 256, 109th Cong., 1st Sess. (2005) pp. 62–63, 142; available at 2005 U.S.C.C.A.N. 88, at 132, 201.)

## § 111. *Nonprofit budget and credit counseling agencies; financial management instructional courses*

*(a) The clerk shall maintain a publicly available list of—*

*(1) nonprofit budget and credit counseling agencies that provide 1 or more services described in section 109(h) currently approved by the United States trustee (or the bankruptcy administrator, if any); and*

*(2) instructional courses concerning personal financial management currently approved by the United States trustee (or the bankruptcy administrator, if any), as applicable.*

*(b) The United States trustee (or bankruptcy administrator, if any) shall only approve a nonprofit budget and credit counseling agency or an instructional course concerning personal financial management as follows:*

*(1) The United States trustee (or bankruptcy administrator, if any) shall have thoroughly reviewed the qualifications of the nonprofit budget and credit counseling agency or of the provider of the instructional course under the standards set forth in this section, and the services or instructional courses that will be offered by such agency or such provider, and may require such agency or such provider that has sought approval to provide information with respect to such review.*

*(2) The United States trustee (or bankruptcy administrator, if any) shall have determined that such agency or such instructional course fully satisfies the applicable standards set forth in this section.*

*(3) If a nonprofit budget and credit counseling agency or instruc-*

*tional course did not appear on the approved list for the district under subsection (a) immediately before approval under this section, approval under this subsection of such agency or such instructional course shall be for a probationary period not to exceed 6 months.*

*(4) At the conclusion of the applicable probationary period under paragraph (3), the United States trustee (or bankruptcy administrator, if any) may only approve for an additional 1-year period, and for successive 1-year periods thereafter, an agency or instructional course that has demonstrated during the probationary or applicable subsequent period of approval that such agency or instructional course—*

*(A) has met the standards set forth under this section during such period; and*

*(B) can satisfy such standards in the future.*

*(5) Not later than 30 days after any final decision under paragraph (4), an interested person may seek judicial review of such decision in the appropriate district court of the United States.*

*(c) (1) The United States trustee (or the bankruptcy administrator, if any) shall only approve a nonprofit budget and credit counseling agency that demonstrates that it will provide qualified counselors, maintain adequate provision for safekeeping and payment of client funds, provide adequate counseling with respect to client credit problems, and deal responsibly and effectively with other matters relating to the quality, effectiveness, and financial security of the services it provides.*

*(2) To be approved by the United States trustee (or the bankruptcy administrator, if any), a nonprofit budget and credit counseling agency shall, at a minimum—*

*(A) have a board of directors the majority of which—*

*(i) are not employed by such agency; and*

*(ii) will not directly or indirectly benefit financially from the outcome of the counseling services provided by such agency;*

*(B) if a fee is charged for counseling services, charge a reasonable fee, and provide services without regard to ability to pay the fee;*

*(C) provide for safekeeping and payment of client funds, including an annual audit of the trust accounts and appropriate employee bonding;*

*(D) provide full disclosures to a client, including funding sources, counselor qualifications, possible impact on credit reports, and any costs of such program that will be paid by such client and how such costs will be paid;*

*(E) provide adequate counseling with respect to a client's credit problems that includes an analysis of such client's current financial condition, factors that caused such financial condition, and how such client can develop a plan to respond to the problems without incurring negative amortization of debt;*

*(F) provide trained counselors who receive no commissions or bonuses based on the outcome of the counseling services provided by such agency, and who have adequate experience, and have been adequately trained to provide counseling services to individuals in financial difficulty, including the matters described in subparagraph (E);*

*(G) demonstrate adequate experience and background in providing credit counseling; and*

*(H) have adequate financial resources to provide continuing support services for budgeting plans over the life of any repayment plan.*

*(d) The United States trustee (or the bankruptcy administrator, if any) shall only approve an instructional course concerning personal financial management—*

*(1) for an initial probationary period under subsection (b)(3) if the course will provide at a minimum—*

*(A) trained personnel with adequate experience and training in providing effective instruction and services;*

*(B) learning materials and teaching methodologies designed to assist debtors in understanding personal financial management and that are consistent with stated objectives directly related to the goals of such instructional course;*

*(C) adequate facilities situated in reasonably convenient locations at which such instructional course is offered, except that such facilities may include the provision of such instructional course by telephone or through the Internet, if such instructional course is effective;*

*(D) the preparation and retention of reasonable records (which shall include the debtor's bankruptcy case number) to permit evaluation of the effectiveness of such instructional course, including any evaluation of satisfaction of instructional course requirements for each debtor attending such instructional course, which shall be available for inspection and evaluation by the Executive Office for United States Trustees, the United States trustee (or the bankruptcy administrator, if any), or the chief bankruptcy judge for the district in which such instructional course is offered; and*

*(E) if a fee is charged for the instructional course, charge a reasonable fee, and provide services without regard to ability to pay the fee.*

*(2) for any 1-year period if the provider thereof has demonstrated that the course meets the standards of paragraph (1) and, in addition—*

*(A) has been effective in assisting a substantial number of debtors to understand personal financial management; and*

*(B) is otherwise likely to increase substantially the debtor's understanding of personal financial management.*

*(e) The district court may, at any time, investigate the qualifications*

*of a nonprofit budget and credit counseling agency referred to in subsection (a), and request production of documents to ensure the integrity and effectiveness of such agency. The district court may, at any time, remove from the approved list under subsection (a) a nonprofit budget and credit counseling agency upon finding such agency does not meet the qualifications of subsection (b).*

*(f) The United States trustee (or the bankruptcy administrator, if any) shall notify the clerk that a nonprofit budget and credit counseling agency or an instructional course is no longer approved, in which case the clerk shall remove it from the list maintained under subsection (a).*

*(g) (1) No nonprofit budget and credit counseling agency may provide to a credit reporting agency information concerning whether a debtor has received or sought instruction concerning personal financial management from such agency.*

*(2) A nonprofit budget and credit counseling agency that willfully or negligently fails to comply with any requirement under this title with respect to a debtor shall be liable for damages in an amount equal to the sum of—*

*(A) any actual damages sustained by the debtor as a result of the violation; and*

*(B) any court costs or reasonable attorneys' fees (as determined by the court) incurred in an action to recover those damages.*

**Section 111**

(April 20, 2005, P. L. 109-8, Title I, § 106(e), 119 Stat. 23)

## HISTORY: ANCILLARY LAWS AND DIRECTIVES

**Amendments:**

**2005.** Act April 20, 2005 (effective 180 days after enactment of April 20, 2005, as provided by § 1501(a) of P. L. 109-8), adds new 11 USC § 111, defining the duties and requirements for nonprofit budget and credit counseling agencies that will provide the required financial management instructional courses for individual debtors.

**Other provisions:**

**Effective date and application of amendments made by Act April 20, 2005.** Act April 20, 2005, P.L. 109-8, Title XV, § 1501(a), 119 Stat. 23, provided that the amendments made to this section would be effective 180 days after enactment of April 20, 2005.

**Abridged Legislative History**

Section 106(e) of the Act adds section 111 to the Bankruptcy Code requiring the clerk to maintain a publicly available list of approved: (1) credit counseling agencies that provide the services described in section 109(h) of the Bankruptcy Code; and (2) personal financial management instructional courses. Section 106(e) further provides that the United States trustee or bankruptcy administrator may only approve an agency or course provider under this provision pursuant to certain specified criteria. These include, for example, if a fee is charged for such services by the agency or course provider, the fee must be reasonable, and such services must be provided without regard to ability to pay the fee. If such agency or provider course is approved, the approval may only be for a probationary period of up to six months. At the conclusion of the probationary period, the United States trustee or bankruptcy administrator may only approve such agency or instructional course for an additional one-year period, and thereafter for successive one-year periods, that has demonstrated during such period that it met the standards set forth in this provision and can satisfy such

standards in the future.
(H. Report No. 109-31 to accompany S. 256, 109th Cong., 1st Sess. (2005) p. 55–6; available at 2005 U.S.C.C.A.N. 88, at 125–26.)

## *§ 112. Prohibition on disclosure of name of minor children*

*The debtor may be required to provide information regarding a minor child involved in matters under this title but may not be required to disclose in the public records in the case the name of such minor child. The debtor may be required to disclose the name of such minor child in a nonpublic record that is maintained by the court and made available by the court for examination by the United States trustee, the trustee, and the auditor (if any) serving under section 586(f) of title 28, in the case. The court, the United States trustee, the trustee, and such auditor shall not disclose the name of such minor child maintained in such nonpublic record.*

**Section 112**

(April 20, 2005, P. L. 109-8, Title IIC, § 233(a), 119 Stat. 23)

### HISTORY: ANCILLARY LAWS AND DIRECTIVES

**Amendments:**

**2005.** Act April 20, 2005 (effective 180 days after enactment of April 20, 2005, as provided by § 1501(a) of P. L. 109-8), adds new 11 USC § 112, providing for protection of the name of a debtor's minor child.

**Other provisions:**

**Effective date and application of amendments made by Act April 20, 2005.** Act April 20, 2005, P.L. 109-8, Title XV, § 1501(a), 119 Stat. 23, provided that the amendments made to this section would be effective 180 days after enactment of April 20, 2005.

**Abridged Legislative History**

(H. Report No. 109-31 to accompany S. 256, 109th Cong., 1st Sess. (2005) p. 68; available at 2005 U.S.C.C.A.N. 88, at 137.)

# Chapter 3
# —Case Administration

## Subchapter I——Commencement of a Case

## Subchapter I——Commencement of a Case

### § 301. Voluntary cases

*(a)* A voluntary case under a chapter of this title is commenced by the filing with the bankruptcy court of a petition under such chapter by an entity that may be a debtor under such chapter. ~~The commencement of a voluntary case under a chapter of this title constitutes an order for relief under such chapter.~~

*(b) The commencement of a voluntary case under a chapter of this title constitutes an order for relief under such chapter.*

**Section 301**

(April 20, 2005, P. L. 109-8, Title V, § 501(b), April 20, 2005, 119 Stat. 23)

#### HISTORY: ANCILLARY LAWS AND DIRECTIVES

**Amendments:**

**2005.** Act April 20, 2005(effective 180 days after enactment of April 20, 2005, as provided by § 1501(a) of P. L. 109-8), amends 11 USC § 301 to move the last sentence to a new subsection 301(b). No substantive change results.

**Other provisions:**

**Effective date and application of amendments made by Act April 20, 2005.** Act April 20, 2005, P.L. 109-8, Title XV, § 1501(a), 119 Stat. 23, provided that the amendments made to this section would be effective 180 days after enactment on April 20, 2005.

### § 302. Joint cases

(a) A joint case under a chapter of this title is commenced by the filing with the bankruptcy court of a single petition under such chapter by an individual that may be a debtor under such chapter and such individual's spouse. The commencement of a joint case under a chapter of this title constitutes an order for relief under such chapter.

(b) After the commencement of a joint case, the court shall determine the extent, if any, to which the debtors' estates shall be consolidated.

### § 303. Involuntary cases

(a) An involuntary case may be commenced only under chapter 7 or 11 of this title, and only against a person, except a farmer, family farmer, or a corporation that is not a moneyed, business, or commercial corporation, that may be a debtor under the chapter under which such case is commenced.

(b) An involuntary case against a person is commenced by the filing with the bankruptcy court of a petition under chapter 7 or 11 of this title—

(1) by three or more entities, each of which is either a holder of a claim against such person that is not contingent as to liability or the subject of a bona fide dispute *as to liability or amount,* or an indenture trustee representing such a holder, ~~if such claims~~ *if such noncontingent, undisputed claims* aggregate at least $12,300 more than the value of any lien on property of the debtor securing such claims held by the holders of such claims;

(2) if there are fewer than 12 such holders, excluding any employee or insider of such person and any transferee of a transfer that is voidable under section 544, 545, 547, 548, 549, or 724(a) of this title, by one or more of such holders that hold in the aggregate at least $12,300 of such claims;

(3) if such person is a partnership—

(A) by fewer than all of the general partners in such partnership; or

(B) if relief has been ordered under this title with respect to all of the general partners in such partnership, by a general partner in such partnership, the trustee of such a general partner, or a holder of a claim against such partnership; or

(4) by a foreign representative of the estate in a foreign proceeding concerning such person.

(c) After the filing of a petition under this section but before the case is dismissed or relief is ordered, a creditor holding an unsecured claim that is not contingent, other than a creditor filing under subsection (b) of this section, may join in the petition with the same effect as if such joining creditor were a petitioning creditor under subsection (b) of this section.

(d) The debtor, or a general partner in a partnership debtor that did not join in the petition, may file an answer to a petition under this section.

(e) After notice and a hearing, and for cause, the court may require the petitioners under this section to file a bond to indemnify the debtor for such amounts as the court may later allow under subsection (i) of this section.

(f) Notwithstanding section 363 of this title, except to the extent that the court orders otherwise, and until an order for relief in the case, any business of the debtor may continue to operate, and the debtor may continue to use, acquire, or dispose of property as if an involuntary case concerning the debtor had not been commenced.

(g) At any time after the commencement of an involuntary case under chapter 7 of this title but before an order for relief in the case, the court, on request of a party in interest, after notice to the debtor and a hearing, and if necessary to preserve the property of the estate or to prevent loss to the estate, may order the United States trustee to appoint an interim trustee under section 701 of this title to take possession of the property of the estate and to operate any business of the debtor. Before an order for relief, the debtor may regain possession of property in the possession of a trustee ordered appointed under this subsection if the debtor files such bond as the court requires, conditioned on the debtor's accounting for and delivering to the trustee, if there is an order for relief in the case, such property, or the value, as of the date the debtor regains possession, of such property.

(h) If the petition is not timely controverted, the court shall order relief against the debtor in an involuntary case under the chapter under which the petition was filed. Otherwise, after trial, the court shall order relief against the debtor in an involuntary case under the chapter under which the petition was filed, only if—

(1) the debtor is generally not paying such debtor's debts as such debts become due unless such debts are the subject of a bona fide dispute *as to liability or amount;* or

(2) within 120 days before the date of the filing of the petition, a custodian, other than a trustee, receiver, or agent appointed or authorized to take charge of less than substantially all of the property of the debtor for the purpose of enforcing a lien against such property, was appointed or took possession.

(i) If the court dismisses a petition under this section other than on consent of all petitioners and the debtor, and if the debtor does not waive the right to judgment under this subsection, the court may grant judgment—

(1) against the petitioners and in favor of the debtor for—

(A) costs; or

(B) a reasonable attorney's fee; or

(2) against any petitioner that filed the petition in bad faith, for—

(A) any damages proximately caused by such filing; or

(B) punitive damages.

(j) Only after notice to all creditors and a hearing may the court dismiss a petition filed under this section—

(1) on the motion of a petitioner;

(2) on consent of all petitioners and the debtor; or

(3) for want of prosecution.

~~(k) Notwithstanding subsection (a) of this section, an involuntary case may be commenced against a foreign bank that is not engaged in such business in the United States only under chapter 7 of this title and only if a foreign proceeding concerning such bank is pending.~~

*(l) (1) If—*

*(A) the petition under this section is false or contains any materially false, fictitious, or fraudulent statement;*

*(B) the debtor is an individual; and*

*(C) the court dismisses such petition,*

*the court, upon the motion of the debtor, shall seal all the records of the court relating to such petition, and all references to such petition.*

*(2) If the debtor is an individual and the court dismisses a petition under this section, the court may enter an order prohibiting all consumer reporting agencies (as defined in section 603(f) of the Fair Credit Reporting Act (15 U.S.C. 1681a(f))) from making any consumer report (as defined in section 603(d) of that Act) that contains any information relating to such petition or to the case commenced by the filing of such petition.*

*(3) Upon the expiration of the statute of limitations described in section 3282 of title 18, for a violation of section 152 or 157 of such title, the court, upon the motion of the debtor and for good cause,*

*may expunge any records relating to a petition filed under this section.*

**Section 303**

(April 20, 2005, P. L. 109-8, Title III, § 332(b); Title VIII, § 802(d)(2); Title XII, § 1234, 119 Stat. 23)

## HISTORY: ANCILLARY LAWS AND DIRECTIVES

**Amendments:**

**2005.** Act April 20, 2005(effective 180 days after enactment of April 20, 2005, as provided by § 1501(a) of P. L. 109-8), deletes 11 USC § 303(k) and adds (l) to provide remedies for false or fraudulent involuntary petitions. The Act (effective upon enactment, as provided by § 1234(b) of P.L. 109-8), amends 11 USC § 303(b) to add a threshold to filing an involuntary petition that there be no dispute "as to liability or amount."

**Other provisions:**

**Effective date and application of amendments made by Act April 20, 2005.** Act April 20, 2005, P.L. 109-8, Title XV, § 1501(a), 119 Stat. 23, provided that the amendments made to § 303(k) and (l) would be effective 180 days after enactment on April 20, 2005. Amendment by Pub.L. 109-8 to § 303(b) is effective "on the date of enactment of this Act [April 20, 2005] and shall apply with respect to cases commenced under title 11 of the United States Code before, on, and after such date." See § 1234(b) of Pub. L. 109-8.

**Abridged Legislative History**

Section 1234 of the Act amends the Bankruptcy Code's criteria for commencing an involuntary bankruptcy case. Current law renders a creditor ineligible if its claim is contingent as to liability or the subject of a bona fide dispute. This provision amends section 303(b)(1) to specify that a creditor would be ineligible to file an involuntary petition if the creditor's claim was the subject of a bona fide dispute as to liability or amount. It further provides that the claims needed to meet the monetary threshold must be undisputed. The provision makes a conforming revision to section 303(h)(1). Section 1234 becomes effective on the date of enactment of this Act and applies to cases commenced before, on, and after such date. (H. Report No. 109-31 to accompany S. 256, 109th Cong., 1st Sess. (2005) pp. 84–86, 148; available at 2005 U.S.C.C.A.N. 88, at 151–52, 206.)

## ~~§ 304. Cases ancillary to foreign proceedings~~

~~(a) A case ancillary to a foreign proceeding is commenced by the filing with the bankruptcy court of a petition under this section by a foreign representative.~~

~~(b) Subject to the provisions of subsection (c) of this section, if a party in interest does not timely controvert the petition, or after trial, the court may—~~

~~(1) enjoin the commencement or continuation of—~~

~~(A) any action against—~~

~~(i) a debtor with respect to property involved in such foreign proceeding; or~~

~~(ii) such property; or~~

~~(B) the enforcement of any judgment against the debtor with respect to such property, or any act or the commencement or continuation of any judicial proceeding to create or enforce a lien against the property of such estate;~~

~~(2) order turnover of the property of such estate, or the proceeds of such property, to such foreign representative; or~~

~~(3) order other appropriate relief.~~

~~(c) In determining whether to grant relief under subsection (b) of this section, the court shall be guided by what will best assure an economical and expeditious administration of such estate, consistent with—~~

~~(1) just treatment of all holders of claims against or interests in such estate;~~

~~(2) protection of claim holders in the United States against prejudice and inconvenience in the processing of claims in such foreign proceeding;~~

~~(3) prevention of preferential or fraudulent dispositions of property of such estate;~~

~~(4) distribution of proceeds of such estate substantially in accordance with the order prescribed by this title;~~

~~(5) comity; and~~

~~(6) if appropriate, the provision of an opportunity for a fresh start for the individual that such foreign proceeding concerns.~~

**Section 304**

(April 20, 2005, P. L. 109-8, Title VIII, § 802(d)(3), 119 Stat. 23)

## HISTORY: ANCILLARY LAWS AND DIRECTIVES

**Amendments:**

**2005.** Act April 20, 2005(effective 180 days after enactment of April 20, 2005, as provided by § 1501(a) of P. L. 109-8), deletes 11 USC § 304.

**Other provisions:**

**Effective date and application of amendments made by Act April 20, 2005.** Act April 20, 2005, P.L. 109-8, Title XV, § 1501(a), 119 Stat. 23, provides that the amendments made to this section would be effective 180 days after enactment on April 20, 2005.

**Abridged Legislative History**

(H. Report No. 109-31 to accompany S. 256, 109th Cong., 1st Sess. (2005) p. 119; available at 2005 U.S.C.C.A.N. 88, at 181.)

## § 305. Abstention

(a) The court, after notice and a hearing, may dismiss a case under this title, or may suspend all proceedings in a case under this title, at any time if—

(1) the interests of creditors and the debtor would be better served by such dismissal or suspension; or

(2) (A) ~~there is pending a foreign proceeding; and~~*a petition under section 1515 for recognition of a foreign proceeding has been granted; and*

(B) ~~the factors specified in section 304(c) of this title warrant such dismissal or suspension.~~*the purposes of chapter 15 of this title would be best served by such dismissal or suspension.*

(b) A foreign representative may seek dismissal or suspension under subsection (a)(2) of this section.

(c) An order under subsection (a) of this section dismissing a case or suspending all proceedings in a case, or a decision not so to dismiss or suspend, is not reviewable by appeal or otherwise by the court of appeals under section 158(d), 1291, or 1292 of title 28 or by the Supreme Court of the United States under section 1254 of title 28.

**Section 305**

(April 20, 2005, P. L. 109-8, Title VIII, § 802(d)(6), 119 Stat. 23)

## HISTORY: ANCILLARY LAWS AND DIRECTIVES

**Amendments:**

**2005.** Act April 20, 2005(effective 180 days after enactment of April 20, 2005, as provided by § 1501(a) of P. L. 109-8), amends 11 USC § 305(a)(2) to strengthen grounds for abstention in a foreign proceeding under new § 1515.

**Other provisions:**

**Effective date and application of amendments made by Act April 20, 2005.** Act April 20, 2005, P.L. 109-8, Title XV, § 1501(a), 119 Stat. 23, provides that the amendments made to this section would be effective 180 days after enactment on April 20, 2005.

# § 306. Limited appearance

An appearance in a bankruptcy court by a foreign representative in connection with a petition or request under section 303~~, 304,~~ or 305 of this title does not submit such foreign representative to the jurisdiction of any court in the United States for any other purpose, but the bankruptcy court may condition any order under section 303~~, 304,~~ or 305 of this title on compliance by such foreign representative with the orders of such bankruptcy court.

**Section 306**

(April 20, 2005, P. L. 109-8, Title VIII, § 802(d)(5), 119 Stat. 23)

## HISTORY: ANCILLARY LAWS AND DIRECTIVES

**Amendments:**

**2005.** Act April 20, 2005(effective 180 days after enactment of April 20, 2005, as provided by § 1501(a) of P. L. 109-8), amends 11 USC § 306 to strike reference to deleted § 304.

**Other provisions:**

**Effective date and application of amendments made by Act April 20, 2005.** Act April 20, 2005, P.L. 109-8, Title XV, § 1501(a), 119 Stat. 23, provides that the amendments made to this section would be effective 180 days after enactment on April 20, 2005.

# § 307. United States trustee

The United States trustee may raise and may appear and be heard on any issue in any case or proceeding under this title but may not file a plan pursuant to section 1121(c) of this title.

# § 308. *Debtor Reporting Requirements*

*(a) For purposes of this section, the term "profitability" means, with respect to a debtor, the amount of money that the debtor has earned or lost during current and recent fiscal periods.*

*(b) A small business debtor shall file periodic financial and other reports containing information including—*

*(1) the debtor's profitability;*

*(2) reasonable approximations of the debtor's projected cash receipts and cash disbursements over a reasonable period;*

*(3) comparisons of actual cash receipts and disbursements with projections in prior reports;*

*(4) (A) whether the debtor is—*

*(i) in compliance in all material respects with postpetition requirements imposed by this title and the Federal Rules of Bankruptcy Procedure; and*

*(ii) timely filing tax returns and other required government filings and paying taxes and other administrative expenses when due;*

*(B) if the debtor is not in compliance with the requirements referred to in subparagraph (A)(i) or filing tax returns and other required government filings and making the payments referred to in subparagraph (A)(ii), what the failures are and how, at what cost, and when the debtor intends to remedy such failures; and*

*(C) such other matters as are in the best interests of the debtor and creditors, and in the public interest in fair and efficient procedures under chapter 11 of this title.*

**Section 308**

(April 20, 2005, P. L. 109-8, Title IVB, § 434(a), 119 Stat. 23)

## HISTORY: ANCILLARY LAWS AND DIRECTIVES

**Amendments:**

**2005.** Act April 20, 2005(effective "60 days after the date on which rules are prescribed under section 2075 of title 28, United States Code, to establish forms to be used to comply with section 308 of title 11, United States Code," as provided by § 434(b) of P. L. 109-8), adds 11 USC § 308 reporting requirements for a small business debtor.

**Other provisions:**

**Effective date and application of amendments made by Act April 20, 2005.** Act April 20, 2005, P.L. 109-8, Title IV, § 434(b), 119 Stat. 23, provides that the amendments made to this section is effective "60 days after the date on which rules are prescribed under section 2075 of title 28, United States Code, to establish forms to be used to comply with section 308 of title 11, United States Code."

**Abridged Legislative History**

Subsection (a) of section 434 of the Act adds a provision to the Bankruptcy Code mandating additional reporting requirements for small business debtors. It requires a small business debtor to file periodic financial reports and other documents containing the following information with respect to the debtor's business operations: (1) profitability; (2) reasonable approximations of projected cash receipts and disbursements; (3) comparisons of actual cash receipts and disbursements with projections in prior reports; (4) whether the debtor is complying with postpetition requirements pursuant to the Bankruptcy Code and Federal Rules of Bankruptcy Procedure; (5) whether the debtor is timely filing tax returns and other government filings; and (6) whether the debtor is paying taxes and other administrative expenses when due. In addition, the debtor must report on such other matters that are in the best interests of the debtor and the creditors and in the public interest. If the debtor is not in compliance with any postpetition requirements pursuant to the Bankruptcy Code and Federal Rules of Bankruptcy Procedure, or is not filing tax returns or other required governmental filings, paying taxes and other administrative expenses when due, the debtor must report: (1) what the failures are, (2) how they will be cured; (3) the cost

of their cure; and (4) when they will be cured. Section 434(b) specifies that the effective date of this provision is 60 days after the date on which the rules required under this provision are promulgated.
(H. Report No. 109-31 to accompany S. 256, 109th Cong., 1st Sess. (2005) pp. 91–92; available at 2005 U.S.C.C.A.N. 88, at 156–57.)

## § 321. Eligibility to serve as trustee

(a) A person may serve as trustee in a case under this title only if such person is—

(1) an individual that is competent to perform the duties of trustee and, in a case under chapter 7, 12, or 13 of this title, resides or has an office in the judicial district within which the case is pending, or in any judicial district adjacent to such district; or

(2) a corporation authorized by such corporation's charter or bylaws to act as trustee, and, in a case under chapter 7, 12, or 13 of this title, having an office in at least one of such districts.

(b) A person that has served as an examiner in the case may not serve as trustee in the case.

(c) The United States trustee for the judicial district in which the case is pending is eligible to serve as trustee in the case if necessary.

## § 322. Qualification of trustee

(a) Except as provided in subsection (b)(1), a person selected under section 701, 702, 703, 1104, 1163, 1202, or 1302 of this title to serve as trustee in a case under this title qualifies if before five days after such selection, and before beginning official duties, such person has filed with the court a bond in favor of the United States conditioned on the faithful performance of such official duties.

(b) (1) The United States trustee qualifies wherever such trustee serves as trustee in a case under this title.

(2) The United States trustee shall determine—

(A) the amount of a bond required to be filed under subsection (a) of this section; and

(B) the sufficiency of the surety on such bond.

(c) A trustee is not liable personally or on such trustee's bond in favor of the United States for any penalty or forfeiture incurred by the debtor.

(d) A proceeding on a trustee's bond may not be commenced after two years after the date on which such trustee was discharged.

## § 323. Role and capacity of trustee

(a) The trustee in a case under this title is the representative of the estate.

(b) The trustee in a case under this title has capacity to sue and be sued.

## § 324. Removal of trustee or examiner

(a) The court, after notice and a hearing, may remove a trustee, other than the United States trustee, or an examiner, for cause.

(b) Whenever the court removes a trustee or examiner under subsection (a) in a case under this title, such trustee or examiner shall thereby be removed in all other cases under this title in which such trustee or examiner is then serving unless the court orders otherwise.

## § 325. Effect of vacancy

A vacancy in the office of trustee during a case does not abate any pending action or proceeding, and the successor trustee shall be substituted as a party in such action or proceeding.

## § 326. Limitation on compensation of trustee

(a) In a case under chapter 7 or 11, the court may allow reasonable compensation under section 330 of this title of the trustee for the trustee's services, payable after the trustee renders such services, not to exceed 25 percent on the first $5,000 or less, 10 percent on any amount in excess of $5,000 but not in excess of $50,000, 5 percent on any amount in excess of $50,000 but not in excess of $1,000,000, and reasonable compensation not to exceed 3 percent of such moneys in excess of $1,000,000, upon all moneys disbursed or turned over in the case by the trustee to parties in interest, excluding the debtor, but including holders of secured claims.

(b) In a case under chapter 12 or 13 of this title, the court may not allow compensation for services or reimbursement of expenses of the United States trustee or of a standing trustee appointed under section 586(b) of title 28, but may allow reasonable compensation under section 330 of this title of a trustee appointed under section 1202(a) or 1302(a) of this title for the trustee's services, payable after the trustee renders such services, not to exceed five percent upon all payments under the plan.

(c) If more than one person serves as trustee in the case, the aggregate compensation of such persons for such service may not exceed the maximum compensation prescribed for a single trustee by subsection (a) or (b) of this section, as the case may be.

(d) The court may deny allowance of compensation for services or reimbursement of expenses of the trustee if the trustee failed to make diligent inquiry into facts that would permit denial of allowance under section 328(c) of this title or, with knowledge of such facts, employed a professional person under section 327 of this title.

## § 327. Employment of professional persons

(a) Except as otherwise provided in this section, the trustee, with the court's approval, may employ one or more attorneys, accountants, appraisers, auctioneers, or other professional persons, that do not hold or represent an interest adverse to the estate, and that are disinterested persons, to represent or assist the trustee in carrying out the trustee's duties under this title.

(b) If the trustee is authorized to operate the business of the debtor under section 721, 1202, or 1108 of this title, and if the debtor has regularly employed attorneys, accountants, or other professional persons on salary, the trustee may retain or replace such professional persons if necessary in the operation of such business.

(c) In a case under chapter 7, 12, or 11 of this title, a person is not disqualified for employment under this section solely because of such person's employment by or representation of a creditor, unless there is objection by another creditor or the United States trustee, in which case the court shall disapprove such employment if there is an actual conflict of interest.

(d) The court may authorize the trustee to act as attorney or accountant for the estate if such authorization is in the best interest of the estate.

(e) The trustee, with the court's approval, may employ, for a specified special purpose, other than to represent the trustee in conducting the case, an attorney that has represented the debtor, if in the best interest of the estate, and if such attorney does not represent or hold any interest adverse to the debtor or to the estate with respect to the matter on which such attorney is to be employed.

(f) The trustee may not employ a person that has served as an examiner in the case.

## § 328. Limitation on compensation of professional persons

(a) The trustee, or a committee appointed under section 1102 of this title, with the court's approval, may employ or authorize the employment of a professional person under section 327 or 1103 of this title, as the case may be, on any reasonable terms and conditions of employment, including on a retainer, on an hourly basis, *on a fixed or percentage fee basis,* or on a contingent fee basis. Notwithstanding such terms and conditions, the court may allow compensation different from the compensation provided under such terms and conditions after the conclusion of such employment, if such terms and conditions prove to have been improvident in light of developments not capable of being anticipated at the time of the fixing of such terms and conditions.

(b) If the court has authorized a trustee to serve as an attorney or accountant for the estate under section 327(d) of this title, the court may allow compensation for the trustee's services as such attorney or accountant only to the extent that the trustee performed services as attorney or accountant for the estate and not for performance of any of the trustee's duties that are generally performed by a trustee without the assistance of an attorney or accountant for the estate.

(c) Except as provided in section 327(c), 327(e), or 1107(b) of this title, the court may deny allowance of compensation for services and reimbursement of expenses of a professional person employed under section 327 or 1103 of this title if, at any time during such professional person's employment under section 327 or 1103 of this title, such professional person is not a disinterested person, or represents or holds an interest adverse to the interest of the estate with respect to the matter on which such professional person is employed.

**Section 328**

(April 20, 2005, P. L. 109-8, Title XII, § 1206, 119 Stat. 23)

## HISTORY: ANCILLARY LAWS AND DIRECTIVES

**Amendments:**

**2005.** Act April 20, 2005(effective 180 days after enactment of April 20, 2005, as provided by § 1501(a) of P. L. 109-8), amends 11 USC § 328(a) to include compensation "on a fixed or percentage fee basis" in addition to the other specified forms of reimbursement.

**Other provisions:**

**Effective date and application of amendments made by Act April 20, 2005.** Act April 20, 2005, P.L. 109-8, Title XV, § 1501(a), 119 Stat. 23, provided that the amendments made to this section would be effective 180 days after enactment on April 20, 2005.

**Abridged Legislative History**

Section 328(a) of the Bankruptcy Code provides that a trustee or a creditors' and equity security holders' committee may, with court approval, obtain the services of a professional person on any reasonable terms and conditions of employment, including on a retainer, on an hourly basis, or on a contingent fee basis. Section 1206 of the Act amends section 328(a) to include compensation "on a fixed or percentage fee basis" in addition to the other specified forms of reimbursement. (H. Report No. 109-31 to accompany S. 256, 109th Cong., 1st Sess. (2005) p. 142; available at 2005 U.S.C.C.A.N. 88, at 201)

# § 329. Debtor's transactions with attorneys

(a) Any attorney representing a debtor in a case under this title, or in connection with such a case, whether or not such attorney applies for compensation under this title, shall file with the court a statement of the compensation paid or agreed to be paid, if such payment or agreement was made after one year before the date of the filing of the petition, for services rendered or to be rendered in contemplation of or in connection with the case by such attorney, and the source of such compensation.

(b) If such compensation exceeds the reasonable value of any such services, the court may cancel any such agreement, or order the return of any such payment, to the extent excessive, to—

(1) the estate if the property transferred—

(A) would have been property of the estate; or

(B) was to be paid by or on behalf of the debtor under a plan under chapter 11, 12, or 13 of this title; or

(2) the entity that made such payment.

# § 330. Compensation of officers

(a) (1) After notice to the parties in interest and the United States

Trustee and a hearing, and subject to sections 326, 328, and 329, the court may award to a trustee, *a consumer privacy ombudsman appointed under section 332,* an examiner, *an ombudsman appointed under section 333,* or a professional person employed under section 327 or 1103—

(A) reasonable compensation for actual, necessary services rendered by the trustee, examiner, *ombudsman,* professional person, or attorney and by any paraprofessional person employed by any such person; and

(B) reimbursement for actual, necessary expenses.

(2) The court may, on its own motion or on the motion of the United States Trustee, the United States Trustee for the District or Region, the trustee for the estate, or any other party in interest, award compensation that is less than the amount of compensation that is requested.

(3) ~~(A)~~ In determining the amount of reasonable compensation to be awarded *to an examiner, trustee under chapter 11, or professional person,* the court shall consider the nature, the extent, and the value of such services, taking into account all relevant factors, including—

(A) the time spent on such services;

(B) the rates charged for such services;

(C) whether the services were necessary to the administration of, or beneficial at the time at which the service was rendered toward the completion of, a case under this title;

(D) whether the services were performed within a reasonable amount of time commensurate with the complexity, importance, and nature of the problem, issue, or task addressed; ~~and~~

*(E) with respect to a professional person, whether the person is board certified or otherwise has demonstrated skill and experience in the bankruptcy field; and*

(~~E~~ *F*) whether the compensation is reasonable based on the customary compensation charged by comparably skilled practitioners in cases other than cases under this title.

(4) (A) Except as provided in subparagraph (B), the court shall not allow compensation for—

(i) unnecessary duplication of services; or

(ii) services that were not—

(I) reasonably likely to benefit the debtor's estate; or

(II) necessary to the administration of the case.

(B) In a chapter 12 or chapter 13 case in which the debtor is an individual, the court may allow reasonable compensation to the debtor's attorney for representing the interests of the debtor in connection with the bankruptcy case based on a consideration of the benefit and necessity of such services to the debtor and the other factors set forth in this section.

(5) The court shall reduce the amount of compensation awarded

under this section by the amount of any interim compensation awarded under section 331, and, if the amount of such interim compensation exceeds the amount of compensation awarded under this section, may order the return of the excess to the estate.

(6) Any compensation awarded for the preparation of a fee application shall be based on the level and skill reasonably required to prepare the application.

*(7) In determining the amount of reasonable compensation to be awarded to a trustee, the court shall treat such compensation as a commission, based on section 326.*

(b) (1) There shall be paid from the filing fee in a case under chapter 7 of this title $45 to the trustee serving in such case, after such trustee's services are rendered.

(2) The Judicial Conference of the United States—

(A) shall prescribe additional fees of the same kind as prescribed under section 1914(b) of title 28; and

(B) may prescribe notice of appearance fees and fees charged against distributions in cases under this title;to pay $15 to trustees serving in cases after such trustees' services are rendered. Beginning 1 year after the date of the enactment of the Bankruptcy Reform Act of 1994, such $15 shall be paid in addition to the amount paid under paragraph (1).

(c) Unless the court orders otherwise, in a case under chapter 12 or 13 of this title the compensation paid to the trustee serving in the case shall not be less than $5 per month from any distribution under the plan during the administration of the plan.

(d) In a case in which the United States trustee serves as trustee, the compensation of the trustee under this section shall be paid to the clerk of the bankruptcy court and deposited by the clerk into the United States Trustee System Fund established by section 589a of title 28.

**Section 330**

(April 20, 2005, P. L. 109-8, Title IIC, § 232(b); Title IVA, §§ 407, 415; Title XI, § 1104 (b), 119 Stat. 23)

## HISTORY: ANCILLARY LAWS AND DIRECTIVES

**Amendments:**

**2005.** Act April 20, 2005(effective 180 days after enactment of April 20, 2005, as provided by § 1501(a) of P. L. 109-8), amends 11 USC § 330(a) to provide for reasonable compensation to a § 332 consumer privacy ombudsman; to clarify that the section's compensation standards apply to a trustee, examiner or other professional persons; to require that trustee compensation be based on a § 326 commission; and to permit the court to consider a professional's certification of other skill or experience in making a compensation award.

**Other provisions:**

**Effective date and application of amendments made by Act April 20, 2005.** Act April 20, 2005, P.L. 109-8, Title XV, § 1501(a), 119 Stat. 23, provided that the amendments made to this section would be effective 180 days after enactment on April 20, 2005.

**Abridged Legislative History**

Section 232(b) amends Bankruptcy Code section 330(a)(1) to permit an ombudsman [see §§ 332–333] to be compensated.

Section 407 amends section 330(a)(3) of the Bankruptcy Code to clarify that this provision applies to examiners, chapter 11 trustees, and professional persons. This section also amends section 330(a) to add a provision that requires a court, in determining the amount of reasonable compensation to award to a trustee, to treat such compensation as a commission pursuant to section 326 of the Bankruptcy Code.

Section 415 amends section 330(a)(3) of the Bankruptcy Code to permit the court to consider, in awarding compensation to a professional person, whether such person is board certified or otherwise has demonstrated skill and experience in the practice of bankruptcy law.

(H. Report No. 109-31 to accompany S. 256, 109th Cong., 1st Sess. (2005) pp. 68, 87, 89, 139–140; available at 2005 U.S.C.C.A.N. 88, at 136–37, 153, 155, 199.)

## § 331. Interim compensation

A trustee, an examiner, a debtor's attorney, or any professional person employed under section 327 or 1103 of this title may apply to the court not more than once every 120 days after an order for relief in a case under this title, or more often if the court permits, for such compensation for services rendered before the date of such an application or reimbursement for expenses incurred before such date as is provided under section 330 of this title. After notice and a hearing, the court may allow and disburse to such applicant such compensation or reimbursement.

## *§ 332. Consumer privacy ombudsman*

*(a) If a hearing is required under section 363(b)(1)(B), the court shall order the United States trustee to appoint, not later than 5 days before the commencement of the hearing, 1 disinterested person (other than the United States trustee) to serve as the consumer privacy ombudsman in the case and shall require that notice of such hearing be timely given to such ombudsman.*

*(b) The consumer privacy ombudsman may appear and be heard at such hearing and shall provide to the court information to assist the court in its consideration of the facts, circumstances, and conditions of the proposed sale or lease of personally identifiable information under section 363(b)(1)(B). Such information may include presentation of—*

*(1) the debtor's privacy policy;*

*(2) the potential losses or gains of privacy to consumers if such sale or such lease is approved by the court;*

*(3) the potential costs or benefits to consumers if such sale or such lease is approved by the court; and*

*(4) the potential alternatives that would mitigate potential privacy losses or potential costs to consumers.*

*(c) A consumer privacy ombudsman shall not disclose any personally identifiable information obtained by the ombudsman under this title.*

**Section 332**

(April 20, 2005, P. L. 109-8, Title IIC, § 232(a), 119 Stat. 23)

## HISTORY: ANCILLARY LAWS AND DIRECTIVES

**Amendments:**

**2005.** Act April 20, 2005(effective 180 days after enactment of April 20, 2005, as provided by § 1501(a) of P. L. 109-8), adds 11 USC § 332 to provide for appointment of a consumer privacy ombudsman when a hearing is required under § 363(b)(1)(B).

**Other provisions:**

**Effective date and application of amendments made by Act April 20, 2005.** Act April 20, 2005, P.L. 109-8, Title XV, § 1501(a), 119 Stat. 23, provided that the amendments made to this section would be effective 180 days after enactment on April 20, 2005.

**Abridged Legislative History**

Section 232 implements the [provision of section 231 of the] Act with respect to the appointment and responsibilities of a consumer privacy ombudsman.(H. Report No. 109-31 to accompany S. 256, 109th Cong., 1st Sess. (2005) p. 68; available at 2005 U.S.C.C.A.N. 88, at 136–37.)

## *§ 333. Appointment of patient care ombudsman*

*(a) (1) If the debtor in a case under chapter 7, 9, or 11 is a health care business, the court shall order, not later than 30 days after the commencement of the case, the appointment of an ombudsman to monitor the quality of patient care and to represent the interests of the patients of the health care business unless the court finds that the appointment of such ombudsman is not necessary for the protection of patients under the specific facts of the case.*

*(2) (A) If the court orders the appointment of an ombudsman under paragraph (1), the United States trustee shall appoint 1 disinterested person (other than the United States trustee) to serve as such ombudsman.*

*(B) If the debtor is a health care business that provides long-term care, then the United States trustee may appoint the State Long-Term Care Ombudsman appointed under the Older Americans Act of 1965 for the State in which the case is pending to serve as the ombudsman required by paragraph (1).*

*(C) If the United States trustee does not appoint a State Long-Term Care Ombudsman under subparagraph (B), the court shall notify the State Long-Term Care Ombudsman appointed under the Older Americans Act of 1965 for the State in which the case is pending, of the name and address of the person who is appointed under subparagraph (A).*

*(b) An ombudsman appointed under subsection (a) shall—*

*(1) monitor the quality of patient care provided to patients of the debtor, to the extent necessary under the circumstances, including interviewing patients and physicians;*

*(2) not later than 60 days after the date of appointment, and not less frequently than at 60-day intervals thereafter, report to the court after notice to the parties in interest, at a hearing or in writing, regarding the quality of patient care provided to patients of the debtor; and*

*(3) if such ombudsman determines that the quality of patient care*

*provided to patients of the debtor is declining significantly or is otherwise being materially compromised, file with the court a motion or a written report, with notice to the parties in interest immediately upon making such determination.*

*(c) (1) An ombudsman appointed under subsection (a) shall maintain any information obtained by such ombudsman under this section that relates to patients (including information relating to patient records) as confidential information. Such ombudsman may not review confidential patient records unless the court approves such review in advance and imposes restrictions on such ombudsman to protect the confidentiality of such records.*

*(2) An ombudsman appointed under subsection (a)(2)(B) shall have access to patient records consistent with authority of such ombudsman under the Older Americans Act of 1965 and under non-Federal laws governing the State Long-Term Care Ombudsman program.*

**Section 333**

(April 20, 2005, P. L. 109-8, Title XI, § 1104(a)(1), 119 Stat. 23)

## HISTORY: ANCILLARY LAWS AND DIRECTIVES

**Amendments:**

**2005.** Act April 20, 2005(effective 180 days after enactment of April 20, 2005, as provided by § 1501(a) of P. L. 109-8), adds 11 USC § 333 to provide for appointment of a patient care ombudsman when the debtor is a health care business.

**Other provisions:**

**Effective date and application of amendments made by Act April 20, 2005.** Act April 20, 2005, P.L. 109-8, Title XV, § 1501(a), 119 Stat. 23, provided that the amendments made to this section would be effective 180 days after enactment on April 20, 2005.

**Abridged Legislative History**

Section 1104 of the Act adds a provision to the Bankruptcy Code requiring the court to order the appointment of an ombudsman to monitor the quality of patient care within 30 days after commencement of a chapter 7, 9, or 11 health care business bankruptcy case, unless the court finds that such appointment is not necessary for the protection of patients under the specific facts of the case. (H. Report No. 109-31 to accompany S. 256, 109th Cong., 1st Sess. (2005) pp. 139–140; available at 2005 U.S.C.C.A.N. 88, at 198–99.)

# § 341. Meetings of creditors and equity security holders

(a) Within a reasonable time after the order for relief in a case under this title, the United States trustee shall convene and preside at a meeting of creditors.

(b) The United States trustee may convene a meeting of any equity security holders.

(c) The court may not preside at, and may not attend, any meeting under this section including any final meeting of creditors. *Notwithstanding any local court rule, provision of a State constitution, any otherwise applicable nonbankruptcy law, or any other requirement that representation at the meeting of creditors under subsection (a) be by an attorney, a creditor holding a consumer debt or any representative of the creditor (which may include an entity or an employee of an entity and may be a representative for more than 1 creditor) shall be permitted to appear at and participate in the meeting of creditors in a case under chapter 7 or 13, either alone or in conjunction with an attorney for the creditor. Nothing in this subsection shall be construed to require any creditor to be represented by an attorney at any meeting of creditors.*

(d) Prior to the conclusion of the meeting of creditors or equity security holders, the trustee shall orally examine the debtor to ensure that the debtor in a case under chapter 7 of this title is aware of—

(1) the potential consequences of seeking a discharge in bankruptcy, including the effects on credit history;

(2) the debtor's ability to file a petition under a different chapter of this title;

(3) the effect of receiving a discharge of debts under this title; and

(4) the effect of reaffirming a debt, including the debtor's knowledge of the provisions of section 524(d) of this title.

*(e) Notwithstanding subsections (a) and (b), the court, on the request of a party in interest and after notice and a hearing, for cause may order that the United States trustee not convene a meeting of creditors or equity security holders if the debtor has filed a plan as to which the debtor solicited acceptances prior to the commencement of the case.*

**Section 341**

(April 20, 2005, P. L. 109-8, Title IVA, §§ 402, 413, 119 Stat. 23)

## HISTORY: ANCILLARY LAWS AND DIRECTIVES

**Amendments:**

**2005.** Act April 20, 2005(effective 180 days after enactment of April 20, 2005, as provided by § 1501(a) of P. L. 109-8), amends 11 USC § 341(c) to permit a creditor holding a consumer debt or any representative of such creditor to appear at and participate in a section 341 meeting of creditors and adds new § 341(e) to permit a court to order the United States trustee not to convene a meeting of creditors or equity security holders if a debtor has filed a plan for which the debtor solicited acceptances prior to the commencement of the case.

**Other provisions:**

**Effective date and application of amendments made by Act April 20, 2005.** Act April 20, 2005, P.L. 109-8, Title XV, § 1501(a), 119 Stat. 23, provided that the amendments made to this section would be effective 180 days after enactment on April 20, 2005.

**Abridged Legislative History**

Section 413 amends section 341(c) of the Bankruptcy Code to permit a creditor holding a consumer debt or any representative of such creditor, notwithstanding any local court rule, provision of a state constitution, or any otherwise applicable nonbankruptcy law, or any other requirement that such creditor must be represented by counsel, to appear at and participate in a section 341 meeting of creditors in chapter 7 and chapter 13 cases either alone or in conjunction with an attorney. (H. Report No. 109-31 to accompany S. 256, 109th Cong., 1st Sess. (2005) pp. 86, 88; available at 2005 U.S.C.C.A.N. 88, at 152, 154.)

## § 342. Notice

(a) There shall be given such notice as is appropriate, including notice to any holder of a community claim, of an order for relief in a case under this title.

(b) ~~Prior to the commencement of a case under this title by an individual whose debts are primarily consumer debts, the clerk shall give written notice to such individual that indicates each chapter of this title under which such individual may proceed.~~*Before the commencement of a case under this title by an individual whose debts are primarily consumer debts, the clerk shall give to such individual written notice containing—*

*(1) a brief description of—*

*(A) chapters 7, 11, 12, and 13 and the general purpose, benefits, and costs of proceeding under each of those chapters; and*

*(B) the types of services available from credit counseling agencies; and*

*(2) statements specifying that—*

*(A) a person who knowingly and fraudulently conceals assets or makes a false oath or statement under penalty of perjury in connection with a case under this title shall be subject to fine, imprisonment, or both; and*

*(B) all information supplied by a debtor in connection with a case under this title is subject to examination by the Attorney General.*

(c) *(1)* If notice is required to be given by the debtor to a creditor under this title, any rule, any applicable law, or any order of the court, such notice shall contain the name, address, and *last four digits of the* taxpayer identification number of the debtor~~, but the failure of such notice to contain such information shall not invalidate the legal effect of such notice~~. *If the notice concerns an amendment that adds a creditor to the schedules of assets and liabilities, the debtor shall include the full taxpayer identification number in the notice sent to that creditor, but the debtor shall include only the last 4 digits of the taxpayer identification number in the copy of the notice filed with the court.*

*(2) (A) If, within the 90 days before the commencement of a voluntary case, a creditor supplies the debtor in at least 2 communications sent to the debtor with the current account number of the debtor and the address at which such creditor requests to receive correspondence, then any notice required by this title to be sent by the debtor to such creditor shall be sent to such address and shall include such account number.*

*(B) If a creditor would be in violation of applicable nonbankruptcy law by sending any such communication within such 90-day period and if such creditor supplies the debtor in the last 2 communications with the current account number of the debtor and the address at which such creditor requests to receive correspondence, then any notice required by this title to be sent by the debtor to such creditor shall be sent to such address and shall include such account number.*

*(d) In a case under chapter 7 of this title in which the debtor is an individual and in which the presumption of abuse arises under section 707(b), the clerk shall give written notice to all creditors not later than 10 days after the date of the filing of the petition that the presumption of abuse has arisen.*

*(e) (1) In a case under chapter 7 or 13 of this title of a debtor who is an individual, a creditor at any time may both file with the court and serve on the debtor a notice of address to be used to provide notice in such case to such creditor.*

*(2) Any notice in such case required to be provided to such creditor by the debtor or the court later than 5 days after the court and the debtor receive such creditor's notice of address, shall be provided to such address.*

*(f) (1) An entity may file with any bankruptcy court a notice of address to be used by all the bankruptcy courts or by particular bankruptcy courts, as so specified by such entity at the time such notice is filed, to provide notice to such entity in all cases under chapters 7 and 13 pending in the courts with respect to which such notice is filed, in which such entity is a creditor.*

*(2) In any case filed under chapter 7 or 13, any notice required to be provided by a court with respect to which a notice is filed under paragraph (1), to such entity later than 30 days after the filing of such notice under paragraph (1) shall be provided to such address unless with respect to a particular case a different address is specified in a notice filed and served in accordance with subsection (e).*

*(3) A notice filed under paragraph (1) may be withdrawn by such entity.*

*(g) (1) Notice provided to a creditor by the debtor or the court other than in accordance with this section (excluding this subsection) shall not be effective notice until such notice is brought to the attention of such creditor. If such creditor designates a person or an organizational subdivision of such creditor to be responsible for receiving notices under this title and establishes reasonable procedures so that such notices receivable by such creditor are to be delivered to such person or such subdivision, then a notice provided to such creditor other than in accordance with this section (excluding this subsection) shall not be considered to have been brought to the attention of such creditor until such notice is received by such person or such subdivision.*

*(2) A monetary penalty may not be imposed on a creditor for a violation of a stay in effect under section 362(a) (including a monetary penalty imposed under section 362(k)) or for failure to comply with section 542 or 543 unless the conduct that is the basis of such violation or of such failure occurs after such creditor receives notice effective under this section of the order for relief.*

**Section 342**

(April 20, 2005, P. L. 109-8, Title I, §§ 102(d), 104; Title IIC, § 234(b); Title III, § 315(a), 119 Stat. 23)

## HISTORY: ANCILLARY LAWS AND DIRECTIVES

**Amendments:**

**2005.** Act April 20, 2005(effective 180 days after enactment of April 20, 2005, as provided by § 1501(a) of P. L. 109-8), amends 11 USC § 342(c) in several noticing requirements: the clerk's duty to notice abuse under § 707(b), the clerk's duty to supply notices to consumer debtors, the restriction to the last four digits of the debtor's social security number, a creditor's ability to specify an address for notices, and the debtor's duty to use the creditor's designated address for notices.

**Other provisions:**

**Effective date and application of amendments made by Act April 20, 2005.** Act April 20, 2005, P.L. 109-8, Title XV, § 1501(a), 119 Stat. 23, provided that the amendments made to this section would be effective 180 days after enactment on April 20, 2005.

**Abridged Legislative History**

In a chapter 7 case where the presumption of abuse applies under [Bankruptcy Code] section 707(b), section 102(d) of the Act amends Bankruptcy Code section 342 to require the clerk to provide written notice to all creditors within ten days after commencement of the case stating that the presumption of abuse applies in such case.

Section 104 of the Act amends section 342(b) of the Bankruptcy Code to require the clerk, before the commencement of a bankruptcy case by an individual whose debts are primarily consumer debts, to supply such individual with a written notice containing: (1) a brief description of chapters 7, 11, 12, and 13 and the general purpose, benefits, and costs of proceeding under each of these chapters; (2) the types of services available from credit counseling agencies; (3) a statement advising that a person who knowingly and fraudulently conceals assets or makes a false oath or statement under penalty of perjury in connection with a bankruptcy case shall be subject to fine, imprisonment, or both; and (4) a statement warning that all information supplied by a debtor in connection with the case is subject to examination by the Attorney General.

In addition, section 315(a) specifies that an entity may file a notice with the court stating an address to be used generally by all bankruptcy courts for chapter 7 and 13 cases, or by particular bankruptcy courts, as specified by such entity. This address must be used by the court to supply notice in such cases within 30 days following the filing of such notice where the entity is a creditor. Notice given other than as provided in section 342 is not effective until it has been brought to the creditor's attention. (H. Report No. 109-31 to accompany S. 256, 109th Cong., 1st Sess. (2005) pp. 52, 53–54, 69, 77–78; available at 2005 U.S.C.C.A.N. 88, at 123–24, 137, 144–45.)

# § 343. Examination of the debtor

The debtor shall appear and submit to examination under oath at the meeting of creditors under section 341(a) of this title. Creditors, any indenture trustee, any trustee or examiner in the case, or the United States trustee may examine the debtor. The United States trustee may administer the oath required under this section.

# § 344. Self-incrimination; immunity

Immunity for persons required to submit to examination, to testify, or to provide information in a case under this title may be granted under part V of title 18.

# § 345. Money of estates

(a) A trustee in a case under this title may make such deposit or investment of the money of the estate for which such trustee serves as will yield the maximum reasonable net return on such money, taking into account the safety of such deposit or investment.

(b) Except with respect to a deposit or investment that is insured or guaranteed by the United States or by a department, agency, or instrumentality of the United States or backed by the full faith and credit of the United States, the trustee shall require from an entity with which such money is deposited or invested—

(1) a bond—

(A) in favor of the United States;

(B) secured by the undertaking of a corporate surety approved by the United States trustee for the district in which the case is pending; and

(C) conditioned on—

(i) a proper accounting for all money so deposited or invested and for any return on such money;

(ii) prompt repayment of such money and return; and

(iii) faithful performance of duties as a depository; or

(2) the deposit of securities of the kind specified in section 9303 of title 31;

unless the court for cause orders otherwise.

(c) An entity with which such moneys are deposited or invested is authorized to deposit or invest such moneys as may be required under this section.

## ~~§ 346. Special tax provisions~~

~~(a) Except to the extent otherwise provided in this section, subsections (b), (c), (d), (e), (g), (h), (i), and (j) of this section apply notwithstanding any State or local law imposing a tax, but subject to the Internal Revenue Code of 1986.~~

~~(b) (1) In a case under chapter 7, 12, or 11 of this title concerning an individual, any income of the estate may be taxed under a State or local law imposing a tax on or measured by income only to the estate, and may not be taxed to such individual. Except as provided in section 728 of this title, if such individual is a partner in a partnership, any gain or loss resulting from a distribution of property from such partnership, or any distributive share of income, gain, loss, deduction, or credit of such individual that is distributed, or considered distributed, from such partnership, after the commencement of the case is gain, loss, income, deduction, or credit, as the case may be, of the estate.~~

~~(2) Except as otherwise provided in this section and in section 728 of this title, any income of the estate in such a case, and any State or local tax on or measured by such income, shall be computed in the same manner as the income and the tax of an estate.~~

~~(3) The estate in such a case shall use the same accounting method as the debtor used immediately before the commencement of the case.~~

(c) (1) The commencement of a case under this title concerning a corporation or a partnership does not effect a change in the status of such corporation or partnership for the purposes of any State or local law imposing a tax on or measured by income. Except as otherwise provided in this section and in section 728 of this title, any income of the estate in such case may be taxed only as though such case had not been commenced.

(2) In such a case, except as provided in section 728 of this title, the trustee shall make any tax return otherwise required by State or local law to be filed by or on behalf of such corporation or partnership in the same manner and form as such corporation or partnership, as the case may be, is required to make such return.

(d) In a case under chapter 13 of this title, any income of the estate or the debtor may be taxed under a State or local law imposing a tax on or measured by income only to the debtor, and may not be taxed to the estate.

(e) A claim allowed under section 502(f) or 503 of this title, other than a claim for a tax that is not otherwise deductible or a capital expenditure that is not otherwise deductible, is deductible by the entity to which income of the estate is taxed unless such claim was deducted by another entity, and a deduction for such a claim is deemed to be a deduction attributable to a business.

(f) The trustee shall withhold from any payment of claims for wages, salaries, commissions, dividends, interest, or other payments, or collect, any amount required to be withheld or collected under applicable State or local tax law, and shall pay such withheld or collected amount to the appropriate governmental unit at the time and in the manner required by such tax law, and with the same priority as the claim from which such amount was withheld was paid.

(g) (1) Neither gain nor loss shall be recognized on a transfer—

(A) by operation of law, of property to the estate;

(B) other than a sale, of property from the estate to the debtor; or

(C) in a case under chapter 11 or 12 of this title concerning a corporation, of property from the estate to a corporation that is an affiliate participating in a joint plan with the debtor, or that is a successor to the debtor under the plan, except that gain or loss may be recognized to the same extent that such transfer results in the recognition of gain or loss under section 371 of the Internal Revenue Code of 1986.

(2) The transferee of a transfer of a kind specified in this subsection shall take the property transferred with the same character, and with the transferor's basis, as adjusted under subsection (j)(5) of this section, and holding period.

(h) Notwithstanding sections 728(a) and 1146(a) of this title, for the purpose of determining the number of taxable periods during which the debtor or the estate may use a loss carryover or a loss carryback, the taxable period of the debtor during which the case is commenced is deemed not to have been terminated by such commencement.

(i) (1) In a case under chapter 7, 12, or 11 of this title concerning an individual, the estate shall succeed to the debtor's tax attributes, including—

(A) any investment credit carryover;

(B) any recovery exclusion;

(C) any loss carryover;

(D) any foreign tax credit carryover;

(E) any capital loss carryover; and

(F) any claim of right.

(2) After such a case is closed or dismissed, the debtor shall succeed to any tax attribute to which the estate succeeded under paragraph (1) of this subsection but that was not utilized by the estate. The debtor may utilize such tax attributes as though any applicable time limitations on such utilization by the debtor were suspended during the time during which the case was pending.

(3) In such a case, the estate may carry back any loss of the estate to a taxable period of the debtor that ended before the order for relief under such chapter the same as the debtor could have carried back such loss had the debtor incurred such loss and the case under this title had not been commenced, but the debtor may not carry back any loss of the debtor from a taxable period that ends after such order to any taxable period of the debtor that ended before such order until after the case is closed.

(j) (1) Except as otherwise provided in this subsection, income is not realized by the estate, the debtor, or a successor to the debtor by reason of forgiveness or discharge of indebtedness in a case under this title.

(2) For the purposes of any State or local law imposing a tax on or measured by income, a deduction with respect to a liability may not be allowed for any taxable period during or after which such liability is forgiven or discharged under this title. In this paragraph, "a deduction with respect to a liability" includes a capital loss incurred on the disposition of a capital asset with respect to a liability that was incurred in connection with the acquisition of such asset.

(3) Except as provided in paragraph (4) of this subsection, for the purpose of any State or local law imposing a tax on or measured by income, any net operating loss of an individual or corporate debtor, including a net operating loss carryover to such debtor, shall be reduced by the amount of indebtedness forgiven or discharged in a case under this title, except to the extent that such forgiveness or discharge resulted in a disallowance under paragraph (2) of this subsection.

(4) A reduction of a net operating loss or a net operating loss carryover under paragraph (3) of this subsection or of basis under paragraph (5) of this subsection is not required to the extent that the indebtedness of an individual or corporate debtor forgiven or discharged—

(A) consisted of items of a deductible nature that were not deducted by such debtor; or

(B) resulted in an expired net operating loss carryover or other deduction that—

(i) did not offset income for any taxable period; and

(ii) did not contribute to a net operating loss in or a net operating loss carryover to the taxable period during or after which such indebtedness was discharged.

(5) For the purposes of a State or local law imposing a tax on or measured by income, the basis of the debtor's property or of property transferred to an entity required to use the debtor's basis in whole or in part shall be reduced by the lesser of—

(A) (i) the amount by which the indebtedness of the debtor has been forgiven or discharged in a case under this title; minus

(ii) the total amount of adjustments made under paragraphs (2) and (3) of this subsection; and

(B) the amount by which the total basis of the debtor's assets that were property of the estate before such forgiveness or discharge exceeds the debtor's total liabilities that were liabilities both before and after such forgiveness or discharge.

(6) Notwithstanding paragraph (5) of this subsection, basis is not required to be reduced to the extent that the debtor elects to treat as taxable income, of the taxable period in which indebtedness is forgiven or discharged, the amount of indebtedness forgiven or discharged that otherwise would be applied in reduction of basis under paragraph (5) of this subsection.

(7) For the purposes of this subsection, indebtedness with respect to which an equity security, other than an interest of a limited partner in a limited partnership, is issued to the creditor to whom such indebtedness was owed, or that is forgiven as a contribution to capital by an equity security holder other than a limited partner in the debtor, is not forgiven or discharged in a case under this title—

(A) to any extent that such indebtedness did not consist of items of a deductible nature; or

(B) if the issuance of such equity security has the same consequences under a law imposing a tax on or measured by income to such creditor as a payment in cash to such creditor in an amount equal to the fair market value of such equity security, then to the lesser of—

(i) the extent that such issuance has the same such consequences; and

(ii) the extent of such fair market value.

## *§ 346. Special provisions related to the treatment of State and local taxes*

*(a) Whenever the Internal Revenue Code of 1986 provides that a separate taxable estate or entity is created in a case concerning a debtor*

*under this title, and the income, gain, loss, deductions, and credits of such estate shall be taxed to or claimed by the estate, a separate taxable estate is also created for purposes of any State and local law imposing a tax on or measured by income and such income, gain, loss, deductions, and credits shall be taxed to or claimed by the estate and may not be taxed to or claimed by the debtor. The preceding sentence shall not apply if the case is dismissed. The trustee shall make tax returns of income required under any such State or local law.*

*(b) Whenever the Internal Revenue Code of 1986 provides that no separate taxable estate shall be created in a case concerning a debtor under this title, and the income, gain, loss, deductions, and credits of an estate shall be taxed to or claimed by the debtor, such income, gain, loss, deductions, and credits shall be taxed to or claimed by the debtor under a State or local law imposing a tax on or measured by income and may not be taxed to or claimed by the estate. The trustee shall make such tax returns of income of corporations and of partnerships as are required under any State or local law, but with respect to partnerships, shall make such returns only to the extent such returns are also required to be made under such Code. The estate shall be liable for any tax imposed on such corporation or partnership, but not for any tax imposed on partners or members.*

*(c) With respect to a partnership or any entity treated as a partnership under a State or local law imposing a tax on or measured by income that is a debtor in a case under this title, any gain or loss resulting from a distribution of property from such partnership, or any distributive share of any income, gain, loss, deduction, or credit of a partner or member that is distributed, or considered distributed, from such partnership, after the commencement of the case, is gain, loss, income, deduction, or credit, as the case may be, of the partner or member, and if such partner or member is a debtor in a case under this title, shall be subject to tax in accordance with subsection (a) or (b).*

*(d) For purposes of any State or local law imposing a tax on or measured by income, the taxable period of a debtor in a case under this title shall terminate only if and to the extent that the taxable period of such debtor terminates under the Internal Revenue Code of 1986.*

*(e) The estate in any case described in subsection (a) shall use the same accounting method as the debtor used immediately before the commencement of the case, if such method of accounting complies with applicable nonbankruptcy tax law.*

*(f) For purposes of any State or local law imposing a tax on or measured by income, a transfer of property from the debtor to the estate or from the estate to the debtor shall not be treated as a disposition for purposes of any provision assigning tax consequences to a disposition, except to the extent that such transfer is treated as a disposition under the Internal Revenue Code of 1986.*

*(g) Whenever a tax is imposed pursuant to a State or local law imposing a tax on or measured by income pursuant to subsection (a) or (b),*

*such tax shall be imposed at rates generally applicable to the same types of entities under such State or local law.*

*(h) The trustee shall withhold from any payment of claims for wages, salaries, commissions, dividends, interest, or other payments, or collect, any amount required to be withheld or collected under applicable State or local tax law, and shall pay such withheld or collected amount to the appropriate governmental unit at the time and in the manner required by such tax law, and with the same priority as the claim from which such amount was withheld or collected was paid.*

*(i) (1) To the extent that any State or local law imposing a tax on or measured by income provides for the carryover of any tax attribute from one taxable period to a subsequent taxable period, the estate shall succeed to such tax attribute in any case in which such estate is subject to tax under subsection (a).*

*(2) After such a case is closed or dismissed, the debtor shall succeed to any tax attribute to which the estate succeeded under paragraph (1) to the extent consistent with the Internal Revenue Code of 1986.*

*(3) The estate may carry back any loss or tax attribute to a taxable period of the debtor that ended before the date of the order for relief under this title to the extent that—*

*(A) applicable State or local tax law provides for a carryback in the case of the debtor; and*

*(B) the same or a similar tax attribute may be carried back by the estate to such a taxable period of the debtor under the Internal Revenue Code of 1986.*

*(j) (1) For purposes of any State or local law imposing a tax on or measured by income, income is not realized by the estate, the debtor, or a successor to the debtor by reason of discharge of indebtedness in a case under this title, except to the extent, if any, that such income is subject to tax under the Internal Revenue Code of 1986.*

*(2) Whenever the Internal Revenue Code of 1986 provides that the amount excluded from gross income in respect of the discharge of indebtedness in a case under this title shall be applied to reduce the tax attributes of the debtor or the estate, a similar reduction shall be made under any State or local law imposing a tax on or measured by income to the extent such State or local law recognizes such attributes. Such State or local law may also provide for the reduction of other attributes to the extent that the full amount of income from the discharge of indebtedness has not been applied.*

*(k) (1) Except as provided in this section and section 505, the time and manner of filing tax returns and the items of income, gain, loss, deduction, and credit of any taxpayer shall be determined under applicable nonbankruptcy law.*

*(2) For Federal tax purposes, the provisions of this section are subject to the Internal Revenue Code of 1986 and other applicable Federal nonbankruptcy law.*

**Section 346**

(April 20, 2005, P. L. 109-8, Title VII, § 719(a), 119 Stat. 23)

## HISTORY: ANCILLARY LAWS AND DIRECTIVES

**Amendments:**

**2005.** Act April 20, 2005(effective 180 days after enactment of April 20, 2005, as provided by § 1501(a) of P. L. 109-8), amends 11 USC § 346 to conform state and local income tax administrative issues to the Internal Revenue Code.

**Other provisions:**

**Effective date and application of amendments made by Act April 20, 2005.** Act April 20, 2005, P.L. 109-8, Title XV, § 1501(a), 119 Stat. 23, provided that the amendments made to this section would be effective 180 days after enactment on April 20, 2005.

**Abridged Legislative History**

(H. Report No. 109-31 to accompany S. 256, 109th Cong., 1st Sess. (2005) p. 105; available at 2005 U.S.C.C.A.N. 88, at 168–69.)

# § 347. Unclaimed property

(a) Ninety days after the final distribution under section 726, 1226, or 1326 of this title in a case under chapter 7, 12, or 13 of this title, as the case may be, the trustee shall stop payment on any check remaining unpaid, and any remaining property of the estate shall be paid into the court and disposed of under chapter 129 of title 28.

(b) Any security, money, or other property remaining unclaimed at the expiration of the time allowed in a case under chapter 9, 11, or 12 of this title for the presentation of a security or the performance of any other act as a condition to participation in the distribution under any plan confirmed under section 943(b), 1129, 1173, or 1225 of this title, as the case may be, becomes the property of the debtor or of the entity acquiring the assets of the debtor under the plan, as the case may be.

# § 348. Effect of conversion

(a) Conversion of a case from a case under one chapter of this title to a case under another chapter of this title constitutes an order for relief under the chapter to which the case is converted, but, except as provided in subsections (b) and (c) of this section, does not effect a change in the date of the filing of the petition, the commencement of the case, or the order for relief.

(b) Unless the court for cause orders otherwise, in sections 701(a), 727(a)(10), 727(b), 728(a), 728(b), 1102(a), 1110(a)(1), 1121(b), 1121(c), 1141(d)(4), 1146(a), 1146(b), 1201(a), 1221, 1228(a), 1301(a), and 1305(a) of this title, "the order for relief under this chapter" in a chapter to which a case has been converted under section 706, 1112, 1208, or 1307 of this title means the conversion of such case to such chapter.

(c) Sections 342 and 365(d) of this title apply in a case that has been converted under section 706, 1112, 1208, or 1307 of this title, as if the conversion order were the order for relief.

(d) A claim against the estate or the debtor that arises after the order for relief but before conversion in a case that is converted under section 1112, 1208, or 1307 of this title, other than a claim specified in section 503(b) of this title, shall be treated for all purposes as if such claim had arisen immediately before the date of the filing of the petition.

(e) Conversion of a case under section 706, 1112, 1208, or 1307 of this title terminates the service of any trustee or examiner that is serving in the case before such conversion.

(f) (1) Except as provided in paragraph (2), when a case under chapter 13 of this title is converted to a case under another chapter under this title—

(A) property of the estate in the converted case shall consist of property of the estate, as of the date of filing of the petition, that remains in the possession of or is under the control of the debtor on the date of conversion; ~~and~~

(B) valuations of property and of allowed secured claims in the chapter 13 case shall apply ~~in the converted case, with allowed secured claims~~ *only in a case converted to a case under chapter 11 or 12, but not in a case converted to a case under chapter 7, with allowed secured claims in cases under chapters 11 and 12* reduced to the extent that they have been paid in accordance with the chapter 13 plan~~.~~*; and*

*(C) with respect to cases converted from chapter 13—*

*(i) the claim of any creditor holding security as of the date of the petition shall continue to be secured by that security unless the full amount of such claim determined under applicable non-bankruptcy law has been paid in full as of the date of conversion, notwithstanding any valuation or determination of the amount of an allowed secured claim made for the purposes of the case under chapter 13; and*

*(ii) unless a prebankruptcy default has been fully cured under the plan at the time of conversion, in any proceeding under this title or otherwise, the default shall have the effect given under applicable nonbankruptcy law.*

(2) If the debtor converts a case under chapter 13 of this title to a case under another chapter under this title in bad faith, the property *of the estate* in the converted case shall consist of the property of the estate as of the date of conversion.

**Section 348**

(April 20, 2005, P. L. 109-8, Title III, § 309(a); Title XII, § 1207, 119 Stat. 23)

## HISTORY: ANCILLARY LAWS AND DIRECTIVES

**Amendments:**

**2005.** Act April 20, 2005(effective 180 days after enactment of April 20, 2005, as provided by § 1501(a) of P. L. 109-8), amends 11 USC § 348(f)(1)(B) to provide that valuations of property and allowed secured claims in a chapter 13 case only apply if the case is subsequently converted to one under chapter 11 or 12.

**Other provisions:**

**Effective date and application of amendments made by Act April 20, 2005.** Act April 20, 2005, P.L. 109-8, Title XV, § 1501(a), 119 Stat. 23, provided that the amendments made to this section would be effective 180 days after enactment on

April 20, 2005.

**Abridged Legislative History**

Section 309(a) of the Act amends Bankruptcy Code section 348(f)(1)(B) to provide that valuations of property and allowed secured claims in a chapter 13 case only apply if the case is subsequently converted to one under chapter 11 or 12. If the chapter 13 case is converted to one under chapter 7, then the creditor holding security as of the petition date shall continue to be secured unless its claim was paid in full as of the conversion date. In addition, unless a prebankruptcy default has been fully cured at the time of conversion, then the default in any bankruptcy proceeding shall have the effect given under applicable nonbankruptcy law.

(H. Report No. 109-31 to accompany S. 256, 109th Cong., 1st Sess. (2005) pp. 73, 142; available at 2005 U.S.C.C.A.N. 88, at 140–41, 201.)

## § 349. Effect of dismissal

(a) Unless the court, for cause, orders otherwise, the dismissal of a case under this title does not bar the discharge, in a later case under this title, of debts that were dischargeable in the case dismissed; nor does the dismissal of a case under this title prejudice the debtor with regard to the filing of a subsequent petition under this title, except as provided in section 109 (g) of this title.

(b) Unless the court, for cause, orders otherwise, a dismissal of a case other than under section 742 of this title—

(1) reinstates—

(A) any proceeding or custodianship superseded under section 543 of this title;

(B) any transfer avoided under section 522, 544, 545, 547, 548, 549, or 724(a) of this title, or preserved under section 510(c)(2), 522(i)(2), or 551 of this title; and

(C) any lien voided under section 506(d) of this title;

(2) vacates any order, judgment, or transfer ordered, under section 522(i)(1), 542, 550, or 553 of this title; and

(3) revests the property of the estate in the entity in which such property was vested immediately before the commencement of the case under this title.

## § 350. Closing and reopening cases

(a) After an estate is fully administered and the court has discharged the trustee, the court shall close the case.

(b) A case may be reopened in the court in which such case was closed to administer assets, to accord relief to the debtor, or for other cause.

## *§ 351. Disposal of patient records*

*If a health care business commences a case under chapter 7, 9, or 11, and the trustee does not have a sufficient amount of funds to pay for the storage of patient records in the manner required under applicable Federal or State law, the following requirements shall apply:*

*(1) The trustee shall—*

*(A) promptly publish notice, in 1 or more appropriate newspa-*

*pers, that if patient records are not claimed by the patient or an insurance provider (if applicable law permits the insurance provider to make that claim) by the date that is 365 days after the date of that notification, the trustee will destroy the patient records; and*

*(B) during the first 180 days of the 365-day period described in subparagraph (A), promptly attempt to notify directly each patient that is the subject of the patient records and appropriate insurance carrier concerning the patient records by mailing to the most recent known address of that patient, or a family member or contact person for that patient, and to the appropriate insurance carrier an appropriate notice regarding the claiming or disposing of patient records.*

*(2) If, after providing the notification under paragraph (1), patient records are not claimed during the 365-day period described under that paragraph, the trustee shall mail, by certified mail, at the end of such 365-day period a written request to each appropriate Federal agency to request permission from that agency to deposit the patient records with that agency, except that no Federal agency is required to accept patient records under this paragraph.*

*(3) If, following the 365-day period described in paragraph (2) and after providing the notification under paragraph (1), patient records are not claimed by a patient or insurance provider, or request is not granted by a Federal agency to deposit such records with that agency, the trustee shall destroy those records by—*

*(A) if the records are written, shredding or burning the records; or*

*(B) if the records are magnetic, optical, or other electronic records, by otherwise destroying those records so that those records cannot be retrieved.*

**Section 351**

(April 20, 2005, P. L. 109-8, Title XI, § 1102(a), 119 Stat. 23)

## HISTORY: ANCILLARY LAWS AND DIRECTIVES

**Amendments:**

**2005.** Act April 20, 2005(effective 180 days after enactment of April 20, 2005, as provided by § 1501(a) of P. L. 109-8), adds 11 USC § 351, specifying requirements for the disposal of patient records in a chapter 7, 9, or 11 case of a health care business where the trustee lacks sufficient funds to pay for the storage of such records in accordance with applicable Federal or state law.

**Other provisions:**

**Effective date and application of amendments made by Act April 20, 2005.** Act April 20, 2005, P.L. 109-8, Title XV, § 1501(a), 119 Stat. 23, provided that the amendments made to this section would be effective 180 days after enactment on April 20, 2005.

**Abridged Legislative History**

(H. Report No. 109-31 to accompany S. 256, 109th Cong., 1st Sess. (2005) pp. 138–139; available at 2005 U.S.C.C.A.N. 88, at 198.)

## § 361. Adequate protection

When adequate protection is required under section 362, 363, or

364 of this title of an interest of an entity in property, such adequate protection may be provided by—

(1) requiring the trustee to make a cash payment or periodic cash payments to such entity, to the extent that the stay under section 362 of this title, use, sale, or lease under section 363 of this title, or any grant of a lien under section 364 of this title results in a decrease in the value of such entity's interest in such property;

(2) providing to such entity an additional or replacement lien to the extent that such stay, use, sale, lease, or grant results in a decrease in the value of such entity's interest in such property; or

(3) granting such other relief, other than entitling such entity to compensation allowable under section 503(b)(1) of this title as an administrative expense, as will result in the realization by such entity of the indubitable equivalent of such entity's interest in such property.

## § 362. Automatic stay

(a) Except as provided in subsection (b) of this section, a petition filed under section 301, 302, or 303 of this title, or an application filed under section 5(a)(3) of the Securities Investor Protection Act of 1970, operates as a stay, applicable to all entities, of—

(1) the commencement or continuation, including the issuance or employment of process, of a judicial, administrative, or other action or proceeding against the debtor that was or could have been commenced before the commencement of the case under this title, or to recover a claim against the debtor that arose before the commencement of the case under this title;

(2) the enforcement, against the debtor or against property of the estate, of a judgment obtained before the commencement of the case under this title;

(3) any act to obtain possession of property of the estate or of property from the estate or to exercise control over property of the estate;

(4) any act to create, perfect, or enforce any lien against property of the estate;

(5) any act to create, perfect, or enforce against property of the debtor any lien to the extent that such lien secures a claim that arose before the commencement of the case under this title;

(6) any act to collect, assess, or recover a claim against the debtor that arose before the commencement of the case under this title;

(7) the setoff of any debt owing to the debtor that arose before the commencement of the case under this title against any claim against the debtor; and

(8) the commencement or continuation of a proceeding before the United States Tax Court concerning ~~the debtor~~ *a corporate debtor's tax liability for a taxable period the bankruptcy court may determine or concerning the tax liability of a debtor who is an individual for a*

*taxable period ending before the date of the order for relief under this title.*

(b) The filing of a petition under section 301, 302, or 303 of this title, or of an application under section 5(a)(3) of the Securities Investor Protection Act of 1970, does not operate as a stay—

(1) under subsection (a) of this section, of the commencement or continuation of a criminal action or proceeding against the debtor;

(2) under subsection (a)~~ of this section—~~

~~(A) of the commencement or continuation of an action or proceeding for—~~

~~(i) the establishment of paternity; or~~

~~(ii) the establishment or modification of an order for alimony, maintenance, or support; or~~

~~(B) of the collection of alimony, maintenance, or support from property that is not property of the estate;~~

*(A) of the commencement or continuation of a civil action or proceeding—*

*(i) for the establishment of paternity;*

*(ii) for the establishment or modification of an order for domestic support obligations;*

*(iii) concerning child custody or visitation;*

*(iv) for the dissolution of a marriage, except to the extent that such proceeding seeks to determine the division of property that is property of the estate; or*

*(v) regarding domestic violence;*

*(B) of the collection of a domestic support obligation from property that is not property of the estate;*

*(C) with respect to the withholding of income that is property of the estate or property of the debtor for payment of a domestic support obligation under a judicial or administrative order or a statute;*

*(D) of the withholding, suspension, or restriction of a driver's license, a professional or occupational license, or a recreational license, under State law, as specified in section 466(a)(16) of the Social Security Act;*

*(E) of the reporting of overdue support owed by a parent to any consumer reporting agency as specified in section 466(a)(7) of the Social Security Act;*

*(F) of the interception of a tax refund, as specified in sections 464 and 466(a)(3) of the Social Security Act or under an analogous State law; or*

*(G) of the enforcement of a medical obligation, as specified under title IV of the Social Security Act;*

(3) under subsection (a) of this section, of any act to perfect, or to maintain or continue the perfection of, an interest in property to the extent that the trustee's rights and powers are subject to such

perfection under section 546(b) of this title or to the extent that such act is accomplished within the period provided under section 547(e)(2)(A) of this title;

(4) under paragraph (1), (2), (3), or (6) of subsection (a) of this section, of the commencement or continuation of an action or proceeding by a governmental unit or any organization exercising authority under the Convention on the Prohibition of the Development, Production, Stockpiling and Use of Chemical Weapons and on Their Destruction, opened for signature on January 13, 1993, to enforce such governmental unit's or organization's police and regulatory power, including the enforcement of a judgment other than a money judgment, obtained in an action or proceeding by the governmental unit to enforce such governmental unit's or organization's police or regulatory power;

[(5) Repealed. Pub.L. 105-277, Div. I, Title VI, § 603(1), Oct. 21, 1998, 112 Stat. 2681–886]

(6) under subsection (a) of this section, of the setoff by a commodity broker, forward contract merchant, stockbroker, financial institution~~s~~, *financial participant,* or securities clearing agency of any mutual debt and claim under or in connection with commodity contracts, as defined in section 761 of this title, forward contracts, or securities contracts, as defined in section 741 of this title, that constitutes the setoff of a claim against the debtor for a margin payment, as defined in section 101, 741, or 761 of this title, or settlement payment, as defined in section 101 or 741 of this title, arising out of commodity contracts, forward contracts, or securities contracts against cash, securities, or other property held by*, pledged to, under the control of,* or due from such commodity broker, forward contract merchant, stockbroker, financial institution~~s~~, *financial participant,* or securities clearing agency to margin, guarantee, secure, or settle commodity contracts, forward contracts, or securities contracts;

(7) under subsection (a) of this section, of the setoff by a repo participant *or financial participant,* of any mutual debt and claim under or in connection with repurchase agreements that constitutes the setoff of a claim against the debtor for a margin payment, as defined in section 741 or 761 of this title, or settlement payment, as defined in section 741 of this title, arising out of repurchase agreements against cash, securities, or other property held by*, pledged to, under the control of,* or due from such repo participant *or financial participant* to margin, guarantee, secure or settle repurchase agreements;

(8) under subsection (a) of this section, of the commencement of any action by the Secretary of Housing and Urban Development to foreclose a mortgage or deed of trust in any case in which the mortgage or deed of trust held by the Secretary is insured or was formerly insured under the National Housing Act and covers property, or combinations of property, consisting of five or more living units;

(9) under subsection (a), of—

(A) an audit by a governmental unit to determine tax liability;

(B) the issuance to the debtor by a governmental unit of a notice of tax deficiency;

(C) a demand for tax returns; or

(D) the making of an assessment for any tax and issuance of a notice and demand for payment of such an assessment (but any tax lien that would otherwise attach to property of the estate by reason of such an assessment shall not take effect unless such tax is a debt of the debtor that will not be discharged in the case and such property or its proceeds are transferred out of the estate to, or otherwise revested in, the debtor).

(10) under subsection (a) of this section, of any act by a lessor to the debtor under a lease of nonresidential real property that has terminated by the expiration of the stated term of the lease before the commencement of or during a case under this title to obtain possession of such property;

(11) under subsection (a) of this section, of the presentment of a negotiable instrument and the giving of notice of and protesting dishonor of such an instrument;

(12) under subsection (a) of this section, after the date which is 90 days after the filing of such petition, of the commencement or continuation, and conclusion to the entry of final judgment, of an action which involves a debtor subject to reorganization pursuant to chapter 11 of this title and which was brought by the Secretary of Transportation under section 31325 of title 46 (including distribution of any proceeds of sale) to foreclose a preferred ship or fleet mort gage, or a security interest in or relating to a vessel or vessel under construction, held by the Secretary of Transportation under section 207 or title XI of the Merchant Marine Act, 1936, or under applicable State law;

(13) under subsection (a) of this section, after the date which is 90 days after the filing of such petition, of the commencement or continuation, and conclusion to the entry of final judgment, of an action which involves a debtor subject to reorganization pursuant to chapter 11 of this title and which was brought by the Secretary of Commerce under section 31325 of title 46 (including distribution of any proceeds of sale) to foreclose a preferred ship or fleet mortgage in a vessel or a mortgage, deed of trust, or other security interest in a fishing facility held by the Secretary of Commerce under section 207 or title XI of the Merchant Marine Act, 1936;

(14) under subsection (a) of this section, of any action by an accrediting agency regarding the accreditation status of the debtor as an educational institution;

(15) under subsection (a) of this section, of any action by a State licensing body regarding the licensure of the debtor as an educational institution;

(16) under subsection (a) of this section, of any action by a

guaranty agency, as defined in section 435(j) of the Higher Education Act of 1965 or the Secretary of Education regarding the eligibility of the debtor to participate in programs authorized under such Act;

(17) ~~under subsection (a) of this section, of the setoff by a swap participant, of any mutual debt and claim under or in connection with any swap agreement that constitutes the setoff of a claim against the debtor for any payment due from the debtor under or in connection with any swap agreement against any payment due to the debtor from the swap participant under or in connection with any swap agreement or against cash, securities, or other property of the debtor held by or due from such swap participant to guarantee, secure or settle any swap agreement; or~~*under subsection (a), of the setoff by a swap participant or financial participant of a mutual debt and claim under or in connection with one or more swap agreements that constitutes the setoff of a claim against the debtor for any payment or other transfer of property due from the debtor under or in connection with any swap agreement against any payment due to the debtor from the swap participant or financial participant under or in connection with any swap agreement or against cash, securities, or other property held by, pledged to, under the control of, or due from such swap participant or financial participant to margin, guarantee, secure, or settle any swap agreement;*

~~(18) under subsection (a) of the creation or perfection of a statutory lien for an ad valorem property tax imposed by the District of Columbia, or a political subdivision of a State, if such tax comes due after the filing of the petition.~~ *under subsection (a) of the creation or perfection of a statutory lien for an ad valorem property tax, or a special tax or special assessment on real property whether or not ad valorem, imposed by a governmental unit, if such tax or assessment comes due after the date of the filing of the petition;*

*(19) under subsection (a), of withholding of income from a debtor's wages and collection of amounts withheld, under the debtor's agreement authorizing that withholding and collection for the benefit of a pension, profit-sharing, stock bonus, or other plan established under section 401, 403, 408, 408A, 414, 457, or 501(c) of the Internal Revenue Code of 1986, that is sponsored by the employer of the debtor, or an affiliate, successor, or predecessor of such employer—*

*(A) to the extent that the amounts withheld and collected are used solely for payments relating to a loan from a plan under section 408(b)(1) of the Employee Retirement Income Security Act of 1974 or is subject to section 72(p) of the Internal Revenue Code of 1986; or*

*(B) a loan from a thrift savings plan permitted under subchapter III of chapter 84 of title 5, that satisfies the requirements of section 8433(g) of such title;*

*but nothing in this paragraph may be construed to provide that any loan made under a governmental plan under section 414(d), or a contract or account under section 403(b), of the Internal Revenue Code of 1986 constitutes a claim or a debt under this title;*

*(20) under subsection (a), of any act to enforce any lien against or security interest in real property following entry of the order under subsection (d)(4) as to such real property in any prior case under this title, for a period of 2 years after the date of the entry of such an order, except that the debtor, in a subsequent case under this title, may move for relief from such order based upon changed circumstances or for other good cause shown, after notice and a hearing;*

*(21) under subsection (a), of any act to enforce any lien against or security interest in real property—*

*(A) if the debtor is ineligible under section 109(g) to be a debtor in a case under this title; or*

*(B) if the case under this title was filed in violation of a bankruptcy court order in a prior case under this title prohibiting the debtor from being a debtor in another case under this title;*

*(22) subject to subsection (l), under subsection (a)(3), of the continuation of any eviction, unlawful detainer action, or similar proceeding by a lessor against a debtor involving residential property in which the debtor resides as a tenant under a lease or rental agreement and with respect to which the lessor has obtained before the date of the filing of the bankruptcy petition, a judgment for possession of such property against the debtor;*

*(23) subject to subsection (m), under subsection (a)(3), of an eviction action that seeks possession of the residential property in which the debtor resides as a tenant under a lease or rental agreement based on endangerment of such property or the illegal use of controlled substances on such property, but only if the lessor files with the court, and serves upon the debtor, a certification under penalty of perjury that such an eviction action has been filed, or that the debtor, during the 30-day period preceding the date of the filing of the certification, has endangered property or illegally used or allowed to be used a controlled substance on the property;*

*(24) under subsection (a), of any transfer that is not avoidable under section 544 and that is not avoidable under section 549;*

*(25) under subsection (a), of—*

*(A) the commencement or continuation of an investigation or action by a securities self regulatory organization to enforce such organization's regulatory power;*

*(B) the enforcement of an order or decision, other than for monetary sanctions, obtained in an action by such securities self regulatory organization to enforce such organization's regulatory power; or*

*(C) any act taken by such securities self regulatory organization to delist, delete, or refuse to permit quotation of any stock that does not meet applicable regulatory requirements;*

*(26) under subsection (a), of the setoff under applicable nonbank-*

*ruptcy law of an income tax refund, by a governmental unit, with respect to a taxable period that ended before the date of the order for relief against an income tax liability for a taxable period that also ended before the date of the order for relief, except that in any case in which the setoff of an income tax refund is not permitted under applicable nonbankruptcy law because of a pending action to determine the amount or legality of a tax liability, the governmental unit may hold the refund pending the resolution of the action, unless the court, on the motion of the trustee and after notice and a hearing, grants the taxing authority adequate protection (within the meaning of section 361) for the secured claim of such authority in the setoff under section 506(a);*

*(27) under subsection (a), of the setoff by a master netting agreement participant of a mutual debt and claim under or in connection with one or more master netting agreements or any contract or agreement subject to such agreements that constitutes the setoff of a claim against the debtor for any payment or other transfer of property due from the debtor under or in connection with such agreements or any contract or agreement subject to such agreements against any payment due to the debtor from such master netting agreement participant under or in connection with such agreements or any contract or agreement subject to such agreements or against cash, securities, or other property held by, pledged to, under the control of, or due from such master netting agreement participant to margin, guarantee, secure, or settle such agreements or any contract or agreement subject to such agreements, to the extent that such participant is eligible to exercise such offset rights under paragraph (6), (7), or (17) for each individual contract covered by the master netting agreement in issue; and*

*(28) under subsection (a), of the exclusion by the Secretary of Health and Human Services of the debtor from participation in the medicare program or any other Federal health care program (as defined in section 1128B(f) of the Social Security Act pursuant to title XI or XVIII of such Act).*

The provisions of paragraphs (12) and (13) of this subsection shall apply with respect to any such petition filed on or before December 31, 1989.

(c) Except as provided in subsections (d), (e), ~~and~~ (f), *and (h)* of this section—

(1) the stay of an act against property of the estate under subsection (a) of this section continues until such property is no longer property of the estate;~~and~~

(2) the stay of any other act under subsection (a) of this section continues until the earliest of—

(A) the time the case is closed;

(B) the time the case is dismissed; or

(C) if the case is a case under chapter 7 of this title concerning an individual or a case under chapter 9, 11, 12, or 13 of this title, the time a discharge is granted or denied~~.~~

*(3) if a single or joint case is filed by or against debtor who is an individual in a case under chapter 7, 11, or 13, and if a single or joint case of the debtor was pending within the preceding 1-year period but was dismissed, other than a case refiled under a chapter other than chapter 7 after dismissal under section 707(b)—*

*(A) the stay under subsection (a) with respect to any action taken with respect to a debt or property securing such debt or with respect to any lease shall terminate with respect to the debtor on the 30th day after the filing of the later case;*

*(B) on the motion of a party in interest for continuation of the automatic stay and upon notice and a hearing, the court may extend the stay in particular cases as to any or all creditors (subject to such conditions or limitations as the court may then impose) after notice and a hearing completed before the expiration of the 30-day period only if the party in interest demonstrates that the filing of the later case is in good faith as to the creditors to be stayed; and*

*(C) for purposes of subparagraph (B), a case is presumptively filed not in good faith (but such presumption may be rebutted by clear and convincing evidence to the contrary)—*

*(i) as to all creditors, if—*

*(I) more than 1 previous case under any of chapters 7, 11, and 13 in which the individual was a debtor was pending within the preceding 1-year period;*

*(II) a previous case under any of chapters 7, 11, and 13 in which the individual was a debtor was dismissed within such 1-year period, after the debtor failed to—*

*(aa) file or amend the petition or other documents as required by this title or the court without substantial excuse (but mere inadvertence or negligence shall not be a substantial excuse unless the dismissal was caused by the negligence of the debtor's attorney);*

*(bb) provide adequate protection as ordered by the court; or*

*(cc) perform the terms of a plan confirmed by the court; or*

*(III) there has not been a substantial change in the financial or personal affairs of the debtor since the dismissal of the next most previous case under chapter 7, 11, or 13 or any other reason to conclude that the later case will be concluded—*

*(aa) if a case under chapter 7, with a discharge; or*

*(bb) if a case under chapter 11 or 13, with a confirmed plan that will be fully performed; and*

*(ii) as to any creditor that commenced an action under subsection (d) in a previous case in which the individual was a debtor if, as of the date of dismissal of such case, that action was still pending or had been resolved by terminating, conditioning, or limiting the stay as to actions of such creditor; and*

*(4) (A) (i) if a single or joint case is filed by or against a debtor who is an individual under this title, and if 2 or more single or joint cases of the debtor were pending within the previous year but were dismissed, other than a case refiled under section 707 (b), the stay under subsection (a) shall not go into effect upon the filing of the later case; and*

*(ii) on request of a party in interest, the court shall promptly enter an order confirming that no stay is in effect;*

*(B) if, within 30 days after the filing of the later case, a party in interest requests the court may order the stay to take effect in the case as to any or all creditors (subject to such conditions or limitations as the court may impose), after notice and a hearing, only if the party in interest demonstrates that the filing of the later case is in good faith as to the creditors to be stayed;*

*(C) a stay imposed under subparagraph (B) shall be effective on the date of the entry of the order allowing the stay to go into effect; and*

*(D) for purposes of subparagraph (B), a case is presumptively filed not in good faith (but such presumption may be rebutted by clear and convincing evidence to the contrary)—*

*(i) as to all creditors if—*

*(I) 2 or more previous cases under this title in which the individual was a debtor were pending within the 1-year period;*

*(II) a previous case under this title in which the individual was a debtor was dismissed within the time period stated in this paragraph after the debtor failed to file or amend the petition or other documents as required by this title or the court without substantial excuse (but mere inadvertence or negligence shall not be substantial excuse unless the dismissal was caused by the negligence of the debtor's attorney), failed to provide adequate protection as ordered by the court, or failed to perform the terms of a plan confirmed by the court; or*

*(III) there has not been a substantial change in the financial or personal affairs of the debtor since the dismissal of the next most previous case under this title, or any other reason to conclude that the later case will not be concluded, if a case under chapter 7, with a discharge, and if a case under chapter 11 or 13, with a confirmed plan that will be fully performed; or*

*(ii) as to any creditor that commenced an action under subsection (d) in a previous case in which the individual was a debtor if, as of the date of dismissal of such case, such action was still pending or had been resolved by terminating, conditioning, or limiting the stay as to such action of such creditor.*

(d) On request of a party in interest and after notice and a hearing, the court shall grant relief from the stay provided under subsection (a) of this section, such as by terminating, annulling, modifying, or conditioning such stay—

(1) for cause, including the lack of adequate protection of an interest in property of such party in interest;

(2) with respect to a stay of an act against property under subsection (a) of this section, if—

(A) the debtor does not have an equity in such property; and

(B) such property is not necessary to an effective reorganization; ~~or~~

(3) with respect to a stay of an act against single asset real estate under subsection (a), by a creditor whose claim is secured by an interest in such real estate, unless, not later than the date that is 90 days after the entry of the order for relief (or such later date as the court may determine for cause by order entered within that 90-day period) *or 30 days after the court determines that the debtor is subject to this paragraph, whichever is later*—

(A) the debtor has filed a plan of reorganization that has a reasonable possibility of being confirmed within a reasonable time; or

(B) ~~the debtor has commenced monthly payments to each creditor whose claim is secured by such real estate (other than a claim secured by a judgment lien or by an unmatured statutory lien), which payments are in an amount equal to interest at a current fair market rate on the value of the creditor's interest in the real estate.~~*the debtor has commenced monthly payments that—*

*(i) may, in the debtor's sole discretion, notwithstanding section 363(c)(2), be made from rents or other income generated before, on, or after the date of the commencement of the case by or from the property to each creditor whose claim is secured by such real estate (other than a claim secured by a judgment lien or by an unmatured statutory lien); and*

*(ii) are in an amount equal to interest at the then applicable nondefault contract rate of interest on the value of the creditor's interest in the real estate; or*

*(4) with respect to a stay of an act against real property under subsection (a), by a creditor whose claim is secured by an interest in such real property, if the court finds that the filing of the petition was part of a scheme to delay, hinder, and defraud creditors that involved either—*

*(A) transfer of all or part ownership of, or other interest in, such real property without the consent of the secured creditor or court approval; or*

*(B) multiple bankruptcy filings affecting such real property.*

*If recorded in compliance with applicable State laws governing notices of interests or liens in real property, an order entered under paragraph (4) shall be binding in any other case under this title purporting to affect such real property filed not later than 2 years after the date of the entry of such order by the court, except that a debtor in a subsequent case under this title may move for relief from such order based upon changed circumstances or for good cause shown, after notice and a hearing. Any Federal, State, or local governmental unit that accepts notices of interests or liens in real property shall accept any certified copy of an order described in this subsection for indexing and recording.*

(e) *(1)* Thirty days after a request under subsection (d) of this section for relief from the stay of any act against property of the estate under subsection (a) of this section, such stay is terminated with respect to the party in interest making such request, unless the court, after notice and a hearing, orders such stay continued in effect pending the conclusion of, or as a result of, a final hearing and determination under subsection (d) of this section. A hearing under this subsection may be a preliminary hearing, or may be consolidated with the final hearing under subsection (d) of this section. The court shall order such stay continued in effect pending the conclusion of the final hearing under subsection (d) of this section if there is a reasonable likelihood that the party opposing relief from such stay will prevail at the conclusion of such final hearing. If the hearing under this subsection is a preliminary hearing, then such final hearing shall be concluded not later than thirty days after the conclusion of such preliminary hearing, unless the 30-day period is extended with the consent of the parties in interest or for a specific time which the court finds is required by compelling circumstances.

*(2) Notwithstanding paragraph (1), in a case under chapter 7, 11, or 13 in which the debtor is an individual, the stay under subsection (a) shall terminate on the date that is 60 days after a request is made by a party in interest under subsection (d), unless—*

*(A) a final decision is rendered by the court during the 60-day period beginning on the date of the request; or*

*(B) such 60-day period is extended—*

*(i) by agreement of all parties in interest; or*

*(ii) by the court for such specific period of time as the court finds is required for good cause, as described in findings made by the court.*

(f) Upon request of a party in interest, the court, with or without a hearing, shall grant such relief from the stay provided under subsection (a) of this section as is necessary to prevent irreparable damage to the interest of an entity in property, if such interest will suffer such damage before there is an opportunity for notice and a hearing under subsection (d) or (e) of this section.

(g) In any hearing under subsection (d) or (e) of this section concerning relief from the stay of any act under subsection (a) of this section—

(1) the party requesting such relief has the burden of proof on the issue of the debtor's equity in property; and

(2) the party opposing such relief has the burden of proof on all other issues.

*(h) (1) In a case in which the debtor is an individual, the stay provided by subsection (a) is terminated with respect to personal property of the estate or of the debtor securing in whole or in part a claim, or subject to an unexpired lease, and such personal property shall no longer be property of the estate if the debtor fails within the applicable time set by section 521(a)(2)—*

*(A) to file timely any statement of intention required under section 521(a)(2) with respect to such personal property or to indicate in such statement that the debtor will either surrender such personal property or retain it and, if retaining such personal property, either redeem such personal property pursuant to section 722, enter into an agreement of the kind specified in section 524(c) applicable to the debt secured by such personal property, or assume such unexpired lease pursuant to section 365(p) if the trustee does not do so, as applicable; and*

*(B) to take timely the action specified in such statement, as it may be amended before expiration of the period for taking action, unless such statement specifies the debtor's intention to reaffirm such debt on the original contract terms and the creditor refuses to agree to the reaffirmation on such terms.*

*(2) Paragraph (1) does not apply if the court determines, on the motion of the trustee filed before the expiration of the applicable time set by section 521(a)(2), after notice and a hearing, that such personal property is of conse quential value or benefit to the estate, and orders appropriate adequate protection of the creditor's interest, and orders the debtor to deliver any collateral in the debtor's possession to the trustee. If the court does not so determine, the stay provided by subsection (a) shall terminate upon the conclusion of the hearing on the motion.*

~~(h) An individual injured by any willful violation of a stay provided by this section shall recover actual damages, including costs and attorneys' fees, and, in appropriate circumstances, may recover punitive damages.~~

*(i) If a case commenced under chapter 7, 11, or 13 is dismissed due to the creation of a debt repayment plan, for purposes of subsection (c)(3), any subsequent case commenced by the debtor under any such chapter shall not be presumed to be filed not in good faith.*

*(j) On request of a party in interest, the court shall issue an order under subsection (c) confirming that the automatic stay has been terminated.*

*(k) (1) Except as provided in paragraph (2), an individual injured by any willful violation of a stay provided by this section shall recover actual damages, including costs and attorneys' fees, and, in appropriate circumstances, may recover punitive damages.*

*(2) If such violation is based on an action taken by an entity in the good faith belief that subsection (h) applies to the debtor, the recovery under paragraph (1) of this subsection against such entity shall be limited to actual damages.*

*(l) (1) Except as otherwise provided in this subsection, subsection (b)(22) shall apply on the date that is 30 days after the date on which the bankruptcy petition is filed, if the debtor files with the petition and serves upon the lessor a certification under penalty of perjury that—*

*(A) under nonbankruptcy law applicable in the jurisdiction, there are circumstances under which the debtor would be permitted to cure the entire monetary default that gave rise to the judgment for possession, after that judgment for possession was entered; and*

*(B) the debtor (or an adult dependent of the debtor) has deposited with the clerk of the court, any rent that would become due during the 30-day period after the filing of the bankruptcy petition.*

*(2) If, within the 30-day period after the filing of the bankruptcy petition, the debtor (or an adult dependent of the debtor) complies with paragraph (1) and files with the court and serves upon the lessor a further certification under penalty of perjury that the debtor (or an adult dependent of the debtor) has cured, under nonbankrupcty law applicable in the jurisdiction, the entire monetary default that gave rise to the judgment under which possession is sought by the lessor, subsection (b)(22) shall not apply, unless ordered to apply by the court under paragraph (3).*

*(3) (A) If the lessor files an objection to any certification filed by the debtor under paragraph (1) or (2), and serves such objection upon the debtor, the court shall hold a hearing within 10 days after the filing and service of such objection to determine if the certification filed by the debtor under paragraph (1) or (2) is true.*

*(B) If the court upholds the objection of the lessor filed under subparagraph (A)—*

*(i) subsection (b)(22) shall apply immediately and relief from the stay provided under subsection (a)(3) shall not be required to enable the lessor to complete the process to recover full possession of the property; and*

*(ii) the clerk of the court shall immediately serve upon the lessor and the debtor a certified copy of the court's order upholding the lessor's objection.*

*(4) If a debtor, in accordance with paragraph (5), indicates on the petition that there was a judgment for possession of the residential rental property in which the debtor resides and does not file a certification under paragraph (1) or (2)—*

*(A) subsection (b)(22) shall apply immediately upon failure to file such certification, and relief from the stay provided under subsection (a)(3) shall not be required to enable the lessor to complete the process to recover full possession of the property; and*

*(B) the clerk of the court shall immediately serve upon the lessor and the debtor a certified copy of the docket indicating the absence of a filed certification and the applicability of the exception to the stay under subsection (b)(22).*

*(5) (A) Where a judgment for possession of residential property in which the debtor resides as a tenant under a lease or rental agreement has been obtained by the lessor, the debtor shall so indicate on the bankruptcy petition and shall provide the name and address of the lessor that obtained that prepetition judgment on the petition and on any certification filed under this subsection.*

*(B) The form of certification filed with the petition, as specified in this subsection, shall provide for the debtor to certify, and the debtor shall certify—*

*(i) whether a judgment for possession of residential rental housing in which the debtor resides has been obtained against the debtor before the date of the filing of the petition; and*

*(ii) whether the debtor is claiming under paragraph (1) that under nonbankruptcy law applicable in the jurisdiction, there are circumstances under which the debtor would be permitted to cure the entire monetary default that gave rise to the judgment for possession, after that judgment of possession was entered, and has made the appropriate deposit with the court.*

*(C) The standard forms (electronic and otherwise) used in a bankruptcy proceeding shall be amended to reflect the requirements of this subsection.*

*(D) The clerk of the court shall arrange for the prompt transmittal of the rent deposited in accordance with paragraph (1)(B) to the lessor.*

*(m) (1) Except as otherwise provided in this subsection, subsection (b)(23) shall apply on the date that is 15 days after the date on which the lessor files and serves a certification described in subsection (b)(23).*

*(2) (A) If the debtor files with the court an objection to the truth or legal sufficiency of the certification described in subsection (b)(23) and serves such objection upon the lessor, subsection (b)(23) shall not apply, unless ordered to apply by the court under this subsection.*

*(B) If the debtor files and serves the objection under subparagraph (A), the court shall hold a hearing within 10 days after the filing and service of such objection to determine if the situation giving rise to the lessor's certification under paragraph (1) existed or has been remedied.*

*(C) If the debtor can demonstrate to the satisfaction of the court that the situation giving rise to the lessor's certification under paragraph (1) did not exist or has been remedied, the stay provided under subsection (a)(3) shall remain in effect until the termination of the stay under this section.*

*(D) If the debtor cannot demonstrate to the satisfaction of the court that the situation giving rise to the lessor's certification under paragraph (1) did not exist or has been remedied—*

*(i) relief from the stay provided under subsection (a)(3) shall*

*not be required to enable the lessor to proceed with the eviction; and*

*(ii) the clerk of the court shall immediately serve upon the lessor and the debtor a certified copy of the court's order upholding the lessor's certification.*

*(3) If the debtor fails to file, within 15 days, an objection under paragraph (2)(A)—*

*(A) subsection (b)(23) shall apply immediately upon such failure and relief from the stay provided under subsection (a)(3) shall not be required to enable the lessor to complete the process to recover full possession of the property; and*

*(B) the clerk of the court shall immediately serve upon the lessor and the debtor a certified copy of the docket indicating such failure.*

*(n) (1) Except as provided in paragraph (2), subsection (a) does not apply in a case in which the debtor—*

*(A) is a debtor in a small business case pending at the time the petition is filed;*

*(B) was a debtor in a small business case that was dismissed for any reason by an order that became final in the 2-year period ending on the date of the order for relief entered with respect to the petition;*

*(C) was a debtor in a small business case in which a plan was confirmed in the 2-year period ending on the date of the order for relief entered with respect to the petition; or*

*(D) is an entity that has acquired substantially all of the assets or business of a small business debtor described in subparagraph (A), (B), or (C), unless such entity establishes by a preponderance of the evidence that such entity acquired substantially all of the assets or business of such small business debtor in good faith and not for the purpose of evading this paragraph.*

*(2) Paragraph (1) does not apply—*

*(A) to an involuntary case involving no collusion by the debtor with creditors; or*

*(B) to the filing of a petition if—*

*(i) the debtor proves by a preponderance of the evidence that the filing of the petition resulted from circumstances beyond the control of the debtor not foreseeable at the time the case then pending was filed; and*

*(ii) it is more likely than not that the court will confirm a feasible plan, but not a liquidating plan, within a reasonable period of time.*

*(o) The exercise of rights not subject to the stay arising under subsection (a) pursuant to paragraph (6), (7), (17), or (27) of subsection (b) shall not be stayed by any order of a court or administrative agency in any proceeding under this title.*

**Section 362**

(April 20, 2005, P.L. 109-8, Title I, § 106(f); Title IIB, § 214; Title IIC, § 224(b); Title III, §§ 302, 303(a), 303(b), 305(1), 311(a), 311 (b), 320; Title IVA, § 401(b); Title IVB,

§§ 441, 444; Title VII, §§ 709, 718; Title IX, § 907(d)(1), (2), (o)(1), (2); Title XI, § 1106; Title XII, § 1225, 119 Stat. 23)

# HISTORY: ANCILLARY LAWS AND DIRECTIVES

**Amendments:**

**2005.** Act April 20, 2005(effective 180 days after enactment of April 20, 2005, as provided by § 1501(a) of P. L. 109-8), amends 11 USC § 362(b), by amending § 362(b)(2), § 362(b)(6), § 362(b)(7), § 362(b)(17), § 362(b)(18), and by adding new §§ 362(b)(19)–(28). The Act also amends § 362(c) by adding §§ 362(c)(3) and (4). Further, the Act amends § 362(d)(3)(B) and adds § 362(d)(4). The Act adds § 362(e)(2) and §§ 362(h)–(o), while deleting former section § 362(h).

**Other provisions:**

**Effective date and application of amendments made by Act April 20, 2005.** Act April 20, 2005, P.L. 109-8, Title XV, § 1501(a), 119 Stat. 23, provided that the amendments made to this section would be effective 180 days after enactment on April 20, 2005.

**Abridged Legislative History:**

Exceptions To Automatic Stay in Domestic Support Proceedings. Under current law, section 362(b)(2) of the Bankruptcy Code excepts from the automatic stay the commencement or continuation of an action or proceeding: (1) for the establishment of paternity; or (2) the establishment or modification of an order for alimony, maintenance or support. It also permits the collection of such obligations from property that is not property of the estate. Section 214 makes several revisions to Bankruptcy Code section 362(b)(2).

Section 224(b) amends section 362(b) of the Bankruptcy Code to except from the automatic stay the withholding of income from a debtor's wages pursuant to an agreement authorizing such withholding for the benefit of a pension, profit-sharing, stock bonus, or other employer-sponsored plan established under Internal Revenue Code section 401, 403, 408, 408A, 414, 457, or 501(c) to the extent that the amounts withheld are used solely to repay a loan from a plan as authorized by section 408(b)(1) of the Employee Retirement Income Security Act of 1974 or subject to Internal Revenue Code section 72(p) or with respect to a loan from certain thrift savings plans.

Discouraging Bad Faith Repeat Filings. Section 302 of the Act amends section 362(c) of the Bankruptcy Code to terminate the automatic stay within 30 days in a chapter 7, 11, or 13 case filed by or against an individual if such individual was a debtor in a previously dismissed case pending within the preceding one-year period.

For purposes of this provision, a case is presumptively not filed in good faith as to all creditors (but such presumption may be rebutted by clear and convincing evidence) if: (1) more than one bankruptcy case under chapter 7, 11 or 13 was previously filed by the debtor within the preceding one-year period; (2) the prior chapter 7, 11, or 13 case was dismissed within the preceding year for the debtor's failure to (a) file or amend without substantial excuse a document required under the Bankruptcy Code or court order, (b) provide adequate protection ordered by the court, or (c) perform the terms of a confirmed plan; or (3) there has been no substantial change in the debtor's financial or personal affairs since the dismissal of the prior case, or there is no reason to conclude that the pending case will conclude either with a discharge (if a chapter 7 case) or confirmation (if a chapter 11 or 13 case). In addition, section 302 provides that a case is presumptively deemed not to be filed in good faith as to any creditor who obtained relief from the automatic stay in the prior case or sought such relief in the prior case and such action was pending at the time of the prior case's dismissal. The presumption may be rebutted by clear and convincing evidence. A similar presumption applies if two or more bankruptcy cases were pending in the one-year preceding the filing of the pending case.

Curbing Abusive Filings. Section 303 of the Act is intended to reduce abusive filings. Subsection (a) amends Bankruptcy Code section 362(d) to add a new ground for relief from the automatic stay. Under this provision, cause for relief from the automatic stay may be established for a creditor whose claim is secured by an interest in real property, if the court finds that the filing of the bankruptcy case was part of a scheme to delay, hinder and defraud creditors that involved either: (1) a transfer of all or part of an ownership interest in real property without such creditor's consent or without court approval; or (2) multiple bankruptcy filings affecting the real property.

Section 303(b) amends Bankruptcy Code section 362(b) to except from the automatic stay an act to enforce any lien against or security interest in real property within two years following the entry of an order entered under section 362(d)(4).

Relief from the Automatic Stay When the Debtor Does Not Complete Intended Surrender of Consumer Debt Collateral. Paragraph (1) of section 305 of the Act amends Bankruptcy Code section 362 to terminate the automatic stay with respect to personal property of the estate or of the debtor in a chapter 7, 11, or 13 case (where the debtor is an individual) that secures a claim (in whole or in part) or is subject to an unexpired lease if the debtor fails to: (1) file timely a statement of intention as required by section 521(a)(2) of the Bankruptcy Code with respect to such property; or (2) indicate in such statement whether the property will be surrendered or retained, and if retained, whether the debtor will redeem the property or reaffirm the debt, or assume an unexpired lease, if the trustee does not. Likewise, the automatic stay is terminated if the debtor fails to take the action specified in the statement of intention in a timely manner, unless the statement specifies reaffirmation and the creditor refuses to enter into the reaffirmation agreement on the original contract terms.

Automatic Stay. Section 311 of the Act amends section 362(b) of the Bankruptcy Code to except from the automatic stay a judgment of eviction with respect to a residential leasehold under certain circumstances.

Section 311 also excepts from the automatic stay a transfer that is not avoidable under Bankruptcy Code section 544 and that is not avoidable under Bankruptcy Code section 549.

Prompt Relief from Stay in Individual Cases. Section 320 of the Act amends section 362(e) of the Bankruptcy Code to terminate the automatic stay in a chapter 7, 11, or 13 case of an individual debtor within 60 days following a request for relief from the stay, unless the bankruptcy court renders a final decision prior to the expiration of the 60-day time period, such period is extended pursuant to agreement of all parties in interest, or a specific extension of time is required for good cause as described in findings made by the court.

Section 401(b) amends section 362 of the Bankruptcy Code to except from the automatic stay certain enforcement actions by a securities self regulatory organization.

Serial Filer Provisions. Paragraph (1) of section 441 of the Act amends section 362 of the Bankruptcy Code to provide that a court may award only actual damages for a violation of the automatic stay committed by an entity in the good faith belief that subsection (h) of section 362 (as amended) applies to the debtor. Section 441(2) adds a new subsection to section 362 of the Bankruptcy Code specifying that the automatic stay does not apply where the chapter 11 debtor: (1) is a debtor in a small business case pending at the time the subsequent case is filed; (2) was a debtor in a small business case dismissed for any reason pursuant to an order that became final in the two-year period ending on the date of the order for relief entered in the pending case; (3) was a debtor in small business case in which a plan was confirmed in the two-year period ending on the date of the order for relief entered in the pending case; or (4) is an entity that has acquired substantially all of the assets or business of a small business debtor described in the preceding paragraphs, unless such entity establishes by a preponderance of the evidence that it acquired the assets or business in good faith and not for the purpose of evading this provision.

Stay of Tax Proceedings Limited to Prepetition Taxes. Under current law, the filing of a petition for relief under the Bankruptcy Code activates an automatic stay that enjoins the commencement or continuation of a case in the United States Tax Court. This rule was arguably extended in Halpern v. Commissioner, 96 T.C. 895 (1991), which held that the tax court did not have jurisdiction to hear a case involving a postpetition year. To address this issue, section 709 of the Act amends section

362(a)(8) of the Bankruptcy Code to specify that the automatic stay is limited to an individual debtor's prepetition taxes (taxes incurred before entering bankruptcy).

Setoff of Tax Refunds. Under current law, the filing of a bankruptcy petition automatically stays the setoff of a prepetition tax refund against a prepetition tax obligation unless the bankruptcy court approves the setoff. Interest and penalties that may continue to accrue may also be nondischargeable pursuant to section 523(a)(1) of the Bankruptcy Code and cause individual debtors undue hardship. Section 718 of the Act amends section 362(b) of the Bankruptcy Code to create an exception to the automatic stay whereby such setoff could occur without court order unless it would not be permitted under applicable nonbankruptcy law because of a pending action to determine the amount or legality of the tax liability.

Subsection (d) [of section 907] amends section 362(b) of the Bankruptcy Code to protect enforcement, free from the automatic stay, of setoff or netting provisions in swap agreements and in master netting agreements and security agreements or arrangements related to one or more swap agreements or master netting agreements.

Subsection (d) also clarifies that the provisions protecting setoff and foreclosure in relation to securities contracts, commodity contracts, forward contracts, repurchase agreements, swap agreements, and master netting agreements free from the automatic stay apply to collateral pledged by the debtor but that cannot technically be "held by" the creditor, such as receivables and book-entry securities, and to collateral that has been repledged by the creditor and securities re-sold pursuant to repurchase agreements.

Section 907(o), as well as other subsections of the Act, adds references to "financial participant" in all the provisions of the Bankruptcy Code relating to securities, forward and commodity contracts and repurchase and swap agreements.

Exclusion from Program Participation Not Subject to Automatic Stay. Section 1106 amends section 362(b) of the Bankruptcy Code to except from the automatic stay the exclusion by the Secretary of Health and Human Services of a debtor from participation in the Medicare program or other specified Federal health care programs.

Amendment to Section 362 of Title 11, United States Code. Section 1225 of the Act amends section 362(b) of the Bankruptcy Code to except from the automatic stay the creation or perfection of a statutory lien for an ad valorem property tax or for a special tax or special assessment on real property (whether or not ad valorem) that is imposed by a governmental unit, if such tax or assessment becomes due after the filing of the petition.

(H. Report No. 109-31 to accompany S. 256, 109th Cong., 1st Sess. (2005) pp. 56, 61, 64, 69–71, 74–75, 80, 86, 93–96, 102, 104–05, 132–33, 140; available at 2005 U.S.C.C.A.N. 88, at 126, 130, 133, 138–39, 142–43, 147, 152, 158–60, 166, 168, 192–94, 199.)

## § 363. Use, sale, or lease of property

(a) In this section, "cash collateral" means cash, negotiable instruments, documents of title, securities, deposit accounts, or other cash equivalents whenever acquired in which the estate and an entity other than the estate have an interest and includes the proceeds, products, offspring, rents, or profits of property and the fees, charges, accounts or other payments for the use or occupancy of rooms and other public facilities in hotels, motels, or other lodging properties subject to a security interest as provided in section 552(b) of this title, whether existing before or after the commencement of a case under this title.

(b) (1) The trustee, after notice and a hearing, may use, sell, or lease, other than in the ordinary course of business, property of the estate~~.~~, *except that if the debtor in connection with offering a product or a service discloses to an individual a policy prohibiting the transfer of personally identifiable information about individuals to persons that are not affiliated with the debtor and if such policy is in effect on the date of the commencement of the case, then the trustee may not sell or lease personally identifiable information to any person unless—*

*(A) such sale or such lease is consistent with such policy; or*

*(B) after appointment of a consumer privacy ombudsman in accordance with section 332, and after notice and a hearing, the court approves such sale or such lease—*

*(i) giving due consideration to the facts, circumstances, and conditions of such sale or such lease; and*

*(ii) finding that no showing was made that such sale or such lease would violate applicable nonbankruptcy law.*

(2) If notification is required under subsection (a) of section 7A of the Clayton Act in the case of a transaction under this subsection, then—

(A) notwithstanding subsection (a) of such section, the notification required by such subsection to be given by the debtor shall be given by the trustee; and

(B) notwithstanding subsection (b) of such section, the required waiting period shall end on the 15th day after the date of the receipt, by the Federal Trade Commission and the Assistant Attorney General in charge of the Antitrust Division of the Department of Justice, of the notification required under such subsection (a), unless such waiting period is extended—

(i) pursuant to subsection (e)(2) of such section, in the same manner as such subsection (e)(2) applies to a cash tender offer;

(ii) pursuant to subsection (g)(2) of such section; or

(iii) by the court after notice and a hearing.

(c) (1) If the business of the debtor is authorized to be operated under section 721, 1108, 1203, 1204, or 1304 of this title and unless the court orders otherwise, the trustee may enter into transactions, including the sale or lease of property of the estate, in the ordinary course of business, without notice or a hearing, and may use property of the estate in the ordinary course of business without notice or a hearing.

(2) The trustee may not use, sell, or lease cash collateral under paragraph (1) of this subsection unless—

(A) each entity that has an interest in such cash collateral consents; or

(B) the court, after notice and a hearing, authorizes such use, sale, or lease in accordance with the provisions of this section.

(3) Any hearing under paragraph (2)(B) of this subsection may be a preliminary hearing or may be consolidated with a hearing under subsection (e) of this section, but shall be scheduled in accordance with the needs of the debtor. If the hearing under paragraph (2)(B) of this subsection is a preliminary hearing, the court may authorize

such use, sale, or lease only if there is a reasonable likelihood that the trustee will prevail at the final hearing under subsection (e) of this section. The court shall act promptly on any request for authorization under paragraph (2)(B) of this subsection.

(4) Except as provided in paragraph (2) of this subsection, the trustee shall segregate and account for any cash collateral in the trustee's possession, custody, or control.

(d) The trustee may use, sell, or lease property under subsection (b) or (c) of this section only — ~~to the extent not inconsistent with any relief granted under section 362(c), 362(d), 362(e), or 362(f) of this title.~~

*(1) in accordance with applicable nonbankruptcy law that governs the transfer of property by a corporation or trust that is not a moneyed, business, or commercial corporation or trust; and*

*(2) to the extent not inconsistent with any relief granted under subsection (c), (d), (e), or (f) of section 362.*

(e) Notwithstanding any other provision of this section, at any time, on request of an entity that has an interest in property used, sold, or leased, or proposed to be used, sold, or leased, by the trustee, the court, with or without a hearing, shall prohibit or condition such use, sale, or lease as is necessary to provide adequate protection of such interest. This subsection also applies to property that is subject to any unexpired lease of personal property (to the exclusion of such property being subject to an order to grant relief from the stay under section 362).

(f) The trustee may sell property under subsection (b) or (c) of this section free and clear of any interest in such property of an entity other than the estate, only if—

(1) applicable nonbankruptcy law permits sale of such property free and clear of such interest;

(2) such entity consents;

(3) such interest is a lien and the price at which such property is to be sold is greater than the aggregate value of all liens on such property;

(4) such interest is in bona fide dispute; or

(5) such entity could be compelled, in a legal or equitable proceeding, to accept a money satisfaction of such interest.

(g) Notwithstanding subsection (f) of this section, the trustee may sell property under subsection (b) or (c) of this section free and clear of any vested or contingent right in the nature of dower or curtesy.

(h) Notwithstanding subsection (f) of this section, the trustee may sell both the estate's interest, under subsection (b) or (c) of this section, and the interest of any co-owner in property in which the debtor had, at the time of the commencement of the case, an undivided interest as a tenant in common, joint tenant, or tenant by the entirety, only if—

(1) partition in kind of such property among the estate and such co-owners is impracticable;

(2) sale of the estate's undivided interest in such property would realize significantly less for the estate than sale of such property free of the interests of such co-owners;

(3) the benefit to the estate of a sale of such property free of the interests of co-owners outweighs the detriment, if any, to such co-owners; and

(4) such property is not used in the production, transmission, or distribution, for sale, of electric energy or of natural or synthetic gas for heat, light, or power.

(i) Before the consummation of a sale of property to which subsection (g) or (h) of this section applies, or of property of the estate that was community property of the debtor and the debtor's spouse immediately before the commencement of the case, the debtor's spouse, or a co-owner of such property, as the case may be, may purchase such property at the price at which such sale is to be consummated.

(j) After a sale of property to which subsection (g) or (h) of this section applies, the trustee shall distribute to the debtor's spouse or the co-owners of such property, as the case may be, and to the estate, the proceeds of such sale, less the costs and expenses, not including any compensation of the trustee, of such sale, according to the interests of such spouse or co-owners, and of the estate.

(k) At a sale under subsection (b) of this section of property that is subject to a lien that secures an allowed claim, unless the court for cause orders otherwise the holder of such claim may bid at such sale, and, if the holder of such claim purchases such property, such holder may offset such claim against the purchase price of such property.

(l) Subject to the provisions of section 365, the trustee may use, sell, or lease property under subsection (b) or (c) of this section, or a plan under chapter 11, 12, or 13 of this title may provide for the use, sale, or lease of property, notwithstanding any provision in a contract, a lease, or applicable law that is conditioned on the insolvency or financial condition of the debtor, on the commencement of a case under this title concerning the debtor, or on the appointment of or the taking possession by a trustee in a case under this title or a custodian, and that effects, or gives an option to effect, a forfeiture, modification, or termination of the debtor's interest in such property.

(m) The reversal or modification on appeal of an authorization under subsection (b) or (c) of this section of a sale or lease of property does not affect the validity of a sale or lease under such authorization to an entity that purchased or leased such property in good faith, whether or not such entity knew of the pendency of the appeal, unless such authorization and such sale or lease were stayed pending appeal.

(n) The trustee may avoid a sale under this section if the sale price was controlled by an agreement among potential bidders at such sale, or may recover from a party to such agreement any amount by which the value of the property sold exceeds the price at which such sale was consummated, and may recover any costs, attorneys' fees, or expenses incurred in avoiding such sale or recovering such amount. In addition to any recovery under the preceding sentence, the court may grant judgment for punitive damages in favor of the estate and against any such party that entered into such an agreement in willful disregard of this subsection.

*(o) Notwithstanding subsection (f), if a person purchases any interest in a consumer credit transaction that is subject to the Truth in Lending Act or any interest in a consumer credit contract (as defined in section 433.1 of title 16 of the Code of Federal Regulations (January 1, 2004), as amended from time to time), and if such interest is purchased through a sale under this section, then such person shall remain subject to all claims and defenses that are related to such consumer credit transaction or such consumer credit contract, to the same extent as such person would be subject to such claims and defenses of the consumer had such interest been purchased at a sale not under this section.*

(~~o~~*p*) In any hearing under this section—

(1) the trustee has the burden of proof on the issue of adequate protection; and

(2) the entity asserting an interest in property has the burden of proof on the issue of the validity, priority, or extent of such interest.

**Section 363**

(April 20, 2005, P.L. 109-8, Title IIA, § 204; Title IIC, § 231(a); Title XII, § 1221(a), 119 Stat. 23)

## HISTORY: ANCILLARY LAWS AND DIRECTIVES

**Amendments:**

**2005.** Act April 20, 2005(effective 180 days after enactment of April 20, 2005, as provided by § 1501(a) of P. L. 109-8), amends 11 USC § 363(b)(1) to restrict a trustee's sale of personally identifiable information, and adds § 363(o) with respect to sales of any interest in a consumer transaction that is subject to the Truth in Lending Act or any interest in a consumer credit contract. Such Act (effective upon enactment and applicable to cases pending on or after that date, as provided by § 1221(a) of P.L. 109-8), amends 11 USC § 363(d) to require that a sale by a trustee of property held by a corporation or trust that is not a moneyed, business or commercial corporation or trust, requiring that a sale must be in compliance with nonbankruptcy law concerning such corporations or trusts.

**Other provisions:**

**Effective date and application of amendments made by Act April 20, 2005.** Act April 20, 2005, P.L. 109-8, Title XV, § 1501(a), 119 Stat. 23, provided that the amendments made to §§ 363(b) and (o) would be effective 180 days after enactment on April 20, 2005. The amendments made by the Act's 1221(a) to Code § 363(d) apply to cases pending on the date of enactment or to cases filed after such date. See Act, Title XII, § 1221(a).

**Abridged Legislative History**

Preservation of Claims and Defenses Upon Sale of Predatory Loans. Section 204 of the Act adds a provision to section 363 of the Bankruptcy Code with respect to sales of any interest in a consumer transaction that is subject to the Truth in Lending Act or any interest in a consumer credit contract (as defined in section 433.1 of title 16 of the Code of Federal Regulations).

Protection of Personally Identifiable Information. Section 231 of the Act clarifies that it applies to personally identifiable information and does not preempt applicable nonbankruptcy law.

Subsection (a) amends Bankruptcy Code section 363(b)(1) to provide that if a debtor, in connection with offering a product or service, discloses to an individual a policy prohibiting the transfer of personally identifiable information to persons unaffiliated with the debtor, and the policy is in effect at the time of the bankruptcy filing, then the trustee may not sell or lease such information unless either of the following conditions is satisfied: (1) the sale is consistent with such policy; or (2) the court, after appointment of a consumer privacy ombudsman (pursuant to section 332 of the Bankruptcy Code, as amended) and notice and hearing, the court approves the sale or lease upon due consideration of the facts, circumstances, and conditions of the sale or lease.

Transfers Made by Nonprofit Charitable Corporations. Section 1221 of the Act amends section 363(d) of the Bankruptcy Code to restrict the authority of a trustee to use, sell, or lease property by a nonprofit corporation or trust. First, the use, sell or lease of such property must be in accordance with applicable nonbankruptcy law and to the extent it is not inconsistent with any relief granted under certain specified provisions of section 362 of the Bankruptcy Code concerning the applicability of the automatic stay. Second, section 1221 imposes similar restrictions with regard to plan confirmation requirements for chapter 11 cases. Third, it amends section 541 of the Bankruptcy Code to provide that any property of a bankruptcy estate in which the debtor is a nonprofit corporation (as described in certain provisions of the Internal Revenue Code) may not be transferred to an entity that is not such a corporation, but only under the same conditions that would apply if the debtor was not in bankruptcy. The amendments made by this section apply to cases pending on the date of enactment or to cases filed after such date. Section 1221 provides that a court may not confirm a plan without considering whether this provision would substantially affect the rights of a party in interest who first acquired rights with respect to the debtor postpetition. Nothing in this provision may be construed to require the court to remand or refer any proceeding, issue, or controversy to any other court or to require the approval of any other court for the transfer of property. (H. Report No. 109-31 to accompany S. 256, 109th Cong., 1st Sess. (2005) pp. 59, 67–68, 145; available at 2005 U.S.C.C.A.N. 88, at 128, 136, 203–04.)

## § 364. Obtaining credit

(a) If the trustee is authorized to operate the business of the debtor under section 721, 1108, 1203, 1204, or 1304 of this title, unless the court orders otherwise, the trustee may obtain unsecured credit and incur unsecured debt in the ordinary course of business allowable under section 503(b)(1) of this title as an administrative expense.

(b) The court, after notice and a hearing, may authorize the trustee to obtain unsecured credit or to incur unsecured debt other than under subsection (a) of this section, allowable under section 503(b)(1) of this title as an administrative expense.

(c) If the trustee is unable to obtain unsecured credit allowable under section 503(b)(1) of this title as an administrative expense, the court, after notice and a hearing, may authorize the obtaining of credit or the incurring of debt—

(1) with priority over any or all administrative expenses of the kind specified in section 503(b) or 507(b) of this title;

(2) secured by a lien on property of the estate that is not otherwise subject to a lien; or

(3) secured by a junior lien on property of the estate that is subject to a lien.

(d) (1) The court, after notice and a hearing, may authorize the obtaining of credit or the incurring of debt secured by a senior or equal lien on property of the estate that is subject to a lien only if—

(A) the trustee is unable to obtain such credit otherwise; and

(B) there is adequate protection of the interest of the holder of the lien on the property of the estate on which such senior or equal lien is proposed to be granted.

(2) In any hearing under this subsection, the trustee has the burden of proof on the issue of adequate protection.

(e) The reversal or modification on appeal of an authorization under this section to obtain credit or incur debt, or of a grant under this section of a priority or a lien, does not affect the validity of any debt so incurred, or any priority or lien so granted, to an entity that extended such credit in good faith, whether or not such entity knew of the pendency of the appeal, unless such authorization and the incurring of such debt, or the granting of such priority or lien, were stayed pending appeal.

(f) Except with respect to an entity that is an underwriter as defined in section 1145(b) of this title, section 5 of the Securities Act of 1933, the Trust Indenture Act of 1939, and any State or local law requiring registration for offer or sale of a security or registration or licensing of an issuer of, underwriter of, or broker or dealer in, a security does not apply to the offer or sale under this section of a security that is not an equity security.

## § 365. Executory contracts and unexpired leases

(a) Except as provided in sections 765 and 766 of this title and in subsections (b), (c), and (d) of this section, the trustee, subject to the court's approval, may assume or reject any executory contract or unexpired lease of the debtor.

(b) (1) If there has been a default in an executory contract or unexpired lease of the debtor, the trustee may not assume such contract or lease unless, at the time of assumption of such contract or lease, the trustee—

(A) cures, or provides adequate assurance that the trustee will promptly cure, such default~~;~~ *other than a default that is a breach of a provision relating to the satisfaction of any provision (other than a penalty rate or penalty provision) relating to a default arising from any failure to perform nonmonetary obligations under an unexpired lease of real property, if it is impossible for the trustee to cure such default by performing nonmonetary acts at and after the time of assumption, except that if such default arises from a failure to operate in accordance with a nonresidential real property lease, then such default shall be cured by performance at and after the time of assumption in accordance with such lease, and pecuniary losses resulting from such default shall be compensated in accordance with the provisions of this paragraph;*

(B) compensates, or provides adequate assurance that the trustee will promptly compensate, a party other than the debtor to such contract or lease, for any actual pecuniary loss to such party resulting from such default; and

(C) provides adequate assurance of future performance under such contract or lease.

(2) Paragraph (1) of this subsection does not apply to a default that is a breach of a provision relating to—

(A) the insolvency or financial condition of the debtor at any time before the closing of the case;

(B) the commencement of a case under this title;

(C) the appointment of or taking possession by a trustee in a case under this title or a custodian before such commencement; or

(D) the satisfaction of any ~~penalty rate or provision~~ *penalty rate or penalty provision* relating to a default arising from any failure by the debtor to perform nonmonetary obligations under the executory contract or unexpired lease.

(3) For the purposes of paragraph (1) of this subsection and paragraph (2)(B) of subsection (f), adequate assurance of future performance of a lease of real property in a shopping center includes adequate assurance—

(A) of the source of rent and other consideration due under such lease, and in the case of an assignment, that the financial condition and operating performance of the proposed assignee and its guarantors, if any, shall be similar to the financial condition and operating performance of the debtor and its guarantors, if any, as of the time the debtor became the lessee under the lease;

(B) that any percentage rent due under such lease will not decline substantially;

(C) that assumption or assignment of such lease is subject to all the provisions thereof, including (but not limited to) provisions such as a radius, location, use, or exclusivity provision, and will not breach any such provision contained in any other lease, financing agreement, or master agreement relating to such shopping center; and

(D) that assumption or assignment of such lease will not disrupt any tenant mix or balance in such shopping center.

(4) Notwithstanding any other provision of this section, if there has been a default in an unexpired lease of the debtor, other than a default of a kind specified in paragraph (2) of this subsection, the trustee may not require a lessor to provide services or supplies incidental to such lease before assumption of such lease unless the lessor is compensated under the terms of such lease for any services and supplies provided under such lease before assumption of such lease.

(c) The trustee may not assume or assign any executory contract or unexpired lease of the debtor, whether or not such contract or lease prohibits or restricts assignment of rights or delegation of duties, if—

(1) (A) applicable law excuses a party, other than the debtor, to

such contract or lease from accepting performance from or rendering performance to an entity other than the debtor or the debtor in possession, whether or not such contract or lease prohibits or restricts assignment of rights or delegation of duties; and

(B) such party does not consent to such assumption or assignment; or

(2) such contract is a contract to make a loan, or extend other debt financing or financial accommodations, to or for the benefit of the debtor, or to issue a security of the debtor; *or*

(3) such lease is of nonresidential real property and has been terminated under applicable nonbankruptcy law prior to the order for relief~~; or~~.

~~(4) such lease is of nonresidential real property under which the debtor is the lessee of an aircraft terminal or aircraft gate at an airport at which the debtor is the lessee under one or more additional nonresidential leases of an aircraft terminal or aircraft gate and the trustee, in connection with such assumption or assignment, does not assume all such leases or does not assume and assign all of such leases to the same person, except that the trustee may assume or assign less than all of such leases with the airport operator's written consent.~~

(d) (1) In a case under chapter 7 of this title, if the trustee does not assume or reject an executory contract or unexpired lease of residential real property or of personal property of the debtor within 60 days after the order for relief, or within such additional time as the court, for cause, within such 60- day period, fixes, then such contract or lease is deemed rejected.

(2) In a case under chapter 9, 11, 12, or 13 of this title, the trustee may assume or reject an executory contract or unexpired lease of residential real property or of personal property of the debtor at any time before the confirmation of a plan but the court, on the request of any party to such contract or lease, may order the trustee to determine within a specified period of time whether to assume or reject such contract or lease.

(3) The trustee shall timely perform all the obligations of the debtor, except those specified in section 365(b)(2), arising from and after the order for relief under any unexpired lease of nonresidential real property, until such lease is assumed or rejected, notwithstanding section 503(b)(1) of this title. The court may extend, for cause, the time for performance of any such obligation that arises within 60 days after the date of the order for relief, but the time for performance shall not be extended beyond such 60-day period. This subsection shall not be deemed to affect the trustee's obligations under the provisions of subsection (b) or (f) of this section. Acceptance of any such performance does not constitute waiver or relinquishment of the lessor's rights under such lease or under this title.

(4) ~~Notwithstanding paragraphs (1) and (2), in a case under any~~

~~chapter of this title, if the trustee does not assume or reject an unexpired lease of nonresidential real property under which the debtor is the lessee within 60 days after the date of the order for relief, or within such additional time as the court, for cause, within such 60-day period, fixes, then such lease is deemed rejected, and the trustee shall immediately surrender such nonresidential real property to the lessor.~~*(A) Subject to subparagraph (B), an unexpired lease of nonresidential real property under which the debtor is the lessee shall be deemed rejected, and the trustee shall immediately surrender that nonresidential real property to the lessor, if the trustee does not assume or reject the unexpired lease by the earlier of—*

*(i) the date that is 120 days after the date of the order for relief; or*

*(ii) the date of the entry of an order confirming a plan.*

*(B) (i) The court may extend the period determined under subparagraph (A), prior to the expiration of the 120-day period, for 90 days on the motion of the trustee or lessor for cause.*

*(ii) If the court grants an extension under clause (i), the court may grant a subsequent extension only upon prior written consent of the lessor in each instance.*

~~(5) Notwithstanding paragraphs (1) and (4) of this subsection, in a case under any chapter of this title, if the trustee does not assume or reject an unexpired lease of nonresidential real property under which the debtor is an affected air carrier that is the lessee of an aircraft terminal or aircraft gate before the occurrence of a termination event, then (unless the court orders the trustee to assume such unexpired leases within 5 days after the termination event), at the option of the airport operator, such lease is deemed rejected 5 days after the occurrence of a termination event and the trustee shall immediately surrender possession of the premises to the airport operator; except that the lease shall not be deemed to be rejected unless the airport operator first waives the right to damages related to the rejection. In the event that the lease is deemed to be rejected under this paragraph, the airport operator shall provide the affected air carrier adequate opportunity after the surrender of the premises to remove the fixtures and equipment installed by the affected air carrier.~~

~~(6) For the purpose of paragraph (5) of this subsection and paragraph (f)(1) of this section, the occurrence of a termination event means, with respect to a debtor which is an affected air carrier that is the lessee of an aircraft terminal or aircraft gate—~~

~~(A) the entry under section 301 or 302 of this title of an order for relief under chapter 7 of this title;~~

~~(B) the conversion of a case under any chapter of this title to a case under chapter 7 of this title; or~~

~~(C) the granting of relief from the stay provided under section 362(a) of this title with respect to aircraft, aircraft engines, propel-~~

~~lers, appliances, or spare parts, as defined in section 40102(a) of title 49, except for property of the debtor found by the court not to be necessary to an effective reorganization.~~

~~(7) Any order entered by the court pursuant to paragraph (4) extending the period within which the trustee of an affected air carrier must assume or reject an unexpired lease of nonresidential real property shall be without prejudice to—~~

~~(A) the right of the trustee to seek further extensions within such additional time period granted by the court pursuant to paragraph (4); and~~

~~(B) the right of any lessor or any other party in interest to request, at any time, a shortening or termination of the period within which the trustee must assume or reject an unexpired lease of nonresidential real property.~~

~~(8) The burden of proof for establishing cause for an extension by an affected air carrier under paragraph (4) or the maintenance of a previously granted extension under paragraph (7)(A) and (B) shall at all times remain with the trustee.~~

~~(9) For purposes of determining cause under paragraph (7) with respect to an unexpired lease of nonresidential real property between the debtor that is an affected air carrier and an airport operator under which such debtor is the lessee of an airport terminal or an airport gate, the court shall consider, among other relevant factors, whether substantial harm will result to the airport operator or airline passengers as a result of the extension or the maintenance of a previously granted extension. In making the determination of substantial harm, the court shall consider, among other relevant factors, the level of actual use of the terminals or gates which are the subject of the lease, the public interest in actual use of such terminals or gates, the existence of competing demands for the use of such terminals or gates, the effect of the court's extension or termination of the period of time to assume or reject the lease on such debtor's ability to successfully reorganize under chapter 11 of this title, and whether the trustee of the affected air carrier is capable of continuing to comply with its obligations under section 365(d)(3) of this title.~~

(~~10~~ *5*) The trustee shall timely perform all of the obligations of the debtor, except those specified in section 365(b)(2), first arising from or after 60 days after the order for relief in a case under chapter 11 of this title under an unexpired lease of personal property (other than personal property leased to an individual primarily for personal, family, or household purposes), until such lease is assumed or rejected notwithstanding section 503(b)(1) of this title, unless the court, after notice and a hearing and based on the equities of the case, orders otherwise with respect to the obligations or timely performance thereof. This subsection shall not be deemed to affect the trustee's obligations under the provisions of subsection (b) or (f). Acceptance of any such performance does not constitute waiver or relinquishment of the lessor's rights under such lease or under this title.

(e) (1) Notwithstanding a provision in an executory contract or unexpired lease, or in applicable law, an executory contract or unexpired lease of the debtor may not be terminated or modified, and any right or obligation under such contract or lease may not be terminated or modified, at any time after the commencement of the case solely because of a provision in such contract or lease that is conditioned on—

(A) the insolvency or financial condition of the debtor at any time before the closing of the case;

(B) the commencement of a case under this title; or

(C) the appointment of or taking possession by a trustee in a case under this title or a custodian before such commencement.

(2) Paragraph (1) of this subsection does not apply to an executory contract or unexpired lease of the debtor, whether or not such contract or lease prohibits or restricts assignment of rights or delegation of duties, if—

(A) (i) applicable law excuses a party, other than the debtor, to such contract or lease from accepting performance from or rendering performance to the trustee or to an assignee of such contract or lease, whether or not such contract or lease prohibits or restricts assignment of rights or delegation of duties; and

(ii) such party does not consent to such assumption or assignment; or

(B) such contract is a contract to make a loan, or extend other debt financing or financial accommodations, to or for the benefit of the debtor, or to issue a security of the debtor.

(f) (1) Except as provided in subsections *(b) and (c)* of this section, notwithstanding a provision in an executory contract or unexpired lease of the debtor, or in applicable law, that prohibits, restricts, or conditions the assignment of such contract or lease, the trustee may assign such contract or lease under paragraph (2) of this subsection~~; except that the trustee may not assign an unexpired lease of nonresidential real property under which the debtor is an affected air carrier that is the lessee of an aircraft terminal or aircraft gate if there has occurred a termination event~~.

(2) The trustee may assign an executory contract or unexpired lease of the debtor only if—

(A) the trustee assumes such contract or lease in accordance with the provisions of this section; and

(B) adequate assurance of future performance by the assignee of such contract or lease is provided, whether or not there has been a default in such contract or lease.

(3) Notwithstanding a provision in an executory contract or unexpired lease of the debtor, or in applicable law that terminates or modifies, or permits a party other than the debtor to terminate or

modify, such contract or lease or a right or obligation under such contract or lease on account of an assignment of such contract or lease, such contract, lease, right, or obligation may not be terminated or modified under such provision because of the assumption or assignment of such contract or lease by the trustee.

(g) Except as provided in subsections (h)(2) and (i)(2) of this section, the rejection of an executory contract or unexpired lease of the debtor constitutes a breach of such contract or lease—

(1) if such contract or lease has not been assumed under this section or under a plan confirmed under chapter 9, 11, 12, or 13 of this title, immediately before the date of the filing of the petition; or

(2) if such contract or lease has been assumed under this section or under a plan confirmed under chapter 9, 11, 12, or 13 of this title—

(A) if before such rejection the case has not been converted under section 1112, 1208, or 1307 of this title, at the time of such rejection; or

(B) if before such rejection the case has been converted under section 1112, 1208, or 1307 of this title—

(i) immediately before the date of such conversion, if such contract or lease was assumed before such conversion; or

(ii) at the time of such rejection, if such contract or lease was assumed after such conversion.

(h) (1) (A) If the trustee rejects an unexpired lease of real property under which the debtor is the lessor and—

(i) if the rejection by the trustee amounts to such a breach as would entitle the lessee to treat such lease as terminated by virtue of its terms, applicable nonbankruptcy law, or any agreement made by the lessee, then the lessee under such lease may treat such lease as terminated by the rejection; or

(ii) if the term of such lease has commenced, the lessee may retain its rights under such lease (including rights such as those relating to the amount and timing of payment of rent and other amounts payable by the lessee and any right of use, possession, quiet enjoyment, subletting, assignment, or hypothecation) that are in or appurtenant to the real property for the balance of the term of such lease and for any renewal or extension of such rights to the extent that such rights are enforceable under applicable nonbankruptcy law.

(B) If the lessee retains its rights under subparagraph (A)(ii), the lessee may offset against the rent reserved under such lease for the balance of the term after the date of the rejection of such lease and for the term of any renewal or extension of such lease, the value of any damage caused by the nonperformance after the date of such rejection, of any obligation of the debtor under such lease, but the lessee shall not have any other right against the estate or the debtor on account of any damage occurring after such date caused by such nonperformance.

(C) The rejection of a lease of real property in a shopping center with respect to which the lessee elects to retain its rights under subparagraph (A)(ii) does not affect the enforceability under applicable nonbankruptcy law of any provision in the lease pertaining to radius, location, use, exclusivity, or tenant mix or balance.

(D) In this paragraph, "lessee" includes any successor, assign, or mortgagee permitted under the terms of such lease.

(2) (A) If the trustee rejects a timeshare interest under a timeshare plan under which the debtor is the timeshare interest seller and—

(i) if the rejection amounts to such a breach as would entitle the timeshare interest purchaser to treat the timeshare plan as terminated under its terms, applicable nonbankruptcy law, or any agreement made by timeshare interest purchaser, the timeshare interest purchaser under the timeshare plan may treat the timeshare plan as terminated by such rejection; or

(ii) if the term of such timeshare interest has commenced, then the timeshare interest purchaser may retain its rights in such timeshare interest for the balance of such term and for any term of renewal or extension of such timeshare interest to the extent that such rights are enforceable under applicable nonbankruptcy law.

(B) If the timeshare interest purchaser retains its rights under subparagraph (A), such timeshare interest purchaser may offset against the moneys due for such timeshare interest for the balance of the term after the date of the rejection of such timeshare interest, and the term of any renewal or extension of such timeshare interest, the value of any damage caused by the nonperformance after the date of such rejection, of any obligation of the debtor under such timeshare plan, but the timeshare interest purchaser shall not have any right against the estate or the debtor on account of any damage occurring after such date caused by such nonperformance.

(i) (1) If the trustee rejects an executory contract of the debtor for the sale of real property or for the sale of a timeshare interest under a timeshare plan, under which the purchaser is in possession, such purchaser may treat such contract as terminated, or, in the alternative, may remain in possession of such real property or timeshare interest.

(2) If such purchaser remains in possession—

(A) such purchaser shall continue to make all payments due under such contract, but may offset against such payments any damages occurring after the date of the rejection of such contract caused by the nonperformance of any obligation of the debtor after such date, but such purchaser does not have any rights against the estate on account of any damages arising after such date from such rejection, other than such offset; and

(B) the trustee shall deliver title to such purchaser in accordance with the provisions of such contract, but is relieved of all other obligations to perform under such contract.

(j) A purchaser that treats an executory contract as terminated under subsection (i) of this section, or a party whose executory contract to purchase real property from the debtor is rejected and under which such party is not in possession, has a lien on the interest of the debtor in such property for the recovery of any portion of the purchase price that such purchaser or party has paid.

(k) Assignment by the trustee to an entity of a contract or lease assumed under this section relieves the trustee and the estate from any liability for any breach of such contract or lease occurring after such assignment.

(l) If an unexpired lease under which the debtor is the lessee is assigned pursuant to this section, the lessor of the property may require a deposit or other security for the performance of the debtor's obligations under the lease substantially the same as would have been required by the landlord upon the initial leasing to a similar tenant.

(m) For purposes of this section 365 and sections 541(b)(2) and 362 (b)(10), leases of real property shall include any rental agreement to use real property.

(n) (1) If the trustee rejects an executory contract under which the debtor is a licensor of a right to intellectual property, the licensee under such contract may elect—

(A) to treat such contract as terminated by such rejection if such rejection by the trustee amounts to such a breach as would entitle the licensee to treat such contract as terminated by virtue of its own terms, applicable nonbankruptcy law, or an agreement made by the licensee with another entity; or

(B) to retain its rights (including a right to enforce any exclusivity provision of such contract, but excluding any other right under applicable nonbankruptcy law to specific performance of such contract) under such contract and under any agreement supplementary to such contract, to such intellectual property (including any embodiment of such intellectual property to the extent protected by applicable nonbankruptcy law), as such rights existed immediately before the case commenced, for—

(i) the duration of such contract; and

(ii) any period for which such contract may be extended by the licensee as of right under applicable nonbankruptcy law.

(2) If the licensee elects to retain its rights, as described in paragraph (1)(B) of this subsection, under such contract—

(A) the trustee shall allow the licensee to exercise such rights;

(B) the licensee shall make all royalty payments due under such contract for the duration of such contract and for any period described in paragraph (1)(B) of this subsection for which the licensee extends such contract; and

(C) the licensee shall be deemed to waive—

(i) any right of setoff it may have with respect to such contract under this title or applicable nonbankruptcy law; and

(ii) any claim allowable under section 503(b) of this title arising from the performance of such contract.

(3) If the licensee elects to retain its rights, as described in paragraph (1)(B) of this subsection, then on the written request of the licensee the trustee shall—

(A) to the extent provided in such contract, or any agreement supplementary to such contract, provide to the licensee any intellectual property (including such embodiment) held by the trustee; and

(B) not interfere with the rights of the licensee as provided in such contract, or any agreement supplementary to such contract, to such intellectual property (including such embodiment) including any right to obtain such intellectual property (or such embodiment) from another entity.

(4) Unless and until the trustee rejects such contract, on the written request of the licensee the trustee shall—

(A) to the extent provided in such contract or any agreement supplementary to such contract—

(i) perform such contract; or

(ii) provide to the licensee such intellectual property (including any embodiment of such intellectual property to the extent protected by applicable nonbankruptcy law) held by the trustee; and

(B) not interfere with the rights of the licensee as provided in such contract, or any agreement supplementary to such contract, to such intellectual property (including such embodiment), including any right to obtain such intellectual property (or such embodiment) from another entity.

(o) In a case under chapter 11 of this title, the trustee shall be deemed to have assumed (consistent with the debtor's other obligations under section 507), and shall immediately cure any deficit under, any commitment by the debtor to a Federal depository institutions regulatory agency (or predecessor to such agency) to maintain the capital of an insured depository institution, and any claim for a subsequent breach of the obligations thereunder shall be entitled to priority under section 507. This subsection shall not extend any commitment that would otherwise be terminated by any act of such an agency.

*(p) (1) If a lease of personal property is rejected or not timely assumed by the trustee under subsection (d), the leased property is no longer property of the estate and the stay under section 362(a) is automatically terminated.*

*(2) (A) If the debtor in a case under chapter 7 is an individual, the debtor may notify the creditor in writing that the debtor desires to assume the lease. Upon being so notified, the creditor may, at its*

*option, notify the debtor that it is willing to have the lease assumed by the debtor and may condition such assumption on cure of any outstanding default on terms set by the contract.*

*(B) If, not later than 30 days after notice is provided under subparagraph (A), the debtor notifies the lessor in writing that the lease is assumed, the liability under the lease will be assumed by the debtor and not by the estate.*

*(C) The stay under section 362 and the injunction under section 524(a)(2) shall not be violated by notification of the debtor and negotiation of cure under this subsection.*

*(3) In a case under chapter 11 in which the debtor is an individual and in a case under chapter 13, if the debtor is the lessee with respect to personal property and the lease is not assumed in the plan confirmed by the court, the lease is deemed rejected as of the conclusion of the hearing on confirmation. If the lease is rejected, the stay under section 362 and any stay under section 1301 is automatically terminated with respect to the property subject to the lease.*

**Section 365**

(April 20, 2005, P.L. 109-8, Title III, §§ 309(b), 328(a); Title IVA, § 404(a), 119 Stat. 23)

## HISTORY: ANCILLARY LAWS AND DIRECTIVES

**Amendments:**

**2005.** Act April 20, 2005(effective 180 days after enactment of April 20, 2005, as provided by § 1501(a) of P. L. 109-8), amends 11 USC § 365(b) to provide that a trustee does not have to cure a default that is a breach of a provision (other than a penalty rate or penalty provision) relating to a default arising from any failure to perform a nonmonetary obligation under an unexpired lease of real property, if it is impossible for the trustee to cure the default by performing such nonmonetary act at and after the time of assumption. Such Act amends 11 USC § 365(c) and adds § (p) to provide that if a lease of personal property is rejected or not assumed by the trustee in a timely manner, such property is no longer property of the estate and the automatic stay under Bankruptcy Code section 362 with respect to such property is terminated, and amends § 365(d)(4) of the Bankruptcy Code to establish a firm, bright line deadline by which an unexpired lease of nonresidential real property must be assumed or rejected. Such Act amends section 365(f)(1) to assure that section 365(f) does not override any part of section 365(b).

**Other provisions:**

**Effective date and application of amendments made by Act April 20, 2005.** Act April 20, 2005, P.L. 109-8, Title XV, § 1501(a), 119 Stat. 23, provided that the amendments made to this section would be effective 180 days after enactment on April 20, 2005.

**Abridged Legislative History**

Section 309(b) amends section 365 of the Bankruptcy Code to provide that if a lease of personal property is rejected or not assumed by the trustee in a timely manner, such property is no longer property of the estate and the automatic stay under Bankruptcy Code section 362 with respect to such property is terminated. With regard to a chapter 7 case in which the debtor is an individual, the debtor may notify the creditor in writing of his or her desire to assume the lease.

Defaults Based on Nonmonetary Obligations. Subsection (a)(1) of section 328 of the Act amends section 365(b) to provide that a trustee does not have to cure a default that is a breach of a provision (other than a penalty rate or penalty provision) relating to a default arising from any failure to perform a nonmonetary obligation under an unexpired lease of real property, if it is impossible for the trustee to cure the default by performing such nonmonetary act at and after the time of assumption. If the default arises from a failure to operate in accordance with a nonresidential real property lease, the default must be cured by performance at and after the time of assumption in accordance with the lease. Pecuniary losses resulting from such default must be compensated pursuant to section 365(b)(1).

Executory Contracts and Unexpired Leases. Subsection (a) of section 404 of the Act amends section 365(d)(4) of the Bankruptcy Code to establish a firm, bright line deadline by which an unexpired lease of nonresidential real property must be assumed or rejected. If such lease is not assumed or rejected by such deadline, then such lease shall be deemed rejected, and the trustee shall immediately surrender such property to the lessor. Section 404(a) permits a bankruptcy trustee to assume or reject a lease on a date that is the earlier of the date of confirmation of a plan or the date, which is 120 days after the date of the order for relief. An extension of time may be granted, within the 120-day period, for an additional 90 days, for cause, upon motion of the trustee or lessor. Any subsequent extension can only be granted by the judge upon the prior written consent of the lessor either by the lessor's motion for an extension or on motion of the trustee, provided that the trustee has the prior written approval of the lessor. This provision is designed to remove the bankruptcy judge's discretion to grant extensions of the time for the retail debtor to decide whether to assume or reject a lease after a maximum possible period of 210 days from the time of entry of the order of relief. Beyond that maximum period, the judge has no authority to grant further time unless the lessor has agreed in writing to the extension.

Section 404(b) amends section 365(f)(1) to assure that section 365(f) does not override any part of section 365(b). (H. Report No. 109-31 to accompany S. 256, 109th Cong., 1st Sess. (2005) pp. 73, 83, 86–87; available at 2005 U.S.C.C.A.N. 88, at 141, 149–50, 152–53.)

## § 366. Utility service

(a) Except as provided in subsection*s* (b) *and (c)* of this section, a utility may not alter, refuse, or discontinue service to, or discriminate against, the trustee or the debtor solely on the basis of the commencement of a case under this title or that a debt owed by the debtor to such utility for service rendered before the order for relief was not paid when due.

(b) Such utility may alter, refuse, or discontinue service if neither the trustee nor the debtor, within 20 days after the date of the order for relief, furnishes adequate assurance of payment, in the form of a deposit or other security, for service after such date. On request of a party in interest and after notice and a hearing, the court may order reasonable modification of the amount of the deposit or other security necessary to provide adequate assurance of payment.

*(c) (1) (A) For purposes of this subsection, the term 'assurance of payment' means—*

*(i) a cash deposit;*

*(ii) a letter of credit;*

*(iii) a certificate of deposit;*

*(iv) a surety bond;*

*(v) a prepayment of utility consumption; or*

*(vi) another form of security that is mutually agreed on between the utility and the debtor or the trustee.*

*(B) For purposes of this subsection an administrative expense priority shall not constitute an assurance of payment.*

*(2) Subject to paragraphs (3) and (4), with respect to a case filed under chapter 11, a utility referred to in subsection (a) may alter, refuse, or discontinue utility service, if during the 30-day period beginning on the date of the filing of the petition, the utility does not receive from the debtor or the trustee adequate assurance of payment for utility service that is satisfactory to the utility.*

*(3) (A) On request of a party in interest and after notice and a hearing, the court may order modification of the amount of an assurance of payment under paragraph (2).*

*(B) In making a determination under this paragraph whether an assurance of payment is adequate, the court may not consider—*

*(i) the absence of security before the date of the filing of the petition;*

*(ii) the payment by the debtor of charges for utility service in a timely manner before the date of the filing of the petition; or*

*(iii) the availability of an administrative expense priority.*

*(4) Notwithstanding any other provision of law, with respect to a case subject to this subsection, a utility may recover or set off against a security deposit provided to the utility by the debtor before the date of the filing of the petition without notice or order of the court.*

**Section 366**

(April 20, 2005, P.L. 109-8, Title IVA, § 417, 119 Stat. 23)

## HISTORY: ANCILLARY LAWS AND DIRECTIVES

**Amendments:**

**2005.** Act April 20, 2005(effective 180 days after enactment of April 20, 2005, as provided by § 1501(a) of P. L. 109-8), amends 11 USC § 366 to provide that assurance of payment, for purposes of this provision, includes a cash deposit, letter of credit, certificate of deposit, surety bond, prepayment of utility consumption, or other form of security that is mutually agreed upon by the debtor or trustee and the utility.

**Other provisions:**

**Effective date and application of amendments made by Act April 20, 2005.** Act April 20, 2005, P.L. 109-8, Title XV, § 1501(a), 119 Stat. 23, provided that the amendments made to this section would be effective 180 days after enactment on April 20, 2005.

**Abridged Legislative History**

Utility Service. Section 417 amends section 366 of the Bankruptcy Code to provide that assurance of payment, for purposes of this provision, includes a cash deposit, letter of credit, certificate of deposit, surety bond, prepayment of utility consumption, or other form of security that is mutually agreed upon by the debtor or trustee and the utility. It also specifies that an administrative expense priority does not constitute an assurance of payment. (H. Report No. 109-31 to accompany S. 256, 109th Cong., 1st Sess. (2005) p.89; available at 2005 U.S.C.C.A.N. 88, at 155.)

# Chapter 5
# —Creditors, the Debtor, and the Estate

## Subchapter I—Creditors and Claims

§ 501. Filing of proofs of claims or interests
§ 502. Allowance of claims or interests
§ 503. Allowance of administrative expenses
§ 504. Sharing of compensation
§ 505. Determination of tax liability
§ 506. Determination of secured status
§ 507. Priorities
§ 508. Effect of distribution other than under this title
§ 509. Claims of codebtors
§ 510. Subordination
***§ 511. Rate of interest on tax claims***

## Subchapter II—Debtor's Duties and Benefits

§ 521. Debtor's duties
§ 522. Exemptions
§ 523. Exceptions to discharge
§ 524. Effect of discharge
§ 525. Protection against discriminatory treatment
***§ 526. Restrictions on debt relief agencies***
***§ 527. Disclosures***
***§ 528. Requirements for debt relief agencies***

## Subchapter III—The Estate

§ 541. Property of the estate
§ 542. Turnover of property to the estate
§ 543. Turnover of property by a custodian
§ 544. Trustee as lien creditor and as successor to certain creditors and purchasers
§ 545. Statutory liens
§ 546. Limitations on avoiding powers
§ 547. Preferences
§ 548. Fraudulent transfers and obligations
§ 549. Postpetition transactions
§ 550. Liability of transferee of avoided transfer
§ 551. Automatic preservation of avoided transfer
§ 552. Postpetition effect of security interest
§ 553. Setoff
§ 554. Abandonment of property of the estate
§ 555. ~~**Contractual right to liquidate a securities**~~

## Subchapter I——Creditors and Claims

### § 501. Filing of proofs of claims or interests

(a) A creditor or an indenture trustee may file a proof of claim. An equity security holder may file a proof of interest.

(b) If a creditor does not timely file a proof of such creditor's claim, an entity that is liable to such creditor with the debtor, or that has secured such creditor, may file a proof of such claim.

(c) If a creditor does not timely file a proof of such creditor's claim, the debtor or the trustee may file a proof of such claim.

(d) A claim of a kind specified in section 502(e)(2), 502(f), 502(g), 502(h) or 502(i) of this title may be filed under subsection (a), (b), or (c) of this section the same as if such claim were a claim against the debtor and had arisen before the date of the filing of the petition.

*(e) A claim arising from the liability of a debtor for fuel use tax assessed consistent with the requirements of section 31705 of title 49 may be filed by the base jurisdiction designated pursuant to the International Fuel Tax Agreement (as defined in section 31701 of title 49) and, if so filed, shall be allowed as a single claim.*

**Section 501**

(April 20, 2005, P. L. 109-8, Title VII, § 702, 119 Stat. 23)

### HISTORY: ANCILLARY LAWS AND DIRECTIVES

**Amendments:**

**2005.** Act April 20, 2005(effective 180 days after enactment of April 20, 2005, as provided by § 1501(a) of P. L. 109-8), amends 11 USC § 501 to add new subsection (e) concerning fuel taxes.

**Other provisions:**

**Effective date and application of amendments made by Act April 20, 2005.** Act April 20, 2005, P.L. 109-8, Title XV, § 1501(a), 119 Stat. 23, provided that the amendments made to this section would be effective 180 days after enactment on April 20, 2005.

**Abridged Legislative History**

Treatment of Fuel Tax Claims. Section 702 of the Act amends section 501 of the Bankruptcy Code to simplify the process for filing of claims by states for certain fuel taxes. (H. Report No. 109-31 to accompany S. 256, 109th Cong., 1st Sess. (2005) pp. 84–86, 148; available at 2005 U.S.C.C.A.N. 88, at 151–52, 206.)

## § 502. Allowance of claims or interests

(a) A claim or interest, proof of which is filed under section 501 of this title, is deemed allowed, unless a party in interest, including a creditor of a general partner in a partnership that is a debtor in a case under chapter 7 of this title, objects.

(b) Except as provided in subsections (e)(2), (f), (g), (h) and (i) of this section, if such objection to a claim is made, the court, after notice and a hearing, shall determine the amount of such claim in lawful currency of the United States as of the date of the filing of the petition, and shall allow such claim in such amount, except to the extent that—

(1) such claim is unenforceable against the debtor and property of the debtor, under any agreement or applicable law for a reason other than because such claim is contingent or unmatured;

(2) such claim is for unmatured interest;

(3) if such claim is for a tax assessed against property of the estate, such claim exceeds the value of the interest of the estate in such property;

(4) if such claim is for services of an insider or attorney of the debtor, such claim exceeds the reasonable value of such services;

(5) such claim is for a debt that is unmatured on the date of the filing of the petition and that is excepted from discharge under section 523(a)(5) of this title;

(6) if such claim is the claim of a lessor for damages resulting from the termination of a lease of real property, such claim exceeds—

(A) the rent reserved by such lease, without acceleration, for the greater of one year, or 15 percent, not to exceed three years, of the remaining term of such lease, following the earlier of—

(i) the date of the filing of the petition; and

(ii) the date on which such lessor repossessed, or the lessee surrendered, the leased property; plus

(B) any unpaid rent due under such lease, without acceleration, on the earlier of such dates;

(7) if such claim is the claim of an employee for damages resulting from the termination of an employment contract, such claim exceeds—

(A) the compensation provided by such contract, without acceleration, for one year following the earlier of—

(i) the date of the filing of the petition; or

(ii) the date on which the employer directed the employee to terminate, or such employee terminated, performance under such contract; plus

(B) any unpaid compensation due under such contract, without acceleration, on the earlier of such dates;

(8) such claim results from a reduction, due to late payment, in the amount of an otherwise applicable credit available to the debtor in connection with an employment tax on wages, salaries, or commissions earned from the debtor; or

(9) proof of such claim is not timely filed, except to the extent tardily filed as permitted under paragraph (1), (2), or (3) of section 726(a) of this title or under the Federal Rules of Bankruptcy Procedure, except that a claim of a governmental unit shall be timely filed if it is filed before 180 days after the date of the order for relief or such later time as the Federal Rules of Bankruptcy Procedure may provide, *and except that in a case under chapter 13, a claim of a governmental unit for a tax with respect to a return filed under section 1308 shall be timely if the claim is filed on or before the date that is 60 days after the date on which such return was filed as required.*

(c) There shall be estimated for purpose of allowance under this section—

(1) any contingent or unliquidated claim, the fixing or liquidation of which, as the case may be, would unduly delay the administration of the case; or

(2) any right to payment arising from a right to an equitable remedy for breach of performance.

(d) Notwithstanding subsections (a) and (b) of this section, the court shall disallow any claim of any entity from which property is recoverable under section 542, 543, 550, or 553 of this title or that is a transferee of a transfer avoidable under section 522(f), 522(h), 544, 545, 547, 548, 549, or 724(a) of this title, unless such entity or transferee has paid the amount, or turned over any such property, for which such entity or transferee is liable under section 522(i), 542, 543, 550, or 553 of this title.

(e) (1) Notwithstanding subsections (a), (b), and (c) of this section and paragraph (2) of this subsection, the court shall disallow any claim for reimbursement or contribution of an entity that is liable with the debtor on or has secured the claim of a creditor, to the extent that—

(A) such creditor's claim against the estate is disallowed;

(B) such claim for reimbursement or contribution is contingent as of the time of allowance or disallowance of such claim for reimbursement or contribution; or

(C) such entity asserts a right of subrogation to the rights of such creditor under section 509 of this title.

(2) A claim for reimbursement or contribution of such an entity that becomes fixed after the commencement of the case shall be determined, and shall be allowed under subsection (a), (b), or (c) of this section, or disallowed under subsection (d) of this section, the same as if such claim had become fixed before the date of the filing of the petition.

(f) In an involuntary case, a claim arising in the ordinary course of the debtor's business or financial affairs after the commencement of the case but before the earlier of the appointment of a trustee and the order for relief shall be determined as of the date such claim arises, and shall be allowed under subsection (a), (b), or (c) of this section or disallowed under subsection (d) or (e) of this section, the same as if such claim had arisen before the date of the filing of the petition.

(g) *(1)* A claim arising from the rejection, under section 365 of this title or under a plan under chapter 9, 11, 12, or 13 of this title, of an executory contract or unexpired lease of the debtor that has not been assumed shall be determined, and shall be allowed under subsection (a), (b), or (c) of this section or disallowed under subsection (d) or (e) of this section, the same as if such claim had arisen before the date of the filing of the petition.

*(2) A claim for damages calculated in accordance with section 562 shall be allowed under subsection (a), (b), or (c), or disallowed under subsection (d) or (e), as if such claim had arisen before the date of the filing of the petition.*

(h) A claim arising from the recovery of property under section 522, 550, or 553 of this title shall be determined, and shall be allowed under subsection (a), (b), or (c) of this section, or disallowed under subsection (d) or (e) of this section, the same as if such claim had arisen before the date of the filing of the petition.

(i) A claim that does not arise until after the commencement of the case for a tax entitled to priority under section 507(a)(8) of this title shall be determined, and shall be allowed under subsection (a), (b), or (c) of this section, or disallowed under subsection (d) or (e) of this section, the same as if such claim had arisen before the date of the filing of the petition.

(j) A claim that has been allowed or disallowed may be reconsidered for cause. A reconsidered claim may be allowed or disallowed according to the equities of the case. Reconsideration of a claim under this subsection does not affect the validity of any payment or transfer from the estate made to a holder of an allowed claim on account of such allowed claim that is not reconsidered, but if a reconsidered claim is allowed and is of the same class as such holder's claim, such holder may not receive any additional payment or transfer from the estate on account of such holder's allowed claim until the holder of such reconsidered and allowed claim receives payment on account of such claim proportionate in value to that already received by such other holder. This subsection does not alter or modify the trustee's right to recover from a creditor any excess payment or transfer made to such creditor.

*(k) (1) The court, on the motion of the debtor and after a hearing, may reduce a claim filed under this section based in whole on an unsecured consumer debt by not more than 20 percent of the claim, if—*

*(A) the claim was filed by a creditor who unreasonably refused to negotiate a reasonable alternative repayment schedule proposed on behalf of the debtor by an approved nonprofit budget and credit counseling agency described in section 111;*

*(B) the offer of the debtor under subparagraph (A)—*

*(i) was made at least 60 days before the date of the filing of the petition; and*

*(ii) provided for payment of at least 60 percent of the amount of the debt over a period not to exceed the repayment period of the loan, or a reasonable extension thereof; and*

*(C) no part of the debt under the alternative repayment schedule is nondischargeable.*

*(2) The debtor shall have the burden of proving, by clear and convincing evidence, that—*

*(A) the creditor unreasonably refused to consider the debtor's proposal; and*

*(B) the proposed alternative repayment schedule was made prior to expiration of the 60-day period specified in paragraph (1)(B)(i).*

**Section 502**

(April 20, 2005, P. L. 109-8, Title IIA, § 201(a); Title VII, § 716(d); Title IX, § 910(b), 119 Stat. 23)

## HISTORY: ANCILLARY LAWS AND DIRECTIVES

**Amendments:**

**2005.** Act April 20, 2005(effective 180 days after enactment of April 20, 2005, as provided by § 1501(a) of P. L. 109-8), amends 11 USC § 502(b)(7) concerning timeliness of governmental claims in chapter 13; § 502(g)(2) concerning calculation of damage claims under § 562; and adds § 502(k) providing for potential reduction of claims by unsecured creditors.

**Other provisions:**

**Effective date and application of amendments made by Act April 20, 2005.** Act April 20, 2005, P.L. 109-8, Title XV, § 1501(a), 119 Stat. 23, provided that the amendments made to this section would be effective 180 days after enactment on April 20, 2005.

**Abridged Legislative History**

Section 716(d) amends section 502(b)(9) of the Bankruptcy Code to provide that in a chapter 13 case, a governmental unit's tax claim based on a return filed under section 1308 shall be deemed to be timely filed if the claim is filed within 60 days from the date on which such return is filed. Section 716(e) states the sense of the Congress that the Judicial Conference of the United States should propose for adoption official rules with respect an objection by a governmental unit to confirmation of a chapter 13 plan when such claim pertains to a tax return filed pursuant to section 1308.

(H. Report No. 109-31 to accompany S. 256, 109th Cong., 1st Sess. (2005) pp. 57, 104, 134–35; available at 2005 U.S.C.C.A.N. 88, at 127, 167–68, 194)

# § 503. Allowance of administrative expenses

(a) An entity may timely file a request for payment of an administrative expense, or may tardily file such request if permitted by the court for cause.

(b) After notice and a hearing, there shall be allowed administrative expenses, other than claims allowed under section 502(f) of this title, including—

(1) (A) ~~the actual, necessary costs and expenses of preserving the estate, including wages, salaries, or commissions for services rendered after the commencement of the case;~~ *the actual, necessary costs and expenses of preserving the estate including—*

*(i) wages, salaries, and commissions for services rendered after the commencement of the case; and*

*(ii) wages and benefits awarded pursuant to a judicial proceeding or a proceeding of the National Labor Relations Board as back pay attributable to any period of time occurring after commencement of the case under this title, as a result of a violation of Federal or State law by the debtor, without regard to the time of the occurrence of unlawful conduct on which such award is based or to whether any services were rendered, if the court determines that payment of wages and benefits by reason of the operation of this clause will not substantially increase the probability of layoff or termination of current employees, or of nonpayment of domestic support obligations, during the case under this title;*

(B) any tax—

(i) incurred by the estate, *whether secured or unsecured, including property taxes for which liability is in rem, in personam, or both,* except a tax of a kind specified in section 507(a)(8) of this title; or

(ii) attributable to an excessive allowance of a tentative carryback adjustment that the estate received, whether the taxable year to which such adjustment relates ended before or after the commencement of the case;~~and~~

(C) any fine, penalty, or reduction in credit relating to a tax of a kind specified in subparagraph (B) of this paragraph*; and*

*(D) notwithstanding the requirements of subsection (a), a governmental unit shall not be required to file a request for the payment of an expense described in subparagraph (B) or (C), as a condition of its being an allowed administrative expense;*

(2) compensation and reimbursement awarded under section 330(a) of this title;

(3) the actual, necessary expenses, other than compensation and reimbursement specified in paragraph (4) of this subsection, incurred by—

(A) a creditor that files a petition under section 303 of this title;

(B) a creditor that recovers, after the court's approval, for the benefit of the estate any property transferred or concealed by the debtor;

(C) a creditor in connection with the prosecution of a criminal offense relating to the case or to the business or property of the debtor;

(D) a creditor, an indenture trustee, an equity security holder, or a committee representing creditors or equity security holders other than a committee appointed under section 1102 of this title, in making a substantial contribution in a case under chapter 9 or 11 of this title;

(E) a custodian superseded under section 543 of this title, and compensation for the services of such custodian; or

(F) a member of a committee appointed under section 1102 of this title, if such expenses are incurred in the performance of the duties of such committee;

(4) reasonable compensation for professional services rendered by an attorney or an accountant of an entity whose expense is allowable under *subparagraph (A), (B), (C), (D), or (E) of* paragraph (3) of this subsection, based on the time, the nature, the extent, and the value of such services, and the cost of comparable services other than in a case under this title, and reimbursement for actual, necessary expenses incurred by such attorney or accountant;

(5) reasonable compensation for services rendered by an indenture trustee in making a substantial contribution in a case under chapter 9 or 11 of this title, based on the time, the nature, the extent, and the value of such services, and the cost of comparable services other than in a case under this title;~~ and~~

(6) the fees and mileage payable under chapter 119 of title 28;~~.~~

*(7) with respect to a nonresidential real property lease previously assumed under section 365, and subsequently rejected, a sum equal to all monetary obligations due, excluding those arising from or relating to a failure to operate or a penalty provision, for the period of 2 years following the later of the rejection date or the date of actual turnover of the premises, without reduction or setoff for any reason whatsoever except for sums actually received or to be received from an entity other than the debtor, and the claim for remaining sums due for the balance of the term of the lease shall be a claim under section 502(b)(6);*

*(8) the actual, necessary costs and expenses of closing a health care business incurred by a trustee or by a Federal agency (as defined in section 551(1) of title 5) or a department or agency of a State or political subdivision thereof, including any cost or expense incurred—*

*(A) in disposing of patient records in accordance with section 351; or*

*(B) in connection with transferring patients from the health care business that is in the process of being closed to another health care business; and*

*(9) the value of any goods received by the debtor within 20 days before the date of commencement of a case under this title in which*

*the goods have been sold to the debtor in the ordinary course of such debtor's business.*

*(c) Notwithstanding subsection (b), there shall neither be allowed, nor paid—*

*(1) a transfer made to, or an obligation incurred for the benefit of, an insider of the debtor for the purpose of inducing such person to remain with the debtor's business, absent a finding by the court based on evidence in the record that—*

*(A) the transfer or obligation is essential to retention of the person because the individual has a bona fide job offer from another business at the same or greater rate of compensation;*

*(B) the services provided by the person are essential to the survival of the business; and*

*(C) either—*

*(i) the amount of the transfer made to, or obligation incurred for the benefit of, the person is not greater than an amount equal to 10 times the amount of the mean transfer or obligation of a similar kind given to nonmanagement employees for any purpose during the calendar year in which the transfer is made or the obligation is incurred; or*

*(ii) if no such similar transfers were made to, or obligations were incurred for the benefit of, such nonmanagement employees during such calendar year, the amount of the transfer or obligation is not greater than an amount equal to 25 percent of the amount of any similar transfer or obligation made to or incurred for the benefit of such insider for any purpose during the calendar year before the year in which such transfer is made or obligation is incurred;*

*(2) a severance payment to an insider of the debtor, unless—*

*(A) the payment is part of a program that is generally applicable to all full-time employees; and*

*(B) the amount of the payment is not greater than 10 times the amount of the mean severance pay given to nonmanagement employees during the calendar year in which the payment is made; or*

*(3) other transfers or obligations that are outside the ordinary course of business and not justified by the facts and circumstances of the case, including transfers made to, or obligations incurred for the benefit of, officers, managers, or consultants hired after the date of the filing of the petition.*

**Section 503**

(April 20, 2005, P. L. 109-8, Title III, §§ 329, 331; Title IVB, § 445; Title VII, § 712(b), (c); Title XI, § 1103; Title XII, §§ 1208, 1227(b), 119 Stat. 23)

## HISTORY: ANCILLARY LAWS AND DIRECTIVES

**Amendments:**

**2005.** Act April 20, 2005(effective 180 days after enactment of April 20, 2005, as provided by § 1501(a) of P. L. 109-8), amends 11 USC § 503(b) concerning administrative claims; adds § 503(b)(7) concerning claims for nonresidential real property leases and (8) related to costs of health care businesses; and adds § 503(c) concerning insider claims.

**Other provisions:**

**Effective date and application of amendments made by Act April 20, 2005.** Act April 20, 2005, P.L. 109-8, Title XV, § 1501(a), 119 Stat. 23, provided that the amendments made to this section would be effective 180 days after enactment on April 20, 2005.

**Abridged Legislative History**

Clarification of Postpetition Wages and Benefits. Section 329 amends Bankruptcy Code section 503(b)(1)(A) to accord administrative expense status to certain back pay awards.

Priority for Administrative Expenses. Section 445 of the Act amends section 503(b) of the Bankruptcy Code to add a new administrative expense priority for a nonresidential real property lease that is assumed under section 365 and then subsequently rejected.

Section 712(b) amends section 503(b)(1)(B)(i) of the Bankruptcy Code to clarify that this provision applies to secured as well as unsecured tax claims, including property taxes based on liability that is in rem, in personam or both. Section 712(c) amends section 503(b)(1) to exempt a governmental unit from the requirement to file a request for payment of an administrative expense.

Health Care Business and Other Administrative Expenses. Section 1103 of the Act amends section 503(b) of the Bankruptcy Code to provide that the actual, necessary costs and expenses of closing a health care business (including the disposal of patient records or transferral of patients) incurred by a trustee, Federal agency, or a department or agency of a state are allowed administrative expenses.

Allowance of Administrative Expenses. Section 1208 of the Act amends section 503(b)(4) of the Bankruptcy Code to limit the types of compensable professional services rendered by an attorney or accountant that can qualify as administrative expenses in a bankruptcy case.

Section 1227(b) amends Bankruptcy Code section 503(b) to provide that the value of any goods received by a debtor not later than within 20 days prior to the commencement of a bankruptcy case in which the goods have been sold to the debtor in the ordinary course of the debtor's business is an allowed administrative expense. (H. Report No. 109-31 to accompany S. 256, 109th Cong., 1st Sess. (2005) pp. 84, 96, 103, 139, 142, 146; available at 2005 U.S.C.C.A.N. 88, at 150, 160–61, 167, 198, 201, 205)

## § 504. Sharing of compensation

(a) Except as provided in subsection (b) of this section, a person receiving compensation or reimbursement under section 503(b)(2) or 503(b)(4) of this title may not share or agree to share—

(1) any such compensation or reimbursement with another person; or

(2) any compensation or reimbursement received by another person under such sections.

(b) (1) A member, partner, or regular associate in a professional association, corporation, or partnership may share compensation or reimbursement received under section 503(b)(2) or 503(b)(4) of this title with another member, partner, or regular associate in such association, corporation, or partnership, and may share in any compensation or reimbursement received under such sections by another member, partner, or regular associate in such association, corporation, or partnership.

(2) An attorney for a creditor that files a petition under section

303 of this title may share compensation and reimbursement received under section 503(b)(4) of this title with any other attorney contributing to the services rendered or expenses incurred by such creditor's attorney.

*(c) This section shall not apply with respect to sharing, or agreeing to share, compensation with a bona fide public service attorney referral program that operates in accordance with non-Federal law regulating attorney referral services and with rules of professional responsibility applicable to attorney acceptance of referrals.*

**Section 504**

(April 20, 2005, P. L. 109-8, Title III, § 326, 119 Stat. 23)

## HISTORY: ANCILLARY LAWS AND DIRECTIVES

**Amendments:**

**2005.** Act April 20, 2005(effective 180 days after enactment of April 20, 2005, as provided by § 1501(a) of P. L. 109-8), adds 11 USC § 504(c) restricting the application of § 504 as to bona fide public service attorney referral programs.

**Other provisions:**

**Effective date and application of amendments made by Act April 20, 2005.** Act April 20, 2005, P.L. 109-8, Title XV, § 1501(a), 119 Stat. 23, provided that the amendments made to this section would be effective 180 days after enactment on April 20, 2005.

**Abridged Legislative History**

Sharing of Compensation. Section 326 amends Bankruptcy Code section 504 to create a limited exception to the prohibition against fee sharing. (H. Report No. 109-31 to accompany S. 256, 109th Cong., 1st Sess. (2005) p. 83; available at 2005 U.S.C.C.A.N. 88, at 149)

# § 505. Determination of tax liability

(a) (1) Except as provided in paragraph (2) of this subsection, the court may determine the amount or legality of any tax, any fine or penalty relating to a tax, or any addition to tax, whether or not previously assessed, whether or not paid, and whether or not contested before and adjudicated by a judicial or administrative tribunal of competent jurisdiction.

(2) The court may not so determine—

(A) the amount or legality of a tax, fine, penalty, or addition to tax if such amount or legality was contested before and adjudicated by a judicial or administrative tribunal of competent jurisdiction before the commencement of the case under this title; ~~or~~

(B) any right of the estate to a tax refund, before the earlier of—

(i) 120 days after the trustee properly requests such refund from the governmental unit from which such refund is claimed; or

(ii) a determination by such governmental unit of such request~~.~~*; or*

*(C) the amount or legality of any amount arising in connection with an ad valorem tax on real or personal property of the estate, if the applicable period for contesting or redetermining that amount under any law (other than a bankruptcy law) has expired.*

*(b) (1) (A) The clerk shall maintain a list under which a Federal, State, or local governmental unit responsible for the collection of taxes within the district may—*

*(i) designate an address for service of requests under this subsection; and*

*(ii) describe where further information concerning additional requirements for filing such requests may be found.*

*(B) If such governmental unit does not designate an address and provide such address to the clerk under subparagraph (A), any request made under this subsection may be served at the address for the filing of a tax return or protest with the appropriate taxing authority of such governmental unit.*

(~~b~~2) A trustee may request a determination of any unpaid liability of the estate for any tax incurred during the administration of the case by submitting a tax return for such tax and a request for such a determination to the governmental unit charged with responsibility for collection or determination of such tax *at the address and in the manner designated in paragraph (1)*. Unless such return is fraudulent, or contains a material misrepresentation, *the estate,* the trustee, the debtor, and any successor to the debtor are discharged from any liability for such tax—

(~~1~~*A*) upon payment of the tax shown on such return, if—

(~~A~~*i*) such governmental unit does not notify the trustee, within 60 days after such request, that such return has been selected for examination; or

(~~B~~*ii*) such governmental unit does not complete such an examination and notify the trustee of any tax due, within 180 days after such request or within such additional time as the court, for cause, permits;

(~~2~~*B*) upon payment of the tax determined by the court, after notice and a hearing, after completion by such governmental unit of such examination; or

(~~3~~*C*) upon payment of the tax determined by such governmental unit to be due.

(c) Notwithstanding section 362 of this title, after determination by the court of a tax under this section, the governmental unit charged with responsibility for collection of such tax may assess such tax against the estate, the debtor, or a successor to the debtor, as the case may be, subject to any otherwise applicable law.

**Section 505**

(April 20, 2005, P. L. 109-8, Title VII, §§ 701(b), 703, 715, 119 Stat. 23)

## HISTORY: ANCILLARY LAWS AND DIRECTIVES

**Amendments:**

**2005.** Act April 20, 2005(effective 180 days after enactment of April 20, 2005, as provided by § 1501(a) of P. L. 109-8), adds 11 USC § 505(a)(2)(C) for determining ad valorem taxes; adds § 505(b) requiring the clerk to maintain a list of tax units and addresses; and amends § 505(b)(2) to make noticing consistent with the additions.

**Other provisions:**
**Effective date and application of amendments made by Act April 20, 2005.** Act April 20, 2005, P.L. 109-8, Title XV, § 1501(a), 119 Stat. 23, provided that the amendments made to this section would be effective 180 days after enactment on April 20, 2005.

**Abridged Legislative History**

Section 701(b) amends section 505(a)(2) of the Bankruptcy Code to prevent a bankruptcy court from determining the amount or legality of an ad valorem tax on real or personal property if the applicable period for contesting or redetermining the amount of the claim under nonbankruptcy law has expired.

Notice of Request for a Determination of Taxes. Section 703 of the Act amends section 505(b) of the Bankruptcy Code to require the clerk of each district to maintain a list of addresses designated by governmental units for service of section 505 requests.

Discharge of the Estate's Liability for Unpaid Taxes. Under the Bankruptcy Code, a trustee or debtor in possession may request a prompt audit to determine postpetition tax liabilities incurred by the bankruptcy estate. (H. Report No. 109-31 to accompany S. 256, 109th Cong., 1st Sess. (2005) pp. 100, 103; available at 2005 U.S.C.C.A.N. 88, at 164–65, 167)

## § 506. Determination of secured status

(a) *(1)* An allowed claim of a creditor secured by a lien on property in which the estate has an interest, or that is subject to ~~set off~~ *setoff* under section 553 of this title, is a secured claim to the extent of the value of such creditor's interest in the estate's interest in such property, or to the extent of the amount subject to setoff, as the case may be, and is an unsecured claim to the extent that the value of such creditor's interest or the amount so subject to setoff is less than the amount of such allowed claim. Such value shall be determined in light of the purpose of the valuation and of the proposed disposition or use of such property, and in conjunction with any hearing on such disposition or use or on a plan affecting such creditor's interest.

*(2) If the debtor is an individual in a case under chapter 7 or 13, such value with respect to personal property securing an allowed claim shall be determined based on the replacement value of such property as of the date of the filing of the petition without deduction for costs of sale or marketing. With respect to property acquired for personal, family, or household purposes, replacement value shall mean the price a retail merchant would charge for property of that kind considering the age and condition of the property at the time value is determined.*

(b) To the extent that an allowed secured claim is secured by property the value of which, after any recovery under subsection (c) of this section, is greater than the amount of such claim, there shall be allowed to the holder of such claim, interest on such claim, and any reasonable fees, costs, or charges provided for under the agreement *or State statute* under which such claim arose.

(c) The trustee may recover from property securing an allowed secured claim the reasonable, necessary costs and expenses of preserving, or disposing of, such property to the extent of any benefit to the holder of such claim, *including the payment of all ad valorem property taxes with respect to the property*.

(d) To the extent that a lien secures a claim against the debtor that is not an allowed secured claim, such lien is void, unless—

(1) such claim was disallowed only under section 502(b)(5) or 502(e) of this title; or

(2) such claim is not an allowed secured claim due only to the failure of any entity to file a proof of such claim under section 501 of this title.

**Section 506**

(April 20, 2005, P. L. 109-8, Title III, § 327; Title VII, § 712(d), 119 Stat. 23)

## HISTORY: ANCILLARY LAWS AND DIRECTIVES

**Amendments:**

**2005.** Act April 20, 2005(effective 180 days after enactment of April 20, 2005, as provided by § 1501(a) of P. L. 109-8), adds 11 USC § 506(a)(2) to establish that value in chapter 7 or 13 cases will be determined on replacement value, and amends § 506(c) to provide for recovery of the costs of ad valorem taxes paid by the trustee.

**Other provisions:**

**Effective date and application of amendments made by Act April 20, 2005.** Act April 20, 2005, P.L. 109-8, Title XV, § 1501(a), 119 Stat. 23, provided that the amendments made to this section would be effective 180 days after enactment on April 20, 2005.

**Abridged Legislative History**

Fair Valuation of Collateral. Section 327 of the Act amends section 506(a) of the Bankruptcy Code to provide that the value of an allowed claim secured by personal property that is an asset in an individual debtor's chapter 7 or 13 case is determined based on the replacement value of such property as of the filing date of the bankruptcy case without deduction for selling or marketing costs. With respect to property acquired for personal, family, or household purposes, replacement value is the price a retail merchant would charge for property of that kind considering the age and condition of the property at the time its value is determined.

712(d)(1) amends section 506(b) to provide that to the extent that an allowed claim is oversecured, the holder is entitled to interest and any reasonable fees, costs, or charges provided for under state law. (H. Report No. 109-31 to accompany S. 256, 109th Cong., 1st Sess. (2005) pp. 83, 103; available at 2005 U.S.C.C.A.N. 88, at 149, 167)

# § 507. Priorities

(a) The following expenses and claims have priority in the following order:

*(1) First:*

*(A) Allowed unsecured claims for domestic support obligations that, as of the date of the filing of the petition in a case under this title, are owed to or recoverable by a spouse, former spouse, or child of the debtor, or such child's parent, legal guardian, or responsible relative, without regard to whether the claim is filed by such person or is filed by a governmental unit on behalf of such person, on the condition that funds received under this paragraph by a governmental unit under this title after the date of the filing of the petition shall be applied and distributed in accordance with applicable nonbankruptcy law.*

*(B) Subject to claims under subparagraph (A), allowed unsecured claims for domestic support obligations that, as of the date of the filing of the petition, are assigned by a spouse, former spouse, child of the debtor, or such child's parent, legal guardian, or responsible relative to a governmental unit (unless such obligation is assigned voluntarily by the spouse, former spouse, child, parent, legal guardian, or responsible relative of the child for the purpose of collecting the debt) or are owed directly to or recoverable by a governmental unit under applicable nonbankruptcy law, on the condition that funds received under this paragraph by a governmental unit under this title after the date of the filing of the petition be applied and distributed in accordance with applicable nonbankruptcy law.*

*(C) If a trustee is appointed or elected under section 701, 702, 703, 1104, 1202, or 1302, the administrative expenses of the trustee allowed under paragraphs (1)(A), (2), and (6) of section 503(b) shall be paid before payment of claims under subparagraphs (A) and (B), to the extent that the trustee administers assets that are otherwise available for the payment of such claims.*

(~~1~~*2*) ~~First~~ *Second*, administrative expenses allowed under section 503(b) of this title, and any fees and charges assessed against the estate under chapter 123 of title 28.

(~~2~~*3*) ~~Second~~ *Third*, unsecured claims allowed under section 502(f) of this title.

(~~3~~*4*) ~~Third~~ *Fourth*, allowed unsecured claims, but only to the extent of ~~$4,925~~ ~~[$4,000]~~*$10,000* for each individual or corporation, as the case may be, earned within *180* ~~90~~ days before the date of the filing of the petition or the date of the cessation of the debtor's business, whichever occurs first, for—

(A) wages, salaries, or commissions, including vacation, severance, and sick leave pay earned by an individual; or

(B) sales commissions earned by an individual or by a corporation with only 1 employee, acting as an independent contractor in the sale of goods or services for the debtor in the ordinary course of the debtor's business if, and only if, during the 12 months preceding that date, at least 75 percent of the amount that the individual or corporation earned by acting as an independent contractor in the sale of goods or services was earned from the debtor~~;~~.

(~~4~~*5*) ~~Fourth~~ *Fifth*, allowed unsecured claims for contributions to an employee benefit plan—

(A) arising from services rendered within 180 days before the date of the filing of the petition or the date of the cessation of the debtor's business, whichever occurs first; but only

(B) for each such plan, to the extent of—

(i) the number of employees covered by each such plan multiplied by ~~$4,925~~[~~$4,000~~] *$10,000*; less

(ii) the aggregate amount paid to such employees under

paragraph (*4*~~3~~) of this subsection, plus the aggregate amount paid by the estate on behalf of such employees to any other employee benefit plan.

(~~5~~*6*) ~~Fifth~~ *Sixth*, allowed unsecured claims of persons—

(A) engaged in the production or raising of grain, as defined in section 557(b) of this title, against a debtor who owns or operates a grain storage facility, as defined in section 557(b) of this title, for grain or the proceeds of grain, or

(B) engaged as a United States fisherman against a debtor who has acquired fish or fish produce from a fisherman through a sale or conversion, and who is engaged in operating a fish produce storage or processing facility—

but only to the extent of [$4,000] for each such individual.

(~~6~~*7*) ~~Sixth~~ *Seventh*, allowed unsecured claims of individuals, to the extent of $1,800 [$2,225] for each such individual, arising from the deposit, before the commencement of the case, of money in connection with the purchase, lease, or rental of property, or the purchase of services, for the personal, family, or household use of such individuals, that were not delivered or provided.

~~(7) Seventh, allowed claims for debts to a spouse, former spouse, or child of the debtor, for alimony to, maintenance for, or support of such spouse or child, in connection with a separation agreement, divorce decree or other order of a court of record, determination made in accordance with State or territorial law by a governmental unit, or property settlement agreement, but not to the extent that such debt—~~

~~(A) is assigned to another entity, voluntarily, by operation of law, or otherwise; or~~

~~(B) includes a liability designated as alimony, maintenance, or support, unless such liability is actually in the nature of alimony, maintenance or support.~~

(8) Eighth, allowed unsecured claims of governmental units, only to the extent that such claims are for—

(A) a tax on or measured by income or gross receipts *for a taxable year ending on or before the date of the filing of the petition* —

(i) ~~for a taxable year ending on or before the date of the filing of the petition~~ for which a return, if required, is last due, including extensions, after three years before the date of the filing of the petition;

(ii) ~~assessed within 240 days, plus any time plus 30 days during which an offer in compromise with respect to such tax that was made within 240 days after such assessment was pending, before the date of the filing of the petition; or~~*assessed within 240 days before the date of the filing of the petition, exclusive of—*

*(I) any time during which an offer in compromise with re-*

*spect to that tax was pending or in effect during that 240-day period, plus 30 days; and*

*(II) any time during which a stay of proceedings against collections was in effect in a prior case under this title during that 240-day period, plus 90 days.*

(iii) other than a tax of a kind specified in section 523(a)(1)(B) or 523(a)(1)(C) of this title, not assessed before, but assessable, under applicable law or by agreement, after, the commencement of the case;

(B) a property tax ~~assessed~~ *incurred* before the commencement of the case and last payable without penalty after one year before the date of the filing of the petition;

(C) a tax required to be collected or withheld and for which the debtor is liable in whatever capacity;

(D) an employment tax on a wage, salary, or commission of a kind specified in paragraph (~~3~~*4*) of this subsection earned from the debtor before the date of the filing of the petition, whether or not actually paid before such date, for which a return is last due, under applicable law or under any extension, after three years before the date of the filing of the petition;

(E) an excise tax on—

(i) a transaction occurring before the date of the filing of the petition for which a return, if required, is last due, under applicable law or under any extension, after three years before the date of the filing of the petition; or

(ii) if a return is not required, a transaction occurring during the three years immediately preceding the date of the filing of the petition;

(F) a customs duty arising out of the importation of merchandise—

(i) entered for consumption within one year before the date of the filing of the petition;

(ii) covered by an entry liquidated or reliquidated within one year before the date of the filing of the petition; or

(iii) entered for consumption within four years before the date of the filing of the petition but unliquidated on such date, if the Secretary of the Treasury certifies that failure to liquidate such entry was due to an investigation pending on such date into assessment of antidumping or countervailing duties or fraud, or if information needed for the proper appraisement or classification of such merchandise was not available to the appropriate customs officer before such date; or

(G) a penalty related to a claim of a kind specified in this paragraph and in compensation for actual pecuniary loss.

*An otherwise applicable time period specified in this paragraph shall be suspended for any period during which a governmental unit is prohibited under applicable nonbankruptcy law from collecting a tax as a result of a request by the debtor for a hearing and an appeal of any collection action taken or proposed against the debtor, plus 90 days; plus any time during which the stay of proceedings was in effect in a prior case under this title or during which collection was precluded by the existence of 1 or more confirmed plans under this title, plus 90 days.*

(9) Ninth, allowed unsecured claims based upon any commitment by the debtor to a Federal depository institutions regulatory agency (or predecessor to such agency) to maintain the capital of an insured depository institution.

*(10) Tenth, allowed claims for death or personal injury resulting from the operation of a motor vehicle or vessel if such operation was unlawful because the debtor was intoxicated from using alcohol, a drug, or another substance.*

(b) If the trustee, under section 362, 363, or 364 of this title, provides adequate protection of the interest of a holder of a claim secured by a lien on property of the debtor and if, notwithstanding such protection, such creditor has a claim allowable under subsection (a)(2~~1~~) of this section arising from the stay of action against such property under section 362 of this title, from the use, sale, or lease of such property under section 363 of this title, or from the granting of a lien under section 364(d) of this title, then such creditor's claim under such subsection shall have priority over every other claim allowable under such subsection.

(c) For the purpose of subsection (a) of this section, a claim of a governmental unit arising from an erroneous refund or credit of a tax has the same priority as a claim for the tax to which such refund or credit relates.

(d) An entity that is subrogated to the rights of a holder of a claim of a kind specified in subsection (a)(1~~3~~), (a)(4), (a)(5), (a)(6), (a)(7), (a)(8), or (a)(9) of this section is not subrogated to the right of the holder of such claim to priority under such subsection.

**Section 507**

(April 20, 2005, P. L. 109-8, Title IIB, § 212; Title IIC, § 223; Title VII, §§ 705, 706; Title XIV, § 1401; Title XV, § 1502(a)(1), 119 Stat. 23)

## HISTORY: ANCILLARY LAWS AND DIRECTIVES

**Amendments:**

**2005.** Act April 20, 2005(effective 180 days after enactment of April 20, 2005, as provided by § 1501(a) of P. L. 109-8), adds 11 USC § 507's priorities, principally moving domestic support obligations to § 507(a)(1), but also increasing the amount of priority under § 507(a)(5) and (6), and adding to § 507(a)(8) clarification that tax periods are tolled by pending bankruptcy cases and tax collection appeals.

**Other provisions:**

**Effective date and application of amendments made by Act April 20, 2005.** Act April 20, 2005, P.L. 109-8, Title XV, § 1501(a), 119 Stat. 23, provided that the amendments made to this section would be effective 180 days after enactment on April 20, 2005.

**Abridged Legislative History**

Priorities for Claims for Domestic Support Obligations. Section 212 of the Act amends section 507(a) of the Bankruptcy Code to accord first priority in payment to allowed unsecured claims for domestic support obligations that, as of the petition date, are owed to or recoverable by a spouse, former spouse, or child of the debtor, or the parent, legal guardian, or responsible relative of such child, without regard to whether such claim is filed by the claimant or by a governmental unit on behalf of such claimant, on the condition that funds received by such unit under this provision be applied and distributed in accordance with nonbankruptcy law.

Additional Amendments to Title 11, United States Code. Section 223 of the Act amends section 507(a) of the Bankruptcy Code to accord a tenth-level priority to claims for death or personal injuries resulting from the debtor's operation of a motor vehicle or vessel while intoxicated.

Priority of Tax Claims. Under current law, a tax claim is entitled to be treated as a priority claim if it arises within certain specified time periods. In the case of income taxes, a priority arises, among other time periods, if the tax return was due within three years of the filing of the bankruptcy petition or if the assessment of the tax was made within 240 days of the filing of the petition. The 240-day period is tolled during the time that an offer in compromise is pending (plus 30 days).

Employee Wage and Benefit Priorities. Section 1401 of the Act amends Bankruptcy Code section 507(a) to provide heightened protections for employees by increasing the monetary cap on wage and employee benefit claims entitled to priority under the Bankruptcy Code from $4,650 to $10,000 and lengthens the reachback period for wage claims from 90 days to 180 days.

(H. Report No. 109-31 to accompany S. 256, 109th Cong., 1st Sess. (2005) pp. 59–60, 63, 101, 154–55; available at 2005 U.S.C.C.A.N. 88, at 129, 132, 165, 211–12)

# § 508. Effect of distribution other than under this title

~~(a) If a creditor receives, in a foreign proceeding, payment of, or a transfer of property on account of, a claim that is allowed under this title, such creditor may not receive any payment under this title on account of such claim until each of the other holders of claims on account of which such holders are entitled to share equally with such creditor under this title has received payment under this title equal in value to the consideration received by such creditor in such foreign proceeding.~~

~~(b)~~ If a creditor of a partnership debtor receives, from a general partner that is not a debtor in a case under chapter 7 of this title, payment of, or a transfer of property on account of, a claim that is allowed under this title and that is not secured by a lien on property of such partner, such creditor may not receive any payment under this title on account of such claim until each of the other holders of claims on account of which such holders are entitled to share equally with such creditor under this title has received payment under this title equal in value to the consideration received by such creditor from such general partner.

**Section 508**

(April 20, 2005, P. L. 109-8, Title VIII, § 802(d)(7), 119 Stat. 23)

## HISTORY: ANCILLARY LAWS AND DIRECTIVES

**Amendments:**

**2005.** Act April 20, 2005(effective 180 days after enactment of April 20, 2005, as provided by § 1501(a) of P. L. 109-8), deletes 11 USC § 507(a).

**Other provisions:**

**Effective date and application of amendments made by Act April 20, 2005.** Act April 20, 2005, P.L. 109-8, Title XV, § 1501(a), 119 Stat. 23, provided that the amendments made to this section would be effective 180 days after enactment on April 20, 2005.

**Abridged Legislative History**

Section 802(d) amends section 109 of the Bankruptcy Code to permit recognition of foreign proceedings involving foreign insurance companies and involving foreign banks which do not have a branch or agency in the United States (as defined in 12 U.S.C. 3101). (H. Report No. 109-31 to accompany S. 256, 109th Cong., 1st Sess. (2005) pp. 118–19; available at 2005 U.S.C.C.A.N. 88, at 181)

## § 509. Claims of codebtors

(a) Except as provided in subsection (b) or (c) of this section, an entity that is liable with the debtor on, or that has secured, a claim of a creditor against the debtor, and that pays such claim, is subrogated to the rights of such creditor to the extent of such payment.

(b) Such entity is not subrogated to the rights of such creditor to the extent that—

(1) a claim of such entity for reimbursement or contribution on account of such payment of such creditor's claim is—

(A) allowed under section 502 of this title;

(B) disallowed other than under section 502(e) of this title; or

(C) subordinated under section 510 of this title; or

(2) as between the debtor and such entity, such entity received the consideration for the claim held by such creditor.

(c) The court shall subordinate to the claim of a creditor and for the benefit of such creditor an allowed claim, by way of subrogation under this section, or for reimbursement or contribution of an entity that is liable with the debtor on, or that has secured, such creditor's claim, until such creditor's claim is paid in full, either through payments under this title or otherwise.

## § 510. Subordination

(a) A subordination agreement is enforceable in a case under this title to the same extent that such agreement is enforceable under applicable nonbankruptcy law.

(b) For the purpose of distribution under this title, a claim arising from rescission of a purchase or sale of a security of the debtor or of an affiliate of the debtor, for damages arising from the purchase or sale of such a security, or for reimbursement or contribution allowed under section 502 on account of such a claim, shall be subordinated to all claims or interests that are senior to or equal the claim or interest represented by such security, except that if such security is common stock, such claim has the same priority as common stock.

(c) Notwithstanding subsections (a) and (b) of this section, after notice and a hearing, the court may—

(1) under principles of equitable subordination, subordinate for purposes of distribution all or part of an allowed claim to all or part of another allowed claim or all or part of an allowed interest to all or part of another allowed interest; or

(2) order that any lien securing such a subordinated claim be transferred to the estate.

## *§ 511. Rate of interest on tax claims*

*(a) If any provision of this title requires the payment of interest on a tax claim or on an administrative expense tax, or the payment of interest to enable a creditor to receive the present value of the allowed amount of a tax claim, the rate of interest shall be the rate determined under applicable nonbankruptcy law.*

*(b) In the case of taxes paid under a confirmed plan under this title, the rate of interest shall be determined as of the calendar month in which the plan is confirmed.*

**Section 511**

(April 20, 2005, P. L. 109-8, Title VII, § 704(a), 119 Stat. 23)

### HISTORY: ANCILLARY LAWS AND DIRECTIVES

**Amendments:**

**2005.** Act April 20, 2005(effective 180 days after enactment of April 20, 2005, as provided by § 1501(a) of P. L. 109-8), adds new 11 USC § 511.

**Other provisions:**

**Effective date and application of amendments made by Act April 20, 2005.** Act April 20, 2005, P.L. 109-8, Title XV, § 1501(a), 119 Stat. 23, provided that the amendments made to this section would be effective 180 days after enactment on April 20, 2005.

**Abridged Legislative History**

Rate of Interest on Tax Claims. Section 704 of the Act amends the Bankruptcy Code to add section 511 for the purpose of simplifying the interest rate calculation. It provides that for all tax claims (federal, state, and local), including administrative expense taxes, the interest rate shall be determined in accordance with applicable nonbankruptcy law. (H. Report No. 109-31 to accompany S. 256, 109th Cong., 1st Sess. (2005) p. 101; available at 2005 U.S.C.C.A.N. 88, at 165)

# Subchapter II——Debtor's Duties and Benefits

## § 521. Debtor's duties

*(a)* The debtor shall—

(1) file ~~a list of creditors, and unless the court orders otherwise, a schedule of assets and liabilities, a schedule of current income and current expenditures, and a statement of the debtor's financial affairs;—~~

*(A) a list of creditors; and*

*(B) unless the court orders otherwise—*

*(i) a schedule of assets and liabilities;*

*(ii) a schedule of current income and current expenditures;*

*(iii) a statement of the debtor's financial affairs and, if section 342(b) applies, a certificate—*

*(I) of an attorney whose name is indicated on the petition as the attorney for the debtor, or a bankruptcy petition preparer signing the petition under section 110(b)(1), indicat-*

*ing that such attorney or the bankruptcy petition preparer delivered to the debtor the notice required by section 342(b); or*

*(II) if no attorney is so indicated, and no bankruptcy petition preparer signed the petition, of the debtor that such notice was received and read by the debtor;*

*(iv) copies of all payment advices or other evidence of payment received within 60 days before the date of the filing of the petition, by the debtor from any employer of the debtor;*

*(v) a statement of the amount of monthly net income, itemized to show how the amount is calculated; and*

*(vi) a statement disclosing any reasonably anticipated increase in income or expenditures over the 12-month period following the date of the filing of the petition;*

(2) if an individual debtor's schedule of assets and liabilities includes ~~consumer~~ debts which are secured by property of the estate—

(A) within thirty days after the date of the filing of a petition under chapter 7 of this title or on or before the date of the meeting of creditors, whichever is earlier, or within such additional time as the court, for cause, within such period fixes, the debtor shall file with the clerk a statement of his intention with respect to the retention or surrender of such property and, if applicable, specifying that such property is claimed as exempt, that the debtor intends to redeem such property, or that the debtor intends to reaffirm debts secured by such property;

(B) within *30 days after the first date set for the meeting of creditors under section 341(a)*~~forty-five days after the filing of a notice of intent under this section~~, or within such additional time as the court, for cause, within such ~~forty-five~~ *30*-day period fixes, the debtor shall perform his intention with respect to such property, as specified by subparagraph (A) of this paragraph; and

(C) nothing in subparagraphs (A) and (B) of this paragraph shall alter the debtor's or the trustee's rights with regard to such property under this title, *except as provided in section 362(h)*;

(3) if a trustee is serving in the case *or an auditor serving under section 586(f) of title 28*, cooperate with the trustee as necessary to enable the trustee to perform the trustee's duties under this title;

(4) if a trustee is serving in the case *or an auditor serving under section 586(f) of title 28*, surrender to the trustee all property of the estate and any recorded information, including books, documents, records, and papers, relating to property of the estate, whether or not immunity is granted under section 344 of this title;~~ and~~

(5) appear at the hearing required under section 524(d) of this title~~.~~*; and*

*(6) in a case under chapter 7 of this title in which the debtor is an individual, not retain possession of personal property as to which a creditor has an allowed claim for the purchase price secured in*

*whole or in part by an interest in such personal property unless the debtor, not later than 45 days after the first meeting of creditors under section 341(a), either—*

*(A) enters into an agreement with the creditor pursuant to section 524(c) with respect to the claim secured by such property; or*

*(B) redeems such property from the security interest pursuant to section 722.*

*If the debtor fails to so act within the 45-day period referred to in paragraph (6), the stay under section 362(a) is terminated with respect to the personal property of the estate or of the debtor which is affected, such property shall no longer be property of the estate, and the creditor may take whatever action as to such property as is permitted by applicable nonbankruptcy law, unless the court determines on the motion of the trustee filed before the expiration of such 45-day period, and after notice and a hearing, that such property is of consequential value or benefit to the estate, orders appropriate adequate protection of the creditor's interest, and orders the debtor to deliver any collateral in the debtor's possession to the trustee; and*

*(7) unless a trustee is serving in the case, continue to perform the obligations required of the administrator (as defined in section 3 of the Employee Retirement Income Security Act of 1974) of an employee benefit plan if at the time of the commencement of the case the debtor (or any entity designated by the debtor) served as such administrator.*

*(b) In addition to the requirements under subsection (a), a debtor who is an individual shall file with the court—*

*(1) a certificate from the approved nonprofit budget and credit counseling agency that provided the debtor services under section 109(h) describing the services provided to the debtor; and*

*(2) a copy of the debt repayment plan, if any, developed under section 109(h) through the approved nonprofit budget and credit counseling agency referred to in paragraph (1).*

*(c) In addition to meeting the requirements under subsection (a), a debtor shall file with the court a record of any interest that a debtor has in an education individual retirement account (as defined in section 530(b)(1) of the Internal Revenue Code of 1986) or under a qualified State tuition program (as defined in section 529(b)(1) of such Code).*

*(d) If the debtor fails timely to take the action specified in subsection (a)(6) of this section, or in paragraphs (1) and (2) of section 362(h), with respect to property which a lessor or bailor owns and has leased, rented, or bailed to the debtor or as to which a creditor holds a security interest not otherwise voidable under section 522(f), 544, 545, 547, 548, or 549, nothing in this title shall prevent or limit the operation of a provision in the underlying lease or agreement that has the effect of placing the debtor in default under such lease or agreement by reason*

*of the occurrence, pendency, or existence of a proceeding under this title or the insolvency of the debtor. Nothing in this subsection shall be deemed to justify limiting such a provision in any other circumstance.*

*(e) (1) If the debtor in a case under chapter 7 or 13 is an individual and if a creditor files with the court at any time a request to receive a copy of the petition, schedules, and statement of financial affairs filed by the debtor, then the court shall make such petition, such schedules, and such statement available to such creditor.*

*(2) (A) The debtor shall provide—*

*(i) not later than 7 days before the date first set for the first meeting of creditors, to the trustee a copy of the Federal income tax return required under applicable law (or at the election of the debtor, a transcript of such return) for the most recent tax year ending immediately before the commencement of the case and for which a Federal income tax return was filed; and*

*(ii) at the same time the debtor complies with clause (i), a copy of such return (or if elected under clause (i), such transcript) to any creditor that timely requests such copy.*

*(B) If the debtor fails to comply with clause (i) or (ii) of subparagraph (A), the court shall dismiss the case unless the debtor demonstrates that the failure to so comply is due to circumstances beyond the control of the debtor.*

*(C) If a creditor requests a copy of such tax return or such transcript and if the debtor fails to provide a copy of such tax return or such transcript to such creditor at the time the debtor provides such tax return or such transcript to the trustee, then the court shall dismiss the case unless the debtor demonstrates that the failure to provide a copy of such tax return or such transcript is due to circumstances beyond the control of the debtor.*

*(3) If a creditor in a case under chapter 13 files with the court at any time a request to receive a copy of the plan filed by the debtor, then the court shall make available to such creditor a copy of the plan—*

*(A) at a reasonable cost; and*

*(B) not later than 5 days after such request is filed.*

*(f) At the request of the court, the United States trustee, or any party in interest in a case under chapter 7, 11, or 13, a debtor who is an individual shall file with the court—*

*(1) at the same time filed with the taxing authority, a copy of each Federal income tax return required under applicable law (or at the election of the debtor, a transcript of such tax return) with respect to each tax year of the debtor ending while the case is pending under such chapter;*

*(2) at the same time filed with the taxing authority, each Federal income tax return required under applicable law (or at the election of the debtor, a transcript of such tax return) that had not been filed with such authority as of the date of the commencement of the case*

*and that was subsequently filed for any tax year of the debtor ending in the 3-year period ending on the date of the commencement of the case;*

*(3) a copy of each amendment to any Federal income tax return or transcript filed with the court under paragraph (1) or (2); and*

*(4) in a case under chapter 13—*

*(A) on the date that is either 90 days after the end of such tax year or 1 year after the date of the commencement of the case, whichever is later, if a plan is not confirmed before such later date; and*

*(B) annually after the plan is confirmed and until the case is closed, not later than the date that is 45 days before the anniversary of the confirmation of the plan;*

*a statement, under penalty of perjury, of the income and expenditures of the debtor during the tax year of the debtor most recently concluded before such statement is filed under this paragraph, and of the monthly income of the debtor, that shows how income, expenditures, and monthly income are calculated.*

*(g) (1) A statement referred to in subsection (f)(4) shall disclose—*

*(A) the amount and sources of the income of the debtor;*

*(B) the identity of any person responsible with the debtor for the support of any dependent of the debtor; and*

*(C) the identity of any person who contributed, and the amount contributed, to the household in which the debtor resides.*

*(2) The tax returns, amendments, and statement of income and expenditures described in subsections (e)(2)(A) and (f) shall be available to the United States trustee (or the bankruptcy administrator, if any), the trustee, and any party in interest for inspection and copying, subject to the requirements of section 315(c) of the Bankruptcy Abuse Prevention and Consumer Protection Act of 2005.*

*(h) If requested by the United States trustee or by the trustee, the debtor shall provide—*

*(1) a document that establishes the identity of the debtor, including a driver's license, passport, or other document that contains a photograph of the debtor; or*

*(2) such other personal identifying information relating to the debtor that establishes the identity of the debtor.*

*(i) (1) Subject to paragraphs (2) and (4) and notwithstanding section 707(a), if an individual debtor in a voluntary case under chapter 7 or 13 fails to file all of the information required under subsection (a)(1) within 45 days after the date of the filing of the petition, the case shall be automatically dismissed effective on the 46th day after the date of the filing of the petition.*

*(2) Subject to paragraph (4) and with respect to a case described in paragraph (1), any party in interest may request the court to enter an order dismissing the case. If requested, the court shall enter an order of dismissal not later than 5 days after such request.*

*(3) Subject to paragraph (4) and upon request of the debtor made within 45 days after the date of the filing of the petition described in paragraph (1), the court may allow the debtor an additional period of not to exceed 45 days to file the information required under subsection (a)(1) if the court finds justification for extending the period for the filing.*

*(4) Notwithstanding any other provision of this subsection, on the motion of the trustee filed before the expiration of the applicable period of time specified in paragraph (1), (2), or (3), and after notice and a hearing, the court may decline to dismiss the case if the court finds that the debtor attempted in good faith to file all the information required by subsection (a)(1)(B)(iv) and that the best interests of creditors would be served by administration of the case.*

*(j) (1) Notwithstanding any other provision of this title, if the debtor fails to file a tax return that becomes due after the commencement of the case or to properly obtain an extension of the due date for filing such return, the taxing authority may request that the court enter an order converting or dismissing the case.*

*(2) If the debtor does not file the required return or obtain the extension referred to in paragraph (1) within 90 days after a request is filed by the taxing authority under that paragraph, the court shall convert or dismiss the case, whichever is in the best interests of creditors and the estate.*

**Section 521**

(April 20, 2005, P. L. 109-8, Title I, § 106(d); Title IIC, § 225(b); Title III, §§ 304(1), 305(2), 315(b), 316; Title IV, § 446(a); Title VI, § 603(c); Title VII, § 720, 119 Stat. 23)

## HISTORY: ANCILLARY LAWS AND DIRECTIVES

**Amendments:**

**2005.** Act April 20, 2005(effective 180 days after enactment of April 20, 2005, as provided by § 1501(a) of P. L. 109-8), makes numerous amendments and additions to the debtor's duties under 11 USC § 521.

**Other provisions:**

**Effective date and application of amendments made by Act April 20, 2005.** Act April 20, 2005, P.L. 109-8, Title XV, § 1501(a), 119 Stat. 23, provided that the amendments made to this section would be effective 180 days after enactment on April 20, 2005.

**Abridged Legislative History**

Section 106(d) of the Act amends section 521 of the Bankruptcy Code to require a debtor who is an individual to file with the court: (1) a certificate from an approved nonprofit budget and credit counseling agency describing the services it provided the debtor pursuant to section 109(h); and (2) a copy of the repayment plan, if any, that was developed by the agency pursuant to section 109(h).

Section 225(b) amends Bankruptcy Code section 521 to require a debtor to file with the court a record of any interest that the debtor has in an education individual retirement account or qualified state tuition program.

Debtor Retention of Personal Property Security. Section 304(1) of the Act amends section 521(a) of the Bankruptcy Code to provide that an individual who is a chapter 7 debtor may not retain possession of personal property securing, in whole or in part, a purchase money security interest unless the debtor, within 45 days after the first meeting of creditors, enters into a reaffirmation agreement with the creditor, or redeems the property.

Section 305(2) amends section 521 of the Bankruptcy Code to make the requirement to file a statement of intention applicable to all secured debts, not just secured consumer debts.

Section 315(b) amends section 521 to specify additional duties of a debtor. This provision requires the debtor to file a certificate executed by the debtor's attorney or bankruptcy petition preparer stating that the attorney or preparer supplied the debtor with the notice required under Bankruptcy Code section 342(b).

In addition, section 315(b) requires such debtor to provide the trustee not later than seven days before the date first set for the meeting of creditors a copy of his or her Federal income tax return or transcript (at the election of the debtor) for the latest taxable period ending prior to the filing of the bankruptcy case for which a tax return was filed.

During the pendency of a chapter 7, 11 or 13 case, the debtor must file with the court, at the request of the judge, United States trustee, or any party in interest, at the time filed with the taxing authority, copies of any Federal income tax returns (or transcripts thereof) that were not filed for the three-year period preceding the date on which the order for relief was entered.

In a chapter 13 case, the debtor must file a statement, under penalty of perjury, of income and expenditures in the preceding tax year and monthly income showing how the amounts were calculated.

Dismissal for Failure To Timely File Schedules or Provide Required Information. Section 316 of the Act amends section 521 of the Bankruptcy Code to provide that if an individual debtor in a voluntary chapter 7 or chapter 13 case fails to file all of the information required under section 521(a)(1) within 45 days of the date on which the case is filed, the case must be automatically dismissed, effective on the 46th day. The 45-day period may be extended for an additional 45-day period providing the debtor requests such extension prior to the expiration of the original 45-day period and the court finds justification for such extension.

Section 603(c) amends section 521 of the Bankruptcy Code to make it a duty of the debtor to cooperate with an auditor.

Dismissal for Failure to Timely File Tax Returns. Section 720 of the Act amends section 521 of the Bankruptcy Code to allow a taxing authority to request that the court dismiss or convert a bankruptcy case if the debtor fails to file a postpetition tax return or obtain an extension. (H. Report No. 109-31 to accompany S. 256, 109th Cong., 1st Sess. (2005) pp. 55, 65, 70–71, 78–79, 96, 99, 105; available at 2005 U.S.C. C.A.N. 88, at 125–26, 134, 139, 145–46, 161, 163–64, 168–69)

## § 522. Exemptions

(a) In this section—

(1) "dependent" includes spouse, whether or not actually dependent; and

(2) "value" means fair market value as of the date of the filing of the petition or, with respect to property that becomes property of the estate after such date, as of the date such property becomes property of the estate.

(b) *(1)* Notwithstanding section 541 of this title, an individual debtor may exempt from property of the estate the property listed in either ~~paragraph (1)~~*paragraph (2)* or, in the alternative, ~~paragraph (2)~~*paragraph (3)* of this subsection. In joint cases filed under section 302 of this title and individual cases filed under section 301 or 303 of this title by or against debtors who are husband and wife, and whose estates are ordered to be jointly administered under Rule 1015(b) of the Federal Rules of Bankruptcy Procedure, one debtor may not elect to exempt property listed in ~~paragraph (1)~~*paragraph*

*(2)* and the other debtor elect to exempt property listed in ~~paragraph (2)~~*paragraph (3)* of this subsection. If the parties cannot agree on the alternative to be elected, they shall be deemed to elect ~~paragraph (1)~~*paragraph (2)*, where such election is permitted under the law of the jurisdiction where the case is filed. ~~Such property is—~~

(~~1~~2) ~~property that is specified under subsection (d) of this section, unless the State law that is applicable to the debtor under paragraph (2)(A) of this subsection specifically does not so authorize; or, in the alternative,~~*Property listed in this paragraph is property that is specified under subsection (d), unless the State law that is applicable to the debtor under paragraph (3)(A) specifically does not so authorize.*

(3~~2~~) *Property listed in this paragraph is*

(A) *subject to subsections (o) and (p),* any property that is exempt under Federal law, other than subsection (d) of this section, or State or local law that is applicable on the date of the filing of the petition at the place in which the debtor's domicile has been located for the ~~180~~*730* days immediately preceding the date of the filing of the petition~~, or for a longer portion of such 180-day period than in any other place~~ *or if the debtor's domicile has not been located at a single State for such 730-day period, the place in which the debtor's domicile was located for 180 days immediately preceding the 730-day period or for a longer portion of such 180-day period than in any other place;* ~~and~~

(B) any interest in property in which the debtor had, immediately before the commencement of the case, an interest as a tenant by the entirety or joint tenant to the extent that such interest as a tenant by the entirety or joint tenant is exempt from process under applicable nonbankruptcy law~~.~~*; and*

*(C) retirement funds to the extent that those funds are in a fund or account that is exempt from taxation under section 401, 403, 408, 408A, 414, 457, or 501(a) of the Internal Revenue Code of 1986.*

*If the effect of the domiciliary requirement under subparagraph (A) is to render the debtor ineligible for any exemption, the debtor may elect to exempt property that is specified under subsection (d).*

*(4) For purposes of paragraph (3)(C) and subsection (d)(12), the following shall apply:*

*(A) If the retirement funds are in a retirement fund that has received a favorable determination under section 7805 of the Internal Revenue Code of 1986, and that determination is in effect as of the date of the filing of the petition in a case under this title, those funds shall be presumed to be exempt from the estate.*

*(B) If the retirement funds are in a retirement fund that has not received a favorable determination under such section 7805, those funds are exempt from the estate if the debtor demonstrates that—*

*(i) no prior determination to the contrary has been made by a court or the Internal Revenue Service; and*

*(ii) (I) the retirement fund is in substantial compliance with the applicable requirements of the Internal Revenue Code of 1986; or*

*(II) the retirement fund fails to be in substantial compliance with the applicable requirements of the Internal Revenue Code of 1986 and the debtor is not materially responsible for that failure.*

*(C) A direct transfer of retirement funds from 1 fund or account that is exempt from taxation under section 401, 403, 408, 408A, 414, 457, or 501(a) of the Internal Revenue Code of 1986, under section 401(a)(31) of the Internal Revenue Code of 1986, or otherwise, shall not cease to qualify for exemption under paragraph (3)(C) or subsection (d)(12) by reason of such direct transfer.*

*(D) (i) Any distribution that qualifies as an eligible rollover distribution within the meaning of section 402(c) of the Internal Revenue Code of 1986 or that is described in clause (ii) shall not cease to qualify for exemption under paragraph (3)(C) or subsection (d)(12) by reason of such distribution.*

*(ii) A distribution described in this clause is an amount that—*

*(I) has been distributed from a fund or account that is exempt from taxation under section 401, 403, 408, 408A, 414, 457, or 501(a) of the Internal Revenue Code of 1986; and*

*(II) to the extent allowed by law, is deposited in such a fund or account not later than 60 days after the distribution of such amount.*

(c) Unless the case is dismissed, property exempted under this section is not liable during or after the case for any debt of the debtor that arose, or that is determined under section 502 of this title as if such debt had arisen, before the commencement of the case, except—

(1) ~~a debt of a kind specified in section 523(a)(1) or 523(a)(5) of this title;~~*a debt of a kind specified in paragraph (1) or (5) of section 523(a) (in which case, notwithstanding any provision of applicable nonbankruptcy law to the contrary, such property shall be liable for a debt of a kind specified in section 523(a)(5));*

(2) a debt secured by a lien that is—

(A) (i) not avoided under subsection (f) or (g) of this section or under section 544, 545, 547, 548, 549, or 724(a) of this title; and

(ii) not void under section 506(d) of this title;

(B) a tax lien, notice of which is properly filed; or

(3) a debt of a kind specified in section 523(a)(4) or 523(a)(6) of this title owed by an institution-affiliated party of an insured depository institution to a Federal depository institutions regulatory agency acting in its capacity as conservator, receiver, or liquidating agent for such institution; or

(4) a debt in connection with fraud in the obtaining or providing of any scholarship, grant, loan, tuition, discount, award, or other

financial assistance for purposes of financing an education at an institution of higher education (as that term is defined in section 101 of the Higher Education Act of 1965 (20 U.S.C. 1001)).

(d) The following property may be exempted under ~~subsection (b)(1)~~ *subsection (b)(2)* of this section:

(1) The debtor's aggregate interest, not to exceed $18,450 in value, in real property or personal property that the debtor or a dependent of the debtor uses as a residence, in a cooperative that owns property that the debtor or a dependent of the debtor uses as a residence, or in a burial plot for the debtor or a dependent of the debtor.

(2) The debtor's interest, not to exceed $2,950 in value, in one motor vehicle.

(3) The debtor's interest, not to exceed $475 in value in any particular item or $9,850 in aggregate value, in household furnishings, household goods, wearing apparel, appliances, books, animals, crops, or musical instruments, that are held primarily for the personal, family, or household use of the debtor or a dependent of the debtor.

(4) The debtor's aggregate interest, not to exceed $1,225 in value, in jewelry held primarily for the personal, family, or household use of the debtor or a dependent of the debtor.

(5) The debtor's aggregate interest in any property, not to exceed in value $975 plus up to $9,250 of any unused amount of the exemption provided under paragraph (1) of this subsection.

(6) The debtor's aggregate interest, not to exceed $1,850 in value, in any implements, professional books, or tools, of the trade of the debtor or the trade of a dependent of the debtor.

(7) Any unmatured life insurance contract owned by the debtor, other than a credit life insurance contract.

(8) The debtor's aggregate interest, not to exceed in value $9,850 less any amount of property of the estate transferred in the manner specified in section 542(d) of this title, in any accrued dividend or interest under, or loan value of, any unmatured life insurance contract owned by the debtor under which the insured is the debtor or an individual of whom the debtor is a dependent.

(9) Professionally prescribed health aids for the debtor or a dependent of the debtor.

(10) The debtor's right to receive—

(A) a social security benefit, unemployment compensation, or a local public assistance benefit;

(B) a veterans' benefit;

(C) a disability, illness, or unemployment benefit;

(D) alimony, support, or separate maintenance, to the extent reasonably necessary for the support of the debtor and any dependent of the debtor;

(E) a payment under a stock bonus, pension, profitsharing, annuity, or similar plan or contract on account of illness, disability, death, age, or length of service, to the extent reasonably necessary for the support of the debtor and any dependent of the debtor, unless—

(i) such plan or contract was established by or under the auspices of an insider that employed the debtor at the time the debtor's rights under such plan or contract arose;

(ii) such payment is on account of age or length of service; and

(iii) such plan or contract does not qualify under section 401(a), 403(a), 403(b), or 408 of the Internal Revenue Code of 1986.

(11) The debtor's right to receive, or property that is traceable to—

(A) an award under a crime victim's reparation law;

(B) a payment on account of the wrongful death of an individual of whom the debtor was a dependent, to the extent reasonably necessary for the support of the debtor and any dependent of the debtor;

(C) a payment under a life insurance contract that insured the life of an individual of whom the debtor was a dependent on the date of such individual's death, to the extent reasonably necessary for the support of the debtor and any dependent of the debtor;

(D) a payment, not to exceed $18,450, on account of personal bodily injury, not including pain and suffering or compensation for actual pecuniary loss, of the debtor or an individual of whom the debtor is a dependent; or

(E) a payment in compensation of loss of future earnings of the debtor or an individual of whom the debtor is or was a dependent, to the extent reasonably necessary for the support of the debtor and any dependent of the debtor.

*(12) Retirement funds to the extent that those funds are in a fund or account that is exempt from taxation under section 401, 403, 408, 408A, 414, 457, or 501(a) of the Internal Revenue Code of 1986.*

(e) A waiver of an exemption executed in favor of a creditor that holds an unsecured claim against the debtor is unenforceable in a case under this title with respect to such claim against property that the debtor may exempt under subsection (b) of this section. A waiver by the debtor of a power under subsection (f) or (h) of this section to avoid a transfer, under subsection (g) or (i) of this section to exempt property, or under subsection (i) of this section to recover property or to preserve a transfer, is unenforceable in a case under this title.

(f) (1) Notwithstanding any waiver of exemptions but subject to paragraph (3), the debtor may avoid the fixing of a lien on an interest of the debtor in property to the extent that such lien impairs an exemption to which the debtor would have been entitled under subsection (b) of this section, if such lien is—

(A) a judicial lien, other than a judicial lien that secures a debt *of a kind that is specified in section 523(a)(5); or—*

~~(i) to a spouse, former spouse, or child of the debtor, for~~

~~alimony to, maintenance for, or support of such spouse or child, in connection with a separation agreement, divorce decree or other order of a court of record, determination made in accordance with State or territorial law by a governmental unit, or property settlement agreement; and~~

~~(ii) to the extent that such debt—~~

~~(I) is not assigned to another entity, voluntarily, by operation of law, or otherwise; and~~

~~(II) includes a liability designated as alimony, maintenance, or support, unless such liability is actually in the nature of alimony, maintenance or support.; or~~

(B) a nonpossessory, nonpurchase-money security interest in any—

(i) household furnishings, household goods, wearing apparel, appliances, books, animals, crops, musical instruments, or jewelry that are held primarily for the personal, family, or household use of the debtor or a dependent of the debtor;

(ii) implements, professional books, or tools, of the trade of the debtor or the trade of a dependent of the debtor; or

(iii) professionally prescribed health aids for the debtor or a dependent of the debtor.

(2) (A) For the purposes of this subsection, a lien shall be considered to impair an exemption to the extent that the sum of—

(i) the lien;

(ii) all other liens on the property; and

(iii) the amount of the exemption that the debtor could claim if there were no liens on the property;

exceeds the value that the debtor's interest in the property would have in the absence of any liens.

(B) In the case of a property subject to more than 1 lien, a lien that has been avoided shall not be considered in making the calculation under subparagraph (A) with respect to other liens.

(C) This paragraph shall not apply with respect to a judgment arising out of a mortgage foreclosure.

(3) In a case in which State law that is applicable to the debtor—

(A) permits a person to voluntarily waive a right to claim exemptions under subsection (d) or prohibits a debtor from claiming exemptions under subsection (d); and

(B) either permits the debtor to claim exemptions under State law without limitation in amount, except to the extent that the debtor has permitted the fixing of a consensual lien on any property or prohibits avoidance of a consensual lien on property otherwise eligible to be claimed as exempt property;

the debtor may not avoid the fixing of a lien on an interest of the debtor or a dependent of the debtor in property if the lien is a nonpossessory, nonpurchase-money security interest in implements, professional books, or tools of the trade of the debtor or a dependent of the debtor or farm animals or crops of the debtor or a dependent of the debtor to the extent the value of such implements, professional books, tools of the trade, animals, and crops exceeds $5,000.

*(4) (A) Subject to subparagraph (B), for purposes of paragraph (1)(B), the term 'household goods' means—*

*(i) clothing;*

*(ii) furniture;*

*(iii) appliances;*

*(iv) 1 radio;*

*(v) 1 television;*

*(vi) 1 VCR;*

*(vii) linens;*

*(viii) china;*

*(ix) crockery;*

*(x) kitchenware;*

*(xi) educational materials and educational equipment primarily for the use of minor dependent children of the debtor;*

*(xii) medical equipment and supplies;*

*(xiii) furniture exclusively for the use of minor children, or elderly or disabled dependents of the debtor;*

*(xiv) personal effects (including the toys and hobby equipment of minor dependent children and wedding rings) of the debtor and the dependents of the debtor; and*

*(xv) 1 personal computer and related equipment.*

*(B) The term 'household goods' does not include—*

*(i) works of art (unless by or of the debtor, or any relative of the debtor);*

*(ii) electronic entertainment equipment with a fair market value of more than $500 in the aggregate (except 1 television, 1 radio, and 1 VCR);*

*(iii) items acquired as antiques with a fair market value of more than $500 in the aggregate;*

*(iv) jewelry with a fair market value of more than $500 in the aggregate (except wedding rings); and*

*(v) a computer (except as otherwise provided for in this section), motor vehicle (including a tractor or lawn tractor), boat, or a motorized recreational device, conveyance, vehicle, watercraft, or aircraft.*

(g) Notwithstanding sections 550 and 551 of this title, the debtor may exempt under subsection (b) of this section property that the trustee recovers under section 510(c)(2), 542, 543, 550, 551, or 553 of this title, to the extent that the debtor could have exempted such property under subsection (b) of this section if such property had not been transferred, if—

(1) (A) such transfer was not a voluntary transfer of such property by the debtor; and

(B) the debtor did not conceal such property; or

(2) the debtor could have avoided such transfer under subsection (f)(~~2~~*1)(B)* of this section.

(h) The debtor may avoid a transfer of property of the debtor or recover a setoff to the extent that the debtor could have exempted such property under subsection (g)(1) of this section if the trustee had avoided such transfer, if—

(1) such transfer is avoidable by the trustee under section 544, 545, 547, 548, 549, or 724(a) of this title or recoverable by the trustee under section 553 of this title; and

(2) the trustee does not attempt to avoid such transfer.

(i) (1) If the debtor avoids a transfer or recovers a setoff under subsection (f) or (h) of this section, the debtor may recover in the manner prescribed by, and subject to the limitations of, section 550 of this title, the same as if the trustee had avoided such transfer, and may exempt any property so recovered under subsection (b) of this section.

(2) Notwithstanding section 551 of this title, a transfer avoided under section 544, 545, 547, 548, 549, or 724(a) of this title, under subsection (f) or (h) of this section, or property recovered under section 553 of this title, may be preserved for the benefit of the debtor to the extent that the debtor may exempt such property under subsection (g) of this section or paragraph (1) of this subsection.

(j) Notwithstanding subsections (g) and (i) of this section, the debtor may exempt a particular kind of property under subsections (g) and (i) of this section only to the extent that the debtor has exempted less property in value of such kind than that to which the debtor is entitled under subsection (b) of this section.

(k) Property that the debtor exempts under this section is not liable for payment of any administrative expense except—

(1) the aliquot share of the costs and expenses of avoiding a transfer of property that the debtor exempts under subsection (g) of this section, or of recovery of such property, that is attributable to the value of the portion of such property exempted in relation to the value of the property recovered; and

(2) any costs and expenses of avoiding a transfer under subsection (f) or (h) of this section, or of recovery of property under subsection (i)(1) of this section, that the debtor has not paid.

(l) The debtor shall file a list of property that the debtor claims as exempt under subsection (b) of this section. If the debtor does not file such a list, a dependent of the debtor may file such a list, or may claim property as exempt from property of the estate on behalf of the debtor. Unless a party in interest objects, the property claimed as exempt on such list is exempt.

(m) Subject to the limitation in subsection (b), this section shall apply separately with respect to each debtor in a joint case.

*(n) For assets in individual retirement accounts described in section 408 or 408A of the Internal Revenue Code of 1986, other than a simplified employee pension under section 408(k) of such Code or a simple retirement account under section 408(p) of such Code, the aggregate value of such assets exempted under this section, without regard to amounts attributable to rollover contributions under section 402(c), 402(e)(6), 403(a)(4), 403(a)(5), and 403(b)(8) of the Internal Revenue Code of 1986, and earnings thereon, shall not exceed $1,000,000 in a case filed by a debtor who is an individual, except that such amount may be increased if the interests of justice so require.*

*(o) For purposes of subsection (b)(3)(A), and notwithstanding subsection (a), the value of an interest in—*

*(1) real or personal property that the debtor or a dependent of the debtor uses as a residence;*

*(2) a cooperative that owns property that the debtor or a dependent of the debtor uses as a residence;*

*(3) a burial plot for the debtor or a dependent of the debtor; or*

*(4) real or personal property that the debtor or a dependent of the debtor claims as a homestead;*

*shall be reduced to the extent that such value is attributable to any portion of any property that the debtor disposed of in the 10-year period ending on the date of the filing of the petition with the intent to hinder, delay, or defraud a creditor and that the debtor could not exempt, or that portion that the debtor could not exempt, under subsection (b), if on such date the debtor had held the property so disposed of.*

*(p) (1) Except as provided in paragraph (2) of this subsection and sections 544 and 548, as a result of electing under subsection (b)(3)(A) to exempt property under State or local law, a debtor may not exempt any amount of interest that was acquired by the debtor during the 1215-day period preceding the date of the filing of the petition that exceeds in the aggregate $125,000 in value in—*

*(A) real or personal property that the debtor or a dependent of the debtor uses as a residence;*

*(B) a cooperative that owns property that the debtor or a dependent of the debtor uses as a residence;*

*(C) a burial plot for the debtor or a dependent of the debtor; or*

*(D) real or personal property that the debtor or dependent of the debtor claims as a homestead.*

*(2) (A) The limitation under paragraph (1) shall not apply to an exemption claimed under subsection (b)(3)(A) by a family farmer for the principal residence of such farmer.*

*(B) For purposes of paragraph (1), any amount of such interest does not include any interest transferred from a debtor's previous principal residence (which was acquired prior to the beginning of*

*such 1215-day period) into the debtor's current principal residence, if the debtor's previous and current residences are located in the same State.*

*(q) (1) As a result of electing under subsection (b)(3)(A) to exempt property under State or local law, a debtor may not exempt any amount of an interest in property described in subparagraphs (A), (B), (C), and (D) of subsection (p)(1) which exceeds in the aggregate $125,000 if—*

*(A) the court determines, after notice and a hearing, that the debtor has been convicted of a felony (as defined in section 3156 of title 18), which under the circumstances, demonstrates that the filing of the case was an abuse of the provisions of this title; or*

*(B) the debtor owes a debt arising from—*

*(i) any violation of the Federal securities laws (as defined in section 3(a)(47) of the Securities Exchange Act of 1934), any State securities laws, or any regulation or order issued under Federal securities laws or State securities laws;*

*(ii) fraud, deceit, or manipulation in a fiduciary capacity or in connection with the purchase or sale of any security registered under section 12 or 15(d) of the Securities Exchange Act of 1934 or under section 6 of the Securities Act of 1933;*

*(iii) any civil remedy under section 1964 of title 18; or*

*(iv) any criminal act, intentional tort, or willful or reckless misconduct that caused serious physical injury or death to another individual in the preceding 5 years.*

*(2) Paragraph (1) shall not apply to the extent the amount of an interest in property described in subparagraphs (A), (B), (C), and (D) of subsection (p)(1) is reasonably necessary for the support of the debtor and any dependent of the debtor.*

**Section 522**

(April 20, 2005, P. L. 109-8, Title IIB, § 216; Title IIC, §§ 224(a), 224(e)(1); Title III, §§ 307, 308, 313(a), 322(a), 119 Stat. 23)

## HISTORY: ANCILLARY LAWS AND DIRECTIVES

**Amendments:**

**2005.** Act April 20, 2005(effective 180 days after enactment of April 20, 2005, as provided by § 1501(a) of P. L. 109-8), makes substantial amendments and additions to 11 USC § 522's exemptions. The Act (effective upon enactment on April 20, 2005, as provided by § 1501(a)(2)) adds § 522(o), (p) and (q) limiting the homestead exemption.

**Other provisions:**

**Effective date and application of amendments made by Act April 20, 2005.** Act April 20, 2005, P.L. 109-8, Title XV, § 1501(a)(1), 119 Stat. 23, provided that the amendments made to this section would be effective 180 days after enactment on April 20, 2005, except that the addition of § 522(o), (p) and (q) is effective upon enactment for "cases commenced under title 11, United States Code, on or after the date of the enactment of this Act." P. L. 109-8, § 1501(a)(2), 119 Stat. 23.

**Abridged Legislative History**

Continued Liability of Property. Section 216(1) of the Act amends section 522(c) of the Bankruptcy Code to make exempt property liable for nondischargeable domestic support obligations notwithstanding any contrary provision of applicable nonbankruptcy law.

Protection of Retirement Savings in Bankruptcy. The intent of section 224 is to expand the protection for tax-favored retirement plans or arrangements that may not be already protected under Bankruptcy Code section 541(c)(2) pursuant to Patterson v. Shumate, 504 U.S. 753 (1992) or other state or Federal law. Subsection (a) of section 224 of the Act amends section 522 of the Bankruptcy Code to permit a debtor to exempt certain retirement funds to the extent those monies are in a fund or account that is exempt from taxation under section 401, 403, 408, 408A, 414, 457, or 501(a) of the Internal Revenue Code and that have received a favorable determination pursuant to Internal Revenue Code section 7805 that is in effect as of the date of the commencement of the case.

Section 224(e) amends section 522 of the Bankruptcy Code to impose a $1 million cap (periodically adjusted pursuant to section 104 of the Bankruptcy Code to reflect changes in the Consumer Price Index) on the value of the debtor's interest in an individual retirement account established under either section 408 or 408A of the Internal Revenue Code (other than a simplified employee pension account under section 408(k) or a simple retirement account under section 408(p) of the Internal Revenue Code) that a debtor may claim as exempt property.

Domiciliary Requirements for Exemptions. Section 307 of the Act amends section 522(b)(2)(A) of the Bankruptcy Code to extend the time that a debtor must be domiciled in a state from 180 days to 730 days before he or she may claim that state's exemptions.

Reduction of Homestead Exemption for Fraud. Section 308 amends section 522 of the Bankruptcy Code to reduce the value of a debtor's interest in the following property that may be claimed as exempt under certain circumstances.

Definition of Household Goods and Antiques. Subsection (a) of section 313 of the Act amends section 522(f) of the Bankruptcy Code to codify a modified version of the Federal Trade Commission's definition of "household goods" for purposes of the avoidance of a nonpossessory, nonpurchase money lien in such property.

(H. Report No. 109-31 to accompany S. 256, 109th Cong., 1st Sess. (2005) pp. 61, 64–65, 72–73, 76, 81–81; available at 2005 U.S.C.C.A.N. 88, at 130, 133–34, 140, 143, 148)

## § 523. Exceptions to discharge

(a) A discharge under section 727, 1141, 1228(a), 1228(b), or 1328(b) of this title does not discharge an individual debtor from any debt—

(1) for a tax or a customs duty—

(A) of the kind and for the periods specified in section 507(a)(~~2~~*3*) or 507(a)(8) of this title, whether or not a claim for such tax was filed or allowed;

(B) with respect to which a return, *or equivalent report or notice,* if required—

(i) was not filed *or given*; or

(ii) was filed *or given* after the date on which such return, *report, or notice* was last due, under applicable law or under any extension, and after two years before the date of the filing of the petition; or

(C) with respect to which the debtor made a fraudulent return or willfully attempted in any manner to evade or defeat such tax;

(2) for money, property, services, or an extension, renewal, or refinancing of credit, to the extent obtained by—

(A) false pretenses, a false representation, or actual fraud, other than a statement respecting the debtor's or an insider's financial condition;

(B) use of a statement in writing—

(i) that is materially false;

(ii) respecting the debtor's or an insider's financial condition;

(iii) on which the creditor to whom the debtor is liable for such money, property, services, or credit reasonably relied; and

(iv) that the debtor caused to be made or published with intent to deceive; or

(C) ~~**for purposes of subparagraph (A) of this paragraph, consumer debts owed to a single creditor and aggregating more than $1,225 for "luxury goods or services" incurred by an individual debtor on or within 60 days before the order for relief under this title, or cash advances aggregating more than $1,225 that are extensions of consumer credit under an open end credit plan obtained by an individual debtor on or within 60 days before the order for relief under this title, are presumed to be nondischargeable; "luxury goods or services" do not include goods or services reasonably acquired for the support or maintenance of the debtor or a dependent of the debtor; an extension of consumer credit under an open end credit plan is to be defined for purposes of this subparagraph as it is defined in the Consumer Credit Protection Act;**~~*(i) for purposes of subparagraph (A)—*

*(I) consumer debts owed to a single creditor and aggregating more than $500 for luxury goods or services incurred by an individual debtor on or within 90 days before the order for relief under this title are presumed to be nondischargeable; and*

*(II) cash advances aggregating more than $750 that are extensions of consumer credit under an open end credit plan obtained by an individual debtor on or within 70 days before the order for relief under this title, are presumed to be nondischargeable; and*

*(ii) for purposes of this subparagraph—*

*(I) the terms 'consumer', 'credit', and 'open end credit plan' have the same meanings as in section 103 of the Truth in Lending Act; and*

*(II) the term 'luxury goods or services' does not include goods or services reasonably necessary for the support or maintenance of the debtor or a dependent of the debtor.*

(3) neither listed nor scheduled under section 521(1) of this title, with the name, if known to the debtor, of the creditor to whom such debt is owed, in time to permit—

(A) if such debt is not of a kind specified in paragraph (2), (4), or (6) of this subsection, timely filing of a proof of claim, unless such creditor had notice or actual knowledge of the case in time for such timely filing; or

(B) if such debt is of a kind specified in paragraph (2), (4), or (6) of this subsection, timely filing of a proof of claim and timely request for a determination of dischargeability of such debt under one of such paragraphs, unless such creditor had notice or actual knowledge of the case in time for such timely filing and request;

(4) for fraud or defalcation while acting in a fiduciary capacity, embezzlement, or larceny;

(5) ~~to a spouse, former spouse, or child of the debtor, for alimony to, maintenance for, or support of such spouse or child, in connection with a separation agreement, divorce decree or other order of a court of record, determination made in accordance with State or territorial law by a governmental unit, or property settlement agreement, but not to the extent that—~~*for a domestic support obligation;*

~~(A) such debt is assigned to another entity, voluntarily, by operation of law, or otherwise (other than debts assigned pursuant to section 408(a)(3) of the Social Security Act, or any such debt which has been assigned to the Federal Government or to a State or any political subdivision of such State); or~~

~~(B) such debt includes a liability designated as alimony, maintenance, or support, unless such liability is actually in the nature of alimony, maintenance, or support;~~

(6) for willful and malicious injury by the debtor to another entity or to the property of another entity;

(7) to the extent such debt is for a fine, penalty, or forfeiture payable to and for the benefit of a governmental unit, and is not compensation for actual pecuniary loss, other than a tax penalty—

(A) relating to a tax of a kind not specified in paragraph (1) of this subsection; or

(B) imposed with respect to a transaction or event that occurred before three years before the date of the filing of the petition;

(8) ~~for an educational benefit overpayment or loan made, insured or guaranteed by a governmental unit, or made under any program funded in whole or in part by a governmental unit or nonprofit institution, or for an obligation to repay funds received as an educational benefit, scholarship or stipend, unless excepting such debt from discharge under this paragraph will impose an undue hardship on the debtor and the debtor's dependents;~~*unless excepting such debt from discharge under this paragraph would impose an undue hardship on the debtor and the debtor's dependents, for—*

*(A) (i) an educational benefit overpayment or loan made, insured, or guaranteed by a governmental unit, or made under any program funded in whole or in part by a governmental unit or nonprofit institution; or*

*(ii) an obligation to repay funds received as an educational benefit, scholarship, or stipend; or*

*(B) any other educational loan that is a qualified education loan, as defined in section 221(d)(1) of the Internal Revenue Code of 1986, incurred by a debtor who is an individual;*

(9) for death or personal injury caused by the debtor's operation of a motor vehicle*, vessel, or aircraft* if such operation was unlawful because the debtor was intoxicated from using alcohol, a drug, or another substance;

(10) that was or could have been listed or scheduled by the debtor in a prior case concerning the debtor under this title or under the Bankruptcy Act in which the debtor waived discharge, or was denied a discharge under section 727(a)(2), (3), (4), (5), (6), or (7) of this title, or under section 14c(1), (2), (3), (4), (6), or (7) of such Act;

(11) provided in any final judgment, unreviewable order, or consent order or decree entered in any court of the United States or of any State, issued by a Federal depository institutions regulatory agency, or contained in any settlement agreement entered into by the debtor, arising from any act of fraud or defalcation while acting in a fiduciary capacity committed with respect to any depository institution or insured credit union;

(12) for malicious or reckless failure to fulfill any commitment by the debtor to a Federal depository institutions regulatory agency to maintain the capital of an insured depository institution, except that this paragraph shall not extend any such commitment which would otherwise be terminated due to any act of such agency; or

(13) for any payment of an order of restitution issued under title 18, United States Code;

(14) incurred to pay a tax to the United States that would be nondischargeable pursuant to paragraph (1);

*(14A) incurred to pay a tax to a governmental unit, other than the United States, that would be nondischargeable under paragraph (1);*

*(14B) incurred to pay fines or penalties imposed under Federal election law;*

(15) *to a spouse, former spouse, or child of the debtor and* not of the kind described in paragraph (5) that is incurred by the debtor in the course of a divorce or separation or in connection with a separation agreement, divorce decree or other order of a court of record, *or* a determination made in accordance with State or territorial law by a governmental unit; ~~unless—~~

~~(A) the debtor does not have the ability to pay such debt from income or property of the debtor not reasonably necessary to be expended for the maintenance or support of the debtor or a dependent of the debtor and, if the debtor is engaged in a business, for the payment of expenditures necessary for the continuation, preservation, and operation of such business; or~~

~~(B) discharging such debt would result in a benefit to the debtor that outweighs the detrimental consequences to a spouse, former spouse, or child of the debtor;~~

(16) for a fee or assessment that becomes due and payable after the order for relief to a membership association with respect to the debtor's interest in a ~~dwelling~~ unit that has condominium ~~owner-~~

~~ship or~~ *ownership,* in a share of a cooperative ~~housing~~ corporation, ~~but only if such fee or assessment is payable for a period during which—~~

~~(A) the debtor physically occupied a dwelling unit in the condominium or cooperative project; or~~

~~(B) the debtor rented the dwelling unit to a tenant and received payments from the tenant for such period~~ *or a lot in a homeowners association, for as long as the debtor or the trustee has a legal, equitable, or possessory ownership interest in such unit, such corporation, or such lot*~~;~~,

but nothing in this paragraph shall except from discharge the debt of a debtor for a membership association fee or assessment for a period arising before entry of the order for relief in a pending or subsequent bankruptcy case;

(17) for a fee imposed ~~by a court~~ *on a prisoner by any court* for the filing of a case, motion, complaint, or appeal, or for other costs and expenses assessed with respect to such filing, regardless of an assertion of poverty by the debtor under ~~section 1915(b) or (f)~~ *subsection (b) or (f)(2) of section 1915* of title 28 *(or a similar non-Federal law)*, or the debtor's status as a prisoner, as defined in section 1915(h) of title 28 *(or a similar non-Federal law)*;

*(18) owed to a pension, profit-sharing, stock bonus, or other plan established under section 401, 403, 408, 408A, 414, 457, or 501(c) of the Internal Revenue Code of 1986, under—*

*(A) a loan permitted under section 408(b)(1) of the Employee Retirement Income Security Act of 1974, or subject to section 72(p) of the Internal Revenue Code of 1986; or*

*(B) a loan from a thrift savings plan permitted under subchapter III of chapter 84 of title 5, that satisfies the requirements of section 8433(g) of such title;*

*but nothing in this paragraph may be construed to provide that any loan made under a governmental plan under section 414(d), or a contract or account under section 403(b), of the Internal Revenue Code of 1986 constitutes a claim or a debt under this title; or*

~~(18) owed under State law to a State or municipality that is—~~

~~(A) in the nature of support, and~~

~~(B) enforceable under part D of title IV of the Social Security Act (42 U.S.C. 601 et seq.); or~~

(19) that—

(A) is for—

(i) the violation of any of the Federal securities laws (as that term is defined in section 3(a)(47) of the Securities Exchange Act of 1934), any of the State securities laws, or any regulation or order issued under such Federal or State securities laws; or

(ii) common law fraud, deceit, or manipulation in connection with the purchase or sale of any security; and

(B) results, *before, on, or after the date on which the petition was filed,* from—

(i) any judgment, order, consent order, or decree entered in any Federal or State judicial or administrative proceeding;

(ii) any settlement agreement entered into by the debtor; or

(iii) any court or administrative order for any damages, fine, penalty, citation, restitutionary payment, disgorgement payment, attorney fee, cost, or other payment owed by the debtor.

*For purposes of this subsection, the term 'return' means a return that satisfies the requirements of applicable nonbankruptcy law (including applicable filing requirements). Such term includes a return prepared pursuant to section 6020(a) of the Internal Revenue Code of 1986, or similar State or local law, or a written stipulation to a judgment or a final order entered by a nonbankruptcy tribunal, but does not include a return made pursuant to section 6020(b) of the Internal Revenue Code of 1986, or a similar State or local law.*

(b) Notwithstanding subsection (a) of this section, a debt that was excepted from discharge under subsection (a)(1), (a)(3), or (a)(8) of this section, under section 17a(1), 17a(3), or 17a(5) of the Bankruptcy Act, under section 439A of the Higher Education Act of 1965, or under section 733(g) of the Public Health Service Act in a prior case concerning the debtor under this title, or under the Bankruptcy Act, is dischargeable in a case under this title unless, by the terms of subsection (a) of this section, such debt is not dischargeable in the case under this title.

(c) (1) Except as provided in subsection (a)(3)(B) of this section, the debtor shall be discharged from a debt of a kind specified in paragraph (2), (4), ~~(6), or (15)~~*or (6)* of subsection (a) of this section, unless, on request of the creditor to whom such debt is owed, and after notice and a hearing, the court determines such debt to be excepted from discharge under paragraph (2), (4), ~~(6), or (15)~~*or (6)*, as the case may be, of subsection (a) of this section.

(2) Paragraph (1) shall not apply in the case of a Federal depository institutions regulatory agency seeking, in its capacity as conservator, receiver, or liquidating agent for an insured depository institution, to recover a debt described in subsection (a)(2), (a)(4), (a)(6), or (a)(11) owed to such institution by an institution-affiliated party unless the receiver, conservator, or liquidating agent was appointed in time to reasonably comply, or for a Federal depository institutions regulatory agency acting in its corporate capacity as a successor to such receiver, conservator, or liquidating agent to reasonably comply, with subsection (a)(3)(B) as a creditor of such institution-affiliated party with respect to such debt.

(d) If a creditor requests a determination of dischargeability of a consumer debt under subsection (a)(2) of this section, and such debt is discharged, the court shall grant judgment in favor of the debtor for the costs of, and a reasonable attorney's fee for, the proceeding if the court finds that the position of the creditor was not substantially justified, except that the court shall not award such costs and fees if special circumstances would make the award unjust.

(e) Any institution-affiliated party of an insured depository institution shall be considered to be acting in a fiduciary capacity with respect to the purposes of subsection (a)(4) or (11).

**Section 523**

(April 20, 2005, P. L. 109-8, Title IIB, §§ 215, 220; Title IIC, § 224(c); Title III, §§ 301, 310, 314(a); Title IVA, § 412; Title VII, § 714; Title XII, §§ 1209, 1235; Title XIV, § 1404(a); Title XV, § 1502(a)(2), 119 Stat. 23)

## HISTORY: ANCILLARY LAWS AND DIRECTIVES

**Amendments:**

**2005.** Act April 20, 2005(effective 180 days after enactment of April 20, 2005, as provided by § 1501(a) of P. L. 109-8), makes substantial amendments and additions to 11 USC § 523's exceptions from discharge. The amendment to § 523(a)(19)(B) is effective on July 30, 2002, the date of enactment of the Sarbanes-Oxley Act. See P. L. 109-8, § 1404(b), 119 Stat. 23.

**Other provisions:**

**Effective date and application of amendments made by Act April 20, 2005.** Act April 20, 2005, P.L. 109-8, Title XV, § 1501(a), 119 Stat. 23, provided that the amendments made to this section would be effective 180 days after enactment on April 20, 2005, except that the amendment to § 523(a)(19)(B) is effective on July 30, 2002, the date of enactment of the Sarbanes-Oxley Act. See P. L. 109-8, § 1404(b), 119 Stat. 23.

**Abridged Legislative History**

Nondischargeability of Certain Debts for Alimony, Maintenance, and Support. Section 215 of the Act amends Bankruptcy Code section 523(a)(5) to provide that a "domestic support obligation" (as defined in section 211 of the Act) is nondischargeable and eliminates Bankruptcy Code section 523(a)(18). Section 215(2) amends Bankruptcy Code section 523(c) to delete the reference to section 523(a)(15) in that provision.

Nondischargeability of Certain Educational Benefits and Loans. Section 220 of the Act amends section 523(a)(8) of the Bankruptcy Code to provide that a debt for a qualified education loan (as defined in section 221(e)(1) of the Internal Revenue Code) is nondischargeable, unless excepting such debt from discharge would impose an undue hardship on the debtor and the debtor's dependents.

Section 224(c) amends Bankruptcy Code section 523(a) to except from discharge any amount owed by the debtor to a pension, profit-sharing, stock bonus, or other plan established under the Internal Revenue Code.

Limitation on Luxury Goods. Section 310 amends section 523(a)(2)(C) of the Bankruptcy Code.

Fees Arising from Certain Ownership Interests. Section 412 amends section 523(a)(16) of the Bankruptcy Code to broaden the protections accorded to community associations with respect to fees or assessments arising from the debtor's interest in a condominium, cooperative, or homeowners' association.

Debts Nondischargeable If Incurred in Violation of Securities Fraud Laws. Bankruptcy Code section 523(a)(19) makes certain debts nondischargeable that result from the violation of Federal securities law, state securities law, or any regulation or order issued under such Federal or state securities law nondischargeable.

(H. Report No. 109-31 to accompany S. 256, 109th Cong., 1st Sess. (2005) pp. 61–62, 64, 69, 74, 76–77, 88, 103, 142–43, 148, 154–55; available at 2005 U.S.C.C.A.N. 88, at 130, 132–33, 137–38, 141–42, 144, 154, 167, 201–02, 206, 212)

# § 524. Effect of discharge

(a) A discharge in a case under this title—

(1) voids any judgment at any time obtained, to the extent that such judgment is a determination of the personal liability of the

debtor with respect to any debt discharged under section 727, 944, 1141, 1228, or 1328 of this title, whether or not discharge of such debt is waived;

(2) operates as an injunction against the commencement or continuation of an action, the employment of process, or an act, to collect, recover or offset any such debt as a personal liability of the debtor, whether or not discharge of such debt is waived; and

(3) operates as an injunction against the commencement or continuation of an action, the employment of process, or an act, to collect or recover from, or offset against, property of the debtor of the kind specified in section 541(a)(2) of this title that is acquired after the commencement of the case, on account of any allowable community claim, except a community claim that is excepted from discharge under ~~section 523, 1228(a)(1), or 1328(a)(1) of this title, or that~~ *section 523, 1228(a)(1), or 1328(a)(1), or that* would be so excepted, determined in accordance with the provisions of sections 523(c) and 523(d) of this title, in a case concerning the debtor's spouse commenced on the date of the filing of the petition in the case concerning the debtor, whether or not discharge of the debt based on such community claim is waived.

(b) Subsection (a)(3) of this section does not apply if—

(1) (A) the debtor's spouse is a debtor in a case under this title, or a bankrupt or a debtor in a case under the Bankruptcy Act, commenced within six years of the date of the filing of the petition in the case concerning the debtor; and

(B) the court does not grant the debtor's spouse a discharge in such case concerning the debtor's spouse; or

(2) (A) the court would not grant the debtor's spouse a discharge in a case under chapter 7 of this title concerning such spouse commenced on the date of the filing of the petition in the case concerning the debtor; and

(B) a determination that the court would not so grant such discharge is made by the bankruptcy court within the time and in the manner provided for a determination under section 727 of this title of whether a debtor is granted a discharge.

(c) An agreement between a holder of a claim and the debtor, the consideration for which, in whole or in part, is based on a debt that is dischargeable in a case under this title is enforceable only to any extent enforceable under applicable nonbankruptcy law, whether or not discharge of such debt is waived, only if—

(1) such agreement was made before the granting of the discharge under section 727, 1141, 1228, or 1328 of this title;

~~(2) (A) such agreement contains a clear and conspicuous statement which advises the debtor that the agreement may be rescinded at any time prior to discharge or within sixty days after such agreement is filed with the court, whichever occurs later, by giving notice of rescission to the holder of such claim; and~~

~~(B) such agreement contains a clear and conspicuous statement~~

~~which advises the debtor that such agreement is not required under this title, under nonbankruptcy law, or under any agreement not in accordance with the provisions of this subsection;~~

*(2) the debtor received the disclosures described in subsection (k) at or before the time at which the debtor signed the agreement;*

(3) such agreement has been filed with the court and, if applicable, accompanied by a declaration or an affidavit of the attorney that represented the debtor during the course of negotiating an agreement under this subsection, which states that—

(A) such agreement represents a fully informed and voluntary agreement by the debtor;

(B) such agreement does not impose an undue hardship on the debtor or a dependent of the debtor; and

(C) the attorney fully advised the debtor of the legal effect and consequences of—

(i) an agreement of the kind specified in this subsection; and

(ii) any default under such an agreement;

(4) the debtor has not rescinded such agreement at any time prior to discharge or within sixty days after such agreement is filed with the court, whichever occurs later, by giving notice of rescission to the holder of such claim;

(5) the provisions of subsection (d) of this section have been complied with; and

(6) (A) in a case concerning an individual who was not represented by an attorney during the course of negotiating an agreement under this subsection, the court approves such agreement as—

(i) not imposing an undue hardship on the debtor or a dependent of the debtor; and

(ii) in the best interest of the debtor.

(B) Subparagraph (A) shall not apply to the extent that such debt is a consumer debt secured by real property.

(d) In a case concerning an individual, when the court has determined whether to grant or not to grant a discharge under section 727, 1141, 1228, or 1328 of this title, the court may hold a hearing at which the debtor shall appear in person. At any such hearing, the court shall inform the debtor that a discharge has been granted or the reason why a discharge has not been granted. If a discharge has been granted and if the debtor desires to make an agreement of the kind specified in subsection (c) of this section and was not represented by an attorney during the course of negotiating such agreement, then the court shall hold a hearing at which the debtor shall appear in person and at such hearing the court shall—

(1) inform the debtor—

(A) that such an agreement is not required under this title, under nonbankruptcy law, or under any agreement not made in accordance with the provisions of subsection (c) of this section; and

(B) of the legal effect and consequences of—

(i) an agreement of the kind specified in subsection (c) of this section; and

(ii) a default under such an agreement; and

(2) determine whether the agreement that the debtor desires to make complies with the requirements of subsection (c)(6) of this section, if the consideration for such agreement is based in whole or in part on a consumer debt that is not secured by real property of the debtor.

(e) Except as provided in subsection (a)(3) of this section, discharge of a debt of the debtor does not affect the liability of any other entity on, or the property of any other entity for, such debt.

(f) Nothing contained in subsection (c) or (d) of this section prevents a debtor from voluntarily repaying any debt.

(g) (1) (A) After notice and hearing, a court that enters an order confirming a plan of reorganization under chapter 11 may issue, in connection with such order, an injunction in accordance with this subsection to supplement the injunctive effect of a discharge under this section.

(B) An injunction may be issued under subparagraph (A) to enjoin entities from taking legal action for the purpose of directly or indirectly collecting, recovering, or receiving payment or recovery with respect to any claim or demand that, under a plan of reorganization, is to be paid in whole or in part by a trust described in paragraph (2)(B)(i), except such legal actions as are expressly allowed by the injunction, the confirmation order, or the plan of reorganization.

(2) (A) Subject to subsection (h), if the requirements of subparagraph (B) are met at the time an injunction described in paragraph (1) is entered, then after entry of such injunction, any proceeding that involves the validity, application, construction, or modification of such injunction, or of this subsection with respect to such injunction, may be commenced only in the district court in which such injunction was entered, and such court shall have exclusive jurisdiction over any such proceeding without regard to the amount in controversy.

(B) The requirements of this subparagraph are that—

(i) the injunction is to be implemented in connection with a trust that, pursuant to the plan of reorganization—

(I) is to assume the liabilities of a debtor which at the time of entry of the order for relief has been named as a defendant in personal injury, wrongful death, or property-damage actions seeking recovery for damages allegedly caused by the presence of, or exposure to, asbestos or asbestos-containing products;

(II) is to be funded in whole or in part by the securities of 1 or more debtors involved in such plan and by the obligation of such debtor or debtors to make future payments, including dividends;

(III) is to own, or by the exercise of rights granted under such plan would be entitled to own if specified contingencies occur, a majority of the voting shares of—

(aa) each such debtor;

(bb) the parent corporation of each such debtor; or

(cc) a subsidiary of each such debtor that is also a debtor; and

(IV) is to use its assets or income to pay claims and demands; and

(ii) subject to subsection (h), the court determines that—

(I) the debtor is likely to be subject to substantial future demands for payment arising out of the same or similar conduct or events that gave rise to the claims that are addressed by the injunction;

(II) the actual amounts, numbers, and timing of such future demands cannot be determined;

(III) pursuit of such demands outside the procedures prescribed by such plan is likely to threaten the plan's purpose to deal equitably with claims and future demands;

(IV) as part of the process of seeking confirmation of such plan—

(aa) the terms of the injunction proposed to be issued under paragraph (1)(A), including any provisions barring actions against third parties pursuant to paragraph (4)(A), are set out in such plan and in any disclosure statement supporting the plan; and

(bb) a separate class or classes of the claimants whose claims are to be addressed by a trust described in clause (i) is established and votes, by at least 75 percent of those voting, in favor of the plan; and

(V) subject to subsection (h), pursuant to court orders or otherwise, the trust will operate through mechanisms such as structured, periodic, or supplemental payments, pro rata distributions, matrices, or periodic review of estimates of the numbers and values of present claims and future demands, or other comparable mechanisms, that provide reasonable assurance that the trust will value, and be in a financial position to pay, present claims and future demands that involve similar claims in substantially the same manner.

(3) (A) If the requirements of paragraph (2)(B) are met and the order confirming the plan of reorganization was issued or affirmed by the district court that has jurisdiction over the reorganization case, then after the time for appeal of the order that issues or affirms the plan—

(i) the injunction shall be valid and enforceable and may not be revoked or modified by any court except through appeal in accordance with paragraph (6);

(ii) no entity that pursuant to such plan or thereafter becomes a direct or indirect transferee of, or successor to any assets of, a debtor or trust that is the subject of the injunction shall be liable with respect to any claim or demand made against such entity by reason of its becoming such a transferee or successor; and

(iii) no entity that pursuant to such plan or thereafter makes a loan to such a debtor or trust or to such a successor or transferee shall, by reason of making the loan, be liable with respect to any claim or demand made against such entity, nor shall any pledge of assets made in connection with such a loan be upset or impaired for that reason;

(B) Subparagraph (A) shall not be construed to—

(i) imply that an entity described in subparagraph (A)(ii) or (iii) would, if this paragraph were not applicable, necessarily be liable to any entity by reason of any of the acts described in subparagraph (A);

(ii) relieve any such entity of the duty to comply with, or of liability under, any Federal or State law regarding the making of a fraudulent conveyance in a transaction described in subparagraph (A)(ii) or (iii); or

(iii) relieve a debtor of the debtor's obligation to comply with the terms of the plan of reorganization, or affect the power of the court to exercise its authority under sections 1141 and 1142 to compel the debtor to do so.

(4) (A) (i) Subject to subparagraph (B), an injunction described in paragraph (1) shall be valid and enforceable against all entities that it addresses.

(ii) Notwithstanding the provisions of section 524(e), such an injunction may bar any action directed against a third party who is identifiable from the terms of such injunction (by name or as part of an identifiable group) and is alleged to be directly or indirectly liable for the conduct of, claims against, or demands on the debtor to the extent such alleged liability of such third party arises by reason of—

(I) the third party's ownership of a financial interest in the debtor, a past or present affiliate of the debtor, or a predecessor in interest of the debtor;

(II) the third party's involvement in the management of the debtor or a predecessor in interest of the debtor, or service as an officer, director or employee of the debtor or a related party;

(III) the third party's provision of insurance to the debtor or a related party; or

(IV) the third party's involvement in a transaction changing the corporate structure, or in a loan or other financial transaction affecting the financial condition, of the debtor or a related party, including but not limited to—

(aa) involvement in providing financing (debt or equity), or advice to an entity involved in such a transaction; or

(bb) acquiring or selling a financial interest in an entity as part of such a transaction.

(iii) As used in this subparagraph, the term "related party" means—

(I) a past or present affiliate of the debtor;

(II) a predecessor in interest of the debtor; or

(III) any entity that owned a financial interest in—

(aa) the debtor;

(bb) a past or present affiliate of the debtor; or

(cc) a predecessor in interest of the debtor.

(B) Subject to subsection (h), if, under a plan of reorganization, a kind of demand described in such plan is to be paid in whole or in part by a trust described in paragraph (2)(B)(i) in connection with which an injunction described in paragraph (1) is to be implemented, then such injunction shall be valid and enforceable with respect to a demand of such kind made, after such plan is confirmed, against the debtor or debtors involved, or against a third party described in subparagraph (A)(ii), if—

(i) as part of the proceedings leading to issuance of such injunction, the court appoints a legal representative for the purpose of protecting the rights of persons that might subsequently assert demands of such kind, and

(ii) the court determines, before entering the order confirming such plan, that identifying such debtor or debtors, or such third party (by name or as part of an identifiable group), in such injunction with respect to such demands for purposes of this subparagraph is fair and equitable with respect to the persons that might subsequently assert such demands, in light of the benefits provided, or to be provided, to such trust on behalf of such debtor or debtors or such third party.

(5) In this subsection, the term "demand" means a demand for payment, present or future, that—

(A) was not a claim during the proceedings leading to the confirmation of a plan of reorganization;

(B) arises out of the same or similar conduct or events that gave rise to the claims addressed by the injunction issued under paragraph (1); and

(C) pursuant to the plan, is to be paid by a trust described in paragraph (2)(B)(i).

(6) Paragraph (3)(A)(i) does not bar an action taken by or at the

direction of an appellate court on appeal of an injunction issued under paragraph (1) or of the order of confirmation that relates to the injunction.

(7) This subsection does not affect the operation of section 1144 or the power of the district court to refer a proceeding under section 157 of title 28 or any reference of a proceeding made prior to the date of the enactment of this subsection.

(h) Application to existing injunctions.—For purposes of subsection (g)—

(1) subject to paragraph (2), if an injunction of the kind described in subsection (g)(1)(B) was issued before the date of the enactment of this Act, as part of a plan of reorganization confirmed by an order entered before such date, then the injunction shall be considered to meet the requirements of subsection (g)(2)(B) for purposes of subsection (g)(2)(A), and to satisfy subsection (g)(4)(A)(ii), if—

(A) the court determined at the time the plan was confirmed that the plan was fair and equitable in accordance with the requirements of section 1129(b);

(B) as part of the proceedings leading to issuance of such injunction and confirmation of such plan, the court had appointed a legal representative for the purpose of protecting the rights of persons that might subsequently assert demands described in subsection (g)(4)(B) with respect to such plan; and

(C) such legal representative did not object to confirmation of such plan or issuance of such injunction; and

(2) for purposes of paragraph (1), if a trust described in subsection (g)(2)(B)(i) is subject to a court order on the date of the enactment of this Act staying such trust from settling or paying further claims—

(A) the requirements of subsection (g)(2)(B)(ii)(V) shall not apply with respect to such trust until such stay is lifted or dissolved; and

(B) if such trust meets such requirements on the date such stay is lifted or dissolved, such trust shall be considered to have met such requirements continuously from the date of the enactment of this Act.

*(i) The willful failure of a creditor to credit payments received under a plan confirmed under this title, unless the order confirming the plan is revoked, the plan is in default, or the creditor has not received payments required to be made under the plan in the manner required by the plan (including crediting the amounts required under the plan), shall constitute a violation of an injunction under subsection (a)(2) if the act of the creditor to collect and failure to credit payments in the manner required by the plan caused material injury to the debtor.*

*(j) Subsection (a)(2) does not operate as an injunction against an act by a creditor that is the holder of a secured claim, if—*

*(1) such creditor retains a security interest in real property that is the principal residence of the debtor;*

*(2) such act is in the ordinary course of business between the creditor and the debtor; and*

*(3) such act is limited to seeking or obtaining periodic payments associated with a valid security interest in lieu of pursuit of in rem relief to enforce the lien.*

*(k) (1) The disclosures required under subsection (c)(2) shall consist of the disclosure statement described in paragraph (3), completed as required in that paragraph, together with the agreement specified in subsection (c), statement, declaration, motion and order described, respectively, in paragraphs (4) through (8), and shall be the only disclosures required in connection with entering into such agreement.*

*(2) Disclosures made under paragraph (1) shall be made clearly and conspicuously and in writing. The terms 'Amount Reaffirmed' and 'Annual Percentage Rate' shall be disclosed more conspicuously than other terms, data or informa tion provided in connection with this disclosure, except that the phrases 'Before agreeing to reaffirm a debt, review these important disclosures' and 'Summary of Reaffirmation Agreement' may be equally conspicuous. Disclosures may be made in a different order and may use terminology different from that set forth in paragraphs (2) through (8), except that the terms 'Amount Reaffirmed' and 'Annual Percentage Rate' must be used where indicated.*

*(3) The disclosure statement required under this paragraph shall consist of the following:*

*(A) The statement: 'Part A: Before agreeing to reaffirm a debt, review these important disclosures:';*

*(B) Under the heading 'Summary of Reaffirmation Agreement', the statement: 'This Summary is made pursuant to the requirements of the Bankruptcy Code';*

*(C) The 'Amount Reaffirmed', using that term, which shall be—*

*(i) the total amount of debt that the debtor agrees to reaffirm by entering into an agreement of the kind specified in subsection (c), and*

*(ii) the total of any fees and costs accrued as of the date of the disclosure statement, related to such total amount.*

*(D) In conjunction with the disclosure of the 'Amount Reaffirmed', the statements—*

*(i) 'The amount of debt you have agreed to reaffirm'; and*

*(ii) 'Your credit agreement may obligate you to pay additional amounts which may come due after the date of this disclosure. Consult your credit agreement.'.*

*(E) The 'Annual Percentage Rate', using that term, which shall be disclosed as—*

*(i) if, at the time the petition is filed, the debt is an extension of credit under an open end credit plan, as the terms 'credit' and 'open end credit plan' are defined in section 103 of the Truth in Lending Act, then—*

*(I) the annual percentage rate determined under paragraphs (5) and (6) of section 127(b) of the Truth in Lending Act, as applicable, as disclosed to the debtor in the most recent periodic statement prior to entering into an agreement of the kind specified in subsection (c) or, if no such periodic statement has been given to the debtor during the prior 6 months, the annual percentage rate as it would have been so disclosed at the time the disclosure statement is given to the debtor, or to the extent this annual percentage rate is not readily available or not applicable, then*

*(II) the simple interest rate applicable to the amount reaffirmed as of the date the disclosure statement is given to the debtor, or if different simple interest rates apply to different balances, the simple interest rate applicable to each such balance, identifying the amount of each such balance included in the amount reaffirmed, or*

*(III) if the entity making the disclosure elects, to disclose the annual percentage rate under subclause (I) and the simple interest rate under subclause (II); or*

*(ii) if, at the time the petition is filed, the debt is an extension of credit other than under an open end credit plan, as the terms 'credit' and 'open end credit plan' are defined in section 103 of the Truth in Lending Act, then—*

*(I) the annual percentage rate under section 128(a)(4) of the Truth in Lending Act, as disclosed to the debtor in the most recent disclosure statement given to the debtor prior to the entering into an agreement of the kind specified in subsection (c) with respect to the debt, or, if no such disclosure statement was given to the debtor, the annual percentage rate as it would have been so disclosed at the time the disclosure statement is given to the debtor, or to the extent this annual percentage rate is not readily available or not applicable, then*

*(II) the simple interest rate applicable to the amount reaffirmed as of the date the disclosure statement is given to the debtor, or if different simple interest rates apply to different balances, the simple interest rate applicable to each such balance, identifying the amount of such balance included in the amount reaffirmed, or*

*(III) if the entity making the disclosure elects, to disclose the annual percentage rate under (I) and the simple interest rate under (II).*

*(F) If the underlying debt transaction was disclosed as a variable rate transaction on the most recent disclosure given under the Truth in Lending Act, by stating 'The interest rate on your loan may be a variable interest rate which changes from time to time, so that the annual percentage rate disclosed here may be higher or lower.'.*

*(G) If the debt is secured by a security interest which has not*

*been waived in whole or in part or determined to be void by a final order of the court at the time of the disclosure, by disclosing that a security interest or lien in goods or property is asserted over some or all of the debts the debtor is reaffirming and listing the items and their original purchase price that are subject to the asserted security interest, or if not a purchase-money security interest then listing by items or types and the original amount of the loan.*

*(H) At the election of the creditor, a statement of the repayment schedule using 1 or a combination of the following—*

*(i) by making the statement: 'Your first payment in the amount of $XXX is due on XXX but the future payment amount may be different. Consult your reaffirmation agreement or credit agreement, as applicable.', and stating the amount of the first payment and the due date of that payment in the places provided;*

*(ii) by making the statement: 'Your payment schedule will be:', and describing the repayment schedule with the number, amount, and due dates or period of payments scheduled to repay the debts reaffirmed to the extent then known by the disclosing party; or*

*(iii) by describing the debtor's repayment obligations with reasonable specificity to the extent then known by the disclosing party.*

*(I) The following statement: 'Note: When this disclosure refers to what a creditor 'may' do, it does not use the word 'may' to give the creditor specific permission. The word 'may' is used to tell you what might occur if the law permits the creditor to take the action. If you have questions about your reaffirming a debt or what the law requires, consult with the attorney who helped you negotiate this agreement reaffirming a debt. If you don't have an attorney helping you, the judge will explain the effect of your reaffirming a debt when the hearing on the reaffirmation agreement is held.'.*

*(J) (i) The following additional statements: Reaffirming a debt is a serious financial decision. The law requires you to take certain steps to make sure the decision is in your best interest. If these steps are not completed, the reaffirmation agreement is not effective, even though you have signed it.*

*1. Read the disclosures in this Part A carefully. Consider the decision to reaffirm carefully. Then, if you want to reaffirm, sign the reaffirmation agreement in Part B (or you may use a separate agreement you and your creditor agree on).*

*2. Complete and sign Part D and be sure you can afford to make the payments you are agreeing to make and have received a copy of the disclosure statement and a completed and signed reaffirmation agreement.*

*3. If you were represented by an attorney during the negotiation of your reaffirmation agreement, the attorney must have signed the certification in Part C.*

*4. If you were not represented by an attorney during the*

*negotiation of your reaffirmation agreement, you must have completed and signed Part E.*

*5. The original of this disclosure must be filed with the court by you or your creditor. If a separate reaffirmation agreement (other than the one in Part B) has been signed, it must be attached.*

*6. If you were represented by an attorney during the negotiation of your reaffirmation agreement, your reaffirmation agreement becomes effective upon filing with the court unless the reaffirmation is presumed to be an undue hardship as explained in Part D.*

*7. If you were not represented by an attorney during the negotiation of your reaffirmation agreement, it will not be effective unless the court approves it. The court will notify you of the hearing on your reaffirmation agreement. You must attend this hearing in bankruptcy court where the judge will review your reaffirmation agreement. The bankruptcy court must approve your reaffirmation agreement as consistent with your best interests, except that no court approval is required if your reaffirmation agreement is for a consumer debt secured by a mortgage, deed of trust, security deed, or other lien on your real property, like your home.Your right to rescind (cancel) your reaffirmation agreement. You may rescind (cancel) your reaffirmation agreement at any time before the bankruptcy court enters a discharge order, or before the expiration of the 60-day period that begins on the date your reaffirmation agreement is filed with the court, whichever occurs later. To rescind (cancel) your reaffirmation agreement, you must notify the creditor that your reaffirmation agreement is rescinded (or canceled).What are your obligations if you reaffirm the debt? A reaffirmed debt remains your personal legal obligation. It is not discharged in your bankruptcy case. That means that if you default on your reaffirmed debt after your bankruptcy case is over, your creditor may be able to take your property or your wages. Otherwise, your obligations will be determined by the reaffirmation agreement which may have changed the terms of the original agreement. For example, if you are reaffirming an open end credit agreement, the creditor may be permitted by that agreement or applicable law to change the terms of that agreement in the future under certain conditions.Are you required to enter into a reaffirmation agreement by any law? No, you are not required to reaffirm a debt by any law. Only agree to reaffirm a debt if it is in your best interest. Be sure you can afford the payments you agree to make.What if your creditor has a security interest or lien? Your bankruptcy discharge does not eliminate any lien on your property. A 'lien' is often referred to as a security interest, deed of trust, mortgage or security deed. Even if you do not reaffirm and your personal liability on the debt is discharged, because of the lien your creditor may still have the right to take the security property if you do not pay the debt or default on it. If the lien is on an item of personal property that is exempt under your State's law or that the trustee has abandoned, you may be able to redeem the item rather than reaffirm the debt. To redeem, you make a single payment to the creditor equal to the current value of the security property, as agreed by the parties or determined by the court.*

*(ii) In the case of a reaffirmation under subsection (m)(2), numbered paragraph 6 in the disclosures required by clause (i) of this subparagraph shall read as follows:*

*6. If you were represented by an attorney during the negotiation of your reaffirmation agreement, your reaffirmation agreement becomes effective upon filing with the court.*

*(4) The form of such agreement required under this paragraph shall consist of the following:*

*Part B: Reaffirmation Agreement. I (we) agree to reaffirm the debts arising under the credit agreement described below.*

*Brief description of credit agreement:*

*Description of any changes to the credit agreement made as part of this reaffirmation agreement:*

*Signature: Date:*

*Borrower:*

*Co-borrower, if also reaffirming these debts:*

*Accepted by creditor:*

*Date of creditor acceptance:.*

*(5) The declaration shall consist of the following:*

*(A) The following certification:*

*Part C: Certification by Debtor's Attorney (If Any).*

*I hereby certify that (1) this agreement represents a fully informed and voluntary agreement by the debtor; (2) this agreement does not impose an undue hardship on the debtor or any dependent of the debtor; and (3) I have fully advised the debtor of the legal effect and consequences of this agreement and any default under this agreement.*

*Signature of Debtor's Attorney: Date:.*

*(B) If a presumption of undue hardship has been established with respect to such agreement, such certification shall state that in the opinion of the attorney, the debtor is able to make the payment.*

*(C) In the case of a reaffirmation agreement under subsection (m)(2), subparagraph (B) is not applicable.*

*(6) (A) The statement in support of such agreement, which the debtor shall sign and date prior to filing with the court, shall consist of the following:*

*Part D: Debtor's Statement in Support of Reaffirmation Agreement.*

*1. I believe this reaffirmation agreement will not impose an undue hardship on my dependents or me. I can afford to make the payments on the reaffirmed debt because my monthly income (take home pay plus any other income received) is $XXX, and my actual current monthly expenses including monthly payments on post-bankruptcy debt and other reaffirmation agreements total $XXX, leaving $XXXX to make the required payments on this reaffirmed debt. I understand that if my income less my monthly expenses does not leave enough to make the payments, this reaffirmation agreement is presumed to be an undue hardship on me and must be reviewed by the court. However, this presumption may be overcome if I explain to the satisfaction of the court how I can afford to make the payments here: XXX.*

*2. I received a copy of the Reaffirmation Disclosure Statement in Part A and a completed and signed reaffirmation agreement.*

*(B) Where the debtor is represented by an attorney and is reaffirming a debt owed to a creditor defined in section 19(b)(1)(A)(iv) of the Federal Reserve Act, the statement of support of the reaffirmation agreement, which the debtor shall sign and date prior to filing with the court, shall consist of the following:I believe this reaffirmation agreement is in my financial interest. I can afford to make the payments on the reaffirmed debt. I received a copy of the Reaffirmation Disclosure Statement in Part A and a completed and signed reaffirmation agreement.*

*(7) The motion that may be used if approval of such agreement by the court is required in order for it to be effective, shall be signed and dated by the movant and shall consist of the following:*

*Part E: Motion for Court Approval (To be completed only if the debtor is not represented by an attorney.) I (we), the debtor(s), affirm the following to be true and correct:*

*I am not represented by an attorney in connection with this reaffirmation agreement.*

*I believe this reaffirmation agreement is in my best interest based on the income and expenses I have disclosed in my Statement in Support of this reaffirmation agreement, and because (provide any additional relevant reasons the court should consider):*

*Therefore, I ask the court for an order approving this reaffirmation agreement.'.*

*(8) The court order, which may be used to approve such agreement, shall consist of the following:*

*Court Order: The court grants the debtor's motion and approves the reaffirmation agreement described above.*

*(l) Notwithstanding any other provision of this title the following shall apply:*

*(1) A creditor may accept payments from a debtor before and after*

*the filing of an agreement of the kind specified in subsection (c) with the court.*

*(2) A creditor may accept payments from a debtor under such agreement that the creditor believes in good faith to be effective.*

*(3) The requirements of subsections (c)(2) and (k) shall be satisfied if disclosures required under those subsections are given in good faith.*

*(m) (1) Until 60 days after an agreement of the kind specified in subsection (c) is filed with the court (or such additional period as the court, after notice and a hearing and for cause, orders before the expiration of such period), it shall be presumed that such agreement is an undue hardship on the debtor if the debtor's monthly income less the debtor's monthly expenses as shown on the debtor's completed and signed statement in support of such agreement required under subsection (k)(6)(A) is less than the scheduled payments on the reaffirmed debt. This presumption shall be reviewed by the court. The presumption may be rebutted in writing by the debtor if the statement includes an explanation that identifies additional sources of funds to make the payments as agreed upon under the terms of such agreement. If the presumption is not rebutted to the satisfaction of the court, the court may disapprove such agreement. No agreement shall be disapproved without notice and a hearing to the debtor and creditor, and such hearing shall be concluded before the entry of the debtor's discharge.*

*(2) This subsection does not apply to reaffirmation agreements where the creditor is a credit union, as defined in section 19(b)(1)(A)(iv) of the Federal Reserve Act.*

**Section 524**

(April 20, 2005, P. L. 109-8, Title IIA, §§ 202, 203(a); Title XII, § 1210, 119 Stat. 23)

## HISTORY: ANCILLARY LAWS AND DIRECTIVES

**Amendments:**

**2005.** Act April 20, 2005(effective 180 days after enactment of April 20, 2005, as provided by § 1501(a) of P. L. 109-8), amends 11 USC § 524(a)'s discharge injunction, makes technical amendments, and adds new §§ 524(i), (j) and (k), with the latter making substantial changes in the minimal requirements for an enforceable reaffirmation agreement.

**Other provisions:**

**Effective date and application of amendments made by Act April 20, 2005.** Act April 20, 2005, P.L. 109-8, Title XV, § 1501(a), 119 Stat. 23, provided that the amendments made to this section would be effective 180 days after enactment on April 20, 2005.

**Abridged Legislative History**

Effect of Discharge. Section 202 of the Act amends section 524 of the Bankruptcy Code in two respects. First, it provides that the willful failure of a creditor to credit payments received under a confirmed chapter 11, 12, or 13 plan constitutes a violation of the discharge injunction if the creditor's action to collect and failure to credit payments in the manner required by the plan caused material injury to the debtor. This provision does not apply if the order confirming the plan is revoked, the plan is in default, or the creditor has not received payments required to be made under the plan in the manner prescribed by the plan. Second, section 202 amends section 524 of the Bankruptcy Code to provide that the discharge injunction does not apply to a creditor having a claim secured by an interest in real property that is the debtor's principal residence if the creditor communicates with the debtor in the ordinary course of business between the creditor and the debtor and such communication is limited to seeking or obtaining periodic payments associated with a valid security interest in lieu of the pursuit of in rem relief to enforce the lien.

Discouraging Abuse of Reaffirmation Agreement Practices. Section 203 of the Act effectuates a comprehensive overhaul of the law applicable to reaffirmation agreements.

Notwithstanding any other provision of the Bankruptcy Code, section 203(a) permits a creditor to accept payments from a debtor: (1) before and after the filing of a reaffirmation agreement with the court; or (2) pursuant to a reaffirmation agreement that the creditor believes in good faith to be effective. It further provides that the requirements specified in subsections (c)(2) and (k) of section 524 are satisfied if the disclosures required by these provisions are given in good faith.

Where the amount of the scheduled payments due on the reaffirmed debt (as disclosed in the debtor's statement) exceeds the debtor's available income, it is presumed for 60 days from the date on which the reaffirmation agreement is filed with the court that the agreement presents an undue hardship.

(H. Report No. 109-31 to accompany S. 256, 109th Cong., 1st Sess. (2005) pp. 57–58, 143; available at 2005 U.S.C.C.A.N. 88, at 127–28, 202)

## § 525. Protection against discriminatory treatment

(a) Except as provided in the Perishable Agricultural Commodities Act, 1930, the Packers and Stockyards Act, 1921, and section 1 of the Act entitled "An Act making appropriations for the Department of Agriculture for the fiscal year ending June 30, 1944, and for other purposes," approved July 12, 1943, a governmental unit may not deny, revoke, suspend, or refuse to renew a license, permit, charter, franchise, or other similar grant to, condition such a grant to, discriminate with respect to such a grant against, deny employment to, terminate the employment of, or discriminate with respect to employment against, a person that is or has been a debtor under this title or a bankrupt or a debtor under the Bankruptcy Act, or another person with whom such bankrupt or debtor has been associated, solely because such bankrupt or debtor is or has been a debtor under this title or a bankrupt or debtor under the Bankruptcy Act, has been insolvent before the commencement of the case under this title, or during the case but before the debtor is granted or denied a discharge, or has not paid a debt that is dischargeable in the case under this title or that was discharged under the Bankruptcy Act.

(b) No private employer may terminate the employment of, or discriminate with respect to employment against, an individual who is or has been a debtor under this title, a debtor or bankrupt under the Bankruptcy Act, or an individual associated with such debtor or bankrupt, solely because such debtor or bankrupt—

(1) is or has been a debtor under this title or a debtor or bankrupt under the Bankruptcy Act;

(2) has been insolvent before the commencement of a case under this title or during the case but before the grant or denial of a discharge; or

(3) has not paid a debt that is dischargeable in a case under this title or that was discharged under the Bankruptcy Act.

(c) (1) A governmental unit that operates a student grant or loan program and a person engaged in a business that includes the making of loans guaranteed or insured under a student loan program may not deny a student grant, loan, loan guarantee, or loan insurance to a person that is or has been a debtor under this title or a bankrupt or debtor under the Bankruptcy Act, or another person with whom the debtor or bankrupt has been associated, because the debtor or bankrupt is or has been a debtor under this title or a bankrupt or debtor under the Bankruptcy Act, has been insolvent before the commencement of a case under this title or during the pendency of the case but before the debtor is granted or denied a discharge, or has not paid a debt that is dischargeable in the case under this title or that was discharged under the Bankruptcy Act.

(2) In this section, "student loan program" means ~~the program operated under part B, D, or E of~~ *any program operated under* title IV of the Higher Education Act of 1965 or a similar program operated under State or local law.

**Section 525**

(April 20, 2005, P. L. 109-8, Title XII, § 1211, 119 Stat. 23)

## HISTORY: ANCILLARY LAWS AND DIRECTIVES

**Amendments:**

**2005.** Act April 20, 2005(effective 180 days after enactment of April 20, 2005, as provided by § 1501(a) of P. L. 109-8), amends 11 USC § 525 to conform a reference to its antecedent reference in section 525(c).

**Other provisions:**

**Effective date and application of amendments made by Act April 20, 2005.** Act April 20, 2005, P.L. 109-8, Title XV, § 1501(a), 119 Stat. 23, provided that the amendments made to this section would be effective 180 days after enactment on April 20, 2005.

**Abridged Legislative History**

(H. Report No. 109-31 to accompany S. 256, 109th Cong., 1st Sess. (2005) p. 143; available at 2005 U.S.C.C.A.N. 88, at 202)

## *§ 526. Restrictions on debt relief agencies*

*(a) A debt relief agency shall not—*

*(1) fail to perform any service that such agency informed an assisted person or prospective assisted person it would provide in connection with a case or proceeding under this title;*

*(2) make any statement, or counsel or advise any assisted person or prospective assisted person to make a statement in a document filed in a case or proceeding under this title, that is untrue and misleading, or that upon the exercise of reasonable care, should have been known by such agency to be untrue or misleading;*

*(3) misrepresent to any assisted person or prospective assisted person, directly or indirectly, affirmatively or by material omission, with respect to—*

*(A) the services that such agency will provide to such person; or*

*(B) the benefits and risks that may result if such person becomes a debtor in a case under this title; or*

*(4) advise an assisted person or prospective assisted person to incur more debt in contemplation of such person filing a case under this title or to pay an attorney or bankruptcy petition preparer fee or charge for services performed as part of preparing for or representing a debtor in a case under this title.*

*(b) Any waiver by any assisted person of any protection or right provided under this section shall not be enforceable against the debtor by any Federal or State court or any other person, but may be enforced against a debt relief agency.*

*(c) (1) Any contract for bankruptcy assistance between a debt relief agency and an assisted person that does not comply with the material requirements of this section, section 527, or section 528 shall be void and may not be enforced by any Federal or State court or by any other person, other than such assisted person.*

*(2) Any debt relief agency shall be liable to an assisted person in the amount of any fees or charges in connection with providing bankruptcy assistance to such person that such debt relief agency has received, for actual damages, and for reasonable attorneys' fees and costs if such agency is found, after notice and a hearing, to have—*

*(A) intentionally or negligently failed to comply with any provision of this section, section 527, or section 528 with respect to a case or proceeding under this title for such assisted person;*

*(B) provided bankruptcy assistance to an assisted person in a case or proceeding under this title that is dismissed or converted to a case under another chapter of this title because of such agency's intentional or negligent failure to file any required document including those specified in section 521; or*

*(C) intentionally or negligently disregarded the material requirements of this title or the Federal Rules of Bankruptcy Procedure applicable to such agency.*

*(3) In addition to such other remedies as are provided under State law, whenever the chief law enforcement officer of a State, or an official or agency designated by a State, has reason to believe that any person has violated or is violating this section, the State—*

*(A) may bring an action to enjoin such violation;*

*(B) may bring an action on behalf of its residents to recover the actual damages of assisted persons arising from such violation, including any liability under paragraph (2); and*

*(C) in the case of any successful action under subparagraph (A) or (B), shall be awarded the costs of the action and reasonable attorneys' fees as determined by the court.*

*(4) The district courts of the United States for districts located in the State shall have concurrent jurisdiction of any action under subparagraph (A) or (B) of paragraph (3).*

*(5) Notwithstanding any other provision of Federal law and in addition to any other remedy provided under Federal or State law, if the court, on its own motion or on the motion of the United States*

*trustee or the debtor, finds that a person intentionally violated this section, or engaged in a clear and consistent pattern or practice of violating this section, the court may—*

*(A) enjoin the violation of such section; or*

*(B) impose an appropriate civil penalty against such person.*

*(d) No provision of this section, section 527, or section 528 shall—*

*(1) annul, alter, affect, or exempt any person subject to such sections from complying with any law of any State except to the extent that such law is inconsistent with those sections, and then only to the extent of the inconsistency; or*

*(2) be deemed to limit or curtail the authority or ability—*

*(A) of a State or subdivision or instrumentality thereof, to determine and enforce qualifications for the practice of law under the laws of that State; or*

*(B) of a Federal court to determine and enforce the qualifications for the practice of law before that court.*

**Section 526**

(April 20, 2005, P. L. 109-8, Title IIC, § 227(a), 119 Stat. 23)

## HISTORY: ANCILLARY LAWS AND DIRECTIVES

**Amendments:**

**2005.** Act April 20, 2005(effective 180 days after enactment of April 20, 2005, as provided by § 1501(a) of P. L. 109-8), adds new 11 USC § 526 for restrictions on debt relief agencies.

**Other provisions:**

**Effective date and application of amendments made by Act April 20, 2005.** Act April 20, 2005, P.L. 109-8, Title XV, § 1501(a), 119 Stat. 23, provided that the amendments made to this section would be effective 180 days after enactment on April 20, 2005.

**Abridged Legislative History**

Restrictions on Debt Relief Agencies. Section 227 of the Act creates a new provision in the Bankruptcy Code intended to proscribe certain activities of a debt relief agency.

In addition, section 227 imposes penalties for the violation of section 526, 527 or 528 of the Bankruptcy Code. (H. Report No. 109-31 to accompany S. 256, 109th Cong., 1st Sess. (2005) p. 66; available at 2005 U.S.C.C.A.N. 88, at 135)

## *§ 527. Disclosures*

*(a) A debt relief agency providing bankruptcy assistance to an assisted person shall provide—*

*(1) the written notice required under section 342(b)(1); and*

*(2) to the extent not covered in the written notice described in paragraph (1), and not later than 3 business days after the first date on which a debt relief agency first offers to provide any bankruptcy assistance services to an assisted person, a clear and conspicuous written notice advising assisted persons that—*

*(A) all information that the assisted person is required to provide with a petition and thereafter during a case under this title is required to be complete, accurate, and truthful;*

*(B) all assets and all liabilities are required to be completely*

*and accurately disclosed in the documents filed to commence the case, and the replacement value of each asset as defined in section 506 must be stated in those documents where requested after reasonable inquiry to establish such value;*

*(C) current monthly income, the amounts specified in section 707(b)(2), and, in a case under chapter 13 of this title, disposable income (determined in accordance with section 707(b)(2)), are required to be stated after reasonable inquiry; and*

*(D) information that an assisted person provides during their case may be audited pursuant to this title, and that failure to provide such information may result in dismissal of the case under this title or other sanction, including a criminal sanction.*

*(b) A debt relief agency providing bankruptcy assistance to an assisted person shall provide each assisted person at the same time as the notices required under subsection (a)(1) the following statement, to the extent applicable, or one substantially similar. The statement shall be clear and conspicuous and shall be in a single document separate from other documents or notices provided to the assisted person:*

*IMPORTANT INFORMATION ABOUT BANKRUPTCY ASSISTANCE SERVICES FROM AN ATTORNEY OR BANKRUPTCY PETITION PREPARER.*

*If you decide to seek bankruptcy relief, you can represent yourself, you can hire an attorney to represent you, or you can get help in some localities from a bankruptcy petition preparer who is not an attorney. THE LAW REQUIRES AN ATTORNEY OR BANKRUPTCY PETITION PREPARER TO GIVE YOU A WRITTEN CONTRACT SPECIFYING WHAT THE ATTORNEY OR BANKRUPTCY PETITION PREPARER WILL DO FOR YOU AND HOW MUCH IT WILL COST. Ask to see the contract before you hire anyone.*

*The following information helps you understand what must be done in a routine bankruptcy case to help you evaluate how much service you need. Although bankruptcy can be complex, many cases are routine.*

*Before filing a bankruptcy case, either you or your attorney should analyze your eligibility for different forms of debt relief available under the Bankruptcy Code and which form of relief is most likely to be beneficial for you. Be sure you understand the relief you can obtain and its limitations. To file a bankruptcy case, documents called a Petition, Schedules and Statement of Financial Affairs, as well as in some cases a Statement of Intention need to be prepared correctly and filed with the bankruptcy court. You will have to pay a filing fee to the bankruptcy court. Once your case starts, you will have to attend the required first meeting of creditors where you may be questioned by a court official called a 'trustee' and by creditors.*

*If you choose to file a chapter 7 case, you may be asked by a creditor to reaffirm a debt. You may want help deciding whether to do so. A creditor is not permitted to coerce you into reaffirming your debts.*

*If you choose to file a chapter 13 case in which you repay your creditors what you can afford over 3 to 5 years, you may also want help with preparing your chapter 13 plan and with the confirmation hearing on your plan which will be before a bankruptcy judge.*

*If you select another type of relief under the Bankruptcy Code other than chapter 7 or chapter 13, you will want to find out what should be done from someone familiar with that type of relief.*

*Your bankruptcy case may also involve litigation. You are generally permitted to represent yourself in litigation in bankruptcy court, but only attorneys, not bankruptcy petition preparers, can give you legal advice.*

*(c) Except to the extent the debt relief agency provides the required information itself after reasonably diligent inquiry of the assisted person or others so as to obtain such information reasonably accurately for inclusion on the petition, schedules or statement of financial affairs, a debt relief agency providing bankruptcy assistance to an assisted person, to the extent permitted by nonbankruptcy law, shall provide each assisted person at the time required for the notice required under subsection (a)(1) reasonably sufficient information (which shall be provided in a clear and conspicuous writing) to the assisted person on how to provide all the information the assisted person is required to provide under this title pursuant to section 521, including—*

*(1) how to value assets at replacement value, determine current monthly income, the amounts specified in section 707(b)(2) and, in a chapter 13 case, how to determine disposable income in accordance with section 707(b)(2) and related calculations;*

*(2) how to complete the list of creditors, including how to determine what amount is owed and what address for the creditor should be shown; and*

*(3) how to determine what property is exempt and how to value exempt property at replacement value as defined in section 506.*

*(d) A debt relief agency shall maintain a copy of the notices required under subsection (a) of this section for 2 years after the date on which the notice is given the assisted person.*

**Section 527**

(April 20, 2005, P. L. 109-8, Title IIC, § 228(a), 119 Stat. 23)

## HISTORY: ANCILLARY LAWS AND DIRECTIVES

**Amendments:**

**2005.** Act April 20, 2005(effective 180 days after enactment of April 20, 2005, as provided by § 1501(a) of P. L. 109-8), adds new 11 USC § 527 disclosures for the debt relief agencies created in § 526.

**Other provisions:**

**Effective date and application of amendments made by Act April 20, 2005.** Act April 20, 2005, P.L. 109-8, Title XV, § 1501(a), 119 Stat. 23, provided that the amendments made to this section would be effective 180 days after enactment on April 20, 2005.

**Abridged Legislative History**

Disclosures. Section 228 of the Act requires a debt relief agency to provide certain specified written notices to an assisted person. (H. Report No. 109-31 to accompany S.

256, 109th Cong., 1st Sess. (2005) pp. 66–67; available at 2005 U.S.C.C.A.N. 88, at 135)

## § 528. Requirements for debt relief agencies

*(a) A debt relief agency shall—*

*(1) not later than 5 business days after the first date on which such agency provides any bankruptcy assistance services to an assisted person, but prior to such assisted person's petition under this title being filed, execute a written contract with such assisted person that explains clearly and conspicuously—*

*(A) the services such agency will provide to such assisted person; and*

*(B) the fees or charges for such services, and the terms of payment;*

*(2) provide the assisted person with a copy of the fully executed and completed contract;*

*(3) clearly and conspicuously disclose in any advertisement of bankruptcy assistance services or of the benefits of bankruptcy directed to the general public (whether in general media, seminars or specific mailings, telephonic or electronic messages, or otherwise) that the services or benefits are with respect to bankruptcy relief under this title; and*

*(4) clearly and conspicuously use the following statement in such advertisement: 'We are a debt relief agency. We help people file for bankruptcy relief under the Bankruptcy Code.' or a substantially similar statement.*

*(b) (1) An advertisement of bankruptcy assistance services or of the benefits of bankruptcy directed to the general public includes—*

*(A) descriptions of bankruptcy assistance in connection with a chapter 13 plan whether or not chapter 13 is specifically mentioned in such advertisement; and*

*(B) statements such as 'federally supervised repayment plan' or 'Federal debt restructuring help' or other similar statements that could lead a reasonable consumer to believe that debt counseling was being offered when in fact the services were directed to providing bankruptcy assistance with a chapter 13 plan or other form of bankruptcy relief under this title.*

*(2) An advertisement, directed to the general public, indicating that the debt relief agency provides assistance with respect to credit defaults, mortgage foreclosures, eviction proceedings, excessive debt, debt collection pressure, or inability to pay any consumer debt shall—*

*(A) disclose clearly and conspicuously in such advertisement that the assistance may involve bankruptcy relief under this title; and*

*(B) include the following statement: 'We are a debt relief agency. We help people file for bankruptcy relief under the Bankruptcy Code.' or a substantially similar statement.*

**Section 528**
(April 20, 2005, P. L. 109-8, Title IIC, § 229(a), 119 Stat. 23)

## HISTORY: ANCILLARY LAWS AND DIRECTIVES

**Amendments:**
**2005.** Act April 20, 2005(effective 180 days after enactment of April 20, 2005, as provided by § 1501(a) of P. L. 109-8), adds new 11 USC § 528 describing requirements for the debt relief agencies created in new § 526.

**Other provisions:**
**Effective date and application of amendments made by Act April 20, 2005.** Act April 20, 2005, P.L. 109-8, Title XV, § 1501(a), 119 Stat. 23, provided that the amendments made to this section would be effective 180 days after enactment on April 20, 2005.

**Abridged Legislative History**
Requirements for Debt Relief Agencies. (H. Report No. 109-31 to accompany S. 256, 109th Cong., 1st Sess. (2005) pp. 67; available at 2005 U.S.C.C.A.N. 88, at 135–36)

# Subchapter III——The Estate

## § 541. Property of the estate

(a) The commencement of a case under section 301, 302, or 303 of this title creates an estate. Such estate is comprised of all the following property, wherever located and by whomever held:

(1) Except as provided in subsections (b) and (c)(2) of this section, all legal or equitable interests of the debtor in property as of the commencement of the case.

(2) All interests of the debtor and the debtor's spouse in community property as of the commencement of the case that is—

(A) under the sole, equal, or joint management and control of the debtor; or

(B) liable for an allowable claim against the debtor, or for both an allowable claim against the debtor and an allowable claim against the debtor's spouse, to the extent that such interest is so liable.

(3) Any interest in property that the trustee recovers under section 329(b), 363(n), 543, 550, 553, or 723 of this title.

(4) Any interest in property preserved for the benefit of or ordered transferred to the estate under section 510(c) or 551 of this title.

(5) Any interest in property that would have been property of the estate if such interest had been an interest of the debtor on the date of the filing of the petition, and that the debtor acquires or becomes entitled to acquire within 180 days after such date—

(A) by bequest, devise, or inheritance;

(B) as a result of a property settlement agreement with the debtor's spouse, or of an interlocutory or final divorce decree; or

(C) as a beneficiary of a life insurance policy or of a death benefit plan.

(6) Proceeds, product, offspring, rents, or profits of or from property of the estate, except such as are earnings from services

performed by an individual debtor after the commencement of the case.

(7) Any interest in property that the estate acquires after the commencement of the case.

(b) Property of the estate does not include—

(1) any power that the debtor may exercise solely for the benefit of an entity other than the debtor;

(2) any interest of the debtor as a lessee under a lease of nonresidential real property that has terminated at the expiration of the stated term of such lease before the commencement of the case under this title, and ceases to include any interest of the debtor as a lessee under a lease of nonresidential real property that has terminated at the expiration of the stated term of such lease during the case;

(3) any eligibility of the debtor to participate in programs authorized under the Higher Education Act of 1965 (20 U.S.C. 1001 et seq.; 42 U.S.C. 2751 et seq.), or any accreditation status or State licensure of the debtor as an educational institution;

(4) any interest of the debtor in liquid or gaseous hydrocarbons to the extent that—

(A) (i) the debtor has transferred or has agreed to transfer such interest pursuant to a farmout agreement or any written agreement directly related to a farmout agreement; and

(ii) but for the operation of this paragraph, the estate could include the interest referred to in clause (i) only by virtue of section 365 or 544(a)(3) of this title; ~~or~~

(B) (i) the debtor has transferred such interest pursuant to a written conveyance of a production payment to an entity that does not participate in the operation of the property from which such production payment is transferred; and

(ii) but for the operation of this paragraph, the estate could include the interest referred to in clause (i) only by virtue of section *365 or* 542 of this title; or

*(5) funds placed in an education individual retirement account (as defined in section 530(b)(1) of the Internal Revenue Code of 1986) not later than 365 days before the date of the filing of the petition in a case under this title, but—*

*(A) only if the designated beneficiary of such account was a child, stepchild, grandchild, or stepgrandchild of the debtor for the taxable year for which funds were placed in such account;*

*(B) only to the extent that such funds—*

*(i) are not pledged or promised to any entity in connection with any extension of credit; and*

*(ii) are not excess contributions (as described in section 4973(e) of the Internal Revenue Code of 1986); and*

*(C) in the case of funds placed in all such accounts having the same designated beneficiary not earlier than 720 days nor later*

*than 365 days before such date, only so much of such funds as does not exceed $5,000;*

*(6) funds used to purchase a tuition credit or certificate or contributed to an account in accordance with section 529(b)(1)(A) of the Internal Revenue Code of 1986 under a qualified State tuition program (as defined in section 529(b)(1) of such Code) not later than 365 days before the date of the filing of the petition in a case under this title, but—*

*(A) only if the designated beneficiary of the amounts paid or contributed to such tuition program was a child, stepchild, grandchild, or stepgrandchild of the debtor for the taxable year for which funds were paid or contributed;*

*(B) with respect to the aggregate amount paid or contributed to such program having the same designated beneficiary, only so much of such amount as does not exceed the total contributions permitted under section 529(b)(7) of such Code with respect to such beneficiary, as adjusted beginning on the date of the filing of the petition in a case under this title by the annual increase or decrease (rounded to the nearest tenth of 1 percent) in the education expenditure category of the Consumer Price Index prepared by the Department of Labor; and*

*(C) in the case of funds paid or contributed to such program having the same designated beneficiary not earlier than 720 days nor later than 365 days before such date, only so much of such funds as does not exceed $5,000;*

*(7) any amount—*

*(A) withheld by an employer from the wages of employees for payment as contributions—*

*(i) to—*

*(I) an employee benefit plan that is subject to title I of the Employee Retirement Income Security Act of 1974 or under an employee benefit plan which is a governmental plan under section 414(d) of the Internal Revenue Code of 1986;*

*(II) a deferred compensation plan under section 457 of the Internal Revenue Code of 1986; or*

*(III) a tax-deferred annuity under section 403(b) of the Internal Revenue Code of 1986;except that such amount under this subparagraph shall not constitute disposable income as defined in section 1325(b)(2); or*

*(ii) to a health insurance plan regulated by State law whether or not subject to such title; or*

*(B) received by an employer from employees for payment as contributions—*

*(i) to—*

*(I) an employee benefit plan that is subject to title I of the Employee Retirement Income Security Act of 1974 or under an employee benefit plan which is a governmental plan under section 414(d) of the Internal Revenue Code of 1986;*

*(II) a deferred compensation plan under section 457 of the Internal Revenue Code of 1986; or*

*(III) a tax-deferred annuity under section 403(b) of the Internal Revenue Code of 1986;except that such amount under this subparagraph shall not constitute disposable income, as defined in section 1325(b)(2); or*

*(ii) to a health insurance plan regulated by State law whether or not subject to such title;*

*(8) subject to subchapter III of chapter 5, any interest of the debtor in property where the debtor pledged or sold tangible personal property (other than securities or written or printed evidences of indebtedness or title) as collateral for a loan or advance of money given by a person licensed under law to make such loans or advances, where—*

*(A) the tangible personal property is in the possession of the pledgee or transferee;*

*(B) the debtor has no obligation to repay the money, redeem the collateral, or buy back the property at a stipulated price; and*

*(C) neither the debtor nor the trustee have exercised any right to redeem provided under the contract or State law, in a timely manner as provided under State law and section 108(b); or*

(~~5~~*9*) any interest in cash or cash equivalents that constitute proceeds of a sale by the debtor of a money order that is made—

(A) on or after the date that is 14 days prior to the date on which the petition is filed; and

(B) under an agreement with a money order issuer that prohibits the commingling of such proceeds with property of the debtor (notwithstanding that, contrary to the agreement, the proceeds may have been commingled with property of the debtor),

unless the money order issuer had not taken action, prior to the filing of the petition, to require compliance with the prohibition.

Paragraph (4) shall not be construed to exclude from the estate any consideration the debtor retains, receives, or is entitled to receive for transferring an interest in liquid or gaseous hydrocarbons pursuant to a farmout agreement.

(c) (1) Except as provided in paragraph (2) of this subsection, an interest of the debtor in property becomes property of the estate under subsection (a)(1), (a)(2), or (a)(5) of this section notwithstanding any provision in an agreement, transfer instrument, or applicable nonbankruptcy law—

(A) that restricts or conditions transfer of such interest by the debtor; or

(B) that is conditioned on the insolvency or financial condition of the debtor, on the commencement of a case under this title, or on the appointment of or taking possession by a trustee in a case under this title or a custodian before such commencement, and that effects or gives an option to effect a forfeiture, modification, or termination of the debtor's interest in property.

(2) A restriction on the transfer of a beneficial interest of the debtor in a trust that is enforceable under applicable nonbankruptcy law is enforceable in a case under this title.

(d) Property in which the debtor holds, as of the commencement of the case, only legal title and not an equitable interest, such as a mortgage secured by real property, or an interest in such a mortgage, sold by the debtor but as to which the debtor retains legal title to service or supervise the servicing of such mortgage or interest, becomes property of the estate under subsection (a)(1) or (2) of this section only to the extent of the debtor's legal title to such property, but not to the extent of any equitable interest in such property that the debtor does not hold.

*(e) In determining whether any of the relationships specified in paragraph (5)(A) or (6)(A) of subsection (b) exists, a legally adopted child of an individual (and a child who is a member of an individual's household, if placed with such individual by an authorized placement agency for legal adoption by such individual), or a foster child of an individual (if such child has as the child's principal place of abode the home of the debtor and is a member of the debtor's household) shall be treated as a child of such individual by blood.*

*(f) Notwithstanding any other provision of this title, property that is held by a debtor that is a corporation described in section 501(c)(3) of the Internal Revenue Code of 1986 and exempt from tax under section 501(a) of such Code may be transferred to an entity that is not such a corporation, but only under the same conditions as would apply if the debtor had not filed a case under this title.*

**Section 541**

(April 20, 2005, P. L. 109-8, Title IIC, § 225(a); Title III, § 323; Title XII, §§ 1212, 1221(c), 1230, 119 Stat. 23)

## HISTORY: ANCILLARY LAWS AND DIRECTIVES

**Amendments:**

**2005.** Act April 20, 2005(effective 180 days after enactment of April 20, 2005, as provided by § 1501(a) of P. L. 109-8), amends 11 USC § 541 to add new exclusions from property of the bankruptcy estate in §§ 541(b)(5), (6), (7) and (8).

The addition of § 541(f) is effective upon enactment and applies to cases pending on the date of enactment or to cases filed after such date. See P. L. 109-8, § 1221(d), 119 Stat. 23.

**Other provisions:**

**Effective date and application of amendments made by Act April 20, 2005.** Act April 20, 2005, P.L. 109-8, Title XV, § 1501(a), 119 Stat. 23, provided that the amendments made to this section would be effective 180 days after enactment on April 20, 2005, except that the addition of § 541(f) is effective upon enactment and applies to cases pending on the date of enactment or to cases filed after such date. See P. L. 109-8, § 1221(d), 119 Stat. 23.

**Abridged Legislative History**

Protection of Education Savings in Bankruptcy. Subsection (a) of section 225 of the Act amends section 541 of the Bankruptcy Code to provide that funds placed not later than 365 days before the filing of the bankruptcy case in an education individual retirement account are not property of the estate if certain criteria are met.

Excluding Employee Benefit Plan Participant Contributions and Other Property from the Estate. Section 323 of the Act amends section 541(b) of the Bankruptcy Code to exclude as property of the estate funds withheld or received by an employer from its employees' wages for payment as contributions to specified employee retirement plans, deferred compensation plans, and tax-deferred annuities.

Section 1221(c) amends section 541 of the Bankruptcy Code to provide that any property of a bankruptcy estate in which the debtor is a nonprofit corporation (as described in certain provisions of the Internal Revenue Code) may not be transferred to an entity that is not such a corporation, but only under the same conditions that would apply if the debtor was not in bankruptcy. The amendments made by this section apply to cases pending on the date of enactment or to cases filed after such date.

Property No Longer Subject to Redemption. Section 1230 of the Act amends section 541(b) of the Bankruptcy Code to provide that, under certain circumstances, an interest of the debtor in tangible personal property (other than securities, or written or printed evidences of indebtedness or title) that the debtor pledged or sold as collateral for a loan or advance of money given by a person licensed under law to make such loan or advance is not property of the estate.

(H. Report No. 109-31 to accompany S. 256, 109th Cong., 1st Sess. (2005) pp. 65, 82, 143, 145, 147; available at 2005 U.S.C.C.A.N. 88, at 134, 149, 202, 204–205)

## § 542. Turnover of property to the estate

(a) Except as provided in subsection (c) or (d) of this section, an entity, other than a custodian, in possession, custody, or control, during the case, of property that the trustee may use, sell, or lease under section 363 of this title, or that the debtor may exempt under section 522 of this title, shall deliver to the trustee, and account for, such property or the value of such property, unless such property is of inconsequential value or benefit to the estate.

(b) Except as provided in subsection (c) or (d) of this section, an entity that owes a debt that is property of the estate and that is matured, payable on demand, or payable on order, shall pay such debt to, or on the order of, the trustee, except to the extent that such debt may be offset under section 553 of this title against a claim against the debtor.

(c) Except as provided in section 362(a)(7) of this title, an entity that has neither actual notice nor actual knowledge of the commencement of the case concerning the debtor may transfer property of the estate, or pay a debt owing to the debtor, in good faith and other than in the manner specified in subsection (d) of this section, to an entity other than the trustee, with the same effect as to the entity making such transfer or payment as if the case under this title concerning the debtor had not been commenced.

(d) A life insurance company may transfer property of the estate or property of the debtor to such company in good faith, with the same effect with respect to such company as if the case under this title concerning the debtor had not been commenced, if such transfer is to pay a premium or to carry out a nonforfeiture insurance option, and is required to be made automatically, under a life insurance contract with such company that was entered into before the date of the filing of the petition and that is property of the estate.

(e) Subject to any applicable privilege, after notice and a hearing, the court may order an attorney, accountant, or other person that holds recorded information, including books, documents, records, and papers, relating to the debtor's property or financial affairs, to turn over or disclose such recorded information to the trustee.

## § 543. Turnover of property by a custodian

(a) A custodian with knowledge of the commencement of a case under this title concerning the debtor may not make any disbursement from, or take any action in the administration of, property of the debtor, proceeds, product, offspring, rents or profits of such property, or property of the estate, in the possession, custody, or control of such custodian, except such action as is necessary to preserve such property.

(b) A custodianshall—

(1) deliver to the trustee any property of the debtor held by or transferred to such custodian, or proceeds, product, offspring, rents, or profits of such property, that is in such custodian's possession, custody, or control on the date that such custodian acquires knowledge of the commencement of the case; and

(2) file an accounting of any property of the debtor, or proceeds, product, offspring, rents, or profits of such property, that, at any time, came into the possession, custody, or control of such custodian.

(c) The court, after notice and a hearing, shall—

(1) protect all entities to which a custodian has become obligated with respect to such property or proceeds, product, offspring, rents, or profits of such property;

(2) provide for payment of reasonable compensation for services rendered and costs and expenses incurred by such custodian; and

(3) surcharge such custodian, other than an assignee for the benefit of the debtor's creditors that was appointed or took possession more than 120 days before the date of the filing of the petition, for any improper or excessive disbursement, other than a disbursement that has been made in accordance with applicable law or that has been approved, after notice and a hearing, by a court of competent jurisdiction before the commencement of the case under this title.

(d) After notice and hearing, the bankruptcy court—

(1) may excuse compliance with subsection (a), (b), or (c) of this section if the interests of creditors and, if the debtor is not insolvent, of equity security holders would be better served by permitting a custodian to continue in possession, custody, or control of such property, and

(2) shall excuse compliance with subsections (a) and (b)(1) of this section if the custodian is an assignee for the benefit of the debtor's creditors that was appointed or took possession more than 120 days before the date of the filing of the petition, unless compliance with such subsections is necessary to prevent fraud or injustice.

## § 544. Trustee as lien creditor and as successor to certain creditors and purchasers

(a) The trustee shall have, as of the commencement of the case, and without regard to any knowledge of the trustee or of any creditor, the rights and powers of, or may avoid any transfer of property of the debtor or any obligation incurred by the debtor that is voidable by—

(1) a creditor that extends credit to the debtor at the time of the commencement of the case, and that obtains, at such time and with respect to such credit, a judicial lien on all property on which a creditor on a simple contract could have obtained such a judicial lien, whether or not such a creditor exists;

(2) a creditor that extends credit to the debtor at the time of the commencement of the case, and obtains, at such time and with respect to such credit, an execution against the debtor that is returned unsatisfied at such time, whether or not such a creditor exists; or

(3) a bona fide purchaser of real property, other than fixtures, from the debtor, against whom applicable law permits such transfer to be perfected, that obtains the status of a bona fide purchaser and has perfected such transfer at the time of the commencement of the case, whether or not such a purchaser exists.

(b) (1) Except as provided in paragraph (2), the trustee may avoid any transfer of an interest of the debtor in property or any obligation incurred by the debtor that is voidable under applicable law by a creditor holding an unsecured claim that is allowable under section 502 of this title or that is not allowable only under section 502(e) of this title.(2) Paragraph (1) shall not apply to a transfer of a charitable contribution (as that term is defined in section 548(d)(3)) that is not covered under section 548(a)(1)(B), by reason of section 548(a)(2). Any claim by any person to recover a transferred contribution described in the preceding sentence under Federal or State law in a Federal or State court shall be preempted by the commencement of the case.

## § 545. Statutory liens

The trustee may avoid the fixing of a statutory lien on property of the debtor to the extent that such lien—

(1) first becomes effective against the debtor—

(A) when a case under this title concerning the debtor is commenced;

(B) when an insolvency proceeding other than under this title concerning the debtor is commenced;

(C) when a custodian is appointed or authorized to take or takes possession;

(D) when the debtor becomes insolvent;

(E) when the debtor's financial condition fails to meet a specified standard; or

(F) at the time of an execution against property of the debtor levied at the instance of an entity other than the holder of such statutory lien;

(2) is not perfected or enforceable at the time of the commencement of the case against a bona fide purchaser that purchases such property at the time of the commencement of the case, whether or not such a purchaser exists, *except in any case in which a purchaser is a purchaser described in section 6323 of the Internal Revenue Code of 1986, or in any other similar provision of State or local law;*

(3) is for rent; or

(4) is a lien of distress for rent.

**Section 545**

(April 20, 2005, P. L. 109-8, Title VII, § 711, 119 Stat. 23)

## HISTORY: ANCILLARY LAWS AND DIRECTIVES

**Amendments:**

**2005.** Act April 20, 2005(effective 180 days after enactment of April 20, 2005, as provided by § 1501(a) of P. L. 109-8), amends 11 USC § 545(2) to prevent the Internal Revenue Code's special protections for certain purchasers of securities and vehicles from being used to avoid an otherwise valid lien.

**Other provisions:**

**Effective date and application of amendments made by Act April 20, 2005.** Act April 20, 2005, P.L. 109-8, Title XV, § 1501(a), 119 Stat. 23, provided that the amendments made to this section would be effective 180 days after enactment on April 20, 2005.

**Abridged Legislative History**

(H. Report No. 109-31 to accompany S. 256, 109th Cong., 1st Sess. (2005) p. 102; available at 2005 U.S.C.C.A.N. 88, at 166)

## § 546. Limitations on avoiding powers

(a) An action or proceeding under section 544, 545, 547, 548, or 553 of this title may not be commenced after the earlier of—

(1) the later of—

(A) 2 years after the entry of the order for relief; or

(B) 1 year after the appointment or election of the first trustee under section 702, 1104, 1163, 1202, or 1302 of this title if such appointment or such election occurs before the expiration of the period specified in subparagraph (A); or

(2) the time the case is closed or dismissed.

(b) (1) The rights and powers of a trustee under sections 544, 545, and 549 of this title are subject to any generally applicable law that—

(A) permits perfection of an interest in property to be effective against an entity that acquires rights in such property before the date of perfection; or

(B) provides for the maintenance or continuation of perfection of an interest in property to be effective against an entity that acquires rights in such property before the date on which action is taken to effect such maintenance or continuation.

(2) If—

(A) a law described in paragraph (1) requires seizure of such property or commencement of an action to accomplish such perfection, or maintenance or continuation of perfection of an interest in property; and

(B) such property has not been seized or such an action has not been commenced before the date of the filing of the petition;

such interest in such property shall be perfected, or perfection of such interest shall be maintained or continued, by giving notice within the time fixed by such law for such seizure or such commencement.

~~(c) Except as provided in subsection (d) of this section, the rights and powers of a trustee under sections 544(a), 545, 547, and 549 of this title are subject to any statutory or common-law right of a seller of goods that has sold goods to the debtor, in the ordinary course of such seller's business, to reclaim such goods if the debtor has received such goods while insolvent, but—~~

~~(1) such a seller may not reclaim any such goods unless such seller demands in writing reclamation of such goods—~~

~~(A) before 10 days after receipt of such goods by the debtor; or~~

~~(B) if such 10-day period expires after the commencement of the case, before 20 days after receipt of such goods by the debtor; and~~

~~(2) the court may deny reclamation to a seller with such a right of reclamation that has made such a demand only if the court—~~

~~(A) grants the claim of such a seller priority as a claim of a kind specified in section 503(b) of this title; or~~

~~(B) secures such claim by a lien.~~

*(c) (1) Except as provided in subsection (d) of this section and in section 507(c), and subject to the prior rights of a holder of a security interest in such goods or the proceeds thereof, the rights and powers of the trustee under sections 544(a), 545, 547, and 549 are subject to the right of a seller of goods that has sold goods to the debtor, in the ordinary course of such seller's business, to reclaim such goods if the debtor has received such goods while insolvent, within 45 days before the date of the commencement of a case under this title, but such seller may not reclaim such goods unless such seller demands in writing reclamation of such goods—*

*(A) not later than 45 days after the date of receipt of such goods by the debtor; or*

*(B) not later than 20 days after the date of commencement of the case, if the 45-day period expires after the commencement of the case.*

*(2) If a seller of goods fails to provide notice in the manner described in paragraph (1), the seller still may assert the rights contained in section 503(b)(9).*

(d) In the case of a seller who is a producer of grain sold to a grain storage facility, owned or operated by the debtor, in the ordinary course of such seller's business (as such terms are defined in section 557 of this title) or in the case of a United States fisherman who has caught fish sold to a fish processing facility owned or operated by the debtor in the ordinary course of such fisherman's business, the rights and powers of the trustee under sections 544(a), 545, 547, and 549 of this title are subject to any statutory or common law right of such producer or fisherman to reclaim such grain or fish if the debtor has received such grain or fish while insolvent, but—

(1) such producer or fisherman may not reclaim any grain or fish unless such producer or fisherman demands, in writing, reclamation of such grain or fish before ten days after receipt thereof by the debtor; and

(2) the court may deny reclamation to such a producer or fisherman with a right of reclamation that has made such a demand only if the court secures such claim by a lien.

(e) Notwithstanding sections 544, 545, 547, 548(a)(1)(B), and 548(b) of this title, the trustee may not avoid a transfer that is a margin payment, as defined in section 101, 741, or 761 of this title, or settlement payment, as defined in section 101 or 741 of this title, made by or to a commodity broker, forward contract merchant, stockbroker, financial institution, *financial participant*, or securities clearing agency, that is made before the commencement of the case, except under section 548(a)(1)(A) of this title.

(f) Notwithstanding sections 544, 545, 547, 548(a)(1)(B), and 548(b) of this title, the trustee may not avoid a transfer that is a margin payment, as defined in section 741 or 761 of this title, or settlement payment, as defined in section 741 of this title, made by or to a repo participant *or financial participant*, in connection with a repurchase agreement and that is made before the commencement of the case, except under section 548(a)(1)(A) of this title.

(g) Notwithstanding sections 544, 545, 547, 548(a)(1)(B) and 548(b) of this title, the trustee may not avoid a transfer ~~under a swap agreement~~, made by or to a swap participant *or financial participant,* ~~in connection with a swap agreement~~ *under or in connection with any swap agreement* and that is made before the commencement of the case, except under section 548(a)(1)(A) of this title.

(~~g~~*h*) Notwithstanding the rights and powers of a trustee under sections 544(a), 545, 547, 549, and 553, if the court determines on a motion by the trustee made not later than 120 days after the date of the order for relief in a case under chapter 11 of this title and after notice and a hearing, that a return is in the best interests of the estate, the debtor, with the consent of a creditor *and subject to the prior rights of holders of security interests in such goods or the proceeds of such goods*, may return goods shipped to the debtor by the creditor before the commencement of the case, and the creditor may offset the purchase price of such goods against any claim of the creditor against the debtor that arose before the commencement of the case.

*(i) (1) Notwithstanding paragraphs (2) and (3) of section 545, the*

*trustee may not avoid a warehouseman's lien for storage, transportation, or other costs incidental to the storage and handling of goods.*

*(2) The prohibition under paragraph (1) shall be applied in a manner consistent with any State statute applicable to such lien that is similar to section 7-209 of the Uniform Commercial Code, as in effect on the date of enactment of the Bankruptcy Abuse Prevention and Consumer Protection Act of 2005, or any successor to such section 7-209.*

*(j) Notwithstanding sections 544, 545, 547, 548(a)(1)(B), and 548(b) the trustee may not avoid a transfer made by or to a master netting agreement participant under or in connection with any master netting agreement or any individual contract covered thereby that is made before the commencement of the case, except under section 548(a)(1)(A) and except to the extent that the trustee could otherwise avoid such a transfer made under an individual contract covered by such master netting agreement.*

**Section 546**

(April 20, 2005, P. L. 109-8, Title IVA, § 406; Title IX, §§ 907(e), (o)(2), (3); Title XII, § 1227(a), 119 Stat. 23)

## HISTORY: ANCILLARY LAWS AND DIRECTIVES

**Amendments:**

**2005.** Act April 20, 2005(effective 180 days after enactment of April 20, 2005, as provided by § 1501(a) of P. L. 109-8), amends 11 USC § 546 to conform to the Uniform Commercial Code and to other changes in financial transactions. Reclamation and warehouse lien amendments are also made.

**Other provisions:**

**Effective date and application of amendments made by Act April 20, 2005.** Act April 20, 2005, P.L. 109-8, Title XV, § 1501(a), 119 Stat. 23, provided that the amendments made to this section would be effective 180 days after enactment on April 20, 2005.

**Abridged Legislative History**

Amendment to Section 546 of Title 11, United States Code. Further, section 406 adds a new provision to section 546 that prohibits a trustee from avoiding a warehouse lien for storage, transportation, or other costs incidental to the storage and handling of goods.

Subsections (e) and (f) of section 907 of the Act amend sections 546 and 548(d) of the Bankruptcy Code to provide that transfers made under or in connection with a master netting agreement may not be avoided by a trustee except where such transfer is made with actual intent to hinder, delay or defraud and not taken in good faith.

Section 907(o), as well as other subsections of the Act, adds references to "financial participant" in all the provisions of the Bankruptcy Code relating to securities, forward and commodity contracts and repurchase and swap agreements.

Reclamation. Section 1227 of the Act amends section 546(c) of the Bankruptcy Code to provide that the rights of a trustee under sections 544(a), 545, 547, and 549 are subject to the rights of a seller of goods to reclaim goods sold in the ordinary course of business to the debtor.

(H. Report No. 109-31 to accompany S. 256, 109th Cong., 1st Sess. (2005) pp. 87, 132, 146; available at 2005 U.S.C.C.A.N. 88, at 153, 192, 204–05)

# § 547. Preferences

(a) In this section—

(1) "inventory" means personal property leased or furnished, held

for sale or lease, or to be furnished under a contract for service, raw materials, work in process, or materials used or consumed in a business, including farm products such as crops or livestock, held for sale or lease;

(2) "new value" means money or money's worth in goods, services, or new credit, or release by a transferee of property previously transferred to such transferee in a transaction that is neither void nor voidable by the debtor or the trustee under any applicable law, including proceeds of such property, but does not include an obligation substituted for an existing obligation;

(3) "receivable" means right to payment, whether or not such right has been earned by performance; and

(4) a debt for a tax is incurred on the day when such tax is last payable without penalty, including any extension.

(b) Except as provided in subsections (c) *and (i)* of this section, the trustee may avoid any transfer of an interest of the debtor in property—

(1) to or for the benefit of a creditor;

(2) for or on account of an antecedent debt owed by the debtor before such transfer was made;

(3) made while the debtor was insolvent;

(4) made—

(A) on or within 90 days before the date of the filing of the petition; or

(B) between ninety days and one year before the date of the filing of the petition, if such creditor at the time of such transfer was an insider; and

(5) that enables such creditor to receive more than such creditor would receive if—

(A) the case were a case under chapter 7 of this title;

(B) the transfer had not been made; and

(C) such creditor received payment of such debt to the extent provided by the provisions of this title.

(c) The trustee may not avoid under this section a transfer—

(1) to the extent that such transfer was—

(A) intended by the debtor and the creditor to or for whose benefit such transfer was made to be a contemporaneous exchange for new value given to the debtor; and

(B) in fact a substantially contemporaneous exchange;

(2) ~~to the extent that such transfer was—~~

~~(A) in payment of a debt incurred by the debtor in the ordinary course of business or financial affairs of the debtor and the transferee;~~

~~(B) made in the ordinary course of business or financial affairs of the debtor and the transferee; and~~

~~(C) made according to ordinary business terms;~~ *to the extent that such transfer was in payment of a debt incurred by the debtor in the ordinary course of business or financial affairs of the debtor and the transferee, and such transfer was—*

*(A) made in the ordinary course of business or financial affairs of the debtor and the transferee; or*

*(B) made according to ordinary business terms;*

(3) that creates a security interest in property acquired by the debtor—

(A) to the extent such security interest secures new value that was—

(i) given at or after the signing of a security agreement that contains a description of such property as collateral;

(ii) given by or on behalf of the secured party under such agreement;

(iii) given to enable the debtor to acquire such property; and

(iv) in fact used by the debtor to acquire such property; and

(B) that is perfected on or before ~~20~~*30* days after the debtor receives possession of such property;

(4) to or for the benefit of a creditor, to the extent that, after such transfer, such creditor gave new value to or for the benefit of the debtor—

(A) not secured by an otherwise unavoidable security interest; and

(B) on account of which new value the debtor did not make an otherwise unavoidable transfer to or for the benefit of such creditor;

(5) that creates a perfected security interest in inventory or a receivable or the proceeds of either, except to the extent that the aggregate of all such transfers to the transferee caused a reduction, as of the date of the filing of the petition and to the prejudice of other creditors holding unsecured claims, of any amount by which the debt secured by such security interest exceeded the value of all security interests for such debt on the later of—

(A) (i) with respect to a transfer to which subsection (b)(4)(A) of this section applies, 90 days before the date of the filing of the petition; or

(ii) with respect to a transfer to which subsection (b)(4)(B) of this section applies, one year before the date of the filing of the petition; or

(B) the date on which new value was first given under the security agreement creating such security interest;

(6) that is the fixing of a statutory lien that is not avoidable under section 545 of this title;

(7) to the extent such transfer was a bona fide payment of a debt *for a domestic support obligation;* ~~to a spouse, former spouse, or child of the debtor, for alimony to, maintenance for, or support of~~

~~such spouse or child, in connection with a separation agreement, divorce decree or other order of a court of record, determination made in accordance with State or territorial law by a governmental unit, or property settlement agreement, but not to the extent that such debt—~~

~~(A) is assigned to another entity, voluntarily, by operation of law, or otherwise; or~~

~~(B) includes a liability designated as alimony, maintenance, or support, unless such liability is actually in the nature of alimony, maintenance or support; or~~

(8) if, in a case filed by an individual debtor whose debts are primarily consumer debts, the aggregate value of all property that constitutes or is affected by such transfer is less than $600~~.~~; or

*(9) if, in a case filed by a debtor whose debts are not primarily consumer debts, the aggregate value of all property that constitutes or is affected by such transfer is less than $5,000.*

(d) The trustee may avoid a transfer of an interest in property of the debtor transferred to or for the benefit of a surety to secure reimbursement of such a surety that furnished a bond or other obligation to dissolve a judicial lien that would have been avoidable by the trustee under subsection (b) of this section. The liability of such surety under such bond or obligation shall be discharged to the extent of the value of such property recovered by the trustee or the amount paid to the trustee.

(e) (1) For the purposes of this section—

(A) a transfer of real property other than fixtures, but including the interest of a seller or purchaser under a contract for the sale of real property, is perfected when a bona fide purchaser of such property from the debtor against whom applicable law permits such transfer to be perfected cannot acquire an interest that is superior to the interest of the transferee; and

(B) a transfer of a fixture or property other than real property is perfected when a creditor on a simple contract cannot acquire a judicial lien that is superior to the interest of the transferee.

(2) For the purposes of this section, except as provided in paragraph (3) of this subsection, a transfer is made—

(A) at the time such transfer takes effect between the transferor and the transferee, if such transfer is perfected at, or within ~~10~~*30* days after, such time, except as provided in subsection (c)(3)(B);

(B) at the time such transfer is perfected, if such transfer is perfected after such ~~10~~ *30* days; or

(C) immediately before the date of the filing of the petition, if such transfer is not perfected at the later of—

(i) the commencement of the case; or

(ii) ~~10~~ *30* days after such transfer takes effect between the transferor and the transferee.

(3) For the purposes of this section, a transfer is not made until the debtor has acquired rights in the property transferred.

(f) For the purposes of this section, the debtor is presumed to have been insolvent on and during the 90 days immediately preceding the date of the filing of the petition.

(g) For the purposes of this section, the trustee has the burden of proving the avoidability of a transfer under subsection (b) of this section, and the creditor or party in interest against whom recovery or avoidance is sought has the burden of proving the nonavoidability of a transfer under subsection (c) of this section.

*(h) The trustee may not avoid a transfer if such transfer was made as a part of an alternative repayment schedule between the debtor and any creditor of the debtor created by an approved nonprofit budget and credit counseling agency.*

*(i) If the trustee avoids under subsection (b) a transfer made between 90 days and 1 year before the date of the filing of the petition, by the debtor to an entity that is not an insider for the benefit of a creditor that is an insider, such transfer shall be considered to be avoided under this section only with respect to the creditor that is an insider.*

**Section 547**

(April 20, 2005, P. L. 109-8, Title IIA, § 201(b); Title IIB, § 217; Title IVA, §§ 403, 409; Title XII, §§ 1213, 1222, 119 Stat. 23)

## HISTORY: ANCILLARY LAWS AND DIRECTIVES

**Amendments:**

**2005.** Act April 20, 2005(effective 180 days after enactment of April 20, 2005, as provided by § 1501(a) of P. L. 109-8), amends 11 USC § 547(c)(2)'s provisions for ordinary course of business, (c)(7)'s provision for domestic support obligations, and adds (c)(9). Also, § 547(h) and (i) are added concerning payments made under an alternative repayment schedule and insider transfers.

**Other provisions:**

**Effective date and application of amendments made by Act April 20, 2005.** Act April 20, 2005, P.L. 109-8, Title XV, § 1501(a), 119 Stat. 23, provided that the amendments made to this section would be effective 180 days after enactment on April 20, 2005.

**Abridged Legislative History**

Section 201(b) amends section 547 of the Bankruptcy Code to prohibit the avoidance as a preferential transfer a payment by a debtor to a creditor pursuant to an alternative repayment plan created by an approved credit counseling agency.

Protection of Domestic Support Claims Against Preferential Protection of Refinance of Security Interest. Section 403 amends section 547(e)(2) of the Bankruptcy Code to increase the perfection period from ten to 30 days for the purpose of determining whether a transfer is an avoidable preference.

Protection of Refinance of Security Interest. Section 403 amends section 547(e)(2) of the Bankruptcy Code to increase the perfection period from ten to 30 days for the purpose of determining whether a transfer is an avoidable preference.

Preferences. Section 409 amends section 547(c)(2) of the Bankruptcy Code to provide that a trustee may not avoid a transfer to the extent such transfer was in payment of a debt incurred by the debtor in the ordinary course of the business or financial affairs of the debtor and the transferee and such transfer was made either: (1) in the ordinary course of the debtor's and the transferee's business or financial affairs; or (2) in accordance with ordinary business terms.

Preferences. Section 1213 of the Act makes a perfecting amendment to section 547 to provide that if the trustee avoids a transfer given by the debtor to a noninsider for the benefit of an insider creditor between 90 days and one year before filing, that avoidance is valid only with respect to the insider creditor. Thus both the previous amendment to section 550 and the perfecting amendment to section 547 protect the noninsider from the avoiding powers of the trustee exercised with respect to transfers made during the 90-day to one-year pre-filing period. This provision is intended to apply to any case, including any adversary proceeding, that is pending or commenced on or after the date of enactment of this Act.

Protection of Valid Purchase Money Security Interests. Section 1222 of the Act extends the applicable perfection period for a security interest in property of the debtor in section 547(c)(3)(B) of the Bankruptcy Code from 20 to 30 days. (H. Report No. 109-31 to accompany S. 256, 109th Cong., 1st Sess. (2005) pp. 57, 61, 86, 88, 144–45; available at 2005 U.S.C.C.A.N. 88, at 127, 130, 152, 154, 202–03, 204)

## § 548. Fraudulent transfers and obligations

(a) (1) The trustee may avoid any transfer *(including any transfer to or for the benefit of an insider under an employment contract)* of an interest of the debtor in property, or any obligation *(including any obligation to or for the benefit of an insider under an employment contract)* incurred by the debtor, that was made or incurred on or within ~~one year~~*2 years* before the date of the filing of the petition, if the debtor voluntarily or involuntarily—

(A) made such transfer or incurred such obligation with actual intent to hinder, delay, or defraud any entity to which the debtor was or became, on or after the date that such transfer was made or such obligation was incurred, indebted; or

(B) (i) received less than a reasonably equivalent value in exchange for such transfer or obligation; and

(ii) (I) was insolvent on the date that such transfer was made or such obligation was incurred, or became insolvent as a result of such transfer or obligation;

(II) was engaged in business or a transaction, or was about to engage in business or a transaction, for which any property remaining with the debtor was an unreasonably small capital; ~~or~~

(III) intended to incur, or believed that the debtor would incur, debts that would be beyond the debtor's ability to pay as such debts matured~~.~~*; or*

*(IV) made such transfer to or for the benefit of an insider, or incurred such obligation to or for the benefit of an insider, under an employment contract and not in the ordinary course of business.*

(2) A transfer of a charitable contribution to a qualified religious or charitable entity or organization shall not be considered to be a transfer covered under paragraph (1)(B) in any case in which.—

(A) the amount of that contribution does not exceed 15 percent of the gross annual income of the debtor for the year in which the transfer of the contribution is made; or

(B) the contribution made by a debtor exceeded the percentage amount of gross annual income specified in subparagraph (A), if the transfer was consistent with the practices of the debtor in making charitable contributions.

(b) The trustee of a partnership debtor may avoid any transfer of an interest of the debtor in property, or any obligation incurred by the debtor, that was made or incurred on or within ~~one year~~*2 years* before the date of the filing of the petition, to a general partner in the debtor, if the debtor was insolvent on the date such transfer was made or such obligation was incurred, or became insolvent as a result of such transfer or obligation.

(c) Except to the extent that a transfer or obligation voidable under this section is voidable under section 544, 545, or 547 of this title, a transferee or obligee of such a transfer or obligation that takes for value and in good faith has a lien on or may retain any interest transferred or may enforce any obligation incurred, as the case may be, to the extent that such transferee or obligee gave value to the debtor in exchange for such transfer or obligation.

(d) (1) For the purposes of this section, a transfer is made when such transfer is so perfected that a bona fide purchaser from the debtor against whom applicable law permits such transfer to be perfected cannot acquire an interest in the property transferred that is superior to the interest in such property of the transferee, but if such transfer is not so perfected before the commencement of the case, such transfer is made immediately before the date of the filing of the petition.

(2) In this section—

(A) "value" means property, or satisfaction or securing of a present or antecedent debt of the debtor, but does not include an unperformed promise to furnish support to the debtor or to a relative of the debtor;

(B) a commodity broker, forward contract merchant, stockbroker, financial institution, *financial participant,* or securities clearing agency that receives a margin payment, as defined in section 101, 741, or 761 of this title, or settlement payment, as defined in section 101 or 741 of this title, takes for value to the extent of such payment;

(C) a repo participant *or financial participant* that receives a margin payment, as defined in section 741 or 761 of this title, or settlement payment, as defined in section 741 of this title, in connection with a repurchase agreement, takes for value to the extent of such payment; ~~and~~

(D) a swap participant *or financial participant* that receives a transfer in connection with a swap agreement takes for value to the extent of such transfer~~.~~*; and*

*(E) a master netting agreement participant that receives a transfer in connection with a master netting agreement or any individual contract covered thereby takes for value to the extent of such transfer, except that, with respect to a transfer under any in-*

*dividual contract covered thereby, to the extent that such master netting agreement participant otherwise did not take (or is otherwise not deemed to have taken) such transfer for value.*

(3) In this section, the term "charitable contribution" means a charitable contribution, as that term is defined in section 170(c) of the Internal Revenue Code of 1986, if that contribution—

(A) is made by a natural person; and

(B) consists of.—

(i) a financial instrument (as that term is defined in section 731(c)(2)(C) of the Internal Revenue Code of 1986); or

(ii) cash.

(4) In this section, the term "qualified religious or charitable entity or organization" means—

(A) an entity described in section 170(c)(1) of the Internal Revenue Code of 1986; or

(B) an entity or organization described in section 170(c)(2) of the Internal Revenue Code of 1986.

*(e) (1) In addition to any transfer that the trustee may otherwise avoid, the trustee may avoid any transfer of an interest of the debtor in property that was made on or within 10 years before the date of the filing of the petition, if—*

*(A) such transfer was made to a self-settled trust or similar device;*

*(B) such transfer was by the debtor;*

*(C) the debtor is a beneficiary of such trust or similar device; and*

*(D) the debtor made such transfer with actual intent to hinder, delay, or defraud any entity to which the debtor was or became, on or after the date that such transfer was made, indebted.*

*(2) For the purposes of this subsection, a transfer includes a transfer made in anticipation of any money judgment, settlement, civil penalty, equitable order, or criminal fine incurred by, or which the debtor believed would be incurred by—*

*(A) any violation of the securities laws (as defined in section 3(a)(47) of the Securities Exchange Act of 1934 (15 U.S.C. 78c(a)(47))), any State securities laws, or any regulation or order issued under Federal securities laws or State securities laws; or*

*(B) fraud, deceit, or manipulation in a fiduciary capacity or in connection with the purchase or sale of any security registered under section 12 or 15(d) of the Securities Exchange Act of 1934 (15 U.S.C. 78l and 78o(d)) or under section 6 of the Securities Act of 1933 (15 U.S.C. 77f).*

**Section 548**

(April 20, 2005, P. L. 109-8, Title IX, §§ 907(f), (o)(4), (5), (6); Title XIV, § 1402, 119 Stat. 23)

## HISTORY: ANCILLARY LAWS AND DIRECTIVES

**Amendments:**

**2005.** Act April 20, 2005(effective 180 days after enactment of April 20, 2005, as provided by § 1501(a) of P. L. 109-8), amends 11 USC § 548 to add references to "financial participant" in all the provisions of the Bankruptcy Code relating to securities, forward and commodity contracts and repurchase and swap agreements. The other amendments to § 548 are effective upon enactment for cases commenced on or after April 20,2005, with the change from 1 to 2 years in § 548(a)(1) effective one year following enactment.

**Other provisions:**

**Effective date and application of amendments made by Act April 20, 2005.** Act April 20, 2005, P.L. 109-8, Title XV, § 1501(a), 119 Stat. 23, provided that the amendments made to this section as to addition of references to "financial participant" would be effective 180 days after enactment on April 20, 2005. The other changes, made by § 1402 of P. L. 109-8 are effective upon enactment, except for the change from 1 to 2 years in § 548(a)(1) effective one year following enactment, as provided by § 1406, P. L. 109-8:

SEC. 1406. EFFECTIVE DATE; APPLICATION OF AMENDMENTS.

(a) EFFECTIVE DATE- Except as provided in subsection (b), this title and the amendments made by this title shall take effect on the date of the enactment of this Act.

(b) APPLICATION OF AMENDMENTS-

1) IN GENERAL- Except as provided in paragraph (2), the amendments made by this title shall apply only with respect to cases commenced under title 11 of the United States Code on or after the date of the enactment of this Act.

(2) AVOIDANCE PERIOD- The amendment made by section 1402(1) shall apply only with respect to cases commenced under title 11 of the United States Code more than 1 year after the date of the enactment of this Act.

**Abridged Legislative History**

Subsections (e) and (f) of section 907 of the Act amend sections 546 and 548(d) of the Bankruptcy Code to provide that transfers made under or in connection with a master netting agreement may not be avoided by a trustee except where such transfer is made with actual intent to hinder, delay or defraud and not taken in good faith.

Fraudulent Transfers and Obligations. Section 1402 of the Act amends section 548 of the Bankruptcy Code to enhance the recovery of avoidable transfers and excessive prepetition compensation, such as bonuses, paid to insiders of a debtor. It effectuates two changes to current law that would make it easier for a trustee to avoid prepetition transfers. First, section 1402(1) extends the one-year reachback period for fraudulent transfers to two years. Second, section 1402(2) amends Bankruptcy Code section 548(a) to clarify that it permits the recovery of any transfer to or an obligation incurred for the benefit of an insider under an employment contract, under certain conditions. In addition, section 1402 adds a new provision to section 548 authorizing a bankruptcy trustee to avoid any transfer of an interest of the debtor in property that was made on or within the ten-year period preceding the filing of the debtor's bankruptcy case if: (a) the transfer was made to a self-settled trust or similar device; (b) the transfer was made by the debtor; (c) the debtor is a beneficiary of such trust or similar device; and (d) the debtor made such transfer with actual intent to hinder, delay, or defraud any entity to which the debtor was or became, on or after the date of such transfer, indebted.

(H. Report No. 109-31 to accompany S. 256, 109th Cong., 1st Sess. (2005) pp. 132, 134, 154; available at 2005 U.S.C.C.A.N. 88, at 192, 194, 211)

# § 549. Postpetition transactions

(a) Except as provided in subsection (b) or (c) of this section, the trustee may avoid a transfer of property of the estate—

(1) that occurs after the commencement of the case; and

(2) (A) that is authorized only under section 303(f) or 542(c) of this title; or

(B) that is not authorized under this title or by the court.

(b) In an involuntary case, the trustee may not avoid under subsection (a) of this section a transfer made after the commencement of such case but before the order for relief to the extent any value, including services, but not including satisfaction or securing of a debt that arose before the commencement of the case, is given after the commencement of the case in exchange for such transfer, notwithstanding any notice or knowledge of the case that the transferee has.

(c) The trustee may not avoid under subsection (a) of this section a transfer of *an interest in* real property to a good faith purchaser without knowledge of the commencement of the case and for present fair equivalent value unless a copy or notice of the petition was filed, where a transfer of *an interest in* such real property may be recorded to perfect such transfer, before such transfer is so perfected that a bona fide purchaser of such *real* property, against whom applicable law permits such transfer to be perfected, could not acquire an interest that is superior to *such* ~~the~~ interest of such good faith purchaser. A good faith purchaser without knowledge of the commencement of the case and for less than present fair equivalent value has a lien on the property transferred to the extent of any present value given, unless a copy or notice of the petition was so filed before such transfer was so perfected.

(d) An action or proceeding under this section may not be commenced after the earlier of—

(1) two years after the date of the transfer sought to be avoided; or

(2) the time the case is closed or dismissed.

**Section 549**

(April 20, 2005, P. L. 109-8, Title XII, § 1214, 119 Stat. 23)

## HISTORY: ANCILLARY LAWS AND DIRECTIVES

**Amendments:**

**2005.** Act April 20, 2005(effective 180 days after enactment of April 20, 2005, as provided by § 1501(a) of P. L. 109-8), amends 11 USC § 549(c) with technical changes in wording.

**Other provisions:**

**Effective date and application of amendments made by Act April 20, 2005.** Act April 20, 2005, P.L. 109-8, Title XV, § 1501(a), 119 Stat. 23, provided that the amendments made to this section would be effective 180 days after enactment on April 20, 2005.

**Abridged Legislative History**

(H. Report No. 109-31 to accompany S. 256, 109th Cong., 1st Sess. (2005) p. 144; available at 2005 U.S.C.C.A.N. 88, at 203)

## § 550. Liability of transferee of avoided transfer

(a) Except as otherwise provided in this section, to the extent that a transfer is avoided under section 544, 545, 547, 548, 549, 553(b), or

724(a) of this title, the trustee may recover, for the benefit of the estate, the property transferred, or, if the court so orders, the value of such property, from—

(1) the initial transferee of such transfer or the entity for whose benefit such transfer was made; or

(2) any immediate or mediate transferee of such initial transferee.

(b) The trustee may not recover under section (a)(2) of this section from—

(1) a transferee that takes for value, including satisfaction or securing of a present or antecedent debt, in good faith, and without knowledge of the voidability of the transfer avoided; or

(2) any immediate or mediate good faith transferee of such transferee.

(c) If a transfer made between 90 days and one year before the filing of the petition—

(1) is avoided under section 547(b) of this title; and

(2) was made for the benefit of a creditor that at the time of such transfer was an insider;

the trustee may not recover under subsection (a) from a transferee that is not an insider.

(d) The trustee is entitled to only a single satisfaction under subsection (a) of this section.

(e) (1) A good faith transferee from whom the trustee may recover under subsection (a) of this section has a lien on the property recovered to secure the lesser of—

(A) the cost, to such transferee, of any improvement made after the transfer, less the amount of any profit realized by or accruing to such transferee from such property; and

(B) any increase in the value of such property as a result of such improvement, of the property transferred.

(2) In this subsection, "improvement" includes—

(A) physical additions or changes to the property transferred;

(B) repairs to such property;

(C) payment of any tax on such property;

(D) payment of any debt secured by a lien on such property that is superior or equal to the rights of the trustee; and

(E) preservation of such property.

(f) An action or proceeding under this section may not be commenced after the earlier of—

(1) one year after the avoidance of the transfer on account of which recovery under this section is sought; or

(2) the time the case is closed or dismissed.

## § 551. Automatic preservation of avoided transfer

Any transfer avoided under section 522, 544, 545, 547, 548, 549, or

724(a) of this title, or any lien void under section 506(d) of this title, is preserved for the benefit of the estate but only with respect to property of the estate.

## § 552. Postpetition effect of security interest

(a) Except as provided in subsection (b) of this section, property acquired by the estate or by the debtor after the commencement of the case is not subject to any lien resulting from any security agreement entered into by the debtor before the commencement of the case.

(b) (1) Except as provided in sections 363, 506(c), 522, 544, 545, 547, and 548 of this title, if the debtor and an entity entered into a security agreement before the commencement of the case and if the security interest created by such security agreement extends to property of the debtor acquired before the commencement of the case and to proceeds, ~~product~~*products*, offspring, or profits of such property, then such security interest extends to such proceeds, ~~product~~*products*, offspring, or profits acquired by the estate after the commencement of the case to the extent provided by such security agreement and by applicable nonbankruptcy law, except to any extent that the court, after notice and a hearing and based on the equities of the case, orders otherwise.

(2) Except as provided in sections 363, 506(c), 522, 544, 545, 547, and 548 of this title, and notwithstanding section 546(b) of this title, if the debtor and an entity entered into a security agreement before the commencement of the case and if the security interest created by such security agreement extends to property of the debtor acquired before the commencement of the case and to amounts paid as rents of such property or the fees, charges, accounts, or other payments for the use or occupancy of rooms and other public facilities in hotels, motels, or other lodging properties, then such security interest extends to such rents and such fees, charges, accounts, or other payments acquired by the estate after the commencement of the case to the extent provided in such security agreement, except to any extent that the court, after notice and a hearing and based on the equities of the case, orders otherwise.

**Section 552**

(April 20, 2005, P. L. 109-8, Title XII, § 1204(2), 119 Stat. 23)

## HISTORY: ANCILLARY LAWS AND DIRECTIVES

**Amendments:**

**2005.** Act April 20, 2005(effective 180 days after enactment of April 20, 2005, as provided by § 1501(a) of P. L. 109-8), amends 11 USC § 552(b) with technical changes in wording.

**Other provisions:**

**Effective date and application of amendments made by Act April 20, 2005.** Act April 20, 2005, P.L. 109-8, Title XV, § 1501(a), 119 Stat. 23, provided that the amendments made to this section would be effective 180 days after enactment on April 20, 2005.

**Abridged Legislative History**

(H. Report No. 109-31 to accompany S. 256, 109th Cong., 1st Sess. (2005) p. 142; available at 2005 U.S.C.C.A.N. 88, at 201)

## § 553. Setoff

(a) Except as otherwise provided in this section and in sections 362 and 363 of this title, this title does not affect any right of a creditor to offset a mutual debt owing by such creditor to the debtor that arose before the commencement of the case under this title against a claim of such creditor against the debtor that arose before the commencement of the case, except to the extent that—

(1) the claim of such creditor against the debtor is disallowed;

(2) such claim was transferred, by an entity other than the debtor, to such creditor—

(A) after the commencement of the case; or

(B) (i) after 90 days before the date of the filing of the petition; and

(ii) while the debtor was insolvent *(except for a setoff of a kind described in section 362(b)(6), 362(b)(7), 362(b)(17), 362(b)(27), 555, 556, 559, 560, or 561)*; or

(3) the debt owed to the debtor by such creditor was incurred by such creditor—

(A) after 90 days before the date of the filing of the petition;

(B) while the debtor was insolvent; and

(C) for the purpose of obtaining a right of setoff against the debtor *(except for a setoff of a kind described in section 362(b)(6), 362(b)(7), 362(b)(17), 362(b)(27), 555, 556, 559, 560, or 561)*.

(b) (1) Except with respect to a setoff of a kind described in section 362(b)(6), 362(b)(7), ~~362(b)(14)~~ *362(b)(17), 362(b)(27), 555, 556, 559, 560, 561*,~~;~~ 365(h), 546(h), or 365(i)(2) of this title, if a creditor offsets a mutual debt owing to the debtor against a claim against the debtor on or within 90 days before the date of the filing of the petition, then the trustee may recover from such creditor the amount so offset to the extent that any insufficiency on the date of such setoff is less than the insufficiency on the later of—

(A) 90 days before the date of the filing of the petition; and

(B) the first date during the 90 days immediately preceding the date of the filing of the petition on which there is an insufficiency.

(2) In this subsection, "insufficiency" means amount, if any, by which a claim against the debtor exceeds a mutual debt owing to the debtor by the holder of such claim.

(c) For the purposes of this section, the debtor is presumed to have been insolvent on and during the 90 days immediately preceding the date of the filing of the petition.

**Section 553**

(April 20, 2005, P. L. 109-8, Title IX, § 907(n), 119 Stat. 23)

## HISTORY: ANCILLARY LAWS AND DIRECTIVES

**Amendments:**

**2005.** Act April 20, 2005(effective 180 days after enactment of April 20, 2005, as provided by § 1501(a) of P. L. 109-8), amends 11 USC § 553(b) to clarify that the acquisition by a creditor of setoff rights in connection with swap agreements, repurchase agreements, securities contracts, forward contracts, commodity contracts and master netting agreements cannot be avoided as a preference.

**Other provisions:**

**Effective date and application of amendments made by Act April 20, 2005.** Act April 20, 2005, P.L. 109-8, Title XV, § 1501(a), 119 Stat. 23, provided that the amendments made to this section would be effective 180 days after enactment on April 20, 2005.

**Abridged Legislative History**

(H. Report No. 109-31 to accompany S. 256, 109th Cong., 1st Sess. (2005) p. 134; available at 2005 U.S.C.C.A.N. 88, at 194)

# § 554. Abandonment of property of the estate

(a) After notice and a hearing, the trustee may abandon any property of the estate that is burdensome to the estate or that is of inconsequential value and benefit to the estate.

(b) On request of a party in interest and after notice and a hearing, the court may order the trustee to abandon any property of the estate that is burdensome to the estate or that is of inconsequential value and benefit to the estate.

(c) Unless the court orders otherwise, any property scheduled under section 521(1) of this title not otherwise administered at the time of the closing of a case is abandoned to the debtor and administered for purposes of section 350 of this title.

(d) Unless the court orders otherwise, property of the estate that is not abandoned under this section and that is not administered in the case remains property of the estate.

# § 555. ~~Contractual right to liquidate a securities contract~~*Contractual right to liquidate, terminate, or accelerate a securities contract*

The exercise of a contractual right of a stockbroker, financial institution, *financial participant,* or securities clearing agency to cause the liquidation, *termination, or acceleration* of a securities contract, as defined in section 741 of this title, because of a condition of the kind specified in section 365(e)(1) of this title shall not be stayed, avoided, or otherwise limited by operation of any provision of this title or by order of a court or administrative agency in any proceeding under this title unless such order is authorized under the provisions of the Securities Investor Protection Act of 1970 or any statute administered by the Securities and Exchange Commission. As used in this section, the term "contractual right" includes a right set forth in a rule or bylaw of a *derivatives clearing organization (as defined in the Commodity Exchange Act), a multilateral clearing organization (as defined in the Federal Deposit Insurance Corporation Improvement Act of*

*1991),* a national securities exchange, a national securities association, ~~or~~ a securities clearing agency~~.~~*, a contract market designated under the Commodity Exchange Act, a derivatives transaction execution facility registered under the Commodity Exchange Act, or a board of trade (as defined in the Commodity Exchange Act), or in a resolution of the governing board thereof, and a right, whether or not in writing, arising under common law, under law merchant, or by reason of normal business practice.*

**Section 555**

(April 20, 2005, P. L. 109-8, Title IX, §§ 907(g), (o)(7), 119 Stat. 23)

## HISTORY: ANCILLARY LAWS AND DIRECTIVES

**Amendments:**

**2005.** Act April 20, 2005(effective 180 days after enactment of April 20, 2005, as provided by § 1501(a) of P. L. 109-8), amends 11 USC § 555, including its caption, to conform to other financial transaction amendments.

**Other provisions:**

**Effective date and application of amendments made by Act April 20, 2005.** Act April 20, 2005, P.L. 109-8, Title XV, § 1501(a), 119 Stat. 23, provided that the amendments made to this section would be effective 180 days after enactment on April 20, 2005.

**Abridged Legislative History**

(H. Report No. 109-31 to accompany S. 256, 109th Cong., 1st Sess. (2005) pp. 132, 134; available at 2005 U.S.C.C.A.N. 88, at 193–94)

## § 556. ~~Contractual right to liquidate a commodities contract or forward contract~~ *Contractual right to liquidate, terminate, or accelerate a commodities contract or forward contract*

The contractual right of a commodity broker, *financial participant,* or forward contract merchant to cause the ~~liquidation~~ *liquidation, termination, or acceleration* of a commodity contract, as defined in section 761 of this title, or forward contract because of a condition of the kind specified in section 365(e)(1) of this title, and the right to a variation or maintenance margin payment received from a trustee with respect to open commodity contracts or forward contracts, shall not be stayed, avoided, or otherwise limited by operation of any provision of this title or by the order of a court in any proceeding under this title. ~~As used in this section, the term "contractual right" includes a right set forth in a rule or bylaw of a clearing organization or contract market or in a resolution of the governing board thereof and a right,~~ *As used in this section, the term 'contractual right' includes a right set forth in a rule or bylaw of a derivatives clearing organization (as defined in the Commodity Exchange Act), a multilateral clearing organization (as defined in the Federal Deposit Insurance Corporation Improvement Act of 1991), a national securities exchange, a national securities association, a securities clearing agency, a contract market designated under the Commodity Exchange Act, a derivatives transaction execution facility registered under the Commodity Exchange Act, or a board of trade (as defined in the Commodity Exchange Act) or in a resolution of the governing board thereof and a right,* whether or not evidenced in writing, arising under common law, under law merchant or by reason of normal business practice.

**Section 556**

(April 20, 2005, P. L. 109-8, Title IX, §§ 907(h), (o)(8), 119 Stat. 23)

## HISTORY: ANCILLARY LAWS AND DIRECTIVES

**Amendments:**

**2005.** Act April 20, 2005(effective 180 days after enactment of April 20, 2005, as provided by § 1501(a) of P. L. 109-8), amends 11 USC § 556 including its caption, to conform to other financial transaction amendments.

**Other provisions:**

**Effective date and application of amendments made by Act April 20, 2005.** Act April 20, 2005, P.L. 109-8, Title XV, § 1501(a), 119 Stat. 23, provided that the amendments made to this section would be effective 180 days after enactment on April 20, 2005.

**Abridged Legislative History**

(H. Report No. 109-31 to accompany S. 256, 109th Cong., 1st Sess. (2005) pp. 132, 134; available at 2005 U.S.C.C.A.N. 88, at 193–94)

## § 557. Expedited determination of interests in, and abandonment or other disposition of grain assets

(a) This section applies only in a case concerning a debtor that owns or operates a grain storage facility and only with respect to grain and the proceeds of grain. This section does not affect the application of any other section of this title to property other than grain and proceeds of grain.

(b) In this section—

(1) "grain" means wheat, corn, flaxseed, grain sorghum, barley, oats, rye, soybeans, other dry edible beans, or rice;

(2) "grain storage facility" means a site or physical structure regularly used to store grain for producers, or to store grain acquired from producers for resale; and

(3) "producer" means an entity which engages in the growing of grain.

(c) (1) Notwithstanding sections 362, 363, 365, and 554 of this title, on the court's own motion the court may, and on the request of the trustee or an entity that claims an interest in grain or the proceeds of grain the court shall, expedite the procedures for the determination of interests in and the disposition of grain and the proceeds of grain, by shortening to the greatest extent feasible such time periods as are otherwise applicable for such procedures and by establishing, by order, a timetable having a duration of not to exceed 120 days for the completion of the applicable procedure specified in subsection (d) of this section. Such time periods and such timetable may be modified by the court, for cause, in accordance with subsection (f) of this section.

(2) The court shall determine the extent to which such time periods shall be shortened, based upon—

(A) any need of an entity claiming an interest in such grain or the proceeds of grain for a prompt determination of such interest;

(B) any need of such entity for a prompt disposition of such grain;

(C) the market for such grain;

(D) the conditions under which such grain is stored;

(E) the costs of continued storage or disposition of such grain;

(F) the orderly administration of the estate;

(G) the appropriate opportunity for an entity to assert an interest in such grain; and

(H) such other considerations as are relevant to the need to expedite such procedures in the case.

(d) The procedures that may be expedited under subsection (c) of this section include—

(1) the filing of and response to—

(A) a claim of ownership;

(B) a proof of claim;

(C) a request for abandonment;

(D) a request for relief from the stay of action against property under section 362(a) of this title;

(E) a request for determination of secured status;

(F) a request for determination of whether such grain or the proceeds of grain—

(i) is property of the estate;

(ii) must be turned over to the estate; or

(iii) may be used, sold, or leased; and

(G) any other request for determination of an interest in such grain or the proceeds of grain;

(2) the disposition of such grain or the proceeds of grain, before or after determination of interests in such grain or the proceeds of grain, by way of—

(A) sale of such grain;

(B) abandonment;

(C) distribution; or

(D) such other method as is equitable in the case;

(3) subject to sections 701, 702, 703, 1104, 1202, and 1302 of this title, the appointment of a trustee or examiner and the retention and compensation of any professional person required to assist with respect to matters relevant to the determination of interests in or disposition of such grain or the proceeds of grain; and

(4) the determination of any dispute concerning a matter specified in paragraph (1), (2), or (3) of this subsection.

(e) (1) Any governmental unit that has regulatory jurisdiction over the operation or liquidation of the debtor or the debtor's business shall be given notice of any request made or order entered under subsection (c) of this section.

(2) Any such governmental unit may raise, and may appear and be heard on, any issue relating to grain or the proceeds of grain in a case in which a request is made, or an order is entered, under subsection (c) of this section.

(3) The trustee shall consult with such governmental unit before taking any action relating to the disposition of grain in the possession, custody, or control of the debtor or the estate.

(f) The court may extend the period for final disposition of grain or the proceeds of grain under this section beyond 120 days if the court finds that—

(1) the interests of justice so require in light of the complexity of the case; and

(2) the interests of those claimants entitled to distribution of grain or the proceeds of grain will not be materially injured by such additional delay.

(g) Unless an order establishing an expedited procedure under subsection (c) of this section, or determining any interest in or approving any disposition of grain or the proceeds of grain, is stayed pending appeal—

(1) the reversal or modification of such order on appeal does not affect the validity of any procedure, determination, or disposition that occurs before such reversal or modification, whether or not any entity knew of the pendency of the appeal; and

(2) neither the court nor the trustee may delay, due to the appeal of such order, any proceeding in the case in which such order is issued.

(h) (1) The trustee may recover from grain and the proceeds of grain the reasonable and necessary costs and expenses allowable under section 503(b) of this title attributable to preserving or disposing of grain or the proceeds of grain, but may not recover from such grain or the proceeds of grain any other costs or expenses.

(2) Notwithstanding section 326(a) of this title, the dollar amounts of money specified in such section include the value, as of the date of disposition, of any grain that the trustee distributes in kind.

(i) In all cases where the quantity of a specific type of grain held by a debtor operating a grain storage facility exceeds ten thousand bushels, such grain shall be sold by the trustee and the assets thereof distributed in accordance with the provisions of this section.

## § 558. Defenses of the estate

The estate shall have the benefit of any defense available to the debtor as against any entity other than the estate, including statutes of limitation, statutes of frauds, usury, and other personal defenses. A waiver of any such defense by the debtor after the commencement of the case does not bind the estate.

## § 559. ~~Contractual right to liquidate a repurchase agreement~~ *Contractual right to liquidate, terminate, or accelerate a repurchase agreement*

The exercise of a contractual right of a repo participant *or financial participant* to cause the ~~liquidation~~ *liquidation, termination, or acceleration* of a repurchase agreement because of a condition of the kind specified in section 365(e)(1) of this title shall not be stayed, avoided, or otherwise limited by operation of any provision of this title or by order of a court or administrative agency in any proceeding under this title, unless, where the debtor is a stockbroker or securities clearing agency, such order is authorized under the provisions of the Securities Investor Protection Act of 1970 or any statute administered by the Securities and Exchange Commission. In the event that a repo participant *or financial participant* liquidates one or more repurchase agreements with a debtor and under the terms of one or more such agreements has agreed to deliver assets subject to repurchase agreements to the debtor, any excess of the market prices received on liquidation of such assets (or if any such assets are not disposed of on the date of liquidation of such repurchase agreements, at the prices available at the time of liquidation of such repurchase agreements from a generally recognized source or the most recent closing bid quotation from such a source) over the sum of the stated repurchase prices and all expenses in connection with the liquidation of such repurchase agreements shall be deemed property of the estate, subject to the available rights of setoff. ~~As used in this section, the term "contractual right" includes a right set forth in a rule or bylaw, applicable to each party to the repurchase agreement, of a national securities exchange, a national securities association, or a securities clearing agency, and a right,~~ *As used in this section, the term 'contractual right' includes a right set forth in a rule or bylaw of a derivatives clearing organization (as defined in the Commodity Exchange Act), a multilateral clearing organization (as defined in the Federal Deposit Insurance Corporation Improvement Act of 1991), a national securities exchange, a national securities association, a securities clearing agency, a contract market designated under the Commodity Exchange Act, a derivatives transaction execution facility registered under the Commodity Exchange Act, or a board of trade (as defined in the Commodity Exchange Act) or in a resolution of the governing board thereof and a right,* whether or not evidenced in writing, arising under common law, under law merchant or by reason of normal business practice.

**Section 559**

(April 20, 2005, P. L. 109-8, Title IX, §§ 907(i), (o)(9), 119 Stat. 23)

### HISTORY: ANCILLARY LAWS AND DIRECTIVES

**Amendments:**

**2005.** Act April 20, 2005(effective 180 days after enactment of April 20, 2005, as provided by § 1501(a) of P. L. 109-8), amends 11 USC § 559, including its caption, to conform to other financial transaction amendments.

**Other provisions:**

**Effective date and application of amendments made by Act April 20, 2005.** Act April 20, 2005, P.L. 109-8, Title XV, § 1501(a), 119 Stat. 23, provided that the amendments made to this section would be effective 180 days after enactment on April 20, 2005.

**Abridged Legislative History**

(H. Report No. 109-31 to accompany S. 256, 109th Cong., 1st Sess. (2005) pp. 132,134; available at 2005 U.S.C.C.A.N. 88, at 193–94)

## § 560. *Contractual right to liquidate, terminate, or accelerate a swap agreement* ~~Contractual right to terminate a swap agreement~~

The exercise of any contractual right of any swap participant *or financial participant* to cause the ~~termination of a swap agreement~~ *liquidation, termination, or acceleration of one or more swap agreements* because of a condition of the kind specified in section 365(e)(1) of this title or to offset or net out any termination values or payment amounts arising under or ~~in connection with any swap agreement~~ *in connection with the termination, liquidation, or acceleration of one or more swap agreements* shall not be stayed, avoided, or otherwise limited by operation of any provision of this title or by order of a court or administrative agency in any proceeding under this title. ~~As used in this section, the term "contractual right" includes a right,~~ *As used in this section, the term 'contractual right' includes a right set forth in a rule or bylaw of a derivatives clearing organization (as defined in the Commodity Exchange Act), a multilateral clearing organization (as defined in the Federal Deposit Insurance Corporation Improvement Act of 1991), a national securities exchange, a national securities association, a securities clearing agency, a contract market designated under the Commodity Exchange Act, a derivatives transaction execution facility registered under the Commodity Exchange Act, or a board of trade (as defined in the Commodity Exchange Act) or in a resolution of the governing board thereof and a right,* whether or not evidenced in writing, arising under common law, under law merchant, or by reason of normal business practice.

**Section 560**

(April 20, 2005, P. L. 109-8, Title IX, §§ 907(j), (o)(10), 119 Stat. 23)

### HISTORY: ANCILLARY LAWS AND DIRECTIVES

**Amendments:**

**2005.** Act April 20, 2005(effective 180 days after enactment of April 20, 2005, as provided by § 1501(a) of P. L. 109-8), amends 11 USC § 560, including its caption, to conform to other financial transaction amendments.

**Other provisions:**

**Effective date and application of amendments made by Act April 20, 2005.** Act April 20, 2005, P.L. 109-8, Title XV, § 1501(a), 119 Stat. 23, provided that the amendments made to this section would be effective 180 days after enactment on April 20, 2005.

**Abridged Legislative History**

(H. Report No. 109-31 to accompany S. 256, 109th Cong., 1st Sess. (2005) pp. 132,134; available at 2005 U.S.C.C.A.N. 88, at 193–94)

## *§ 561. Contractual right to terminate, liquidate, accelerate, or offset under a master netting agreement and across contracts; proceedings under chapter 15*

*(a) Subject to subsection (b), the exercise of any contractual right, because of a condition of the kind specified in section 365(e)(1), to cause the termination, liquidation, or acceleration of or to offset or net termination values, payment amounts, or other transfer obligations arising under or in connection with one or more (or the termination, liquidation, or acceleration of one or more)—*

*(1) securities contracts, as defined in section 741(7);*

*(2) commodity contracts, as defined in section 761(4);*

*(3) forward contracts;*

*(4) repurchase agreements;*

*(5) swap agreements; or*

*(6) master netting agreements,*

*shall not be stayed, avoided, or otherwise limited by operation of any provision of this title or by any order of a court or administrative agency in any proceeding under this title.*

*(b) (1) A party may exercise a contractual right described in subsection (a) to terminate, liquidate, or accelerate only to the extent that such party could exercise such a right under section 555, 556, 559, or 560 for each individual contract covered by the master netting agreement in issue.*

*(2) If a debtor is a commodity broker subject to subchapter IV of chapter 7—*

*(A) a party may not net or offset an obligation to the debtor arising under, or in connection with, a commodity contract traded on or subject to the rules of a contract market designated under the Commodity Exchange Act or a derivatives transaction execution facility registered under the Commodity Exchange Act against any claim arising under, or in connection with, other instruments, contracts, or agreements listed in subsection (a) except to the extent that the party has positive net equity in the commodity accounts at the debtor, as calculated under such subchapter; and*

*(B) another commodity broker may not net or offset an obligation to the debtor arising under, or in connection with, a commodity contract entered into or held on behalf of a customer of the debtor and traded on or subject to the rules of a contract market designated under the Commodity Exchange Act or a derivatives transaction execution facility registered under the Commodity Exchange Act against any claim arising under, or in connection with, other instruments, contracts, or agreements listed in subsection (a).*

*(3) No provision of subparagraph (A) or (B) of paragraph (2) shall prohibit the offset of claims and obligations that arise under—*

*(A) a cross-margining agreement or similar arrangement that has been approved by the Commodity Futures Trading Commission or submitted to the Commodity Futures Trading Commission under paragraph (1) or (2) of section 5c(c) of the Commodity Exchange Act and has not been abrogated or rendered ineffective by the Commodity Futures Trading Commission; or*

*(B) any other netting agreement between a clearing organization (as defined in section 761) and another entity that has been approved by the Commodity Futures Trading Commission.*

*(c) As used in this section, the term 'contractual right' includes a right set forth in a rule or bylaw of a derivatives clearing organization (as defined in the Commodity Exchange Act), a multilateral clearing organization (as defined in the Federal Deposit Insurance Corporation Improvement Act of 1991), a national securities exchange, a national securities association, a securities clearing agency, a contract market designated under the Commodity Exchange Act, a derivatives transaction execution facility registered under the Commodity Exchange Act, or a board of trade (as defined in the Commodity Exchange Act) or in a resolution of the governing board thereof, and a right, whether or not evidenced in writing, arising under common law, under law merchant, or by reason of normal business practice.*

*(d) Any provisions of this title relating to securities contracts, commodity contracts, forward contracts, repurchase agreements, swap agreements, or master netting agreements shall apply in a case under chapter 15, so that enforcement of contractual provisions of such contracts and agreements in accordance with their terms will not be stayed or otherwise limited by operation of any provision of this title or by order of a court in any case under this title, and to limit avoidance powers to the same extent as in a proceeding under chapter 7 or 11 of this title (such enforcement not to be limited based on the presence or absence of assets of the debtor in the United States).*

**Section 561**

(April 20, 2005, P. L. 109-8, Title *I*X, § 907(k)(1), 119 Stat. 23)

## HISTORY: ANCILLARY LAWS AND DIRECTIVES

**Amendments:**

**2005.** Act April 20, 2005(effective 180 days after enactment of April 20, 2005, as provided by § 1501(a) of P. L. 109-8), adds new 11 USC § 561 concerning contract rights under new chapter 15.

**Other provisions:**

**Effective date and application of amendments made by Act April 20, 2005.** Act April 20, 2005, P.L. 109-8, Title XV, § 1501(a), 119 Stat. 23, provided that the amendments made to this section would be effective 180 days after enactment on April 20, 2005.

**Abridged Legislative History**

(H. Report No. 109-31 to accompany S. 256, 109th Cong., 1st Sess. (2005) pp. 132–34; available at 2005 U.S.C.C.A.N. 88, at 193–94)

## *§ 562. Timing of damage measurement in connection with swap agreements, securities contracts, forward contracts, commodity contracts, repurchase agreements, and master netting agreements*

*(a) If the trustee rejects a swap agreement, securities contract (as defined in section 741), forward contract, commodity contract (as defined in section 761), repurchase agreement, or master netting agreement pursuant to section 365(a), or if a forward contract merchant, stockbroker, financial institution, securities clearing agency, repo participant, financial participant, master netting agreement participant, or swap participant liquidates, terminates, or accelerates such contract or agreement, damages shall be measured as of the earlier of—*

*(1) the date of such rejection; or*

*(2) the date or dates of such liquidation, termination, or acceleration.*

*(b) If there are not any commercially reasonable determinants of value as of any date referred to in paragraph (1) or (2) of subsection (a), damages shall be measured as of the earliest subsequent date or dates on which there are commercially reasonable determinants of value.*

*(c) For the purposes of subsection (b), if damages are not measured as of the date or dates of rejection, liquidation, termination, or acceleration, and the forward contract merchant, stockbroker, financial institution, securities clearing agency, repo participant, financial participant, master netting agreement participant, or swap participant or the trustee objects to the timing of the measurement of damages—*

*(1) the trustee, in the case of an objection by a forward contract merchant, stockbroker, financial institution, securities clearing agency, repo participant, financial participant, master netting agreement participant, or swap participant; or*

*(2) the forward contract merchant, stockbroker, financial institution, securities clearing agency, repo participant, financial participant, master netting agreement participant, or swap participant, in the case of an objection by the trustee,*

*has the burden of proving that there were no commercially reasonable determinants of value as of such date or dates.*

**Section 562**

(April 20, 2005, P. L. 109-8, Title IX, § 910(a)(1), 119 Stat. 23)

## HISTORY: ANCILLARY LAWS AND DIRECTIVES

**Amendments:**

**2005.** Act April 20, 2005(effective 180 days after enactment of April 20, 2005, as provided by § 1501(a) of P. L. 109-8), adds new 11 USC § 562 concerning damages under new chapter 15.

**Other provisions:**

**Effective date and application of amendments made by Act April 20, 2005.** Act April 20, 2005, P.L. 109-8, Title XV, § 1501(a), 119 Stat. 23, provided that the amendments made to this section would be effective 180 days after enactment on

April 20, 2005.

**Abridged Legislative History**

(H. Report No. 109-31 to accompany S. 256, 109th Cong., 1st Sess. (2005) pp. 134–35; available at 2005 U.S.C.C.A.N. 88, at 194–95).

# Chapter 7
# —Liquidation

## Subchapter I——Officers and Administration



## Subchapter II——Collection, Liquidation, and Distribution of the Estate



## Subchapter III——Stockbroker Liquidation



## Subchapter IV——Commodity Broker

## Liquidation



**SUBCHAPTER V CLEARING BANK LIQUIDATION**



## Subchapter I——Officers and Administration

## § 701. Interim trustee

(a)

(1) Promptly after the order for relief under this chapter, the United States trustee shall appoint one disinterested person that is a member of the panel of private trustees established under section 586(a)(1) of title 28 or that is serving as trustee in the case immediately before the order for relief under this chapter to serve as interim trustee in the case.

(2) If none of the members of such panel is willing to serve as interim trustee in the case, then the United States trustee may serve as interim trustee in the case.

(b) The service of an interim trustee under this section terminates when a trustee elected or designated under section 702 of this title to serve as trustee in the case qualifies under section 322 of this title.

(c) An interim trustee serving under this section is a trustee in a case under this title.

## § 702. Election of trustee

(a) A creditor may vote for a candidate for trustee only if such creditor—

(1) holds an allowable, undisputed, fixed, liquidated, unsecured claim of a kind entitled to distribution under section 726(a)(2), 726 (a)(3), 726(a)(4), 752(a), 766(h), or 766(i) of this title;

(2) does not have an interest materially adverse, other than an equity interest that is not substantial in relation to such creditor's interest as a creditor, to the interest of creditors entitled to such distribution; and

(3) is not an insider.

(b) At the meeting of creditors held under section 341 of this title, creditors may elect one person to serve as trustee in the case if election of a trustee is requested by creditors that may vote under subsection (a) of this section, and that hold at least 20 percent in amount of the claims specified in subsection (a)(1) of this section that are held by creditors that may vote under subsection (a) of this section.

(c) A candidate for trustee is elected trustee if—

(1) creditors holding at least 20 percent in amount of the claims of a kind specified in subsection (a)(1) of this section that are held by creditors that may vote under subsection (a) of this section vote; and

(2) such candidate receives the votes of creditors holding a majority in amount of claims specified in subsection (a)(1) of this section that are held by creditors that vote for a trustee.

(d) If a trustee is not elected under this section, then the interim trustee shall serve as trustee in the case.

## § 703. Successor trustee

(a) If a trustee dies or resigns during a case, fails to qualify under section 322 of this title, or is removed under section 324 of this title, creditors may elect, in the manner specified in section 702 of this title, a person to fill the vacancy in the office of trustee.

(b) Pending election of a trustee under subsection (a) of this section, if necessary to preserve or prevent loss to the estate, the United States trustee may appoint an interim trustee in the manner specified in section 701(a).

(c) If creditors do not elect a successor trustee under subsection (a) of this section or if a trustee is needed in a case reopened under section 350 of this title, then the United States trustee—

(1) shall appoint one disinterested person that is a member of the panel of private trustees established under section 586(a)(1) of title 28 to serve as trustee in the case; or

(2) may, if none of the disinterested members of such panel is willing to serve as trustee, serve as trustee in the case.

## § 704. Duties of trustee

*(a)* The trustee shall—

(1) collect and reduce to money the property of the estate for which such trustee serves, and close such estate as expeditiously as is compatible with the best interests of parties in interest;

(2) be accountable for all property received;

(3) ensure that the debtor shall perform his intention as specified in section 521(2)(B) of this title;

(4) investigate the financial affairs of the debtor;

(5) if a purpose would be served, examine proofs of claims and object to the allowance of any claim that is improper;

(6) if advisable, oppose the discharge of the debtor;

(7) unless the court orders otherwise, furnish such information concerning the estate and the estate's administration as is requested by a party in interest;

(8) if the business of the debtor is authorized to be operated, file with the court, with the United States trustee, and with any governmental unit charged with responsibility for collection or determination of any tax arising out of such operation, periodic reports and summaries of the operation of such business, including a statement of receipts and disbursements, and such other information as the United States trustee or the court requires; ~~and~~

(9) make a final report and file a final account of the administration of the estate with the court and with the United States trustee~~.~~;

*(10) if with respect to the debtor there is a claim for a domestic support obligation, provide the applicable notice specified in subsection (c);*

*(11) if, at the time of the commencement of the case, the debtor (or any entity designated by the debtor) served as the administrator (as defined in section 3 of the Employee Retirement Income Security Act of 1974) of an employee benefit plan, continue to perform the obligations required of the administrator; and*

*(12) use all reasonable and best efforts to transfer patients from a health care business that is in the process of being closed to an appropriate health care business that—*

*(A) is in the vicinity of the health care business that is closing;*

*(B) provides the patient with services that are substantially similar to those provided by the health care business that is in the process of being closed; and*

*(C) maintains a reasonable quality of care.*

*(b) (1) With respect to a debtor who is an individual in a case under this chapter—*

*(A) the United States trustee (or the bankruptcy administrator, if any) shall review all materials filed by the debtor and, not later than 10 days after the date of the first meeting of creditors, file with the court a statement as to whether the debtor's case would be presumed to be an abuse under section 707(b); and*

*(B) not later than 5 days after receiving a statement under subparagraph (A), the court shall provide a copy of the statement to all creditors.*

*(2) The United States trustee (or bankruptcy administrator, if any) shall, not later than 30 days after the date of filing a statement under paragraph (1), either file a motion to dismiss or convert under section 707(b) or file a statement setting forth the reasons the United States trustee (or the bankruptcy administrator, if any) does not consider such a motion to be appropriate, if the United States trustee (or the bankruptcy administrator, if any) determines that the debtor's case should be presumed to be an abuse under section 707(b) and the*

*product of the debtor's current monthly income, multiplied by 12 is not less than—*

*(A) in the case of a debtor in a household of 1 person, the median family income of the applicable State for 1 earner; or*

*(B) in the case of a debtor in a household of 2 or more individuals, the highest median family income of the applicable State for a family of the same number or fewer individuals.*

*(c) (1) In a case described in subsection (a)(10) to which subsection (a)(10) applies, the trustee shall—*

*(A) (i) provide written notice to the holder of the claim described in subsection (a)(10) of such claim and of the right of such holder to use the services of the State child support enforcement agency established under sections 464 and 466 of the Social Security Act for the State in which such holder resides, for assistance in collecting child support during and after the case under this title;*

*(ii) include in the notice provided under clause (i) the address and telephone number of such State child support enforcement agency; and*

*(iii) include in the notice provided under clause (i) an explanation of the rights of such holder to payment of such claim under this chapter;*

*(B) (i) provide written notice to such State child support enforcement agency of such claim; and*

*(ii) include in the notice provided under clause (i) the name, address, and telephone number of such holder; and*

*(C) at such time as the debtor is granted a discharge under section 727, provide written notice to such holder and to such State child support enforcement agency of—*

*(i) the granting of the discharge;*

*(ii) the last recent known address of the debtor;*

*(iii) the last recent known name and address of the debtor's employer; and*

*(iv) the name of each creditor that holds a claim that—*

*(I) is not discharged under paragraph (2), (4), or (14A) of section 523(a); or*

*(II) was reaffirmed by the debtor under section 524(c).*

*(2) (A) The holder of a claim described in subsection (a)(10) or the State child support enforcement agency of the State in which such holder resides may request from a creditor described in paragraph (1)(C)(iv) the last known address of the debtor.*

*(B) Notwithstanding any other provision of law, a creditor that makes a disclosure of a last known address of a debtor in connection with a request made under subparagraph (A) shall not be liable by reason of making such disclosure.*

**Section 704**
(April 20, 2005, P. L. 109-8, Title I, § 102(c); Title IIB, § 219(a); Title IVB, § 446(b); Title XI, § 1105(a), 119 Stat. 23)

## HISTORY: ANCILLARY LAWS AND DIRECTIVES

**Amendments:**

**2005.** Act April 20, 2005(effective 180 days after enactment of April 20, 2005, as provided by § 1501(a) of P. L. 109-8), amends 11 USC § 704 to add new duties for the chapter 7 trustee.

**Other provisions:**

**Effective date and application of amendments made by Act April 20, 2005.** Act April 20, 2005, P.L. 109-8, Title XV, § 1501(a), 119 Stat. 23, provided that the amendments made to this section would be effective 180 days after enactment on April 20, 2005.

**Abridged Legislative History**

Section 102(c) of the Act amends section 704 of the Bankruptcy Code to require the United States trustee or bankruptcy administrator in a chapter 7 case where the debtor is an individual to: (1) review all materials filed by the debtor; and (2) file a statement with the court (within ten days following the meeting of creditors held pursuant to section 341 of the Bankruptcy Code) as to whether or not the debtor's case should be presumed to be an abuse under section 707(b). The court must provide a copy of such statement to all creditors within five days after its filing. Within 30 days of the filing of such statement, the United States trustee or bankruptcy administrator must file either: (1) a motion under section 707(b); or (2) a statement setting forth the reasons why such motion is not appropriate in any case where the debtor's filing should be presumed to be an abuse and the debtor's current monthly income exceeds certain monetary thresholds.

Section 219(a) requires a chapter 7 trustee to provide written notice to a domestic support claimant of the right to use the services of a state child support enforcement agency established under sections 464 and 466 of the Social Security Act in the state where the claimant resides for assistance in collecting child support during and after the bankruptcy case.

(H. Report No. 109-31 to accompany S. 256, 109th Cong., 1st Sess. (2005) p. 52, 62, 96, 141; available at 2005 U.S.C.C.A.N. 88, at 122–23, 131, 161, 199)

## § 705. Creditor's committee

(a) At the meeting under section 341(a) of this title, creditors that may vote for a trustee under section 702(a) of this title may elect a committee of not fewer than three, and not more than eleven, creditors, each of whom holds an allowable unsecured claim of a kind entitled to distribution under section 726(a)(2) of this title.

(b) A committee elected under subsection (a) of this section may consult with the trustee or the United States trustee in connection with the administration of the estate, make recommendations to the trustee or the United States trustee respecting the performance of the trustee's duties, and submit to the court or the United States trustee any question affecting the administration of the estate.

## § 706. Conversion

(a) The debtor may convert a case under this chapter to a case under chapter 11, 12, or 13 of this title at any time, if the case has not been converted under section 1112, 1208, or 1307 of this title. Any waiver of the right to convert a case under this subsection is unenforceable.

(b) On request of a party in interest and after notice and a hearing, the court may convert a case under this chapter to a case under chapter 11 of this title at any time.

(c) The court may not convert a case under this chapter to a case under chapter 12 or 13 of this title unless the debtor requests *or consents to* such conversion.

(d) Notwithstanding any other provision of this section, a case may not be converted to a case under another chapter of this title unless the debtor may be a debtor under such chapter.

**Section 706**

(April 20, 2005, P. L. 109-8, Title I, § 101, 119 Stat. 23)

## HISTORY: ANCILLARY LAWS AND DIRECTIVES

**Amendments:**

**2005.** Act April 20, 2005(effective 180 days after enactment of April 20, 2005, as provided by § 1501(a) of P. L. 109-8), amends 11 USC § 706(c) to add "or consents."

**Other provisions:**

**Effective date and application of amendments made by Act April 20, 2005.** Act April 20, 2005, P.L. 109-8, Title XV, § 1501(a), 119 Stat. 23, provided that the amendments made to this section would be effective 180 days after enactment on April 20, 2005.

**Abridged Legislative History**

Section 101 of the Act amends this provision to allow a chapter 7 case to be converted to a case under chapter 12 or chapter 13 on request or consent of the debtor. (H. Report No. 109-31 to accompany S. 256, 109th Cong., 1st Sess. (2005) p. 47, available at 2005 U.S.C.C.A.N. 88, at 119)

# § 707. Dismissal *of a case or conversion to a case under Chapter 11 or 13*

(a) The court may dismiss a case under this chapter only after notice and a hearing and only for cause, including—

(1) unreasonable delay by the debtor that is prejudicial to creditors;

(2) nonpayment of any fees or charges required under chapter 123 of title 28; and

(3) failure of the debtor in a voluntary case to file, within fifteen days or such additional time as the court may allow after the filing of the petition commencing such case, the information required by paragraph (1) of section 521, but only on a motion by the United States trustee.

(b) *(1)* After notice and a hearing, the court, on its own motion or on a motion by the United States trustee, ~~but not at the request or suggestion of~~ *trustee (or bankruptcy administrator, if any), or* any party in interest, may dismiss a case filed by an individual debtor under this chapter whose debts are primarily consumer debts, *or, with the debtor's consent, convert such a case to a case under chapter 11 or 13 of this title,* if it finds that the granting of relief would be ~~a substantial abuse~~ *an abuse* of the provisions of this chapter. ~~There shall be a presumption in favor of granting the relief requested by~~

~~the debtor.~~ In making a determination whether to dismiss a case under this section, the court may not take into consideration whether a debtor has made, or continues to make, charitable contributions (that meet the definition of "charitable contribution" under section 548(d)(3)) to any qualified religious or charitable entity or organization (as that term is defined in section 548(d)(4)).

*(2) (A) (i) In considering under paragraph (1) whether the granting of relief would be an abuse of the provisions of this chapter, the court shall presume abuse exists if the debtor's current monthly income reduced by the amounts determined under clauses (ii), (iii), and (iv), and multiplied by 60 is not less than the lesser of—*

*(I) 25 percent of the debtor's nonpriority unsecured claims in the case, or $6,000, whichever is greater; or*

*(II) $10,000.*

*(ii) (I) The debtor's monthly expenses shall be the debtor's applicable monthly expense amounts specified under the National Standards and Local Standards, and the debtor's actual monthly expenses for the categories specified as Other Necessary Expenses issued by the Internal Revenue Service for the area in which the debtor resides, as in effect on the date of the order for relief, for the debtor, the dependents of the debtor, and the spouse of the debtor in a joint case, if the spouse is not otherwise a dependent. Such expenses shall include reasonably necessary health insurance, disability insurance, and health savings account expenses for the debtor, the spouse of the debtor, or the dependents of the debtor. Notwithstanding any other provision of this clause, the monthly expenses of the debtor shall not include any payments for debts. In addition, the debtor's monthly expenses shall include the debtor's reasonably necessary expenses incurred to maintain the safety of the debtor and the family of the debtor from family violence as identified under section 309 of the Family Violence Prevention and Services Act, or other applicable Federal law. The expenses included in the debtor's monthly expenses described in the preceding sentence shall be kept confidential by the court. In addition, if it is demonstrated that it is reasonable and necessary, the debtor's monthly expenses may also include an additional allowance for food and clothing of up to 5 percent of the food and clothing categories as specified by the National Standards issued by the Internal Revenue Service.*

*(II) In addition, the debtor's monthly expenses may include, if applicable, the continuation of actual expenses paid by the debtor that are reasonable and necessary for care and support of an elderly, chronically ill, or disabled household member or member of the debtor's immediate family (including parents, grandparents, siblings, children, and grandchildren of the debtor, the dependents of the debtor, and the spouse of the*

*debtor in a joint case who is not a dependent) and who is unable to pay for such reasonable and necessary expenses.*

*(III) In addition, for a debtor eligible for chapter 13, the debtor's monthly expenses may include the actual administrative expenses of administering a chapter 13 plan for the district in which the debtor resides, up to an amount of 10 percent of the projected plan payments, as determined under schedules issued by the Executive Office for United States Trustees.*

*(IV) In addition, the debtor's monthly expenses may include the actual expenses for each dependent child less than 18 years of age, not to exceed $1,500 per year per child, to attend a private or public elementary or secondary school if the debtor provides documentation of such expenses and a detailed explanation of why such expenses are reasonable and necessary, and why such expenses are not already accounted for in the National Standards, Local Standards, or Other Necessary Expenses referred to in subclause (I).*

*(V) In addition, the debtor's monthly expenses may include an allowance for housing and utilities, in excess of the allowance specified by the Local Standards for housing and utilities issued by the Internal Revenue Service, based on the actual expenses for home energy costs if the debtor provides documentation of such actual expenses and demonstrates that such actual expenses are reasonable and necessary.*

*(iii) The debtor's average monthly payments on account of secured debts shall be calculated as the sum of—*

*(I) the total of all amounts scheduled as contractually due to secured creditors in each month of the 60 months following the date of the petition; and*

*(II) any additional payments to secured creditors necessary for the debtor, in filing a plan under chapter 13 of this title, to maintain possession of the debtor's primary residence, motor vehicle, or other property necessary for the support of the debtor and the debtor's dependents, that serves as collateral for secured debts;*

*divided by 60.*

*(iv) The debtor's expenses for payment of all priority claims (including priority child support and alimony claims) shall be calculated as the total amount of debts entitled to priority, divided by 60.*

*(B) (i) In any proceeding brought under this subsection, the presumption of abuse may only be rebutted by demonstrating special circumstances, such as a serious medical condition or a call or order to active duty in the Armed Forces, to the extent such special circumstances that justify additional expenses or adjustments of current monthly income for which there is no reasonable alternative.*

*(ii) In order to establish special circumstances, the debtor shall be required to itemize each additional expense or adjustment of income and to provide—*

*(I) documentation for such expense or adjustment to income; and*

*(II) a detailed explanation of the special circumstances that make such expenses or adjustment to income necessary and reasonable.*

*(iii) The debtor shall attest under oath to the accuracy of any information provided to demonstrate that additional expenses or adjustments to income are required.*

*(iv) The presumption of abuse may only be rebutted if the additional expenses or adjustments to income referred to in clause (i) cause the product of the debtor's current monthly income reduced by the amounts determined under clauses (ii), (iii), and (iv) of subparagraph (A) when multiplied by 60 to be less than the lesser of—*

*(I) 25 percent of the debtor's nonpriority unsecured claims, or $6,000, whichever is greater; or*

*(II) $10,000.*

*(C) As part of the schedule of current income and expenditures required under section 521, the debtor shall include a statement of the debtor's current monthly income, and the calculations that determine whether a presumption arises under subparagraph (A)(i), that show how each such amount is calculated.*

*(D) Subparagraphs (A) through (C) shall not apply, and the court may not dismiss or convert a case based on any form of means testing, if the debtor is a disabled veteran (as defined in section 3741(1) of title 38), and the indebtedness occurred primarily during a period during which he or she was—*

*(i) on active duty (as defined in section 101(d)(1) of title 10); or*

*(ii) performing a homeland defense activity (as defined in section 901(1) of title 32).*

*(3) In considering under paragraph (1) whether the granting of relief would be an abuse of the provisions of this chapter in a case in which the presumption in subparagraph (A)(i) of such paragraph does not arise or is rebutted, the court shall consider—*

*(A) whether the debtor filed the petition in bad faith; or*

*(B) the totality of the circumstances (including whether the debtor seeks to reject a personal services contract and the financial need for such rejection as sought by the debtor) of the debtor's financial situation demonstrates abuse.*

*(4) (A) The court, on its own initiative or on the motion of a party in interest, in accordance with the procedures described in rule 9011 of the Federal Rules of Bankruptcy Procedure, may order the attorney for the debtor to reimburse the trustee for all reasonable costs in prosecuting a motion filed under section 707(b), including reasonable attorneys' fees, if—*

*(i) a trustee files a motion for dismissal or conversion under this subsection; and*

*(ii) the court—*

*(I) grants such motion; and*

*(II) finds that the action of the attorney for the debtor in filing a case under this chapter violated rule 9011 of the Federal Rules of Bankruptcy Procedure.*

*(B) If the court finds that the attorney for the debtor violated rule 9011 of the Federal Rules of Bankruptcy Procedure, the court, on its own initiative or on the motion of a party in interest, in accordance with such procedures, may order—*

*(i) the assessment of an appropriate civil penalty against the attorney for the debtor; and*

*(ii) the payment of such civil penalty to the trustee, the United States trustee (or the bankruptcy administrator, if any).*

*(C) The signature of an attorney on a petition, pleading, or written motion shall constitute a certification that the attorney has—*

*(i) performed a reasonable investigation into the circumstances that gave rise to the petition, pleading, or written motion; and*

*(ii) determined that the petition, pleading, or written motion—*

*(I) is well grounded in fact; and*

*(II) is warranted by existing law or a good faith argument for the extension, modification, or reversal of existing law and does not constitute an abuse under paragraph (1).*

*(D) The signature of an attorney on the petition shall constitute a certification that the attorney has no knowledge after an inquiry that the information in the schedules filed with such petition is incorrect.*

*(5) (A) Except as provided in subparagraph (B) and subject to paragraph (6), the court, on its own initiative or on the motion of a party in interest, in accordance with the procedures described in rule 9011 of the Federal Rules of Bankruptcy Procedure, may award a debtor all reasonable costs (including reasonable attorneys' fees) in contesting a motion filed by a party in interest (other than a trustee or United States trustee (or bankruptcy administrator, if any)) under this subsection if—*

*(i) the court does not grant the motion; and*

*(ii) the court finds that—*

*(I) the position of the party that filed the motion violated rule 9011 of the Federal Rules of Bankruptcy Procedure; or*

*(II) the attorney (if any) who filed the motion did not comply with the requirements of clauses (i) and (ii) of paragraph (4)(C), and the motion was made solely for the purpose of coercing a debtor into waiving a right guaranteed to the debtor under this title.*

*(B) A small business that has a claim of an aggregate amount less than $1,000 shall not be subject to subparagraph (A)(ii)(I).*

*(C) For purposes of this paragraph—*

*(i) the term "small business" means an unincorporated business, partnership, corporation, association, or organization that—*

*(I) has fewer than 25 full-time employees as determined on the date on which the motion is filed; and*

*(II) is engaged in commercial or business activity; and*

*(ii) the number of employees of a wholly owned subsidiary of a corporation includes the employees of—*

*(I) a parent corporation; and*

*(II) any other subsidiary corporation of the parent corporation.*

*(6) Only the judge or United States trustee (or bankruptcy administrator, if any) may file a motion under section 707(b), if the current monthly income of the debtor, or in a joint case, the debtor and the debtor's spouse, as of the date of the order for relief, when multiplied by 12, is equal to or less than—*

*(A) in the case of a debtor in a household of 1 person, the median family income of the applicable State for 1 earner;*

*(B) in the case of a debtor in a household of 2, 3, or 4 individuals, the highest median family income of the applicable State for a family of the same number or fewer individuals; or*

*(C) in the case of a debtor in a household exceeding 4 individuals, the highest median family income of the applicable State for a family of 4 or fewer individuals, plus $525 per month for each individual in excess of 4.*

*(7) (A) No judge, United States trustee (or bankruptcy administrator, if any), trustee, or other party in interest may file a motion under paragraph (2) if the current monthly income of the debtor, including a veteran (as that term is defined in section 101 of title 38), and the debtor's spouse combined, as of the date of the order for relief when multiplied by 12, is equal to or less than—*

*(i) in the case of a debtor in a household of 1 person, the median family income of the applicable State for 1 earner;*

*(ii) in the case of a debtor in a household of 2, 3, or 4 individuals, the highest median family income of the applicable State for a family of the same number or fewer individuals; or*

*(iii) in the case of a debtor in a household exceeding 4 individuals, the highest median family income of the applicable State for a family of 4 or fewer individuals, plus $525 per month for each individual in excess of 4.*

*(B) In a case that is not a joint case, current monthly income of the debtor's spouse shall not be considered for purposes of subparagraph (A) if—*

*(i) (I) the debtor and the debtor's spouse are separated under applicable nonbankruptcy law; or*

*(II) the debtor and the debtor's spouse are living separate*

*and apart, other than for the purpose of evading subparagraph (A); and*

*(ii) the debtor files a statement under penalty of perjury—*

*(I) specifying that the debtor meets the requirement of subclause (I) or (II) of clause (i); and*

*(II) disclosing the aggregate, or best estimate of the aggregate, amount of any cash or money payments received from the debtor's spouse attributed to the debtor's current monthly income.*

*(c) (1) In this subsection—*

*(A) the term 'crime of violence' has the meaning given such term in section 16 of title 18; and*

*(B) the term 'drug trafficking crime' has the meaning given such term in section 924(c)(2) of title 18.*

*(2) Except as provided in paragraph (3), after notice and a hearing, the court, on a motion by the victim of a crime of violence or a drug trafficking crime, may when it is in the best interest of the victim dismiss a voluntary case filed under this chapter by a debtor who is an individual if such individual was convicted of such crime.*

*(3) The court may not dismiss a case under paragraph (2) if the debtor establishes by a preponderance of the evidence that the filing of a case under this chapter is necessary to satisfy a claim for a domestic support obligation.*

**Section 707**

(April 20, 2005, P. L. 109-8, Title I, §§ 102(a), (f), 119 Stat. 23)

## HISTORY: ANCILLARY LAWS AND DIRECTIVES

**Amendments:**

**2005.** Act April 20, 2005(effective 180 days after enactment of April 20, 2005, as provided by § 1501(a) of P. L. 109-8), amends 11 USC § 707 to add a financial means test to determine eligibility under that chapter of relief.

**Other provisions:**

**Effective date and application of amendments made by Act April 20, 2005.** Act April 20, 2005, P.L. 109-8, Title XV, § 1501(a), 119 Stat. 23, provided that the amendments made to this section would be effective 180 days after enactment on April 20, 2005.

**Abridged Legislative History**

Dismissal or Conversion.

Section 102 of the Act revises current law in several significant respects. First, it amends section 707(b) of the Bankruptcy Code to permit-in addition to the court and the United States trustee-a trustee, bankruptcy administrator, or a party in interest to seek dismissal or conversion of a chapter 7 case to one under chapter 11 or 13 on consent of the debtor, under certain circumstances. In addition, section 102 of the Act changes the current standard for dismissal from "substantial abuse" to "abuse." Section 102 of the Act also amends Bankruptcy Code section 707(b) to mandate a presumption of abuse if the debtor's current monthly income (reduced by certain specified amounts) when multiplied by 60 is not less than the lesser of 25 percent of the debtor's nonpriority unsecured claims or $6,000 (whichever is greater), or $10,000.

To determine whether the presumption of abuse applies under section 707(b) of the Bankruptcy Code, section 102(a) of the Act specifies certain monthly expense amounts that are to be deducted from the debtor's "current monthly income" (a defined term).

With respect to secured debts, Section 102(a)(2)(C) of the Act specifies that the debtor's average monthly payments on account of secured debts is calculated as the sum of the following divided by 60: (1) all amounts scheduled as contractually due to secured creditors for each month of the 60- month period following filing of the case; and (2) any additional payments necessary, in filing a plan under chapter 13, to maintain possession of the debtor's primary residence, motor vehicle or other property necessary for the support of the debtor and the debtor's dependents, that serves as collateral for secured debts.

With respect to priority claims, section 102(a)(2)(C) of the Act specifies that the debtor's expenses for payment of such claims (including child support and alimony claims) is calculated as the total of such debts divided by 60.

To implement these needs-based reforms, the Act requires the debtor to file, as part of the schedules of current income and current expenditures, a statement of current monthly income. This statement must show: (1) the calculations that determine whether a presumption of abuse arises under section 707(b) (as amended), and (2) how each amount is calculated.

In a case where the presumption of abuse does not apply or has been rebutted, section 102(a)(2)(C) of the Act amends Bankruptcy Code section 707(b) to require a court to consider whether: (1) the debtor filed the chapter 7 case in bad faith; or (2) the totality of the circumstances of the debtor's financial situation demonstrates abuse, including whether the debtor wants to reject a personal services contract and the debtor's financial need for such rejection.

While the Act replaces the current law's presumption in favor of granting relief requested by a chapter 7 debtor with a presumption of abuse (if applicable under the income and expense analysis previously described), it does provide that this presumption may be rebutted under certain circumstances.

Section 102(a)(2)(C) of the Act provides that the signature of an attorney on a petition, pleading or written motion shall constitute a certification that the attorney has: (1) performed a reasonable investigation into the circumstances that gave rise to such document; and (2) determined that such document is well-grounded in fact and warranted by existing law or a good faith argument for the extension, modification, or reversal of existing law and does not constitute an abuse under section 707(b)(1).

The Act includes two "safe harbors" with respect to its needs-based reforms. One safe harbor allows only a judge, United States trustee, or bankruptcy administrator to file a section 707(b) motion (based on the debtor's ability to repay, bad faith, or the totality of the circumstances) if the chapter 7 debtor's current monthly income (or in a joint case, the income of the debtor and the debtor's spouse) falls below the state median family income for a family of equal or lesser size (adjusted for larger sized families), or the state median family income for one earner in the case of a one-person household.

The Act's second safe harbor only pertains to a motion under section 707(b)(2), that is, a motion to dismiss based on a debtor's ability to repay. It does not allow a judge, United States trustee, bankruptcy administrator or party in interest to file such motion if the income of the debtor (including a veteran, as that term is defined in 38 U.S.C. S 101) and the debtor's spouse is less than certain monetary thresholds.

(H. Report No. 109-31 to accompany S. 256, 109th Cong., 1st Sess. (2005) pp. 48–51, 52, available at 2005 U.S.C.C.A.N. 88, at 119–22, 123)

# Subchapter II——Collection, Liquidation, and Distribution of the Estate

## § 721. Authorization to operate business

The court may authorize the trustee to operate the business of the debtor for a limited period, if such operation is in the best interest of the estate and consistent with the orderly liquidation of the estate.

## § 722. Redemption

An individual debtor may, whether or not the debtor has waived the right to redeem under this section, redeem tangible personal property intended primarily for personal, family, or household use, from a lien securing a dischargeable consumer debt, if such property is exempted under section 522 of this title or has been abandoned under section 554 of this title, by paying the holder of such lien the amount of the allowed secured claim of such holder that is secured by such lien *in full at the time of redemption.*

**Section 722**

(April 20, 2005, P. L. 109-8, Title III, § 304(2), 119 Stat. 23)

### HISTORY: ANCILLARY LAWS AND DIRECTIVES

**Amendments:**

**2005.** Act April 20, 2005(effective 180 days after enactment of April 20, 2005, as provided by § 1501(a) of P. L. 109-8), amends 11 USC § 722 to clarify that a chapter 7 debtor must pay the redemption value in full.

**Other provisions:**

**Effective date and application of amendments made by Act April 20, 2005.** Act April 20, 2005, P.L. 109-8, Title XV, § 1501(a), 119 Stat. 23, provided that the amendments made to this section would be effective 180 days after enactment on April 20, 2005.

**Abridged Legislative History**

Section 304(2) amends section 722 to clarify that a chapter 7 debtor must pay the redemption value in full at the time of redemption. (H. Report No. 109-31 to accompany S. 256, 109th Cong., 1st Sess. (2005) p. 71, available at 2005 U.S.C.C.A.N. 88, at 139)

## § 723. Rights of partnership trustee against general partners

(a) If there is a deficiency of property of the estate to pay in full all claims which are allowed in a case under this chapter concerning a partnership and with respect to which a general partner of the partnership is personally liable, the trustee shall have a claim against such general partner to the extent that under applicable nonbankruptcy law such general partner is personally liable for such deficiency.

(b) To the extent practicable, the trustee shall first seek recovery of such deficiency from any general partner in such partnership that is not a debtor in a case under this title. Pending determination of such deficiency, the court may order any such partner to provide the estate with indemnity for, or assurance of payment of, any deficiency recoverable from such partner, or not to dispose of property.

(c) Notwithstanding section 728(c) of this title, the trustee has a claim against the estate of each general partner in such partnership that is a debtor in a case under this title for the full amount of all claims of creditors allowed in the case concerning such partnership. Notwithstanding section 502 of this title, there shall not be allowed in such partner's case a claim against such partner on which both such partner and such partnership are liable, except to any extent that such claim is secured only by property of such partner and not by property of such partnership. The claim of the trustee under this subsection is entitled to distribution in such partner's case under section 726(a) of this title the same as any other claim of a kind specified in such section.

(d) If the aggregate that the trustee recovers from the estates of general partners under subsection (c) of this section is greater than any deficiency not recovered under subsection (b) of this section, the court, after notice and a hearing, shall determine an equitable distribution of the surplus so recovered, and the trustee shall distribute such surplus to the estates of the general partners in such partnership according to such determination.

## § 724. Treatment of certain liens

(a) The trustee may avoid a lien that secures a claim of a kind specified in section 726(a)(4) of this title.

(b) Property in which the estate has an interest and that is subject to a lien that is not avoidable under this title *(other than to the extent that there is a properly perfected unavoidable tax lien arising in connection with an ad valorem tax on real or personal property of the estate)* and that secures an allowed claim for a tax, or proceeds of such property, shall be distributed—

(1) first, to any holder of an allowed claim secured by a lien on such property that is not avoidable under this title and that is senior to such tax lien;

(2) second, to any holder of a claim of a kind specified in section 507(a)(1) *(except that such expenses, other than claims for wages, salaries, or commissions that arise after the date of the filing of the petition, shall be limited to expenses incurred under chapter 7 of this title and shall not include expenses incurred under chapter 11 of this title)*, 507(a)(2), 507(a)(3), 507(a)(4), 507(a)(5), 507(a)(6), or 507(a)(7) of this title, to the extent of the amount of such allowed tax claim that is secured by such tax lien;

(3) third, to the holder of such tax lien, to any extent that such holder's allowed tax claim that is secured by such tax lien exceeds any amount distributed under paragraph (2) of this subsection;

(4) fourth, to any holder of an allowed claim secured by a lien on such property that is not avoidable under this title and that is junior to such tax lien;

(5) fifth, to the holder of such tax lien, to the extent that such holder's allowed claim secured by such tax lien is not paid under paragraph (3) of this subsection; and

(6) sixth, to the estate.

(c) If more than one holder of a claim is entitled to distribution under a particular paragraph of subsection (b) of this section, distribution to such holders under such paragraph shall be in the same order as distribution to such holders would have been other than under this section.

(d) A statutory lien the priority of which is determined in the same manner as the priority of a tax lien under section 6323 of the Internal Revenue Code of 1986 shall be treated under subsection (b) of this section the same as if such lien were a tax lien.

*(e) Before subordinating a tax lien on real or personal property of the estate, the trustee shall—*

*(1) exhaust the unencumbered assets of the estate; and*

*(2) in a manner consistent with section 506(c), recover from property securing an allowed secured claim the reasonable, necessary costs and expenses of preserving or disposing of such property.*

*(f) Notwithstanding the exclusion of ad valorem tax liens under this section and subject to the requirements of subsection (e), the following may be paid from property of the estate which secures a tax lien, or the proceeds of such property:*

*(1) Claims for wages, salaries, and commissions that are entitled to priority under section 507(a)(4).*

*(2) Claims for contributions to an employee benefit plan entitled to priority under section 507(a)(5).*

**Section 724**

(April 20, 2005, P. L. 109-8, Title VII, § 701(a), 119 Stat. 23)

## HISTORY: ANCILLARY LAWS AND DIRECTIVES

**Amendments:**

**2005.** Act April 20, 2005(effective 180 days after enactment of April 20, 2005, as provided by § 1501(a) of P. L. 109-8), amends 11 USC § 724 to provide greater protection for holders of tax liens on real or personal property of the estate, particularly holders of ad valorem tax liens.

**Other provisions:**

**Effective date and application of amendments made by Act April 20, 2005.** Act April 20, 2005, P.L. 109-8, Title XV, § 1501(a), 119 Stat. 23, provided that the amendments made to this section would be effective 180 days after enactment on April 20, 2005.

**Abridged Legislative History**

Treatment of Certain Tax Liens. Subsection (a) of section 701 of the Act makes several amendments to section 724 of the Bankruptcy Code to provide greater protection for holders of tax liens on real or personal property of the estate, particularly holders of ad valorem tax liens.

(H. Report No. 109-31 to accompany S. 256, 109th Cong., 1st Sess. (2005) p. 100, available at 2005 U.S.C.C.A.N. 88, at 164)

## § 725. Disposition of certain property

After the commencement of a case under this chapter, but before final distribution of property of the estate under section 726 of this title, the trustee, after notice and a hearing, shall dispose of any property in which an entity other than the estate has an interest, such as a lien, and that has not been disposed of under another section of this title.

## § 726. Distribution of property of the estate

(a) Except as provided in section 510 of this title, property of the estate shall be distributed—

(1) first, in payment of claims of the kind specified in, and in the order specified in, section 507 of this title, proof of which is timely filed under section 501 of this title or tardily filed ~~before the date on which the trustee commences distribution under this section;~~ *on or before the earlier of—*

*(A) the date that is 10 days after the mailing to creditors of the summary of the trustee's final report; or*

*(B) the date on which the trustee commences final distribution under this section;*

(2) second, in payment of any allowed unsecured claim, other than a claim of a kind specified in paragraph (1), (3), or (4) of this subsection, proof of which is—

(A) timely filed under section 501(a) of this title;

(B) timely filed under section 501(b) or 501(c) of this title; or

(C) tardily filed under section 501(a) of this title, if—

(i) the creditor that holds such claim did not have notice or actual knowledge of the case in time for timely filing of a proof of such claim under section 501(a) of this title; and

(ii) proof of such claim is filed in time to permit payment of such claim;

(3) third, in payment of any allowed unsecured claim proof of which is tardily filed under section 501(a) of this title, other than a claim of the kind specified in paragraph (2)(C) of this subsection;

(4) fourth, in payment of any allowed claim, whether secured or unsecured, for any fine, penalty, or forfeiture, or for multiple, exemplary, or punitive damages, arising before the earlier of the order for relief or the appointment of a trustee, to the extent that such fine, penalty, forfeiture, or damages are not compensation for actual pecuniary loss suffered by the holder of such claim;

(5) fifth, in payment of interest at the legal rate from the date of the filing of the petition, on any claim paid under paragraph (1), (2), (3), or (4) of this subsection; and

(6) sixth, to the debtor.

(b) Payment on claims of a kind specified in paragraph (1), (2), (3), (4), (5), (6), (7), or (8) of section 507(a) of this title, or in paragraph (2), (3), (4), or (5) of subsection (a) of this section, shall be made pro rata among claims of the kind specified in each such particular paragraph, except that in a case that has been converted to this chapter under section ~~1009,~~ 1112, 1208, or 1307 of this title, a claim allowed under section 503(b) of this title incurred under this chapter after such conversion has priority over a claim allowed under section 503(b) of this title incurred under any other chapter of this title or under this chapter before such conversion and over any expenses of a custodian superseded under section 543 of this title.

(c) Notwithstanding subsections (a) and (b) of this section, if there is property of the kind specified in section 541(a)(2) of this title, or proceeds of such property, in the estate, such property or proceeds shall be segregated from other property of the estate, and such property or proceeds and other property of the estate shall be distributed as follows:

(1) Claims allowed under section 503 of this title shall be paid either from property of the kind specified in section 541(a)(2) of this title, or from other property of the estate, as the interest of justice requires.

(2) Allowed claims, other than claims allowed under section 503 of this title, shall be paid in the order specified in subsection (a) of this section, and, with respect to claims of a kind specified in a particular paragraph of section 507 of this title or subsection (a) of this section, in the following order and manner:

(A) First, community claims against the debtor or the debtor's spouse shall be paid from property of the kind specified in section 541(a)(2) of this title, except to the extent that such property is solely liable for debts of the debtor.

(B) Second, to the extent that community claims against the debtor are not paid under subparagraph (A) of this paragraph, such community claims shall be paid from property of the kind specified in section 541(a)(2) of this title that is solely liable for debts of the debtor.

(C) Third, to the extent that all claims against the debtor including community claims against the debtor are not paid under subparagraph (A) or (B) of this paragraph such claims shall be paid from property of the estate other than property of the kind specified in section 541(a)(2) of this title.

(D) Fourth, to the extent that community claims against the debtor or the debtor's spouse are not paid under subparagraph (A), (B), or (C) of this paragraph, such claims shall be paid from all remaining property of the estate.

**Section 726**

(April 20, 2005, P. L. 109-8, Title VII, § 713; Title XII, § 1215, 119 Stat. 23)

## HISTORY: ANCILLARY LAWS AND DIRECTIVES

**Amendments:**

**2005.** Act April 20, 2005(effective 180 days after enactment of April 20, 2005, as provided by § 1501(a) of P. L. 109-8), amends 11 USC § 726(a)(1) concerning allowance of certain tardily filed claims.

**Other provisions:**

**Effective date and application of amendments made by Act April 20, 2005.** Act April 20, 2005, P.L. 109-8, Title XV, § 1501(a), 119 Stat. 23, provided that the amendments made to this section would be effective 180 days after enactment on April 20, 2005.

**Abridged Legislative History**

(H. Report No. 109-31 to accompany S. 256, 109th Cong., 1st Sess. (2005) pp. 103, 144; available at 2005 U.S.C.C.A.N. 88, at 167, 203)

# § 727. Discharge

(a) The court shall grant the debtor a discharge, unless—

(1) the debtor is not an individual;

(2) the debtor, with intent to hinder, delay, or defraud a creditor or an officer of the estate charged with custody of property under this title, has transferred, removed, destroyed, mutilated, or concealed, or has permitted to be transferred, removed, destroyed, mutilated, or concealed—

(A) property of the debtor, within one year before the date of the filing of the petition; or

(B) property of the estate, after the date of the filing of the petition;

(3) the debtor has concealed, destroyed, mutilated, falsified, or failed to keep or preserve any recorded information, including books, documents, records, and papers, from which the debtor's financial condition or business transactions might be ascertained, unless such act or failure to act was justified under all of the circumstances of the case;

(4) the debtor knowingly and fraudulently, in or in connection with the case—

(A) made a false oath or account;

(B) presented or used a false claim;

(C) gave, offered, received, or attempted to obtain money, property, or advantage, or a promise of money, property, or advantage, for acting or forbearing to act; or

(D) withheld from an officer of the estate entitled to possession under this title, any recorded information, including books, documents, records, and papers, relating to the debtor's property or financial affairs;

(5) the debtor has failed to explain satisfactorily, before determination of denial of discharge under this paragraph, any loss of assets or deficiency of assets to meet the debtor's liabilities;

(6) the debtor has refused, in the case—

(A) to obey any lawful order of the court, other than an order to respond to a material question or to testify;

(B) on the ground of privilege against self-incrimination, to respond to a material question approved by the court or to testify, after the debtor has been granted immunity with respect to the matter concerning which such privilege was invoked; or

(C) on a ground other than the properly invoked privilege against self-incrimination, to respond to a material question approved by the court or to testify;

(7) the debtor has committed any act specified in paragraph (2), (3), (4), (5), or (6) of this subsection, on or within one year before the date of the filing of the petition, or during the case, in connection with another case, under this title or under the Bankruptcy Act, concerning an insider;

(8) the debtor has been granted a discharge under this section, under section 1141 of this title, or under section 14, 371, or 476 of

the Bankruptcy Act, in a case commenced within ~~six~~ *8* years before the date of the filing of the petition;

(9) the debtor has been granted a discharge under section 1228 or 1328 of this title, or under section 660 or 661 of the Bankruptcy Act, in a case commenced within six years before the date of the filing of the petition, unless payments under the plan in such case totaled at least—

(A) 100 percent of the allowed unsecured claims in such case; or

(B) (i) 70 percent of such claims; and

(ii) the plan was proposed by the debtor in good faith, and was the debtor's best effort; ~~or~~

(10) the court approves a written waiver of discharge executed by the debtor after the order for relief under this chapter~~.~~*;*

*(11) after filing the petition, the debtor failed to complete an instructional course concerning personal financial management described in section 111, except that this paragraph shall not apply with respect to a debtor who is a person described in section 109(h)(4) or who resides in a district for which the United States trustee (or the bankruptcy administrator, if any) determines that the approved instructional courses are not adequate to service the additional individuals who would otherwise be required to complete such instructional courses under this section (The United States trustee (or the bankruptcy administrator, if any) who makes a determination described in this paragraph shall review such determination not later than 1 year after the date of such determination, and not less frequently than annually thereafter.); or*

*(12) the court after notice and a hearing held not more than 10 days before the date of the entry of the order granting the discharge finds that there is reasonable cause to believe that—*

*(A) section 522(q)(1) may be applicable to the debtor; and*

*(B) there is pending any proceeding in which the debtor may be found guilty of a felony of the kind described in section 522(q)(1)(A) or liable for a debt of the kind described in section 522(q)(1)(B).*

(b) Except as provided in section 523 of this title, a discharge under subsection (a) of this section discharges the debtor from all debts that arose before the date of the order for relief under this chapter, and any liability on a claim that is determined under section 502 of this title as if such claim had arisen before the com mencement of the case, whether or not a proof of claim based on any such debt or liability is filed under section 501 of this title, and whether or not a claim based on any such debt or liability is allowed under section 502 of this title.

(c) (1) The trustee, a creditor, or the United States trustee may object to the granting of a discharge under subsection (a) of this section.

(2) On request of a party in interest, the court may order the

trustee to examine the acts and conduct of the debtor to determine whether a ground exists for denial of discharge.

(d) On request of the trustee, a creditor, or the United States trustee, and after notice and a hearing, the court shall revoke a discharge granted under subsection (a) of this section if—

(1) such discharge was obtained through the fraud of the debtor, and the requesting party did not know of such fraud until after the granting of such discharge;

(2) the debtor acquired property that is property of the estate, or became entitled to acquire property that would be property of the estate, and knowingly and fraudulently failed to report the acquisition of or entitlement to such property, or to deliver or surrender such property to the trustee; ~~or~~

(3) the debtor committed an act specified in subsection (a)(6) of this section*; or*

*(4) the debtor has failed to explain satisfactorily—*

*(A) a material misstatement in an audit referred to in section 586(f) of title 28; or*

*(B) a failure to make available for inspection all necessary accounts, papers, documents, financial records, files, and all other papers, things, or property belonging to the debtor that are requested for an audit referred to in section 586(f) of title 28.*

(e) The trustee, a creditor, or the United States trustee may request a revocation of a discharge—

(1) under subsection (d)(1) of this section within one year after such discharge is granted; or

(2) under subsection (d)(2) or (d)(3) of this section before the later of—

(A) one year after the granting of such discharge; and

(B) the date the case is closed.

**Section 727**

(April 20, 2005, P. L. 109-8, Title I, § 106(b); Title III, §§ 312(1), 330(a); Title VI, § 603(d), 119 Stat. 23)

## HISTORY: ANCILLARY LAWS AND DIRECTIVES

**Amendments:**

**2005.** Act April 20, 2005(effective 180 days after enactment of April 20, 2005, as provided by § 1501(a) of P. L. 109-8), amends 11 USC § 727's discharge restrictions, adding requirements to complete a financial management course and cooperate with any audit. The Act changes the time between discharges from 6 to 8 years. The Act also adds new § 1228(f) which is related to new § 522(q), and this amendment is effective upon enactment. See P.L. 109-8, §§ 330(c)(3), 1501(b)(2).

**Other provisions:**

**Effective date and application of amendments made by Act April 20, 2005.** Act April 20, 2005, P.L. 109-8, Title XV, § 1501(a), 119 Stat. 23, provided that the amendments made to this section would be effective 180 days after enactment on April 20, 2005. New § 522(q), which is related to new § 727(a)(12), is effective upon enactment, according to § 1501(b)(2) of P.L. 109-8; therefore, § 727(a)(12) is effective upon enactment.

**Abridged Legislative History**
Section 106(b) of the Act amends section 727(a) of the Bankruptcy Code to deny a discharge to a chapter 7 debtor who fails to complete a personal financial management instructional course.

Extension of Period Between Bankruptcy Discharges. Section 312 of the Act amends section 727(a)(8) of the Bankruptcy Code to extend the period before which a chapter 7 debtor may receive a subsequent chapter 7 discharge from six to eight years. It also amends section 1328 to prohibit the issuance of a discharge in a subsequent chapter 13 case if the debtor received a discharge in a prior chapter 7, 11, or 12 case within four years preceding the filing of the subsequent chapter 13 case. In addition, it prohibits the issuance of a discharge in a subsequent chapter 13 case if the debtor received a discharge in a chapter 13 case filed during the two-year period preceding the date of the filing of the subsequent chapter 13 case.

Delay of Discharge During Pendency of Certain Proceedings. Section 330(a) of the Act amends section 727(a) of the Bankruptcy Code to require the court to withhold the entry of a debtor's discharge order if the court, after notice and a hearing, finds that there is reasonable cause to believe that there is a pending proceeding in which the debtor may be found guilty of a felony of the kind described in Bankruptcy Code section 522(q)(1) or liable for a debt of the kind described in Bankruptcy Code section 522(q)(2).

(H. Report No. 109-31 to accompany S. 256, 109th Cong., 1st Sess. (2005) pp. 55, 76, 84, 99; available at 2005 U.S.C.C.A.N. 88, at 125, 143, 150, 163)

## ~~§ 728. Special tax provisions~~

~~(a) For the purposes of any State or local law imposing a tax on or measured by income, the taxable period of a debtor that is an individual shall terminate on the date of the order for relief under this chapter, unless the case was converted under section 1112 or 1208 of this title.~~

~~(b) Notwithstanding any State or local law imposing a tax on or measured by income, the trustee shall make tax returns of income for the estate of an individual debtor in a case under this chapter or for a debtor that is a corporation in a case under this chapter only if such estate or corporation has net taxable income for the entire period after the order for relief under this chapter during which the case is pending. If such entity has such income, or if the debtor is a partnership, then the trustee shall make and file a return of income for each taxable period during which the case was pending after the order for relief under this chapter.~~

~~(c) If there are pending a case under this chapter concerning a partnership and a case under this chapter concerning a partner in such partnership, a governmental unit's claim for any unpaid liability of such partner for a State or local tax on or measured by income, to the extent that such liability arose from the inclusion in such partner's taxable income of earnings of such partnership that were not withdrawn by such partner, is a claim only against such partnership.~~

~~(d) Notwithstanding section 541 of this title, if there are pending a case under this chapter concerning a partnership and a case under this chapter concerning a partner in such partnership, then any State or local tax refund or reduction of tax of such partner that would have otherwise been property of the estate of such partner under section 541 of this title—~~

~~(1) is property of the estate of such partnership to the extent that such tax refund or reduction of tax is fairly apportionable to losses sustained by such partnership and not reimbursed by such partner;~~ and

~~(2) is otherwise property of the estate of such partner.~~

**Section 728**

(April 20, 2005, P. L. 109-8, Title VII, § 719(b)(1), 119 Stat. 23)

## HISTORY: ANCILLARY LAWS AND DIRECTIVES

**Amendments:**

**2005.** Act April 20, 2005(effective 180 days after enactment of April 20, 2005, as provided by § 1501(a) of P. L. 109-8), deletes 11 USC § 728.

**Other provisions:**

**Effective date and application of amendments made by Act April 20, 2005.** Act April 20, 2005, P.L. 109-8, Title XV, § 1501(a), 119 Stat. 23, provided that the amendments made to this section would be effective 180 days after enactment on April 20, 2005.

**Abridged Legislative History**

(H. Report No. 109-31 to accompany S. 256, 109th Cong., 1st Sess. (2005) p. 105; available at 2005 U.S.C.C.A.N. 88, at 168)

# Subchapter III——Stockbroker Liquidation

## § 741. Definitions for this subchapter

In this subchapter—

(1) "Commission" means Securities and Exchange Commission;

(2) "customer" includes—

(A) entity with whom a person deals as principal or agent and that has a claim against such person on account of a security received, acquired, or held by such person in the ordinary course of such person's business as a stockbroker, from or for the securities account or accounts of such entity—

(i) for safekeeping;

(ii) with a view to sale;

(iii) to cover a consummated sale;

(iv) pursuant to a purchase;

(v) as collateral under a security agreement; or

(vi) for the purpose of effecting registration of transfer; and

(B) entity that has a claim against a person arising out of—

(i) a sale or conversion of a security received, acquired, or held as specified in subparagraph (A) of this paragraph; or

(ii) a deposit of cash, a security, or other property with such person for the purpose of purchasing or selling a security;

(3) "customer name security" means security—

(A) held for the account of a customer on the date of the filing of the petition by or on behalf of the debtor;

(B) registered in such customer's name on such date or in the process of being so registered under instructions from the debtor; and

(C) not in a form transferable by delivery on such date;

(4) "customer property" means cash, security, or other property, and proceeds of such cash, security, or property, received, acquired, or held by or for the account of the debtor, from or for the securities account of a customer—

(A) including—

(i) property that was unlawfully converted from and that is the lawful property of the estate;

(ii) a security held as property of the debtor to the extent such security is necessary to meet a net equity claim of a customer based on a security of the same class and series of an issuer;

(iii) resources provided through the use or realization of a customer's debit cash balance or a debit item includible in the Formula for Determination of Reserve Requirement for Brokers and Dealers as promulgated by the Commission under the Securities Exchange Act of 1934; and

(iv) other property of the debtor that any applicable law, rule, or regulation requires to be set aside or held for the benefit of a customer, unless including such property as customer property would not significantly increase customer property; but

(B) not including—

(i) a customer name security delivered to or reclaimed by a customer under section 751 of this title; or

(ii) property to the extent that a customer does not have a claim against the debtor based on such property;

(5) "margin payment" means payment or deposit of cash, a security, or other property, that is commonly known to the securities trade as original margin, initial margin, maintenance margin, or variation margin, or as a mark-to-market payment, or that secures an obligation of a participant in a securities clearing agency;

(6) "net equity" means, with respect to all accounts of a customer that such customer has in the same capacity—

(A) (i) aggregate dollar balance that would remain in such accounts after the liquidation, by sale or purchase, at the time of the filing of the petition, of all securities positions in all such accounts, except any customer name securities of such customer; minus

(ii) any claim of the debtor against such customer in such capacity that would have been owing immediately after such liquidation; plus

(B) any payment by such customer to the trustee, within 60 days after notice under section 342 of this title, of any business related claim of the debtor against such customer in such capacity;

(7) 'securities contract' ~~means contract for the purchase, sale, or loan of a security, including an option for the purchase or sale of a security, certificate of deposit, or group or index of securities (including any interest therein or based on the value thereof), or any option entered into on a national securities exchange relating to foreign currencies, or the guarantee of any settlement of cash or securities by or to a securities clearing agency;—~~

*(A) means—*

*(i) a contract for the purchase, sale, or loan of a security, a certificate of deposit, a mortgage loan or any interest in a mortgage loan, a group or index of securities, certificates of deposit, or mortgage loans or interests therein (including an interest therein or based on the value thereof), or option on any of the foregoing, including an option to purchase or sell any such security, certificate of deposit, mortgage loan, interest, group or index, or option, and including any repurchase or reverse repurchase transaction on any such security, certificate of deposit, mortgage loan, interest, group or index, or option;*

*(ii) any option entered into on a national securities exchange relating to foreign currencies;*

*(iii) the guarantee by or to any securities clearing agency of a settlement of cash, securities, certificates of deposit, mortgage loans or interests therein, group or index of securities, or mortgage loans or interests therein (including any interest therein or based on the value thereof), or option on any of the foregoing, including an option to purchase or sell any such security, certificate of deposit, mortgage loan, interest, group or index, or option;*

*(iv) any margin loan;*

*(v) any other agreement or transaction that is similar to an agreement or transaction referred to in this subparagraph;*

*(vi) any combination of the agreements or transactions referred to in this subparagraph;*

*(vii) any option to enter into any agreement or transaction referred to in this subparagraph;*

*(viii) a master agreement that provides for an agreement or transaction referred to in clause (i), (ii), (iii), (iv), (v), (vi), or (vii), together with all supplements to any such master agreement, without regard to whether the master agreement provides for an agreement or transaction that is not a securities contract under this subparagraph, except that such master agreement shall be considered to be a securities contract under this subparagraph only with respect to each agreement or transaction under such master agreement that is referred to in clause (i), (ii), (iii), (iv), (v), (vi), or (vii); or*

*(ix) any security agreement or arrangement or other credit enhancement related to any agreement or transaction referred to in this subparagraph, including any guarantee or reimburse-*

*ment obligation by or to a stockbroker, securities clearing agency, financial institution, or financial participant in connection with any agreement or transaction referred to in this subparagraph, but not to exceed the damages in connection with any such agreement or transaction, measured in accordance with section 562; and*

*(B) does not include any purchase, sale, or repurchase obligation under a participation in a commercial mortgage loan;*

(8) "settlement payment" means a preliminary settlement payment, a partial settlement payment, an interim settlement payment, a settlement payment on account, a final settlement payment, or any other similar payment commonly used in the securities trade; and

(9) "SIPC" means Securities Investor Protection Corporation.

**Section 741**

(April 20, 2005, P. L. 109-8, Title IX, § 907(a)(2), 119 Stat. 23)

## HISTORY: ANCILLARY LAWS AND DIRECTIVES

**Amendments:**

**2005.** Act April 20, 2005(effective 180 days after enactment of April 20, 2005, as provided by § 1501(a) of P. L. 109-8), amends 11 USC § 741's definition of "securities contract" to conform to the definition in the Federal Deposit Insurance Act.

**Other provisions:**

**Effective date and application of amendments made by Act April 20, 2005.** Act April 20, 2005, P.L. 109-8, Title XV, § 1501(a), 119 Stat. 23, provided that the amendments made to this section would be effective 180 days after enactment on April 20, 2005.

**Abridged Legislative History**

Subsections (a)(2) and (a)(3) amend the Bankruptcy Code definitions of "securities contract" and "commodity contract," respectively, to conform them to the definitions in the Federal Deposit Insurance Act.

Subsection (a)(2), like the amendments to the FDIA and the FCUA, amends the definition of "securities contract" expressly to encompass margin loans, to clarify the coverage of securities options and to clarify the coverage of repurchase and reverse repurchase transactions.

Subsection (a)(2) also specifies that purchase, sale and repurchase obligations under a participation in a commercial mortgage loan do not constitute "securities contracts."

(H. Report No. 109-31 to accompany S. 256, 109th Cong., 1st Sess. (2005) pp. 129–30; available at 2005 U.S.C.C.A.N. 88, at 190–91)

## § 742. Effect of section 362 of this title in this chapter

Notwithstanding section 362 of this title, SIPC may file an application for a protective decree under the Securities Investor Protection Act of 1970. The filing of such application stays all proceedings in the case under this title unless and until such application is dismissed. If SIPC completes the liquidation of the debtor, then the court shall dismiss the case.

## § 743. Notice

The clerk shall give the notice required by section 342 of this title to SIPC and to the Commission.

## § 744. Executory contracts

Notwithstanding section 365(d)(1) of this title, the trustee shall assume or reject, under section 365 of this title, any executory contract of the debtor for the purchase or sale of a security in the ordinary course of the debtor's business, within a reasonable time after the date of the order for relief, but not to exceed 30 days. If the trustee does not assume such a contract within such time, such contract is rejected.

## § 745. Treatment of accounts

(a) Accounts held by the debtor for a particular customer in separate capacities shall be treated as accounts of separate customers.

(b) If a stockbroker or a bank holds a customer net equity claim against the debtor that arose out of a transaction for a customer of such stockbroker or bank, each such customer of such stockbroker or bank shall be treated as a separate customer of the debtor.

(c) Each trustee's account specified as such on the debtor's books, and supported by a trust deed filed with, and qualified as such by, the Internal Revenue Service, and under the Internal Revenue Code of 1986, shall be treated as a separate customer account for each beneficiary under such trustee account.

## § 746. Extent of customer claims

(a) If, after the date of the filing of the petition, an entity enters into a transaction with the debtor, in a manner that would have made such entity a customer had such transaction occurred before the date of the filing of the petition, and such transaction was entered into by such entity in good faith and before the qualification under section 322 of this title of a trustee, such entity shall be deemed a customer, and the date of such transaction shall be deemed to be the date of the filing of the petition for the purpose of determining such entity's net equity.

(b) An entity does not have a claim as a customer to the extent that such entity transferred to the debtor cash or a security that, by contract, agreement, understanding, or operation of law, is—

(1) part of the capital of the debtor; or

(2) subordinated to the claims of any or all creditors.

## § 747. Subordination of certain customer claims

Except as provided in section 510 of this title, unless all other customer net equity claims have been paid in full, the trustee may not pay in full or in part, directly or indirectly, any net equity claim of a customer that was, on the date the transaction giving rise to such claim occurred—

(1) an insider;

(2) a beneficial owner of at least five percent of any class of equity securities of the debtor, other than—

(A) nonconvertible stock having fixed preferential dividend and liquidation rights; or

(B) interests of limited partners in a limited partnership;

(3) a limited partner with a participation of at least five percent in the net assets or net profits of the debtor; or

(4) an entity that, directly or indirectly, through agreement or otherwise, exercised or had the power to exercise control over the management or policies of the debtor.

## § 748. Reduction of securities to money

As soon as practicable after the date of the order for relief, the trustee shall reduce to money, consistent with good market practice, all securities held as property of the estate, except for customer name securities delivered or reclaimed under section 751 of this title.

## § 749. Voidable transfers

(a) Except as otherwise provided in this section, any transfer of property that, but for such transfer, would have been customer property, may be avoided by the trustee, and such property shall be treated as customer property, if and to the extent that the trustee avoids such transfer under section 544, 545, 547, 548, or 549 of this title. For the purpose of such sections, the property so transferred shall be deemed to have been property of the debtor and, if such transfer was made to a customer or for a customer's benefit such customer shall be deemed, for the purposes of this section, to have been a creditor.

(b) Notwithstanding sections 544, 545, 547, 548, and 549 of this title, the trustee may not avoid a transfer made before five days after the order for relief if such transfer is approved by the Commission by rule or order, either before or after such transfer, and if such transfer is—

(1) a transfer of a securities contract entered into or carried by or through the debtor on behalf of a customer, and of any cash, security, or other property margining or securing such securities contract; or

(2) the liquidation of a securities contract entered into or carried by or through the debtor on behalf of a customer.

## § 750. Distribution of securities

The trustee may not distribute a security except under section 751 of this title.

## § 751. Customer name securities

The trustee shall deliver any customer name security to or on behalf of the customer entitled to such security, unless such customer has a negative net equity. With the approval of the trustee, a customer may reclaim a customer name security after payment to the trustee, within such period as the trustee allows, of any claim of the debtor against such customer to the extent that such customer will not have a negative net equity after such payment.

## § 752. Customer property

(a) The trustee shall distribute customer property ratably to customers on the basis and to the extent of such customers' allowed net equity claims and in priority to all other claims, except claims of the kind specified in section 507(a)(~~1~~2) of this title that are attributable to the administration of such customer property.

(b) (1) The trustee shall distribute customer property in excess of that distributed under subsection (a) of this section in accordance with section 726 of this title.

(2) Except as provided in section 510 of this title, if a customer is not paid the full amount of such customer's allowed net equity claim from customer property, the unpaid portion of such claim is a claim entitled to distribution under section 726 of this title.

(c) Any cash or security remaining after the liquidation of a security interest created under a security agreement made by the debtor, excluding property excluded under section 741(4)(B) of this title, shall be apportioned between the general estate and customer property in the same proportion as the general estate of the debtor and customer property were subject to such security interest.

**Section 752**

(April 20, 2005, P. L. 109-8, Title XV, § 1502(a)(3), 119 Stat. 23)

### HISTORY: ANCILLARY LAWS AND DIRECTIVES

**Amendments:**

**2005.** Act April 20, 2005(effective 180 days after enactment of April 20, 2005, as provided by § 1501(a) of P. L. 109-8), amends 11 USC § 752 to make technical corrections to references.

**Other provisions:**

**Effective date and application of amendments made by Act April 20, 2005.** Act April 20, 2005, P.L. 109-8, Title XV, § 1501(a), 119 Stat. 23, provided that the amendments made to this section would be effective 180 days after enactment on April 20, 2005.

**Abridged Legislative History**

(H. Report No. 109-31 to accompany S. 256, 109th Cong., 1st Sess. (2005) p. 155; available at 2005 U.S.C.C.A.N. 88, at 212)

## *§ 753. Stockbroker liquidation and forward contract merchants, commodity brokers, stockbrokers, financial institutions, financial participants, securities clearing agencies, swap participants, repo participants, and master netting agreement participants*

*Notwithstanding any other provision of this title, the exercise of rights by a forward contract merchant, commodity broker, stockbroker, financial institution, financial participant, securities clearing agency, swap participant, repo participant, or master netting agreement participant under this title shall not affect the priority of any unsecured claim it may have after the exercise of such rights.*

**Section 753**

(April 20, 2005, P. L. 109-8, Title IX, § 907(m), 119 Stat. 23)

## HISTORY: ANCILLARY LAWS AND DIRECTIVES

**Amendments:**

**2005.** Act April 20, 2005(effective 180 days after enactment of April 20, 2005, as provided by § 1501(a) of P. L. 109-8), adds new 11 USC § 753.

**Other provisions:**

**Effective date and application of amendments made by Act April 20, 2005.** Act April 20, 2005, P.L. 109-8, Title XV, § 1501(a), 119 Stat. 23, provided that the amendments made to this section would be effective 180 days after enactment on April 20, 2005.

**Abridged Legislative History**

(H. Report No. 109-31 to accompany S. 256, 109th Cong., 1st Sess. (2005) p. 134; available at 2005 U.S.C.C.A.N. 88, at 194)

# Subchapter IV——Commodity Broker Liquidation

## § 761. Definitions for this subchapter

In this subchapter—

(1) "Act" means Commodity Exchange Act;

(2) "clearing organization" means a derivatives clearing organization registered under the Act;

(3) "Commission" means Commodity Futures Trading Commission;

(4) "commodity contract" means—

(A) with respect to a futures commission merchant, contract for the purchase or sale of a commodity for future delivery on, or subject to the rules of, a contract market or board of trade;

(B) with respect to a foreign futures commission merchant, foreign future;

(C) with respect to a leverage transaction merchant, leverage transaction;

(D) with respect to a clearing organization, contract for the purchase or sale of a commodity for future delivery on, or subject to the rules of, a contract market or board of trade that is cleared by such clearing organization, or commodity option traded on, or subject to the rules of, a contract market or board of trade that is cleared by such clearing organization; ~~or~~

(E) with respect to a commodity options dealer, commodity option;

*(F) any other agreement or transaction that is similar to an agreement or transaction referred to in this paragraph;*

*(G) any combination of the agreements or transactions referred to in this paragraph;*

*(H) any option to enter into an agreement or transaction referred to in this paragraph;*

*(I) a master agreement that provides for an agreement or transaction referred to in subparagraph (A), (B), (C), (D), (E), (F), (G), or (H), together with all supplements to such master agreement, without regard to whether the master agreement provides for an agreement or transaction that is not a commodity contract under this paragraph, except that the master agreement shall be considered to be a commodity contract under this paragraph only with respect to each agreement or transaction under the master agreement that is referred to in subparagraph (A), (B), (C), (D), (E), (F), (G), or (H); or*

*(J) any security agreement or arrangement or other credit enhancement related to any agreement or transaction referred to in this paragraph, including any guarantee or reimbursement obligation by or to a commodity broker or financial participant in connection with any agreement or transaction referred to in this paragraph, but not to exceed the damages in connection with any such agreement or transaction, measured in accordance with section 562;*

(5) "commodity option" means agreement or transaction subject to regulation under section 4c(b) of the Act;

(6) "commodity options dealer" means person that extends credit to, or that accepts cash, a security, or other property from, a customer of such person for the purchase or sale of an interest in a commodity option;

(7) "contract market" means a registered entity;

(8) "contract of sale", "commodity", "derivatives clearing organization", "future delivery", "board of trade", "registered entity", and "futures commission merchant" have the meanings assigned to those terms in the Act;

(9) "customer" means—

(A) with respect to a futures commission merchant—

(i) entity for or with whom such futures commission merchant deals and that holds a claim against such futures commission merchant on account of a commodity contract made, received, acquired, or held by or through such futures commission merchant in the ordinary course of such futures commission merchant's business as a futures commission merchant from or for the commodity futures account of such entity; or

(ii) entity that holds a claim against such futures commission merchant arising out of—

(I) the making, liquidation, or change in the value of a commodity contract of a kind specified in clause (i) of this subparagraph;

(II) a deposit or payment of cash, a security, or other property with such futures commission merchant for the purpose of making or margining such a commodity contract; or

(III) the making or taking of delivery on such a commodity contract;

(B) with respect to a foreign futures commission merchant—

(i) entity for or with whom such foreign futures commission merchant deals and that holds a claim against such foreign futures commission merchant on account of a commodity contract made, received, acquired, or held by or through such foreign futures commission merchant in the ordinary course of such foreign futures commission merchant's business as a foreign futures commission merchant from or for the foreign futures account of such entity; or

(ii) entity that holds a claim against such foreign futures commission merchant arising out of—

(I) the making, liquidation, or change in value of a commodity contract of a kind specified in clause (i) of this subparagraph;

(II) a deposit or payment of cash, a security, or other property with such foreign futures commission merchant for the purpose of making or margining such a commodity contract; or

(III) the making or taking of delivery on such a commodity contract;

(C) with respect to a leverage transaction merchant—

(i) entity for or with whom such leverage transaction merchant deals and that holds a claim against such leverage transaction merchant on account of a commodity contract engaged in by or with such leverage transaction merchant in the ordinary course of such leverage transaction merchant's business as a leverage transaction merchant from or for the leverage account of such entity; or

(ii) entity that holds a claim against such leverage transaction merchant arising out of—

(I) the making, liquidation, or change in value of a commodity contract of a kind specified in clause (i) of this subparagraph;

(II) a deposit or payment of cash, a security, or other property with such leverage transaction merchant for the purpose of entering into or margining such a commodity contract; or

(III) the making or taking of delivery on such a commodity contract;

(D) with respect to a clearing organization, clearing member of such clearing organization with whom such clearing organization deals and that holds a claim against such clearing organization on account of cash, a security, or other property received by such clearing organization to margin, guarantee, or secure a commodity contract in such clearing member's proprietary account or customers' account; or

(E) with respect to a commodity options dealer—

(i) entity for or with whom such commodity options dealer deals and that holds a claim on account of a commodity contract made, received, acquired, or held by or through such commodity options dealer in the ordinary course of such commodity options dealer's business as a commodity options dealer from or for the commodity options account of such entity; or

(ii) entity that holds a claim against such commodity options dealer arising out of—

(I) the making of, liquidation of, exercise of, or a change in value of, a commodity contract of a kind specified in clause (i) of this subparagraph; or

(II) a deposit or payment of cash, a security, or other property with such commodity options dealer for the purpose of making, exercising, or margining such a commodity contract;

(10) "customer property" means cash, a security, or other property, or proceeds of such cash, security, or property, received, acquired, or held by or for the account of the debtor, from or for the account of a customer—

(A) including—

(i) property received, acquired, or held to margin, guarantee, secure, purchase, or sell a commodity contract;

(ii) profits or contractual or other rights accruing to a customer as a result of a commodity contract;

(iii) an open commodity contract;

(iv) specifically identifiable customer property;

(v) warehouse receipt or other document held by the debtor evidencing ownership of or title to property to be delivered to fulfill a commodity contract from or for the account of a customer;

(vi) cash, a security, or other property received by the debtor as payment for a commodity to be delivered to fulfill a commodity contract from or for the account of a customer;

(vii) a security held as property of the debtor to the extent such security is necessary to meet a net equity claim based on a security of the same class and series of an issuer;

(viii) property that was unlawfully converted from and that is the lawful property of the estate; and

(ix) other property of the debtor that any applicable law, rule, or regulation requires to be set aside or held for the benefit of a customer, unless including such property as customer property would not significantly increase customer property; but

(B) not including property to the extent that a customer does not have a claim against the debtor based on such property;

(11) "foreign future" means contract for the purchase or sale of a commodity for future delivery on, or subject to the rules of, a board of trade outside the United States;

(12) "foreign futures commission merchant" means entity engaged in soliciting or accepting orders for the purchase or sale of a foreign future or that, in connection with such a solicitation or acceptance, accepts cash, a security, or other property, or extends credit to margin, guarantee, or secure any trade or contract that results from such a solicitation or acceptance;

(13) "leverage transaction" means agreement that is subject to regulation under section 19 of the Commodity Exchange Act, and that is commonly known to the commodities trade as a margin account, margin contract, leverage account, or leverage contract;

(14) "leverage transaction merchant" means person in the business of engaging in leverage transactions;

(15) "margin payment" means payment or deposit of cash, a security, or other property, that is commonly known to the commodities trade as original margin, initial margin, maintenance margin, or variation margin, including mark-to-market payments, settlement payments, variation payments, daily settlement payments, and final settlement payments made as adjustments to settlement prices;

(16) "member property" means customer property received, acquired, or held by or for the account of a debtor that is a clearing organization, from or for the proprietary account of a customer that is a clearing member of the debtor; and

(17) "net equity" means, subject to such rules and regulations as the Commission promulgates under the Act, with respect to the aggregate of all of a customer's accounts that such customer has in the same capacity—

(A) the balance remaining in such customer's accounts immediately after—

(i) all commodity contracts of such customer have been transferred, liquidated, or become identified for delivery; and

(ii) all obligations of such customer in such capacity to the debtor have been offset; plus

(B) the value, as of the date of return under section 766 of this title, of any specifically identifiable customer property actually returned to such customer before the date specified in subparagraph (A) of this paragraph; plus

(C) the value, as of the date of transfer, of—

(i) any commodity contract to which such customer is entitled that is transferred to another person under section 766 of this title; and

(ii) any cash, security, or other property of such customer transferred to such other person under section 766 of this title to margin or secure such transferred commodity contract.

**Section 761**
(April 20, 2005, P. L. 109-8, Title IX § 907(a)(3), 119 Stat. 23)

## HISTORY: ANCILLARY LAWS AND DIRECTIVES

**Amendments:**

**2005.** Act April 20, 2005(effective 180 days after enactment of April 20, 2005, as provided by § 1501(a) of P. L. 109-8), adds 11 USC § 761(4)(F)–(J), to amend the definition of "commodity contract."

**Other provisions:**

**Effective date and application of amendments made by Act April 20, 2005.** Act April 20, 2005, P.L. 109-8, Title XV, § 1501(a), 119 Stat. 23, provided that the amendments made to this section would be effective 180 days after enactment on April 20, 2005.

**Abridged Legislative History**

Bankruptcy Law Amendments. Section 907 of the Act makes a series of amendments to the Bankruptcy Code. Subsection (a)(1) amends the Bankruptcy Code definitions of "repurchase agreement" and "swap agreement" to conform with the amendments to the FDIA contained in sections 901(e) and (f) of the Act.

Subsection (a)(1) also amends the definition of "repurchase agreement" to include those on mortgage-related securities, mortgage loans and interests therein, and to include principal and interest-only U.S. government and agency securities as securities that can be the subject of a "repurchase agreement."

The definition also includes any security agreement or arrangement, or other credit enhancement, related to a swap agreement, including any guarantee or reimbursement obligation related to a swap agreement.

(H. Report No. 109-31 to accompany S. 256, 109th Cong., 1st Sess. (2005) pp. 127–30; available at 2005 U.S.C.C.A.N. 88, at 188–91)

## § 762. Notice to the Commission and right to be heard

(a) The clerk shall give the notice required by section 342 of this title to the Commission.

(b) The Commission may raise and may appear and be heard on any issue in a case under this chapter.

## § 763. Treatment of accounts

(a) Accounts held by the debtor for a particular customer in separate capacities shall be treated as accounts of separate customers.

(b) A member of a clearing organization shall be deemed to hold such member's proprietary account in a separate capacity from such member's customers' account.

(c) The net equity in a customer's account may not be offset against the net equity in the account of any other customer.

## § 764. Voidable transfers

(a) Except as otherwise provided in this section, any transfer by the debtor of property that, but for such transfer, would have been customer property, may be avoided by the trustee, and such property shall be treated as customer property, if and to the extent that the trustee avoids such transfer under section 544, 545, 547, 548, 549, or 724(a) of this title. For the purpose of such sections, the property so transferred shall be deemed to have been property of the debtor, and, if such transfer was made to a customer or for a customer's benefit, such customer shall be deemed, for the purposes of this section, to have been a creditor.

(b) Notwithstanding sections 544, 545, 547, 548, 549, and 724(a) of this title, the trustee may not avoid a transfer made before five days after the order for relief, if such transfer is approved by the Commission by rule or order, either before or after such transfer, and if such transfer is—

(1) a transfer of a commodity contract entered into or carried by or through the debtor on behalf of a customer, and of any cash, securities, or other property margining or securing such commodity contract; or

(2) the liquidation of a commodity contract entered into or carried by or through the debtor on behalf of a customer.

## § 765. Customer instructions

(a) The notice required by section 342 of this title to customers shall instruct each customer—

(1) to file a proof of such customer's claim promptly, and to specify in such claim any specifically identifiable security, property, or commodity contract; and

(2) to instruct the trustee of such customer's desired disposition, including transfer under section 766 of this title or liquidation, of any commodity contract specifically identified to such customer.

(b) The trustee shall comply, to the extent practicable, with any instruction received from a customer regarding such customer's desired disposition of any commodity contract specifically identified to such customer. If the trustee has transferred, under section 766 of this title, such a commodity contract, the trustee shall transmit any such instruction to the commodity broker to whom such commodity contract was so transferred.

## § 766. Treatment of customer property

(a) The trustee shall answer all margin calls with respect to a specifically identifiable commodity contract of a customer until such time as the trustee returns or transfers such commodity contract, but the trustee may not make a margin payment that has the effect of a distribution to such customer of more than that to which such customer is entitled under subsection (h) or (i) of this section.

(b) The trustee shall prevent any open commodity contract from remaining open after the last day of trading in such commodity contract, or into the first day on which notice of intent to deliver on such commodity contract may be tendered, whichever occurs first. With respect to any commodity contract that has remained open after the last day of trading in such commodity contract or with respect to which delivery must be made or accepted under the rules of the contract market on which such commodity contract was made, the trustee may operate the business of the debtor for the purpose of—

(1) accepting or making tender of notice of intent to deliver the physical commodity underlying such commodity contract;

(2) facilitating delivery of such commodity; or

(3) disposing of such commodity if a party to such commodity contract defaults.

(c) The trustee shall return promptly to a customer any specifically identifiable security, property, or commodity contract to which such customer is entitled, or shall transfer, on such customer's behalf, such security, property, or commodity contract to a commodity broker that is not a debtor under this title, subject to such rules or regulations as the Commission may prescribe, to the extent that the value of such security, property, or commodity contract does not exceed the amount to which such customer would be entitled under subsection (h) or (i) of this section if such security, property, or commodity contract were not returned or transferred under this subsection.

(d) If the value of a specifically identifiable security, property, or commodity contract exceeds the amount to which the customer of the debtor is entitled under subsection (h) or (i) of this section, then such customer to whom such security, property, or commodity contract is specifically identified may deposit cash with the trustee equal to the difference between the value of such security, property, or commodity contract and such amount, and the trustee then shall—

(1) return promptly such security, property, or commodity contract to such customer; or

(2) transfer, on such customer's behalf, such security, property, or commodity contract to a commodity broker that is not a debtor under this title, subject to such rules or regulations as the Commission may prescribe.

(e) Subject to subsection (b) of this section, the trustee shall liquidate any commodity contract that—

(1) is identified to a particular customer and with respect to which such customer has not timely instructed the trustee as to the desired disposition of such commodity contract;

(2) cannot be transferred under subsection (c) of this section; or

(3) cannot be identified to a particular customer.

(f) As soon as practicable after the commencement of the case, the trustee shall reduce to money, consistent with good market practice, all securities and other property, other than commodity contracts, held as property of the estate, except for specifically identifiable securities or property distributable under subsection (h) or (i) of this section.

(g) The trustee may not distribute a security or other property except under subsection (h) or (i) of this section.

(h) Except as provided in subsection (b) of this section, the trustee shall distribute customer property ratably to customers on the basis and to the extent of such customers' allowed net equity claims, and in priority to all other claims, except claims of a kind specified in section

507(a)(21) of this title that are attributable to the administration of customer property. Such distribution shall be in the form of—

(1) cash;

(2) the return or transfer, under subsection (c) or (d) of this section, of specifically identifiable customer securities, property, or commodity contracts; or

(3) payment of margin calls under subsection (a) of this section.

Notwithstanding any other provision of this subsection, a customer net equity claim based on a proprietary account, as defined by Commission rule, regulation, or order, may not be paid either in whole or in part, directly or indirectly, out of customer property unless all other customer net equity claims have been paid in full.

(i) If the debtor is a clearing organization, the trustee shall distribute—

(1) customer property, other than member property, ratably to customers on the basis and to the extent of such customers' allowed net equity claims based on such customers' accounts other than proprietary accounts, and in priority to all other claims, except claims of a kind specified in section 507(a)(21) of this title that are attributable to the administration of such customer property; and

(2) member property ratably to customers on the basis and to the extent of such customers' allowed net equity claims based on such customers' proprietary accounts, and in priority to all other claims, except claims of a kind specified in section 507(a)(21) of this title that are attributable to the administration of member property or customer property.

(j) (1) The trustee shall distribute customer property in excess of that distributed under subsection (h) or (i) of this section in accordance with section 726 of this title.

(2) Except as provided in section 510 of this title, if a customer is not paid the full amount of such customer's allowed net equity claim from customer property, the unpaid portion of such claim is a claim entitled to distribution under section 726 of this title.

**Section 766**

(April 20, 2005, P. L. 109-8, Title XV § 1502(a)(4), 119 Stat. 23)

## HISTORY: ANCILLARY LAWS AND DIRECTIVES

**Amendments:**

**2005.** Act April 20, 2005(effective 180 days after enactment of April 20, 2005, as provided by § 1501(a) of P. L. 109-8), amends 11 USC § 766 to make a technical correction to a reference.

**Other provisions:**

**Effective date and application of amendments made by Act April 20, 2005.** Act April 20, 2005, P.L. 109-8, Title XV, § 1501(a), 119 Stat. 23, provided that the amendments made to this section would be effective 180 days after enactment on April 20, 2005.

**Abridged Legislative History**

(H. Report No. 109-31 to accompany S. 256, 109th Cong., 1st Sess. (2005) p. 62, available at 2005 U.S.C.C.A.N. 88, at 131)

## *§ 767. Commodity broker liquidation and forward contract merchants, commodity brokers, stockbrokers, financial institutions, financial participants, securities clearing agencies, swap participants, repo participants, and master netting agreement participants*

*Notwithstanding any other provision of this title, the exercise of rights by a forward contract merchant, commodity broker, stockbroker, financial institution, financial participant, securities clearing agency, swap participant, repo participant, or master netting agreement participant under this title shall not affect the priority of any unsecured claim it may have after the exercise of such rights.*

**Section 767**

(April 20, 2005, P. L. 109-8, Title IX § 907(l), 119 Stat. 23)

### HISTORY: ANCILLARY LAWS AND DIRECTIVES

**Amendments:**

**2005.** Act April 20, 2005(effective 180 days after enactment of April 20, 2005, as provided by § 1501(a) of P. L. 109-8), adds new 11 USC § 767 to clarify that the exercise of termination and netting rights will not otherwise affect the priority of the creditor's claim after the exercise of netting, foreclosure and related rights.

**Other provisions:**

**Effective date and application of amendments made by Act April 20, 2005.** Act April 20, 2005, P.L. 109-8, Title XV, § 1501(a), 119 Stat. 23, provided that the amendments made to this section would be effective 180 days after enactment on April 20, 2005.

**Abridged Legislative History**

(H. Report No. 109-31 to accompany S. 256, 109th Cong., 1st Sess. (2005) p. 134; available at 2005 U.S.C.C.A.N. 88, at 194).

## SUBCHAPTER V CLEARING BANK LIQUIDATION

## § 781. Definitions

For purposes of this subchapter, the following definitions shall apply:

(1) BOARD.—The term 'Board' means the Board of Governors of the Federal Reserve System.

(2) DEPOSITORY INSTITUTION.—The term 'depository institution' has the same meaning as in section 3 of the Federal Deposit Insurance Act.

(3) CLEARING BANK.—The term 'clearing bank' means an uninsured State member bank, or a corporation organized under section 25A of the Federal Reserve Act, which operates, or operates as, a multilateral clearing organization pursuant to section 409 of the Federal Deposit Insurance Corporation Improvement Act of 1991.

## § 782. Selection of trustee

(a) IN GENERAL

(1) APPOINTMENT.—Notwithstanding any other provision of

this title, the conservator or receiver who files the petition shall be the trustee under this chapter, unless the Board designates an alternative trustee.

(2) SUCCESSOR.—The Board may designate a successor trustee if required.

(b) AUTHORITY OF TRUSTEE.—Whenever the Board appoints or designates a trustee, chapter 3 and sections 704 and 705 of this title shall apply to the Board in the same way and to the same extent that they apply to a United States trustee.

## § 783. Additional powers of trustee

(a) DISTRIBUTION OF PROPERTY NOT OF THE ESTATE.—The trustee under this subchapter has power to distribute property not of the estate, including distributions to customers that are mandated by subchapters III and IV of this chapter.

(b) DISPOSITION OF INSTITUTION.—The trustee under this subchapter may, after notice and a hearing—

(1) sell the clearing bank to a depository institution or consortium of depository institutions (which consortium may agree on the allocation of the clearing bank among the consortium);

(2) merge the clearing bank with a depository institution;

(3) transfer contracts to the same extent as could a receiver for a depository institution under paragraphs (9) and (10) of section 11(e) of the Federal Deposit Insurance Act;

(4) transfer assets or liabilities to a depository institution; and

(5) transfer assets and liabilities to a bridge bank as provided in paragraphs (1), (3)(A), (5), and (6) of section 11(n) of the Federal Deposit Insurance Act, paragraphs (9) through (13) of such section, and subparagraphs (A) through (H) and subparagraph (K) of paragraph (4) of such section 11(n), except that—

(A) the bridge bank to which such assets or liabilities are transferred shall be treated as a clearing bank for the purpose of this subsection; and

(B) any references in any such provision of law to the Federal Deposit Insurance Corporation shall be construed to be references to the appointing agency and that references to deposit insurance shall be omitted

(c) CERTAIN TRANSFERS INCLUDED.—Any reference in this section to transfers of liabilities includes a ratable transfer of liabilities within a priority class.

## § 784. Right to be heard

The Board or a Federal reserve bank (in the case of a clearing bank that is a member of that bank) may raise and may appear and be heard on any issue in a case under this subchapter.

# Chapter 9
# —Adjustment of Debts of a Municipality

## Subchapter I——General Provisions



## Subchapter II——Administration



## Subchapter III——The Plan



## Subchapter I——General Provisions

### § 901. Applicability of other sections of this title

(a) Sections 301, 344, 347(b), 349, 350(b), 361, 362, 364(c), 364(d), 364(e), 364(f), 365, 366, 501, 502, 503, 504, 506, 507(a)(2~~1~~), 509, 510, 524(a)(1), 524(a)(2), 544, 545, 546, 547, 548, 549(a), 549(c), 549(d), 550, 551, 552, 553, *555, 556,* 557, *559, 560, 561, 562,* 1102, 1103, 1109, 1111(b), 1122, 1123(a)(1), 1123(a)(2), 1123(a)(3), 1123(a)(4), 1123(a)(5), 1123(b), *1123(d),* 1124, 1125, 1126(a), 1126(b), 1126(c), 1126(e), 1126(f), 1126(g), 1127(d), 1128, 1129(a)(2), 1129(a)(3), 1129(a)(6), 1129(a)(8), 1129(a)(10), 1129(b)(1), 1129(b)(2)(A), 1129(b)(2)(B), 1142(b), 1143, 1144, and 1145 of this title apply in a case under this chapter.

(b) A term used in a section of this title made applicable in a case under this chapter by subsection (a) of this section or section 103(e) of this title has the meaning defined for such term for the purpose of such applicable section, unless such term is otherwise defined in section 902 of this title.

(c) A section made applicable in a case under this chapter by subsection (a) of this section that is operative if the business of the debtor is authorized to be operated is operative in a case under this chapter.

**Section 901**

(April 20, 2005, P. L. 109-8, Title V, § 502; Title XII, § 1216; Title XV, § 1502(a)(5), 119 Stat. 23)

## HISTORY: ANCILLARY LAWS AND DIRECTIVES

**Amendments:**

**2005.** Act April 20, 2005(effective 180 days after enactment of April 20, 2005, as provided by § 1501(a) of P. L. 109-8), amends 11 USC § 901 to make technical corrections in references to other amended Code sections.

**Other provisions:**

**Effective date and application of amendments made by Act April 20, 2005.** Act April 20, 2005, P.L. 109-8, Title XV, § 1501(a), 119 Stat. 23, provided that the amendments made to this section would be effective 180 days after enactment on April 20, 2005.

**Abridged Legislative History**

H. Report No. 109-31 to accompany S. 256, 109th Cong., 1st Sess. (2005) pp. 96–97, 144, 155; available at 2005 U.S.C.C.A.N. 88, at 161, 203, 212

## § 902. Definitions for this chapter

In this chapter—

(1) "property of the estate," when used in a section that is made applicable in a case under this chapter by section 103(e) or 901 of this title, means property of the debtor;

(2) "special revenues" means—

(A) receipts derived from the ownership, operation, or disposition of projects or systems of the debtor that are primarily used or intended to be used primarily to provide transportation, utility, or other services, including the proceeds of borrowings to finance the projects or systems;

(B) special excise taxes imposed on particular activities or transactions;

(C) incremental tax receipts from the benefited area in the case of tax-increment financing;

(D) other revenues or receipts derived from particular functions of the debtor, whether or not the debtor has other functions; or

(E) taxes specifically levied to finance one or more projects or systems, excluding receipts from general property, sales, or income taxes (other than tax-increment financing) levied to finance the general purposes of the debtor;

(3) "special tax payer" means record owner or holder of legal or equitable title to real property against which a special assessment or special tax has been levied the proceeds of which are the sole source of payment of an obligation issued by the debtor to defray the cost of an improvement relating to such real property;

(4) "special tax payer affected by the plan" means special tax payer with respect to whose real property the plan proposes to increase the proportion of special assessments or special taxes referred to in paragraph (2) of this section assessed against such real property; and

(5) "trustee," when used in a section that is made applicable in a case under this chapter by section 103(e) or 901 of this title, means debtor, except as provided in section 926 of this title.

## § 903. Reservation of State power to control municipalities

This chapter does not limit or impair the power of a State to control, by legislation or otherwise, a municipality of or in such State in the exercise of the political or governmental powers of such municipality, including expenditures for such exercise, but—

(1) a State law prescribing a method of composition of indebtedness of such municipality may not bind any creditor that does not consent to such composition; and

(2) a judgment entered under such a law may not bind a creditor that does not consent to such composition.

## § 904. Limitation on jurisdiction and powers of court

Notwithstanding any power of the court, unless the debtor consents or the plan so provides, the court may not, by any stay, order, or decree, in the case or otherwise, interfere with—

(1) any of the political or governmental powers of the debtor;

(2) any of the property or revenues of the debtor; or

(3) the debtor's use or enjoyment of any income-producing property.

# Subchapter II——Administration

## § 921. Petition and proceedings relating to petition

(a) Notwithstanding sections 109(d) and 301 of this title, a case under this chapter concerning an unincorporated tax or special assessment district that does not have such district's own officials is commenced by the filing under section 301 of this title of a petition under this chapter by such district's governing authority or the board or body having authority to levy taxes or assessments to meet the obligations of such district.

(b) The chief judge of the court of appeals for the circuit embracing the district in which the case is commenced shall designate the bankruptcy judge to conduct the case.

(c) After any objection to the petition, the court, after notice and a hearing, may dismiss the petition if the debtor did not file the petition in good faith or if the petition does not meet the requirements of this title.

(d) If the petition is not dismissed under subsection (c) of this section, the court shall order relief under this chapter *notwithstanding section 301(b)*.

(e) The court may not, on account of an appeal from an order for relief, delay any proceeding under this chapter in the case in which the appeal is being taken; nor shall any court order a stay of such proceeding pending such appeal. The reversal on appeal of a finding of jurisdiction does not affect the validity of any debt incurred that is authorized by the court under section 364(c) or 364(d) of this title.

**Section 921**

(April 20, 2005, P. L. 109-8, Title V, § 501(a), 119 Stat. 23)

## HISTORY: ANCILLARY LAWS AND DIRECTIVES

**Amendments:**

**2005.** Act April 20, 2005(effective 180 days after enactment of April 20, 2005, as provided by § 1501(a) of P. L. 109-8), amends 11 USC § 921 to add "notwithstanding section 301(b)" to § 921(d).

**Other provisions:**

**Effective date and application of amendments made by Act April 20, 2005.** Act April 20, 2005, P.L. 109-8, Title XV, § 1501(a), 119 Stat. 23, provided that the amendments made to this section would be effective 180 days after enactment on April 20, 2005.

**Abridged Legislative History**

H. Report No. 109-31 to accompany S. 256, 109th Cong., 1st Sess. (2005) p. 96; available at 2005 U.S.C.C.A.N. 88, at 101

# § 922. Automatic stay of enforcement of claims against the debtor

(a) A petition filed under this chapter operates as a stay, in addition to the stay provided by section 362 of this title, applicable to all entities, of—

(1) the commencement or continuation, including the issuance or employment of process, of a judicial, administrative, or other action or proceeding against an officer or inhabitant of the debtor that seeks to enforce a claim against the debtor; and

(2) the enforcement of a lien on or arising out of taxes or assessments owed to the debtor.

(b) Subsections (c), (d), (e), (f), and (g) of section 362 of this title apply to a stay under subsection (a) of this section the same as such subsections apply to a stay under section 362(a) of this title.

(c) If the debtor provides, under section 362, 364, or 922 of this title, adequate protection of the interest of the holder of a claim secured by a lien on property of the debtor and if, notwithstanding such protection such creditor has a claim arising from the stay of action against such property under section 362 or 922 of this title or from the granting of a lien under section 364(d) of this title, then such claim shall be allowable as an administrative expense under section 503(b) of this title.

(d) Notwithstanding section 362 of this title and subsection (a) of this section, a petition filed under this chapter does not operate as a stay of application of pledged special revenues in a manner consistent with section 927 of this title to payment of indebtedness secured by such revenues.

## § 923. Notice

There shall be given notice of the commencement of a case under this chapter, notice of an order for relief under this chapter, and notice of the dismissal of a case under this chapter. Such notice shall also be published at least once a week for three successive weeks in at least one newspaper of general circulation published within the district in which the case is commenced, and in such other newspaper having a general circulation among bond dealers and bondholders as the court designates.

## § 924. List of creditors

The debtor shall file a list of creditors.

## § 925. Effect of list of claims

A proof of claim is deemed filed under section 501 of this title for any claim that appears in the list filed under section 924 of this title, except a claim that is listed as disputed, contingent, or unliquidated.

## § 926. Avoiding powers

(a) If the debtor refuses to pursue a cause of action under section 544, 545, 547, 548, 549(a), or 550 of this title, then on request of a creditor, the court may appoint a trustee to pursue such cause of action.

(b) A transfer of property of the debtor to or for the benefit of any holder of a bond or note, on account of such bond or note, may not be avoided under section 547 of this title.

## § 927. Limitation on recourse

The holder of a claim payable solely from special revenues of the debtor under applicable nonbankruptcy law shall not be treated as having recourse against the debtor on account of such claim pursuant to section 1111(b) of this title.

## § 928. Post petition effect of security interest

(a) Notwithstanding section 552(a) of this title and subject to subsection (b) of this section, special revenues acquired by the debtor after the commencement of the case shall remain subject to any lien resulting from any security agreement entered into by the debtor before the commencement of the case.

(b) Any such lien on special revenues, other than municipal betterment assessments, derived from a project or system shall be subject to the necessary operating expenses of such project or system, as the case may be.

## § 929. Municipal leases

A lease to a municipality shall not be treated as an executory contract or unexpired lease for the purposes of section 365 or 502(b)(6) of this title solely by reason of its being subject to termination in the event the debtor fails to appropriate rent.

## § 930. Dismissal

(a) After notice and a hearing, the court may dismiss a case under this chapter for cause, including—

(1) want of prosecution;

(2) unreasonable delay by the debtor that is prejudicial to creditors;

(3) failure to propose a plan within the time fixed under section 941 of this title;

(4) if a plan is not accepted within any time fixed by the court;

(5) denial of confirmation of a plan under section 943(b) of this title and denial of additional time for filing another plan or a modification of a plan; or

(6) if the court has retained jurisdiction after confirmation of a plan—

(A) material default by the debtor with respect to a term of such plan; or

(B) termination of such plan by reason of the occurrence of a condition specified in such plan.

(b) The court shall dismiss a case under this chapter if confirmation of a plan under this chapter is refused.

# Subchapter III—The Plan

## § 941. Filing of plan

The debtor shall file a plan for the adjustment of the debtor's debts. If such a plan is not filed with the petition, the debtor shall file such a plan at such later time as the court fixes.

## § 942. Modification of plan

The debtor may modify the plan at any time before confirmation, but may not modify the plan so that the plan as modified fails to meet the requirements of this chapter. After the debtor files a modification, the plan as modified becomes the plan.

## § 943. Confirmation

(a) A special tax payer may object to confirmation of a plan.

(b) The court shall confirm the plan if—

(1) the plan complies with the provisions of this title made applicable by sections 103(e) and 901 of this title;

(2) the plan complies with the provisions of this chapter;

(3) all amounts to be paid by the debtor or by any person for services or expenses in the case or incident to the plan have been fully disclosed and are reasonable;

(4) the debtor is not prohibited by law from taking any action necessary to carry out the plan;

(5) except to the extent that the holder of a particular claim has agreed to a different treatment of such claim, the plan provides that on the effective date of the plan each holder of a claim of a kind specified in section 507(a)(*2*~~1~~) of this title will receive on account of such claim cash equal to the allowed amount of such claim;

(6) any regulatory or electoral approval necessary under applicable nonbankruptcy law in order to carry out any provision of the plan has been obtained, or such provision is expressly conditioned on such approval; and

(7) the plan is in the best interests of creditors and is feasible.

**Section 943**

(April 20, 2005, P. L. 109-8, Title XV, § 1502(a)(6), 119 Stat. 23)

## HISTORY: ANCILLARY LAWS AND DIRECTIVES

**Amendments:**

**2005.** Act April 20, 2005(effective 180 days after enactment of April 20, 2005, as provided by § 1501(a) of P. L. 109-8), amends 11 USC § 943 to make a technical correction in cross-reference numbering.

**Other provisions:**

**Effective date and application of amendments made by Act April 20, 2005.** Act April 20, 2005, P.L. 109-8, Title XV, § 1501(a), 119 Stat. 23, provided that the amendments made to this section would be effective 180 days after enactment on April 20, 2005.

**Abridged Legislative History**

H. Report No. 109-31 to accompany S. 256, 109th Cong., 1st Sess. (2005) p. 155; available at 2005 U.S.C.C.A.N. 88, at 212

# Chapter 11 —Reorganization



## Subchapter II——The Plan



## Subchapter III——Postconfirmation Matters



## Subchapter IV——Railroad Reorganization

## § 1101. Definitions for this chapter

In this chapter—

(1) "debtor in possession" means debtor except when a person that has qualified under section 322 of this title is serving as trustee in the case;

(2) "substantial consummation" means—

(A) transfer of all or substantially all of the property proposed by the plan to be transferred;

(B) assumption by the debtor or by the successor to the debtor under the plan of the business or of the management of all or substantially all of the property dealt with by the plan; and

(C) commencement of distribution under the plan.

## § 1102. Creditors' and equity security holders' committees

(a) (1) Except as provided in paragraph (3), as soon as practicable after the order for relief under [this chapter] chapter 11 of this title, the United States trustee shall appoint a committee of creditors holding unsecured claims and may appoint additional committees of creditors or of equity security holders as the United States trustee deems appropriate.

(2) On request of a party in interest, the court may order the appointment of additional committees of creditors or of equity security holders if necessary to assure adequate representation of creditors or of equity security holders. The United States trustee shall appoint any such committee.

(3) On request of a party in interest in a case in which the debtor is a small business *debtor* and for cause, the court may order that a committee of creditors not be appointed.

*(4) On request of a party in interest and after notice and a hearing, the court may order the United States trustee to change the membership of a committee appointed under this subsection, if the court determines that the change is necessary to ensure adequate representation of creditors or equity security holders. The court may*

*order the United States trustee to increase the number of members of a committee to include a creditor that is a small business concern (as described in section 3(a)(1) of the Small Business Act), if the court determines that the creditor holds claims (of the kind represented by the committee) the aggregate amount of which, in comparison to the annual gross revenue of that creditor, is disproportionately large.*

(b)

(1) A committee of creditors appointed under subsection (a) of this section shall ordinarily consist of the persons, willing to serve, that hold the seven largest claims against the debtor of the kinds represented on such committee, or of the members of a committee organized by creditors before the commencement of the case under this chapter, if such committee was fairly chosen and is representative of the different kinds of claims to be represented.

(2) A committee of equity security holders appointed under subsection (a)(2) of this section shall ordinarily consist of the persons, willing to serve, that hold the seven largest amounts of equity securities of the debtor of the kinds represented on such committee.

*(3) A committee appointed under subsection (a) shall—*

*(A) provide access to information for creditors who—*

*(i) hold claims of the kind represented by that committee; and*

*(ii) are not appointed to the committee;*

*(B) solicit and receive comments from the creditors described in subparagraph (A); and*

*(C) be subject to a court order that compels any additional report or disclosure to be made to the creditors described in subparagraph (A).*

(April 20, 2005, P. L. 109-8, Title IV, § § 405(a), 405(b), 432(b), 119 Stat. 23)

## HISTORY: ANCILLARY LAWS AND DIRECTIVES

**Amendments:**

**2005.** Act April 20, 2005, added "debtor" after "small business" in subsection (a)(3) and added new subsections (a)(4) and (b)(3).

**Abridged Legislative History**

Sec. 405. Creditors and Equity Security Holders Committees. Subsection (a) of section 405 of the Act amends section 1102(a)(2) of the Bankruptcy Code to permit, after notice and a hearing, a court, on request of a party in interest, to order a change in a committee's membership if necessary to ensure adequate representation of creditors or equity security holders in a chapter 11 case.

Section 405(b) requires the committee to give creditors having claims of the kind represented by the committee access to information. In addition, the committee must solicit and receive comments from these creditors and, pursuant to court order, make additional reports or disclosures available to them. (H. Report No. 109-31 to accompany S. 256, 109th Cong., 1st Sess. (2005) p. 87, 90; available at 2005 U.S.C.C.A.N. 88, at 153, 156.)

## § 1103. Powers and duties of committees

(a) At a scheduled meeting of a committee appointed under section 1102 of this title, at which a majority of the members of such committee are present, and with the court's approval, such committee may select and authorize the employment by such committee of one or more attorneys, accountants, or other agents, to represent or perform services for such committee.

(b) An attorney or accountant employed to represent a committee appointed under section 1102 of this title may not, while employed by such committee, represent any other entity having an adverse interest in connection with the case. Representation of one or more creditors of the same class as represented by the committee shall not per se constitute the representation of an adverse interest.

(c) A committee appointed under section 1102 of this title may—

(1) consult with the trustee or debtor in possession concerning the administration of the case;

(2) investigate the acts, conduct, assets, liabilities, and financial condition of the debtor, the operation of the debtor's business and the desirability of the continuance of such business, and any other matter relevant to the case or to the formulation of a plan;

(3) participate in the formulation of a plan, advise those represented by such committee of such committee's determinations as to any plan formulated, and collect and file with the court acceptances or rejections of a plan;

(4) request the appointment of a trustee or examiner under section 1104 of this title; and

(5) perform such other services as are in the interest of those represented.

(d) As soon as practicable after the appointment of a committee under section 1102 of this title, the trustee shall meet with such committee to transact such business as may be necessary and proper.

## § 1104. Appointment of trustee or examiner

(a) At any time after the commencement of the case but before confirmation of a plan, on request of a party in interest or the United States trustee, and after notice and a hearing, the court shall order the appointment of a trustee—

(1) for cause, including fraud, dishonesty, incompetence, or gross mismanagement of the affairs of the debtor by current management, either before or after the commencement of the case, or similar cause, but not including the number of holders of securities of the debtor or the amount of assets or liabilities of the debtor; ~~or~~

(2) if such appointment is in the interests of creditors, any equity security holders, and other interests of the estate, without regard to the number of holders of securities of the debtor or the amount of assets or liabilities of the debtor~~.~~*; or*

*(3) if grounds exist to convert or dismiss the case under section 1112, but the court determines that the appointment of a trustee or an examiner is in the best interests of creditors and the estate.*

(b) *(1)* Except as provided in section 1163 of this title, on the request of a party in interest made not later than 30 days after the court orders the appointment of a trustee under subsection (a), the United States trustee shall convene a meeting of creditors for the purpose of electing one disinterested person to serve as trustee in the case. The election of a trustee shall be conducted in the manner provided in subsections (a), (b), and (c) of section 702 of this title.

*(2) (A) If an eligible, disinterested trustee is elected at a meeting of creditors under paragraph (1), the United States trustee shall file a report certifying that election.*

*(B) Upon the filing of a report under subparagraph (A)—*

*(i) the trustee elected under paragraph (1) shall be considered to have been selected and appointed for purposes of this section; and*

*(ii) the service of any trustee appointed under subsection (d) shall terminate.*

*(C) The court shall resolve any dispute arising out of an election described in subparagraph (A).*

(c) If the court does not order the appointment of a trustee under this section, then at any time before the confirmation of a plan, on request of a party in interest or the United States trustee, and after notice and a hearing, the court shall order the appointment of an examiner to conduct such an investigation of the debtor as is appropriate, including an investigation of any allegations of fraud, dishonesty, incompetence, misconduct, mismanagement, or irregularity in the management of the affairs of the debtor of or by current or former management of the debtor, if—

(1) such appointment is in the interests of creditors, any equity security holders, and other interests of the estate; or

(2) the debtor's fixed, liquidated, unsecured debts, other than debts for goods, services, or taxes, or owing to an insider, exceed $5,000,000.

(d) If the court orders the appointment of a trustee or an examiner, if a trustee or an examiner dies or resigns during the case or is removed under section 324 of this title, or if a trustee fails to qualify under section 322 of this title, then the United States trustee, after consultation with parties in interest, shall appoint, sub ject to the court's approval, one disinterested person other than the United States trustee to serve as trustee or examiner, as the case may be, in the case.

*(e) The United States trustee shall move for the appointment of a trustee under subsection (a) if there are reasonable grounds to suspect that current members of the governing body of the debtor, the debtor's chief executive or chief financial officer, or members of the governing body who selected the debtor's chief executive or chief financial officer, participated in actual fraud, dishonesty, or criminal conduct in the management of the debtor or the debtor's public financial reporting.*

**Section 1104**

(April 20, 2005, P. L. 109-8, Title IV, §§ 416, 442(b); Title XIV, §§ 1405, 1406, 119 Stat. 23)

## HISTORY: ANCILLARY LAWS AND DIRECTIVES

**Amendments:**

**2005**. Act April 20, 2005, added new subsections (a)(3), (b)(2) and (e).

**Other provisions:**

**Effective date and application of Act April 20, 2005.**

Act April 20, 2005, Pub.L. 109-8, Title XV, § 1501, 119 Stat. 23, is generally effective 180 days after enactment [April 20, 2005]. Amendment by Pub. L. 109-8 to § 1104(e) is effective "on the date of enactment of this Act [April 20, 2005]," see § 1406(a) of Pub. L. 109-8, and "shall apply only with respect to cases commenced under title 11 of the United States Code on or after the enactment of this Act." See § 1406(a) of Pub. L. 109-8.

**Abridged Legislative History**

Sec. 416. Appointment of Elected Trustee. Section 416 of the Act amends section 1104(b) of the Bankruptcy Code to clarify the procedure for the election of a trustee in a chapter 11 case.

Section 442(b) creates an additional ground for the appointment of a chapter 11 trustee or examiner under section 1104(a).

Section 442(b) is designed to benefit creditors when a chapter 11 case would otherwise be dismissed or converted to a chapter 7 case pursuant to section 1112 of the Bankruptcy Code. Section 442(b) allows the court to appoint a chapter 11 trustee or examiner, as an alternative to dismissing or converting the case to chapter 7, if in the best interest of creditors and the bankruptcy estate. Section 442(b) is not intended to ease the standards for appointing chapter 11 trustees. Practice under Chapter X of the Bankruptcy Act of 1898 demonstrated that routine appointment of trustees deters the use of reorganization statutes and increases the likelihood that by the time a company resorts to bankruptcy relief, it must liquidate. It is therefore important for section 442(b) to be used only for cases that would otherwise be dismissed or converted to chapter 7, and not as an alternative method for attaining the appointment of a chapter 11 trustee.

Sec. 1406. Effective Date; Application of Amendments. Section 1406 provides that title XIV, with the exception of one provision, takes effect on the date of enactment of this Act and the amendments apply only to cases commenced after such date. The exception applies to section 1402(1) of the Act, which applies only to cases commenced under the Bankruptcy Code more than one year after the date of enactment of this Act. (H. Report No. 109-31 to accompany S. 256, 109th Cong., 1st Sess. (2005) p. 89, 95, 155; available at 2005 U.S.C.C.A.N. 88, at 155, 160, 212.)

# § 1105. Termination of trustee's appointment

At any time before confirmation of a plan, on request of a party in interest or the United States trustee, and after notice and a hearing, the court may terminate the trustee's appointment and restore the debtor to possession and management of the property of the estate and of the operation of the debtor's business.

# § 1106. Duties of trustee and examiner

(a) A trustee shall—

(1) perform the duties of *the* ~~a~~ trustee, *as* specified in *paragraphs* ~~sections~~*(2), (5), (7), (8), (9), (10), (11), and (12) of section* 704~~(2), 704(5), 704(7), 704(8), and 704(9) of this title~~;

(2) if the debtor has not done so, file the list, schedule, and statement required under section 521(1) of this title;

(3) except to the extent that the court orders otherwise, investigate the acts, conduct, assets, liabilities, and financial condition of the

debtor, the operation of the debtor's business and the desirability of the continuance of such business, and any other matter relevant to the case or to the formulation of a plan;

(4) as soon as practicable—

(A) file a statement of any investigation conducted under paragraph (3) of this subsection, including any fact ascertained pertaining to fraud, dishonesty, incompetence, misconduct, mismanagement, or irregularity in the management of the affairs of the debtor, or to a cause of action available to the estate; and

(B) transmit a copy or a summary of any such statement to any creditors' committee or equity security holders' committee, to any indenture trustee, and to such other entity as the court designates;

(5) as soon as practicable, file a plan under section 1121 of this title, file a report of why the trustee will not file a plan, or recommend conversion of the case to a case under chapter 7, 12, or 13 of this title or dismissal of the case;

(6) for any year for which the debtor has not filed a tax return required by law, furnish, without personal liability, such information as may be required by the governmental unit with which such tax return was to be filed, in light of the condition of the debtor's books and records and the availability of such information; ~~and~~

(7) after confirmation of a plan, file such reports as are necessary or as the court orders~~.~~*; and*

*(8) if with respect to the debtor there is a claim for a domestic support obligation, provide the applicable notice specified in subsection (c).*

(b) An examiner appointed under section 1104(d) of this title shall perform the duties specified in paragraphs (3) and (4) of subsection (a) of this section, and, except to the extent that the court orders otherwise, any other duties of the trustee that the court orders the debtor in possession not to perform.

*(c) (1) In a case described in subsection (a)(8) to which subsection (a)(8) applies, the trustee shall—*

*(A) (i) provide written notice to the holder of the claim described in subsection (a)(8) of such claim and of the right of such holder to use the services of the State child support enforcement agency established under sections 464 and 466 of the Social Security Act for the State in which such holder resides, for assistance in collecting child support during and after the case under this title; and*

*(ii) include in the notice required by clause (i) the address and telephone number of such State child support enforcement agency;*

*(B) (i) provide written notice to such State child support enforcement agency of such claim;and*

*(ii) include in the notice required by clause (i) the name, address, and telephone number of such holder; and*

*(C) at such time as the debtor is granted a discharge under section 1141, provide written notice to such holder and to such State child support enforcement agency of—*

*(i) the granting of the discharge;*

*(ii) the last recent known address of the debtor;*

*(iii) the last recent known name and address of the debtor's employer; and*

*(iv) the name of each creditor that holds a claim that—*

*(I) is not discharged under paragraph (2), (4), or (14A) of section 523(a); or*

*(II) was reaffirmed by the debtor under section 524(c).*

*(2) (A) The holder of a claim described in subsection (a)(8) or the State child enforcement support agency of the State in which such holder resides may request from a creditor described in paragraph (1)(C)(iv) the last known address of the debtor.*

*(B) Notwithstanding any other provision of law, a creditor that makes a disclosure of a last known address of a debtor in connection with a request made under subparagraph (A) shall not be liable by reason of making such disclosure.*

**Section 1106**

(April 20, 2005, P. L. 109-8, Title II, § 219(b); Title IV, § 446(c); Title XI, § 1105(b), 119 Stat. 23)

## HISTORY: ANCILLARY LAWS AND DIRECTIVES

**Amendments:**

**2005**. Act April 20, 2005, made stylistic changes and additional changes in cross-references in subsection (a)(1) and added new subsections (a)(8) and (c).

**Other provisions:**

**Effective date and application of Act April 20, 2005.**

Act April 20, 2005, Pub.L. 109-8, Title XV, § 1501, 119 Stat. 23, is generally effective 180 days after enactment [April 20, 2005].

**Abridged Legislative History**

Sec. 219. Collection of Child Support. Section 219 amends sections 704, 1106, 1202, and 1302 of the Bankruptcy Code to require trustees in chapter 7, 11, 12, and 13 cases to provide certain notices to child support claimants and governmental enforcement agencies.

Sec. 446. Duties with Respect to a Debtor Who Is a Plan Administrator of an Employee Benefit Plan. Subsection (a) of section 446 of the Act amends Bankruptcy Code section 521(a) to require a debtor, unless a trustee is serving in the case, to serve as the administrator (as defined in the Employee Retirement Income Security Act of 1974) of an employee benefit plan if the debtor served in such capacity at the time the case was filed.(H. Report No. 109-31 to accompany S. 256, 109th Cong., 1st Sess. (2005) p. 62, 96; available at 2005 U.S.C.C.A.N. 88, at 130, 161.)

# § 1107. Rights, powers, and duties of debtor in possession

(a) Subject to any limitations on a trustee serving in a case under this chapter, and to such limitations or conditions as the court prescribes, a debtor in possession shall have all the rights, other than the right to compensation under section 330 of this title, and powers, and shall perform all the functions and duties, except the duties specified in sections 1106(a)(2), (3), and (4) of this title, of a trustee serving in a case under this chapter.

(b) Notwithstanding section 327(a) of this title, a person is not disqualified for employment under section 327 of this title by a debtor in possession solely because of such person's employment by or representation of the debtor before the commencement of the case.

## § 1108. Authorization to operate business

Unless the court, on request of a party in interest and after notice and a hearing, orders otherwise, the trustee may operate the debtor's business.

## § 1109. Right to be heard

(a) The Securities and Exchange Commission may raise and may appear and be heard on any issue in a case under this chapter, but the Securities and Exchange Commission may not appeal from any judgment, order, or decree entered in the case.

(b) A party in interest, including the debtor, the trustee, a creditors' committee, an equity security holders' committee, a creditor, an equity security holder, or any indenture trustee, may raise and may appear and be heard on any issue in a case under this chapter.

## § 1110. Aircraft equipment and vessels

(a) (1) Except as provided in paragraph (2) and subject to subsection (b), the right of a secured party with a security interest in equipment described in paragraph (3), or of a lessor or conditional vendor of such equipment, to take possession of such equipment in compliance with a security agreement, lease, or conditional sale contract, and to enforce any of its other rights or remedies, under such security agreement, lease, or conditional sale contract, to sell, lease, or otherwise retain or dispose of such equipment, is not limited or otherwise affected by any other provision of this title or by any power of the court.

(2) The right to take possession and to enforce the other rights and remedies described in paragraph (1) shall be subject to section 362 if—

(A) before the date that is 60 days after the date of the order for relief under this chapter, the trustee, subject to the approval of the court, agrees to perform all obligations of the debtor under such security agreement, lease, or conditional sale contract; and

(B) any default, other than a default of a kind specified in section 365(b)(2), under such security agreement, lease, or conditional sale contract—

(i) that occurs before the date of the order is cured before the expiration of such 60-day period;

(ii) that occurs after the date of the order and before the expiration of such 60–day period is cured before the later of—

(I) the date that is 30 days after the date of the default; or

(II) the expiration of such 60-day period; and

(iii) that occurs on or after the expiration of such 60–day period is cured in compliance with the terms of such security agreement, lease, or conditional sale contract, if a cure is permitted under that agreement, lease, or contract.

(3) The equipment described in this paragraph

(A) is—

(i) an aircraft, aircraft engine, propeller, appliance, or spare part (as defined in section 40102 of title 49) that is subject to a security interest granted by, leased to, or conditionally sold to a debtor that, at the time such transaction is entered into, holds an air carrier operating certificate issued by the Secretary of Transportation pursuant to chapter 447 of title 49 for aircraft capable of carrying 10 or more individuals or 6,000 pounds or more of cargo; or

(ii) a documented vessel (as defined in section 30101(1) of title 46) that is subject to a security interest granted by, leased to, or conditionally sold to a debtor that is a water carrier that,at the time such transaction is entered into, holds a certificate of public convenience and necessity or permit issued by the Department of Transportation; and

(B) includes all records and documents relating to such equipment that are required, under the terms of the security agreement, lease, or conditional sale contract, to be surrendered or returned by the debtor in connection with the surrender or return of such equipment.

(4) Paragraph (1) applies to a secured party, lessor, or conditional vendor acting in its own behalf or acting as trustee or otherwise in behalf of another party.

(b) The trustee and the secured party, lessor, or conditional vendor whose right to take possession is protected under subsection (a) may agree, subject to the approval of the court, to extend the 60-day period specified in subsection (a)(1).

(c) (1) In any case under this chapter, the trustee shall immediately surrender and return to a secured party, lessor, or conditional vendor, described in subsection (a)(1), equipment described in subsection (a)(3), if at any time after the date of the order for relief under this chapter such secured party, lessor, or conditional vendor is entitled pursuant to subsection (a)(1) to take possession of such equipment and makes a written demand for such possession to the trustee.

(2) At such time as the trustee is required under paragraph (1) to surrender and return equipment described in subsection (a)(3), any lease of such equipment, and any security agreement or conditional sale contract relating to such equipment, if such security agreement or conditional sale contract is an executory contract, shall be deemed rejected.

(d) With respect to equipment first placed in service on or before October 22, 1994, for purposes of this section—

(1) the term "lease" includes any written agreement with respect to which the lessor and the debtor, as lessee, have expressed in the agreement or in a substantially contemporaneous writing that the agreement is to be treated as a lease for Federal income tax purposes; and

(2) the term "security interest" means a purchase-money equipment security interest.

## § 1111. Claims and interests

(a) A proof of claim or interest is deemed filed under section 501 of this title for any claim or interest that appears in the schedules filed under section 521(1) or 1106(a)(2) of this title, except a claim or interest that is scheduled as disputed, contingent, or unliquidated.

(b) (1) (A) A claim secured by a lien on property of the estate shall be allowed or disallowed under section 502 of this title the same as if the holder of such claim had recourse against the debtor on account of such claim, whether or not such holder has such recourse, unless—

(i) the class of which such claim is a part elects, by at least two-thirds in amount and more than half in number of allowed claims of such class, application of paragraph (2) of this subsection; or

(ii) such holder does not have such recourse and such property is sold under section 363 of this title or is to be sold under the plan.

(B) A class of claims may not elect application of paragraph (2) of this subsection if—

(i) the interest on account of such claims of the holders of such claims in such property is of inconsequential value; or

(ii) the holder of a claim of such class has recourse against the debtor on account of such claim and such property is sold under section 363 of this title or is to be sold under the plan.

(2) If such an election is made, then notwithstanding section 506(a) of this title, such claim is a secured claim to the extent that such claim is allowed.

## § 1112. Conversion or dismissal

(a) The debtor may convert a case under this chapter to a case under chapter 7 of this title unless—

(1) the debtor is not a debtor in possession;

(2) the case originally was commenced as an involuntary case under this chapter; or

(3) the case was converted to a case under this chapter other than on the debtor's request.

~~(b) Except as provided in subsection (c) of this section, on request of~~

~~a party in interest or the United States trustee or bankruptcy administrator, and after notice and a hearing, the court may convert a case under this chapter to a case under chapter 7 of this title or may dismiss a case under this chapter, whichever is in the best interest of creditors and the estate, for cause, including—~~

~~(1) continuing loss to or diminution of the estate and absence of a reasonable likelihood of rehabilitation;~~

~~(2) inability to effectuate a plan;~~

~~(3) unreasonable delay by the debtor that is prejudicial to creditors;~~

~~(4) failure to propose a plan under section 1121 of this title within any time fixed by the court;~~

~~(5) denial of confirmation of every proposed plan and denial of a request made for additional time for filing another plan or a modification of a plan;~~

~~(6) revocation of an order of confirmation under section 1144 of this title, and denial of confirmation of another plan or a modified plan under section 1129 of this title;~~

~~(7) inability to effectuate substantial consummation of a confirmed plan;~~

~~(8) material default by the debtor with respect to a confirmed plan;~~

~~(9) termination of a plan by reason of the occurrence of a condition specified in the plan; or~~

~~(10) nonpayment of any fees or charges required under chapter 123 of title 28 [28 USC §§ 1911 et seq.]~~

*(b) (1) Except as provided in paragraph (2) of this subsection, subsection (c) of this section, and section 1104(a)(3), on request of a party in interest, and after notice and a hearing, absent unusual circumstances specifically identified by the court that establish that the requested conversion or dismissal is not in the best interests of creditors and the estate, the court shall convert a case under this chapter to a case under chapter 7 or dismiss a case under this chapter, whichever is in the best interests of creditors and the estate, if the movant establishes cause.*

*(2) The relief provided in paragraph (1) shall not be granted absent unusual circumstances specifically identified by the court that establish that such relief is not in the best interests of creditors and the estate, if the debtor or another party in interest objects and establishes that—*

*(A) there is a reasonable likelihood that a plan will be confirmed within the timeframes established in sections 1121(e) and 1129(e) of this title, or if such sections do not apply, within a reasonable period of time; and*

*(B) the grounds for granting such relief include an act or omission of the debtor other than under paragraph (4)(A)—*

*(i) for which there exists a reasonable justification for the act or omission; and*

*(ii) that will be cured within a reasonable period of time fixed by the court.*

*(3) The court shall commence the hearing on a motion under this subsection not later than 30 days after filing of the motion, and shall decide the motion not later than 15 days after commencement of such hearing, unless the movant expressly consents to a continuance for a specific period of time or compelling circumstances prevent the court from meeting the time limits established by this paragraph.*

*(4) For purposes of this subsection, the term 'cause' includes—*

*(A) substantial or continuing loss to or diminution of the estate and the absence of a reasonable likelihood of rehabilitation;*

*(B) gross mismanagement of the estate;*

*(C) failure to maintain appropriate insurance that poses a risk to the estate or to the public;*

*(D) unauthorized use of cash collateral substantially harmful to 1 or more creditors;*

*(E) failure to comply with an order of the court;*

*(F) unexcused failure to satisfy timely any filing or reporting requirement established by this title or by any rule applicable to a case under this chapter;*

*(G) failure to attend the meeting of creditors convened under section 341(a) or an examination ordered under rule 2004 of the Federal Rules of Bankruptcy Procedure without good cause shown by the debtor;*

*(H) failure timely to provide information or attend meetings reasonably requested by the United States trustee (or the bankruptcy administrator, if any);*

*(I) failure timely to pay taxes owed after the date of the order for relief or to file tax returns due after the date of the order for relief;*

*(J) failure to file a disclosure statement, or to file or confirm a plan, within the time fixed by this title or by order of the court;*

*(K) failure to pay any fees or charges required under chapter 123 of title 28;*

*(L) revocation of an order of confirmation under section 1144;*

*(M) inability to effectuate substantial consummation of a confirmed plan;*

*(N) material default by the debtor with respect to a confirmed plan;*

*(O) termination of a confirmed plan by reason of the occurrence of a condition specified in the plan; and*

*(P) failure of the debtor to pay any domestic support obligation that first becomes payable after the date of the filing of the petition.*

(c) The court may not convert a case under this chapter to a case under chapter 7 of this title if the debtor is a farmer or a corporation that is not a moneyed, business, or commercial corporation, unless the debtor requests such conversion.

(d) The court may convert a case under this chapter to a case under chapter 12 or 13 of this title only if—

(1) the debtor requests such conversion;

(2) the debtor has not been discharged under section 1141(d) of this title; and

(3) if the debtor requests conversion to chapter 12 of this title, such conversion is equitable.

(e) Except as provided in subsections (c) and (f), the court, on request of the United States trustee, may convert a case under this chapter to a case under chapter 7 of this title or may dismiss a case under this chapter, whichever is in the best interest of creditors and the estate if the debtor in a voluntary case fails to file, within fifteen days after the filing of the petition commencing such case or such additional time as the court may allow, the information required by paragraph (1) of section 521, including a list containing the names and addresses of the holders of the twenty largest unsecured claims (or of all unsecured claims if there are fewer than twenty unsecured claims), and the approximate dollar amounts of each of such claims.

(f) Notwithstanding any other provision of this section, a case may not be converted to a case under another chapter of this title unless the debtor may be a debtor under such chapter.

**Section 1112**

(April 20, 2005, P. L. 109-8, Title IV, § 442(a), 119 Stat. 23)

## HISTORY: ANCILLARY LAWS AND DIRECTIVES

**Amendments:**

**2005**. Act April 20, 2005, replaced subsection (b).

**Other provisions:**

**Effective date and application of Act April 20, 2005.**

Act April 20, 2005, Pub.L. 109-8, Title XV, § 1501, 119 Stat. 23, is generally effective 180 days after enactment [April 20, 2005].

**Abridged Legislative History**

(H. Report No. 109-31 to accompany S. 256, 109th Cong., 1st Sess. (2005) p. 94; available at 2005 U.S.C.C.A.N. 88, at 159.)

# § 1113. Rejection of collective bargaining agreements

(a) The debtor in possession, or the trustee if one has been appointed under the provisions of this chapter, other than a trustee in a case covered by subchapter IV of this chapter and by title I of the Railway Labor Act, may assume or reject a collective bargaining agreement only in accordance with the provisions of this section.

(b) (1) Subsequent to filing a petition and prior to filing an application seeking rejection of a collective bargaining agreement, the debtor in possession or trustee (hereinafter in this section "trustee" shall include a debtor in possession), shall—

(A) make a proposal to the authorized representative of the employees covered by such agreement, based on the most complete and reliable information available at the time of such proposal, which provides for those necessary modifications in the employees benefits and protections that are necessary to permit the reorganization of the debtor and assures that all creditors, the debtor and all of the affected parties are treated fairly and equitably; and

(B) provide, subject to subsection (d)(3), the representative of the employees with such relevant information as is necessary to evaluate the proposal.

(2) During the period beginning on the date of the making of a proposal provided for in paragraph (1) and ending on the date of the hearing provided for in subsection (d)(1), the trustee shall meet, at reasonable times, with the authorized representative to confer in good faith in attempting to reach mutually satisfactory modifications of such agreement.

(c) The court shall approve an application for rejection of a collective bargaining agreement only if the court finds that—

(1) the trustee has, prior to the hearing, made a proposal that fulfills the requirements of subsection (b)(1);

(2) the authorized representative of the employees has refused to accept such proposal without good cause; and

(3) the balance of the equities clearly favors rejection of such agreement.

(d) (1) Upon the filing of an application for rejection the court shall schedule a hearing to be held not later than fourteen days after the date of the filing of such application. All interested parties may appear and be heard at such hearing. Adequate notice shall be provided to such parties at least ten days before the date of such hearing. The court may extend the time for the commencement of such hearing for a period not exceeding seven days where the circumstances of the case, and the interests of justice require such extension, or for additional periods of time to which the trustee and representative agree.

(2) The court shall rule on such application for rejection within thirty days after the date of the commencement of the hearing. In the interests of justice, the court may extend such time for ruling for such additional period as the trustee and the employees' representative may agree to. If the court does not rule on such application within thirty days after the date of the commencement of the hearing, or within such additional time as the trustee and the employees' representative may agree to, the trustee may terminate or alter any provisions of the collective bargaining agreement pending the ruling of the court on such application.

(3) The court may enter such protective orders, consistent with the need of the authorized representative of the employee to evaluate the trustee's proposal and the application for rejection, as may be necessary to prevent disclosure of information provided to such representative where such disclosure could compromise the position

of the debtor with respect to its competitors in the industry in which it is engaged.

(e) If during a period when the collective bargaining agreement continues in effect, and if essential to the continuation of the debtor's business, or in order to avoid irreparable damage to the estate, the court, after notice and a hearing, may authorize the trustee to implement interim changes in the terms, conditions, wages, benefits, or work rules provided by a collective bargaining agreement. Any hearing under this paragraph shall be scheduled in accordance with the needs of the trustee. The implementation of such interim changes shall not render the application for rejection moot.

(f) No provision of this title shall be construed to permit a trustee to unilaterally terminate or alter any provisions of a collective bargaining agreement prior to compliance with the provisions of this section.

## § 1114. Payment of insurance benefits to retired employees

(a) For purposes of this section, the term "retiree benefits" means payments to any entity or person for the purpose of providing or reimbursing payments for retired employees and their spouses and dependents, for medical, surgical, or hospital care benefits, or benefits in the event of sickness, accident, disability, or death under any plan, fund, or program (through the purchase of insurance or otherwise) maintained or established in whole or in part by the debtor prior to filing a petition commencing a case under this title.

(b) (1) For purposes of this section, the term "authorized representative" means the authorized representative designated pursuant to subsection (c) for persons receiving any retiree benefits covered by a collective bargaining agreement or subsection (d) in the case of persons receiving retiree benefits not covered by such an agreement.

(2) Committees of retired employees appointed by the court pursuant to this section shall have the same rights, powers, and duties as committees appointed under sections 1102 and 1103 of this title for the purpose of carrying out the purposes of sections 1114 and 1129(a)(13) and, as permitted by the court, shall have the power to enforce the rights of persons under this title as they relate to retiree benefits.

(c) (1) A labor organization shall be, for purposes of this section, the authorized representative of those persons receiving any retiree benefits covered by any collective bargaining agreement to which that labor organization is signatory, unless (A) such labor organization elects not to serve as the authorized representative of such persons, or (B) the court, upon a motion by any party in interest, after notice and hearing, determines that different representation of such persons is appropriate.

(2) In cases where the labor organization referred to in paragraph (1) elects not to serve as the authorized representative of those persons receiving any retiree benefits covered by any collective

bargaining agreement to which that labor organization is signatory, or in cases where the court, pursuant to paragraph (1) finds different representation of such persons appropriate, the court, upon a motion by any party in interest, and after notice and a hearing, shall appoint a committee of retired employees if the debtor seeks to modify or not pay the retiree benefits or if the court otherwise determines that it is appropriate, from among such persons, to serve as the authorized representative of such persons under this section.

(d) The court, upon a motion by any party in interest, and after notice and a hearing, shall *order the* appoint*ment of* a committee of retired employees if the debtor seeks to modify or not pay the retiree benefits or if the court otherwise determines that it is appropriate, to serve as the authorized representative, under this section, of those persons receiving any retiree benefits not covered by a collective bargaining agreement. *The United States trustee shall appoint any such committee.*

(e) (1) Notwithstanding any other provision of this title, the debtor in possession, or the trustee if one has been appointed under the provisions of this chapter (hereinafter in this section "trustee" shall include a debtor in possession), shall timely pay and shall not modify any retiree benefits, except that—

(A) the court, on motion of the trustee or authorized representative, and after notice and a hearing, may order modification of such payments, pursuant to the provisions of subsections (g) and (h) of this section, or

(B) the trustee and the authorized representative of the recipients of those benefits may agree to modification of such payments, after which such benefits as modified shall continue to be paid by the trustee.

(2) Any payment for retiree benefits required to be made before a plan confirmed under section 1129 of this title is effective has the status of an allowed administrative expense as provided in section 503 of this title.

(f) (1) Subsequent to filing a petition and prior to filing an application seeking modification of the retiree benefits, the trustee shall—

(A) make a proposal to the authorized representative of the retirees, based on the most complete and reliable information available at the time of such proposal, which provides for those necessary modifications in the retiree benefits that are necessary to permit the reorganization of the debtor and assures that all creditors, the debtor and all of the affected parties are treated fairly and equitably; and

(B) provide, subject to subsection (k)(3), the representative of the retirees with such relevant information as is necessary to evaluate the proposal.

(2) During the period beginning on the date of the making of a proposal provided for in paragraph (1), and ending on the date of

the hearing provided for in subsection (k)(1), the trustee shall meet, at reasonable times, with the authorized representative to confer in good faith in attempting to reach mutually satisfactory modifications of such retiree benefits.

(g) The court shall enter an order providing for modification in the payment of retiree benefits if the court finds that—

(1) the trustee has, prior to the hearing, made a proposal that fulfills the requirements of subsection (f);

(2) the authorized representative of the retirees has refused to accept such proposal without good cause; and

(3) such modification is necessary to permit the reorganization of the debtor and assures that all creditors, the debtor, and all of the affected parties are treated fairly and equitably, and is clearly favored by the balance of the equities; except that in no case shall the court enter an order providing for such modification which provides for a modification to a level lower than that proposed by the trustee in the proposal found by the court to have complied with the requirements of this subsection and subsection (f): Provided, however, That at any time after an order is entered providing for modification in the payment of retiree benefits, or at any time after an agreement modifying such benefits is made between the trustee and the authorized representative of the recipients of such benefits, the authorized representative may apply to the court for an order increasing those benefits which order shall be granted if the increase in retiree benefits sought is consistent with the standard set forth in paragraph (3): Provided further, That neither the trustee nor the authorized representative is precluded from making more than one motion for a modification order governed by this subsection.

(h) (1) Prior to a court issuing a final order under subsection (g) of this section, if essential to the continuation of the debtor's business, or in order to avoid irreparable damage to the estate, the court, after notice and a hearing, may authorize the trustee to implement interim modifications in retiree benefits.

(2) Any hearing under this subsection shall be scheduled in accordance with the needs of the trustee.

(3) The implementation of such interim changes does not render the motion for modification moot.

(i) No retiree benefits paid between the filing of the petition and the time a plan confirmed under section 1129 of this title becomes effective shall be deducted or offset from the amounts allowed as claims for any benefits which remain unpaid, or from the amounts to be paid under the plan with respect to such claims for unpaid benefits, whether such claims for unpaid benefits are based upon or arise from a right to future unpaid benefits or from any benefits not paid as a result of modifications allowed pursuant to this section.

(j) No claim for retiree benefits shall be limited by section 502(b)(7) of this title.

(k) (1) Upon the filing of an application for modifying retiree benefits, the court shall schedule a hearing to be held not later than fourteen days after the date of the filing of such application. All interested parties may appear and be heard at such hearing. Adequate notice shall be provided to such parties at least ten days before the date of such hearing. The court may extend the time for the commencement of such hearing for a period not exceeding seven days where the circumstances of the case, and the interests of justice require such extension, or for additional periods of time to which the trustee and the authorized representative agree.

(2) The court shall rule on such application for modification within ninety days after the date of the commencement of the hearing. In the interests of justice, the court may extend such time for ruling for such additional period as the trustee and the authorized representative may agree to. If the court does not rule on such application within ninety days after the date of the commencement of the hearing, or within such additional time as the trustee and the authorized representative may agree to, the trustee may implement the proposed modifications pending the ruling of the court on such application.

(3) The court may enter such protective orders, consistent with the need of the authorized representative of the retirees to evaluate the trustee's proposal and the application for modification, as may be necessary to prevent disclosure of information provided to such representative where such disclosure could compromise the position of the debtor with respect to its competitors in the industry in which it is engaged.

*(l) If the debtor, during the 180-day period ending on the date of the filing of the petition—*

*(1) modified retiree benefits; and*

*(2) was insolvent on the date such benefits were modified; the court, on motion of a party in interest, and after notice and a hearing, shall issue an order reinstating as of the date the modification was made, such benefits as in effect immediately before such date unless the court finds that the balance of the equities clearly favors such modification.*

(~~l~~ *m*) This section shall not apply to any retiree, or the spouse or dependents of such retiree, if such retiree's gross income for the twelve months preceding the filing of the bankruptcy petition equals or exceeds $250,000, unless such retiree can demonstrate to the satisfaction of the court that he is unable to obtain health, medical, life, and disability coverage for himself, his spouse, and his dependents who would otherwise be covered by the employer's insurance plan, comparable to the coverage provided by the employer on the day before the filing of a petition under this title.

**Section 1114**

(April 20, 2005, P. L. 109-8, Title IV, § 447; Title XIV, § 1403, 1406, 119 Stat. 23)

## HISTORY: ANCILLARY LAWS AND DIRECTIVES

**Amendments:**

**2005**. Act April 20, 2005, amended subsection (d) by striking "appoint" and inserting "order the appointment of" and by adding at the end the sentence, "The United States trustee shall appoint any such committee," and added new subsection (*l*).

**Other provisions:**

**Effective date and application of Act April 20, 2005.**

Act April 20, 2005, Pub.L. 109-8, Title XV, § 1501, 119 Stat. 23, is generally effective 180 days after enactment [April 20, 2005]. Amendment by Pub. L. 109-8 to § 1114(*l*) is effective "on the date of enactment of this Act [April 20, 2005]," see § 1406(a) of Pub. L. 109-8, and "shall apply only with respect to cases commenced under title 11 of the United States Code on or after the enactment of this Act." See § 1406(a) of Pub. L. 109-8.

**Abridged Legislative History**

Sec. 447. Appointment of Committee of Retired Employees. This provision amends section 1114(d) of the Bankruptcy Code to clarify that it is the responsibility of the United States trustee to appoint members to a committee of retired employees.

Sec. 1403. Payment of Insurance Benefits to Retired Employees. Section 1403 amends Bankruptcy Code section 1114 to prevent debtors from evading these requirements by terminating retiree benefit plans on the eve of bankruptcy. The amendment would require retroactive reinstatement of retiree benefits that were modified within 180 days before the debtor filed for bankruptcy protection, unless the court finds that the balance of the equities clearly favors the modification.

Sec. 1406. Effective Date; Application of Amendments. Section 1406 provides that title XIV, with the exception of one provision, takes effect on the date of enactment of this Act and the amendments apply only to cases commenced after such date. The exception applies to section 1402(1) of the Act, which applies only to cases commenced under the Bankruptcy Code more than one year after the date of enactment of this Act. (H. Report No. 109-31 to accompany S. 256, 109th Cong., 1st Sess. (2005) p. 96, 154, 155; available at 2005 U.S.C.C.A.N. 88, at 161, 211–12, 212.)

# *§ 1115. Property of the estate*

*(a) In a case in which the debtor is an individual, property of the estate includes, in addition to the property specified in section 541—*

*(1) all property of the kind specified in section 541 that the debtor acquires after the commencement of the case but before the case is closed, dismissed, or converted to a case under chapter 7, 12, or 13, whichever occurs first; and*

*(2) earnings from services performed by the debtor after the commencement of the case but before the case is closed, dismissed, or converted to a case under chapter 7, 12, or 13, whichever occurs first.*

*(b) Except as provided in section 1104 or a confirmed plan or order confirming a plan, the debtor shall remain in possession of all property of the estate.*

**Section 1115**

(April 20, 2005, P. L. 109-8, Title III, § 321(a)(1), 119 Stat. 23)

## HISTORY: ANCILLARY LAWS AND DIRECTIVES

**Amendments:**

**2005**. Act April 20, 2005, added a new § 1115.

**Other provisions:**

**Effective date and application of Act April 20, 2005.**

Act April 20, 2005, Pub.L. 109-8, Title XV, § 1501, 119 Stat. 23, is generally effective

180 days after enactment [April 20, 2005].

**Abridged Legislative History**

(H. Report No. 109-31 to accompany S. 256, 109th Cong., 1st Sess. (2005) p. 80; available at 2005 U.S.C.C.A.N. 88, at 147.)

## *§ 1116. Duties of trustee or debtor in possession in small business cases*

*In a small business case, a trustee or the debtor in possession, in addition to the duties provided in this title and as otherwise required by law, shall—*

*(1) append to the voluntary petition or, in an involuntary case, file not later than 7 days after the date of the order for relief—*

*(A) its most recent balance sheet, statement of operations, cash-flow statement, and Federal income tax return; or*

*(B) a statement made under penalty of perjury that no balance sheet, statement of operations, or cash-flow statement has been prepared and no Federal tax return has been filed;*

*(2) attend, through its senior management personnel and counsel, meetings scheduled by the court or the United States trustee, including initial debtor interviews, scheduling conferences, and meetings of creditors convened under section 341 unless the court, after notice and a hearing, waives that requirement upon a finding of extraordinary and compelling circumstances;*

*(3) timely file all schedules and statements of financial affairs, unless the court, after notice and a hearing, grants an extension, which shall not extend such time period to a date later than 30 days after the date of the order for relief, absent extraordinary and compelling circumstances;*

*(4) file all postpetition financial and other reports required by the Federal Rules of Bankruptcy Procedure or by local rule of the district court;*

*(5) subject to section 363(c)(2), maintain insurance customary and appropriate to the industry;*

*(6) (A) timely file tax returns and other required government filings; and*

*(B) subject to section 363(c)(2), timely pay all taxes entitled to administrative expense priority except those being contested by appropriate proceedings being diligently prosecuted; and*

*(7) allow the United States trustee, or a designated representative of the United States trustee, to inspect the debtor's business premises, books, and records at reasonable times, after reasonable prior written notice, unless notice is waived by the debtor.*

**Section 1116**

(April 20, 2005, P. L. 109-8, Title IV, § 436(a), 119 Stat. 23)

## HISTORY: ANCILLARY LAWS AND DIRECTIVES

**Amendments:**

**2005**. Act April 20, 2005, added a new § 1116.

**Other provisions:**
**Effective date and application of Act April 20, 2005.**
Act April 20, 2005, Pub.L. 109-8, Title XV, § 1501, 119 Stat. 23, is generally effective 180 days after enactment [April 20, 2005].

**Abridged Legislative History**
(H. Report No. 109-31 to accompany S. 256, 109th Cong., 1st Sess. (2005) p. 91–92; available at 2005 U.S.C.C.A.N. 88, at 157.)

# Subchapter II——The Plan

## § 1121. Who may file a plan

(a) The debtor may file a plan with a petition commencing a voluntary case, or at any time in a voluntary case or an involuntary case.

(b) Except as otherwise provided in this section, only the debtor may file a plan until after 120 days after the date of the order for relief under this chapter.

(c) Any party in interest, including the debtor, the trustee, a creditors' committee, an equity security holders' committee, a creditor, an equity security holder, or any indenture trustee, may file a plan if and only if—

(1) a trustee has been appointed under this chapter;

(2) the debtor has not filed a plan before 120 days after the date of the order for relief under this chapter; or

(3) the debtor has not filed a plan that has been accepted, before 180 days after the date of the order for relief under this chapter, by each class of claims or interests that is impaired under the plan.

(d) *(1) Subject to paragraph (2), on* ~~On~~ request of a party in interest made within the respective periods specified in subsections (b) and (c) of this section and after notice and a hearing, the court may for cause reduce or increase the 120-day period or the 180-day period referred to in this section.

*(2) (A) The 120-day period specified in paragraph (1) may not be extended beyond a date that is 18 months after the date of the order for relief under this chapter.*

*(B) The 180-day period specified in paragraph (1) may not be extended beyond a date that is 20 months after the date of the order for relief under this chapter.*

(e) ~~In a case in which the debtor is a small business and elects to be considered a small business~~*In a small business case—*

~~(1) only the debtor may file a plan until after 100 days after the date of the order for relief under this chapter;~~

~~(2) all plans shall be filed within 160 days after the date of the order for relief; and~~

~~(3) on request of a party in interest made within the respective periods specified in paragraphs (1) and (2) and after notice and a hearing, the court may—~~

~~(A) reduce the 100-day period or the 160-day period specified in paragraph (1) or (2) for cause; and~~

~~(B) increase the 100-day period specified in paragraph (1) if the debtor shows that the need for an increase is caused by circumstances for which the debtor should not be held accountable.~~

*(1) only the debtor may file a plan until after 180 days after the date of the order for relief, unless that period is—*

*(A) extended as provided by this subsection, after notice and a hearing; or*

*(B) the court, for cause, orders otherwise;*

*(2) the plan and a disclosure statement (if any) shall be filed not later than 300 days after the date of the order for relief; and*

*(3) the time periods specified in paragraphs (1) and (2), and the time fixed in section 1129(e) within which the plan shall be confirmed, may be extended only if—*

*(A) the debtor, after providing notice to parties in interest (including the United States trustee), demonstrates by a preponderance of the evidence that it is more likely than not that the court will confirm a plan within a reasonable period of time;*

*(B) a new deadline is imposed at the time the extension is granted; and*

*(C) the order extending time is signed before the existing deadline has expired.*

**Section 1121**

(April 20, 2005, P. L. 109-8, Title IV, § 411, 437, 119 Stat. 23)

## HISTORY: ANCILLARY LAWS AND DIRECTIVES

**Amendments:**

**2005**. Act April 20, 2005, added a new subsection (d)(2) and replaced subsection (e).

**Other provisions:**

**Effective date and application of Act April 20, 2005.**

Act April 20, 2005, Pub.L. 109-8, Title XV, § 1501, 119 Stat. 23, is generally effective 180 days after enactment [April 20, 2005].

**Abridged Legislative History**

Sec. 437. Plan Filing and Confirmation Deadlines. Section 437 of the Act amends section 1121(e) of the Bankruptcy Code with respect to the period of time within which a small business debtor must file and confirm a plan of reorganization. (H. Report No. 109-31 to accompany S. 256, 109th Cong., 1st Sess. (2005) p. 88, 92; available at 2005 U.S.C.C.A.N. 88, at 154, 158.)

# § 1122. Classification of claims or interests

(a) Except as provided in subsection (b) of this section, a plan may place a claim or an interest in a particular class only if such claim or interest is substantially similar to the other claims or interests of such class.

(b) A plan may designate a separate class of claims consisting only of every unsecured claim that is less than or reduced to an amount that the court approves as reasonable and necessary for administrative convenience.

## § 1123. Contents of plan

(a) Notwithstanding any otherwise applicable nonbankruptcy law, a plan shall—

(1) designate, subject to section 1122 of this title, classes of claims, other than claims of a kind specified in section 507(a)(*2*~~1~~), 507(a)(*3*~~2~~), or 507(a)(8) of this title, and classes of interests;

(2) specify any class of claims or interests that is not impaired under the plan;

(3) specify the treatment of any class of claims or interests that is impaired under the plan;

(4) provide the same treatment for each claim or interest of a particular class, unless the holder of a particular claim or interest agrees to a less favorable treatment of such particular claim or interest;

(5) provide adequate means for the plan's implementation, such as—

(A) retention by the debtor of all or any part of the property of the estate;

(B) transfer of all or any part of the property of the estate to one or more entities, whether organized before or after the confirmation of such plan;

(C) merger or consolidation of the debtor with one or more persons;

(D) sale of all or any part of the property of the estate, either subject to or free of any lien, or the distribution of all or any part of the property of the estate among those having an interest in such property of the estate;

(E) satisfaction or modification of any lien;

(F) cancellation or modification of any indenture or similar instrument;

(G) curing or waiving of any default;

(H) extension of a maturity date or a change in an interest rate or other term of outstanding securities;

(I) amendment of the debtor's charter; or

(J) issuance of securities of the debtor, or of any entity referred to in subparagraph (B) or (C) of this paragraph, for cash, for property, for existing securities, or in exchange for claims or interests, or for any other appropriate purpose;

(6) provide for the inclusion in the charter of the debtor, if the debtor is a corporation, or of any corporation referred to in paragraph (5)(B) or (5)(C) of this subsection, of a provision prohibiting the issuance of nonvoting equity securities, and providing, as to the several classes of securities possessing voting power, an appropriate distribution of such power among such classes, including, in the case of any class of equity securities having a preference over another class of equity securities with respect to dividends, ade-

quate provisions for the election of directors representing such preferred class in the event of default in the payment of such dividends; ~~and~~

(7) contain only provisions that are consistent with the interests of creditors and equity security holders and with public policy with respect to the manner of selection of any officer, director, or trustee under the plan and any successor to such officer, director, or trustee~~.~~*; and*

*(8) in a case in which the debtor is an individual, provide for the payment to creditors under the plan of all or such portion of earnings from personal services performed by the debtor after the commencement of the case or other future income of the debtor as is necessary for the execution of the plan.*

(b) Subject to subsection (a) of this section, a plan may—

(1) impair or leave unimpaired any class of claims, secured or unsecured, or of interests;

(2) subject to section 365 of this title, provide for the assumption, rejection, or assignment of any executory contract or unexpired lease of the debtor not previously rejected under such section;

(3) provide for—

(A) the settlement or adjustment of any claim or interest belonging to the debtor or to the estate; or

(B) the retention and enforcement by the debtor, by the trustee, or by a representative of the estate appointed for such purpose, of any such claim or interest;

(4) provide for the sale of all or substantially all of the property of the estate, and the distribution of the proceeds of such sale among holders of claims or interests;

(5) modify the rights of holders of secured claims, other than a claim secured only by a security interest in real property that is the debtor's principal residence, or of holders of unsecured claims, or leave unaffected the rights of holders of any class of claims; and

(6) include any other appropriate provision not inconsistent with the applicable provisions of this title.

(c) In a case concerning an individual, a plan proposed by an entity other than the debtor may not provide for the use, sale, or lease of property exempted under section 522 of this title, unless the debtor consents to such use, sale, or lease.

(d) Notwithstanding subsection (a) of this section and sections 506 (b), 1129(a)(7), and 1129(b) of this title, if it is proposed in a plan to cure a default the amount necessary to cure the default shall be determined in accordance with the underlying agreement and applicable nonbankruptcy law.

**Section 1123**

(April 20, 2005, P. L. 109-8, Title III, § 321(b); Title XV, § 1502(a)(7), 119 Stat. 23)

## HISTORY: ANCILLARY LAWS AND DIRECTIVES

**Amendments:**

**2005**. Act April 20, 2005, corrected cross-references in subsection (a)(1) and added a new subsection (a)(8).

**Other provisions:**

**Effective date and application of Act April 20, 2005.**

Act April 20, 2005, Pub.L. 109-8, Title XV, § 1501, 119 Stat. 23, is generally effective 180 days after enactment [April 20, 2005].

**Abridged Legislative History**

Section 321(b) amends Bankruptcy Code section 1123 to require the chapter 11 plan of an individual debtor to provide for the payment to creditors of all or such portion of the debtor's earnings from personal services performed after commencement of the case or other future income that is necessary for the plan's execution.

(H. Report No. 109-31 to accompany S. 256, 109th Cong., 1st Sess. (2005) p. 80, 155; available at 2005 U.S.C.C.A.N. 88, at 147, 212.)

# § 1124. Impairment of claims or interests

Except as provided in section 1123(a)(4) of this title, a class of claims or interests is impaired under a plan unless, with respect to each claim or interest of such class, the plan—

(1) leaves unaltered the legal, equitable, and contractual rights to which such claim or interest entitles the holder of such claim or interest; or

(2) notwithstanding any contractual provision or applicable law that entitles the holder of such claim or interest to demand or receive accelerated payment of such claim or interest after the occurrence of a default—

(A) cures any such default that occurred before or after the commencement of the case under this title, other than a default of a kind specified in section 365(b)(2) of this title *or of a kind that section 365(b)(2) expressly does not require to be cured*;

(B) reinstates the maturity of such claim or interest as such maturity existed before such default;

(C) compensates the holder of such claim or interest for any damages incurred as a result of any reasonable reliance by such holder on such contractual provision or such applicable law; ~~and~~

*(D) if such claim or such interest arises from any failure to perform a nonmonetary obligation, other than a default arising from failure to operate a nonresidential real property lease subject to section 365(b)(1)(A), compensates the holder of such claim or such interest (other than the debtor or an insider) for any actual pecuniary loss incurred by such holder as a result of such failure; and*

(~~D~~ *E*) does not otherwise alter the legal, equitable, or contractual rights to which such claim or interest entitles the holder of such claim or interest.

**Section 1124**

(April 20, 2005, P. L. 109-8, Title III, § 328(b), 119 Stat. 23)

## HISTORY: ANCILLARY LAWS AND DIRECTIVES

**Amendments:**

**2005**. Act April 20, 2005, inserted "or of a kind that section 365(b)(2) expressly does not require to be cured" at the end of subsection (2)(A), added a new subsection (2)(D) and redesignated former subsection (2)(D) as (2)(E).

**Other provisions:**

**Effective date and application of Act April 20, 2005.**

Act April 20, 2005, Pub.L. 109-8, Title XV, § 1501, 119 Stat. 23, is generally effective 180 days after enactment [April 20, 2005].

**Abridged Legislative History**

Section 328(b) amends section 1124(2)(A) of the Bankruptcy Code to clarify that a claim is not impaired if section 365(b)(2) (as amended by this Act) expressly does not require a default with respect to such claim to be cured. In addition, it provides that any claim or interest that arises from the failure to perform a nonmonetary obligation (other than a default arising from the failure to operate a nonresidential real property lease subject to section 365(b)(1)(A)), is impaired unless the holder of such claim or interest (other than the debtor or an insider) is compensated for any actual pecuniary loss incurred by the holder as a result of such failure. (H. Report No. 109-31 to accompany S. 256, 109th Cong., 1st Sess. (2005) p. 83; available at 2005 U.S.C.C.A.N. 88, at 150.)

# § 1125. Postpetition disclosure and solicitation

(a) In this section—

(1) "adequate information" means information of a kind, and in sufficient detail, as far as is reasonably practicable in light of the nature and history of the debtor and the condition of the debtor's books and records, *including a discussion of the potential material Federal tax consequences of the plan to the debtor, any successor to the debtor, and a hypothetical investor typical of the holders of claims or interests in the case,* that would enable ~~a hypothetical reasonable investor typical of holders of claims or interests~~*such a hypothetical investor* of the relevant class to make an informed judgment about the plan, but adequate information need not include such information about any other possible or proposed plan *and in determining whether a disclosure statement provides adequate information, the court shall consider the complexity of the case, the benefit of additional information to creditors and other parties in interest, and the cost of providing additional information*; and

(2) "investor typical of holders of claims or interests of the relevant class" means investor having—

(A) a claim or interest of the relevant class;

(B) such a relationship with the debtor as the holders of other claims or interests of such class generally have; and

(C) such ability to obtain such information from sources other than the disclosure required by this section as holders of claims or interests in such class generally have.

(b) An acceptance or rejection of a plan may not be solicited after the commencement of the case under this title from a holder of a claim or interest with respect to such claim or interest, unless, at the time of or before such solicitation, there is transmitted to such holder the plan or a summary of the plan, and a written disclosure statement approved, after notice and a hearing, by the court as containing adequate information. The court may approve a disclosure statement without a valuation of the debtor or an appraisal of the debtor's assets.

(c) The same disclosure statement shall be transmitted to each holder of a claim or interest of a particular class, but there may be transmitted different disclosure statements, differing in amount, detail, or kind of information, as between classes.

(d) Whether a disclosure statement required under subsection (b) of this section contains adequate information is not governed by any otherwise applicable nonbankruptcy law, rule, or regulation, but an agency or official whose duty is to administer or enforce such a law, rule, or regulation may be heard on the issue of whether a disclosure statement contains adequate information. Such an agency or official may not appeal from, or otherwise seek review of, an order approving a disclosure statement.

(e) A person that solicits acceptance or rejection of a plan, in good faith and in compliance with the applicable provisions of this title, or that participates, in good faith and in compliance with the applicable provisions of this title, in the offer, issuance, sale, or purchase of a security, offered or sold under the plan, of the debtor, of an affiliate participating in a joint plan with the debtor, or of a newly organized successor to the debtor under the plan, is not liable, on account of such solicitation or participation, for violation of any applicable law, rule, or regulation governing solicitation of acceptance or rejection of a plan or the offer, issuance, sale, or purchase of securities.

(f) ~~Notwithstanding subsection (b), in a case in which the debtor has elected under section 1121(e) to be considered a small business~~*Notwithstanding subsection (b), in a small business case—*

~~(1) the court may conditionally approve a disclosure statement subject to final approval after notice and a hearing;~~

~~(2) acceptances and rejections of a plan may be solicited based on a conditionally approved disclosure statement as long as the debtor provides adequate information to each holder of a claim or interest that is solicited, but a conditionally approved disclosure statement shall be mailed at least 10 days prior to the date of the hearing on confirmation of the plan; and~~

~~(3) a hearing on the disclosure statement may be combined with a hearing on confirmation of a plan.~~

*(1) the court may determine that the plan itself provides adequate information and that a separate disclosure statement is not necessary;*

*(2) the court may approve a disclosure statement submitted on standard forms approved by the court or adopted under section 2075 of title 28; and*

*(3) (A) the court may conditionally approve a disclosure statement subject to final approval after notice and a hearing;*

*(B) acceptances and rejections of a plan may be solicited based*

*on a conditionally approved disclosure statement if the debtor provides adequate information to each holder of a claim or interest that is solicited, but a conditionally approved disclosure statement shall be mailed not later than 25 days before the date of the hearing on confirmation of the plan; and*

*(C) the hearing on the disclosure statement may be combined with the hearing on confirmation of a plan.*

*(g) Notwithstanding subsection (b), an acceptance or rejection of the plan may be solicited from a holder of a claim or interest if such solicitation complies with applicable nonbankruptcy law and if such holder was solicited before the commencement of the case in a manner complying with applicable nonbankruptcy law.*

**Section 1125**

(April 20, 2005, P. L. 109-8, Title IV, §§ 408, 423; Title VII, § 717, 119 Stat. 23)

## HISTORY: ANCILLARY LAWS AND DIRECTIVES

**Amendments:**

**2005**. Act April 20, 2005, inserted "and in determining whether a disclosure statement provides adequate information, the court shall consider the complexity of the case, the benefit of additional information to creditors and other parties in interest, and the cost of providing additional information" at the end of subsection (a)(1), replaced subsection (f) and added a new subsection (g).

**Other provisions:**

**Effective date and application of Act April 20, 2005.**

Act April 20, 2005, Pub.L. 109-8, Title XV, § 1501, 119 Stat. 23, is generally effective 180 days after enactment [April 20, 2005].

**Abridged Legislative History**

Sec. 408. Postpetition Disclosure and Solicitation. Section 408 amends section 1125 of the Bankruptcy Code to permit an acceptance or rejection of a chapter 11 plan to be solicited from the holder of a claim or interest if the holder was solicited before the commencement of the case in a manner that complied with applicable nonbankruptcy law.

(H. Report No. 109-31 to accompany S. 256, 109th Cong., 1st Sess. (2005) p. 87, 90, 104; available at 2005 U.S.C.C.A.N. 88, at 154, 156, 168.)

# § 1126. Acceptance of plan

(a) The holder of a claim or interest allowed under section 502 of this title may accept or reject a plan. If the United States is a creditor or equity security holder, the Secretary of the Treasury may accept or reject the plan on behalf of the United States.

(b) For the purposes of subsections (c) and (d) of this section, a holder of a claim or interest that has accepted or rejected the plan before the commencement of the case under this title is deemed to have accepted or rejected such plan, as the case may be, if—

(1) the solicitation of such acceptance or rejection was in compliance with any applicable nonbankruptcy law, rule, or regulation governing the adequacy of disclosure in connection with such solicitation; or

(2) if there is not any such law, rule, or regulation, such acceptance or rejection was solicited after disclosure to such holder of adequate information, as defined in section 1125(a) of this title.

(c) A class of claims has accepted a plan if such plan has been accepted by creditors, other than any entity designated under subsection (e) of this section, that hold at least two-thirds in amount and more than one-half in number of the allowed claims of such class held by creditors, other than any entity designated under subsection (e) of this section, that have accepted or rejected such plan.

(d) A class of interests has accepted a plan if such plan has been accepted by holders of such interests, other than any entity designated under subsection (e) of this section, that hold at least two-thirds in amount of the allowed interests of such class held by holders of such interests, other than any entity designated under subsection (e) of this section, that have accepted or rejected such plan.

(e) On request of a party in interest, and after notice and a hearing, the court may designate any entity whose acceptance or rejection of such plan was not in good faith, or was not solicited or procured in good faith or in accordance with the provisions of this title.

(f) Notwithstanding any other provision of this section, a class that is not impaired under a plan, and each holder of a claim or interest of such class, are conclusively presumed to have accepted the plan, and solicitation of acceptances with respect to such class from the holders of claims or interests of such class is not required.

(g) Notwithstanding any other provision of this section, a class is deemed not to have accepted a plan if such plan provides that the claims or interests of such class do not entitle the holders of such claims or interests to receive or retain any property under the plan on account of such claims or interests.

## § 1127. Modification of plan

(a) The proponent of a plan may modify such plan at any time before confirmation, but may not modify such plan so that such plan as modified fails to meet the requirements of sections 1122 and 1123 of this title. After the proponent of a plan files a modification of such plan with the court, the plan as modified becomes the plan.

(b) The proponent of a plan or the reorganized debtor may modify such plan at any time after confirmation of such plan and before substantial consummation of such plan, but may not modify such plan so that such plan as modified fails to meet the requirements of sections 1122 and 1123 of this title. Such plan as modified under this subsection becomes the plan only if circumstances warrant such modification and the court, after notice and a hearing, confirms such plan as modified, under section 1129 of this title.

(c) The proponent of a modification shall comply with section 1125 of this title with respect to the plan as modified.

(d) Any holder of a claim or interest that has accepted or rejected a plan is deemed to have accepted or rejected, as the case may be, such plan as modified, unless, within the time fixed by the court, such holder changes such holder's previous acceptance or rejection.

*(e) If the debtor is an individual, the plan may be modified at any*

*time after confirmation of the plan but before the completion of payments under the plan, whether or not the plan has been substantially consummated, upon request of the debtor, the trustee, the United States trustee, or the holder of an allowed unsecured claim, to—*

*(1) increase or reduce the amount of payments on claims of a particular class provided for by the plan;*

*(2) extend or reduce the time period for such payments; or*

*(3) alter the amount of the distribution to a creditor whose claim is provided for by the plan to the extent necessary to take account of any payment of such claim made other than under the plan.*

*(f) (1) Sections 1121 through 1128 and the requirements of section 1129 apply to any modification under subsection (a).*

*(2) The plan, as modified, shall become the plan only after there has been disclosure under section 1125 as the court may direct, notice and a hearing, and such modification is approved.*

**Section 1127**

(April 20, 2005, P. L. 109-8, Title III, § 321(e), 119 Stat. 23)

## HISTORY: ANCILLARY LAWS AND DIRECTIVES

**Amendments:**

**2005**. Act April 20, 2005, added new subsections (e) and (f).

**Other provisions:**

**Effective date and application of Act April 20, 2005.**

Act April 20, 2005, Pub.L. 109-8, Title XV, § 1501, 119 Stat. 23, is generally effective 180 days after enactment [April 20, 2005].

**Abridged Legislative History**

Section 321(c) amends Bankruptcy Code section 1129(a) to include an additional requirement for confirmation in a chapter 11 case of an individual debtor upon objection to confirmation by a holder of an allowed unsecured claim. (H. Report No. 109-31 to accompany S. 256, 109th Cong., 1st Sess. (2005) p. 81; available at 2005 U.S.C.C. A.N. 88, at 147–48.)

# § 1128. Confirmation hearing

(a) After notice, the court shall hold a hearing on confirmation of a plan.

(b) A party in interest may object to confirmation of a plan.

# § 1129. Confirmation of plan

(a) The court shall confirm a plan only if all of the following requirements are met:

(1) The plan complies with the applicable provisions of this title.

(2) The proponent of the plan complies with the applicable provisions of this title.

(3) The plan has been proposed in good faith and not by any means forbidden by law.

(4) Any payment made or to be made by the proponent, by the debtor, or by a person issuing securities or acquiring property under the plan, for services or for costs and expenses in or in connection

with the case, or in connection with the plan and incident to the case, has been approved by, or is subject to the approval of, the court as reasonable.

(5) (A) (i) The proponent of the plan has disclosed the identity and affiliations of any individual proposed to serve, after confirmation of the plan, as a director, officer, or voting trustee of the debtor, an affiliate of the debtor participating in a joint plan with the debtor, or a successor to the debtor under the plan; and

(ii) the appointment to, or continuance in, such office of such individual, is consistent with the interests of creditors and equity security holders and with public policy; and

(B) the proponent of the plan has disclosed the identity of any insider that will be employed or retained by the reorganized debtor, and the nature of any compensation for such insider.

(6) Any governmental regulatory commission with jurisdiction, after confirmation of the plan, over the rates of the debtor has approved any rate change provided for in the plan, or such rate change is expressly conditioned on such approval.

(7) With respect to each impaired class of claims or interests—

(A) each holder of a claim or interest of such class—

(i) has accepted the plan; or

(ii) will receive or retain under the plan on account of such claim or interest property of a value, as of the effective date of the plan, that is not less than the amount that such holder would so receive or retain if the debtor were liquidated under chapter 7 of this title on such date; or

(B) if section 1111(b)(2) of this title applies to the claims of such class, each holder of a claim of such class will receive or retain under the plan on account of such claim property of a value, as of the effective date of the plan, that is not less than the value of such holder's interest in the estate's interest in the property that secures such claims.

(8) With respect to each class of claims or interests—

(A) such class has accepted the plan; or

(B) such class is not impaired under the plan.

(9) Except to the extent that the holder of a particular claim has agreed to a different treatment of such claim, the plan provides that—

(A) with respect to a claim of a kind specified in section 507(a)(*2*~~1~~) or 507(a)(*3*~~2~~) of this title, on the effective date of the plan, the holder of such claim will receive on account of such claim cash equal to the allowed amount of such claim;

(B) with respect to a class of claims of a kind specified in section 507(a)(*1*~~3~~), 507(a)(4), 507(a)(5), 507(a)(6), or 507(a)(7) of this title, each holder of a claim of such class will receive—

(i) if such class has accepted the plan, deferred cash payments of a value, as of the effective date of the plan, equal to the allowed amount of such claim; or

(ii) if such class has not accepted the plan, cash on the effective date of the plan equal to the allowed amount of such claim; ~~and~~

(C) with respect to a claim of a kind specified in section 507(a)(8) of this title, the holder of such claim will receive on account of such claim ~~deferred cash payments, over a period not exceeding six years after the date of assessment of such claim, of a value, as of the effective date of the plan, equal to the allowed amount of such claim.~~ *regular installment payments in cash—*

*(i) of a total value, as of the effective date of the plan, equal to the allowed amount of such claim;*

*(ii) over a period ending not later than 5 years after the date of the order for relief under section 301, 302, or 303; and*

*(iii) in a manner not less favorable than the most favored nonpriority unsecured claim provided for by the plan (other than cash payments made to a class of creditors under section 1122(b)); and*

*(D) with respect to a secured claim which would otherwise meet the description of an unsecured claim of a governmental unit under section 507(a)(8), but for the secured status of that claim, the holder of that claim will receive on account of that claim, cash payments, in the same manner and over the same period, as prescribed in subparagraph (C).*

(10) If a class of claims is impaired under the plan, at least one class of claims that is impaired under the plan has accepted the plan, determined without including any acceptance of the plan by any insider.

(11) Confirmation of the plan is not likely to be followed by the liquidation, or the need for further financial reorganization, of the debtor or any successor to the debtor under the plan, unless such liquidation or reorganization is proposed in the plan.

(12) All fees payable under section 1930 of title 28, as determined by the court at the hearing on confirmation of the plan, have been paid or the plan provides for the payment of all such fees on the effective date of the plan.

(13) The plan provides for the continuation after its effective date of payment of all retiree benefits, as that term is defined in section 1114 of this title, at the level established pursuant to subsection (e)(1)(B) or (g) of section 1114 of this title, at any time prior to confirmation of the plan, for the duration of the period the debtor has obligated itself to provide such benefits.

*(14) If the debtor is required by a judicial or administrative order, or by statute, to pay a domestic support obligation, the debtor has paid all amounts payable under such order or such statute for such obligation that first become payable after the date of the filing of the petition.*

*(15) In a case in which the debtor is an individual and in which the holder of an allowed unsecured claim objects to the confirmation of the plan—*

*(A) the value, as of the effective date of the plan, of the property to be distributed under the plan on account of such claim is not less than the amount of such claim; or*

*(B) the value of the property to be distributed under the plan is not less than the projected disposable income of the debtor (as defined in section 1325(b)(2)) to be received during the 5-year period beginning on the date that the first payment is due under the plan, or during the period for which the plan provides payments, whichever is longer.*

*(16) All transfers of property of the plan shall be made in accordance with any applicable provisions of nonbankruptcy law that govern the transfer of property by a corporation or trust that is not a moneyed, business, or commercial corporation or trust.*

(b) (1) Notwithstanding section 510(a) of this title, if all of the applicable requirements of subsection (a) of this section other than paragraph (8) are met with respect to a plan, the court, on request of the proponent of the plan, shall confirm the plan notwithstanding the requirements of such paragraph if the plan does not discriminate unfairly, and is fair and equitable, with respect to each class of claims or interests that is impaired under, and has not accepted, the plan.

(2) For the purpose of this subsection, the condition that a plan be fair and equitable with respect to a class includes the following requirements:

(A) With respect to a class of secured claims, the plan provides—

(i) (I) that the holders of such claims retain the liens securing such claims, whether the property subject to such liens is retained by the debtor or transferred to another entity, to the extent of the allowed amount of such claims; and

(II) that each holder of a claim of such class receive on account of such claim deferred cash payments totaling at least the allowed amount of such claim, of a value, as of the effective date of the plan, of at least the value of such holder's interest in the estate's interest in such property;

(ii) for the sale, subject to section 363(k) of this title, of any property that is subject to the liens securing such claims, free and clear of such liens, with such liens to attach to the proceeds of such sale, and the treatment of such liens on proceeds under clause (i) or (iii) of this subparagraph; or

(iii) for the realization by such holders of the indubitable equivalent of such claims.

(B) With respect to a class of unsecured claims—

(i) the plan provides that each holder of a claim of such class receive or retain on account of such claim property of a value, as of the effective date of the plan, equal to the allowed amount of such claim; or

(ii) the holder of any claim or interest that is junior to the claims of such class will not receive or retain under the plan on account of such junior claim or interest any property, *except that in a case in which the debtor is an individual, the debtor may retain property included in the estate under section 1115, subject to the requirements of subsection (a)(14) of this section.*

(C) With respect to a class of interests—

(i) the plan provides that each holder of an interest of such class receive or retain on account of such interest property of a value, as of the effective date of the plan, equal to the greatest of the allowed amount of any fixed liquidation preference to which such holder is entitled, any fixed redemption price to which such holder is entitled, or the value of such interest; or

(ii) the holder of any interest that is junior to the interests of such class will not receive or retain under the plan on account of such junior interest any property.

(c) Notwithstanding subsections (a) and (b) of this section and except as provided in section 1127(b) of this title, the court may confirm only one plan, unless the order of confirmation in the case has been revoked under section 1144 of this title. If the requirements of subsections (a) and (b) of this section are met with respect to more than one plan, the court shall consider the preferences of creditors and equity security holders in determining which plan to confirm.

(d) Notwithstanding any other provision of this section, on request of a party in interest that is a governmental unit, the court may not confirm a plan if the principal purpose of the plan is the avoidance of taxes or the avoidance of the application of section 5 of the Securities Act of 1933. In any hearing under this subsection, the governmental unit has the burden of proof on the issue of avoidance.

*(e) In a small business case, the court shall confirm a plan that complies with the applicable provisions of this title and that is filed in accordance with section 1121(e) not later than 45 days after the plan is filed unless the time for confirmation is extended in accordance with section 1121(e)(3).*

**Section 1129**

(April 20, 2005, P. L. 109-8, Title II, § 213(1); Title III, §§ 321(c)(1), 321(c)(2); Title IV, § 438; Title VII, § 710; Title XII, § 1221(d); Title XV, § 1502(a)(8), 119 Stat. 23)

## HISTORY: ANCILLARY LAWS AND DIRECTIVES

**Amendments:**

**2005**. Act April 20, 2005, revised subsection (a)(9)(C) by deleting the former language, "deferred cash payments . . .," and inserting "regular installment payments in cash—(i) of a total value, as of the effective date of the plan, equal to the allowed amount of such claim; (ii) over a period ending not later than 5 years after the date of the order for relief under section 301, 302, or 303; and (iii) in a manner not less favorable than the most favored nonpriority unsecured claim provided for by the plan (other than cash payments made to a class of creditors under section 1122(b)," added subsections (a)(9)(D) and (a)(14) through (16), added an exception to (b)(2)(B)(ii) "that in a case in which the debtor is an individual, the debtor may retain property included in the estate under section 1115, subject to the requirements of subsection (a)(14) of this section," and added a new subsection (e)

**Other provisions:**

**Effective date and application of Act April 20, 2005.**

Act April 20, 2005, Pub.L. 109-8, Title XV, § 1501, 119 Stat. 23, is generally effective 180 days after enactment [April 20, 2005]. Amendment by Pub. L. 109-8 to add § 1129 (a)(16) applies "to cases pending on the date of enactment or to cases filed after such date," but "a court may not confirm a plan without considering whether this provision would substantially affect the rights of a party in interest who first acquired rights with respect to the debtor postpetition." See § 1221(d) of Pub. L. 109-8.

**Abridged Legislative History**

Sec. 1501. Effective Date; Application of Amendments. Subsection (a) of section 1501 of the Act provides that the Act shall take effect 180 days after the date of enactment, unless otherwise specified in this Act. Section 1501(b) provides that the amendments made by this Act shall not apply to cases commenced under the Bankruptcy Code before the Act's effective date, unless otherwise specified in this Act. The provision specifies that the amendments made by sections 308, 322 and 330 shall apply to cases commenced on or after the date of enactment of this Act. (H. Report No. 109-31 to accompany S. 256, 109th Cong., 1st Sess. (2005) p. 60, 80, 92, 102, 145, 155; available at 2005 U.S.C.C.A.N. 88, at 129, 147, 157, 166, 203–04, 212.)

# Subchapter III——Postconfirmation Matters

## § 1141. Effect of confirmation

(a) Except as provided in subsections (d)(2) and (d)(3) of this section, the provisions of a confirmed plan bind the debtor, any entity issuing securities under the plan, any entity acquiring property under the plan, and any creditor, equity security holder, or general partner in the debtor, whether or not the claim or interest of such creditor, equity security holder, or general partner is impaired under the plan and whether or not such creditor, equity security holder, or general partner has accepted the plan.

(b) Except as otherwise provided in the plan or the order confirming the plan, the confirmation of a plan vests all of the property of the estate in the debtor.

(c) Except as provided in subsections (d)(2) and (d)(3) of this section and except as otherwise provided in the plan or in the order confirming the plan, after confirmation of a plan, the property dealt with by the plan is free and clear of all claims and interests of creditors, equity security holders, and of general partners in the debtor.

(d) (1) Except as otherwise provided in this subsection, in the plan, or in the order confirming the plan, the confirmation of a plan—

(A) discharges the debtor from any debt that arose before the date of such confirmation, and any debt of a kind specified in section 502(g), 502(h), or 502(i) of this title, whether or not—

(i) a proof of the claim based on such debt is filed or deemed filed under section 501 of this title;

(ii) such claim is allowed under section 502 of this title; or

(iii) the holder of such claim has accepted the plan; and

(B) terminates all rights and interests of equity security holders and general partners provided for by the plan.

(2~~)~~ ~~The confirmation of a plan does not discharge an individual debtor~~*A discharge under this chapter does not discharge a debtor who is an individual* from any debt excepted from discharge under section 523 of this title.

(3) The confirmation of a plan does not discharge a debtor if—

(A) the plan provides for the liquidation of all or substantially all of the property of the estate;

(B) the debtor does not engage in business after consummation of the plan; and

(C) the debtor would be denied a discharge under section 727(a) of this title if the case were a case under chapter 7 of this title.

(4) The court may approve a written waiver of discharge executed by the debtor after the order for relief under this chapter.

*(5) In a case in which the debtor is an individual—*

*(A) unless after notice and a hearing the court orders otherwise for cause, confirmation of the plan does not discharge any debt provided for in the plan until the court grants a discharge on completion of all payments under the plan;*

*(B) at any time after the confirmation of the plan, and after notice and a hearing, the court may grant a discharge to the debtor who has not completed payments under the plan if—*

*(i) the value, as of the effective date of the plan, of property actually distributed under the plan on account of each allowed unsecured claim is not less than the amount that would have been paid on such claim if the estate of the debtor had been liquidated under chapter 7 on such date; and*

*(ii) modification of the plan under section 1127 is not practicable; and*

*(C) unless after notice and a hearing held not more than 10 days before the date of the entry of the order granting the discharge, the court finds that there is no reasonable cause to believe that—*

*(i) section 522(q)(1) may be applicable to the debtor; and*

*(ii) there is pending any proceeding in which the debtor may be found guilty of a felony of the kind described in section 522(q)(1)(A) or liable for a debt of the kind described in section 522(q)(1)(B).*

*(6) Notwithstanding paragraph (1), the confirmation of a plan does not discharge a debtor that is a corporation from any debt—*

*(A) of a kind specified in paragraph (2)(A) or (2)(B) of section 523(a) that is owed to a domestic governmental unit, or owed to a person as the result of an action filed under subchapter III of chapter 37 of title 31 or any similar State statute; or*

*(B) for a tax or customs duty with respect to which the debtor—*

*(i) made a fraudulent return; or*

*(ii) willfully attempted in any manner to evade or to defeat such tax or such customs duty.*

**Section 1141**

(April 20, 2005, P. L. 109-8, Title III, § 321(d), 330(b); Title VII, § 708; Title XV, § 1501(b), 119 Stat. 23)

## HISTORY: ANCILLARY LAWS AND DIRECTIVES

**Amendments:**

**2005**. Act April 20, 2005, replaced "The confirmation of a plan does not discharge an individual debtor," with "A discharge under this chapter does not discharge a debtor who is an individual," in subsection (d)(2) and added new subsections (d)(5) and (6).

**Other provisions:**

**Effective date and application of Act April 20, 2005.**

Act April 20, 2005, Pub.L. 109-8, Title XV, § 1501, 119 Stat. 23, is generally effective 180 days after enactment [April 20, 2005]. Amendment by Pub. L. 109-8 to add § 1141 (d)(5)(C) "shall apply with respect to cases commenced under title 11, United States Code, on or after the enactment of this Act [April 20, 2005]." See § 1501(b)(2) of Pub.L. 109-8.

**Abridged Legislative History**

Sec. 708. No Discharge of Fraudulent Taxes in Chapter 11. Under current law, the confirmation of a chapter 11 plan discharges a corporate debtor from most debts. Section 708 amends section 1141(d) of the Bankruptcy Code to except from discharge in a corporate chapter 11 case a debt specified in subsections 523(a)(2)(A) or (B) of the Bankruptcy Code owed to a domestic governmental unit. In addition, it excepts from discharge a debt owed to a person as the result of an action filed under subchapter III of chapter 37 of title 31 of the United States Code or any similar state statute. Section 708 excepts from discharge a debt for a tax or customs duty with respect to which the debtor made a fraudulent tax return or willfully attempted in any manner to evade or defeat such tax.

Section 1501(b) provides that the amendments made by this Act shall not apply to cases commenced under the Bankruptcy Code before the Act's effective date, unless otherwise specified in this Act. The provision specifies that the amendments made by sections 308, 322 and 330 shall apply to cases commenced on or after the date of enactment of this Act.

(H. Report No. 109-31 to accompany S. 256, 109th Cong., 1st Sess. (2005) p. 80–1, 84, 102, 155; available at 2005 U.S.C.C.A.N. 88, at 147, 150, 166, 212.)

# § 1142. Implementation of plan

(a) Notwithstanding any otherwise applicable nonbankruptcy law, rule, or regulation relating to financial condition, the debtor and any entity organized or to be organized for the purpose of carrying out the plan shall carry out the plan and shall comply with any orders of the court.

(b) The court may direct the debtor and any other necessary party to execute or deliver or to join in the execution or delivery of any instrument required to effect a transfer of property dealt with by a confirmed plan, and to perform any other act, including the satisfaction of any lien, that is necessary for the consummation of the plan.

# § 1143. Distribution

If a plan requires presentment or surrender of a security or the performance of any other act as a condition to participation in distribution under the plan, such action shall be taken not later than five years after the date of the entry of the order of confirmation. Any entity that has not within such time presented or surrendered such entity's security or taken any such other action that the plan requires may not participate in distribution under the plan.

## § 1144. Revocation of an order of confirmation

On request of a party in interest at any time before 180 days after the date of the entry of the order of confirmation, and after notice and a hearing, the court may revoke such order if and only if such order was procured by fraud. An order under this section revoking an order of confirmation shall—

(1) contain such provisions as are necessary to protect any entity acquiring rights in good faith reliance on the order of confirmation; and

(2) revoke the discharge of the debtor.

## § 1145. Exemption from securities laws

(a) Except with respect to an entity that is an underwriter as defined in subsection (b) of this section, section 5 of the Securities Act of 1933 and any State or local law requiring registration for offer or sale of a security or registration or licensing of an issuer of, underwriter of, or broker or dealer in, a security do not apply to—

(1) the offer or sale under a plan of a security of the debtor, of an affiliate participating in a joint plan with the debtor, or of a successor to the debtor under the plan—

(A) in exchange for a claim against, an interest in, or a claim for an administrative expense in the case concerning, the debtor or such affiliate; or

(B) principally in such exchange and partly for cash or property;

(2) the offer of a security through any warrant, option, right to subscribe, or conversion privilege that was sold in the manner specified in paragraph (1) of this subsection, or the sale of a security upon the exercise of such a warrant, option, right, or privilege;

(3) the offer or sale, other than under a plan, of a security of an issuer other than the debtor or an affiliate, if—

(A) such security was owned by the debtor on the date of the filing of the petition;

(B) the issuer of such security is—

(i) required to file reports under section 13 or 15(d) of the Securities Exchange Act of 1934; and

(ii) in compliance with the disclosure and reporting provision of such applicable section; and

(C) such offer or sale is of securities that do not exceed—

(i) during the two-year period immediately following the date of the filing of the petition, four percent of the securities of such class outstanding on such date; and

(ii) during any 180-day period following such two-year period, one percent of the securities outstanding at the beginning of such 180-day period; or

(4) a transaction by a stockbroker in a security that is executed after a transaction of a kind specified in paragraph (1) or (2) of this subsection in such security and before the expiration of 40 days after the first date on which such security was bona fide offered to the public by the issuer or by or through an underwriter, if such stockbroker provides, at the time of or before such transaction by such stockbroker, a disclosure statement approved under section 1125 of this title, and, if the court orders, information supplementing such disclosure statement.

(b) (1) Except as provided in paragraph (2) of this subsection and except with respect to ordinary trading transactions of an entity that is not an issuer, an entity is an underwriter under section 2(11) of the Securities Act of 1933, if such entity—

(A) purchases a claim against, interest in, or claim for an administrative expense in the case concerning, the debtor, if such purchase is with a view to distribution of any security received or to be received in exchange for such a claim or interest;

(B) offers to sell securities offered or sold under the plan for the holders of such securities;

(C) offers to buy securities offered or sold under the plan from the holders of such securities, if such offer to buy is—

(i) with a view to distribution of such securities; and

(ii) under an agreement made in connection with the plan, with the consummation of the plan, or with the offer or sale of securities under the plan; or

(D) is an issuer, as used in such section 2(11), with respect to such securities.

(2) An entity is not an underwriter under section 2(11) of the Securities Act of 1933 or under paragraph (1) of this subsection with respect to an agreement that provides only for—

(A) (i) the matching or combining of fractional interests in securities offered or sold under the plan into whole interests; or

(ii) the purchase or sale of such fractional interests from or to entities receiving such fractional interests under the plan; or

(B) the purchase or sale for such entities of such fractional or whole interests as are necessary to adjust for any remaining fractional interests after such matching.

(3) An entity other than an entity of the kind specified in paragraph (1) of this subsection is not an underwriter under section 2(11) of the Securities Act of 1933 with respect to any securities offered or sold to such entity in the manner specified in subsection (a)(1) of this section.

(c) An offer or sale of securities of the kind and in the manner specified under subsection (a)(1) of this section is deemed to be a public offering.

(d) The Trust Indenture Act of 1939 does not apply to a note issued under the plan that matures not later than one year after the effective date of the plan.

## § 1146. Special tax provisions

~~(a) For the purposes of any State or local law imposing a tax on or measured by income, the taxable period of a debtor that is an individual shall terminate on the date of the order for relief under this chapter, unless the case was converted under section 706 of this title.~~

~~(b) The trustee shall make a State or local tax return of income for the estate of an individual debtor in a case under this chapter for each taxable period after the order for relief under this chapter during which the case is pending.~~

(*a* ~~c~~) The issuance, transfer, or exchange of a security, or the making or delivery of an instrument of transfer under a plan confirmed under section 1129 of this title, may not be taxed under any law imposing a stamp tax or similar tax.

(*b* ~~d~~) The court may authorize the proponent of a plan to request a determination, limited to questions of law, by a State or local governmental unit charged with responsibility for collection or determination of a tax on or measured by income, of the tax effects, under section 346 of this title and under the law imposing such tax, of the plan. In the event of an actual controversy, the court may declare such effects after the earlier of—

(1) the date on which such governmental unit responds to the request under this subsection; or

(2) 270 days after such request.

**Section 1146**

(April 20, 2005, P. L. 109-8, Title VII, § 719(b)(3), 119 Stat. 23)

### HISTORY: ANCILLARY LAWS AND DIRECTIVES

**Amendments:**

**2005**. Act April 20, 2005, entirely replaced former § 1146.

**Other provisions:**

**Effective date and application of Act April 20, 2005.**

Act April 20, 2005, Pub.L. 109-8, Title XV, § 1501, 119 Stat. 23, is generally effective 180 days after enactment [April 20, 2005].

**Abridged Legislative History**

Sec. 719. Special Provisions Related to the Treatment of State and Local Taxes. Section 719 of the Act conforms state and local income tax administrative issues to the Internal Revenue Code. (H. Report No. 109-31 to accompany S. 256, 109th Cong., 1st Sess. (2005) p. 105; available at 2005 U.S.C.C.A.N. 88, at 168.)

# Subchapter IV—Railroad Reorganization

## § 1161. Inapplicability of other sections

Sections 341, 343, 1102(a)(1), 1104, 1105, 1107, 1129(a)(7), and 1129(c) of this title do not apply in a case concerning a railroad.

## § 1162. Definition

In this subchapter, "Board" means the "Surface Transportation Board".

## § 1163. Appointment of trustee

As soon as practicable after the order for relief the Secretary of Transportation shall submit a list of five disinterested persons that are qualified and willing to serve as trustees in the case. The United States trustee shall appoint one of such persons to serve as trustee in the case.

## § 1164. Right to be heard

The Board, the Department of Transportation, and any State or local commission having regulatory jurisdiction over the debtor may raise and may appear and be heard on any issue in a case under this chapter, but may not appeal from any judgment, order, or decree entered in the case.

## § 1165. Protection of the public interest

In applying sections 1166, 1167, 1169, 1170, 1171, 1172, 1173, and 1174 of this title, the court and the trustee shall consider the public interest in addition to the interests of the debtor, creditors, and equity security holders.

## § 1166. Effect of subtitle IV of title 49 and of Federal, State, or local regulations

Except with respect to abandonment under section 1170 of this title, or merger, modification of the financial structure of the debtor, or issuance or sale of securities under a plan, the trustee and the debtor are subject to the provisions of subtitle IV of title 49 that are applicable to railroads, and the trustee is subject to orders of any Federal, State, or local regulatory body to the same extent as the debtor would be if a petition commencing the case under this chapter had not been filed, but—

(1) any such order that would require the expenditure, or the incurring of an obligation for the expenditure, of money from the estate is not effective unless approved by the court; and

(2) the provisions of this chapter are subject to section 601(b) of the Regional Rail Reorganization Act of 1973.

## § 1167. Collective bargaining agreements

Notwithstanding section 365 of this title, neither the court nor the trustee may change the wages or working conditions of employees of the debtor established by a collective bargaining agreement that is subject to the Railway Labor Act except in accordance with section 6 of such Act.

## § 1168. Rolling stock equipment

(a) (1) The right of a secured party with a security interest in or of a lessor or conditional vendor of equipment described in paragraph (2) to take possession of such equipment in compliance with an equipment security agreement, lease, or conditional sale contract, and to enforce any of its other rights or remedies under such security agreement, lease, or conditional sale contract, to sell, lease, or otherwise retain or dispose of such equipment, is not limited or otherwise affected by any other provision of this title or by any power of the court, except that right to take possession and enforce those other rights and remedies shall be subject to section 362, if—(A) before the date that is 60 days after the date of commencement of a case under this chapter, the trustee, subject to the court's approval, agrees to perform all obligations of the debtor under such security agreement, lease, or conditional sale contract; and

(B) any default, other than a default of a kind described in section 365(b)(2), under such security agreement, lease, or conditional sale contract—

(i) that occurs before the date of commencement of the case and is an event of default therewith is cured before the expiration of such 60-day period;

(ii) that occurs or becomes an event of default after the date of commencement of the case and before the expiration of such 60-day period is cured before the later of—

(I) the date that is 30 days after the date of the default or event of default; or

(II) the expiration of such 60-day period; and

(iii) that occurs on or after the expiration of such 60-day period is cured in accordance with the terms of such security agreement, lease, or conditional sale contract, if cure is permitted under that agreement, lease, or conditional sale contract.

(2) The equipment described in this paragraph—

(A) is rolling stock equipment or accessories used on equipment, including superstructures or racks, that is subject to a security interest granted by, leased to, or conditionally sold to a debtor; and

(B) includes all records and documents relating to such equipment that are required, under the terms of the security agreement, lease, or conditional sale contract, that is to be surrendered or returned by the debtor in connection with the surrender or return of such equipment.

(3) Paragraph (1) applies to a secured party, lessor, or conditional vendor acting in its own behalf or acting as trustee or otherwise in behalf of another party.

(b) The trustee and the secured party, lessor, or conditional vendor whose right to take possession is protected under subsection (a) may agree, subject to the court's approval, to extend the 60-day period specified in subsection (a)(1).

(c) (1) In any case under this chapter, the trustee shall immediately surrender and return to a secured party, lessor, or conditional vendor, described in subsection (a)(1), equipment described in subsection (a)(2), if at any time after the date of commencement of the case under this chapter such secured party, lessor, or conditional vendor is entitled pursuant to subsection (a)(1) to take possession of such equipment and makes a written demand for such possession of the trustee.

(2) At such time as the trustee is required under paragraph (1) to surrender and return equipment described in subsection (a)(2), any lease of such equipment, and any security agreement or conditional sale contract relating to such equipment, if such security agreement or conditional sale contract is an executory contract, shall be deemed rejected.

(d) With respect to equipment first placed in service on or prior to October 22, 1994, for purposes of this section—(1) the term "lease" includes any written agreement with respect to which the lessor and the debtor, as lessee, have expressed in the agreement or in a substantially contemporaneous writing that the agreement is to be treated as a lease for Federal income tax purposes; and

(2) the term "security interest" means a purchase-money equipment security interest.

(e) With respect to equipment first placed in service after October 22, 1994, for purposes of this section, the term "rolling stock equipment" includes rolling stock equipment that is substantially rebuilt and accessories used on such equipment.

## § 1169. Effect of rejection of lease of railroad line

(a) Except as provided in subsection (b) of this section, if a lease of a line of railroad under which the debtor is the lessee is rejected under section 365 of this title, and if the trustee, within such time as the court fixes, and with the court's approval, elects not to operate the leased line, the lessor under such lease, after such approval, shall operate the line.

(b) If operation of such line by such lessor is impracticable or contrary to the public interest, the court, on request of such lessor, and after notice and a hearing, shall order the trustee to continue operation of such line for the account of such lessor until abandonment is ordered under section 1170 of this title, or until such operation is otherwise lawfully terminated, whichever occurs first.

(c) During any such operation, such lessor is deemed a carrier subject to the provisions of subtitle IV of title 49 that are applicable to railroads.

## § 1170. Abandonment of railroad line

(a) The court, after notice and a hearing, may authorize the abandonment of all or a portion of a railroad line if such abandonment is—

(1) (A) in the best interest of the estate; or

(B) essential to the formulation of a plan; and

(2) consistent with the public interest.

(b) If, except for the pendency of the case under this chapter, such abandonment would require approval by the Board under a law of the United States, the trustee shall initiate an appropriate application for such abandonment with the Board. The court may fix a time within which the Board shall report to the court on such application.

(c) After the court receives the report of the Board, or the expiration of the time fixed under subsection (b) of this section, whichever occurs first, the court may authorize such abandonment, after notice to the Board, the Secretary of Transportation, the trustee, any party in interest that has requested notice, any affected shipper or community, and any other entity prescribed by the court, and a hearing.

(d) (1) Enforcement of an order authorizing such abandonment shall be stayed until the time for taking an appeal has expired, or, if an appeal is timely taken, until such order has become final.

(2) If an order authorizing such abandonment is appealed, the court, on request of a party in interest, may authorize suspension of service on a line or a portion of a line pending the determination of such appeal, after notice to the Board, the Secretary of Transportation, the trustee, any party in interest that has requested notice, any affected shipper or community, and any other entity prescribed by the court, and a hearing. An appellant may not obtain a stay of the enforcement of an order authorizing such suspension by the giving of a supersedeas bond or otherwise, during the pendency of such appeal.

(e) (1) In authorizing any abandonment of a railroad line under this section, the court shall require the rail carrier to provide a fair arrangement at least as protective of the interests of employees as that established under section ~~11347~~*11326(a)* of title 49.

(2) Nothing in this subsection shall be deemed to affect the priorities or timing of payment of employee protection which might have existed in the absence of this subsection.

**Section 1170**

(April 20, 2005, P. L. 109-8, Title XII, § 1217, 119 Stat. 23)

## HISTORY: ANCILLARY LAWS AND DIRECTIVES

**Amendments:**

**2005**. Act April 20, 2005, inserted "11326(a)" in subsection (e)(1) instead of "11347."

**Other provisions:**

**Effective date and application of Act April 20, 2005.**

Act April 20, 2005, Pub.L. 109-8, Title XV, § 1501, 119 Stat. 23, is generally effective 180 days after enactment [April 20, 2005].

**Abridged Legislative History**

(H. Report No. 109-31 to accompany S. 256, 109th Cong., 1st Sess. (2005) p. 144; available at 2005 U.S.C.C.A.N. 88, at 203.)

## § 1171. Priority claims

(a) There shall be paid as an administrative expense any claim of an individual or of the personal representative of a deceased individual against the debtor or the estate, for personal injury to or death of such individual arising out of the operation of the debtor or the estate, whether such claim arose before or after the commencement of the case.

(b) Any unsecured claim against the debtor that would have been entitled to priority if a receiver in equity of the property of the debtor had been appointed by a Federal court on the date of the order for relief under this title shall be entitled to the same priority in the case under this chapter.

## § 1172. Contents of plan

(a) In addition to the provisions required or permitted under section 1123 of this title, a plan—

(1) shall specify the extent to and the means by which the debtor's rail service is proposed to be continued, and the extent to which any of the debtor's rail service is proposed to be terminated; and

(2) may include a provision for—

(A) the transfer of any or all of the operating railroad lines of the debtor to another operating railroad; or

(B) abandonment of any railroad line in accordance with section 1170 of this title.

(b) If, except for the pendency of the case under this chapter, transfer of, or operation of or over, any of the debtor's rail lines by an entity other than the debtor or a successor to the debtor under the plan would require approval by the Board under a law of the United States, then a plan may not propose such a transfer or such operation unless the proponent of the plan initiates an appropriate application for such a transfer or such operation with the Board and, within such time as the court may fix, not exceeding 180 days, the Board, with or without a hearing, as the Board may determine, and with or without modification or condition, approves such application, or does not act on such application. Any action or order of the Board approving, modifying, conditioning, or disapproving such application is subject to review by the court only under sections 706(2)(A), 706(2)(B), 706(2)(C), and 706(2)(D) of title 5.

(c) (1) In approving an application under subsection (b) of this section, the Board shall require the rail carrier to provide a fair arrangement at least as protective of the interests of employees as that established under section ~~11347~~*11326(a)* of title 49.

(2) Nothing in this subsection shall be deemed to affect the priorities or timing of payment of employee protection which might have existed in the absence of this subsection.

**Section 1172**

(April 20, 2005, P. L. 109-8, Title XII, § 1218, 119 Stat. 23)

## HISTORY: ANCILLARY LAWS AND DIRECTIVES

**Amendments:**

**2005**. Act April 20, 2005, inserted "11326(a)" in subsection (c)(1) instead of "11347."

**Other provisions:**

**Effective date and application of Act April 20, 2005.**

Act April 20, 2005, Pub.L. 109-8, Title XV, § 1501, 119 Stat. 23, is generally effective 180 days after enactment [April 20, 2005].

**Abridged Legislative History**

(H. Report No. 109-31 to accompany S. 256, 109th Cong., 1st Sess. (2005) p. 144–45; available at 2005 U.S.C.C.A.N. 88, at 203.)

# § 1173. Confirmation of plan

(a) The court shall confirm a plan if—

(1) the applicable requirements of section 1129 of this title have been met;

(2) each creditor or equity security holder will receive or retain under the plan property of a value, as of the effective date of the plan, that is not less than the value of property that each such creditor or equity security holder would so receive or retain if all of the operating railroad lines of the debtor were sold, and the proceeds of such sale, and the other property of the estate, were distributed under chapter 7 of this title on such date;

(3) in light of the debtor's past earnings and the probable prospective earnings of the reorganized debtor, there will be adequate coverage by such prospective earnings of any fixed charges, such as interest on debt, amortization of funded debt, and rent for leased railroads, provided for by the plan; and

(4) the plan is consistent with the public interest.

(b) If the requirements of subsection (a) of this section are met with respect to more than one plan, the court shall confirm the plan that is most likely to maintain adequate rail service in the public interest.

# § 1174. Liquidation

On request of a party in interest and after notice and a hearing, the court may, or, if a plan has not been confirmed under section 1173 of this title before five years after the date of the order for relief, the court shall, order the trustee to cease the debtor's operation and to collect and reduce to money all of the property of the estate in the same manner as if the case were a case under chapter 7 of this title.

# Chapter 12
# —Adjustment of Debts of a Family Farmer *or Fisherman* with Regular Annual Income

## Subchapter I——Officers, Administration, and the Estate



## Subchapter II——The Plan



## Subchapter I——Officers, Administration, and the Estate

### § 1201. Stay of action against codebtor

(a) Except as provided in subsections (b) and (c) of this section, after the order for relief under this chapter, a creditor may not act, or commence or continue any civil action, to collect all or any part of a consumer debt of the debtor from any individual that is liable on such debt with the debtor, or that secured such debt, unless—

(1) such individual became liable on or secured such debt in the ordinary course of such individual's business; or

(2) the case is closed, dismissed, or converted to a case under chapter 7 of this title.

(b) A creditor may present a negotiable instrument, and may give notice of dishonor of such an instrument.

(c) On request of a party in interest and after notice and a hearing, the court shall grant relief from the stay provided by subsection (a) of this section with respect to a creditor, to the extent that—

(1) as between the debtor and the individual protected under subsection (a) of this section, such individual received the consideration for the claim held by such creditor;

(2) the plan filed by the debtor proposes not to pay such claim; or

(3) such creditor's interest would be irreparably harmed by continuation of such stay.

(d) Twenty days after the filing of a request under subsection (c)(2) of this section for relief from the stay provided by subsection (a) of this section, such stay is terminated with respect to the party in interest making such request, unless the debtor or any individual that is liable on such debt with the debtor files and serves upon such party in interest a written objection to the taking of the proposed action.

**Section 1201**

(April 20, 2005, P. L. 109-8, Title X, § 1001, 119 Stat. 23)

## HISTORY: ANCILLARY LAWS AND DIRECTIVES

**Amendments:**

**2005.** Act April 20, 2005(makes no change to 11 USC § 1201 but does make chapter 12 a permanent chapter of the Bankruptcy Code, effective July 1, 2005, as provided by § 1001 of P. L. 109-8). Chapter 12 relief is also extended to family fishermen.

**Other provisions:**

**Effective date and application of amendments made by Act April 20, 2005.** Act April 20, 2005, P.L. 109-8, Title X, § 1001, 119 Stat. 23, provided that chapter 12 becomes a permanent chapter of the Bankruptcy Code, effective July 1, 2005, the date of the most recent expiration of a temporary extension of chapter 12.

**Abridged Legislative History**

(H. Report No. 109-31 to accompany S. 256, 109th Cong., 1st Sess. (2005) p. 136, available at 2005 U.S.C.C.A.N. 88, at 195–96.)

## § 1202. Trustee

(a) If the United States trustee has appointed an individual under section 586(b) of title 28 to serve as standing trustee in cases under this chapter and if such individual qualifies as a trustee under section 322 of this title, then such individual shall serve as trustee in any case filed under this chapter. Otherwise, the United States trustee shall appoint one disinterested person to serve as trustee in the case or the United States trustee may serve as trustee in the case if necessary.

(b) The trustee shall—

(1) perform the duties specified in sections 704(2), 704(3), 704(5), 704(6), 704(7), and 704(9) of this title;

(2) perform the duties specified in section 1106(a)(3) and 1106(a)(4) of this title if the court, for cause and on request of a party in interest, the trustee, or the United States trustee, so orders;

(3) appear and be heard at any hearing that concerns—

(A) the value of property subject to a lien;

(B) confirmation of a plan;

(C) modification of the plan after confirmation; or

(D) the sale of property of the estate;

(4) ensure that the debtor commences making timely payments required by a confirmed plan; ~~and~~

(5) if the debtor ceases to be a debtor in possession, perform the duties specified in sections 704(8), 1106(a)(1), 1106(a)(2), 1106(a)(6), 1106(a)(7), and 1203~~.~~*; and*

*(6) if with respect to the debtor there is a claim for a domestic support obligation, provide the applicable notice specified in subsection (c).*

*(c) (1) In a case described in subsection (b)(6) to which subsection (b)(6) applies, the trustee shall—*

*(A) (i) provide written notice to the holder of the claim described in subsection (b)(6) of such claim and of the right of such holder to use the services of the State child support enforcement agency established under sections 464 and 466 of the Social Security Act for the State in which such holder resides, for assistance in collecting child support during and after the case under this title; and*

*(ii) include in the notice provided under clause (i) the address and telephone number of such State child support enforcement agency;*

*(B) (i) provide written notice to such State child support enforcement agency of such claim; and*

*(ii) include in the notice provided under clause (i) the name, address, and telephone number of such holder; and*

*(C) at such time as the debtor is granted a discharge under section 1228, provide written notice to such holder and to such State child support enforcement agency of—*

*(i) the granting of the discharge;*

*(ii) the last recent known address of the debtor;*

*(iii) the last recent known name and address of the debtor's employer; and*

*(iv) the name of each creditor that holds a claim that—*

*(I) is not discharged under paragraph (2), (4), or (14A) of section 523(a); or*

*(II) was reaffirmed by the debtor under section 524(c).*

*(2) (A) The holder of a claim described in subsection (b)(6) or the State child support enforcement agency of the State in which such holder resides may request from a creditor described in paragraph (1)(C)(iv) the last known address of the debtor.*

*(B) Notwithstanding any other provision of law, a creditor that makes a disclosure of a last known address of a debtor in connec-*

*tion with a request made under subparagraph (A) shall not be liable by reason of making that disclosure.*

**Section 1202**

(April 20, 2005, P. L. 109-8, Title IIB, § 219(c), 119 Stat. 23)

## HISTORY: ANCILLARY LAWS AND DIRECTIVES

**Amendments:**

**2005.** Act April 20, 2005(effective 180 days after enactment of April 20, 2005, as provided by § 1501(a) of P. L. 109-8), adds 11 USC § 1202(b)(6) and (c) to provide duties for the trustee concerning domestic support creditors.

**Other provisions:**

**Effective date and application of amendments made by Act April 20, 2005.** Act April 20, 2005, P.L. 109-8, Title X, § 1001, 119 Stat. 23, provided that chapter 12 becomes a permanent chapter of the Bankruptcy Code, effective July 1, 2005, the date of the most recent expiration of a temporary extension of chapter 12. Such Act, § 1501 (a), provided that the amendments made to this section would otherwise be effective 180 days after enactment on April 20, 2005.

**Abridged Legislative History**

(H. Report No. 109-31 to accompany S. 256, 109th Cong., 1st Sess. (2005) p. 62, available at 2005 U.S.C.C.A.N. 88, at 130.)

# § 1203. Rights and powers of debtor

Subject to such limitations as the court may prescribe, a debtor in possession shall have all the rights, other than the right to compensation under section 330, and powers, and shall perform all the functions and duties, except the duties specified in paragraphs (3) and (4) of section 1106(a), of a trustee serving in a case under chapter 11, including operating the debtor's farm *or commercial fishing operation.*

**Section 1203**

(April 20, 2005, P. L. 109-8, Title X, § 1007(c)(2), 119 Stat. 23)

## HISTORY: ANCILLARY LAWS AND DIRECTIVES

**Amendments:**

**2005.** Act April 20, 2005(effective 180 days after enactment of April 20, 2005, as provided by § 1501(a) of P. L. 109-8), amends 11 USC § 1203 to add "or commercial fishing operation."

**Other provisions:**

**Effective date and application of amendments made by Act April 20, 2005.** Act April 20, 2005, P.L. 109-8, Title X, § 1001, 119 Stat. 23, provided that chapter 12 becomes a permanent chapter of the Bankruptcy Code, effective July 1, 2005, the date of the most recent expiration of a temporary extension of chapter 12. Such Act, § 1501 (a), provided that the amendments made to this section would otherwise be effective 180 days after enactment on April 20, 2005.

**Abridged Legislative History**

(H. Report No. 109-31 to accompany S. 256, 109th Cong., 1st Sess. (2005) p. 138, available at 2005 U.S.C.C.A.N. 88, at 197.)

# § 1204. Removal of debtor as debtor in possession

(a) On request of a party in interest, and after notice and a hearing, the court shall order that the debtor shall not be a debtor in possession for cause, including fraud, dishonesty, incompetence, or gross mismanagement of the affairs of the debtor, either before or after the commencement of the case.

(b) On request of a party in interest, and after notice and a hearing, the court may reinstate the debtor in possession.

## § 1205. Adequate protection

(a) Section 361 does not apply in a case under this chapter.

(b) In a case under this chapter, when adequate protection is required under section 362, 363, or 364 of this title of an interest of an entity in property, such adequate protection may be provided by—

(1) requiring the trustee to make a cash payment or periodic cash payments to such entity, to the extent that the stay under section 362 of this title, use, sale, or lease under section 363 of this title, or any grant of a lien under section 364 of this title results in a decrease in the value of property securing a claim or of an entity's ownership interest in property;

(2) providing to such entity an additional or replacement lien to the extent that such stay, use, sale, lease, or grant results in a decrease in the value of property securing a claim or of an entity's ownership interest in property;

(3) paying to such entity for the use of farmland the reasonable rent customary in the community where the property is located, based upon the rental value, net income, and earning capacity of the property; or

(4) granting such other relief, other than entitling such entity to compensation allowable under section 503(b)(1) of this title as an administrative expense, as will adequately protect the value of property securing a claim or of such entity's ownership interest in property.

## § 1206. Sales free of interests

After notice and a hearing, in addition to the authorization contained in section 363(f), the trustee in a case under this chapter may sell property under section 363(b) and (c) free and clear of any interest in such property of an entity other than the estate ~~if the property is farmland or farm equipment~~*if the property is farmland, farm equipment, or property used to carry out a commercial fishing operation (including a commercial fishing vessel)*, except that the proceeds of such sale shall be subject to such interest.

**Section 1206**

(April 20, 2005, P. L. 109-8, Title X, § 1007(c)(3), 119 Stat. 23)

### HISTORY: ANCILLARY LAWS AND DIRECTIVES

**Amendments:**

**2005.** Act April 20, 2005(effective 180 days after enactment of April 20, 2005, as provided by § 1501(a) of P. L. 109-8), amends 11 USC § 1206 to add references to commercial fishing.

**Other provisions:**

**Effective date and application of amendments made by Act April 20, 2005.** Act April 20, 2005, P.L. 109-8, Title X, § 1001, 119 Stat. 23, provided that chapter 12 becomes a permanent chapter of the Bankruptcy Code, effective July 1, 2005, the date of the most recent expiration of a temporary extension of chapter 12. Such Act, § 1501 (a), provided that the amendments made to this section would otherwise be effective 180 days after enactment on April 20, 2005.

**Abridged Legislative History**

(H. Report No. 109-31 to accompany S. 256, 109th Cong., 1st Sess. (2005) p. 138, available at 2005 U.S.C.C.A.N. 88, at 197.)

## § 1207. Property of the estate

(a) Property of the estate includes, in addition to the property specified in section 541 of this title—

(1) all property of the kind specified in such section that the debtor acquires after the commencement of the case but before the case is closed, dismissed, or converted to a case under chapter 7 of this title, whichever occurs first; and

(2) earnings from services performed by the debtor after the commencement of the case but before the case is closed, dismissed, or converted to a case under chapter 7 of this title, whichever occurs first.

(b) Except as provided in section 1204, a confirmed plan, or an order confirming a plan, the debtor shall remain in possession of all property of the estate.

## § 1208. Conversion or dismissal

(a) The debtor may convert a case under this chapter to a case under chapter 7 of this title at any time. Any waiver of the right to convert under this subsection is unenforceable.

(b) On request of the debtor at any time, if the case has not been converted under section 706 or 1112 of this title, the court shall dismiss a case under this chapter. Any waiver of the right to dismiss under this subsection is unenforceable.

(c) On request of a party in interest, and after notice and a hearing, the court may dismiss a case under this chapter for cause, including—

(1) unreasonable delay, or gross mismanagement, by the debtor that is prejudicial to creditors;

(2) nonpayment of any fees and charges required under chapter 123 of title 28;

(3) failure to file a plan timely under section 1221 of this title;

(4) failure to commence making timely payments required by a confirmed plan;

(5) denial of confirmation of a plan under section 1225 of this title and denial of a request made for additional time for filing another plan or a modification of a plan;

(6) material default by the debtor with respect to a term of a confirmed plan;

(7) revocation of the order of confirmation under section 1230 of this title, and denial of confirmation of a modified plan under section 1229 of this title;

(8) termination of a confirmed plan by reason of the occurrence of a condition specified in the plan; ~~or~~

(9) continuing loss to or diminution of the estate and absence of a reasonable likelihood of rehabilitation~~.~~*; and*

*(10) failure of the debtor to pay any domestic support obligation that first becomes payable after the date of the filing of the petition.*

(d) On request of a party in interest, and after notice and a hearing, the court may dismiss a case under this chapter or convert a case under this chapter to a case under chapter 7 of this title upon a showing that the debtor has committed fraud in connection with the case.

(e) Notwithstanding any other provision of this section, a case may not be converted to a case under another chapter of this title unless the debtor may be a debtor under such chapter.

**Section 1208**

(April 20, 2005, P. L. 109-8, Title IIB, § 213(2), 119 Stat. 23)

## HISTORY: ANCILLARY LAWS AND DIRECTIVES

**Amendments:**

**2005.** Act April 20, 2005(effective 180 days after enactment of April 20, 2005, as provided by § 1501(a) of P. L. 109-8), amends 11 USC § 1208(c) to add a basis for dismissal of the case for the debtor's failure to pay post-petition domestic support obligations.

**Other provisions:**

**Effective date and application of amendments made by Act April 20, 2005.** Act April 20, 2005, P.L. 109-8, Title X, § 1001, 119 Stat. 23, provided that chapter 12 becomes a permanent chapter of the Bankruptcy Code, effective July 1, 2005, the date of the most recent expiration of a temporary extension of chapter 12. Such Act, § 1501 (a), provided that the amendments made to this section would otherwise be effective 180 days after enactment on April 20, 2005.

**Abridged Legislative History**

(H. Report No. 109-31 to accompany S. 256, 109th Cong., 1st Sess. (2005) p. 138, available at 2005 U.S.C.C.A.N. 88, at 197.)

# Subchapter II——The Plan

## § 1221. Filing of plan

The debtor shall file a plan not later than 90 days after the order for relief under this chapter, except that the court may extend such period if the need for an extension is attributable to circumstances for which the debtor should not justly be held accountable.

## § 1222. Contents of plan

(a) The plan shall—

(1) provide for the submission of all or such portion of future earnings or other future income of the debtor to the supervision and control of the trustee as is necessary for the execution of the plan;

(2) ~~provide for the full payment, in deferred cash payments, of all claims entitled to priority under section 507 of this title, unless the holder of a particular claim agrees to a different treatment of such~~

~~claim; and~~ *provide for the full payment, in deferred cash payments, of all claims entitled to priority under section 507, unless—*

*(A) the claim is a claim owed to a governmental unit that arises as a result of the sale, transfer, exchange, or other disposition of any farm asset used in the debtor's farming operation, in which case the claim shall be treated as an unsecured claim that is not entitled to priority under section 507, but the debt shall be treated in such manner only if the debtor receives a discharge; or*

*(B) the holder of a particular claim agrees to a different treatment of that claim;*

(3) if the plan classifies claims and interests, provide the same treatment for each claim or interest within a particular class unless the holder of a particular claim or interest agrees to less favorable treatment~~.~~*; and*

*(4) notwithstanding any other provision of this section, a plan may provide for less than full payment of all amounts owed for a claim entitled to priority under section 507(a)(1)(B) only if the plan provides that all of the debtor's projected disposable income for a 5-year period beginning on the date that the first payment is due under the plan will be applied to make payments under the plan.*

(b) Subject to subsections (a) and (c) of this section, the plan may—

(1) designate a class or classes of unsecured claims, as provided in section 1122 of this title, but may not discriminate unfairly against any class so designated; however, such plan may treat claims for a consumer debt of the debtor if an individual is liable on such consumer debt with the debtor differently than other unsecured claims;

(2) modify the rights of holders of secured claims, or of holders of unsecured claims, or leave unaffected the rights of holders of any class of claims;

(3) provide for the curing or waiving of any default;

(4) provide for payments on any unsecured claim to be made concurrently with payments on any secured claim or any other unsecured claim;

(5) provide for the curing of any default within a reasonable time and maintenance of payments while the case is pending on any unsecured claim or secured claim on which the last payment is due after the date on which the final payment under the plan is due;

(6) subject to section 365 of this title, provide for the assumption, rejection, or assignment of any executory contract or unexpired lease of the debtor not previously rejected under such section;

(7) provide for the payment of all or part of a claim against the debtor from property of the estate or property of the debtor;

(8) provide for the sale of all or any part of the property of the estate or the distribution of all or any part of the property of the estate among those having an interest in such property;

(9) provide for payment of allowed secured claims consistent with

section 1225(a)(5) of this title, over a period exceeding the period permitted under section 1222(c);

(10) provide for the vesting of property of the estate, on confirmation of the plan or at a later time, in the debtor or in any other entity; ~~and~~

*(11) provide for the payment of interest accruing after the date of the filing of the petition on unsecured claims that are nondischargeable under section 1228(a), except that such interest may be paid only to the extent that the debtor has disposable income available to pay such interest after making provision for full payment of all allowed claims; and*

(*12*~~11~~) include any other appropriate provision not inconsistent with this title.

(c) Except as provided in subsections (b)(5) and (b)(9), the plan may not provide for payments over a period that is longer than three years unless the court for cause approves a longer period, but the court may not approve a period that is longer than five years.

(d) Notwithstanding subsection (b)(2) of this section and sections 506(b) and 1225(a)(5) of this title, if it is proposed in a plan to cure a default, the amount nec essary to cure the default, shall be determined in accordance with the underlying agreement and applicable nonbankruptcy law.

**Section 1222**

(April 20, 2005, P. L. 109-8, Title IIB, § 213(3), (4); Title X, § 1003(a), 119 Stat. 23)

## HISTORY: ANCILLARY LAWS AND DIRECTIVES

**Amendments:**

**2005.** Act April 20, 2005(effective upon enactment on April 20, 2005, and applies to cases commenced after such effective date, as provided by § 1003(c) of P. L. 109-8, which provides for the amendment to § 1222(a)), amends 11 USC § 1222(a)(2) of the Bankruptcy Code to add an exception with respect to payments to a governmental unit for a debt entitled to priority under section 507; and (effective 180 days after enactment of April 20, 2005, as provided by § 1501(a) of P. L. 109-8) adds § 1222(a)(4) to permit a chapter 12 debtor to propose a plan paying less than full payment of all amounts owed for a claim entitled to priority under Bankruptcy Code section 507(a)(1)(B) if all of the debtor's projected disposable income for a five-year period is applied to make payments under the plan. The Act also amends § 1222(b) to permit a chapter 12 debtor to propose a plan that pays postpetition interest on claims that are nondischargeable under § 1228 (a).

**Other provisions:**

**Effective date and application of amendments made by Act April 20, 2005.** Act April 20, 2005, P.L. 109-8, Title X, § 1001, 119 Stat. 23, provided that chapter 12 becomes a permanent chapter of the Bankruptcy Code, effective July 1, 2005, the date of the most recent expiration of a temporary extension of chapter 12. Such Act, § 1501 (a), provided that the amendments made to this section would otherwise be effective 180 days after enactment on April 20, 2005, but such Act, § 1003(c), provided that the amendments to § 1222(a)(2) are effective upon enactment on April 20, 2005, and apply to cases commenced after such effective date.

**Abridged Legislative History**

(H. Report No. 109-31 to accompany S. 256, 109th Cong., 1st Sess. (2005) pp. 60, 136, available at 2005 U.S.C.C.A.N. 88, at 129–30, 196.)

## § 1223. Modification of plan before confirmation

(a) The debtor may modify the plan at any time before confirmation, but may not modify the plan so that the plan as modified fails to meet the requirements of section 1222 of this title.

(b) After the debtor files a modification under this section, the plan as modified becomes the plan.

(c) Any holder of a secured claim that has accepted or rejected the plan is deemed to have accepted or rejected, as the case may be, the plan as modified, unless the modification provides for a change in the rights of such holder from what such rights were under the plan before modification, and such holder changes such holder's previous acceptance or rejection.

## § 1224. Confirmation hearing

After expedited notice, the court shall hold a hearing on confirmation of the plan. A party in interest, the trustee, or the United States trustee may object to the confirmation of the plan. Except for cause, the hearing shall be concluded not later than 45 days after the filing of the plan.

## § 1225. Confirmation of plan

(a) Except as provided in subsection (b), the court shall confirm a plan if—

(1) the plan complies with the provisions of this chapter and with the other applicable provisions of this title;

(2) any fee, charge, or amount required under chapter 123 of title 28, or by the plan, to be paid before confirmation, has been paid;

(3) the plan has been proposed in good faith and not by any means forbidden by law;

(4) the value, as of the effective date of the plan, of property to be distributed under the plan on account of each allowed unsecured claim is not less than the amount that would be paid on such claim if the estate of the debtor were liquidated under chapter 7 of this title on such date;

(5) with respect to each allowed secured claim provided for by the plan—

(A) the holder of such claim has accepted the plan;

(B) (i) the plan provides that the holder of such claim retain the lien securing such claim; and

(ii) the value, as of the effective date of the plan, of property to be distributed by the trustee or the debtor under the plan on account of such claim is not less than the allowed amount of such claim; or

(C) the debtor surrenders the property securing such claim to such holder;~~ and~~

(6) the debtor will be able to make all payments under the plan and to comply with the plan~~.~~*; and*

*(7) the debtor has paid all amounts that are required to be paid under a domestic support obligation and that first become payable after the date of the filing of the petition if the debtor is required by a judicial or administrative order, or by statute, to pay such domestic support obligation.*

(b) (1) If the trustee or the holder of an allowed unsecured claim objects to the confirmation of the plan, then the court may not approve the plan unless, as of the effective date of the plan—

(A) the value of the property to be distributed under the plan on account of such claim is not less than the amount of such claim; ~~or~~

(B) the plan provides that all of the debtor's projected disposable income to be received in the three-year period, or such longer period as the court may approve under section 1222(c), beginning on the date that the first payment is due under the plan will be applied to make payments under the plan~~.~~*; or*

*(C) the value of the property to be distributed under the plan in the 3-year period, or such longer period as the court may approve under section 1222(c), beginning on the date that the first distribution is due under the plan is not less than the debtor's projected disposable income for such period.*

(2) For purposes of this subsection, "disposable income" means income which is received by the debtor and which is not reasonably necessary to be expended—

(A) for the maintenance or support of the debtor or a dependent of the debtor *or for a domestic support obligation that first becomes payable after the date of the filing of the petition*; or

(B) for the payment of expenditures necessary for the continuation, preservation, and operation of the debtor's business.

(c) After confirmation of a plan, the court may order any entity from whom the debtor receives income to pay all or any part of such income to the trustee.

**Section 1225**

(April 20, 2005, P. L. 109-8, Title IIB, §§ 213(5), 218; Title X, § 1006(a), 119 Stat. 23)

## HISTORY: ANCILLARY LAWS AND DIRECTIVES

**Amendments:**

**2005.** Act April 20, 2005(effective 180 days after enactment of April 20, 2005, as provided by § 1501(a) of P. L. 109-8), amends 11 USC § 1225's provisions for disposable income.

**Other provisions:**

**Effective date and application of amendments made by Act April 20, 2005.** Act April 20, 2005, P.L. 109-8, Title X, § 1001, 119 Stat. 23, provided that chapter 12 becomes a permanent chapter of the Bankruptcy Code, effective July 1, 2005, the date of the most recent expiration of a temporary extension of chapter 12. Such Act, § 1501 (a), provided that the amendments made to this section would otherwise be effective 180 days after enactment on April 20, 2005.

**Abridged Legislative History**

(H. Report No. 109-31 to accompany S. 256, 109th Cong., 1st Sess. (2005) pp. 60, 62, 137, available at 2005 U.S.C.C.A.N. 88, at 130, 131, 197)

## § 1226. Payments

(a) Payments and funds received by the trustee shall be retained by the trustee until confirmation or denial of confirmation of a plan. If a plan is confirmed, the trustee shall distribute any such payment in accordance with the plan. If a plan is not confirmed, the trustee shall return any such payments to the debtor, after deducting—

(1) any unpaid claim allowed under section 503(b) of this title; and

(2) if a standing trustee is serving in the case, the percentage fee fixed for such standing trustee.

(b) Before or at the time of each payment to creditors under the plan, there shall be paid—

(1) any unpaid claim of the kind specified in section 507(a)(2~~1~~) of this title; and

(2) if a standing trustee appointed under section 1202(c) of this title is serving in the case, the percentage fee fixed for such standing trustee under section 1202(d) of this title.

(c) Except as otherwise provided in the plan or in the order confirming the plan, the trustee shall make payments to creditors under the plan.

**Section 1226**

(April 20, 2005, P. L. 109-8, Title XV, § 1502(a)(9), 119 Stat. 23)

### HISTORY: ANCILLARY LAWS AND DIRECTIVES

**Amendments:**

**2005.** Act April 20, 2005(effective 180 days after enactment of April 20, 2005, as provided by § 1501(a) of P. L. 109-8), amends 11 USC § 1226 to make a technical correction for reference to another section.

**Other provisions:**

**Effective date and application of amendments made by Act April 20, 2005.** Act April 20, 2005, P.L. 109-8, Title X, § 1001, 119 Stat. 23, provided that chapter 12 becomes a permanent chapter of the Bankruptcy Code, effective July 1, 2005, the date of the most recent expiration of a temporary extension of chapter 12. Such Act, § 1501 (a), provided that the amendments made to this section would otherwise be effective 180 days after enactment on April 20, 2005.

**Abridged Legislative History**

(H. Report No. 109-31 to accompany S. 256, 109th Cong., 1st Sess. (2005) p. 155, available at 2005 U.S.C.C.A.N. 88, at 212)

## § 1227. Effect of confirmation

(a) Except as provided in section 1228(a) of this title, the provisions of a confirmed plan bind the debtor, each creditor, each equity security holder, and each general partner in the debtor, whether or not the claim of such creditor, such equity security holder, or such general partner in the debtor is provided for by the plan, and whether or not such creditor, such equity security holder, or such general partner in the debtor has objected to, has accepted, or has rejected the plan.

(b) Except as otherwise provided in the plan or the order confirming the plan, the confirmation of a plan vests all of the property of the estate in the debtor.

(c) Except as provided in section 1228(a) of this title and except as otherwise provided in the plan or in the order confirming the plan, the property vesting in the debtor under subsection (b) of this section is free and clear of any claim or interest of any creditor provided for by the plan.

## § 1228. Discharge

(a) ~~As~~ *Subject to subsection (d), as* soon as practicable after completion by the debtor of all payments under the plan, *and in the case of a debtor who is required by a judicial or administrative order, or by statute, to pay a domestic support obligation, after such debtor certifies that all amounts payable under such order or such statute that are due on or before the date of the certification (including amounts due before the petition was filed, but only to the extent provided for by the plan) have been paid*, other than payments to holders of allowed claims provided for under section 1222(b)(5) or 1222(b)(9) of this title, unless the court approves a written waiver of discharge executed by the debtor after the order for relief under this chapter, the court shall grant the debtor a discharge of all debts provided for by the plan allowed under section 503 of this title or disallowed under section 502 of this title, except any debt—

(1) provided for under section 1222(b)(5) or 1222(b)(9) of this title; or

(2) of the kind specified in section 523(a) of this title.

(b) ~~At~~ *Subject to subsection (d), at* any time after the confirmation of the plan and after notice and a hearing, the court may grant a discharge to a debtor that has not completed payments under the plan only if—

(1) the debtor's failure to complete such payments is due to circumstances for which the debtor should not justly be held accountable;

(2) the value, as of the effective date of the plan, of property actually distributed under the plan on account of each allowed unsecured claim is not less than the amount that would have been paid on such claim if the estate of the debtor had been liquidated under chapter 7 of this title on such date; and

(3) modification of the plan under section 1229 of this title is not practicable.

(c) A discharge granted under subsection (b) of this section discharges the debtor from all unsecured debts provided for by the plan or disallowed under section 502 of this title, except any debt—

(1) provided for under section 1222(b)(5) or 1222(b)(9) of this title; or

(2) of a kind specified in section 523(a) of this title.

(d) On request of a party in interest before one year after a discharge under this section is granted, and after notice and a hearing, the court may revoke such discharge only if—

(1) such discharge was obtained by the debtor through fraud; and

(2) the requesting party did not know of such fraud until after such discharge was granted.

(e) After the debtor is granted a discharge, the court shall terminate the services of any trustee serving in the case.

*(f) The court may not grant a discharge under this chapter unless the court after notice and a hearing held not more than 10 days before the date of the entry of the order granting the discharge finds that there is no reasonable cause to believe that —*

*(1) section 522(q)(1) may be applicable to the debtor; and*

*(2) there is pending any proceeding in which the debtor may be found guilty of a felony of the kind described in section 522(q)(1)(A) or liable for a debt of the kind described in section 522(q)(1)(B).*

**Section 1228**

(April 20, 2005, P. L. 109-8, Title XV, § 1502(a)(9), 119 Stat. 23)

## HISTORY: ANCILLARY LAWS AND DIRECTIVES

**Amendments:**

**2005.** Act April 20, 2005(effective 180 days after enactment of April 20, 2005, as provided by § 1501(a) of P. L. 109-8), amends 11 USC § 1228 amends Bankruptcy Code section 1228(a) to condition the granting of a chapter 12 discharge upon the debtor's payment of certain postpetition domestic support obligations and adds new § 1228(f) which is related to new § 522(q).

**Other provisions:**

**Effective date and application of amendments made by Act April 20, 2005.** Act April 20, 2005, P.L. 109-8, Title X, § 1001, 119 Stat. 23, provided that chapter 12 becomes a permanent chapter of the Bankruptcy Code, effective July 1, 2005, the date of the most recent expiration of a temporary extension of chapter 12. Such Act, § 1501 (a), provided that the amendments made to this section would otherwise be effective 180 days after enactment on April 20, 2005. New § 522(q), which is related to new § 1228(f), is effective upon enactment, according to § 308 of P.L. 109-8.

**Abridged Legislative History**

(H. Report No. 109-31 to accompany S. 256, 109th Cong., 1st Sess. (2005) pp. 60, 84, available at 2005 U.S.C.C.A.N. 88, at 130, 150)

# § 1229. Modification of plan after confirmation

(a) At any time after confirmation of the plan but before the completion of payments under such plan, the plan may be modified, on request of the debtor, the trustee, or the holder of an allowed unsecured claim, to—

(1) increase or reduce the amount of payments on claims of a particular class provided for by the plan;

(2) extend or reduce the time for such payments; or

(3) alter the amount of the distribution to a creditor whose claim is provided for by the plan to the extent necessary to take account of any payment of such claim other than under the plan.

(b) (1) Sections 1222(a), 1222(b), and 1223(c) of this title and the requirements of section 1225(a) of this title apply to any modification under subsection (a) of this section.

(2) The plan as modified becomes the plan unless, after notice and a hearing, such modification is disapproved.

(c) A plan modified under this section may not provide for payments over a period that expires after three years after the time that the first payment under the original confirmed plan was due, unless the court, for cause, approves a longer period, but the court may not approve a period that expires after five years after such time.

*(d) A plan may not be modified under this section—*

*(1) to increase the amount of any payment due before the plan as modified becomes the plan;*

*(2) by anyone except the debtor, based on an increase in the debtor's disposable income, to increase the amount of payments to unsecured creditors required for a particular month so that the aggregate of such payments exceeds the debtor's disposable income for such month; or*

*(3) in the last year of the plan by anyone except the debtor, to require payments that would leave the debtor with insufficient funds to carry on the farming operation after the plan is completed.*

**Section 1229**

(April 20, 2005, P. L. 109-8, Title X, § 1006(b), 119 Stat. 23)

## HISTORY: ANCILLARY LAWS AND DIRECTIVES

**Amendments:**

**2005.** Act April 20, 2005(effective 180 days after enactment of April 20, 2005, as provided by § 1501(a) of P. L. 109-8), adds 11 USC § 1229(d) to restrict the bases for modifying a confirmed chapter 12 plan.

**Other provisions:**

**Effective date and application of amendments made by Act April 20, 2005.** Act April 20, 2005, P.L. 109-8, Title X, § 1001, 119 Stat. 23, provided that chapter 12 becomes a permanent chapter of the Bankruptcy Code, effective July 1, 2005, the date of the most recent expiration of a temporary extension of chapter 12. Such Act, § 1501 (a), provided that the amendments made to this section would otherwise be effective 180 days after enactment on April 20, 2005.

**Abridged Legislative History**

(H. Report No. 109-31 to accompany S. 256, 109th Cong., 1st Sess. (2005) p. 137, available at 2005 U.S.C.C.A.N. 88, at 197)

# § 1230. Revocation of an order of confirmation

(a) On request of a party in interest at any time within 180 days after the date of the entry of an order of confirmation under section 1225 of this title, and after notice and a hearing, the court may revoke such order if such order was procured by fraud.

(b) If the court revokes an order of confirmation under subsection (a) of this section, the court shall dispose of the case under section 1207 of this title, unless, within the time fixed by the court, the debtor proposes and the court confirms a modification of the plan under section 1229 of this title.

# § 1231. Special tax provisions

~~(a) For the purpose of any State or local law imposing a tax on or measured by income, the taxable period of a debtor that is an individual shall terminate on the date of the order for relief under this chapter, unless the case was converted under section 706 of this title.~~

~~(b) The trustee shall make a State or local tax return of income for the estate of an individual debtor in a case under this chapter for each taxable period after the order for relief under this chapter during which the case is pending.~~

(*a*~~c~~) The issuance, transfer, or exchange of a security, or the making or delivery of an instrument of transfer under a plan confirmed under section 1225 of this title, may not be taxed under any law imposing a stamp tax or similar tax.

(*b*~~d~~) The court may authorize the proponent of a plan to request a determination, limited to questions of law, by *any* ~~a State or local~~ governmental unit charged with responsibility for collection or determination of a tax on or measured by income, of the tax effects, under section 346 of this title and under the law imposing such tax, of the plan. In the event of an actual controversy, the court may declare such effects after the earlier of—

(1) the date on which such governmental unit responds to the request under this subsection; or

(2) 270 days after such request.

**Section 1231**

(April 20, 2005, P. L. 109-8, Title VII, § 719(b)(4); Title X, § 1003(b), 119 Stat. 23)

## HISTORY: ANCILLARY LAWS AND DIRECTIVES

**Amendments:**

**2005.** Act April 20, 2005(effective upon enactment on April 20, 2005, and applies to cases commenced after such effective date, as provided by § 1003(c) of P. L. 109-8), amends 11 USC § 1231 to conform state and local income tax administrative issues to the Internal Revenue Code.

**Other provisions:**

**Effective date and application of amendments made by Act April 20, 2005.** Act April 20, 2005, P.L. 109-8, Title X, § 1001, 119 Stat. 23, provided that chapter 12 becomes a permanent chapter of the Bankruptcy Code, effective July 1, 2005, the date of the most recent expiration of a temporary extension of chapter 12. Such Act, § 1501 (a), provided that the amendments made to this section would otherwise be effective 180 days after enactment on April 20, 2005, but such Act, § 1003(c), provided that the amendments to § 1231(b) are effective upon enactment on April 20, 2005, and apply to cases commenced after such effective date.

**Abridged Legislative History**

(H. Report No. 109-31 to accompany S. 256, 109th Cong., 1st Sess. (2005) pp. 105, 136–37, available at 2005 U.S.C.C.A.N. 88, at 168, 196).

# Chapter 13
# —Adjustment of Debts of an Individual with Regular Income

## Subchapter I——Officers, Administration, and the Estate



## Subchapter II——The Plan



## Subchapter I——Officers, Administration, and the Estate

### § 1301. Stay of action against codebtor

(a) Except as provided in subsections (b) and (c) of this section, after the order for relief under this chapter, a creditor may not act, or commence or continue any civil action, to collect all or any part of a consumer debt of the debtor from any individual that is liable on such debt with the debtor, or that secured such debt, unless—

(1) such individual became liable on or secured such debt in the ordinary course of such individual's business; or

(2) the case is closed, dismissed, or converted to a case under chapter 7 or 11 of this title.

(b) A creditor may present a negotiable instrument, and may give notice of dishonor of such an instrument.

(c) On request of a party in interest and after notice and a hearing, the court shall grant relief from the stay provided by subsection (a) of this section with respect to a creditor, to the extent that—

(1) as between the debtor and the individual protected under subsection (a) of this section, such individual received the consideration for the claim held by such creditor;

(2) the plan filed by the debtor proposes not to pay such claim; or

(3) such creditor's interest would be irreparably harmed by continuation of such stay.

(d) Twenty days after the filing of a request under subsection (c)(2) of this section for relief from the stay provided by subsection (a) of this section, such stay is terminated with respect to the party in interest making such request, unless the debtor or any individual that is liable on such debt with the debtor files and serves upon such party in interest a written objection to the taking of the proposed action.

## § 1302. Trustee

(a) If the United States trustee appoints an individual under section 586(b) of title 28 to serve as standing trustee in cases under this chapter and if such individual qualifies under section 322 of this title, then such individual shall serve as trustee in the case. Otherwise, the United States trustee shall appoint one disinterested person to serve as trustee in the case or the United States trustee may serve as a trustee in the case.

(b) The trustee shall—

(1) perform the duties specified in sections 704(2), 704(3), 704(4), 704(5), 704(6), 704(7), and 704(9) of this title;

(2) appear and be heard at any hearing that concerns—

(A) the value of property subject to a lien;

(B) confirmation of a plan; or

(C) modification of the plan after confirmation;

(3) dispose of, under regulations issued by the Director of the Administrative Office of the United States Courts, moneys received or to be received in a case under chapter XIII of the Bankruptcy Act;

(4) advise, other than on legal matters, and assist the debtor in performance under the plan;~~ and~~

(5) ensure that the debtor commences making timely payments under section 1326 of this title~~.~~*; and*

*(6) if with respect to the debtor there is a claim for a domestic support obligation, provide the applicable notice specified in subsection (d).*

(c) If the debtor is engaged in business, then in addition to the duties specified in subsection (b) of this section, the trustee shall perform the duties specified in sections 1106(a)(3) and 1106(a)(4) of this title.

*(d) (1) In a case described in subsection (b)(6) to which subsection (b)(6) applies, the trustee shall—*

*(A) (i) provide written notice to the holder of the claim described in subsection (b)(6) of such claim and of the right of such holder to use the services of the State child support enforcement agency established under sections 464 and 466 of the Social Security Act for the State in which such holder resides, for assistance in collecting child support during and after the case under this title; and*

*(ii) include in the notice provided under clause (i) the address and telephone number of such State child support enforcement agency;*

*(B) (i) provide written notice to such State child support enforcement agency of such claim; and*

*(ii) include in the notice provided under clause (i) the name, address, and telephone number of such holder; and*

*(C) at such time as the debtor is granted a discharge under section 1328, provide written notice to such holder and to such State child support enforcement agency of—*

*(i) the granting of the discharge;*

*(ii) the last recent known address of the debtor;*

*(iii) the last recent known name and address of the debtor's employer; and*

*(iv) the name of each creditor that holds a claim that—*

*(I) is not discharged under paragraph (2) or (4) of section 523(a); or*

*(II) was reaffirmed by the debtor under section 524(c).*

*(2) (A) The holder of a claim described in subsection (b)(6) or the State child support enforcement agency of the State in which such holder resides may request from a creditor described in paragraph (1)(C)(iv) the last known address of the debtor.*

*(B) Notwithstanding any other provision of law, a creditor that makes a disclosure of a last known address of a debtor in connection with a request made under subparagraph (A) shall not be liable by reason of making that disclosure.*

**Section 1302**

(April 20, 2005, P. L. 109-8, Title IIB, § 219(d), 119 Stat. 23)

## HISTORY: ANCILLARY LAWS AND DIRECTIVES

**Amendments:**

**2005.** Act April 20, 2005(effective 180 days after enactment of April 20, 2005, as provided by § 1501(a) of P. L. 109-8), amends 11 USC § 1302 to add duties for the trustee to domestic support creditors.

**Other provisions:**

**Effective date and application of amendments made by Act April 20, 2005.** Act April 20, 2005, P.L. 109-8, Title XV, § 1501(a), 119 Stat. 23, provided that the amendments made to this section would be effective 180 days after enactment on April 20, 2005.

**Abridged Legislative History**

(H. Report No. 109-31 to accompany S. 256, 109th Cong., 1st Sess. (2005) p. 62, available at 2005 U.S.C.C.A.N. 88, at 131)

## § 1303. Rights and powers of debtor

Subject to any limitations on a trustee under this chapter, the debtor shall have, exclusive of the trustee, the rights and powers of a trustee under sections 363(b), 363(d), 363(e), 363(f), and 363(l), of this title.

## § 1304. Debtor engaged in business

(a) A debtor that is self-employed and incurs trade credit in the production of income from such employment is engaged in business.

(b) Unless the court orders otherwise, a debtor engaged in business may operate the business of the debtor and, subject to any limitations on a trustee under sections 363(c) and 364 of this title and to such limitations or conditions as the court prescribes, shall have, exclusive of the trustee, the rights and powers of the trustee under such sections.

(c) A debtor engaged in business shall perform the duties of the trustee specified in section 704(8) of this title.

## § 1305. Filing and allowance of postpetition claims

(a) A proof of claim may be filed by any entity that holds a claim against the debtor—

(1) for taxes that become payable to a governmental unit while the case is pending; or

(2) that is a consumer debt, that arises after the date of the order for relief under this chapter, and that is for property or services necessary for the debtor's performance under the plan.

(b) Except as provided in subsection (c) of this section, a claim filed under subsection (a) of this section shall be allowed or disallowed under section 502 of this title, but shall be determined as of the date such claim arises, and shall be allowed under section 502(a), 502(b), or 502(c) of this title, or disallowed under section 502(d) or 502(e) of this title, the same as if such claim had arisen before the date of the filing of the petition.

(c) A claim filed under subsection (a)(2) of this section shall be disallowed if the holder of such claim knew or should have known that prior approval by the trustee of the debtor's incurring the obligation was practicable and was not obtained.

## § 1306. Property of the estate

(a) Property of the estate includes, in addition to the property specified in section 541 of this title—

(1) all property of the kind specified in such section that the debtor acquires after the commencement of the case but before the case is

closed, dismissed, or converted to a case under chapter 7, 11, or 12 of this title, whichever occurs first; and

(2) earnings from services performed by the debtor after the commencement of the case but before the case is closed, dismissed, or converted to a case under chapter 7, 11, or 12 of this title, whichever occurs first.

(b) Except as provided in a confirmed plan or order confirming a plan, the debtor shall remain in possession of all property of the estate.

## § 1307. Conversion or dismissal

(a) The debtor may convert a case under this chapter to a case under chapter 7 of this title at any time. Any waiver of the right to convert under this subsection is unenforceable.

(b) On request of the debtor at any time, if the case has not been converted under section 706, 1112, or 1208 of this title, the court shall dismiss a case under this chapter. Any waiver of the right to dismiss under this subsection is unenforceable.

(c) Except as provided in subsection (e) of this section, on request of a party in interest or the United States trustee and after notice and a hearing, the court may convert a case under this chapter to a case under chapter 7 of this title, or may dismiss a case under this chapter, whichever is in the best interests of creditors and the estate, for cause, including—

(1) unreasonable delay by the debtor that is prejudicial to creditors;

(2) nonpayment of any fees and charges required under chapter 123 of title 28;

(3) failure to file a plan timely under section 1321 of this title;

(4) failure to commence making timely payments under section 1326 of this title;

(5) denial of confirmation of a plan under section 1325 of this title and denial of a request made for additional time for filing another plan or a modification of a plan;

(6) material default by the debtor with respect to a term of a confirmed plan;

(7) revocation of the order of confirmation under section 1330 of this title, and denial of confirmation of a modified plan under section 1329 of this title;

(8) termination of a confirmed plan by reason of the occurrence of a condition specified in the plan other than completion of payments under the plan;

(9) only on request of the United States trustee, failure of the debtor to file, within fifteen days, or such additional time as the court may allow, after the filing of the petition commencing such case, the information required by paragraph (1) of section 521; ~~or~~

(10) only on request of the United States trustee, failure to timely file the information required by paragraph (2) of section 521~~.~~*; or*

*(11) failure of the debtor to pay any domestic support obligation that first becomes payable after the date of the filing of the petition.*

(d) Except as provided in subsection (e) of this section, at any time before the confirmation of a plan under section 1325 of this title, on request of a party in interest or the United States trustee and after notice and a hearing, the court may convert a case under this chapter to a case under chapter 11 or 12 of this title.

*(e) Upon the failure of the debtor to file a tax return under section 1308, on request of a party in interest or the United States trustee and after notice and a hearing, the court shall dismiss a case or convert a case under this chapter to a case under chapter 7 of this title, whichever is in the best interest of the creditors and the estate.*

(~~e~~ *f*) The court may not convert a case under this chapter to a case under chapter 7, 11, or 12 of this title if the debtor is a farmer, unless the debtor requests such conversion.

(~~f~~ *g*) Notwithstanding any other provision of this section, a case may not be converted to a case under another chapter of this title unless the debtor may be a debtor under such chapter.

**Section 1307**

(April 20, 2005, P. L. 109-8, Title IIB, § 213(7); Title VII, § 716(c), 119 Stat. 23)

## HISTORY: ANCILLARY LAWS AND DIRECTIVES

**Amendments:**

**2005.** Act April 20, 2005(effective 180 days after enactment of April 20, 2005, as provided by § 1501(a) of P. L. 109-8), amends 11 USC § 1307 to add as grounds for dismissal or conversion the debtor's failure to pay post-petition domestic support obligations or to file required tax returns.

**Other provisions:**

**Effective date and application of amendments made by Act April 20, 2005.** Act April 20, 2005, P.L. 109-8, Title XV, § 1501(a), 119 Stat. 23, provided that the amendments made to this section would be effective 180 days after enactment on April 20, 2005.

**Abridged Legislative History**

With respect to chapter 13 cases, section 213(7) of the Act amends Bankruptcy Code section 1307(c) to provide that the failure of a debtor to pay any domestic support obligation that first becomes payable postpetition is cause for conversion or dismissal of the debtor's case. Section 213(8) amends Bankruptcy Code section 1322(a) to permit a chapter 13 debtor to propose a plan paying less than the full amount of a claim entitled to priority under Bankruptcy Code section 507(a)(1)(B) if the plan provides that all of the debtor's projected disposable income over a five-year period will be applied to make payments under the plan. Section 213(9) amends Bankruptcy Code section 1322(b) to permit a chapter 13 debtor to propose a plan that pays postpetition interest on nondischargeable debts under section 1328(a), but only to the extent that the debtor has disposable income available to pay such interest after payment in full of all allowed claims. Section 213(10) amends Bankruptcy Code section 1325(a) to provide that if a chapter 13 debtor is required by judicial or administrative order or statute to pay a domestic support obligation, then the debtor must pay all such obligations pursuant to such order or statute that became payable postpetition as a condition of confirmation. Section 213(11) amends Bankruptcy Code section 1328(a) to condition the granting of a chapter 13 discharge on the debtor's payment of certain postpetition domestic support obligations.

Section 716(c) amends section 1307 of the Bankruptcy Code to provide that if a chapter 13 debtor fails to file a tax return as required by section 1308, the court must dismiss the case or convert it to one under chapter 7 (whichever is in the best interests of creditors and the estate) on request of a party in interest or the United States trustee after notice and a hearing.

(H. Report No. 109-31 to accompany S. 256, 109th Cong., 1st Sess. (2005) pp. 60–61, 104; available at 2005 U.S.C.C.A.N. 88, at 130, 168).

## *§ 1308. Filing of prepetition tax returns*

*(a) Not later than the day before the date on which the meeting of the creditors is first scheduled to be held under section 341(a), if the debtor was required to file a tax return under applicable nonbankruptcy law, the debtor shall file with appropriate tax authorities all tax returns for all taxable periods ending during the 4-year period ending on the date of the filing of the petition.*

*(b) (1) Subject to paragraph (2), if the tax returns required by subsection (a) have not been filed by the date on which the meeting of creditors is first scheduled to be held under section 341(a), the trustee may hold open that meeting for a reasonable period of time to allow the debtor an additional period of time to file any unfiled returns, but such additional period of time shall not extend beyond—*

*(A) for any return that is past due as of the date of the filing of the petition, the date that is 120 days after the date of that meeting; or*

*(B) for any return that is not past due as of the date of the filing of the petition, the later of—*

*(i) the date that is 120 days after the date of that meeting; or*

*(ii) the date on which the return is due under the last automatic extension of time for filing that return to which the debtor is entitled, and for which request is timely made, in accordance with applicable nonbankruptcy law.*

*(2) After notice and a hearing, and order entered before the tolling of any applicable filing period determined under this subsection, if the debtor demonstrates by a preponderance of the evidence that the failure to file a return as required under this subsection is attributable to circumstances beyond the control of the debtor, the court may extend the filing period established by the trustee under this subsection for—*

*(A) a period of not more than 30 days for returns described in paragraph (1); and*

*(B) a period not to extend after the applicable extended due date for a return described in paragraph (2).*

*(c) For purposes of this section, the term 'return' includes a return prepared pursuant to subsection (a) or (b) of section 6020 of the Internal Revenue Code of 1986, or a similar State or local law, or a written stipulation to a judgment or a final order entered by a nonbankruptcy tribunal.*

**Section 1308**

(April 20, 2005, P. L. 109-8, Title VII, § 716(b), 119 Stat. 23)

## HISTORY: ANCILLARY LAWS AND DIRECTIVES

**Amendments:**

**2005.** Act April 20, 2005(effective 180 days after enactment of April 20, 2005, as provided by § 1501(a) of P. L. 109-8), adds 11 USC § 1308 with tax return requirements for debtors.

**Other provisions:**

**Effective date and application of amendments made by Act April 20, 2005.** Act April 20, 2005, P.L. 109-8, Title XV, § 1501(a), 119 Stat. 23, provided that the amendments made to this section would be effective 180 days after enactment on April 20, 2005.

**Abridged Legislative History**

(H. Report No. 109-31 to accompany S. 256, 109th Cong., 1st Sess. (2005) p. 104; available at 2005 U.S.C.C.A.N. 88, at 168).

# Subchapter II——The Plan

## § 1321. Filing of plan

The debtor shall file a plan.

## § 1322. Contents of plan

(a) The plan shall—

(1) provide for the submission of all or such portion of future earnings or other future income of the debtor to the supervision and control of the trustee as is necessary for the execution of the plan;

(2) provide for the full payment, in deferred cash payments, of all claims entitled to priority under section 507 of this title, unless the holder of a particular claim agrees to a different treatment of such claim;~~ and~~

(3) if the plan classifies claims, provide the same treatment for each claim within a particular class~~.~~*; and*

*(4) notwithstanding any other provision of this section, a plan may provide for less than full payment of all amounts owed for a claim entitled to priority under section 507(a)(1)(B) only if the plan provides that all of the debtor's projected disposable income for a 5-year period beginning on the date that the first payment is due under the plan will be applied to make payments under the plan.*

(b) Subject to subsections (a) and (c) of this section, the plan may—

(1) designate a class or classes of unsecured claims, as provided in section 1122 of this title, but may not discriminate unfairly against any class so designated; however, such plan may treat claims for a consumer debt of the debtor if an individual is liable on such consumer debt with the debtor differently than other unsecured claims;

(2) modify the rights of holders of secured claims, other than a claim secured only by a security interest in real property that is the debtor's principal residence, or of holders of unsecured claims, or leave unaffected the rights of holders of any class of claims;

(3) provide for the curing or waiving of any default;

(4) provide for payments on any unsecured claim to be made concurrently with payments on any secured claim or any other unsecured claim;

(5) notwithstanding paragraph (2) of this subsection, provide for the curing of any default within a reasonable time and maintenance of payments while the case is pending on any unsecured claim or secured claim on which the last payment is due after the date on which the final payment under the plan is due;

(6) provide for the payment of all or any part of any claim allowed under section 1305 of this title;

(7) subject to section 365 of this title, provide for the assumption, rejection, or assignment of any executory contract or unexpired lease of the debtor not previously rejected under such section;

(8) provide for the payment of all or part of a claim against the debtor from property of the estate or property of the debtor;

(9) provide for the vesting of property of the estate, on confirmation of the plan or at a later time, in the debtor or in any other entity;~~ and~~

*(10) provide for the payment of interest accruing after the date of the filing of the petition on unsecured claims that are nondischargeable under section 1328(a), except that such interest may be paid only to the extent that the debtor has disposable income available to pay such interest after making provision for full payment of all allowed claims; and*

(*11*~~10~~) include any other appropriate provision not inconsistent with this title.

(c) Notwithstanding subsection (b)(2) and applicable nonbankruptcy law—

(1) a default with respect to, or that gave rise to, a lien on the debtor's principal residence may be cured under paragraph (3) or (5) of subsection (b) until such residence is sold at a foreclosure sale that is conducted in accordance with applicable nonbankruptcy law; and

(2) in a case in which the last payment on the original payment schedule for a claim secured only by a security interest in real property that is the debtor's principal residence is due before the date on which the final payment under the plan is due, the plan may provide for the payment of the claim as modified pursuant to section 1325(a)(5) of this title.

(d) ~~The plan may not provide for payments over a period that is longer than three years, unless the court, for cause, approves a longer period, but the court may not approve a period that is longer than five years.~~*(1) If the current monthly income of the debtor and the debtor's spouse combined, when multiplied by 12, is not less than—*

*(A) in the case of a debtor in a household of 1 person, the median family income of the applicable State for 1 earner;*

*(B) in the case of a debtor in a household of 2, 3, or 4 individu-*

*als, the highest median family income of the applicable State for a family of the same number or fewer individuals; or*

*(C) in the case of a debtor in a household exceeding 4 individuals, the highest median family income of the applicable State for a family of 4 or fewer individuals, plus $525 per month for each individual in excess of 4,*

*the plan may not provide for payments over a period that is longer than 5 years.*

*(2) If the current monthly income of the debtor and the debtor's spouse combined, when multiplied by 12, is less than—*

*(A) in the case of a debtor in a household of 1 person, the median family income of the applicable State for 1 earner;*

*(B) in the case of a debtor in a household of 2, 3, or 4 individuals, the highest median family income of the applicable State for a family of the same number or fewer individuals; or*

*(C) in the case of a debtor in a household exceeding 4 individuals, the highest median family income of the applicable State for a family of 4 or fewer individuals, plus $525 per month for each individual in excess of 4,*

*the plan may not provide for payments over a period that is longer than 3 years, unless the court, for cause, approves a longer period, but the court may not approve a period that is longer than 5 years.*

(e) Notwithstanding subsection (b)(2) of this section and sections 506(b) and 1325(a)(5) of this title, if it is proposed in a plan to cure a default, the amount necessary to cure the default, shall be determined in accordance with the underlying agreement and applicable nonbankruptcy law.

*(f) A plan may not materially alter the terms of a loan described in section 362(b)(19) and any amounts required to repay such loan shall not constitute 'disposable income' under section 1325.*

**Section 1322**

(April 20, 2005, P. L. 109-8, Title IIB, §§ 213(8), (9); Title IIC, § 224(d); Title III, § 318(1), 119 Stat. 23)

## HISTORY: ANCILLARY LAWS AND DIRECTIVES

**Amendments:**

**2005.** Act April 20, 2005(effective 180 days after enactment of April 20, 2005, as provided by § 1501(a) of P. L. 109-8), amends 11 USC § 1322's plan requirements.

**Other provisions:**

**Effective date and application of amendments made by Act April 20, 2005.** Act April 20, 2005, P.L. 109-8, Title XV, § 1501(a), 119 Stat. 23, provided that the amendments made to this section would be effective 180 days after enactment on April 20, 2005.

**Abridged Legislative History**

Section 213(8) amends Bankruptcy Code section 1322(a) to permit a chapter 13 debtor to propose a plan paying less than the full amount of a claim entitled to priority under Bankruptcy Code section 507(a)(1)(B) if the plan provides that all of the debtor's projected disposable income over a five-year period will be applied to make payments under the plan.

Section 213(9) amends Bankruptcy Code section 1322(b) to permit a chapter 13 debtor to propose a plan that pays postpetition interest on nondischargeable debts under section 1328(a), but only to the extent that the debtor has disposable income available to pay such interest after payment in full of all allowed claims.

Section 224(d) amends Bankruptcy Code section 1322 to provide that a chapter 13 plan may not materially alter the terms of a loan described in section 362(b)(19) and that any amounts required to repay such loan shall not constitute "disposable income" under section 1325 of the Bankruptcy Code.

Chapter 13 Plans To Have a 5-Year Duration in Certain Cases. Paragraph (1) of section 318 of the Act amends Bankruptcy Code sections 1322(d) and 1325(b) to specify that a chapter 13 plan may not provide for payments over a period that is not less than five years if the current monthly income of the debtor and the debtor's spouse combined exceeds certain monetary thresholds.

(H. Report No. 109-31 to accompany S. 256, 109th Cong., 1st Sess. (2005) pp 60–61, 64, 79; available at 2005 U.S.C.C.A.N. 88, at 130, 133, 146)

## § 1323. Modification of plan before confirmation

(a) The debtor may modify the plan at any time before confirmation, but may not modify the plan so that the plan as modified fails to meet the requirements of section 1322 of this title.

(b) After the debtor files a modification under this section, the plan as modified becomes the plan.

(c) Any holder of a secured claim that has accepted or rejected the plan is deemed to have accepted or rejected, as the case may be, the plan as modified, unless the modification provides for a change in the rights of such holder from what such rights were under the plan before modification, and such holder changes such holder's previous acceptance or rejection.

## § 1324. Confirmation hearing

~~After~~

*(a) Except as provided in subsection (b) and after* notice, the court shall hold a hearing on confirmation of the plan. A party in interest may object to confirmation of the plan.

*(b) The hearing on confirmation of the plan may be held not earlier than 20 days and not later than 45 days after the date of the meeting of creditors under section 341(a), unless the court determines that it would be in the best interests of the creditors and the estate to hold such hearing at an earlier date and there is no objection to such earlier date.*

**Section 1324**

(April 20, 2005, P. L. 109-8, Title III, § 317, 119 Stat. 23)

### HISTORY: ANCILLARY LAWS AND DIRECTIVES

**Amendments:**

**2005.** Act April 20, 2005(effective 180 days after enactment of April 20, 2005, as provided by § 1501(a) of P. L. 109-8), amends 11 USC § 1324 to specify that a confirmation hearing may not be held earlier than 20 days and not later than 45 days after the § 341 meeting of creditors.

**Other provisions:**

**Effective date and application of amendments made by Act April 20, 2005.** Act April 20, 2005, P.L. 109-8, Title XV, § 1501(a), 119 Stat. 23, provided that the amendments made to this section would be effective 180 days after enactment on April 20, 2005.

**Abridged Legislative History**

(H. Report No. 109-31 to accompany S. 256, 109th Cong., 1st Sess. (2005) p. 79; available at 2005 U.S.C.C.A.N. 88, at 146).

## § 1325. Confirmation of plan

(a) Except as provided in subsection (b), the court shall confirm a plan if—

(1) the plan complies with the provisions of this chapter and with the other applicable provisions of this title;

(2) any fee, charge, or amount required under chapter 123 of title 28, or by the plan, to be paid before confirmation, has been paid;

(3) the plan has been proposed in good faith and not by any means forbidden by law;

(4) the value, as of the effective date of the plan, of property to be distributed under the plan on account of each allowed unsecured claim is not less than the amount that would be paid on such claim if the estate of the debtor were liquidated under chapter 7 of this title on such date;

(5) with respect to each allowed secured claim provided for by the plan—

(A) the holder of such claim has accepted the plan;

(B) (i) ~~the plan provides that the holder of such claim retain the lien securing such claim; and~~*the plan provides that—*

*(I) the holder of such claim retain the lien securing such claim until the earlier of—*

*(aa) the payment of the underlying debt determined under nonbankruptcy law; or*

*(bb) discharge under section 1328; and*

*(II) if the case under this chapter is dismissed or converted without completion of the plan, such lien shall also be retained by such holder to the extent recognized by applicable nonbankruptcy law; and*

(ii) the value, as of the effective date of the plan, of property to be distributed under the plan on account of such claim is not less than the allowed amount of such claim;~~or~~ *and*

*(iii) if—*

*(I) property to be distributed pursuant to this subsection is in the form of periodic payments, such payments shall be in equal monthly amounts; and*

*(II) the holder of the claim is secured by personal property, the amount of such payments shall not be less than an amount sufficient to provide to the holder of such claim adequate protection during the period of the plan; or*

(C) the debtor surrenders the property securing such claim to such holder; ~~and~~

(6) the debtor will be able to make all payments under the plan and to comply with the plan~~.~~*;*

*(7) the action of the debtor in filing the petition was in good faith;*

*(8) the debtor has paid all amounts that are required to be paid under a domestic support obligation and that first become payable after the date of the filing of the petition if the debtor is required by a judicial or administrative order, or by statute, to pay such domestic support obligation; and*

*(9) the debtor has filed all applicable Federal, State, and local tax returns as required by section 1308.*

*For purposes of paragraph (5), section 506 shall not apply to a claim described in that paragraph if the creditor has a purchase money security interest securing the debt that is the subject of the claim, the debt was incurred within the 910-day preceding the date of the filing of the petition, and the collateral for that debt consists of a motor vehicle (as defined in section 30102 of title 49) acquired for the personal use of the debtor, or if collateral for that debt consists of any other thing of value, if the debt was incurred during the 1-year period preceding that filing.*

(b) (1) If the trustee or the holder of an allowed unsecured claim objects to the confirmation of the plan, then the court may not approve the plan unless, as of the effective date of the plan—

(A) the value of the property to be distributed under the plan on account of such claim is not less than the amount of such claim; or

(B) the plan provides that all of the debtor's projected disposable income to be received in the ~~three-year period~~ *applicable commitment period* beginning on the date that the first payment is due under the plan will be applied to make payments *to unsecured creditors* under the plan.

(2) ~~For purposes of this subsection, "disposable income" means income which is received by the debtor and which is not reasonably necessary to be expended~~*For purposes of this subsection, the term 'disposable income' means current monthly income received by the debtor (other than child support payments, foster care payments, or disability payments for a dependent child made in accordance with applicable nonbankruptcy law to the extent reasonably necessary to be expended for such child) less amounts reasonably necessary to be expended—*

~~(A) for the maintenance or support of the debtor or a dependent of the debtor, including charitable contributions (that meet the definition of "charitable contribution" under section 548(d)(3)) to a qualified religious or chari table entity or organization (as that term is defined in section 548(d)(4)) in an amount not to exceed 15 percent of the gross income of the debtor for the year in which the contributions are made; and~~

~~(B) if the debtor is engaged in business, for the payment of expenditures necessary for the continuation, preservation, and operation of such business.~~*(A) (i) for the maintenance or support of the debtor or a dependent of the debtor, or for a domestic support obligation, that first becomes payable after the date the petition is filed; and*

*(ii) for charitable contributions (that meet the definition of 'charitable contribution' under section 548(d)(3) to a qualified religious or charitable entity or organization (as defined in section 548(d)(4)) in an amount not to exceed 15 percent of gross income of the debtor for the year in which the contributions are made; and*

*(B) if the debtor is engaged in business, for the payment of expenditures necessary for the continuation, preservation, and operation of such business.*

*(3) Amounts reasonably necessary to be expended under paragraph (2) shall be determined in accordance with subparagraphs (A) and (B) of section 707(b)(2), if the debtor has current monthly income, when multiplied by 12, greater than—*

*(A) in the case of a debtor in a household of 1 person, the median family income of the applicable State for 1 earner;*

*(B) in the case of a debtor in a household of 2, 3, or 4 individuals, the highest median family income of the applicable State for a family of the same number or fewer individuals; or*

*(C) in the case of a debtor in a household exceeding 4 individuals, the highest median family income of the applicable State for a family of 4 or fewer individuals, plus $525 per month for each individual in excess of 4.*

*(4) For purposes of this subsection, the 'applicable commitment period'—*

*(A) subject to subparagraph (B), shall be—*

*(i) 3 years; or*

*(ii) not less than 5 years, if the current monthly income of the debtor and the debtor's spouse combined, when multiplied by 12, is not less than—*

*(I) in the case of a debtor in a household of 1 person, the median family income of the applicable State for 1 earner;*

*(II) in the case of a debtor in a household of 2, 3, or 4 individuals, the highest median family income of the applicable State for a family of the same number or fewer individuals; or*

*(III) in the case of a debtor in a household exceeding 4 individuals, the highest median family income of the applicable State for a family of 4 or fewer individuals, plus $525 per month for each individual in excess of 4; and*

*(B) may be less than 3 or 5 years, whichever is applicable under subparagraph (A), but only if the plan provides for payment in full of all allowed unsecured claims over a shorter period.*

(c) After confirmation of a plan, the court may order any entity from whom the debtor receives income to pay all or any part of such income to the trustee.

**Section 1325**

(April 20, 2005, P. L. 109-8, Title I, §§ 102(g), (h); Title IIB, §§ 213(10); Title III, §§ 306(a), (b), 309(c)(1), 318(2), (3); Title VII, § 716(a), 119 Stat. 23)

## HISTORY: ANCILLARY LAWS AND DIRECTIVES

**Amendments:**

**2005.** Act April 20, 2005(effective 180 days after enactment of April 20, 2005, as provided by § 1501(a) of P. L. 109-8), amends 11 USC § 1325's confirmation requirements, with several new subsections.

**Other provisions:**

**Effective date and application of amendments made by Act April 20, 2005.** Act April 20, 2005, P.L. 109-8, Title XV, § 1501(a), 119 Stat. 23, provided that the amendments made to this section would be effective 180 days after enactment on April 20, 2005.

**Abridged Legislative History**

Section 102(g) of the Act amends section 1325(a) of the Bankruptcy Code to require the court, as a condition of confirming a chapter 13 plan, to find that the debtor's action in filing the case was in good faith.

Section 213(10) amends Bankruptcy Code section 1325(a) to provide that if a chapter 13 debtor is required by judicial or administrative order or statute to pay a domestic support obligation, then the debtor must pay all such obligations pursuant to such order or statute that became payable postpetition as a condition of confirmation.

Giving Secured Creditors Fair Treatment in Chapter 13. Subsection (a) of section 306 of the Act amends Bankruptcy Code section 1325(a)(5)(B)(i) to require-as a condition of confirmation-that a chapter 13 plan provide that a secured creditor retain its lien until the earlier of when the underlying debt is paid or the debtor receives a discharge.

Section 306(b) adds a new paragraph to section 1325(a) of the Bankruptcy Code specifying that Bankruptcy Code section 506 does not apply to a debt incurred within the two and one-half year period preceding the filing of the bankruptcy case if the debt is secured by a purchase money security interest in a motor vehicle acquired for the personal use of the debtor within 910 days preceding the filing of the petition. Where the collateral consists of any other type of property having value, section 306(b) provides that section 506 of the Bankruptcy Code does not apply if the debt was incurred during the one-year period preceding the filing of the bankruptcy case.

Section 309(c)(1) amends Bankruptcy Code section 1325(a)(5)(B) to require that periodic payments pursuant to a chapter 13 plan with respect to a secured claim be made in equal monthly installments.

Chapter 13 Plans To Have a 5-Year Duration in Certain Cases. Paragraph (1) of section 318 of the Act amends Bankruptcy Code sections 1322(d) and 1325(b) to specify that a chapter 13 plan may not provide for payments over a period that is not less than five years if the current monthly income of the debtor and the debtor's spouse combined exceeds certain monetary thresholds.

(H. Report No. 109-31 to accompany S. 256, 109th Cong., 1st Sess. (2005) pp. 52–53, 60–61, 71–71, 73, 79, 104; available at 2005 U.S.C.C.A.N. 88, at 123, 130, 140, 141, 146, 167.)

# § 1326. Payments

(a) (1) ~~Unless the court orders otherwise, the debtor shall commence making the payments proposed by a plan within 30 days after the plan is filed.~~ *Unless the court orders otherwise, the debtor shall commence making payments not later than 30 days after the date of the filing of the plan or the order for relief, whichever is earlier, in the amount—*

*(A) proposed by the plan to the trustee;*

*(B) scheduled in a lease of personal property directly to the lessor for that portion of the obligation that becomes due after the order for relief, reducing the payments under subparagraph (A) by the amount so paid and providing the trustee with evidence of such payment, including the amount and date of payment; and*

*(C) that provides adequate protection directly to a creditor holding an allowed claim secured by personal property to the extent the claim is attributable to the purchase of such property by the debtor for that portion of the obligation that becomes due after the order for relief, reducing the payments under subparagraph (A) by the amount so paid and providing the trustee with evidence of such payment, including the amount and date of payment.*

(2) ~~A payment made under this subsection shall be retained by the trustee until confirmation or denial of confirmation of a plan. If a plan is confirmed, the trustee shall distribute any such payment in accordance with the plan as soon as practicable. If a plan is not confirmed, the trustee shall return any such payment to the debtor, after deducting any unpaid claim allowed under section 503(b) of this title.~~*A payment made under paragraph (1)(A) shall be retained by the trustee until confirmation or denial of confirmation. If a plan is confirmed, the trustee shall distribute any such payment in accordance with the plan as soon as is practicable. If a plan is not confirmed, the trustee shall return any such payments not previously paid and not yet due and owing to creditors pursuant to paragraph (3) to the debtor, after deducting any unpaid claim allowed under section 503(b).*

*(3) Subject to section 363, the court may, upon notice and a hearing, modify, increase, or reduce the payments required under this subsection pending confirmation of a plan.*

*(4) Not later than 60 days after the date of filing of a case under this chapter, a debtor retaining possession of personal property subject to a lease or securing a claim attributable in whole or in part to the purchase price of such property shall provide the lessor or secured creditor reasonable evidence of the maintenance of any required insurance coverage with respect to the use or ownership of such property and continue to do so for so long as the debtor retains possession of such property.*

(b) Before or at the time of each payment to creditors under the plan, there shall be paid—

(1) any unpaid claim of the kind specified in section 507(a)(2~~1~~) of this title;~~ and~~

(2) if a standing trustee appointed under section 586(b) of title 28 is serving in the case, the percentage fee fixed for such standing trustee under section 586(e)(1)(B) of title 28~~.~~*; and*

*(3) if a chapter 7 trustee has been allowed compensation due to the conversion or dismissal of the debtor's prior case pursuant to section 707(b), and some portion of that compensation remains unpaid in a*

*case converted to this chapter or in the case dismissed under section 707(b) and refiled under this chapter, the amount of any such unpaid compensation, which shall be paid monthly—*

*(A) by prorating such amount over the remaining duration of the plan; and*

*(B) by monthly payments not to exceed the greater of—*

*(i) $25; or*

*(ii) the amount payable to unsecured nonpriority creditors, as provided by the plan, multiplied by 5 percent, and the result divided by the number of months in the plan.*

(c) Except as otherwise provided in the plan or in the order confirming the plan, the trustee shall make payments to creditors under the plan.

*(d) Notwithstanding any other provision of this title—*

*(1) compensation referred to in subsection (b)(3) is payable and may be collected by the trustee under that paragraph, even if such amount has been discharged in a prior case under this title; and*

*(2) such compensation is payable in a case under this chapter only to the extent permitted by subsection (b)(3).*

**Section 1326**

(April 20, 2005, P. L. 109-8, Title III, § 309(c)(2); Title XII, § 1224; Title XV, § 1502(a)(10), 119 Stat. 23)

## HISTORY: ANCILLARY LAWS AND DIRECTIVES

**Amendments:**

**2005.** Act April 20, 2005(effective 180 days after enactment of April 20, 2005, as provided by § 1501(a) of P. L. 109-8), amends 11 USC § 1326's requirements for payments to the trustee.

**Other provisions:**

**Effective date and application of amendments made by Act April 20, 2005.** Act April 20, 2005, P.L. 109-8, Title XV, § 1501(a), 119 Stat. 23, provided that the amendments made to this section would be effective 180 days after enactment on April 20, 2005.

**Abridged Legislative History**

Section 309(c)(2) provides that if the plan is confirmed, the trustee must distribute payments received from the debtor as soon as practicable in accordance with the plan. (H. Report No. 109-31 to accompany S. 256, 109th Cong., 1st Sess. (2005) pp. 74, 146, 155; available at 2005 U.S.C.C.A.N. 88, at 141, 204, 212)

# § 1327. Effect of confirmation

(a) The provisions of a confirmed plan bind the debtor and each creditor, whether or not the claim of such creditor is provided for by the plan, and whether or not such creditor has objected to, has accepted, or has rejected the plan.

(b) Except as otherwise provided in the plan or the order confirming the plan, the confirmation of a plan vests all of the property of the estate in the debtor.

(c) Except as otherwise provided in the plan or in the order confirming the plan, the property vesting in the debtor under subsection (b) of this section is free and clear of any claim or interest of any creditor provided for by the plan.

## § 1328. Discharge

(a) ~~As~~ *Subject to subsection (d), as* soon as practicable after completion by the debtor of all payments under the plan, *and in the case of a debtor who is required by a judicial or administrative order, or by statute, to pay a domestic support obligation, after such debtor certifies that all amounts payable under such order or such statute that are due on or before the date of the certification (including amounts due before the petition was filed, but only to the extent provided for by the plan) have been paid,* unless the court approves a written waiver of discharge executed by the debtor after the order for relief under this chapter, the court shall grant the debtor a discharge of all debts provided for by the plan or disallowed under section 502 of this title, except any debt—

(1) ~~provided for under section 1322(b)(5) of this title;~~*provided for under section 1322(b)(5);*

(2) ~~of the kind specified in paragraph (5), (8), or (9) of section 523(a) of this title; or~~*of the kind specified in section 507(a)(8)(C) or in paragraph (1)(B), (1)(C), (2), (3), (4), (5), (8), or (9) of section 523 (a);*

(3) ~~for restitution, or a criminal fine, included in a sentence on the debtor's conviction of a crime.~~*for restitution, or a criminal fine, included in a sentence on the debtor's conviction of a crime; or*

*(4) for restitution, or damages, awarded in a civil action against the debtor as a result of willful or malicious injury by the debtor that caused personal injury to an individual or the death of an individual.*

(b) ~~At~~ *Subject to subsection (d), at* any time after the confirmation of the plan and after notice and a hearing, the court may grant a discharge to a debtor that has not completed payments under the plan only if—

(1) the debtor's failure to complete such payments is due to circumstances for which the debtor should not justly be held accountable;

(2) the value, as of the effective date of the plan, of property actually distributed under the plan on account of each allowed unsecured claim is not less than the amount that would have been paid on such claim if the estate of the debtor had been liquidated under chapter 7 of this title on such date; and

(3) modification of the plan under section 1329 of this title is not practicable.

(c) A discharge granted under subsection (b) of this section discharges the debtor from all unsecured debts provided for by the plan or disallowed under section 502 of this title, except any debt—

(1) provided for under section 1322(b)(5) of this title; or

(2) of a kind specified in section 523(a) of this title.

(d) Notwithstanding any other provision of this section, a discharge granted under this section does not discharge the debtor from any debt based on an allowed claim filed under section 1305(a)(2) of this title if prior approval by the trustee of the debtor's incurring such debt was practicable and was not obtained.

(e) On request of a party in interest before one year after a discharge under this section is granted, and after notice and a hearing, the court may revoke such discharge only if—

(1) such discharge was obtained by the debtor through fraud; and

(2) the requesting party did not know of such fraud until after such discharge was granted.

*(f) Notwithstanding subsections (a) and (b), the court shall not grant a discharge of all debts provided for in the plan or disallowed under section 502, if the debtor has received a discharge—*

*(1) in a case filed under chapter 7, 11, or 12 of this title during the 4-year period preceding the date of the order for relief under this chapter, or*

*(2) in a case filed under chapter 13 of this title during the 2-year period preceding the date of such order.*

*(g) (1) The court shall not grant a discharge under this section to a debtor unless after filing a petition the debtor has completed an instructional course concerning personal financial management described in section 111.*

*(2) Paragraph (1) shall not apply with respect to a debtor who is a person described in section 109(h)(4) or who resides in a district for which the United States trustee (or the bankruptcy administrator, if any) determines that the approved instructional courses are not adequate to service the additional individuals who would otherwise be required to complete such instructional course by reason of the requirements of paragraph (1).*

*(3) The United States trustee (or the bankruptcy administrator, if any) who makes a determination described in paragraph (2) shall review such determination not later than 1 year after the date of such determination, and not less frequently than annually thereafter.*

*(h) The court may not grant a discharge under this chapter unless the court after notice and a hearing held not more than 10 days before the date of the entry of the order granting the discharge finds that there is no reasonable cause to believe that—*

*(1) section 522(q)(1) may be applicable to the debtor; and*

*(2) there is pending any proceeding in which the debtor may be found guilty of a felony of the kind described in section 522(q)(1)(A) or liable for a debt of the kind described in section 522(q)(1)(B).*

**Section 1328**

(April 20, 2005, P. L. 109-8, Title I, § 106(c); Title IIB, §§ 213(11); Title III, §§ 312(2), 314(b), 330(d); Title VII, § 707, 119 Stat. 23)

## HISTORY: ANCILLARY LAWS AND DIRECTIVES

**Amendments:**

**2005.** Act April 20, 2005(effective 180 days after enactment of April 20, 2005, as provided by § 1501(a) of P. L. 109-8), amends 11 USC § 1328's discharge provisions, including the debtor's obligation to pay certain postpetition domestic support obligations and to complete an instructional course prior to discharge. The Act also adds new § 1328(h) which is related to new § 522(q).

**Other provisions:**

**Effective date and application of amendments made by Act April 20, 2005.** Act April 20, 2005, P.L. 109-8, Title XV, § 1501(a), 119 Stat. 23, provided that the amendments made to this section would be effective 180 days after enactment on April 20, 2005. New § 522(q), which is related to new § 1328(h), is effective upon enactment, according to § 308 of P.L. 109-8.

**Abridged Legislative History**

Section 106(c) of the Act amends section 1328 of the Bankruptcy Code to deny a discharge to a chapter 13 debtor who fails to complete a personal financial management instructional course.

Section 213(11) amends Bankruptcy Code section 1328(a) to condition the granting of a chapter 13 discharge on the debtor's payment of certain postpetition domestic support obligations.

No Discharge of Fraudulent Taxes in Chapter 13. Section 707 of the Act amends Bankruptcy Code section 1328(a)(2) to prohibit the discharge of tax claims described in section 523(a)(1)(B) and (C) as well as claims for a tax required to be collected or withheld and for which the debtor is liable in whatever capacity pursuant to section 507(a)(8)(C).

(H. Report No. 109-31 to accompany S. 256, 109th Cong., 1st Sess. (2005) pp. 55, 61, 76–77, 84, 101; available at 2005 U.S.C.C.A.N. 88, at 125, 130, 143–44, 150, 165)

# § 1329. Modification of plan after confirmation

(a) At any time after confirmation of the plan but before the completion of payments under such plan, the plan may be modified, upon request of the debtor, the trustee, or the holder of an allowed unsecured claim, to—

(1) increase or reduce the amount of payments on claims of a particular class provided for by the plan;

(2) extend or reduce the time for such payments; ~~or~~

(3) alter the amount of the distribution to a creditor whose claim is provided for by the plan to the extent necessary to take account of any payment of such claim other than under the plan~~.~~*; or*

*(4) reduce amounts to be paid under the plan by the actual amount expended by the debtor to purchase health insurance for the debtor (and for any dependent of the debtor if such dependent does not otherwise have health insurance coverage) if the debtor documents the cost of such insurance and demonstrates that—*

*(A) such expenses are reasonable and necessary;*

*(B) (i) if the debtor previously paid for health insurance, the amount is not materially larger than the cost the debtor previously paid or the cost necessary to maintain the lapsed policy; or*

*(ii) if the debtor did not have health insurance, the amount is not materially larger than the reasonable cost that would be incurred by a debtor who purchases health insurance, who has*

*similar income, expenses, age, and health status, and who lives in the same geographical location with the same number of dependents who do not otherwise have health insurance coverage; and*

*(C) the amount is not otherwise allowed for purposes of determining disposable income under section 1325(b) of this title;*

*and upon request of any party in interest, files proof that a health insurance policy was purchased.*

(b) (1) Sections 1322(a), 1322(b), and 1323(c) of this title and the requirements of section 1325(a) of this title apply to any modification under subsection (a) of this section.

(2) The plan as modified becomes the plan unless, after notice and a hearing, such modification is disapproved.

(c) A plan modified under this section may not provide for payments over a period that expires after ~~three years~~ *the applicable commitment period under section 1325(b)(1)(B)* after the time that the first payment under the original confirmed plan was due, unless the court, for cause, approves a longer period, but the court may not approve a period that expires after five years after such time.

**Section 1329**

(April 20, 2005, P. L. 109-8, Title I, § 102(i); Title III, § 318(4), 119 Stat. 23)

## HISTORY: ANCILLARY LAWS AND DIRECTIVES

**Amendments:**

**2005.** Act April 20, 2005(effective 180 days after enactment of April 20, 2005, as provided by § 1501(a) of P. L. 109-8), amends 11 USC § 1329's plan modification provisions.

**Other provisions:**

**Effective date and application of amendments made by Act April 20, 2005.** Act April 20, 2005, P.L. 109-8, Title XV, § 1501(a), 119 Stat. 23, provided that the amendments made to this section would be effective 180 days after enactment on April 20, 2005.

**Abridged Legislative History**

Chapter 13 Plans To Have a 5-Year Duration in Certain Cases. Paragraph (1) of section 318 of the Act amends Bankruptcy Code sections 1322(d) and 1325(b) to specify that a chapter 13 plan may not provide for payments over a period that is not less than five years if the current monthly income of the debtor and the debtor's spouse combined exceeds certain monetary thresholds.

(H. Report No. 109-31 to accompany S. 256, 109th Cong., 1st Sess. (2005) pp. 53, 79; available at 2005 U.S.C.C.A.N. 88, at 123–24, 146.)

# § 1330. Revocation of an order of confirmation

(a) On request of a party in interest at any time within 180 days after the date of the entry of an order of confirmation under section 1325 of this title, and after notice and a hearing, the court may revoke such order if such order was procured by fraud.

(b) If the court revokes an order of confirmation under subsection (a) of this section, the court shall dispose of the case under section 1307 of this title, unless, within the time fixed by the court, the debtor proposes and the court confirms a modification of the plan under section 1329 of this title.

# Chapter 15

# —~~Repealed~~ *Ancillary and Other Cross-Border Cases*

***§ 1501. Purpose and scope of application***
***§ 1502. Definitions***
***§ 1503. International obligations of the United States***
***§ 1504. Commencement of ancillary case***
***§ 1505. Authorization to act in a foreign country***
***§ 1506. Public policy exception***
***§ 1507. Additional assistance***
***§ 1508. Interpretation***
***§ 1509. Right of direct access***
***§ 1510. Limited jurisdiction***
***§ 1511. Commencement of case under section 301 or 303***
***§ 1512. Participation of a foreign representative in a case under this title***
***§ 1513. Access of foreign creditors to a case under this title***
***§ 1514. Notification to foreign creditors concerning a case under this title***
***§ 1515. Application for recognition***
***§ 1516. Presumptions concerning recognition***
***§ 1517. Order granting recognition***
***§ 1518. Subsequent information***
***§ 1519. Relief that may be granted upon filing petition for recognition***
***§ 1520. Effects of recognition of a foreign main proceeding***
***§ 1521. Relief that may be granted upon recognition***
***§ 1522. Protection of creditors and other interested persons***
***§ 1523. Actions to avoid acts detrimental to creditors***
***§ 1524. Intervention by a foreign representative***
***§ 1525. Cooperation and direct communication between the court and foreign courts or foreign representatives***
***§ 1526. Cooperation and direct communication between the trustee and foreign courts or foreign representatives***
***§ 1527. Forms of cooperation***
***§ 1528. Commencement of a case under this title after recognition of a foreign main proceeding***
***§ 1529. Coordination of a case under this title and a foreign proceeding***
***§ 1530. Coordination of more than 1 foreign proceeding***
***§ 1531. Presumption of insolvency based on recognition of a foreign main proceeding***
***§ 1532. Rule of payment in concurrent proceedings***

## *§ 1501. Purpose and scope of application*

*(a) The purpose of this chapter is to incorporate the Model Law on Cross-Border Insolvency so as to provide effective mechanisms for dealing with cases of cross-border insolvency with the objectives of—*

*(1) cooperation between—*

*(A) courts of the United States, United States trustees, trustees, examiners, debtors, and debtors in possession; and*

*(B) the courts and other competent authorities of foreign countries involved in cross-border insolvency cases;*

*(2) greater legal certainty for trade and investment;*

*(3) fair and efficient administration of cross-border insolvencies that protects the interests of all creditors, and other interested entities, including the debtor;*

*(4) protection and maximization of the value of the debtor's assets; and*

*(5) facilitation of the rescue of financially troubled businesses, thereby protecting investment and preserving employment.*

*(b) This chapter applies where—*

*(1) assistance is sought in the United States by a foreign court or a foreign representative in connection with a foreign proceeding;*

*(2) assistance is sought in a foreign country in connection with a case under this title;*

*(3) a foreign proceeding and a case under this title with respect to the same debtor are pending concurrently; or*

*(4) creditors or other interested persons in a foreign country have an interest in requesting the commencement of, or participating in, a case or proceeding under this title.*

*(c) This chapter does not apply to—*

*(1) a proceeding concerning an entity, other than a foreign insurance company, identified by exclusion in section 109(b);*

*(2) an individual, or to an individual and such individual's spouse, who have debts within the limits specified in section 109(e) and who are citizens of the United States or aliens lawfully admitted for permanent residence in the United States; or*

*(3) an entity subject to a proceeding under the Securities Investor Protection Act of 1970, a stockbroker subject to subchapter III of chapter 7 of this title, or a commodity broker subject to subchapter IV of chapter 7 of this title.*

*(d) The court may not grant relief under this chapter with respect to any deposit, escrow, trust fund, or other security required or permitted under any applicable State insurance law or regulation for the benefit of claim holders in the United States.*

**Section 1501**

(April 20, 2005, P. L. 109-8, Title VIII, § 801(a), 119 Stat. 23)

### HISTORY: ANCILLARY LAWS AND DIRECTIVES

**Amendments:**

**2005.** Act April 20, 2005, created a new § 1501.

**Other provisions:**

**Effective date and application of Act April 20, 2005.**

Act April 20, 2005, Pub.L. 109-8, Title VIII, § 801(a), 119 Stat. 23, created a new Title 15 and is effective 180 days after enactment [April 20, 2005]. Section 1501 provides:

EFFECTIVE DATE; APPLICATION OF AMENDMENTS.

EFFECTIVE DATE- Except as otherwise provided in this Act, this Act and the amendments made by this Act shall take effect 180 days after the date of enactment of this Act.

(b) APPLICATION OF AMENDMENTS—

(1) IN GENERAL- Except as otherwise provided in this Act and paragraph (2), the amendments made by this Act shall not apply with respect to cases commenced under title 11, United States Code, before the effective date of this Act.

(2) CERTAIN LIMITATIONS APPLICABLE TO DEBTORS— The amendments made by sections 308, 322, and 330 shall apply with respect to cases commenced under title 11, United States Code, on or after the date of the enactment of this Act.

**Abridged Legislative History**

Title VIII of the Act adds a new chapter to the Bankruptcy Code for transnational bankruptcy cases. It incorporates the Model Law on Cross-Border Insolvency to encourage cooperation between the United States and foreign countries with respect to transnational insolvency cases. Title VIII is intended to provide greater legal certainty for trade and investment as well as to provide for the fair and efficient administration of cross-border insolvencies, which protects the interests of creditors and other interested parties, including the debtor. In addition, it serves to protect and maximize the value of the debtor's assets.

(H. Report No. 109-31 to accompany S. 256, 109th Cong., 1st Sess. (2005) p.106; available at 2005 U.S.C.C.A.N. 88, at 169–70.)

## *§ 1502. Definitions*

*For the purposes of this chapter, the term—*

*(1) "debtor" means an entity that is the subject of a foreign proceeding;*

*(2) "establishment" means any place of operations where the debtor carries out a nontransitory economic activity;*

*(3) "foreign court" means a judicial or other authority competent to control or supervise a foreign proceeding;*

*(4) "foreign main proceeding" means a foreign proceeding pending in the country where the debtor has the center of its main interests;*

*(5) "foreign nonmain proceeding" means a foreign proceeding, other than a foreign main proceeding, pending in a country where the debtor has an establishment;*

*(6) "trustee" includes a trustee, a debtor in possession in a case under any chapter of this title, or a debtor under chapter 9 of this title;*

*(7) "recognition" means the entry of an order granting recognition of a foreign main proceeding or foreign nonmain proceeding under this chapter; and*

*(8) "within the territorial jurisdiction of the United States", when used with reference to property of a debtor, refers to tangible property located within the territory of the United States and intangible property deemed under applicable nonbankruptcy law to be located within that territory, including any property subject to attachment or garnishment that may properly be seized or garnished by an action in a Federal or State court in the United States.*

**Section 1502**

(April 20, 2005, P. L. 109-8, Title VIII, § 801(a), 119 Stat. 23)

## HISTORY: ANCILLARY LAWS AND DIRECTIVES

**Amendments:**

**2005.** Act April 20, 2005, created a new § 1502.

**Other provisions:**

**Effective date and application of Act April 20, 2005.**

Act April 20, 2005, Pub.L. 109-8, Title VIII, § 801(a), 119 Stat. 23, created a new Title 15 and is effective 180 days after enactment [April 20, 2005].

**Abridged Legislative History**

Sec. 1502. Definitions. "Debtor" is given a special definition for this chapter. This definition does not come from the Model Law, but is necessary to eliminate the need to refer repeatedly to "the same debtor as in the foreign proceeding."

The definition of "within the territorial jurisdiction of the United States" in subsection (7) is not taken from the Model Law. It has been added because the United States, like some other countries, asserts insolvency jurisdiction over property outside its territorial limits under appropriate circumstances.

Two key definitions of "foreign proceeding" and "foreign representative," are found in sections 101(23) and (24), which have been amended consistent with Model Law article 2. (H. Report No. 109-31 to accompany S. 256, 109th Cong., 1st Sess. (2005) p.107; available at 2005 U.S.C.C.A.N. 88, at 170.)

# *§ 1503. International obligations of the United States*

*To the extent that this chapter conflicts with an obligation of the United States arising out of any treaty or other form of agreement to which it is a party with one or more other countries, the requirements of the treaty or agreement prevail.*

**Section 1503**

(April 20, 2005, P. L. 109-8, Title VIII, § 801(a), 119 Stat. 23)

## HISTORY: ANCILLARY LAWS AND DIRECTIVES

**Amendments:**

**2005.** Act April 20, 2005, created a new § 1503.

**Other provisions:**

**Effective date and application of Act April 20, 2005.**

Act April 20, 2005, Pub.L. 109-8, Title VIII, § 801(a), 119 Stat. 23, created a new Title 15 and is effective 180 days after enactment [April 20, 2005].

**Abridged Legislative History**

Sec. 1503. International obligations of the United States. This section is taken exactly from the Model Law with only minor adaptations of terminology. (H. Report No. 109-31 to accompany S. 256, 109th Cong., 1st Sess. (2005) p.107; available at 2005 U.S.C.C.A.N. 88, at 171.)

# *§ 1504. Commencement of ancillary case*

*A case under this chapter is commenced by the filing of a petition for recognition of a foreign proceeding under section 1515.*

**Section 1504**

(April 20, 2005, P. L. 109-8, Title VIII, § 801(a), 119 Stat. 23)

## HISTORY: ANCILLARY LAWS AND DIRECTIVES

**Amendments:**

**2005.** Act April 20, 2005, created a new § 1504.

**Other provisions:**

**Effective date and application of Act April 20, 2005.**

Act April 20, 2005, Pub.L. 109-8, Title VIII, § 801(a), 119 Stat. 23, created a new Title 15 and is effective 180 days after enactment [April 20, 2005].

**Abridged Legislative History**

Sec. 1504. Commencement of ancillary case. Article 4 of the Model Law is designed for designation of the competent court which will exercise jurisdiction under the Model Law.

(H. Report No. 109-31 to accompany S. 256, 109th Cong., 1st Sess. (2005) p.107–08; available at 2005 U.S.C.C.A.N. 88, at 171.)

## *§ 1505. Authorization to act in a foreign country*

*A trustee or another entity (including an examiner) may be authorized by the court to act in a foreign country on behalf of an estate created under section 541. An entity authorized to act under this section may act in any way permitted by the applicable foreign law.*

**Section 1505**

(April 20, 2005, P. L. 109-8, Title VIII, § 801(a), 119 Stat. 23)

### HISTORY: ANCILLARY LAWS AND DIRECTIVES

**Amendments:**

**2005.** Act April 20, 2005, created a new § 1505.

**Other provisions:**

**Effective date and application of Act April 20, 2005.**

Act April 20, 2005, Pub.L. 109-8, Title VIII, § 801(a), 119 Stat. 23, created a new Title 15 and is effective 180 days after enactment [April 20, 2005].

**Abridged Legislative History**

Sec. 1505. Authorization to act in a foreign country. The language in this section varies from the wording of article 5 of the Model Law as necessary to comport with United States law and terminology.

The related amendment to section 586(a)(3) of title 28 makes acting pursuant to authorization under this section an additional power of a trustee or debtor in possession.

This section also contemplates the designation of an examiner or other natural person to act for the estate in one or more foreign countries where appropriate. (H. Report No. 109-31 to accompany S. 256, 109th Cong., 1st Sess. (2005) p.108–09; available at 2005 U.S.C.C.A.N. 88, at 171–72.)

## *§ 1506. Public policy exception*

*Nothing in this chapter prevents the court from refusing to take an action governed by this chapter if the action would be manifestly contrary to the public policy of the United States.*

**Section 1506**

(April 20, 2005, P. L. 109-8, Title VIII, § 801(a), 119 Stat. 23)

### HISTORY: ANCILLARY LAWS AND DIRECTIVES

**Amendments:**

**2005.** Act April 20, 2005, created a new § 1506.

**Other provisions:**

**Effective date and application of Act April 20, 2005.**

Act April 20, 2005, Pub.L. 109-8, Title VIII, § 801(a), 119 Stat. 23, created a new Title 15 and is effective 180 days after enactment [April 20, 2005].

**Abridged Legislative History**

Sec. 1506. Public policy exception. This provision follows the Model Law article 5 exactly. (H. Report No. 109-31 to accompany S. 256, 109th Cong., 1st Sess. (2005) p. 109; available at 2005 U.S.C.C.A.N. 88, at 172.)

## *§ 1507. Additional assistance*

*(a) Subject to the specific limitations stated elsewhere in this chapter the court, if recognition is granted, may provide additional assistance to a foreign representative under this title or under other laws of the United States.*

*(b) In determining whether to provide additional assistance under this title or under other laws of the United States, the court shall consider whether such additional assistance, consistent with the principles of comity, will reasonably assure—*

*(1) just treatment of all holders of claims against or interests in the debtor's property;*

*(2) protection of claim holders in the United States against prejudice and inconvenience in the processing of claims in such foreign proceeding;*

*(3) prevention of preferential or fraudulent dispositions of property of the debtor;*

*(4) distribution of proceeds of the debtor's property substantially in accordance with the order prescribed by this title; and*

*(5) if appropriate, the provision of an opportunity for a fresh start for the individual that such foreign proceeding concerns.*

**Section 1507**

(April 20, 2005, P. L. 109-8, Title VIII, § 801(a), 119 Stat. 23)

### HISTORY: ANCILLARY LAWS AND DIRECTIVES

**Amendments:**

**2005.** Act April 20, 2005, created a new § 1507.

**Other provisions:**

**Effective date and application of Act April 20, 2005.**

Act April 20, 2005, Pub.L. 109-8, Title VIII, § 801(a), 119 Stat. 23, created a new Title 15 and is effective 180 days after enactment [April 20, 2005].

**Abridged Legislative History**

Sec. 1507. Additional assistance. Subsection (1) follows the language of Model Law article 7. (H. Report No. 109-31 to accompany S. 256, 109th Cong., 1st Sess. (2005) p.109; available at 2005 U.S.C.C.A.N. 88, at 172.)

## *§ 1508. Interpretation*

*In interpreting this chapter, the court shall consider its international origin, and the need to promote an application of this chapter that is consistent with the application of similar statutes adopted by foreign jurisdictions.*

**Section 1508**

(April 20, 2005, P. L. 109-8, Title VIII, § 801(a), 119 Stat. 23)

### HISTORY: ANCILLARY LAWS AND DIRECTIVES

**Amendments:**

**2005.** Act April 20, 2005, created a new § 1508.

**Other provisions:**

**Effective date and application of Act April 20, 2005.**

Act April 20, 2005, Pub.L. 109-8, Title VIII, § 801(a), 119 Stat. 23, created a new Title 15 and is effective 180 days after enactment [April 20, 2005].

**Abridged Legislative History**

Sec. 1508. Interpretation. This provision follows conceptually Model Law article 8. (H. Report No. 109-31 to accompany S. 256, 109th Cong., 1st Sess. (2005) p.109–10; available at 2005 U.S.C.C.A.N. 88, at 172–73.)

## *§ 1509. Right of direct access*

*(a) A foreign representative may commence a case under section 1504 by filing directly with the court a petition for recognition of a foreign proceeding under section 1515.*

*(b) If the court grants recognition under section 1517, and subject to any limitations that the court may impose consistent with the policy of this chapter—*

*(1) the foreign representative has the capacity to sue and be sued in a court in the United States;*

*(2) the foreign representative may apply directly to a court in the United States for appropriate relief in that court; and*

*(3) a court in the United States shall grant comity or cooperation to the foreign representative.*

*(c) A request for comity or cooperation by a foreign representative in a court in the United States other than the court which granted recognition shall be accompanied by a certified copy of an order granting recognition under section 1517.*

*(d) If the court denies recognition under this chapter, the court may issue any appropriate order necessary to prevent the foreign representative from obtaining comity or cooperation from courts in the United States.*

*(e) Whether or not the court grants recognition, and subject to sections 306 and 1510, a foreign representative is subject to applicable nonbankruptcy law.*

*(f) Notwithstanding any other provision of this section, the failure of a foreign representative to commence a case or to obtain recognition under this chapter does not affect any right the foreign representative may have to sue in a court in the United States to collect or recover a claim which is the property of the debtor.*

**Section 1509**

(April 20, 2005, P. L. 109-8, Title VIII, § 801(a), 119 Stat. 23)

## HISTORY: ANCILLARY LAWS AND DIRECTIVES

**Amendments:**

**2005.** Act April 20, 2005, created a new § 1509.

**Other provisions:**

**Effective date and application of Act April 20, 2005.**

Act April 20, 2005, Pub.L. 109-8, Title VIII, § 801(a), 119 Stat. 23, created a new Title 15 and is effective 180 days after enactment [April 20, 2005].

**Abridged Legislative History**

Sec. 1509. Right of direct access. This section implements the purpose of article 9 of the Model Law.

(H. Report No. 109-31 to accompany S. 256, 109th Cong., 1st Sess. (2005) p. 110–11; available at 2005 U.S.C.C.A.N. 88, at 173.)

## *§ 1510. Limited jurisdiction*

*The sole fact that a foreign representative files a petition under section 1515 does not subject the foreign representative to the jurisdiction of any court in the United States for any other purpose.*

**Section 1510**

(April 20, 2005, P. L. 109-8, Title VIII, § 801(a), 119 Stat. 23)

### HISTORY: ANCILLARY LAWS AND DIRECTIVES

**Amendments:**

**2005.** Act April 20, 2005, created a new § 1510.

**Other provisions:**

**Effective date and application of Act April 20, 2005.**

Act April 20, 2005, Pub.L. 109-8, Title VIII, § 801(a), 119 Stat. 23, created a new Title 15 and is effective 180 days after enactment [April 20, 2005].

**Abridged Legislative History**

Sec. 1510. Limited jurisdiction. Section 1510, article 10 of the Model Law, is modeled on section 306 of the Bankruptcy Code. (H. Report No. 109-31 to accompany S. 256, 109th Cong., 1st Sess. (2005) p. 111; available at 2005 U.S.C.C.A.N. 88, at 173–74.)

## *§ 1511. Commencement of case under section 301 or 303*

*(a) Upon recognition, a foreign representative may commence—*

*(1) an involuntary case under section 303; or*

*(2) a voluntary case under section 301 or 302, if the foreign proceeding is a foreign main proceeding.*

*(b) The petition commencing a case under subsection (a) must be accompanied by a certified copy of an order granting recognition. The court where the petition for recognition has been filed must be advised of the foreign representative's intent to commence a case under subsection (a) prior to such commencement.*

**Section 1511**

(April 20, 2005, P. L. 109-8, Title VIII, § 801(a), 119 Stat. 23)

### HISTORY: ANCILLARY LAWS AND DIRECTIVES

**Amendments:**

**2005.** Act April 20, 2005, created a new § 1511.

**Other provisions:**

**Effective date and application of Act April 20, 2005.**

Act April 20, 2005, Pub.L. 109-8, Title VIII, § 801(a), 119 Stat. 23, created a new Title 15 and is effective 180 days after enactment [April 20, 2005].

**Abridged Legislative History**

Sec. 1511. Commencement of Case Under Section 301 or 303. This section reflects the intent of article 11 of the Model Law, but adds language that conforms to United States law or that is otherwise necessary in the United States given its many bankruptcy court districts and the importance of full information and coordination among them. (H. Report No. 109-31 to accompany S. 256, 109th Cong., 1st Sess. (2005) p. 111; available at 2005 U.S.C.C.A.N. 88, at 174.)

## *§ 1512. Participation of a foreign representative in a case under this title*

*Upon recognition of a foreign proceeding, the foreign representative in the recognized proceeding is entitled to participate as a party in interest in a case regarding the debtor under this title.*

**Section 1512**

(April 20, 2005, P. L. 109-8, Title VIII, § 801(a), 119 Stat. 23)

### HISTORY: ANCILLARY LAWS AND DIRECTIVES

**Amendments:**

**2005.** Act April 20, 2005, created a new § 1512.

**Other provisions:**

**Effective date and application of Act April 20, 2005.**

Act April 20, 2005, Pub.L. 109-8, Title VIII, § 801(a), 119 Stat. 23, created a new Title 15 and is effective 180 days after enactment [April 20, 2005].

**Abridged Legislative History**

Sec. 1512. Participation of a foreign representative in a case under this title. This section tracks article 12 of the Model Law with a slight alteration to tie into United States procedural terminology. (H. Report No. 109-31 to accompany S. 256, 109th Cong., 1st Sess. (2005) p. 111; available at 2005 U.S.C.C.A.N. 88, at 174.)

## *§ 1513. Access of foreign creditors to a case under this title*

*(a) Foreign creditors have the same rights regarding the commencement of, and participation in, a case under this title as domestic creditors.*

*(b) (1) Subsection (a) does not change or codify present law as to the priority of claims under section 507 or 726, except that the claim of a foreign creditor under those sections shall not be given a lower priority than that of general unsecured claims without priority solely because the holder of such claim is a foreign creditor.*

*(2) (A) Subsection (a) and paragraph (1) do not change or codify present law as to the allowability of foreign revenue claims or other foreign public law claims in a proceeding under this title.*

*(B) Allowance and priority as to a foreign tax claim or other foreign public law claim shall be governed by any applicable tax treaty of the United States, under the conditions and circumstances specified therein.*

**Section 1513**

(April 20, 2005, P. L. 109-8, Title VIII, § 801(a), 119 Stat. 23)

### HISTORY: ANCILLARY LAWS AND DIRECTIVES

**Amendments:**

**2005.** Act April 20, 2005, created a new § 1513.

**Other provisions:**

**Effective date and application of Act April 20, 2005.**

Act April 20, 2005, Pub.L. 109-8, Title VIII, § 801(a), 119 Stat. 23, created a new Title

15 and is effective 180 days after enactment [April 20, 2005].

**Abridged Legislative History**

Sec. 1513. Access of foreign creditors to a case under this title. This section mandates nondiscriminatory or "national" treatment for foreign creditors, except as provided in subsection (b) and section 1514. It follows the intent of Model Law article 13, but the language required alteration to fit into the Bankruptcy Code. (H. Report No. 109-31 to accompany S. 256, 109th Cong., 1st Sess. (2005) p. 111–12; available at 2005 U.S.C.C.A.N. 88, at 174.)

## *§ 1514. Notification to foreign creditors concerning a case under this title*

*(a) Whenever in a case under this title notice is to be given to creditors generally or to any class or category of creditors, such notice shall also be given to the known creditors generally, or to creditors in the notified class or category, that do not have addresses in the United States. The court may order that appropriate steps be taken with a view to notifying any creditor whose address is not yet known.*

*(b) Such notification to creditors with foreign addresses described in subsection (a) shall be given individually, unless the court considers that, under the circumstances, some other form of notification would be more appropriate. No letter or other formality is required.*

*(c) When a notification of commencement of a case is to be given to foreign creditors, such notification shall—*

*(1) indicate the time period for filing proofs of claim and specify the place for filing such proofs of claim;*

*(2) indicate whether secured creditors need to file proofs of claim; and*

*(3) contain any other information required to be included in such notification to creditors under this title and the orders of the court.*

*(d) Any rule of procedure or order of the court as to notice or the filing of a proof of claim shall provide such additional time to creditors with foreign addresses as is reasonable under the circumstances.*

**Section 1514**

(April 20, 2005, P. L. 109-8, Title VIII, § 801(a), 119 Stat. 23)

### HISTORY: ANCILLARY LAWS AND DIRECTIVES

**Amendments:**

**2005.** Act April 20, 2005, created a new § 1514.

**Other provisions:**

**Effective date and application of Act April 20, 2005.**

Act April 20, 2005, Pub.L. 109-8, Title VIII, § 801(a), 119 Stat. 23, created a new Title 15 and is effective 180 days after enactment [April 20, 2005].

**Abridged Legislative History**

Sec. 1514. Notification of foreign creditors concerning a case under title 11. This section ensures that foreign creditors receive proper notice of cases in the United States. (H. Report No. 109-31 to accompany S. 256, 109th Cong., 1st Sess. (2005) p. 112; available at 2005 U.S.C.C.A.N. 88, at 174–75.)

## *§ 1515. Application for recognition*

*(a) A foreign representative applies to the court for recognition of a*

*foreign proceeding in which the foreign representative has been appointed by filing a petition for recognition.*

*(b) A petition for recognition shall be accompanied by—*

*(1) a certified copy of the decision commencing such foreign proceeding and appointing the foreign representative;*

*(2) a certificate from the foreign court affirming the existence of such foreign proceeding and of the appointment of the foreign representative; or*

*(3) in the absence of evidence referred to in paragraphs (1) and (2), any other evidence acceptable to the court of the existence of such foreign proceeding and of the appointment of the foreign representative.*

*(c) A petition for recognition shall also be accompanied by a statement identifying all foreign proceedings with respect to the debtor that are known to the foreign representative.*

*(d) The documents referred to in paragraphs (1) and (2) of subsection (b) shall be translated into English. The court may require a translation into English of additional documents.*

**Section 1515**

(April 20, 2005, P. L. 109-8, Title VIII, § 801(a), 119 Stat. 23)

## HISTORY: ANCILLARY LAWS AND DIRECTIVES

**Amendments:**

**2005.** Act April 20, 2005, created a new § 1515.

**Other provisions:**

**Effective date and application of Act April 20, 2005.**

Act April 20, 2005, Pub.L. 109-8, Title VIII, § 801(a), 119 Stat. 23, created a new Title 15 and is effective 180 days after enactment [April 20, 2005].

**Abridged Legislative History**

Sec. 1515. Application for recognition of a foreign proceeding. This section follows article 15 of the Model Law with minor changes. (H. Report No. 109-31 to accompany S. 256, 109th Cong., 1st Sess. (2005) p. 112; available at 2005 U.S.C.C.A.N. 88, at 175.)

# *§ 1516. Presumptions concerning recognition*

*(a) If the decision or certificate referred to in section 1515(b) indicates that the foreign proceeding is a foreign proceeding and that the person or body is a foreign representative, the court is entitled to so presume.*

*(b) The court is entitled to presume that documents submitted in support of the petition for recognition are authentic, whether or not they have been legalized.*

*(c) In the absence of evidence to the contrary, the debtor's registered office, or habitual residence in the case of an individual, is presumed to be the center of the debtor's main interests.*

**Section 1516**

(April 20, 2005, P. L. 109-8, Title VIII, § 801(a), 119 Stat. 23)

## HISTORY: ANCILLARY LAWS AND DIRECTIVES

**Amendments:**

**2005.** Act April 20, 2005, created a new § 1516.

**Other provisions:**

**Effective date and application of Act April 20, 2005.**

Act April 20, 2005, Pub.L. 109-8, Title VIII, § 801(a), 119 Stat. 23, created a new Title 15 and is effective 180 days after enactment [April 20, 2005].

**Abridged Legislative History**

Sec. 1516. Presumptions concerning recognition. This section follows article 16 of the Model Law with minor changes. (H. Report No. 109-31 to accompany S. 256, 109th Cong., 1st Sess. (2005) p. 112–13; available at 2005 U.S.C.C.A.N. 88, at 175.)

## *§ 1517. Order granting recognition*

*(a) Subject to section 1506, after notice and a hearing, an order recognizing a foreign proceeding shall be entered if—*

*(1) such foreign proceeding for which recognition is sought is a foreign main proceeding or foreign nonmain proceeding within the meaning of section 1502;*

*(2) the foreign representative applying for recognition is a person or body; and*

*(3) the petition meets the requirements of section 1515.*

*(b) Such foreign proceeding shall be recognized—*

*(1) as a foreign main proceeding if it is pending in the country where the debtor has the center of its main interests; or*

*(2) as a foreign nonmain proceeding if the debtor has an establishment within the meaning of section 1502 in the foreign country where the proceeding is pending.*

*(c) A petition for recognition of a foreign proceeding shall be decided upon at the earliest possible time. Entry of an order recognizing a foreign proceeding constitutes recognition under this chapter.*

*(d) The provisions of this subchapter do not prevent modification or termination of recognition if it is shown that the grounds for granting it were fully or partially lacking or have ceased to exist, but in considering such action the court shall give due weight to possible prejudice to parties that have relied upon the order granting recognition. A case under this chapter may be closed in the manner prescribed under section 350.*

**Section 1517**

(April 20, 2005, P. L. 109-8, Title VIII, § 801(a), 119 Stat. 23)

### HISTORY: ANCILLARY LAWS AND DIRECTIVES

**Amendments:**

**2005.** Act April 20, 2005, created a new § 1517.

**Other provisions:**

**Effective date and application of Act April 20, 2005.**

Act April 20, 2005, Pub.L. 109-8, Title VIII, § 801(a), 119 Stat. 23, created a new Title 15 and is effective 180 days after enactment [April 20, 2005].

**Abridged Legislative History**

Sec. 1517. Order granting recognition. This section closely tracks article 17 of the Model Law, with a few exceptions.

(H. Report No. 109-31 to accompany S. 256, 109th Cong., 1st Sess. (2005) p. 113; available at 2005 U.S.C.C.A.N. 88, at 175–76.)

## *§ 1518. Subsequent information*

*From the time of filing the petition for recognition of a foreign proceeding, the foreign representative shall file with the court promptly a notice of change of status concerning—*

*(1) any substantial change in the status of such foreign proceeding or the status of the foreign representative's appointment; and*

*(2) any other foreign proceeding regarding the debtor that becomes known to the foreign representative.*

**Section 1518**

(April 20, 2005, P. L. 109-8, Title VIII, § 801(a), 119 Stat. 23)

### HISTORY: ANCILLARY LAWS AND DIRECTIVES

**Amendments:**

**2005.** Act April 20, 2005, created a new § 1518.

**Other provisions:**

**Effective date and application of Act April 20, 2005.**

Act April 20, 2005, Pub.L. 109-8, Title VIII, § 801(a), 119 Stat. 23, created a new Title 15 and is effective 180 days after enactment [April 20, 2005].

**Abridged Legislative History**

Sec. 1518. Subsequent information. This section follows the Model Law, except to eliminate the word "same," which is rendered unnecessary by the definition of "debtor" in section 1502, and to provide for a formal document to be filed with the court. (H. Report No. 109-31 to accompany S. 256, 109th Cong., 1st Sess. (2005) p. 114; available at 2005 U.S.C.C.A.N. 88, at 176.)

## *§ 1519. Relief that may be granted upon filing petition for recognition*

*(a) From the time of filing a petition for recognition until the court rules on the petition, the court may, at the request of the foreign representative, where relief is urgently needed to protect the assets of the debtor or the interests of the creditors, grant relief of a provisional nature, including—*

*(1) staying execution against the debtor's assets;*

*(2) entrusting the administration or realization of all or part of the debtor's assets located in the United States to the foreign representative or another person authorized by the court, including an examiner, in order to protect and preserve the value of assets that, by their nature or because of other circumstances, are perishable, susceptible to devaluation or otherwise in jeopardy; and*

*(3) any relief referred to in paragraph (3), (4), or (7) of section 1521(a).*

*(b) Unless extended under section 1521(a)(6), the relief granted under this section terminates when the petition for recognition is granted.*

*(c) It is a ground for denial of relief under this section that such relief would interfere with the administration of a foreign main proceeding.*

*(d) The court may not enjoin a police or regulatory act of a governmental unit, including a criminal action or proceeding, under this section.*

*(e) The standards, procedures, and limitations applicable to an injunction shall apply to relief under this section.*

*(f) The exercise of rights not subject to the stay arising under section 362(a) pursuant to paragraph (6), (7), (17), or (27) of section 362(b) or pursuant to section 362(n) shall not be stayed by any order of a court or administrative agency in any proceeding under this chapter.*

**Section 1519**

(April 20, 2005, P. L. 109-8, Title VIII, § 801(a), 119 Stat. 23)

## HISTORY: ANCILLARY LAWS AND DIRECTIVES

**Amendments:**

**2005.** Act April 20, 2005, created a new § 1519.

**Other provisions:**

**Effective date and application of Act April 20, 2005.**

Act April 20, 2005, Pub.L. 109-8, Title VIII, § 801(a), 119 Stat. 23, created a new Title 15 and is effective 180 days after enactment [April 20, 2005].

**Abridged Legislative History**

Sec. 1519. Relief may be granted upon petition for recognition of a foreign proceeding. This section generally follows article 19 of the Model Law. (H. Report No. 109-31 to accompany S. 256, 109th Cong., 1st Sess. (2005) p. 114; available at 2005 U.S.C.C.A.N. 88, at 176–77.)

## *§ 1520. Effects of recognition of a foreign main proceeding*

*(a) Upon recognition of a foreign proceeding that is a foreign main proceeding—*

*(1) sections 361 and 362 apply with respect to the debtor and the property of the debtor that is within the territorial jurisdiction of the United States;*

*(2) sections 363, 549, and 552 apply to a transfer of an interest of the debtor in property that is within the territorial jurisdiction of the United States to the same extent that the sections would apply to property of an estate;*

*(3) unless the court orders otherwise, the foreign representative may operate the debtor's business and may exercise the rights and powers of a trustee under and to the extent provided by sections 363 and 552; and*

*(4) section 552 applies to property of the debtor that is within the territorial jurisdiction of the United States.*

*(b) Subsection (a) does not affect the right to commence an individual action or proceeding in a foreign country to the extent necessary to preserve a claim against the debtor.*

*(c) Subsection (a) does not affect the right of a foreign representative or an entity to file a petition commencing a case under this title or the right of any party to file claims or take other proper actions in such a case.*

**Section 1520**

(April 20, 2005, P. L. 109-8, Title VIII, § 801(a), 119 Stat. 23)

## HISTORY: ANCILLARY LAWS AND DIRECTIVES

**Amendments:**

**2005.** Act April 20, 2005, created a new § 1520.

**Other provisions:**

**Effective date and application of Act April 20, 2005.**

Act April 20, 2005, Pub.L. 109-8, Title VIII, § 801(a), 119 Stat. 23, created a new Title 15 and is effective 180 days after enactment [April 20, 2005].

**Abridged Legislative History**

Sec. 1520. Effects of recognition of a foreign main proceeding. In general, this chapter sets forth all the relief that is available as a matter of right based upon recognition hereunder, although additional assistance may be provided under section 1507 and this chapter has no effect on any relief currently available under section 105.

(H. Report No. 109-31 to accompany S. 256, 109th Cong., 1st Sess. (2005) p. 114–15; available at 2005 U.S.C.C.A.N. 88, at 177–78.)

# *§ 1521. Relief that may be granted upon recognition*

*(a) Upon recognition of a foreign proceeding, whether main or nonmain, where necessary to effectuate the purpose of this chapter and to protect the assets of the debtor or the interests of the creditors, the court may, at the request of the foreign representative, grant any appropriate relief, including—*

*(1) staying the commencement or continuation of an individual action or proceeding concerning the debtor's assets, rights, obligations or liabilities to the extent they have not been stayed under section 1520(a);*

*(2) staying execution against the debtor's assets to the extent it has not been stayed under section 1520(a);*

*(3) suspending the right to transfer, encumber or otherwise dispose of any assets of the debtor to the extent this right has not been suspended under section 1520(a);*

*(4) providing for the examination of witnesses, the taking of evidence or the delivery of information concerning the debtor's assets, affairs, rights, obligations or liabilities;*

*(5) entrusting the administration or realization of all or part of the debtor's assets within the territorial jurisdiction of the United States to the foreign representative or another person, including an examiner, authorized by the court;*

*(6) extending relief granted under section 1519(a); and*

*(7) granting any additional relief that may be available to a trustee, except for relief available under sections 522, 544, 545, 547, 548, 550, and 724(a).*

*(b) Upon recognition of a foreign proceeding, whether main or nonmain, the court may, at the request of the foreign representative, entrust the distribution of all or part of the debtor's assets located in the United States to the foreign representative or another person, including an examiner, authorized by the court, provided that the court is satisfied that the interests of creditors in the United States are sufficiently protected.*

*(c) In granting relief under this section to a representative of a foreign nonmain proceeding, the court must be satisfied that the relief relates to assets that, under the law of the United States, should be administered in the foreign nonmain proceeding or concerns information required in that proceeding.*

*(d) The court may not enjoin a police or regulatory act of a governmental unit, including a criminal action or proceeding, under this section.*

*(e) The standards, procedures, and limitations applicable to an injunction shall apply to relief under paragraphs (1), (2), (3), and (6) of subsection (a).*

*(f) The exercise of rights not subject to the stay arising under section 362(a) pursuant to paragraph (6), (7), (17), or (27) of section 362(b) or pursuant to section 362(n) shall not be stayed by any order of a court or administrative agency in any proceeding under this chapter.*

**Section 1521**

(April 20, 2005, P. L. 109-8, Title VIII, § 801(a), 119 Stat. 23)

## HISTORY: ANCILLARY LAWS AND DIRECTIVES

**Amendments:**

**2005.** Act April 20, 2005, created a new § 1521.

**Other provisions:**

**Effective date and application of Act April 20, 2005.**

Act April 20, 2005, Pub.L. 109-8, Title VIII, § 801(a), 119 Stat. 23, created a new Title 15 and is effective 180 days after enactment [April 20, 2005].

**Abridged Legislative History**

Sec. 1521. Relief that may be granted upon recognition of a foreign proceeding. This section follows article 21 of the Model Law, with detailed changes to conform to United States law. (H. Report No. 109-31 to accompany S. 256, 109th Cong., 1st Sess. (2005) p. 115–16; available at 2005 U.S.C.C.A.N. 88, at 178.)

## *§ 1522. Protection of creditors and other interested persons*

*(a) The court may grant relief under section 1519 or 1521, or may modify or terminate relief under subsection (c), only if the interests of the creditors and other interested entities, including the debtor, are sufficiently protected.*

*(b) The court may subject relief granted under section 1519 or 1521, or the operation of the debtor's business under section 1520(a)(3), to conditions it considers appropriate, including the giving of security or the filing of a bond.*

*(c) The court may, at the request of the foreign representative or an entity affected by relief granted under section 1519 or 1521, or at its own motion, modify or terminate such relief.*

*(d) Section 1104(d) shall apply to the appointment of an examiner under this chapter. Any examiner shall comply with the qualification requirements imposed on a trustee by section 322.*

**Section 1522**

(April 20, 2005, P. L. 109-8, Title VIII, § 801(a), 119 Stat. 23)

## HISTORY: ANCILLARY LAWS AND DIRECTIVES

**Amendments:**
**2005.** Act April 20, 2005, created a new § 1522.

**Other provisions:**
**Effective date and application of Act April 20, 2005.**
Act April 20, 2005, Pub.L. 109-8, Title VIII, § 801(a), 119 Stat. 23, created a new Title 15 and is effective 180 days after enactment [April 20, 2005].

**Abridged Legislative History**
Sec. 1522. Protection of creditors and other interested persons. This section follows article 22 of the Model Law with changes for United States usage and references to relevant Bankruptcy Code sections. (H. Report No. 109-31 to accompany S. 256, 109th Cong., 1st Sess. (2005) p. 116; available at 2005 U.S.C.C.A.N. 88, at 178.)

# *§ 1523. Actions to avoid acts detrimental to creditors*

*(a) Upon recognition of a foreign proceeding, the foreign representative has standing in a case concerning the debtor pending under another chapter of this title to initiate actions under sections 522, 544, 545, 547, 548, 550, 553, and 724(a).*

*(b) When a foreign proceeding is a foreign nonmain proceeding, the court must be satisfied that an action under subsection (a) relates to assets that, under United States law, should be administered in the foreign nonmain proceeding.*

**Section 1523**
(April 20, 2005, P. L. 109-8, Title VIII, § 801(a), 119 Stat. 23)

## HISTORY: ANCILLARY LAWS AND DIRECTIVES

**Amendments:**
**2005.** Act April 20, 2005, created a new § 1523.

**Other provisions:**
**Effective date and application of Act April 20, 2005.**
Act April 20, 2005, Pub.L. 109-8, Title VIII, § 801(a), 119 Stat. 23, created a new Title 15 and is effective 180 days after enactment [April 20, 2005].

**Abridged Legislative History**
Sec. 1523. Actions to avoid acts detrimental to creditors. This section follows article 23 of the Model Law, with wording to fit it within procedure under this title. (H. Report No. 109-31 to accompany S. 256, 109th Cong., 1st Sess. (2005) p. 116; available at 2005 U.S.C.C.A.N. 88, at 178–79.)

# *§ 1524. Intervention by a foreign representative*

*Upon recognition of a foreign proceeding, the foreign representative may intervene in any proceedings in a State or Federal court in the United States in which the debtor is a party.*

**Section 1524**
(April 20, 2005, P. L. 109-8, Title VIII, § 801(a), 119 Stat. 23)

## HISTORY: ANCILLARY LAWS AND DIRECTIVES

**Amendments:**
**2005.** Act April 20, 2005, created a new § 1524.

**Other provisions:**
**Effective date and application of Act April 20, 2005.**
Act April 20, 2005, Pub.L. 109-8, Title VIII, § 801(a), 119 Stat. 23, created a new Title

15 and is effective 180 days after enactment [April 20, 2005].

**Abridged Legislative History**

Sec. 1524. Intervention by a foreign representative. The wording is the same as the Model Law, except for a few clarifying words. (H. Report No. 109-31 to accompany S. 256, 109th Cong., 1st Sess. (2005) p. 116; available at 2005 U.S.C.C.A.N. 88, at 179.)

## *§ 1525. Cooperation and direct communication between the court and foreign courts or foreign representatives*

*(a) Consistent with section 1501, the court shall cooperate to the maximum extent possible with a foreign court or a foreign representative, either directly or through the trustee.*

*(b) The court is entitled to communicate directly with, or to request information or assistance directly from, a foreign court or a foreign representative, subject to the rights of a party in interest to notice and participation.*

**Section 1525**

(April 20, 2005, P. L. 109-8, Title VIII, § 801(a), 119 Stat. 23)

### HISTORY: ANCILLARY LAWS AND DIRECTIVES

**Amendments:**

**2005.** Act April 20, 2005, created a new § 1525.

**Other provisions:**

**Effective date and application of Act April 20, 2005.**

Act April 20, 2005, Pub.L. 109-8, Title VIII, § 801(a), 119 Stat. 23, created a new Title 15 and is effective 180 days after enactment [April 20, 2005].

**Abridged Legislative History**

Sec. 1525. Cooperation and direct communication between the court and foreign courts or foreign representatives. The wording of this provision is nearly identical to that of the Model Law. (H. Report No. 109-31 to accompany S. 256, 109th Cong., 1st Sess. (2005) p. 117; available at 2005 U.S.C.C.A.N. 88, at 179.)

## *§ 1526. Cooperation and direct communication between the trustee and foreign courts or foreign representatives*

*(a) Consistent with section 1501, the trustee or other person, including an examiner, authorized by the court, shall, subject to the supervision of the court, cooperate to the maximum extent possible with a foreign court or a foreign representative.*

*(b) The trustee or other person, including an examiner, authorized by the court is entitled, subject to the supervision of the court, to communicate directly with a foreign court or a foreign representative.*

**Section 1526**

(April 20, 2005, P. L. 109-8, Title VIII, § 801(a), 119 Stat. 23)

### HISTORY: ANCILLARY LAWS AND DIRECTIVES

**Amendments:**

**2005.** Act April 20, 2005, created a new § 1526.

**Other provisions:**

**Effective date and application of Act April 20, 2005.**

Act April 20, 2005, Pub.L. 109-8, Title VIII, § 801(a), 119 Stat. 23, created a new Title

15 and is effective 180 days after enactment [April 20, 2005].

**Abridged Legislative History**

Sec. 1526 Cooperation and direct communication between the trustee and foreign courts or foreign representatives. This section closely tracks the Model Law. (H. Report No. 109-31 to accompany S. 256, 109th Cong., 1st Sess. (2005) p.117; available at 2005 U.S.C.C.A.N. 88, at 179.)

## *§ 1527. Forms of cooperation*

*Cooperation referred to in sections 1525 and 1526 may be implemented by any appropriate means, including—*

*(1) appointment of a person or body, including an examiner, to act at the direction of the court;*

*(2) communication of information by any means considered appropriate by the court;*

*(3) coordination of the administration and supervision of the debtor's assets and affairs;*

*(4) approval or implementation of agreements concerning the coordination of proceedings; and*

*(5) coordination of concurrent proceedings regarding the same debtor.*

**Section 1527**

(April 20, 2005, P. L. 109-8, Title VIII, § 801(a), 119 Stat. 23)

### HISTORY: ANCILLARY LAWS AND DIRECTIVES

**Amendments:**

**2005.** Act April 20, 2005, created a new § 1527.

**Other provisions:**

**Effective date and application of Act April 20, 2005.**

Act April 20, 2005, Pub.L. 109-8, Title VIII, § 801(a), 119 Stat. 23, created a new Title 15 and is effective 180 days after enactment [April 20, 2005].

**Abridged Legislative History**

Sec. 1527. Forms of cooperation. This section is identical to the Model Law. (H. Report No. 109-31 to accompany S. 256, 109th Cong., 1st Sess. (2005) p. 117; available at 2005 U.S.C.C.A.N. 88, at 179.)

## *§ 1528. Commencement of a case under this title after recognition of a foreign main proceeding*

*After recognition of a foreign main proceeding, a case under another chapter of this title may be commenced only if the debtor has assets in the United States. The effects of such case shall be restricted to the assets of the debtor that are within the territorial jurisdiction of the United States and, to the extent necessary to implement cooperation and coordination under sections 1525, 1526, and 1527, to other assets of the debtor that are within the jurisdiction of the court under sections 541(a) of this title, and 1334(e) of title 28, to the extent that such other assets are not subject to the jurisdiction and control of a foreign proceeding that has been recognized under this chapter.*

**Section 1528**

(April 20, 2005, P. L. 109-8, Title VIII, § 801(a), 119 Stat. 23)

## HISTORY: ANCILLARY LAWS AND DIRECTIVES

**Amendments:**

**2005.** Act April 20, 2005, created a new § 1528.

**Other provisions:**

**Effective date and application of Act April 20, 2005.**

Act April 20, 2005, Pub.L. 109-8, Title VIII, § 801(a), 119 Stat. 23, created a new Title 15 and is effective 180 days after enactment [April 20, 2005].

**Abridged Legislative History**

Sec. 1528. Commencement of a case under title 11 after recognition of a foreign main proceeding. This section follows the Model Law, with specifics of United States law replacing the general clause at the end of the section to cover assets normally included within the jurisdiction of the United States courts in bankruptcy cases, except where assets are subject to the jurisdiction of another recognized proceeding.

(H. Report No. 109-31 to accompany S. 256, 109th Cong., 1st Sess. (2005) p. 117; available at 2005 U.S.C.C.A.N. 88, at 179–80.)

## *§ 1529. Coordination of a case under this title and a foreign proceeding*

*If a foreign proceeding and a case under another chapter of this title are pending concurrently regarding the same debtor, the court shall seek cooperation and coordination under sections 1525, 1526, and 1527, and the following shall apply:*

*(1) If the case in the United States pending at the time the petition for recognition of such foreign proceeding is filed—*

*(A) any relief granted under section 1519 or 1521 must be consistent with the relief granted in the case in the United States; and*

*(B) section 1520 does not apply even if such foreign proceeding is recognized as a foreign main proceeding.*

*(2) If a case in the United States under this title commences after recognition, or after the date of the filing of the petition for recognition, of such foreign proceeding—*

*(A) any relief in effect under section 1519 or 1521 shall be reviewed by the court and shall be modified or terminated if inconsistent with the case in the United States; and*

*(B) if such foreign proceeding is a foreign main proceeding, the stay and suspension referred to in section 1520(a) shall be modified or terminated if inconsistent with the relief granted in the case in the United States.*

*(3) In granting, extending, or modifying relief granted to a representative of a foreign nonmain proceeding, the court must be satisfied that the relief relates to assets that, under the laws of the United States, should be administered in the foreign nonmain proceeding or concerns information required in that proceeding.*

*(4) In achieving cooperation and coordination under sections 1528 and 1529, the court may grant any of the relief authorized under section 305.*

**Section 1529**

(April 20, 2005, P. L. 109-8, Title VIII, § 801(a), 119 Stat. 23)

## HISTORY: ANCILLARY LAWS AND DIRECTIVES

**Amendments:**

**2005.** Act April 20, 2005, created a new § 1529.

**Other provisions:**

**Effective date and application of Act April 20, 2005.**

Act April 20, 2005, Pub.L. 109-8, Title VIII, § 801(a), 119 Stat. 23, created a new Title 15 and is effective 180 days after enactment [April 20, 2005].

**Abridged Legislative History**

Sec. 1529. Coordination of a case under title 11 and a foreign proceeding. This section follows the Model Law almost exactly, but subsection (4) adds a reference to section 305 to make it clear the bankruptcy court may continue to use that section, as under present law, to dismiss or suspend a United States case as part of coordination and cooperation with foreign proceedings. (H. Report No. 109-31 to accompany S. 256, 109th Cong., 1st Sess. (2005) p. 117; available at 2005 U.S.C.C.A.N. 88, at 180.)

# *§ 1530. Coordination of more than 1 foreign proceeding*

*In matters referred to in section 1501, with respect to more than 1 foreign proceeding regarding the debtor, the court shall seek cooperation and coordination under sections 1525, 1526, and 1527, and the following shall apply:*

*(1) Any relief granted under section 1519 or 1521 to a representative of a foreign nonmain proceeding after recognition of a foreign main proceeding must be consistent with the foreign main proceeding.*

*(2) If a foreign main proceeding is recognized after recognition, or after the filing of a petition for recognition, of a foreign nonmain proceeding, any relief in effect under section 1519 or 1521 shall be reviewed by the court and shall be modified or terminated if inconsistent with the foreign main proceeding.*

*(3) If, after recognition of a foreign nonmain proceeding, another foreign nonmain proceeding is recognized, the court shall grant, modify, or terminate relief for the purpose of facilitating coordination of the proceedings.*

**Section 1530**

(April 20, 2005, P. L. 109-8, Title VIII, § 801(a), 119 Stat. 23)

## HISTORY: ANCILLARY LAWS AND DIRECTIVES

**Amendments:**

**2005.** Act April 20, 2005, created a new § 1530.

**Other provisions:**

**Effective date and application of Act April 20, 2005.**

Act April 20, 2005, Pub.L. 109-8, Title VIII, § 801(a), 119 Stat. 23, created a new Title 15 and is effective 180 days after enactment [April 20, 2005].

**Abridged Legislative History**

Sec. 1530. Coordination of more than one foreign proceeding. This section follows article 30 of the Model Law exactly. (H. Report No. 109-31 to accompany S. 256, 109th Cong., 1st Sess. (2005) p. 118; available at 2005 U.S.C.C.A.N. 88, at 180.)

## *§ 1531. Presumption of insolvency based on recognition of a foreign main proceeding*

*In the absence of evidence to the contrary, recognition of a foreign main proceeding is, for the purpose of commencing a proceeding under section 303, proof that the debtor is generally not paying its debts as such debts become due.*

**Section 1531**

(April 20, 2005, P. L. 109-8, Title VIII, § 801(a), 119 Stat. 23)

### HISTORY: ANCILLARY LAWS AND DIRECTIVES

**Amendments:**

**2005.** Act April 20, 2005, created a new § 1531.

**Other provisions:**

**Effective date and application of Act April 20, 2005.**

Act April 20, 2005, Pub.L. 109-8, Title VIII, § 801(a), 119 Stat. 23, created a new Title 15 and is effective 180 days after enactment [April 20, 2005].

**Abridged Legislative History**

Sec. 1531. Presumption of insolvency based on recognition of a foreign main proceeding. This section follows the Model Law exactly, inserting a reference to the standard for an involuntary case under this title. (H. Report No. 109-31 to accompany S. 256, 109th Cong., 1st Sess. (2005) p.118; available at 2005 U.S.C.C.A.N. 88, at 180.)

## *§ 1532. Rule of payment in concurrent proceedings*

*Without prejudice to secured claims or rights in rem, a creditor who has received payment with respect to its claim in a foreign proceeding pursuant to a law relating to insolvency may not receive a payment for the same claim in a case under any other chapter of this title regarding the debtor, so long as the payment to other creditors of the same class is proportionately less than the payment the creditor has already received.*

**Section 1532**

(April 20, 2005, P. L. 109-8, Title VIII, § 801(a), 119 Stat. 23)

### HISTORY: ANCILLARY LAWS AND DIRECTIVES

**Amendments:**

**2005.** Act April 20, 2005, created a new § 1532.

**Other provisions:**

**Effective date and application of Act April 20, 2005.**

Act April 20, 2005, Pub.L. 109-8, Title VIII, § 801(a), 119 Stat. 23, created a new Title 15 and is effective 180 days after enactment [April 20, 2005].

**Abridged Legislative History**

Sec. 1532. Rule of payment in concurrent proceeding. This section follows the Model Law exactly and is very similar to prior section 508(a), which is repealed. (H. Report No. 109-31 to accompany S. 256, 109th Cong., 1st Sess. (2005) p. 118; available at 2005 U.S.C.C.A.N. 88, at 180.)

# Bankruptcy Related Provisions in Title 18 United States Code

## Crimes and Criminal Procedure

## Title 18

## Part I
## Crimes

## Sec. 156. Knowing disregard of bankruptcy law or rule

(a) Definitions- In this section—

*(1) the term* 'bankruptcy petition preparer' means a person, other than the debtor's attorney or an employee of such an attorney, who prepares for compensation a document for filing~~.~~; *and*

*(2) the term* 'document for filing' means a petition or any other document prepared for filing by a debtor in a United States bankruptcy court or a United States district court in connection with a case under ~~this title~~ *title 11.*

(b) Offense- If a bankruptcy case or related proceeding is dismissed because of a knowing attempt by a bankruptcy petition preparer in any manner to disregard the requirements of title 11, United States Code, or the Federal Rules of Bankruptcy Procedure, the bankruptcy petition preparer shall be fined under this title, imprisoned not more than 1 year, or both.

**Section 156**

(April 20, 2005, P. L. 109-8, Title XII, § 1220, 119 Stat. 23)

### HISTORY: ANCILLARY LAWS AND DIRECTIVES

**Amendments:**

2005. Act April 20, 2005, inserted "the term" in subsections (a)(1) and (2) and inserted "title 11" instead of "this title".

**Short Titles:**

Act April 20, 2005, P. L. 109-8, Section 1(a), 119 Stat. 23 [amending substantial sections of Title 11, Chapters 1, 3, 5, 7, 11, 12 and 13, and adding Chapter 15], generally effective 180 following enactment, as provided by § 1501(a) of such Act, provides: "This Act may be cited as the 'Bankruptcy Abuse Prevention and Consumer Protection Act of 2005'."

**Other provisions:**

**Effective date and application of Act April 20, 2005.**

Act April 20, 2005, Pub.L. 109-8, Title XV, § 1501, 119 Stat. 23, is generally effective 180 days after enactment [April 20, 2005]. Section 1501 provides:

EFFECTIVE DATE; APPLICATION OF AMENDMENTS.

(a) EFFECTIVE DATE- Except as otherwise provided in this Act, this Act and the amendments made by this Act shall take effect 180 days after the date of enactment of this Act.

(b) APPLICATION OF AMENDMENTS-

1) IN GENERAL- Except as otherwise provided in this Act and paragraph (2), the amendments made by this Act shall not apply with respect to cases commenced under title 11, United States Code, before the effective date of this Act.

(2) CERTAIN LIMITATIONS APPLICABLE TO DEBTORS- The amendments made by sections 308, 322, and 330 shall apply with respect to cases commenced under title 11, United States Code, on or after the date of the enactment of this Act.

**Abridged Legislative History**

**2005 Act.**

(H. Report No. 109-31 to accompany S. 256, 109th Cong., 1st Sess. (2005) p. 145; available at 2005 U.S.C.C.A.N. 88, at 203.)

# Sec. 157. Bankruptcy fraud

A person who, having devised or intending to devise a scheme or artifice to defraud and for the purpose of executing or concealing such a scheme or artifice or attempting to do so—

(1) files a petition under title 11, *including a fraudulent involuntary bankruptcy petition under section 303 of such title*;

(2) files a document in a proceeding under title 11, *including a fraudulent involuntary bankruptcy petition under section 303 of such title*; or

(3) makes a false or fraudulent representation, claim, or promise concerning or in relation to a proceeding under title 11, *including a fraudulent involuntary bankruptcy petition under section 303 of such title*, at any time before or after the filing of the petition, or in relation to a proceeding falsely asserted to be pending under such title,

shall be fined under this title, imprisoned not more than 5 years, or both.

**Section 157**

(April 20, 2005, P. L. 109-8, Title III, § 332(c), 119 Stat. 23)

## HISTORY: ANCILLARY LAWS AND DIRECTIVES

**Amendments:**

**2005.** Act April 20, 2005 (effective 180 days from enactment on April 20, 2005, as provided by § 1501(a) of P.L. 109-8), inserted "including a fraudulent involuntary bankruptcy petition under section 303 of such title" after "title 11". *The language of the Act is silent as to which paragraph(s) are so amended.

**Other provisions:**

**Effective date and application of amendments made by Act April 20, 2005.** Act April 20, 2005, P.L. 109-8, Title XV, § 1501(a), 119 Stat. 23, provided that the amendments made to this section would be effective 180 days after enactment on April 20, 2005.

**Abridged Legislative History**

(H. Report No. 109-31 to accompany S. 256, 109th Cong., 1st Sess. (2005) p.86; available at 2005 U.S.C.C.A.N. 88, at 152.)

## *Sec. 158. Designation of United States attorneys and agents of the Federal Bureau of Investigation to address abusive reaffirmations of debt and materially fraudulent statements in bankruptcy schedules*

*(a) IN GENERAL- The Attorney General of the United States shall designate the individuals described in subsection (b) to have primary responsibility in carrying out enforcement activities in addressing violations of section 152 or 157 relating to abusive reaffirmations of debt. In addition to addressing the violations referred to in the preceding sentence, the individuals described under subsection (b) shall address violations of section 152 or 157 relating to materially fraudulent statements in bankruptcy schedules that are intentionally false or intentionally misleading.*

*(b) UNITED STATES ATTORNEYS AND AGENTS OF THE FEDERAL BUREAU OF INVESTIGATION— The individuals referred to in subsection (a) are—*

*(1) the United States attorney for each judicial district of the United States; and*

*(2) an agent of the Federal Bureau of Investigation for each field office of the Federal Bureau of Investigation.*

*(c) BANKRUPTCY INVESTIGATIONS— Each United States attorney designated under this section shall, in addition to any other responsibilities, have primary responsibility for carrying out the duties of a United States attorney under section 3057.*

*(d) BANKRUPTCY PROCEDURES— The bankruptcy courts shall establish procedures for referring any case that may contain a materially fraudulent statement in a bankruptcy schedule to the individuals designated under this section.*

**Section 158**

(April 20, 2005, P. L. 109-8, Title IIA, § 203(b), 119 Stat. 23)

## HISTORY: ANCILLARY LAWS AND DIRECTIVES

**Amendments:**

**2005.** Act April 20, 2005 (effective 180 days after enactment on April 20, 2005, as provided by § 1501(a) of P.L. 109-8), inserted new § 158.

**Other provisions:**

**Effective date and application of amendments made by Act April 20, 2005.** Act April 20, 2005, P.L. 109-8, Title XV, § 1501(a), 119 Stat. 23, provided that the amendments made to this section would be effective 180 days after enactment on April 20, 2005.

**Abridged Legislative History**

(H. Report No. 109-31 to accompany S. 256, 109th Cong., 1st Sess. (2005) p.58; available at 2005 U.S.C.C.A.N. 88, at 128.)

# Bankruptcy Related Provisions in Title 28 United States Code

## JUDICIARY AND JUDICIAL PROCEDURE

**TITLE 28 —UNITED STATES CODE**

## Chapter 6 —Bankruptcy Judges

Sec. 152. Appointment of bankruptcy judges
Sec. 157. Procedures
Sec. 158. Appeals
***Sec. 159. Bankruptcy statistics***

## *Part II —Department of Justice*

## Chapter 39 —United States Trustees

Sec. 586. Duties; supervision by Attorney General
Sec. 589a. United States Trustee System Fund
***Sec. 589b. Bankruptcy data***

## *Part III —Court Officers and Employees*

## Chapter 57 —General Provisions Applicable to Court Officers and Employees

Sec. 960. Tax liability

## *Part IV —Jurisdiction and Venue*

## Chapter 85 —District Courts; Jurisdiction

Sec. 1334. Bankruptcy cases and proceedings

## Chapter 87 —District Courts; Venue

Sec. 1409. Venue of proceedings arising under title 11 or arising in or related to cases under title 11
**~~Sec. 1410. Venue of cases ancillary to foreign proceedings~~**
***Sec. 1410. Venue of cases ancillary to foreign proceedings***

## *Part V —Procedure*

## Chapter 123 —Fees and Costs

Sec. 1930. Bankruptcy fees

## Chapter 131 —Rules of Courts

Sec. 2075. Bankruptcy rules

### Title 28 —United States Code

* * * * * * *

## Chapter 6 —Bankruptcy Judges

* * * * * * *

## Sec. 152. Appointment of bankruptcy judges

(a) (1) ~~The United States court of appeals for the circuit shall appoint bankruptcy judges for the judicial districts established in paragraph (2) in such numbers as are established in such paragraph.~~. *Each bankruptcy judge to be appointed for a judicial district, as provided in paragraph (2), shall be appointed by the court of appeals of the United States for the circuit in which such district is located.* Such appointments shall be made after considering the recommendations of the Judicial Conference submitted pursuant to subsection (b). Each bankruptcy judge shall be appointed for a term of fourteen years, subject to the provisions of subsection (e). However, upon the expiration of the term, a bankruptcy judge may, with the approval of the judicial council of the circuit, continue to perform the duties of the office until the earlier of the date which is 180 days after the expiration of the term or the date of the appointment of a successor. Bankruptcy judges shall serve as judicial officers of the United States district court established under Article III of the Constitution.

(2) The bankruptcy judges appointed pursuant to this section shall be appointed for the several judicial districts as follows:

| Districts | Judges | |
|---|---|---|
| Alabama: | | |
| Northern | 5 | |
| Middle | 2 | |
| Southern | 2 | |
| Alaska | 2 | |
| Arizona | 7 | |
| Arkansas: | | |
| Eastern and Western | 3 | |
| California: | | |
| Northern | 9 | |
| Eastern | ~~6~~ | 7 |
| Central | ~~21~~ | *24* |
| Southern | 4 | |

| Districts | Judges | |
|---|---|---|
| Colorado | 5 | |
| Connecticut | 3 | |
| Delaware | ~~1~~ | *5* |
| District of Columbia | 1 | |
| Florida: | | |
| Northern | 1 | |
| Middle | 8 | |
| Southern | ~~5~~ | *7* |
| Georgia: | | |
| Northern | 8 | |
| Middle | ~~2~~ | 3 |
| Southern | ~~2~~ | *3* |
| ~~Middle and Southern~~ | ~~1~~ | |
| Hawaii | 1 | |
| Idaho | 2 | |
| Illinois: | | |
| Northern | 10 | |
| Central | 3 | |
| Southern | 1 | |
| Indiana: | | |
| Northern | 3 | |
| Southern | 4 | |
| Iowa: | | |
| Northern | 2 | |
| Southern | 2 | |
| Kansas | 4 | |
| Kentucky: | | |
| Eastern | 2 | |
| Western | 3 | |
| Louisiana: | | |
| Eastern | 2 | |
| Middle | 1 | |
| Western | 3 | |
| Maine | 2 | |
| Maryland | ~~4~~ | *7* |
| Massachusetts | 5 | |
| Michigan: | | |
| Eastern | ~~4~~ | *5* |
| Western | 3 | |
| Minnesota | 4 | |
| Mississippi: | | |

| Districts | Judges |
|---|---|
| Northern | 1 |
| Southern | ~~2~~ *3* |
| Missouri: | |
| Eastern | 3 |
| Western | 3 |
| Montana | 1 |
| Nebraska | 2 |
| Nevada | ~~3~~ 4 |
| New Hampshire | 1 |
| New Jersey | ~~8~~ *9* |
| New Mexico | 2 |
| New York: | |
| Northern | ~~2~~ 3 |
| Southern | ~~9~~ 10 |
| Eastern | ~~6~~ *7* |
| Western | 3 |
| North Carolina: | |
| Eastern | ~~2~~ 3 |
| Middle | 2 |
| Western | 2 |
| North Dakota | 1 |
| Ohio: | |
| Northern | 8 |
| Southern | 7 |
| Oklahoma: | |
| Northern | 2 |
| Eastern | 1 |
| Western | 3 |
| Oregon | 5 |
| Pennsylvania: | |
| Eastern | ~~5~~ 6 |
| Middle | ~~2~~ 3 |
| Western | 4 |
| Puerto Rico | ~~2~~ 3 |
| Rhode Island | 1 |
| South Carolina | ~~2~~ 3 |
| South Dakota | 2 |
| Tennessee: | |
| Eastern | 3 |
| Middle | 3 |
| Western | ~~4~~ 5 |

| Districts | Judges |
|---|---|
| Texas: | |
| Northern | 6 |
| Eastern | 2 |
| Southern | 6 |
| Western | 4 |
| Utah | 3 |
| Vermont | 1 |
| Virginia: | |
| Eastern | ~~5~~ 6 |
| Western | 3 |
| Washington: | |
| Eastern | 2 |
| Western | 5 |
| West Virginia: | |
| Northern | 1 |
| Southern | 1 |
| Wisconsin: | |
| Eastern | 4 |
| Western | 2 |
| Wyoming | 1 |

(3) Whenever a majority of the judges of any court of appeals cannot agree upon the appointment of a bankruptcy judge, the chief judge of such court shall make such appointment.

(4) The judges of the district courts for the territories shall serve as the bankruptcy judges for such courts. The United States court of appeals for the circuit within which such a territorial district court is located may appoint bankruptcy judges under this chapter for such district if authorized to do so by the Congress of the United States under this section.

(b) (1) The Judicial Conference of the United States shall, from time to time, and after considering the recommendations submitted by the Director of the Administrative Office of the United States Courts after such Director has consulted with the judicial council of the circuit involved, determine the official duty stations of bankruptcy judges and places of holding court.

(2) The Judicial Conference shall, from time to time, submit recommendations to the Congress regarding the number of bankruptcy judges needed and the districts in which such judges are needed.

(3) Not later than December 31, 1994, and not later than the end of each 2-year period thereafter, the Judicial Conference of the United States shall conduct a comprehensive review of all judicial districts to assess the continuing need for the bankruptcy judges

authorized by this section, and shall report to the Congress its findings and any recommendations for the elimination of any authorized position which can be eliminated when a vacancy exists by reason of resignation, retirement, removal, or death.

(c) Each bankruptcy judge may hold court at such places within the judicial district, in addition to the official duty station of such judge, as the business of the court may require.

(d) With the approval of the Judicial Conference and of each of the judicial councils involved, a bankruptcy judge may be designated to serve in any district adjacent to or near the district for which such bankruptcy judge was appointed.

(e) A bankruptcy judge may be removed during the term for which such bankruptcy judge is appointed, only for incompetence, misconduct, neglect of duty, or physical or mental disability and only by the judicial council of the circuit in which the judge's official duty station is located. Removal may not occur unless a majority of all of the judges of such council concur in the order of removal. Before any order of removal may be entered, a full specification of charges shall be furnished to such bankruptcy judge who shall be accorded an opportunity to be heard on such charges.

**Section 152**

(April 20, 2005, P. L. 109-8, Title XII, § 1223, 119 Stat. 23)

## HISTORY: ANCILLARY LAWS AND DIRECTIVES

**Amendments:**

**2005.** Act April 20, 2005 (effective upon enactment on April 20, 2005, as provided by § 1223(e) of P.L. 109-8), amends 28 USC § 152(a) to add the following new judgeships:

(A) One additional bankruptcy judge for the eastern district of California.

(B) Three additional bankruptcy judges for the central district of California.

(C) Four additional bankruptcy judges for the district of Delaware.

(D) Two additional bankruptcy judges for the southern district of Florida.

(E) One additional bankruptcy judge for the southern district of Georgia.

(F) Three additional bankruptcy judges for the district of Maryland.

(G) One additional bankruptcy judge for the eastern district of Michigan.

(H) One additional bankruptcy judge for the southern district of Mississippi.

(I) One additional bankruptcy judge for the district of New Jersey.

(J) One additional bankruptcy judge for the eastern district of New York.

(K) One additional bankruptcy judge for the northern district of New York.

(L) One additional bankruptcy judge for the southern district of New York.

(M) One additional bankruptcy judge for the eastern district of North Carolina.

(N) One additional bankruptcy judge for the eastern district of Pennsylvania.

(O) One additional bankruptcy judge for the middle district of Pennsylvania.

(P) One additional bankruptcy judge for the district of Puerto Rico.

(Q) One additional bankruptcy judge for the western district of Tennessee.

(R) One additional bankruptcy judge for the eastern district of Virginia.

(S) One additional bankruptcy judge for the district of South Carolina.

(T) One additional bankruptcy judge for the district of Nevada.

[In addition, the Act made these temporary judgeships, providing:]

(2) VACANCIES-

(A) DISTRICTS WITH SINGLE APPOINTMENTS- Except as provided in subparagraphs (B), (C), (D), and (E), the first vacancy occurring in the office of bankruptcy judge in each of the judicial districts set forth in paragraph (1)—

(i) occurring 5 years or more after the appointment date of the bankruptcy judge appointed under paragraph (1) to such office; and

(ii) resulting from the death, retirement, resignation, or removal of a bankruptcy judge;

shall not be filled.

(B) CENTRAL DISTRICT OF CALIFORNIA- The 1st, 2d, and 3d vacancies in the office of bankruptcy judge in the central district of California—

(i) occurring 5 years or more after the respective 1st, 2d, and 3d appointment dates of the bankruptcy judges appointed under paragraph (1)(B); and

(ii) resulting from the death, retirement, resignation, or removal of a bankruptcy judge;

shall not be filled.

(C) DISTRICT OF DELAWARE- The 1st, 2d, 3d, and 4th vacancies in the office of bankruptcy judge in the district of Delaware—

(i) occurring 5 years or more after the respective 1st, 2d, 3d, and 4th appointment dates of the bankruptcy judges appointed under paragraph (1)(F); and

(ii) resulting from the death, retirement, resignation, or removal of a bankruptcy judge;

shall not be filled.

(D) SOUTHERN DISTRICT OF FLORIDA— The 1st and 2d vacancies in the office of bankruptcy judge in the southern district of Florida—

(i) occurring 5 years or more after the respective 1st and 2d appointment dates of the bankruptcy judges appointed under paragraph (1)(D); and

(ii) resulting from the death, retirement, resignation, or removal of a bankruptcy judge;

shall not be filled.

(E) DISTRICT OF MARYLAND- The 1st, 2d, and 3d vacancies in the office of bankruptcy judge in the district of Maryland—

(i) occurring 5 years or more after the respective 1st, 2d, and 3d appointment dates of the bankruptcy judges appointed under paragraph (1)(F); and

(ii) resulting from the death, retirement, resignation, or removal of a bankruptcy judge;

shall not be filled.

[Further, the Act extended some prior temporary judgeships:]

(c) EXTENSIONS-

(1) IN GENERAL- The temporary office of bankruptcy judges authorized for the northern district of Alabama, the district of Delaware, the district of Puerto Rico, and the eastern district of Tennessee under paragraphs (1), (3), (7), and (9) of section 3(a) of the Bankruptcy Judgeship Act of 1992 (28 U.S.C. 152 note) are extended until the first vacancy occurring in the office of a bankruptcy judge in the applicable district resulting from the death, retirement, resignation, or removal of a bankruptcy judge and occurring 5 years after the date of the enactment of this Act.

(2) APPLICABILITY OF OTHER PROVISIONS- All other provisions of section 3 of the Bankruptcy Judgeship Act of 1992 (28 U.S.C. 152 note) remain applicable to the temporary office of bankruptcy judges referred to in this subsection.

[The Act made the following technical amendments:]

(d) TECHNICAL AMENDMENTS- Section 152(a) of title 28, United States Code, is amended—

(1) in paragraph (1), by striking the first sentence and inserting the following: 'Each bankruptcy judge to be appointed for a judicial district, as provided in paragraph (2), shall be appointed by the court of appeals of the United States for the circuit in which such district is located.'; and

(2) in paragraph (2)—

(A) in the item relating to the middle district of Georgia, by striking '2' and inserting '3'; and

(B) in the collective item relating to the middle and southern districts of Georgia, by striking 'Middle and Southern. . . . 1'.

[The Act's effective date provides:]

(e) EFFECTIVE DATE- The amendments made by this section shall take effect on the date of the enactment of this Act.

**Short Titles:**

Act April 20, 2005, P. L. 109-8, Section 1223(a), 119 Stat. 23 [amending substantial sections of Titles 11, 12, 15, 18, and 28], effective upon enactment for this section, as provided by § 1223(e) of such Act, provides: "This section may be cited as the 'Bankruptcy Judgeship Act of 2005."

**Other provisions:**

**Effective date and application of amendments made by Act April 20, 2005.** Act April 20, 2005, P.L. 109-8, Title XII, § 1223(e), 119 Stat. 23, provided that the amendments made to this section would be effective upon enactment on April 20, 2005.

**Abridged Legislative History**

(H. Report No. 109-31 to accompany S. 256, 109th Cong., 1st Sess. (2005) p.145–46; available at 2005 U.S.C.C.A.N. 88, at 204.)

## Sec. 157. Procedures

(a) Each district court may provide that any or all cases under title

11 and any or all proceedings arising under title 11 or arising in or related to a case under title 11 shall be referred to the bankruptcy judges for the district.

(b) (1) Bankruptcy judges may hear and determine all cases under title 11 and all core proceedings arising under title 11, or arising in a case under title 11, referred under subsection (a) of this section, and may enter appropriate orders and judgments, subject to review under section 158 of this title.

(2) Core proceedings include, but are not limited to—

(A) matters concerning the administration of the estate;

(B) allowance or disallowance of claims against the estate or exemptions from property of the estate, and estimation of claims or interests for the purposes of confirming a plan under chapter 11, 12, or 13 of title 11 but not the liquidation or estimation of contingent or unliquidated personal injury tort or wrongful death claims against the estate for purposes of distribution in a case under title 11;

(C) counterclaims by the estate against persons filing claims against the estate;

(D) orders in respect to obtaining credit;

(E) orders to turn over property of the estate;

(F) proceedings to determine, avoid, or recover preferences;

(G) motions to terminate, annul, or modify the automatic stay;

(H) proceedings to determine, avoid, or recover fraudulent conveyances;

(I) determinations as to the dischargeability of particular debts;

(J) objections to discharges;

(K) determinations of the validity, extent, or priority of liens;

(L) confirmations of plans;

(M) orders approving the use or lease of property, including the use of cash collateral;

(N) orders approving the sale of property other than property resulting from claims brought by the estate against persons who have not filed claims against the estate; ~~and~~

(O) other proceedings affecting the liquidation of the assets of the estate or the adjustment of the debtor-creditor or the equity security holder relationship, except personal injury tort or wrongful death claims~~.~~*; and*

*(P) recognition of foreign proceedings and other matters under chapter 15 of title 11.*

(3) The bankruptcy judge shall determine, on the judge's own motion or on timely motion of a party, whether a proceeding is a core proceeding under this subsection or is a proceeding that is otherwise related to a case under title 11. A determination that a proceeding is not a core proceeding shall not be made solely on the basis that its resolution may be affected by State law.

(4) Non-core proceedings under section 157(b)(2)(B) of title 28, United States Code, shall not be subject to the mandatory abstention provisions of section 1334(c)(2).

(5) The district court shall order that personal injury tort and wrongful death claims shall be tried in the district court in which the bankruptcy case is pending, or in the district court in the district in which the claim arose, as determined by the district court in which the bankruptcy case is pending.

(c) (1) A bankruptcy judge may hear a proceeding that is not a core proceeding but that is otherwise related to a case under title 11. In such proceeding, the bankruptcy judge shall submit proposed findings of fact and conclusions of law to the district court, and any final order or judgment shall be entered by the district judge after considering the bankruptcy judge's proposed findings and conclusions and after reviewing de novo those matters to which any party has timely and specifically objected.

(2) Notwithstanding the provisions of paragraph (1) of this subsection, the district court, with the consent of all the parties to the proceeding, may refer a proceeding related to a case under title 11 to a bankruptcy judge to hear and determine and to enter appropriate orders and judgments, subject to review under section 158 of this title.

(d) The district court may withdraw, in whole or in part, any case or proceeding referred under this section, on its own motion or on timely motion of any party, for cause shown. The district court shall, on timely motion of a party, so withdraw a proceeding if the court determines that resolution of the proceeding requires consideration of both title 11 and other laws of the United States regulating organizations or activities affecting interstate commerce.

(e) If the right to a jury trial applies in a proceeding that may be heard under this section by a bankruptcy judge, the bankruptcy judge may conduct the jury trial if specially designated to exercise such jurisdiction by the district court and with the express consent of all the parties.

**Section 157**

(April 20, 2005, P. L. 109-8, Title VIII, § 802(c)(1), 119 Stat. 23)

## HISTORY: ANCILLARY LAWS AND DIRECTIVES

**Amendments:**

**2005.** Act April 20, 2005 (effective 180 days after enactment on April 20, 2005, as provided by § 1501(a) of P.L. 109-8), inserted foreign proceedings and matters under new chapter 15 of title 11 as core proceedings.

**Other provisions:**

**Effective date and application of Act April 20, 2005.**

Act April 20, 2005, Pub.L. 109-8, Title XV, § 1501, 119 Stat. 23, is generally effective 180 days after enactment [April 20, 2005]. Section 1501 provides:

EFFECTIVE DATE; APPLICATION OF AMENDMENTS.

(a) EFFECTIVE DATE- Except as otherwise provided in this Act, this Act and the amendments made by this Act shall take effect 180 days after the date of enactment of this Act.

(b) APPLICATION OF AMENDMENTS-

(1) IN GENERAL- Except as otherwise provided in this Act and paragraph (2), the amendments made by this Act shall not apply with respect to cases commenced under title 11, United States Code, before the effective date of this Act.

(2) CERTAIN LIMITATIONS APPLICABLE TO DEBTORS- The amendments made by sections 308, 322, and 330 shall apply with respect to cases commenced under title 11, United States Code, on or after the date of the enactment of this Act.

**Abridged Legislative History**

(H. Report No. 109-31 to accompany S. 256, 109th Cong., 1st Sess. (2005) p.118; available at 2005 U.S.C.C.A.N. 88, at 180–81.)

# Sec. 158. Appeals

(a) The district courts of the United States shall have jurisdiction to hear appeals

(1) from final judgments, orders, and decrees;

(2) from interlocutory orders and decrees issued under section 1121(d) of title 11 increasing or reducing the time periods referred to in section 1121 of such title; and

(3) with leave of the court, from other interlocutory orders and decrees; and, with leave of the court, from interlocutory orders and decrees, of bankruptcy judges entered in cases and proceedings referred to the bankruptcy judges under section 157 of this title. An appeal under this subsection shall be taken only to the district court for the judicial district in which the bankruptcy judge is serving.

(b) (1) The judicial council of a circuit shall establish a bankruptcy appellate panel service composed of bankruptcy judges of the districts in the circuit who are appointed by the judicial council in accordance with paragraph (3), to hear and determine, with the consent of all the parties, appeals under subsection (a) unless the judicial council finds that—

(A) there are insufficient judicial resources available in the circuit; or

(B) establishment of such service would result in undue delay or increased cost to parties in cases under title 11. Not later than 90 days after making the finding, the judicial council shall submit to the Judicial Conference of the United States a report containing the factual basis of such finding.

(2) (A) A judicial council may reconsider, at any time, the finding described in paragraph (1).

(B) On the request of a majority of the district judges in a circuit for which a bankruptcy appellate panel service is established under paragraph (1), made after the expiration of the 1-year period beginning on the date such service is established, the judicial council of the circuit shall determine whether a circumstance specified in subparagraph (A) or (B) of such paragraph exists.

(C) On its own motion, after the expiration of the 3-year period beginning on the date a bankruptcy appellate panel service is established under paragraph (1), the judicial council of the circuit may determine whether a circumstance specified in subparagraph (A) or (B) of such paragraph exists.

(D) If the judicial council finds that either of such circumstances exists, the judicial council may provide for the completion of the appeals then pending before such service and the orderly termination of such service.

(3) Bankruptcy judges appointed under paragraph (1) shall be appointed and may be reappointed under such paragraph.

(4) If authorized by the Judicial Conference of the United States, the judicial councils of 2 or more circuits may establish a joint bankruptcy appellate panel comprised of bankruptcy judges from the districts within the circuits for which such panel is established, to hear and determine, upon the consent of all the parties, appeals under subsection (a) of this section.

(5) An appeal to be heard under this subsection shall be heard by a panel of 3 members of the bankruptcy appellate panel service, except that a member of such service may not hear an appeal originating in the district for which such member is appointed or designated under section 152 of this title.

(6) Appeals may not be heard under this subsection by a panel of the bankruptcy appellate panel service unless the district judges for the district in which the appeals occur, by majority vote, have authorized such service to hear and determine appeals originating in such district.

(c) (1) Subject to ~~subsection (b),~~ *subsections (b) and (d)(2),* each appeal under subsection (a) shall be heard by a 3-judge panel of the bankruptcy appellate panel service established under subsection (b)(1) unless—

(A) the appellant elects at the time of filing the appeal; or

(B) any other party elects, not later than 30 days after service of notice of the appeal; to have such appeal heard by the district court.

(2) An appeal under subsections (a) and (b) of this section shall be taken in the same manner as appeals in civil proceedings generally are taken to the courts of appeals from the district courts and in the time provided by Rule 8002 of the Bankruptcy Rules.

(d) *(1)* The courts of appeals shall have jurisdiction of appeals from all final decisions, judgments, orders, and decrees entered under subsections (a) and (b) of this section.

*(2) (A) The appropriate court of appeals shall have jurisdiction of appeals described in the first sentence of subsection (a) if the bankruptcy court, the district court, or the bankruptcy appellate panel involved, acting on its own motion or on the request of a party to the judgment, order, or decree described in such first sentence, or all the appellants and appellees (if any) acting jointly, certify that —*

*(i) the judgment, order, or decree involves a question of law as*

*to which there is no controlling decision of the court of appeals for the circuit or of the Supreme Court of the United States, or involves a matter of public importance;*

*(ii) the judgment, order, or decree involves a question of law requiring resolution of conflicting decisions; or*

*(iii) an immediate appeal from the judgment, order, or decree may materially advance the progress of the case or proceeding in which the appeal is taken; and if the court of appeals authorizes the direct appeal of the judgment, order, or decree.*

*(B) If the bankruptcy court, the district court, or the bankruptcy appellate panel —*

*(i) on its own motion or on the request of a party, determines that a circumstance specified in clause (i), (ii), or (iii) of subparagraph (A) exists; or*

*(ii) receives a request made by a majority of the appellants and a majority of appellees (if any) to make the certification described in subparagraph (A); then the bankruptcy court, the district court, or the bankruptcy appellate panel shall make the certification described in subparagraph (A).*

*(C) The parties may supplement the certification with a short statement of the basis for the certification.*

*(D) An appeal under this paragraph does not stay any proceeding of the bankruptcy court, the district court, or the bankruptcy appellate panel from which the appeal is taken, unless the respective bankruptcy court, district court, or bankruptcy appellate panel, or the court of appeals in which the appeal in pending, issues a stay of such proceeding pending the appeal.*

*(E) Any request under subparagraph (B) for certification shall be made not later than 60 days after the entry of the judgment, order, or decree.*

**Section 158**

(April 20, 2005, P. L. 109-8, Title XII, § 1233, 119 Stat. 23)

## HISTORY: ANCILLARY LAWS AND DIRECTIVES

**Amendments:**

**2005.** Act April 20, 2005 (effective 180 days after enactment on April 20, 2005, as provided by § 1501(a) of P.L. 109-8), creates a potential direct appeal to the circuit court.

**Other provisions:**

**Effective date and application of amendments made by Act April 20, 2005.** Act April 20, 2005, P.L. 109-8, Title XV, § 1501(a), 119 Stat. 23, provided that the amendments made to this section would be effective 180 days after enactment on April 20, 2005.

**Abridged Legislative History**

(H. Report No. 109-31 to accompany S. 256, 109th Cong., 1st Sess. (2005) p. 148; available at 2005 U.S.C.C.A.N. 88, at 206.)

## *Sec. 159. Bankruptcy statistics*

*(a) The clerk of the district court, or the clerk of the bankruptcy court*

*if one is certified pursuant to section 156(b) of this title, shall collect statistics regarding debtors who are individuals with primarily consumer debts seeking relief under chapters 7, 11, and 13 of title 11. Those statistics shall be in a standardized format prescribed by the Director of the Administrative Office of the United States Courts (referred to in this section as the "Director").*

*(b) The Director shall—*

*(1) compile the statistics referred to in subsection (a);*

*(2) make the statistics available to the public; and*

*(3) not later than July 1, 2008, and annually thereafter, prepare, and submit to Congress a report concerning the information collected under subsection (a) that contains an analysis of the information.*

*(c) The compilation required under subsection (b) shall—*

*(1) be itemized, by chapter, with respect to title 11;*

*(2) be presented in the aggregate and for each district; and*

*(3) include information concerning—*

*(A) the total assets and total liabilities of the debtors described in subsection (a), and in each category of assets and liabilities, as reported in the schedules prescribed pursuant to section 2075 of this title and filed by debtors;*

*(B) the current monthly income, average income, and average expenses of debtors as reported on the schedules and statements that each such debtor files under sections 521 and 1322 of title 11;*

*(C) the aggregate amount of debt discharged in cases filed during the reporting period, determined as the difference between the total amount of debt and obligations of a debtor reported on the schedules and the amount of such debt reported in categories which are predominantly nondischargeable;*

*(D) the average period of time between the date of the filing of the petition and the closing of the case for cases closed during the reporting period;*

*(E) for cases closed during the reporting period—*

*(i) the number of cases in which a reaffirmation agreement was filed; and*

*(ii) (I) the total number of reaffirmation agreements filed;*

*(II) of those cases in which a reaffirmation agreement was filed, the number of cases in which the debtor was not represented by an attorney; and*

*(III) of those cases in which a reaffirmation agreement was filed, the number of cases in which the reaffirmation agreement was approved by the court;*

*(F) with respect to cases filed under chapter 13 of title 11, for the reporting period—*

*(i) (I) the number of cases in which a final order was entered determining the value of property securing a claim in an amount less than the amount of the claim; and*

*(II) the number of final orders entered determining the value of property securing a claim;*

*(ii) the number of cases dismissed, the number of cases dismissed for failure to make payments under the plan, the number of cases refiled after dismissal, and the number of cases in which the plan was completed, separately itemized with respect to the number of modifications made before completion of the plan, if any; and*

*(iii) the number of cases in which the debtor filed another case during the 6-year period preceding the filing;*

*(G) the number of cases in which creditors were fined for misconduct and any amount of punitive damages awarded by the court for creditor misconduct; and*

*(H) the number of cases in which sanctions under rule 9011 of the Federal Rules of Bankruptcy Procedure were imposed against debtor's attorney or damages awarded under such Rule.*

**Section 159**

(April 20, 2005, P. L. 109-8, Title VI, § 601(a), 119 Stat. 23)

## HISTORY: ANCILLARY LAWS AND DIRECTIVES

**Amendments:**

**2005.** Act April 20, 2005 (effective 18 months after the date of enactment of this Act on April 20, 2005, as provided by § 601(c) of P.L. 109-8), creates a new section concerning bankruptcy statistics.

**Other provisions:**

**Effective date and application of amendments made by Act April 20, 2005.** Act April 20, 2005, P.L. 109-8, Title VI, § 601(c), 119 Stat. 23, provided that the amendments made to this section would take effect 18 months after the date of enactment of this Act, on April 20, 2005.

**Abridged Legislative History**

Improved Bankruptcy Statistics. This provision amends chapter 6 of title 28 of the United States Code to require the clerk for each district (or the bankruptcy court clerk if one has been certified pursuant to section 156(b) of title 28 of the United States Code) to collect certain statistics for chapter 7, 11, and 13 cases in a standardized format prescribed by the Director of the Administrative Office of the United States Courts and to make this information available to the public. Not later than July 1, 2008, the Director must submit a report to Congress concerning the statistical information collected and then must report annually thereafter. The statistics must be itemized by chapter of the Bankruptcy Code and be presented in the aggregate for each district.

Section 601 provides that the amendments in this provision take effect 18 months after the date of enactment of this Act. (H. Report No. 109-31 to accompany S. 256, 109th Cong., 1st Sess. (2005) p. 97–98; available at 2005 U.S.C.C.A.N. 88, at 161–62.)

* * * * * * *

## *Part II*
## *—Department of Justice*

* * * * * * *

# Chapter 39
# —United States Trustees

## Sec. 586. Duties; supervision by Attorney General

(a) Each United States trustee, within the region for which such United States trustee is appointed, shall—

(1) establish, maintain, and supervise a panel of private trustees that are eligible and available to serve as trustees in cases under chapter 7 of title 11;

(2) serve as and perform the duties of a trustee in a case under title 11 when required under title 11 to serve as trustee in such a case;

(3) supervise the administration of cases and trustees in cases under chapter 7, 11, 12, ~~or~~ 13*, or 15* of title 11 by, whenever the United States trustee considers it to be appropriate—(A) (i) reviewing, in accordance with procedural guidelines adopted by the Executive Office of the United States Trustee (which guidelines shall be applied uniformly by the United States trustee except when circumstances warrant different treatment), applications filed for compensation and reimbursement under section 330 of title 11; and

(ii) filing with the court comments with respect to such application and, if the United States Trustee considers it to be appropriate, objections to such application.

(B) monitoring plans and disclosure statements filed in cases under chapter 11 of title 11 and filing with the court, in connection with hearings under sections 1125 and 1128 of such title, comments with respect to such plans and disclosure statements;

(C) monitoring plans filed under chapters 12 and 13 of title 11 and filing with the court, in connection with hearings under sections 1224, 1229, 1324, and 1329 of such title, comments with respect to such plans;

(D) taking such action as the United States trustee deems to be appropriate to ensure that all reports, schedules, and fees required to be filed under title 11 and this title by the debtor are properly and timely filed;

(E) monitoring creditors' committees appointed under title 11;

(F) notifying the appropriate United States attorney of matters which relate to the occurrence of any action which may constitute a crime under the laws of the United States and, on the request of the United States attorney, assisting the United States attorney in carrying out prosecutions based on such action;

(G) monitoring the progress of cases under title 11 and taking such actions as the United States trustee deems to be appropriate to prevent undue delay in such progress; ~~and~~

*(H) in small business cases (as defined in section 101 of title 11), performing the additional duties specified in title 11 pertaining to such cases; and*

~~(H)~~ *(I)* monitoring applications filed under section 327 of title 11 and, whenever the United States trustee deems it to be appropriate, filing with the court comments with respect to the approval of such applications;

(4) deposit or invest under section 345 of title 11 money received as trustee in cases under title 11;

(5) perform the duties prescribed for the United States trustee under title 11 and this title, and such duties consistent with title 11 and this title as the Attorney General may prescribe; ~~and~~

(6) make such reports as the Attorney General directs*, including the results of audits performed under section 603(a) of the Bankruptcy Abuse Prevention and Consumer Protection Act of 2005;*

*(7) in each of such small business cases —*

*(A) conduct an initial debtor interview as soon as practicable after the date of the order for relief but before the first meeting scheduled under section 341(a) of title 11, at which time the United States trustee shall —*

*(i) begin to investigate the debtor's viability;*

*(ii) inquire about the debtor's business plan;*

*(iii) explain the debtor's obligations to file monthly operating reports and other required reports;*

*(iv) attempt to develop an agreed scheduling order; and*

*(v) inform the debtor of other obligations;*

*(B) if determined to be appropriate and advisable, visit the appropriate business premises of the debtor, ascertain the state of the debtor's books and records, and verify that the debtor has filed its tax returns; and*

*(C) review and monitor diligently the debtor's activities, to identify as promptly as possible whether the debtor will be unable to confirm a plan; and*

*(8) in any case in which the United States trustee finds material grounds for any relief under section 1112 of title 11, the United States trustee shall apply promptly after making that finding to the court for relief.*

(b) If the number of cases under chapter 12 or 13 of title 11 commenced in a particular region so warrants, the United States trustee for such region may, subject to the approval of the Attorney General, appoint one or more individuals to serve as standing trustee, or designate one or more assistant United States trustees to serve in cases under such chapter. The United States trustee for such region shall supervise any such individual appointed as standing trustee in the performance of the duties of standing trustee.

(c) Each United States trustee shall be under the general supervision of the Attorney General, who shall provide general coordination and assistance to the United States trustees.

(d) *(1)* The Attorney General shall prescribe by rule qualifications for membership on the panels established by United States trustees under paragraph (a)(1) of this section, and qualifications for appointment under subsection (b) of this section to serve as standing trustee in cases under chapter 12 or 13 of title 11. The Attorney General may not require that an individual be an attorney in order to qualify for appointment under subsection (b) of this section to serve as standing trustee in cases under chapter 12 or 13 of title 11.

*(2) A trustee whose appointment under subsection (a)(1) or under subsection (b) is terminated or who ceases to be assigned to cases filed under title 11, United States Code, may obtain judicial review of the final agency decision by commencing an action in the district court of the United States for the district for which the panel to which the trustee is appointed under subsection (a)(1), or in the district court of the United States for the district in which the trustee is appointed under subsection (b) resides, after first exhausting all available administrative remedies, which if the trustee so elects, shall also include an administrative hearing on the record. Unless the trustee elects to have an administrative hearing on the record, the trustee shall be deemed to have exhausted all administrative remedies for purposes of this paragraph if the agency fails to make a final agency decision within 90 days after the trustee requests administrative remedies. The Attorney General shall prescribe procedures to implement this paragraph. The decision of the agency shall be affirmed by the district court unless it is unreasonable and without cause based on the administrative record before the agency.*

(e) (1) The Attorney General, after consultation with a United States trustee that has appointed an individual under subsection (b) of this section to serve as standing trustee in cases under chapter 12 or 13 of title 11, shall fix—

(A) a maximum annual compensation for such individual consisting of—

(i) an amount not to exceed the highest annual rate of basic pay in effect for level V of the Executive Schedule; and

(ii) the cash value of employment benefits comparable to the employment benefits provided by the United States to individuals who are employed by the United States at the same rate of basic pay to perform similar services during the same period of time; and

(B) a percentage fee not to exceed—

(i) in the case of a debtor who is not a family farmer, ten percent; or

(ii) in the case of a debtor who is a family farmer, the sum of—

(I) not to exceed ten percent of the payments made under the plan of such debtor, with respect to payments in an aggregate amount not to exceed $450,000; and

(II) three percent of payments made under the plan of such debtor, with respect to payments made after the aggregate amount of payments made under the plan exceeds $450,000;

based on such maximum annual compensation and the actual, necessary expenses incurred by such individual as standing trustee.

(2) Such individual shall collect such percentage fee from all payments received by such individual under plans in the cases under chapter 12 or 13 of title 11 for which such individual serves as standing trustee. Such individual shall pay to the United States trustee, and the United States trustee shall deposit in the United States Trustee System Fund—

(A) any amount by which the actual compensation of such individual exceeds 5 per centum upon all payments received under plans in cases under chapter 12 or 13 of title 11 for which such individual serves as standing trustee; and

(B) any amount by which the percentage for all such cases exceeds—

(i) such individual's actual compensation for such cases, as adjusted under subparagraph (A) of paragraph (1); plus

(ii) the actual, necessary expenses incurred by such individual as standing trustee in such cases. Subject to the approval of the Attorney General, any or all of the interest earned from the deposit of payments under plans by such individual may be utilized to pay actual, necessary expenses without regard to the percentage limitation contained in subparagraph (d)(1)(B) of this section.

*(3) After first exhausting all available administrative remedies, an individual appointed under subsection (b) may obtain judicial review of final agency action to deny a claim of actual, necessary expenses under this subsection by commencing an action in the district court of the United States for the district where the individual resides. The decision of the agency shall be affirmed by the district court unless it is unreasonable and without cause based upon the administrative record before the agency.*

*(4) The Attorney General shall prescribe procedures to implement this subsection.*

*(f) (1) The United States trustee for each district is authorized to contract with auditors to perform audits in cases designated by the United States trustee, in accordance with the procedures established under section 603(a) of the Bankruptcy Abuse Prevention and Consumer Protection Act of 2005.*

*(2) (A) The report of each audit referred to in paragraph (1) shall*

*be filed with the court and transmitted to the United States trustee. Each report shall clearly and conspicuously specify any material misstatement of income or expenditures or of assets identified by the person performing the audit. In any case in which a material misstatement of income or expenditures or of assets has been reported, the clerk of the district court (or the clerk of the bankruptcy court if one is certified under section 156(b) of this title) shall give notice of the misstatement to the creditors in the case.*

*(B) If a material misstatement of income or expenditures or of assets is reported, the United States trustee shall—*

*(i) report the material misstatement, if appropriate, to the United States Attorney pursuant to section 3057 of title 18; and*

*(ii) if advisable, take appropriate action, including but not limited to commencing an adversary proceeding to revoke the debtor's discharge pursuant to section 727(d) of title 11.*

**Section 586**

(April 20, 2005, P. L. 109-8, Title IVB, § 439; Title VI, § 603(b); Title VII, § 802(c)(3); Title XII, § 1231(a), (b), 119 Stat. 23)

## HISTORY: ANCILLARY LAWS AND DIRECTIVES

**Amendments:**

**2005.** Act April 20, 2005 (as to section 586(a)(6), effective 18 months after the date of enactment of this Act on April 20, 2005, as provided by § 603(e) of P.L. 109-8; as to the amendments to other parts of section 586, effective 180 days following enactment on April 20, 2005, as provided by § 1501(a) of P.L. 109-8), adds new duties for the United States trustee concerning small business debtors, audit procedures and new title 15. The Act also adds a level of judicial review concerning some actions taken against panel trustees.

**Other provisions:**

**Effective date and application of amendments made by Act April 20, 2005.** Act April 20, 2005, P.L. 109-8, Title XV, § 1501(a), 119 Stat. 23, provided that the amendments made to this section would be effective 180 days after enactment on April 20, 2005, except that the amendments to § 586(a)(6) are effective 18 months after the enactment, as provided by § 603(e) of P.L. 109-8.

**Abridged Legislative History**

(H. Report No. 109-31 to accompany S. 256, 109th Cong., 1st Sess. (2005) pp. 93, 99, 118, 147–148; available at 2005 U.S.C.C.A.N. 88, at 158, 163, 180–81, 205–06.)

# Sec. 589a. United States Trustee System Fund

(a) There is hereby established in the Treasury of the United States a special fund to be known as the "United States Trustee System Fund" (hereinafter in this section referred to as the "Fund"). Monies in the Fund shall be available to the Attorney General without fiscal year limitation in such amounts as may be specified in appropriations Acts for the following purposes in connection with the operations of United States trustees—

(1) salaries and related employee benefits;

(2) travel and transportation;

(3) rental of space;

(4) communication, utilities, and miscellaneous computer charges;

(5) security investigations and audits;

(6) supplies, books, and other materials for legal research;

(7) furniture and equipment;

(8) miscellaneous services, including those obtained by contract; and

(9) printing.

(b) For the purpose of recovering the cost of services of the United States Trustee System, there shall be deposited as offsetting collections to the appropriation "United States Trustee System Fund", to remain available until expended, the following—

~~(1) 27.42 percent of the fees collected under section 1930(a)(1) of this title;~~

*(1) (A) 40.46 percent of the fees collected under section 1930(a)(1)(A) of this title; and*

*(B) 28.33 percent of the fees collected under section 1930(a)(1)(B);*

(2) ~~one-half~~ *55 percent* of the fees collected under section 1930(a)(3) of this title;

(3) one-half of the fees collected under section 1930(a)(4) of this title;

(4) one-half of the fees collected under section 1930(a)(5) of this title;

(5) 100 percent of the fees collected under section 1930(a)(6) of this title;

(6) three-fourths of the fees collected under the last sentence of section 1930(a) of this title;

(7) the compensation of trustees received under section 330(d) of title 11 by the clerks of the bankruptcy courts; and

(8) excess fees collected under section 586(e)(2) of this title.

(c) Amounts in the Fund which are not currently needed for the purposes specified in subsection (a) shall be kept on deposit or invested in obligations of, or guaranteed by, the United States.

(d) The Attorney General shall transmit to the Congress, not later than 120 days after the end of each fiscal year, a detailed report on the amounts deposited in the Fund and a description of expenditures made under this section.

(e) There are authorized to be appropriated to the Fund for any fiscal year such sums as may be necessary to supplement amounts deposited under subsection (b) for the purposes specified in subsection (a).

**Section 589a**

(April 20, 2005, P. L. 109-8, Title III, § 325(b), 119 Stat. 23; May 11, 2005, P. O. 109-13, Title VI, § 6058(b), 119 Stat. 231)

## HISTORY: ANCILLARY LAWS AND DIRECTIVES

**Amendments:**

Act April 20, 2005 and Act May 11, 2005 (effective immediately upon enactment on April 20, 2005, as provided by § 6058(b) of P.L. 109-13), altered the percentages of fees allocated to the United States Trustee System. There was a drafting error in the original Act, P.L. 109-8, and that error was corrected in P.L. 109-13, 119 Stat. 231.

**Other provisions**

**Effective date and application of amendments made by Act April 20, 2005.** Act April 20, 2005 and Act May 11, 2005(effective immediately upon enactment on April 20, 2005, as provided by § 6058(b) of P.L. 109-13)

**Abridged Legislative History**

(H. Report No. 109-31 to accompany S. 256, 109th Cong., 1st Sess. (2005) pp. 82–3; available at 2005 U.S.C.C.A.N. 88, at 149.)

Due to a drafting error in the percentage allocations, which totaled more than 100%, the error was corrected in P.L. 109-13, § 6058(a), 119 Stat. 231.

## *Sec. 589b. Bankruptcy data*

*(a) RULES— The Attorney General shall, within a reasonable time after the effective date of this section, issue rules requiring uniform forms for (and from time to time thereafter to appropriately modify and approve)—*

*(1) final reports by trustees in cases under chapters 7, 12, and 13 of title 11; and*

*(2) periodic reports by debtors in possession or trustees in cases under chapter 11 of title 11.*

*(b) REPORTS— Each report referred to in subsection (a) shall be designed (and the requirements as to place and manner of filing shall be established) so as to facilitate compilation of data and maximum possible access of the public, both by physical inspection at one or more central filing locations, and by electronic access through the Internet or other appropriate media.*

*(c) REQUIRED INFORMATION— The information required to be filed in the reports referred to in subsection (b) shall be that which is in the best interests of debtors and creditors, and in the public interest in reasonable and adequate information to evaluate the efficiency and practicality of the Federal bankruptcy system. In issuing rules proposing the forms referred to in subsection (a), the Attorney General shall strike the best achievable practical balance between—*

*(1) the reasonable needs of the public for information about the operational results of the Federal bankruptcy system;*

*(2) economy, simplicity, and lack of undue burden on persons with a duty to file reports; and*

*(3) appropriate privacy concerns and safeguards.*

*(d) FINAL REPORTS— The uniform forms for final reports required under subsection (a) for use by trustees under chapters 7, 12, and 13 of title 11 shall, in addition to such other matters as are required by law or as the Attorney General in the discretion of the Attorney General shall propose, include with respect to a case under such title—*

*(1) information about the length of time the case was pending;*

*(2) assets abandoned;*

*(3) assets exempted;*

*(4) receipts and disbursements of the estate;*

*(5) expenses of administration, including for use under section 707 (b), actual costs of administering cases under chapter 13 of title 11;*

*(6) claims asserted;*

*(7) claims allowed; and*

*(8) distributions to claimants and claims discharged without payment,*

*in each case by appropriate category and, in cases under chapters 12 and 13 of title 11, date of confirmation of the plan, each modification thereto, and defaults by the debtor in performance under the plan.*

*(e) PERIODIC REPORTS— The uniform forms for periodic reports required under subsection (a) for use by trustees or debtors in possession under chapter 11 of title 11 shall, in addition to such other matters as are required by law or as the Attorney General in the discretion of the Attorney General shall propose, include—*

*(1) information about the industry classification, published by the Department of Commerce, for the businesses conducted by the debtor;*

*(2) length of time the case has been pending;*

*(3) number of full-time employees as of the date of the order for relief and at the end of each reporting period since the case was filed;*

*(4) cash receipts, cash disbursements and profitability of the debtor for the most recent period and cumulatively since the date of the order for relief;*

*(5) compliance with title 11, whether or not tax returns and tax payments since the date of the order for relief have been timely filed and made;*

*(6) all professional fees approved by the court in the case for the most recent period and cumulatively since the date of the order for relief (separately reported, for the professional fees incurred by or on behalf of the debtor, between those that would have been incurred absent a bankruptcy case and those not); and*

*(7) plans of reorganization filed and confirmed and, with respect thereto, by class, the recoveries of the holders, expressed in aggregate dollar values and, in the case of claims, as a percentage of total claims of the class allowed.*

**Section 589b**

(April 20, 2005, P. L. 109-8, Title VI, § 602(a), 119 Stat. 23)

## HISTORY: ANCILLARY LAWS AND DIRECTIVES

**Amendments:**

**2005.** Act April 20, 2005 (effective 180 days after enactment on April 20, 2005, as provided by § 1501(a) of P.L. 109-8), adds a new § 589b.

**Other provisions:**

**Effective date and application of amendments by Act April 20, 2005.** Act April 20, 2005, P.L. 109-8, Title XV, § 1501(a), 119 Stat. 23, provided that the amendments made to this section would be effective 180 days after enactment on April 20, 2005; however, new § 589b(a) provides that the Attorney General shall, "within a reasonable time after the effective date of this section, issue rules requiring uniform forms for" complying with this new section.

**Abridged Legislative History**

Uniform Rules for the Collection of Bankruptcy Data. Section 602 of the Act amends chapter 39 of title 28 of the United States Code to require the Attorney General to promulgate rules mandating the establishment of uniform forms for final reports in chapter 7, 12 and 13 cases and periodic reports in chapter 11 cases. (H. Report No. 109-31 to accompany S. 256, 109th Cong., 1st Sess. (2005) p. 98; available at 2005 U.S.C.C.A.N. 88, at 162–63.)

## *Part III*
## *—Court Officers and Employees*

# Chapter 57
# —General Provisions Applicable to Court Officers and Employees

## Sec. 960. Tax liability

*(a)* Any officers and agents conducting any business under authority of a United States court shall be subject to all Federal, State and local taxes applicable to such business to the same extent as if it were conducted by an individual or corporation.

*(b) A tax under subsection (a) shall be paid on or before the due date of the tax under applicable nonbankruptcy law, unless—*

*(1) the tax is a property tax secured by a lien against property that is abandoned under section 554 of title 11, within a reasonable period of time after the lien attaches, by the trustee in a case under title 11; or*

*(2) payment of the tax is excused under a specific provision of title 11.*

*(c) In a case pending under chapter 7 of title 11, payment of a tax may be deferred until final distribution is made under section 726 of title 11, if—*

*(1) the tax was not incurred by a trustee duly appointed or elected under chapter 7 of title 11; or*

*(2) before the due date of the tax, an order of the court makes a finding of probable insufficiency of funds of the estate to pay in full the administrative expenses allowed under section 503(b) of title 11 that have the same priority in distribution under section 726(b) of title 11 as the priority of that tax.*

**Section 960**

(April 20, 2005, P. L. 109-8, Title VII, § 712, 119 Stat. 23)

## HISTORY: ANCILLARY LAWS AND DIRECTIVES

**Amendments:**

**2005.** Act April 20, 2005 (effective 180 days after enactment on April 20, 2005, as provided by § 1501(a) of P.L. 109-8), adds a new § 960(b) to clarify that postpetition taxes in the ordinary course of business must generally be paid by the normal due date.

**Other provisions:**

**Effective date and application of amendments by Act April 20, 2005.** Act April 20, 2005, P.L. 109-8, Title XV, § 1501(a), 119 Stat. 23, provided that the amendments made to this section would be effective 180 days after enactment on April 20, 2005.

**Abridged Legislative History**

Payment of Taxes in the Conduct of Business. Although current law generally requires trustees and receivers to pay taxes in the ordinary course of the debtor's business, the payment of administrative expenses must first be authorized by the court. Section 712(a) of the Act amends section 960 of title 28 of the United States Code to clarify that postpetition taxes in the ordinary course of business must be paid on or before when such tax is due under applicable nonbankruptcy law, with certain exceptions. (H. Report No. 109-31 to accompany S. 256, 109th Cong., 1st Sess. (2005) pp. 102–03; available at 2005 U.S.C.C.A.N. 88, at 166–67.)

*Part IV*
# *—Jurisdiction and Venue*

# Chapter 85
# —District Courts; Jurisdiction

## Sec. 1334. Bankruptcy cases and proceedings

(a) Except as provided in subsection (b) of this section, the district court shall have original and exclusive jurisdiction of all cases under title 11.

(b) ~~Notwithstanding~~ *Except as provided in subsection (e)(2) and notwithstanding* any Act of Congress that confers exclusive jurisdiction on a court or courts other than the district courts, the district courts shall have original but not exclusive jurisdiction of all civil proceedings arising under title 11, or arising in or related to cases under title 11.

(c) (1) ~~Nothing in~~ *Except with respect to a case under chapter 15 of title 11, nothing in* this section prevents a district court in the interest of justice, or in the interest of comity with State courts or respect for State law, from abstaining from hearing a particular proceeding arising under title 11 or arising in or related to a case under title 11.

(2) Upon timely motion of a party in a proceeding based upon a State law claim or State law cause of action, related to a case under title 11 but not arising under title 11 or arising in a case under title 11, with respect to which an action could not have been commenced in a court of the United States absent jurisdiction under this section, the district court shall abstain from hearing such proceeding if an action is commenced, and can be timely adjudicated, in a State forum of appropriate jurisdiction.

(d) Any decision to abstain or not to abstain ~~made under this subsection~~ *made under subsection (c)* (other than a decision not to abstain in a proceeding described in subsection (c)(2)) is not reviewable by appeal or otherwise by the court of appeals under section 158(d), 1291, or 1292 of this title or by the Supreme Court of the United States under section 1254 of this title. ~~This subsection~~ *Subsection (c) and this subsection* shall not be construed to limit the applicability of the stay provided for by section 362 of title 11, United States Code, as such section applies to an action affecting the property of the estate in bankruptcy.

(e) The district court in which a case under title 11 is commenced or is pending shall have exclusive jurisdiction ~~of all of the property, wherever located, of the debtor as of the commencement of such case, and of property of the estate.~~—

*(1) of all the property, wherever located, of the debtor as of the commencement of such case, and of property of the estate; and*

*(2) over all claims or causes of action that involve construction of section 327 of title 11, United States Code, or rules relating to disclosure requirements under section 327.*

**Section 1334**

(April 20, 2005, P. L. 109-8, Title III, § 324; Title VIII, § 802(c); Title XII, § 1219, 119 Stat. 23)

## HISTORY: ANCILLARY LAWS AND DIRECTIVES

**Amendments:**

**2005.** Act April 20, 2005 (as to the amendment to § 1334(e), effective upon enactment on April 20, 2005, but only applicable to cases filed after the date of enactment, as provided by § 324(b) of P.L. 109-8), and as to other amendments, effective 180 days after enactment, as provided by § 1501(a) of P.L. 109-8) amends the bankruptcy court's jurisdiction as to new title 15 and as to all matters related to § 327.

**Other provisions:**

**Effective date and application of amendments by Act April 20, 2005.** Act April 20, 2005, P.L. 109-8, Title XV, § 1501(a), 119 Stat. 23, provided that the amendments made to this section would be effective 180 days after enactment on April 20, 2005, except that the amendment to § 1334(e) is effective upon enactment but only applicable to cases filed after the date of enactment, as provided by § 324(b) of P.L. 109-8, 119 Stat. 23.

**Abridged Legislative History**

Exclusive Jurisdiction in Matters Involving Bankruptcy Professionals. Section 324 of the Act amends section 1334 of title 28 of the United State Code to give a district court exclusive jurisdiction of all claims or causes of action involving the construction of section 327 of the Bankruptcy Code or rules relating to disclosure requirements under such provision.

Section 802(c) amends section 157(b)(2) of title 28 to provide that proceedings under chapter 15 will be core proceedings while other amendments to title 28 provide that the United States trustee's standing extends to cases under chapter 15 and that the United States trustee's duties include acting in chapter 15 cases.

(H. Report No. 109-31 to accompany S. 256, 109th Cong., 1st Sess. (2005) pp. 82, 118, 145; available at 2005 U.S.C.C.A.N. 88, at 149, 180–81,203.)

# Chapter 87 —District Courts; Venue

## Sec. 1409. Venue of proceedings arising under title 11 or arising in or related to cases under title 11

(a) Except as otherwise provided in subsections (b) and (d), a proceeding arising under title 11 or arising in or related to a case under title 11 may be commenced in the district court in which such case is pending.

(b) Except as provided in subsection (d) of this section, a trustee in a case under title 11 may commence a proceeding arising in or related to such case to recover a money judgment of or property worth less than $1,000 or a consumer debt of less than ~~$5,000~~ *$15,000, or a debt (excluding a consumer debt) against a noninsider of less than $10,000,* only in the district court for the district in which the defendant resides.

(c) Except as provided in subsection (b) of this section, a trustee in a case under title 11 may commence a proceeding arising in or related to such case as statutory successor to the debtor or creditors under section 541 or 544(b) of title 11 in the district court for the district where the State or Federal court sits in which, under applicable nonbankruptcy venue provisions, the debtor or creditors, as the case may be, may have commenced an action on which such proceeding is based if the case under title 11 had not been commenced.

(d) A trustee may commence a proceeding arising under title 11 or arising in or related to a case under title 11 based on a claim arising after the commencement of such case from the operation of the business of the debtor only in the district court for the district where a State or Federal court sits in which, under applicable nonbankruptcy venue provisions, an action on such claim may have been brought.

(e) A proceeding arising under title 11 or arising in or related to a case under title 11, based on a claim arising after the commencement of such case from the operation of the business of the debtor, may be commenced against the representative of the estate in such case in the district court for the district where the State or Federal court sits in which the party commencing such proceeding may, under applicable nonbankruptcy venue provisions, have brought an action on such claim, or in the district court in which such case is pending.

**Section 1409**

(April 20, 2005, P. L. 109-8, Title IVA, § 410, 119 Stat. 23)

### HISTORY: ANCILLARY LAWS AND DIRECTIVES

**Amendments:**

**2005.** Act April 20, 2005 (effective 180 days after enactment, as provided by § 1501(a) of P.L. 109-8) amends the bankruptcy court's venue for trustee's avoidance actions.

**Other provisions:**

**Effective date and application of amendments by Act April 20, 2005.** Act April 20, 2005, P.L. 109-8, Title XV, § 1501(a), 119 Stat. 23, provided that the amendments made to this section would be effective 180 days after enactment on April 20, 2005.

**Abridged Legislative History**

Venue of Certain Proceedings. Section 1409(b) of title 28 of the United States Code provides that a proceeding to recover a money judgment of, or property worth less than, certain specified amounts must be commenced in the district where the defendant resides. (H. Report No. 109-31 to accompany S. 256, 109th Cong., 1st Sess. (2005) p. 88; available at 2005 U.S.C.C.A.N. 88, at 154.)

## ~~Sec. 1410. Venue of cases ancillary to foreign proceedings~~

~~(a) A case under section 304 of title 11 to enjoin the commencement or continuation of an action or proceeding in a State or Federal court, or the enforcement of a judgment, may be commenced only in the district court for the district where the State or Federal court sits in which is pending the action or proceeding against which the injunction is sought.~~

~~(b) A case under section 304 of title 11 to enjoin the enforcement of a lien against a property, or to require the turnover of property of an estate, may be commenced only in the district court for the district in which such property is found.~~

~~(c) A case under section 304 of title 11, other than a case specified in subsection (a) or (b) of this section, may be commenced only in the district court for the district in which is located the principal place of business in the United States, or the principal assets in the United States, of the estate that is the subject of such case.~~

## *Sec. 1410. Venue of cases ancillary to foreign proceedings*

*A case under chapter 15 of title 11 may be commenced in the district court of the United States for the district—*

*(1) in which the debtor has its principal place of business or principal assets in the United States;*

*(2) if the debtor does not have a place of business or assets in the United States, in which there is pending against the debtor an action or proceeding in a Federal or State court; or*

*(3) in a case other than those specified in paragraph (1) or (2), in which venue will be consistent with the interests of justice and the convenience of the parties, having regard to the relief sought by the foreign representative.*

**Section 1410**

(April 20, 2005, P. L. 109-8, Title VIII, § 802(c)(4), 119 Stat. 23)

## HISTORY: ANCILLARY LAWS AND DIRECTIVES

**Amendments:**

**2005.** Act April 20, 2005 (effective 180 days after enactment, as provided by § 1501(a) of P.L. 109-8) amends the bankruptcy court's venue for foreign proceedings to make it consistent with new chapter 15.

**Other provisions:**

**Effective date and application of amendments by Act April 20, 2005.** Act April 20, 2005, P.L. 109-8, Title XV, § 1501(a), 119 Stat. 23, provided that the amendments made to this section would be effective 180 days after enactment on April 20, 2005.

**Abridged Legislative History**

Section 802(c) amends section 157(b)(2) of title 28 to provide that proceedings under chapter 15 will be core proceedings while other amendments to title 28 provide that the United States trustee's standing extends to cases under chapter 15 and that the United States trustee's duties include acting in chapter 15 cases. (H. Report No. 109-31 to accompany S. 256, 109th Cong., 1st Sess. (2005) p. 118; available at 2005 U.S.C.C.A.N. 88, at 180–81.)

*Part V*
***—Procedure***

# Chapter 123
# —Fees and Costs

## Sec. 1930. Bankruptcy fees

(a) ~~Notwithstanding section 1915 of this title, the~~ *The* parties commencing a case under title 11 shall pay to the clerk of the district court or the clerk of the bankruptcy court, if one has been certified pursuant to section 156(b) of this title, the following filing fees:

(1) ~~For a case commenced under chapter 7 or 13 of title 11, $155.~~ *For a case commenced under—*

*(A) chapter 7 of title 11, $220; and*

*(B) chapter 13 of title 11, $150.*

(2) For a case commenced under chapter 9 of title 11, equal to the fee specified in paragraph (3) for filing a case under chapter 11 of title 11. The amount by which the fee payable under this paragraph exceeds $300 shall be deposited in the fund established under section 1931 of this title.

(3) For a case commenced under chapter 11 of title 11 that does not concern a railroad, as defined in section 101 of title 11, ~~$800~~ *$1000.*

(4) For a case commenced under chapter 11 of title 11 concerning a railroad, as so defined, $1,000.

(5) For a case commenced under chapter 12 of title 11, $200.

(6) In addition to the filing fee paid to the clerk, a quarterly fee shall be paid to the United States trustee, for deposit in the Treasury, in each case under chapter 11 of title 11 for each quarter (including any fraction thereof) until the case is converted or dismissed, whichever occurs first. The fee shall be $250 for each quarter in which disbursements total less than $15,000; $500 for each quarter in which disbursements total $15,000 or more but less than $75,000; $750 for each quarter in which disbursements total $75,000 or more but less than $150,000; $1,250 for each quarter in which disbursements total $150,000 or more but less than $225,000; $1,500 for each quarter in which disbursements total $225,000 or more but less than $300,000; $3,750 for each quarter in which disbursements total $300,000 or more but less than $1,000,000; $5,000 for each quarter in which disbursements total $1,000,000 or more but less than $2,000,000; $7,500 for each quarter in which disbursements total $2,000,000 or more but less than $3,000,000; $8,000 for each quarter in which disbursements total $3,000,000 or more but less than $5,000,000; $10,000 for each quarter in which

disbursements total $5,000,000 or more. The fee shall be payable on the last day of the calendar month following the calendar quarter for which the fee is owed.

(7) In districts that are not part of a United States trustee region as defined in section 581 of this title, the Judicial Conference of the United States may require the debtor in a case under chapter 11 of title 11 to pay fees equal to those imposed by paragraph (6) of this subsection. Such fees shall be deposited as offsetting receipts to the fund established under section 1931 of this title and shall remain available until expended.

An individual commencing a voluntary case or a joint case under title 11 may pay such fee in installments. For converting, on request of the debtor, a case under chapter 7, or 13 of title 11, to a case under chapter 11 of title 11, the debtor shall pay to the clerk of the district court or the clerk of the bankruptcy court, if one has been certified pursuant to section 156(b) of this title, a fee of the amount equal to the difference between the fee specified in paragraph (3) and the fee specified in paragraph (1).

(b) The Judicial Conference of the United States may prescribe additional fees in cases under title 11 of the same kind as the Judicial Conference prescribes under section 1914(b) of this title.

(c) Upon the filing of any separate or joint notice of appeal or application for appeal or upon the receipt of any order allowing, or notice of the allowance of, an appeal or a writ of certiorari $5 shall be paid to the clerk of the court, by the appellant or petitioner.

(d) Whenever any case or proceeding is dismissed in any bankruptcy court for want of jurisdiction, such court may order the payment of just costs.

(e) The clerk of the court may collect only the fees prescribed under this section.

*(f) (1) Under the procedures prescribed by the Judicial Conference of the United States, the district court or the bankruptcy court may waive the filing fee in a case under chapter 7 of title 11 for an individual if the court determines that such individual has income less than 150 percent of the income official poverty line (as defined by the Office of Management and Budget, and revised annually in accordance with section 673(2) of the Omnibus Budget Reconciliation Act of 1981) applicable to a family of the size involved and is unable to pay that fee in installments. For purposes of this paragraph, the term 'filing fee' means the filing fee required by subsection (a), or any other fee prescribed by the Judicial Conference under subsections (b) and (c) that is payable to the clerk upon the commencement of a case under chapter 7.*

*(2) The district court or the bankruptcy court may waive for such debtors other fees prescribed under subsections (b) and (c).*

*(3) This subsection does not restrict the district court or the bankruptcy court from waiving, in accordance with Judicial Conference policy, fees prescribed under this section for other debtors and creditors.*

**Section 1930**

(April 20, 2005, P. L. 109-8, Title III, § 325(a); Title IVA, § 418, 119 Stat. 23; and May 11, 2005, P. L. 109-13, Title VI, § 6058(a), 119 Stat. 231)

## HISTORY: ANCILLARY LAWS AND DIRECTIVES

**Amendments:**

**2005.** Act April 20, 2005 and Act May 11, 2005 (effective 180 days after enactment, as provided by § 1501(a) of P.L. 109-8) amends the filing fees for chapter 7, 11 and 13 cases and adopted a filing fee waiver provision.

**Other provisions:**

**Effective date and application of amendments by Act April 20, 2005.** Act April 20, 2005, P.L. 109-8, Title XV, § 1501(a), 119 Stat. 23, provided that the amendments made to this section would be effective 180 days after enactment on April 20, 2005. There was some confusion about the effective date of these changes to filing fees, but subsequent to further amendment by Act May 11, 2005, P. L. 109-13, § 6058(a), the Administrative Office of United States Courts has opined that the change in filing fees is effective 180 days after April 20, 2005.

**Abridged Legislative History**

(H. Report No. 109-31 to accompany S. 256, 109th Cong., 1st Sess. (2005) pp. 82–3, 89; available at 2005 U.S.C.C.A.N. 88, at 149, 155.) Subsequent to the Act of April 20, 2005, Congress further amended the filing fee for chapter 7 cases in an Act of May 11, 2005, P. L. 109-31, § 6058(a), 119 Stat. 231, changing the chapter 7 fee to $220. See Commentary in Part One at § 4:2 for pending legislation that may increase fees again.

# Chapter 131 —Rules of Courts

## Sec. 2075. Bankruptcy rules

The Supreme Court shall have the power to prescribe by general rules, the forms of process, writs, pleadings, and motions, and the practice and procedure in cases under Title 11.

Such rules shall not abridge, enlarge, or modify any substantive right.

The Supreme Court shall transmit to Congress not later than May 1 of the year in which a rule prescribed under this section is to become effective a copy of the proposed rule. The rule shall take effect no earlier than December 1 of the year in which it is transmitted to Congress unless otherwise provided by law. *The bankruptcy rules promulgated under this section shall prescribe a form for the statement required under section 707(b)(2)(C) of title 11 and may provide general rules on the content of such statement.*

**Section 2075**

(April 20, 2005, P. L. 109-8, Title XII, § 1232, 119 Stat. 23)

### HISTORY: ANCILLARY LAWS AND DIRECTIVES

**Amendments:**

**2005.** Act April 20, 2005 and Act May 11, 2005 (effective 180 days after enactment, as provided by § 1501(a) of P.L. 109-8) provides for a form to be used under amended § 707(b)(2)(C).

**Other provisions:**

**Effective date and application of amendments by Act April 20, 2005.** Act April 20, 2005, P.L. 109-8, Title XV, § 1501(a), 119 Stat. 23, provided that the amendments made to this section would be effective 180 days after enactment on April 20, 2005.

**Abridged Legislative History**

(H. Report No. 109-31 to accompany S. 256, 109th Cong., 1st Sess. (2005) p. 148; available at 2005 U.S.C.C.A.N. 88, at 206.)

## SECTION 406 OF THE JUDICIARY APPROPRIATIONS ACT, 1990

**Sec. 406.**

(a) * * *

(b) All fees as shall be hereafter collected for any service not of a kind described in any of the items enumerated as items 1 through 7 and as items 9 through 18, as in effect on November 21, 1989, of the bankruptcy miscellaneous fee schedule prescribed by the Judicial Conference of the United States ~~pursuant to 28 U.S.C. section 1930(b) and 33.87 percent of the fees hereafter collected under 28 U.S.C. section 1930(a)(1) and 25 percent of the fees hererafter collected under 28 U.S.C. section 1930(a)(3) shall be deposited as offsetting receipts to the fund established under 28 U.S.C. section 1931~~

*under section 1930(b) of title 28, United States Code, 28.87 of the fees collected under section 1930(a)(1)(A) of that title, 35.00 percent of the fees collected under section 1930(a)(1)(B) of that title, and 25 percent of the fees collected under section 1930(a)(3) of that title shall be deposited as offsetting receipts to the fund established under section 1931 of that title* and shall remain available to the Judiciary until expended to reimburse any appropriation for the amount paid out of such appropriation for expenses of the Courts of Appeals, District Courts, and other Judicial Services and the Administrative Office of the United States Courts. The Judicial Conference shall report to the Committees on Appropriations of the House of Representatives and the Senate on a quarterly basis beginning on the first day of each fiscal year regarding the sums deposited in said fund.

**Section 2075**

(April 20, 2005, P. L. 109-8, Title XII, § 1232, 119 Stat. 23 and May 11, 2005, P. L. 109-13, Title VI, § 6058(a), 119 Stat. 231)

## HISTORY: ANCILLARY LAWS AND DIRECTIVES

**Amendments:**

Act April 20, 2005 and Act May 11, 2005 (effective immediately upon enactment on April 20, 2005, as provided by § 6058(b) of P.L. 109-13), altered the percentages of fees allocated to the United States Trustee System. There was a drafting error in the original Act, P.L. 109-8, and that error was corrected in P.L. 109-13, 119 Stat. 231.

**Other provisions**

**Effective date and application of amendments made by Act April 20, 2005.** Act May 11, 2005 (effective immediately upon enactment of P. L. 109-8 on April 20, 2005, as provided by § 6058(b) of P.L. 109-13)

**Abridged Legislative History**

(H. Report No. 109-31 to accompany S. 256, 109th Cong., 1st Sess. (2005) p. 82; available at 2005 U.S.C.C.A.N. 88, at 149.) There was a drafting error in the percentage, which was corrected by the Act of May 11, 2005, P. L. 109-13, § 6058(c), 119 Stat. 231.

# INTERIM FEDERAL RULES OF BANKRUPTCY PROCEDURE

Rule 1006 [Interim]. Filing Fee.
Rule 1007 [Interim]. Lists, Schedules, ~~and~~ Statements,*and Other Documents*; Time Limits.
Rule 1009 [Interim]. Amendments of Voluntary Petitions, Lists, Schedules and Statements.
Rule 1010 [Interim]. Service of Involuntary Petition and Summons; Petition ~~Commencing Ancillary Case~~ *For Recognition of a Foreign Nonmain Proceeding*.
Rule 1011 [Interim]. Responsive Pleading or Motion in Involuntary and ~~Ancillary~~ *Cross-Border* Cases.
Rule 1017 [Interim]. Dismissal or Conversion of Case; Suspension.
Rule 1019 [Interim]. Conversion of Chapter 11 Reorganization Case, Chapter 12 Family Farmer's Debt Adjustment Case, or Chapter 13 Individual's Debt Adjustment Case to a Chapter 7 Liquidation Case.
Rule 1020 [Interim]. ~~Election to be Considered a Small Business in a Chapter 11 Reorganization Case~~ *Small Business Chapter 11 Reorganization Case*.
Rule 1021 [Interim]. *Health Care Business Case.*
Rule 2002 [Interim]. Notices to Creditors, Equity Security Holders, *Administrators in Foreign Proceedings, Persons Against Whom Provisional Relief is Sought in Ancillary and Other Cross-Border Cases,* United States, and United States Trustee.
Rule 2003 [Interim]. Meeting of Creditors or Equity Security Holders.
Rule 2007.1 [Interim]. Appointment of Trustee or Examiner in a Chapter 11 Reorganization Case.
Rule 2007.2 [Interim]. *Appointment of Patient Care Ombudsman in a Health Care Business Case*
Rule 2015 [Interim]. Duty To Keep Records, Make Reports, and Give Notice of Case *or Change of Status*.
Rule 2015.1 [Interim]. *Patient Care Ombudsman*
Rule 2015.2 [Interim]. *Transfer of Patient in Health Care Business Case*
Rule 3002 [Interim]. Filing Proof of Claim or Interest.
Rule 3003 [Interim]. Filing Proof of Claim or Equity Security Interest in Chapter 9 Municipality or Chapter 11 Reorganization Cases.
Rule 3016 [Interim]. Filing of Plan and Disclosure Statement in a Chapter 9 Municipality or Chapter 11 Reorganization Case.
Rule 3017.1 [Interim]. Court Consideration of Disclosure Statement in a Small Business Case.
Rule 3019 [Interim]. Modification of Accepted Plan Before *or After* Confirmation in a Chapter 9 Municipality or Chapter 11 Reorganization Case.
Rule 4002 [Interim]. Duties of Debtor.
Rule 4003 [Interim]. Exemptions.
Rule 4004 [Interim]. Grant or Denial of Discharge.

Rule 4006 [Interim]. Notice of No Discharge.
Rule 4007 [Interim]. Determination of Dischargeability of a Debt.
Rule 4008 [Interim]. Discharge and Reaffirmation Hearing.
Rule 5003 [Interim]. Records Kept By the Clerk.
Rule 5008 [Interim]. *Notice Regarding Presumption of Abuse in Chapter 7 Cases of Individual Debtors.*
Rule 5012 [Interim]. *Communication and Cooperation With Foreign Courts and Foreign Representatives.*
Rule 6004 [Interim]. Use, Sale, or Lease of Property.
Rule 6011 [Interim]. Disposal of Patient Records in Health Care Business Case.
Rule 8001 [Interim]. Manner of Taking Appeal; Voluntary Dismissal; *Certification to Court of Appeals.*
Rule 8003 [Interim]. Leave to Appeal.
Rule 9006 [Interim]. Time.
Rule 9009 [Interim]. Forms.

## Rule 1006 [Interim]. Filing Fee.

**(a) General Requirement.** Every petition shall be accompanied by the filing fee except as provided in subdivisions (b) *and c* of this rule. For the purpose of this rule, "filing fee" means the filing fee prescribed by 28 U.S.C. § 1930(a)(1)–(a)(5) and any other fee prescribed by the Judicial Conference of the United States under 28 U.S.C. § 1930(b) that is payable to the clerk upon the commencement of a case under the Code.

**(b) Payment of Filing Fee in Installments.**

(1) Application ~~for Permission~~ to Pay Filing Fee in Installments. A voluntary petition by an individual shall be accepted for filing if accompanied by the debtor's signed application, *prepared as prescribed by the appropriate Official Form,* stating that the debtor is unable to pay the filing fee except in installments. ~~The application shall state the proposed terms of the installment payments and that the applicant has neither paid any money nor transferred any property to an attorney for services in connection with the case.~~

(2) Action on Application. Prior to the meeting of creditors, the court may order the filing fee paid to the clerk or grant leave to pay in installments and fix the number, amount and dates of payment. The number of installments shall not exceed four, and the final installment shall be payable not later than 120 days after filing the petition. For cause shown, the court may extend the time of any installment, provided the last installment is paid not later than 180 days after filing the petition.

(3) Postponement of Attorney's Fees. ~~The filing fee~~ *All installments of the filing fee* must be paid in full before the debtor or chapter 13 trustee may *make further payments* ~~pay an~~ *to an* attorney or any other person who renders services to the debtor in connection with the case.

***(c) Waiver of Filing Fee.***

*A voluntary chapter 7 petition filed by an individual shall be ac-*

*cepted for filing if accompanied by the debtor's application requesting a waiver under 28 U.S.C. § 1930(f), prepared as prescribed by the appropriate Official Form.*

## Rule 1007 [Interim]. Lists, Schedules, ~~and~~ Statements, *and Other Documents*; Time Limits.

**(a) List of Creditors and Equity Security Holders, and Corporate Ownership Statement.**

(1) Voluntary Case. In a voluntary case, the debtor shall file with the petition a list containing the name and address of each entity included or to be included on Schedules D, E, F, G, and H as prescribed by the Official Forms. If the debtor is a corporation, other than a governmental unit, the debtor shall file with the petition a corporate ownership statement containing the information described in Rule 7007.1. The debtor shall file a supplemental statement promptly upon any change in circumstances that renders the corporate ownership statement inaccurate.

(2) Involuntary Case. In an involuntary case, the debtor shall file within 15 days after entry of the order for relief, a list containing the name and address of each entity included or to be included on Schedules D, E, F, G, and H as prescribed by the Official Forms.

(3) Equity Security Holders. In a chapter 11 reorganization case, unless the court orders otherwise, the debtor shall file within 15 days after entry of the order for relief a list of the debtor's equity security holders of each class showing the number and kind of interests registered in the name of each holder, and the last known address or place of business of each holder.

*(4) Chapter 15 Case. Unless the court orders otherwise, a foreign representative filing a petition for recognition under chapter 15 shall file with the petition a list containing the name and address of all administrators in foreign proceedings of the debtor, all parties to any litigation in which the debtor is a party and that is pending in the United States at the time of the filing of the petition, and all entities against whom provisional relief is being sought under § 1519 of the Code.*

~~(4)~~*(5)* Extension of Time. Any extension of time for the filing of the lists required by this subdivision may be granted only on motion for cause shown and on notice to the United States trustee and to any trustee, committee elected ~~pursuant to~~ *under* § 705 or appointed ~~pursuant to~~ *under* § 1102 of the Code, or other party as the court may direct.

**(b) Schedules, ~~and~~ Statements, *and Other Documents* Required.**

(1) Except in a chapter 9 municipality case, the debtor, unless the court orders otherwise, shall file *the following schedules, statements, and other documents, prepared as prescribed by the appropriate Official Forms, if any:*

*(A)* schedules of assets and liabilities~~,~~ *;*

*(B)* a schedule of current income and expenditures~~,~~ *;*

*(C)* a schedule of executory contracts and unexpired leases~~, and~~ *;*

*(D)* a statement of financial affairs~~, prepared as prescribed by the appropriate Official Forms.~~ *;*

*(E) copies of all payment advices or other evidence of payment, if any, with all but the last four digits of the debtor's social security number redacted, received by the debtor from an employer within 60 days before the filing of the petition; and*

*(F) a record of any interest that the debtor has in an account or program of the type specified in § 521(c) of the Code.*

(2) An individual debtor in a chapter 7 case shall file a statement of intention as required by § *521(a)* ~~521(2)~~ of the Code, prepared as prescribed by the appropriate Official Form. A copy of the statement of intention shall be served on the trustee and creditors named in the statement on or before the filing of the statement.

*(3) Unless the United States trustee has determined that the credit counseling requirement of § 109 does not apply in the district, an individual debtor must file the certificate and debt repayment plan, if any, required by § 521(b), a certification under § 109(h)(3), or a request for a determination by the court under § 109(h)(4).*

*(4) Unless § 707(b)(2)(D) applies, an individual debtor in a chapter 7 case with primarily consumer debts shall file a statement of current monthly income prepared as prescribed by the appropriate Official Form, and, if the debtor has current monthly income greater than the applicable median family income for the applicable state and household size, the calculations in accordance with § 707(b), prepared as prescribed by the appropriate Official Form.*

*(5) An individual debtor in a chapter 11 case shall file a statement of current monthly income, prepared as prescribed by the appropriate Official Form.*

*(6) A debtor in a chapter 13 case shall file a statement of current monthly income, prepared as prescribed by the appropriate Official Form, and, if the debtor has current monthly income greater than the median family income for the applicable state and family size, a calculation of disposable income in accordance with § 1325(b)(3), prepared as prescribed by the appropriate Official Form.*

*(7) An individual debtor in a chapter 7 or chapter 13 case shall file a statement regarding completion of a course in personal financial management, prepared as prescribed by the appropriate Official Form.*

*(8) If an individual debtor in a chapter 11, 12, or 13 case has claimed an exemption under § 522(b)(3)(A) in an amount in excess of the amount set out in § 522(q)(1) in property of the kind described in § 522(p)(1), the debtor shall file a statement as to whether there is pending a proceeding in which the debtor may be found guilty of a felony of a kind described in § 522(q)(1)(A) or found liable for a debt of the kind described in § 522(q)(1)(B).*

**(c) Time Limits.** In a voluntary case, the schedules, ~~and~~ statements *, and other documents required by subdivision (b)(1), (4), (5), and (6)*~~, other than the statement of intention,~~ shall be filed with the petition~~, or~~ within 15 days thereafter, except as otherwise provided in subdivisions (d), (e), (f) and (h) of this rule. In an involuntary case, the list in subdivision (a)(2), and the schedules, ~~and~~ statements, *and other documents required by subdivision (b)(1)* ~~other than the statement of intention,~~ shall be filed by the debtor within 15 days of the entry of the order for relief. *The documents required by subdivision (b)(3) shall be filed with the petition in a voluntary case. The statement required by subdivision (b)(7) shall be filed by the debtor within 45 days after the first date set for the meeting of creditors under § 341 of the Code in a chapter 7 case, and no later than the last payment made by the debtor as required by the plan or the filing of a motion for entry of a discharge under § 1328(b) in a chapter 13 case. The statement required by subdivision (b)(8) shall be filed by the debtor not earlier than the date of the last payment made under the plan or the date of the filing of a motion for entry of a discharge under §§ 1141(d)(5)(B), 1228(b), or 1328(b).* Lists, schedules, ~~and~~ statements*, and other documents* filed prior to the conversion of a case to another chapter shall be deemed filed in the converted case unless the court directs otherwise. *Except as provided in § 1116(3) of the Code, any* ~~Any~~ extension of time for the filing of the schedules, ~~and~~ statements*, and other documents* may be granted only on motion for cause shown and on notice to the United States trustee and to any committee elected under § 705 or appointed under § 1102 of the Code, trustee, examiner, or other party as the court may direct. Notice of an extension shall be given to the United States trustee and to any committee, trustee, or other party as the court may direct.

**(d) List of 20 Largest Creditors in Chapter 9 Municipality Case or Chapter 11 Reorganization Case.** In addition to the list required by subdivision (a) of this rule, a debtor in a chapter 9 municipality case or a debtor in a voluntary chapter 11 reorganization case shall file with the petition a list containing the name, address and claim of the creditors that hold the 20 largest unsecured claims, excluding insiders, as prescribed by the appropriate Official Form. In an involuntary chapter 11 reorganization case, such list shall be filed by the debtor within 2 days after entry of the order for relief under § 303(h) of the Code.

**(e) List in Chapter 9 Municipality Cases.** The list required by subdivision (a) of this rule shall be filed by the debtor in a chapter 9 municipality case within such time as the court shall fix. If a proposed plan requires a revision of assessments so that the proportion of special assessments or special taxes to be assessed against some real property will be different from the proportion in effect at the date the petition is filed, the debtor shall also file a list showing the name and address of each known holder of title, legal or equitable, to real property adversely affected. On motion for cause shown, the court may modify the requirements of this subdivision and subdivision (a) of this rule.

**(f) Statement of Social Security Number.** An individual debtor shall submit a verified statement that sets out the debtor's social security number, or states that the debtor does not have a social security number. In a voluntary case, the debtor shall submit the statement with the petition. In an involuntary case, the debtor shall submit the statement within 15 days after the entry of the order for relief.

**(g) Partnership and Partners.** The general partners of a debtor partnership shall prepare and file the schedules of the assets and liabilities, schedule of current income and expenditures, schedule of executory contracts and unexpired leases, and statement of financial affairs of the partnership. The court may order any general partner to file a statement of personal assets and liabilities within such time as the court may fix.

**(h) Interests Acquired or Arising After Petition.** If, as provided by § 541(a)(5) of the Code, the debtor acquires or becomes entitled to acquire any interest in property, the debtor shall within 10 days after the information comes to the debtor's knowledge or within such further time the court may allow, file a supplemental schedule in the chapter 7 liquidation case, chapter 11 reorganization case, chapter 12 family farmer's debt adjustment case, or chapter 13 individual debt adjustment case. If any of the property required to be reported under this subdivision is claimed by the debtor as exempt, the debtor shall claim the exemptions in the supplemental schedule. The duty to file a supplemental schedule in accordance with this subdivision continues notwithstanding the closing of the case, except that the schedule need not be filed in a chapter 11, chapter 12, or chapter 13 case with respect to property acquired after entry of the order confirming a chapter 11 plan or discharging the debtor in a chapter 12 or chapter 13 case.

**(i) Disclosure of List of Security Holders.** After notice and hearing and for cause shown, the court may direct an entity other than the debtor or trustee to disclose any list of security holders of the debtor in its possession or under its control, indicating the name, address and security held by any of them. The entity possessing this list may be required either to produce the list or a true copy thereof, or permit inspection or copying, or otherwise disclose the information contained on the list.

**(j) Impounding of Lists.** On motion of a party in interest and for cause shown the court may direct the impounding of the lists filed under this rule, and may refuse to permit inspection by any entity. The court may permit inspection or use of the lists, however, by any party in interest on terms prescribed by the court.

**(k) Preparation of List, Schedules, or Statements on Default of Debtor.** If a list, schedule, or statement, other than a statement of intention, is not prepared and filed as required by this rule, the court may order the trustee, a petitioning creditor, committee, or other party to prepare and file any of these papers within a time fixed by the court. The court may approve reimbursement of the cost incurred in complying with such an order as an administrative expense.

**(l) Transmission To United States Trustee.** The clerk shall forthwith transmit to the United States trustee a copy of every list, schedule, and statement filed pursuant to subdivision (a)(1), (a)(2), (b), (d), or (h) of this rule.

**(m) Infants and Incompetent Persons.** If the debtor knows that a person on the list of creditors or schedules is an infant or incompetent person, the debtor also shall include the name, address, and legal relationship of any person upon whom process would be served in an adversary proceeding against the infant or incompetent person in accordance with Rule 7004(b)(2).

## Rule 1009 [Interim]. Amendments of Voluntary Petitions, Lists, Schedules and Statements.

**(a) General Right to Amend.** A voluntary petition, list, schedule, or statement may be amended by the debtor as a matter of course at any time before the case is closed. The debtor shall give notice of the amendment to the trustee and to any entity affected thereby. On motion of a party in interest, after notice and a hearing, the court may order any voluntary petition, list, schedule, or statement to be amended and the clerk shall give notice of the amendment to entities designated by the court.

**(b) Statement of Intention.** The statement of intention may be amended by the debtor at any time before the expiration of the period provided in § *521(a)* ~~521(2)(B)~~ of the Code. The debtor shall give notice of the amendment to the trustee and to any entity affected thereby.

**(c) Transmission To United States Trustee.** The clerk shall forthwith transmit to the United States trustee a copy of every amendment filed pursuant to subdivision (a) or (b) of this rule.

## Rule 1010 [Interim]. Service of Involuntary Petition and Summons; Petition ~~Commencing Ancillary Case~~ *For Recognition of a Foreign Nonmain Proceeding*.

On the filing of an involuntary petition or a petition ~~commencing a case ancillary to~~ *for recognition of* a foreign *nonmain* proceeding the clerk shall forthwith issue a summons for service. When an involuntary petition is filed, service shall be made on the debtor. When a petition ~~commencing an ancillary case~~ *for recognition of a foreign nonmain proceeding* is filed, service shall be made on the ~~parties against whom relief is sought pursuant to § 304(b)~~ *debtor, any entity against whom provisional relief is sought under § 1519* of the Code, and on any other parties as the court may direct. The summons shall be served with a copy of the petition in the manner provided for service of a summons and complaint by Rule 7004(a) or (b). If service cannot be so made, the court may order that the summons and petition be served by mailing copies to the party's last known address, and by at least one publication in a manner and form directed by the court. The summons and petition may be served on the party anywhere.Rule 7004(e) and Rule 4*(l)* FR Civ P apply when service is made or attempted under this rule.

## Rule 1011 [Interim]. Responsive Pleading or Motion in Involuntary and ~~Ancillary~~ *Cross-Border* Cases.

**(a) Who May Contest Petition.** The debtor named in an involuntary petition or a party in interest to a petition ~~commencing a case ancillary to a~~ *for recognition of a* foreign proceeding may contest the petition. In the case of a petition against a partnership under Rule 1004, a nonpetitioning general partner, or a person who is alleged to be a general partner but denies the allegation, may contest the petition.

**(b) Defenses and Objections; When Presented.** Defenses and objections to the petition shall be presented in the manner prescribed by Rule 12 FR Civ P and shall be filed and served within 20 days after service of the summons, except that if service is made by publication on a party or partner not residing or found within the state in which the court sits, the court shall prescribe the time for filing and serving the response.

**(c) Effect of Motion.** Service of a motion under Rule 12(b) FR Civ P shall extend the time for filing and serving a responsive pleading as permitted by Rule 12(a) FR Civ P.

**(d) Claims Against Petitioners.** A claim against a petitioning creditor may not be asserted in the answer except for the purpose of defeating the petition.

(e) Other Pleadings. No other pleadings shall be permitted, except that the court may order a reply to an answer and prescribe the time for filing and service.

## Rule 1017 [Interim]. Dismissal or Conversion of Case; Suspension.

**(a) Voluntary Dismissal; Dismissal for Want of Prosecution or Other Cause.** Except as provided in §§ 707(a)(3), 707(b), 1208(b), and 1307(b) of the Code, and in Rule 1017(b), (c), and (e), a case shall not be dismissed on motion of the petitioner, for want of prosecution or other cause, or by consent of the parties, before a hearing on notice as provided in Rule 2002. For the purpose of the notice, the debtor shall file a list of creditors with their addresses within the time fixed by the court unless the list was previously filed. If the debtor fails to file the list, the court may order the debtor or another entity to prepare and file it.

**(b) Dismissal for Failure To Pay Filing Fee.**

(1) If any installment of the filing fee has not been paid, the court may, after a hearing on notice to the debtor and the trustee, dismiss the case.

(2) If the case is dismissed or closed without full payment of the filing fee, the installments collected shall be distributed in the same manner and proportions as if the filing fee had been paid in full.

**(c) Dismissal of Voluntary Chapter 7 or Chapter 13 Case for Failure to Timely File List of Creditors, Schedules, and Statement of Financial Affairs.** The court may dismiss a voluntary chapter 7 or chapter 13 case under § 707(a)(3) or § 1307(c)(9) after a hearing on notice served by the United States trustee on the debtor, the trustee, and any other entities as the court directs.

**(d) Suspension.** The court shall not dismiss a case or suspend proceedings under § 305 before a hearing on notice as provided in Rule 2002(a).

**(e) Dismissal of an Individual Debtor's Chapter 7 Case *or Conversion to a Case under Chapter 11 or 13* for ~~Substantial~~ Abuse.** The court may dismiss *or, with the debtor's consent, convert* an individual debtor's case for ~~substantial~~ abuse under § 707(b) only on motion ~~by the United States trustee or on the court's own motion~~ and after a hearing on notice to the debtor, the trustee, the United States trustee, and any other entities as the court directs.

(1) *Except as otherwise provided in § 704(b)(2), a* ~~A~~ motion to dismiss a case for ~~substantial~~ abuse *under § 707(b) or (c)* may be filed ~~by the United States trustee~~ only within 60 days after the first date set for the meeting of creditors under § 341(a), unless, on request filed ~~by the United States trustee~~ before the time has expired, the court for cause extends the time for filing the motion to dismiss. The ~~United States trustee~~ *party filing the motion* shall set forth in the motion all matters to be *considered* ~~submitted to the court for its consideration~~ at the hearing. *A motion to dismiss under § 707(b)(1) and (3) shall state with particularity the circumstances alleged to constitute abuse.*

(2) If the hearing is set on the court's own motion, notice of the hearing shall be served on the debtor no later than 60 days after the first date set for the meeting of creditors under § 341(a). The notice shall set forth all matters to be considered by the court at the hearing.

**(f) Procedure for Dismissal, Conversion, or Suspension.**

(1) Rule 9014 governs a proceeding to dismiss or suspend a case, or to convert a case to another chapter, except under §§ 706(a), 1112(a), 1208(a) or (b), or 1307(a) or (b).

(2) Conversion or dismissal under §§ 706(a), 1112(a), 1208(b), or 1307(b) shall be on motion filed and served as required by Rule 9013.

(3) A chapter 12 or chapter 13 case shall be converted without court order when the debtor files a notice of conversion under §§ 1208(a) or 1307(a). The filing date of the notice becomes the date of the conversion order for the purposes of applying § 348(c) and Rule 1019. The clerk shall promptly transmit a copy of the notice to the United States trustee.

## Rule 1019 [Interim]. Conversion of Chapter 11 Reorganization Case, Chapter 12 Family Farmer's Debt Adjustment Case, or Chapter 13 Individual's Debt Adjustment Case to a Chapter 7 Liquidation Case.

When a chapter 11, chapter 12, or chapter 13 case has been converted or reconverted to a chapter 7 case:

(1) Filing of Lists, Inventories, Schedules, Statements.

(A) Lists, inventories, schedules, and statements of financial affairs theretofore filed shall be deemed to be filed in the chapter 7 case, unless the court directs otherwise. If they have not been previously filed, the debtor shall comply with Rule 1007 as if an order for relief had been entered on an involuntary petition on the date of the entry of the order directing that the case continue under chapter 7.

(B) If a statement of intention is required, it shall be filed within 30 days after entry of the order of conversion or before the first date set for the meeting of creditors, whichever is earlier. The court may grant an extension of time for cause only on written motion filed, or oral request made during a hearing, before the time has expired. Notice of an extension shall be given to the United States trustee and to any committee, trustee, or other party as the court may direct.

(2) New Filing Periods. A new time period for filing ~~claims~~ *a motion under § 707(b) or (c), a claim*, a complaint objecting to discharge, or a complaint to obtain a determination of dischargeability of any debt shall commence *under* ~~pursuant to~~ Rules *1017,* 3002, 4004, or 4007, provided that a new time period shall not commence if a chapter 7 case had been converted to a chapter 11, 12, or 13 case and thereafter reconverted to a chapter 7 case and the time for filing ~~claims~~ *a motion under § 707(b) or (c), a claim*, a complaint objecting to discharge, or a complaint to obtain a determination of the dischargeability of any debt, or any extension thereof, expired in the original chapter 7 case.

(3) Claims Filed Before Conversion. All claims actually filed by a creditor before conversion of the case are deemed filed in the chapter 7 case.

(4) Turnover of Records and Property. After qualification of, or assumption of duties by the chapter 7 trustee, any debtor in possession or trustee previously acting in the chapter 11, 12, or 13 case shall, forthwith, unless otherwise ordered, turn over to the chapter 7 trustee all records and property of the estate in the possession or control of the debtor in possession or trustee.

(5) Filing Final Report and Schedule of Postpetition Debts.

(A) Conversion of Chapter 11 or Chapter 12 Case. Unless the court directs otherwise, if a chapter 11 or chapter 12 case in converted to chapter 7, the debtor in possession or, if the debtor is not a debtor in possession, the trustee serving at the time of conversion, shall:

(i) not later than 15 days after conversion of the case, file a schedule of unpaid debts incurred after the filing of the petition and before conversion of the case, including the name and address of each holder of a claim; and

(ii) not later than 30 days after conversion of the case, file and transmit to the United States trustee a final report and account;

(B) Conversion of Chapter 13 Case. Unless the court directs otherwise, if a chapter 13 case in converted to chapter 7,

(i) the debtor, not later than 15 days after conversion of the case, shall file a schedule of unpaid debts incurred after the filing of the petition and before conversion of the case, including the name and address of each holder of a claim; and

(ii) the trustee, not later than 30 days after conversion of the case, shall file and transmit to the United States trustee a final report and account;

(C) Conversion After Confirmation of a Plan. Unless the court orders otherwise, if a chapter 11, chapter 12, or chapter 13 case is converted to chapter 7 after confirmation of a plan, the debtor shall file:

(i) a schedule of property not listed in the final report and account acquired after the filing of the petition but before conversion, except if the case is converted from chapter 13 to chapter 7 and § 348(f)(2) does not apply;

(ii) a schedule of unpaid debts not listed in the final report and account incurred after confirmation but before the conversion; and

(iii) a schedule of executory contracts and unexpired leases entered into or assumed after the filing of the petition but before conversion.

(D) Transmission to United States Trustee. The clerk shall forthwith transmit to the United States trustee a copy of every schedule filed pursuant to Rule 1019(5)

(6) Postpetition Claims; written motion filed, or oral request made during a hearing, Notice. A request for payment of an administrative expense incurred before conversion of the case is timely filed under § 503(a) of the Code if it is filed before conversion or a time fixed by the court. If the request is filed by a governmental unit, it is timely if it is filed before conversion or within the later of a time fixed by the court or 180 days after the date of the conversion. A claim of a kind specified in § 348(d) may be filed in accordance with Rules 3001(a)–(d) and 3002. Upon the filing of the schedule of unpaid debts incurred after commencement of the case and before conversion, the clerk, or some other person as the court may direct, shall give notice to those entities listed on the schedule of the time

for filing a request for payment of an administrative expense and, unless a notice of insufficient assets to pay a dividend is mailed in accordance with Rule 2002(e), the time for filing a claim of a kind specified in § 348(d).

## Rule 1020 [Interim]. ~~Election to be Considered a Small Business in a Chapter 11 Reorganization Case~~ *Small Business Chapter 11 Reorganization Case.*

*(a) Small business debtor designation. In a voluntary chapter 11 case, the debtor shall state in the petition whether the debtor is a small business debtor. In an involuntary chapter 11 case, the debtor shall file within 15 days after entry of the order for relief a statement as to whether the debtor is a small business debtor. Except as provided in subdivision (c), the status of the case with respect to whether it is a small business case shall be in accordance with the debtor's statement under this subdivision, unless and until the court enters an order finding that the debtor's statement is incorrect.*

*(b) Objecting to designation. Except as provided in subdivision (c), the United States trustee or a party in interest may file an objection to the debtor's statement under subdivision (a) not later than 30 days after the conclusion of the meeting of creditors held under § 341(a) of the Code, or within 30 days after any amendment to the statement, whichever is later.*

*(c) Appointment of committee of unsecured creditors. If the United States trustee has appointed a committee of unsecured creditors under § 1102(a)(1), the case shall proceed as a small business case only if, and from the time when, the court enters an order determining that the committee has not been sufficiently active and representative to provide effective oversight of the debtor and that the debtor satisfies all the other requirements for being a small business. A request for a determination under this subdivision may be filed by the United States trustee or a party in interest only within a reasonable time after the failure of the committee to be sufficiently active and representative. The debtor may file a request for a determination at any time as to whether the committee has been sufficiently active and representative.*

*(d) Procedure for objection or determination. Any objection or request for a determination under this rule shall be governed by Rule 9014 and served on the debtor, the debtor's attorney, the United States trustee, the trustee, any committee appointed under § 1102 or its authorized agent, or, if no committee of unsecured creditors has been appointed under § 1102, on the creditors included on the list filed under Rule 1007(d), and on such other entities as the court may direct.*

## Rule 1021 [Interim]. *Health Care Business Case.*

*(a) Health care business designation. Unless the court orders otherwise, if a petition in a case under chapter 7, chapter 9, or*

*chapter 11 states that the debtor is a health care business, the case shall proceed as a case in which the debtor is a health care business.*

*(b) Motion. The United States trustee or a party in interest may file a motion for a determination as to whether the debtor is a health care business. The motion shall be transmitted to the United States trustee and served on the debtor, the trustee, any committee elected under § 705 or appointed under § 1102 of the Code or its authorized agent, or, if the case is a chapter 9 municipality case or a chapter 11 reorganization case and no committee of unsecured creditors has been appointed under § 1102, on the creditors included on the list filed under Rule 1007(d), and such other entities as the court may direct. The motion shall be governed by Rule 9014.*

## Rule 2002 [Interim]. Notices to Creditors, Equity Security Holders, *Administrators in Foreign Proceedings, Persons Against Whom Provisional Relief is Sought in Ancillary and Other Cross-Border Cases,* United States, and United States Trustee.

**(a) Twenty-day Notices to Parties in Interest.** Except as provided in subdivisions (h), (i), ~~and (l)~~ *(l), (p) and (q)* of this rule, the clerk, or some other person as the court may direct, shall give the debtor, the trustee, all creditors and indenture trustees at least 20 days' notice by mail of:

(1) the meeting of creditors under § 341 or § 1104(b) of the Code, *which notice, unless the court orders otherwise, shall include the debtor's employer identification number, Social Security number, and any other federal taxpayer identification number;*

(2) a proposed use, sale, or lease of property of the estate other than in the ordinary course of business, unless the court for cause shown shortens the time or directs another method of giving notice;

(3) the hearing on approval of a compromise or settlement of a controversy other than approval of an agr eement pursuant to Rule 4001(d), unless the court for cause shown directs that notice not be sent;

(4) in a chapter 7 liquidation, a chapter 11 reorganization case, or a chapter 12 family farmer debt adjustment case, the hearing on the dismissal of the case or the conversion of the case to another chapter, unless the hearing is under § 707(a)(3) or § 707(b) or is on dismissal of the case for failure to pay the filing fee;

(5) the time fixed to accept or reject a proposed modification of a plan;

(6) a hearing on any entity's request for compensation or reimbursement of expenses if the request exceeds $1,000;

(7) the time fixed for filing proofs of claims pursuant to Rule 3003 (c); and

(8) the time fixed for filing objections and the hearing to consider confirmation of a chapter 12 plan.

**(b) Twenty-five-day Notices to Parties in Interest.** Except as provided in subdivision (l) of this rule, the clerk, or some other person as the court may direct, shall give the debtor, the trustee, all creditors and indenture trustees not less than 25 days notice by mail of (1) the time fixed for filing objections and the hearing to consider approval of a disclosure statement *or, under § 1125(f), to make a final determination whether the plan provides adequate information so that a separate disclosure statement is not necessary*; and (2) the time fixed for filing objections and the hearing to consider confirmation of a chapter 9, chapter 11, or chapter 13 plan.

**(c) Content of Notice.**

(1) Proposed Use, Sale, or Lease of Property. Subject to Rule 6004 the notice of a proposed use, sale, or lease of property required by subdivision (a)(2) of this rule shall include the time and place of any public sale, the terms and conditions of any private sale and the time fixed for filing objections. The notice of a proposed use, sale, or lease of property, including real estate, is sufficient if it generally describes the property. *The notice of a proposed sale or lease of personally identifiable information under § 363(b)(1)(A) or (B) of the Code shall state whether the sale is consistent with a policy prohibiting the transfer of the information.*

(2) Notice of Hearing on Compensation. The notice of a hearing on an application for compensation or reimbursement of expenses required by subdivision (a)(6) of this rule shall identify the applicant and the amounts requested.

(3) Notice of Hearing on Confirmation When Plan Provides for an Injunction. If a plan provides for an injunction against conduct not otherwise enjoined under the Code, the notice required under Rule 2002(b)(2) shall:

(A) include in conspicuous language (bold, italic, or underlined text) a statement that the plan proposes an injunction;

(B) describe briefly the nature of the injunction; and

(C) identify the entities that would be subject to the injunction.

**(d) Notice to Equity Security Holders.** In a chapter 11 reorganization case, unless otherwise ordered by the court, the clerk, or some other person as the court may direct, shall in the manner and form directed by the court give notice to all equity security holders of (1) the order for relief; (2) any meeting of equity security holders held pursuant to § 341 of the Code; (3) the hearing on the proposed sale of all or substantially all of the debtor's assets; (4) the hearing on the dismissal or conversion of a case to another chapter; (5) the time fixed for filing objections to and the hearing to consider approval of a disclosure statement; (6) the time fixed for filing objections to and the hearing to consider confirmation of a plan; and (7) the time fixed to accept or reject a proposed modification of a plan.

**(e) Notice of No Dividend.** In a chapter 7 liquidation case, if it appears from the schedules that there are no assets from which a dividend can be paid, the notice of the meeting of creditors may include a statement to that effect; that it is unnecessary to file claims; and that if sufficient assets become available for the payment of a dividend, further notice will be given for the filing of claims.

**(f) Other Notices.** Except as provided in subdivision (l) of this rule, the clerk, or some other person as the court may direct, shall give the debtor, all creditors, and indenture trustees notice by mail of: (1) the order for relief; (2) the dismissal or the conversion of the case to another chapter, or the suspension of proceedings under § 305; (3) the time allowed for filing claims pursuant to Rule 3002; (4) the time fixed for filing a complaint objecting to the debtor's discharge pursuant to § 727 of the Code as provided in Rule 4004; (5) the time fixed for filing a complaint to determine the dischargeability of a debt pursuant to § 523 of the Code as provided in Rule 4007; (6) the waiver, denial, or revocation of a discharge as provided in Rule 4006; (7) entry of an order confirming a chapter 9, 11, or 12 plan; ~~and~~ (8) a summary of the trustee's final report in a chapter 7 case if the net proceeds realized exceed $1,500*; (9) a notice under Rule 5008 regarding the presumption of abuse; (10) a statement under § 704(b)(1) as to whether the debtor's case would be presumed to be an abuse under § 707(b); and (11) the time to request a delay in the entry of the discharge under §§ 1141(d)(5)(C), 1228(f), and 1328(h).*. Notice of the time fixed for accepting or rejecting a plan pursuant to Rule 3017(c) shall be given in accordance with Rule 3017(d).

**(g) Addressing Notices.** (1) Notices required to be mailed under Rule 2002 to a creditor, indenture trustee, or equity security holder shall be addressed as such entity or an authorized agent has directed in its last request filed in the particular case. For the purposes of this subdivision —

(A) a proof of claim filed by a creditor or indenture trustee that designates a mailing address constitutes a filed request to mail notices to that address, unless a notice of no dividend has been given under Rule 2002(e) and a later notice of possible dividend under Rule 3002(c)(5) has not been given; and

(B) a proof of interest filed by an equity security holder that designates a mailing address constitutes a filed request to mail notices to that address.

(2) *Except as provided in § 342(f) of the Code, if* ~~If~~ a creditor or indenture trustee has not filed a request designating a mailing address under Rule 2002(g)(1), the notices shall be mailed to the address shown on the list of creditors or schedule of liabilities, whichever is filed later. If an equity security holder has not filed a request designating a mailing address under Rule 2002(g)(1), the notices shall be mailed to the address shown on the list of equity security holders.

(3) If a list or schedule filed under Rule 1007 includes the name and address of a legal representative of an infant or incompetent person, and a person other than that representative files a request or proof of claim designating a name and mailing address that dif-

fers from the name and address of the representative included in the list or schedule, unless the court orders otherwise, notices under Rule 2002 shall be mailed to the representative included in the list or schedules and to the name and address designated in the request or proof of claim.

**(h) Notices to Creditors Whose Claims Are Filed.** In a chapter 7 case, after 90 days following the first date set for the meeting of creditors under § 341 of the Code, the court may direct that all notices required by subdivision (a) of this rule be mailed only to the debtor, the trustee, all indenture trustees, creditors that hold claims for which proofs of claim have been filed, and creditors, if any, that are still permitted to file claims by reason of an extension granted pursuant to Rule 3002(c)(1) or (c)(2). In a case where notice of insufficient assets to pay a dividend has been given to creditors pursuant to subdivision (e) of this rule, after 90 days following the mailing of a notice of the time for filing claims pursuant to Rule 3002(c)(5), the court may direct that notices be mailed only to the entities specified in the preceding sentence.

**(i) Notices to Committees.** Copies of all notices required to be mailed pursuant to this rule shall be mailed to the committees elected under § 705 or appointed under § 1102 of the Code or to their authorized agents. Notwithstanding the foregoing subdivisions, the court may order that notices required by subdivision (a)(2), (3) and (6) of this rule be transmitted to the United States trustee and be mailed only to the committees elected under § 705 or appointed under § 1102 of the Code or to their authorized agents and to the creditors and equity security holders who serve on the trustee or debtor in possession and file a request that all notices be mailed to them. A committee appointed under § 1114 shall receive copies of all notices required by subdivisions (a)(1), (a)(5), (b), (f)(2), and (f)(7), and such other notices as the court may direct.

**(j) Notices to the United States.** Copies of notices required to be mailed to all creditors under this rule shall be mailed (1) in a chapter 11 reorganization case, to the Securities and Exchange Commission at any place the Commission designates, if the Commission has filed either a notice of appearance in the case or a written request to receive notices; (2) in a commodity broker case, to the Commodity Futures Trading Commission at Washington, D.C.; (3) in a chapter 11 case to the ~~District Director of~~ Internal Revenue *Service at its address set out in the register maintained under Rule 5003(e)* for the district in which the case is pending; (4) if the papers in the case disclose a debt to the United States other than for taxes, to the United States attorney for the district in which the case is pending and to the department, agency, or instrumentality of the United States through which the debtor became indebted; or *(5)* if the filed papers disclose a stock interest of the United States, to the Secretary of the Treasury at Washington, D.C.

**(k) Notices to United States Trustee.** Unless the case is a chapter 9 municipality case or unless the United States trustee requests otherwise, the clerk, or some other person as the court may direct, shall transmit to the United States trustee notice of the matters described in subdivisions (a)(2), (a)(3), (a)(4), (a)(8), (b), (f)(1), (f)(2), (f)(4), (f)(6), (f)(7), and (f)(8) of this rule and notice of hearings on all applications for compensation or reimbursement of expenses. Notices to the United States trustee shall be transmitted within the time prescribed in subdivision (a) or (b) of this rule. The United States trustee shall also receive notice of any other matter if such notice is requested by the United States trustee or ordered by the court. Nothing in these rules requires the clerk or any other person to transmit to the United States trustee any notice, schedule, report, application or other document in a case under the Securities Investor Protection Act, 15 U.S.C. §§ 78aaa et seq.

**(l) Notice by Publication.** The court may order notice by publication if it finds that notice by mail is impracticable or that it is desirable to supplement the notice.

**(m) Orders Designating Matter of Notices.** The court may from time to time enter orders designating the matters in respect to which, the entity to whom, and the form and manner in which notices shall be sent except as otherwise provided by these rules.

**(n) Caption.** The caption of every notice given under this rule shall comply with Rule 1005. The caption of every notice required to be given by the debtor to a creditor shall include the information required to be in the notice by § 342(c) of the Code.

**(o) Notice of Order for Relief in Consumer Case.** In a voluntary case commenced by an individual debtor whose debts are primarily consumer debts, the clerk, or some other person as the court may direct, shall give the trustee and all creditors notice by mail of the order for relief within 20 days from the date thereof.

***(p) Notice to a Foreign Creditor.***

*(1) If, at the request of a party in interest or the United States trustee, or on its own initiative, the court finds that a notice mailed within the time prescribed by these rules would not be sufficient to give a creditor with a foreign address to which notices under these rules are mailed reasonable notice under the circumstances, the court may order that the notice be supplemented with notice by other means or that the time prescribed for the notice by mail be enlarged.*

*(2) Unless the court for cause orders otherwise, a creditor with a foreign address to which notices under this rule are mailed shall be given at least 30 days' notice of the time fixed for filing a proof of claim under Rule 3002(c) or Rule 3003(c).*

***(q) Notice of Petition for Recognition of Foreign Proceeding and of Court's Intention to Communicate With Foreign Courts and Foreign Representatives.***

*(1) Notice of Petition for Recognition. The clerk, or some other person as the court may direct, shall forthwith give the debtor, all administrators in foreign proceedings of the debtor, all entities against whom provisional relief is being sought under § 1519 of the*

*Code, all parties to any litigation in which the debtor is a party and that is pending in the United States at the time of the filing of the petition, and such other entities as the court may direct, at least 20 days' notice by mail of the hearing on the petition for recognition of a foreign proceeding. The notice shall state whether the petition seeks recognition as a foreign main proceeding or foreign nonmain proceeding.*

*(2) Notice of Court's Intention to Communicate with Foreign Courts and Foreign Representatives. The clerk, or some other person as the court may direct, shall give the debtor, all administrators in foreign proceedings of the debtor, all entities against whom provisional relief is being sought under § 1519 of the Code, all parties to any litigation in which the debtor is a party and that is pending in the United States at the time of the filing of the petition, and such other entities as the court may direct, notice by mail of the court's intention to communicate with a foreign court or foreign representative as prescribed by Rule 5012.*

## Rule 2003 [Interim]. Meeting of Creditors or Equity Security Holders.

**(a) Date and Place.** *Except as provided in § 341(e) of the Code, in* ~~In~~ a chapter 7 liquidation or a chapter 11 reorganization case, the United States trustee shall call a meeting of creditors to be held no fewer than 20 and no more than 40 days after the order for relief. In a chapter 12 family farmer debt adjustment case, the United States trustee shall call a meeting of creditors to be held no fewer than 20 and no more than 35 days after the order for relief. In a chapter 13 individual's debt adjustment case, the United States trustee shall call a meeting of creditors to be held no fewer than 20 and no more than 50 days after the order for relief. If there is an appeal from or a motion to vacate the order for relief, or if there is a motion to dismiss the case, the United States trustee may set a later date for the meeting. The meeting may be held at a regular place for holding court or at any other place designated by the United States trustee within the district convenient for the parties in interest. If the United States trustee designates a place for the meeting which is not regularly staffed by the United States trustee or an assistant who may preside at the meeting, the meeting may be held not more than 60 days after the order for relief.

**(b) Order of Meeting.**

(1) Meeting of Creditors. The United States trustee shall preside at the meeting of creditors. The business of the meeting shall include the examination of the debtor under oath and, in a chapter 7 liquidation case, may include the election of a creditors' committee and, if the case is not under subchapter V of chapter 7, the election of a trustee. The presiding officer shall have the authority to administer oaths.

(2) Meeting of Equity Security Holders. If the United States

trustee convenes a meeting of equity security holders pursuant to § 341(b) of the Code, the United States trustee shall fix a date for the meeting and shall preside.

(3) Right To Vote. In a chapter 7 liquidation case, a creditor is entitled to vote at a meeting if, at or before the meeting, the creditor has filed a proof of claim or a writing setting forth facts evidencing a right to vote pursuant to § 702(a) of the Code unless objection is made to the claim or the proof of claim is insufficient on its face. A creditor of a partnership may file a proof of claim or writing evidencing a right to vote for the trustee for the estate of a general partner notwithstanding that a trustee for the estate of the partnership has previously qualified. In the event of an objection to the amount or allowability of a claim for the purpose of voting, unless the court orders otherwise, the United States trustee shall tabulate the votes for each alternative presented by the dispute and, if resolution of such dispute is necessary to determine the result of the election, the tabulations for each alternative shall be reported to the court.

**(c) Record of Meeting.** Any examination under oath at the meeting of creditors held pursuant to § 341(a) of the Code shall be recorded verbatim by the United States trustee using electronic sound recording equipment or other means of recording, and such record shall be preserved by the United States trustee and available for public access until two years after the conclusion of the meeting of creditors. Upon request of any entity, the United States trustee shall certify and provide a copy or transcript of such recording at the entity's expense.

**(d) Report of Election and Resolution of Disputes in a Chapter 7 Case.**

(1) Report of Undisputed Election. In a chapter 7 case, if the election of a trustee or a member of a creditors' committee is not disputed, the United States trustee shall promptly file a report of the election, including the name and address of the person or entity elected and a statement that the election is undisputed.

(2) Disputed Election. If the election is disputed, the United States trustee shall promptly file a report stating that the election is disputed, informing the court of the nature of the dispute, and listing the name and address of any candidate elected under any alternative presented by the dispute. No later than the date on which the report is filed, the United States trustee shall mail a copy of the report to any party in interest that has made a request to receive a copy of the report. Pending disposition by the court of a disputed election for trustee, the interim trustee shall continue in office. Unless a motion for the resolution of the dispute is filed no later than 10 days after the United States trustee files a report of a disputed election for trustee, the interim trustee shall serve as trustee in the case.

**(e) Adjournment.** The meeting may be adjourned from time to time by announcement at the meeting of the adjourned date and time without further written notice.

**(f) Special Meetings.** The United States trustee may call a special meeting of creditors on request of a party in interest or on the United States trustee's own initiative.

**(g) Final Meeting.** If the United States trustee calls a final meeting of c reditors in a case in which the net proceeds realized exceed $1,500, the clerk shall mail a summary of the trustee's final account to the creditors with a notice of the meeting, together with a statement of the amount of the claims allowed. The trustee shall attend the final meeting and shall, if requested, report on the administration of the estate.

## Rule 2007.1 [Interim]. Appointment of Trustee or Examiner in a Chapter 11 Reorganization Case.

**(a) Order To Appoint Trustee or Examiner.** In a chapter 11 reorganization case, a motion for an order to appoint a trustee or an examiner under § 1104(a) or § 1104(c) of the Code shall be made in accordance with Rule 9014.

**(b) Election of Trustee.**

(1) Request for an Election. A request to convene a meeting of creditors for the purpose of electing a trustee in a chapter 11 reorganization case shall be filed and transmitted to the United States trustee in accordance with Rule 5005 within the time prescribed by § 1104(b) of the Code. Pending court approval of the person elected, any person appointed by the United States trustee under § 1104(d) and approved in accordance with subdivision (c) of this rule shall serve as trustee.

(2) Manner of Election and Notice. An election of a trustee under § 1104(b) of the Code shall be conducted in the manner provided in Rules 2003(b)(3) and 2006. Notice of the meeting of creditors convened under § 1104(b) shall be given as provided in Rule 2002. The United States trustee shall preside at the meeting. A proxy for the purpose of voting in the election may be solicited only by a committee of creditors appointed under § 1102 of the Code or by any other party entitled to solicit a proxy pursuant to Rule 2006.

(3) Report of Election and Resolution of Disputes.

(A) Report of Undisputed Election. If *no dispute arises out of* the election ~~is not disputed~~, the United States trustee shall promptly file a report ~~of~~ *certifying* the election, including the name and address of the person elected and a statement that the election is undisputed. *The report shall be accompanied by a verified statement of the person elected setting forth the person's connections with the debtor, creditors, any other party in interest, their respective attorneys and accountants, the United States trustee, or any person employed in the office of the United States trustee.* ~~The United States trustee shall file with the report an application for approval of the appointment in accordance with subdivision (c) of this rule. The report constitutes appointment of the elected person to serve as trustee, subject to court approval, as of the date of entry of the order approving the appointment.~~

(B) *Dispute Arising Out of an* ~~Disputed~~ Election. If *a dispute arises out of an* ~~the~~ election ~~is disputed~~, the United States trustee shall promptly file a report stating that the election is disputed, informing the court of the nature of the dispute, and listing the name and address of any candidate elected under any alternative presented by the dispute. The report shall be accompanied by a verified statement by each candidate elected under each alternative presented by the dispute, setting forth the person's connections with the debtor, creditors, any other party in interest, their respective attorneys and accountants, the United States trustee; ~~and~~ *or* any person employed in the office of the United States trustee. Not later than the date on which the report of the disputed election is filed, the United States trustee shall mail a copy of the report and each verified statement to any party in interest that has made a request to convene a meeting under § 1104(b) or to receive a copy of the report, and to any committee appointed under § 1102 of the Code. ~~Unless a motion for the resolution of the dispute is filed not later than 10 days after the United States trustee under § 1104(d) and approved in accordance with subdivision (c) of this rule shall serve as trustee. If a motion for the resolution of the dispute is timely filed, and the court determines the result of the election and approves the person elected, the report will constitute appointment of the elected person as of the date of entry of the order approving the appointment.~~

**(c) Approval of Appointment.** An order approving the appointment of a trustee ~~elected under § 1104(b) or appointed under § 1104(d)~~, or ~~the appointment of~~ an examiner under 1104(d) of the Code, shall be made on application of the United States trustee. The application shall state the name of the person appointed and, to the best of the applicant's knowledge, all the person's connections with the debtor, creditors, any other parties in interest, their respective attorneys and accountants, the United States trustee, ~~and~~ *or* persons employed in the office of the United States trustee. ~~Unless the person has been elected under § 1104(b), the~~ *The* application shall state the names of the parties in interest with whom the United States trustee consulted regarding the appointment. The application shall be accompanied by a verified statement of the person appointed setting forth the person's connections with the debtor, creditors, any other party in interest, their respective attorneys and accountants, the United States trustee, ~~and~~ *or* any person employed in the office of the United States trustee.

## Rule 2007.2 [Interim]. *Appointment of Patient Care Ombudsman in a Health Care Business Case*

***(a) Order to Appoint Patient Care Ombudsman.*** *In a chapter 7, chapter 9, or chapter 11 case in which the debtor is a health care business, the court shall order the appointment of a patient care ombudsman under § 333 of the Code, unless the court, on motion of the United States trustee or a party in interest filed not later than 20 days after* *the commencement of the case or within another time fixed by the court, finds that the appointment of a patient care ombudsman is not necessary for the protection of patients under the specific circumstances of the case.*

***(b) Motion for Order to Appoint Ombudsman.*** *If the court has ordered that the appointment of an ombudsman is not necessary, or has ordered the termination of the appointment of an ombudsman, the court, on motion of the United States trustee or a party in interest, may order the appointment at any time during the case if the court finds that the appointment of an ombudsman has become necessary to protect patients.*

***(c) Appointment of Ombudsman.*** *If a patient care ombudsman is appointed under § 333, the United States trustee shall promptly file a notice of the appointment, including the name and address of the person appointed. Unless the person appointed is a State Long-Term Care Ombudsman, the notice shall be accompanied by a verified statement of the person appointed setting forth the person's connections with the debtor, creditors, patients, any other party in interest, their respective attorneys and accountants, the United States trustee, and any person employed in the office of the United States trustee.*

***(d) Termination of Appointment.*** *On motion of the United States trustee or a party in interest, the court may terminate the appointment of a patient care ombudsman if the court finds that the appointment is not necessary for the protection of patients.*

***(e) Motion.*** *A motion under this rule shall be governed by Rule 9014. The motion shall be transmitted to the United States trustee and served on the debtor, the trustee, any committee elected under § 705 or appointed under § 1102 of the Code or its authorized agent, or, if the case is a chapter 9 municipality case or a chapter 11 reorganization case and no committee of unsecured creditors has been appointed under § 1102, on the creditors included on the list filed under Rule 1007(d), and such other entities as the court may direct.*

## Rule 2015 [Interim]. Duty To Keep Records, Make Reports, and Give Notice of Case *or Change of Status.*

**(a) Trustee or Debtor in Possession.** A trustee or debtor in possession shall (1) in a chapter 7 liquidation, and if the court directs, in a chapter 11 reorganization case file and transmit to the United States trustee a complete inventory of the property of the debtor within 30 days after qualifying as a trustee or debtor in possession, unless such an inventory has already been filed; (2) keep a record of receipts and the disposition of money and property received; (3) file the reports and summaries required by § 704(8) of the Code which shall include a statement, if payments are made to employees, of the amounts of deductions for all taxes required to be withheld or paid for and on behalf of employees and the place where these amounts are deposited; (4) as soon as possible after the commencement of the case, give notice of the case to every entity known to be holding money or property subject to withdrawal or order of the debtor, including every bank, savings or building and loan association, public utility company, and landlord with whom the debtor has a deposit, and to every insurance company which has issued a policy having a cash surrender value payable to the debtor, except that notice need not be given to any entity who has knowledge or has previously been notified of the case; (5) in a chapter 11 reorganization case, on or before the last day of the month after each calendar quarter during which there is a duty to pay fees under 28 U.S.C. § 1930(a)(6) file and transmit to the United States trustee a statement of any disbursements made during that quarter and a statement of the amount of any fees payable under 28 U.S.C. § 1930(a)(6) for that quarter.

**(b) Chapter 12 Trustee and Debtor in Possession.** In a chapter 12 family farmer's debt adjustment case, the debtor in possession shall perform the duties prescribed in clauses (2)–(4) of subdivision (a) of this rule and, if the court directs, shall file and transmit to the United States trustee a complete inventory of the property of the debtor within the time fixed by the court. If the debtor is removed as debtor in possession, the trustee shall perform the duties of the debtor in possession prescribed in this paragraph.

**(c) Chapter 13 Trustee and Debtor.**

(1) Business Cases. In a chapter 13 individual's debt adjustment case, when the debtor is engaged in business, the debtor shall perform the duties prescribed by clauses (2)–(4) of subdivision (a) of this rule and, if the court directs, shall file and transmit to the United States trustee a complete inventory of the property of the debtor within the time fixed by the court.

(2) Nonbusiness Cases. In a chapter 13 individual's debt adjustment case, when the debtor is not engaged in business, the trustee shall perform the duties prescribed by clause (2) of subdivision (a) of this rule.

***(d) Foreign Representative.*** *In a case in which the court has granted recognition of a foreign proceeding under chapter 15, the foreign representative shall file any notice required under § 1518 of the Code within 15 days after the date when the representative becomes aware of the subsequent information.*

~~**(d)**~~***(e)*** **Transmission of Reports**. In a chapter 11 case the court may direct that copies or summaries of annual reports and copies or summaries of other reports shall be mailed to the creditors, equity security holders, and indenture trustees. The court may also direct the publication of summaries of any such reports. A copy of every report or summary mailed or published pursuant to this subdivision shall be transmitted to the United States trustee.

## Rule 2015.1 [Interim]. *Patient Care Ombudsman*

***(a) Reports.*** *Unless the court orders otherwise, a patient care ombudsman, at least 10 days before making a report under § 333(b)(2)* *of the Code, shall give notice that the report will be made to the court. The notice shall be transmitted to the United States trustee, posted conspicuously at the health care facility that is the subject of the report, and served on the debtor, the trustee, all patients, and any committee elected under § 705 or appointed under § 1102 of the Code or its authorized agent, or, if the case is a chapter 9 municipality case or a chapter 11 reorganization case and no committee of unsecured creditors has been appointed under § 1102, on the creditors included on the list filed under Rule 1007(d), and such other entities as the court may direct. The notice shall state the date and time when the report will be made, the manner in which the report will be made, and, if the report is in writing, the name, address, telephone number, email address, and website, if any, of the person from whom a copy of the report may be obtained at the debtor's expense.*

***(b) Authorization to Review Confidential Patient Records.*** *A motion by a health care ombudsman under § 333(c) to review confidential patient records shall be governed by Rule 9014, served on the patient and any family member or other contact person whose name and address has been given to the trustee or the debtor for the purpose of providing information regarding the patient's health care, and transmitted to the United States trustee subject to applicable nonbankruptcy law relating to patient privacy. Unless the court orders otherwise, a hearing on the motion may be commenced no earlier than 15 days after service of the motion.*

## Rule 2015.2 [Interim]. *Transfer of Patient in Health Care Business Case*

*Unless the court orders otherwise, if the debtor is a health care business, the trustee may not transfer a patient to another health care business under § 704(a)(12) of the Code unless the trustee gives at least 10 days' notice of the transfer to the patient care ombudsman, if any, and to the patient and any family member or other contact person whose name and address has been given to the trustee or the debtor for the purpose of providing information regarding the patient's health care subject to applicable nonbankruptcy law relating to patient privacy.*

## Rule 3002 [Interim]. Filing Proof of Claim or Interest.

**(a) Necessity for Filing.** An unsecured creditor or an equity security holder must file a proof of claim or interest for the claim or interest to be allowed, except as provided in Rules 1019(3), 3003, 3004, and 3005.

**(b) Place of Filing.** A proof of claim or interest shall be filed in accordance with Rule 5005.

**(c) Time for Filing.** In a chapter 7 liquidation, chapter 12 family farmer's debt adjustment, or chapter 13 individual's debt adjustment case, a proof of claim is timely filed if it is filed not later than 90 days after the first date set for the meeting of creditors called under § 341(a) of the Code, except as follows:

(1) A proof of claim filed by a governmental unit, *other than for a claim resulting from a tax return filed under § 1308,* is timely filed if it is filed not later than 180 days after the date of the order for relief. On motion of a governmental unit before the expiration of such period and for cause shown, the court may extend the time for filing of a claim by the governmental unit. *A proof of claim filed by a governmental unit for a claim resulting from a tax return filed under § 1308 is timely filed if it is filed not later than 180 days after the date of the order for relief or 60 days after the date of the filing of the tax return, whichever is later.*

(2) In the interest of justice and if it will not unduly delay the administration of the case, the court may extend the time for filing a proof of claim by an infant or incompetent person or the representative of either.

(3) An unsecured claim which arises in favor of an entity or becomes allowable as a result of a judgment may be filed within 30 days after the judgment becomes final if the judgment is for the recovery of money or property from that entity or denies or avoids the entity's interest in property. If the judgment imposes a liability which is not satisfied, or a duty which is not performed within such period or such further time as the court may permit, the claim shall not be allowed.

(4) A claim arising from the rejection of an executory contract or unexpired lease of the debtor may be filed within such time as the court may direct.

(5) If notice of insufficient assets to pay a dividend was given to creditors pursuant to Rule 2002(e), and subsequently the trustee notifies the court that payment of a dividend appears possible, the clerk shall notify the creditors of that fact and that they may file proofs of claim within 90 days after the mailing of the notice.

*(6) If notice of the time for filing a proof of claim has been mailed to a creditor at a foreign address, on motion filed by the creditor before or after the expiration of the time, the court may extend the time by not more than 60 days if the court finds that the notice was not sufficient under the circumstances to give the creditor a reasonable time to file a proof of claim.*

## Rule 3003 [Interim]. Filing Proof of Claim or Equity Security Interest in Chapter 9 Municipality or Chapter 11 Reorganization Cases.

**(a) Applicability of Rule.** This rule applies in chapter 9 and 11 cases.

**(b) Schedule of Liabilities and List of Equity Security Holders.**

(1) Schedule of Liabilities. The schedule of liabilities filed pursuant to § 521(1) of the Code shall constitute prima facie evidence of the validity and amount of the claims of creditors, unless they are scheduled as disputed, contingent, or unliquidated. It shall not be

necessary for a creditor or equity security holder to file a proof of claim or interest except as provided in subdivision (c)(2) of this rule.

(2) List of Equity Security Holders. The list of equity security holders filed pursuant to Rule 1007(a)(3) shall constitute prima facie evidence of the validity and amount of the equity security interests and it shall not be necessary for the holders of such interests to file a proof of interest.

**(c) Filing Proof of Claim.**

(1) Who May File. Any creditor or indenture trustee may file a proof of claim within the time prescribed by subdivision (c)(3) of this rule.

(2) Who Must File. Any creditor or equity security holder whose claim or interest is not scheduled or scheduled as disputed, contingent, or unliquidated shall file a proof of claim or interest within the time prescribed by subdivision (c)(3) of this rule; any creditor who fails to do so shall not be treated as a creditor with respect to such claim for the purposes of voting and distribution.

(3) Time for Filing. The court shall fix and for cause shown may extend the time within which proofs of claim or interest may be filed. Notwithstanding the expiration of such time, a proof of claim may be filed to the extent and under the conditions stated in Rule 3002(c)(2), (c)(3), ~~and~~ (c)(4)*, and (c)(6)*.

(4) Effect of Filing Claim or Interest. A proof of claim or interest executed and filed in accordance with this subdivision shall supersede any scheduling of that claim or interest pursuant to § 521*(a)*(1) of the Code.

(5) Filing by Indenture Trustee. An indenture trustee may file a claim on behalf of all known or unknown holders of securities issued pursuant to the trust instrument under which it is trustee.

**(d) Proof of Right To Record Status.** For the purposes of Rules 3017, 3018 and 3021 and for receiving notices, an entity who is not the record holder of a security may file a statement setting forth facts which entitle that entity to be treated as the record holder. An objection to the statement may be filed by any party in interest.

## Rule 3016 [Interim]. Filing of Plan and Disclosure Statement in a Chapter 9 Municipality or Chapter 11 Reorganization Case.

**(a) Identification of Plan.** Every proposed plan and any modification thereof shall be dated and, in a chapter 11 case, identified with the name of the entity or entities submitting or filing it.

**(b) Disclosure Statement.** In a chapter 9 or 11 case, a disclosure statement under § 1125 or evidence showing compliance with § 1126 (b) of the Code shall be filed with the plan or within a time fixed by the court, *unless the plan is intended to provide adequate information under § 1125(f)(1). If the plan is intended to provide adequate information under § 1125(f)(1), it shall be so designated and Rule 3017.1 shall apply as if the plan is a disclosure statement.*

**(c) Injunction Under a Plan.** If a plan provides for an injunction against conduct not otherwise enjoined under the Code, the plan and disclosure statement shall describe in specific and conspicuous language (bold, italic, or underlined text) all acts to be enjoined and identify the entities that would be subject to the injunction.

## Rule 3017.1 [Interim]. Court Consideration of Disclosure Statement in a Small Business Case.

**(a) Conditional Approval of Disclosure Statement.** ~~If the debtor is~~ *In* a small business *case* ~~and has made a timely election to be considered a small business in a chapter 11 case~~, the court may, on application of the plan proponent *or on its own initiative*, conditionally approve a disclosure statement filed in accordance with Rule 3016~~(b)~~. On or before conditional approval of the disclosure statement, the court shall:

(1) fix a time within which the holders of claims and interests may accept or reject the plan;

(2) fix a time for filing objections to the disclosure statement;

(3) fix a date for the hearing on final approval of the disclosure statement to be held if a timely objection is filed; and

(4) fix a date for the hearing on confirmation.

**(b) Application of Rule 3017.** Rule 3017(a), (b), (c), and (e) do not apply to a conditionally approved disclosure statement. Rule 3017(d) applies to a conditionally approved disclosure statement, except that conditional approval is considered approval of the disclosure statement for the purpose of applying Rule 3017(d).

**(c) Final Approval.**

(1) Notice. Notice of the time fixed for filing objections and the hearing to consider final approval of the disclosure statement shall be given in accordance with Rule 2002 and may be combined with notice of the hearing on confirmation of the plan.

(2) Objections. Objections to the disclosure statement shall be filed, transmitted to the United States trustee, and served on the debtor, the trustee, any committee appointed under the Code and any other entity designated by the court at any time before final approval of the disclosure statement or by an earlier date as the court may fix.

(3) Hearing. If a timely objection to the disclosure statement is filed, the court shall hold a hearing to consider final approval before or combined with the hearing on confirmation of the plan.

## Rule 3019 [Interim]. Modification of Accepted Plan Before *or After* Confirmation in a Chapter 9 Municipality or Chapter 11 Reorganization Case.

*(a)* In a chapter 9 or chapter 11 case, after a plan has been accepted and before its confirmation, the proponent may file a modification of the plan. If the court finds after hearing on notice to the trustee, any

committee appointed under the Code, and any other entity designated by the court that the proposed modification does not adversely change the treatment of the claim of any creditor or the interest of any equity security holder who has not accepted in writing the modification, it shall be deemed accepted by all creditors and equity security holders who have previously accepted the plan.

*(b) If the debtor is an individual, a request to modify the plan under § 1127(e) of the Code shall identify the proponent and shall be filed together with the proposed modification. The clerk, or some other person as the court may direct, shall give the debtor, the trustee, and all creditors not less than 20 days' notice by mail of the time fixed for filing objections and, if an objection is filed, the hearing to consider the proposed modification, unless the court orders otherwise with respect to creditors who are not affected by the proposed modification. A copy of the notice shall be transmitted to the United States trustee. A copy of the proposed modification shall be included with the notice. Any objection to the proposed modification shall be filed and served on the debtor, the proponent of the modification, the trustee, and any other entity designated by the court, and shall be transmitted to the United States trustee. An objection to a proposed modification is governed by Rule 9014.*

## Rule 4002 [Interim]. Duties of Debtor.

**(a) *In General.*** In addition to performing other duties prescribed by the Code and rules, the debtor shall:

(1) attend and submit to an examination at the times ordered by the court;

(2) attend the hearing on a complaint objecting to discharge and testify, if called as a witness;

(3) inform the trustee immediately in writing as to the location of real property in which the debtor has an interest and the name and address of every person holding money or property subject to the debtor's withdrawal or order if a schedule of property has not yet been filed pursuant to Rule 1007;

(4) cooperate with the trustee in the preparation of an inventory, the examination of proofs of claim, and the administration of the estate; and

(5) file a statement of any change of the debtor's address.

***(b) Individual Debtor's Duty to Provide Documentation.***

*(1) Personal Identification. Every individual debtor shall bring to the meeting of creditors under § 341:*

*(A) a picture identification issued by a governmental unit, or other personal identifying information that establishes the debtor's identity; and*

*(B) evidence of social security number(s), or a written statement that such documentation does not exist.*

*(2) Financial Information. Every individual debtor shall bring to*

*the meeting of creditors under § 341 and make available to the trustee the following documents or copies of them, or provide a written statement that the documentation does not exist or is not in the debtor's possession:*

*(A) evidence of current income such as the most recent payment advice;*

*(B) unless the trustee or the United States trustee instructs otherwise, statements for each of the debtor's depository and investment accounts, including checking, savings, and money market accounts, mutual funds and brokerage accounts for the time period that includes the date of the filing of the petition; and*

*(C) documentation of monthly expenses claimed by the debtor when required by § 707(b)(2)(A) or (B).*

*(3) Tax Return. At least 7 days before the first date set for the meeting of creditors under § 341, the debtor shall provide to the trustee a copy of the debtor's Federal income tax return for the most recent tax year ending immediately before the commencement of the case and for which a return was filed, including any attachments, or a transcript of the tax return, or provide a written statement that the documentation does not exist.*

*(4) Tax Returns Provided to Creditors. If a creditor, at least 15 days before the first date set for the meeting of creditors under § 341, requests a copy of the debtor's tax return that is to be provided to the trustee under subdivision (b)(3), the debtor shall provide to the requesting creditor a copy of the return, including any attachments, or a transcript of the tax return, or provide a written statement that the documentation does not exist at least 7 days before the first date set for the meeting of creditors under § 341.*

*(5) The debtor's obligation to provide tax returns under Rule 4002(b)(3) and (b)(4) is subject to procedures for safeguarding the confidentiality of tax information established by the Director of the Administrative Office of the United States Courts.*

## Rule 4003 [Interim]. Exemptions.

**(a) Claim of Exemptions.** A debtor shall list the property claimed as exempt under § 522 of the Code on the schedule of assets required to be filed by Rule 1007. If the debtor fails to claim exemptions or file the schedule within the time specified in Rule 1007, a dependent of the debtor may file the list within 30 days thereafter.

**(b) Objecting to a Claim of Exemptions.** *(1) Except as provided in paragraph (2), a* ~~A~~ party in interest may file an objection to the list of property claimed as exempt ~~only~~ within 30 days after the meeting of creditors held under § 341(a) is concluded or within 30 days after any amendment to the list or supplemental schedules is filed, whichever is later. The court may, for cause, extend the time for filing objections if, before the time to object expires, a party in interest files a request for an extension.

*(2) An objection to a claim of exemption based on § 522(q) shall be*

*filed before the closing of the case. If an exemption is first claimed after a case is reopened, an objection shall be filed before the reopened case is closed.*

*(3)* Copies of the objections shall be delivered or mailed to the trustee, the person filing the list, and the attorney for that person.

**(c) Burden of Proof.** In any hearing under this rule, the objecting party has the burden of proving that the exemptions are not properly claimed. After hearing on notice, the court shall determine the issues presented by the objections.

**(d) Avoidance by Debtor of Transfers of Exempt Property.** A proceeding by the debtor to avoid a lien or other transfer of property exempt under § 522(f) of the Code shall be by motion in accordance with Rule 9014.

## Rule 4004 [Interim]. Grant or Denial of Discharge.

**(a) Time for Filing Complaint Objecting to Discharge; Notice of Time Fixed.** In a chapter 7 liquidation case a complaint objecting to the debtor's discharge under § 727(a) of the Code shall be filed no later than 60 days after the first date set for the meeting of creditors under § 341(a). In a chapter 11 reorganization case, the complaint shall be filed no later than the first date set for the hearing on confirmation. At least 25 days' notice of the time so fixed shall be given to the United States trustee and all creditors as provided in Rule 2002(f) and (k), and to the trustee and the trustee's attorney.

**(b) Extension of Time.** On motion of any party in interest, after hearing on notice, the court may for cause extend the time to file a complaint objecting to discharge. The motion shall be filed before the time has expired.

**(c) Grant of Discharge.**

(1) In a chapter 7 case, on expiration of the time fixed for filing a complaint objecting to discharge and the time fixed for filing a motion to dismiss the case under Rule 1017(e), the court shall forthwith grant the discharge unless:

(A) the debtor is not an individual,

(B) a complaint objecting to the discharge has been filed,

(C) the debtor has filed a waiver under § 727(a)(10),

(D) a motion to dismiss the case under § 707 is pending,

(E) a motion to extend the time for filing a complaint objecting to discharge is pending,

(F) a motion to extend the time for filing a motion to dismiss the case under Rule 1017(e)~~(1)~~ is pending, ~~or~~

(G) the debtor has not paid in full the filing fee prescribed by 28 U.S.C. § 1930(a) and any other fee prescribed by the Judicial Conference of the United States under 28 U.S.C. § 1930(b) that is payable to the clerk upon the commencement of a case under the Code~~.~~*, unless the court has waived the fees under 28 U.S.C. § 1930(f);*

*(H) the debtor has not filed with the court a statement regarding completion of a course in personal financial management as required by Rule 1007(b)(7);*

*(I) a motion to delay or postpone discharge under § 727(a)(12) is pending; or*

*(J) a presumption that a reaffirmation agreement is an undue hardship has arisen under § 524(m); or*

*(K) a motion to delay discharge, alleging that the debtor has not filed with the court all tax documents required to be filed under § 521(f), is pending.*

(2) Notwithstanding Rule 4004(c)(1), on motion of the debtor, the court may defer the entry of an order granting a discharge for 30 days and, on motion within that, the court may defer entry of the order to a date certain.

(3) *If the debtor is required to file a statement under Rule 1007(b)(8), the court shall not grant a discharge earlier than 30 days after the filing of the statement.*

**(d) Applicability of Rules in Part VII.** A proceeding commenced by a complaint objecting to discharge is governed by Part VII of these rules.

**(e) Order of Discharge.** An order of discharge shall conform to the appropriate Official Form.

**(f) Registration in Other Districts.** An order of discharge that has become final may be registered in any other district by filing a certified copy of the order in the office of the clerk of that district. When so registered the order of discharge shall have the same effect as an order of the court of the district where registered.

**(g) Notice of Discharge.** The clerk shall promptly mail a copy of the final order of discharge to those specified in subdivision (a) of this rule.

## Rule 4006 [Interim]. Notice of No Discharge.

If an order is entered denying or revoking a discharge or if a waiver of discharge is filed, the clerk, after the order becomes final or the waiver is filed, *or, in the case of an individual, if the case is closed without the entry of an order of discharge,* shall promptly give notice thereof to all ~~creditors~~ *parties in interest* in the manner provided in Rule 2002.

## Rule 4007 [Interim]. Determination of Dischargeability of a Debt.

**(a) Persons Entitled To File Complaint.** A debtor or any creditor may file a complaint to obtain a determination of the dischargeability of any debt.

**(b) Time for Commencing Proceeding Other Than Under § 523(c) of the Code.** A complaint other than under § 523(c) may be filed at any time. A case may be reopened without payment of an additional filing fee for the purpose of filing a complaint to obtain a determination under this rule.

**(c) Time for Filing Complaint Under § 523(c) in a Chapter 7 Liquidation, Chapter 11 Reorganization,~~or~~ Chapter 12 Family Farmer's Debt Adjustment Case, *or Chapter 13 Individual's Debt Adjustment Case*; Notice of Time Fixed.** *Except as provided in subdivision (d), a* ~~A~~ complaint to determine the dischargeability of a debt under § 523(c) shall be filed no later than 60 days after the first date set for the meeting of creditors under § 341(a). The court shall give all creditors no less than 30 days' notice of the time so fixed in the manner provided in Rule 2002. On motion of a party in interest, after hearing on notice, the court may for cause extend the time fixed under this subdivision. The motion shall be filed before the time has expired.

**(d) Time for Filing Complaint Under § ~~523(c)~~ *523(a)(6)* in a Chapter 13 Individual's Debt Adjustment Case; Notice of Time Fixed.** On motion by a debtor for a discharge under § 1328(b), the court shall enter an order fixing the time to file a complaint to determine the dischargeability of any debt under § ~~523(c)~~ *523(a)(6)* and shall give no less than 30 days' notice of the time fixed to all creditors in the manner provided in Rule 2002. On motion of any party in interest, after hearing on notice, the court may for cause extend the time fixed under this subdivision. The motion shall be filed before the time has expired.

**(e) Applicability of Rules in Part VII.** A proceeding commenced by a complaint filed under this rule is governed by Part VII of these rules.

## Rule 4008 [Interim]. Discharge and Reaffirmation Hearing.

Not more than 30 days following the entry of an order granting or denying a discharge, or confirming a plan in a chapter 11 reorganization case concerning an individual debtor and on not less than 10 days notice to the debtor and the trustee, the court may hold a hearing as provided in § 524(d) of the Code. A motion by the debtor for approval of a reaffirmation agreement shall be filed before or at the hearing. *The debtor's statement required under § 524(k) shall be accompanied by a statement of the total income and total expense amounts stated on schedules I and J. If there is a difference between the income and expense amounts stated on schedules I and J and the statement required under § 524(k), the accompanying statement shall include an explanation of any difference.*

## Rule 5003 [Interim]. Records Kept By the Clerk.

**(a) Bankruptcy Dockets.** The clerk shall keep a docket in each case under the Code and shall enter thereon each judgment, order, and activity in that case as prescribed by the Director of the Administrative Office of the United States Courts. The entry of a judgment or order in a docket shall show the date the entry is made.

**(b) Claims Register.** The clerk shall keep in a claims register a list of claims filed in a case when it appears that there will be a distribution to unsecured creditors.

**(c) Judgments and Orders.** The clerk shall keep, in the form and manner as the Director of the Administrative Office of the United States Courts may prescribe, a correct copy of every final judgment or order affecting title to or lien on real property or for the recovery of money or property, and any other order which the court may direct to be kept. On request of the prevailing party, a correct copy of every judgment or order affecting title to or lien upon real or personal property or for the recovery of money or property shall be kept and indexed with the civil judgments of the district court.

**(d) Index of Cases; Certificate of Search.** The clerk shall keep indices of all cases and adversary proceedings as prescribed by the Director of the Administrative Office of the United States Courts. On request, the clerk shall make a search of any index and papers in the clerk's custody and certify whether a case or proceeding has been filed in or transferred to the court or if a discharge has been entered in its records.

**(e) Register of Mailing Addresses of Federal and State Governmental Units *and Certain Taxing Authorities*.** The United States or the state or territory in which the court is located may file a statement designating its mailing address. *The United States, state, territory, or local governmental unit responsible for the collection of taxes within the district in which the case is pending may file a statement designating an address for service of requests under § 505(b) of the Code, and the designation shall describe where further information concerning additional requirements for filing such requests may be found.* The clerk shall keep, in the form and manner as the Director of the Administrative Office of the United States Courts may prescribe, a register that includes ~~these~~ *the* mailing addresses *designated under this subdivision*, but the clerk is not required to include in the register more than one mailing address for each department, agency, or instrumentality of the United States or the state or territory. If more than one address for a department, agency, or instrumentality is included in the register, the clerk shall also include information that would enable a user of the register to determine the circumstances when each address is applicable, and mailing notice to only one applicable address is sufficient to provide effective notice. The clerk shall update the register annually, effective January 2 of each year. The mailing address in the register is conclusively presumed to be a proper address for the governmental unit, but the failure to use that mailing address does not invalidate any notice that is otherwise effective under applicable law.

**(f) Other Books and Records of the Clerk.** The clerk shall keep any other books and records required by the Director of the Administrative Office of the United States Courts.

## Rule 5008 [Interim]. *Notice Regarding Presumption of Abuse in Chapter 7 Cases of Individual Debtors.*

*In a chapter 7 case of an individual with primarily consumer debts in which a presumption of abuse has arisen under § 707(b), the clerk shall give to creditors notice of the presumption of abuse in accordance with Rule 2002 within 10 days after the date of the filing of the petition. If the debtor has not filed a statement indicating whether a presumption of abuse has arisen, the clerk shall give notice to creditors within 10 days after the date of the filing of the petition that the debtor has not filed the statement and that further notice will be given if a later filed statement indicates that a presumption of abuse has arisen. If a debtor later files a statement indicating that a presumption of abuse has arisen, the clerk shall give notice to creditors of the presumption of abuse as promptly as practicable.*

## Rule 5012 [Interim]. *Communication and Cooperation With Foreign Courts and Foreign Representatives.*

*Except for communications for scheduling and administrative purposes, the court in any case commenced by a foreign representative shall give at least 20 days' notice of its intent to communicate with a foreign court or a foreign representative. The notice shall identify the subject of the anticipated communication and shall be given in the manner provided by Rule 2002(q). Any entity that wishes to participate in the communication shall notify the court of its intention not later than 5 days before the scheduled communication.*

## Rule 6004 [Interim]. Use, Sale, or Lease of Property.

**(a) Notice of Proposed Use, Sale, or Lease of Property.** Notice of a proposed use, sale, or lease of property, other than cash collateral, not in the ordinary course of business shall be given pursuant to Rule 2002(a)(2), (c)(1), (i), and (k) and, if applicable, in accordance with § 363(b)(2) of the Code.

**(b) Objection to Proposal.** Except as provided in subdivisions (c) and (d) of this rule, an objection to a proposed use, sale, or lease of property shall be filed and served not less than five days before the date set for the proposed action or within the time fixed by the court. An objection to the proposed use, sale, or lease of property is governed by Rule 9014.

**(c) Sale Free and Clear of Liens and Other Interests.** A motion for authority to sell property free and clear of liens or other interests shall be made in accordance with Rule 9014 and shall be served on the parties who have liens or other interests in the property to be sold. The notice required by subdivision (a) of this rule shall include the date of the hearing on the motion and the time within which objections may be filed and served on the debtor in possession or trustee.

**(d) Sale of Property Under $2,500.** Notwithstanding subdivision

(a) of this rule, when all of the nonexempt property of the estate has an aggregate gross value less than $2,500, it shall be sufficient to give a general notice of intent to sell such property other than in the ordinary course of business to all creditors, indenture trustees, committees appointed or elected pursuant to the Code, the United States trustee and other persons as the court may direct. An objection to any such sale may be filed and served by a party in interest within 15 days of the mailing of the notice, or within the time fixed by the court. An objection is governed by Rule 9014.

**(e) Hearing.** If a timely objection is made pursuant to subdivision (b) or (d) of this rule, the date of the hearing thereon may be set in the notice given pursuant to subdivision (a) of this rule.

**(f) Conduct of Sale Not in the Ordinary Course of Business.**

(1) Public or Private Sale. All sales not in the ordinary course of business may be by private sale or by public auction. Unless it is impracticable, an itemized statement of the property sold, the name of each purchaser, and the price received for each item or lot or for the property as a whole if sold in bulk shall be filed on completion of a sale. If the property is sold by an auctioneer, the auctioneer shall file the statement, transmit a copy thereof to the United States trustee, and furnish a copy to the trustee, debtor in possession, or chapter 13 debtor. If the property is not sold by an auctioneer, the trustee, debtor in possession, or chapter 13 debtor shall file the statement and transmit a copy thereof to the United States trustee.

(2) Execution of Instruments. After a sale in accordance with this rule the debtor, the trustee, or debtor in possession, as the case may be, shall execute any instrument necessary or ordered by the court to effectuate the transfer to the purchaser.

***(g) Sale of Personally Identifiable Information.***

*(1) Motion. A motion for authority to sell or lease personally identifiable information under § 363(b)(1)(B) shall include a request for an order directing the United States trustee to appoint a consumer privacy ombudsman under § 332. The motion shall be governed by Rule 9014 and shall be served on any committee elected under § 705 or appointed under § 1102 of the Code, or if the case is a chapter 11 reorganization case and no committee of unsecured creditors has been appointed under § 1102, on the creditors included on the list of creditors filed under Rule 1007(d), and on such other entities as the court may direct. The motion shall be transmitted to the United States trustee.*

*(2) Appointment. If a consumer privacy ombudsman is appointed under § 332, no later than 5 days before the hearing on the motion under § 363(b)(1)(B), the United States trustee shall file a notice of the appointment, including the name and address of the person appointed. The United States trustee's notice shall be accompanied by a verified statement of the person appointed setting forth the person's connections with the debtor, creditors, any other party in interest, their respective attorneys and accountants, the United States*

*trustee, or any person employed in the office of the United States trustee.*

**(g *h*) Stay of Order Authorizing Use, Sale, or Lease of Property.** An order authorizing the use, sale, or lease of property other than cash collateral is stayed until the expiration of 10 days after entry of the order, unless the court orders otherwise.

## Rule 6011 [Interim]. Disposal of Patient Records in Health Care Business Case.

*(a) NOTICE BY PUBLICATION UNDER § 351(1)(A). A notice regarding the claiming or disposing of patient records under § 351(1)(A) shall not identify patients by name or other identifying information, but shall:*

*(1) identify with particularity the health care facility whose patient records the trustee proposes to destroy;*

*(2) state the name, address, telephone number, email address, and website, if any, of a person from whom information about the patient records may be obtained and how those records may be claimed; and*

*(3) state the date by which patient records must be claimed, and that if they are not so claimed the records will be destroyed.*

*(b) NOTICE BY MAIL UNDER § 351(1)(B). Subject to applicable nonbankuptcy law relating to patient privacy, a notice regarding the claiming or disposing of patient records under § 351(1)(B) shall, in addition to including the information in subdivision (a), direct that a patient's family member or other representative who receives the notice inform the patient of the notice, and be mailed to the patient and any family member or other contact person whose name and address have been given to the trustee or the debtor for the purpose of providing information regarding the patient's health care, and to insurance companies known to have provided health care insurance to the patient.*

*(c) PROOF OF COMPLIANCE WITH NOTICE REQUIREMENT. Unless the court orders the trustee to file proof of compliance with § 351(1)(B) under seal, the trustee shall not file, but shall maintain, the proof of compliance for a reasonable time.*

*(d) REPORT OF DESTRUCTION OF RECORDS. The trustee shall file, not later than 30 days after the destruction of patient records under § 351(3), a report certifying that the unclaimed records have been destroyed and explaining the method used to effect the destruction. The report shall not identify patients by name or other identifying information.*

## Rule 8001 [Interim]. Manner of Taking Appeal; Voluntary Dismissal; *Certification to Court of Appeals*.

**(a) Appeal as of Right; How Taken.**

An appeal from a judgment, order, or decree of a bankruptcy judge to a district court or bankruptcy appellate panel as permitted by 28 U.S.C. § 158(a)(1) or (a)(2) shall be taken by filing a notice of appeal with the clerk within the time allowed by Rule 8002. An appellant's failure to take any step other than timely filing a notice of appeal does not affect the validity of the appeal, but is ground only for such action as the district court or bankruptcy appellate panel deems appropriate, which may include dismissal of the appeal. The notice of appeal shall (1) conform substantially to the appropriate Official Form, (2) contain the names of all parties to the judgment, order, or decree appealed from and the names, addresses and telephone numbers of their respective attorneys, and (3) be accompanied by the prescribed fee. Each appellant shall file a sufficient number of copies of the notice of appeal to enable the clerk to comply promptly with Rule 8004.

**(b) Appeal by Leave; How Taken.** An appeal from an interlocutory judgment, order or decree of a bankruptcy judge as permitted by 28 U.S.C. § 158(a)(3) shall be taken by filing a notice of appeal, as prescribed in subdivision (a) of this rule, accompanied by a motion for leave to appeal prepared in accordance with Rule 8003 and with proof of service in accordance with Rule 8008.

**(c) Voluntary Dismissal.**

(1) Before Docketing. If an appeal has not been docketed, the appeal may be dismissed by the bankruptcy judge on the filing of a stipulation for dismissal signed by all the parties, or on motion and notice by the appellant.

(2) After Docketing. If an appeal has been docketed and the parties to the appeal sign and file with the clerk of the district court or the clerk of the bankruptcy appellate panel an agreement that the appeal be dismissed and pay any court costs or fees that may be due, the clerk of the district court or the clerk of the bankruptcy appellate panel shall enter an order dismissing the appeal. An appeal may also be dismissed on motion of the appellant on terms and conditions fixed by the district court or bankruptcy appellate panel.

**(d) [Abrogated]**

**(e) Election to Have Appeal Heard by District Court Instead of Bankruptcy Appellate Panel** An election to have an appeal heard by the district court under 28 U.S.C. § 158(c)(1) may be made only by a statement of election contained in a separate writing filed within the time prescribed by 28 U.S.C. § 158(c)(1).

***(f) Certification for Direct Appeal to Court of Appeals***

***(1) Timely Appeal Required.*** *A certification of a judgment, order, or decree of a bankruptcy court to a court of appeals under 28 U.S.C. § 158(d)(2) shall not be treated as a certification entered on the docket within the meaning of § 1233(b)(4)(A) of Public Law No. 109-8 until a timely appeal has been taken in the manner required by subdivisions (a) or (b) of this rule and the notice of appeal has become effective under Rule 8002.*

***(2) Court Where Made.*** *A certification that a circumstance specified in 28 U.S.C. § 158(d)(2)(A)(i)-(iii) exists shall be filed in the* *court in which a matter is pending for purposes of 28 U.S.C. § 158(d)(2) and this rule. A matter is pending in a bankruptcy court until the docketing, in accordance with Rule 8007(b), of an appeal taken under 28 U.S.C. § 158(a)(1) or (2), or the grant of leave to appeal under 28 U.S.C. § 158(a)(3). A matter is pending in a district court or bankruptcy appellate panel after the docketing, in accordance with Rule 8007(b), of an appeal taken under 28 U.S.C. § 158(a)(1) or (2), or the grant of leave to appeal under 28 U.S.C. § 158(a)(3).*

***(A) Certification by Court on Request or Court's Own Initiative.***

***(i) Before Docketing or Grant of Leave to Appeal.*** *Only a bankruptcy court may make a certification on request or on its own initiative while the matter is pending in the bankruptcy court.*

***(ii)*** *After Docketing or Grant of Leave to Appeal*. Only the district court or bankruptcy appellate panel involved may make a certification on request of the parties or on its own initiative while the matter is pending in the district court or bankruptcy appellate panel.

***(B) Certification by All Appellants and Appellees Acting Jointly.*** *A certification by all the appellants and appellees, if any, acting jointly may be made by filing the appropriate Official Form with the clerk of the court in which the matter is pending. The certification may be accompanied by a short statement of the basis for the certification, which may include the information listed in subdivision (f)(3)(C) of this rule.*

***(3) Request for Certification; Filing; Service; Contents.***

*(A) A request for certification shall be filed, within the time specified by 28 U.S.C. § 158(d)(2), with the clerk of the court in which the matter is pending.*

*(B) Notice of the filing of a request for certification shall be served in the manner required for service of a notice of appeal under Rule 8004.*

*(C) A request for certification shall include the following:*

*(i) the facts necessary to understand the question presented;*

*(ii) the question itself;*

*(iii) the relief sought;*

*(iv) the reasons why the appeal should be allowed and is authorized by statute or rule, including why a circumstance specified in 28 U.S.C. § 158(d)(2)(A)(i)-(iii) exists; and*

*(v) an attached copy of the judgment, order, or decree complained of and any related opinion or memorandum.*

*(D) A party may file a response to a request for certification or a cross-request within 10 days after the notice of the request is served, or another time fixed by the court.*

*(E) The request, cross request, and any response shall not be*

*governed by Rule 9014 and shall be submitted without oral argument unless the court otherwise directs.*

*(F) A certification of an appeal under 28 U.S.C. § 158(d)(2) shall be made in a separate document served on the parties.*

***(4) Certification on Court's Own Initiative.***

*(A) A certification of an appeal on the court's own initiative under 28 U.S.C. § 158(d)(2) shall be made in a separate document served on the parties in the manner required for service of a notice of appeal under Rule 8004. The certification shall be accompanied by an opinion or memorandum that contains the information required by subdivision (f)(3)(C)(i)-(iv) of this rule.*

*(B) A party may file a supplementary short statement of the basis for certification within 10 days after the certification.*

## Rule 8003 [Interim]. Leave to Appeal.

**(a) Content of Motion; Answer.** A motion for leave to appeal under 28 U.S.C. § 158(a) shall contain: (1) a statement of the facts necessary to an understanding of the questions to be presented by the appeal; (2) a statement of those questions and of the relief sought; (3) a statement of the reasons why an appeal should be granted; and (4) a copy of the judgment, order, or decree complained of and of any opinion or memorandum relating thereto. Within 10 days after service of the motion an adverse party may file with the clerk an answer in opposition.

**(b) Transmittal; Determination of Motion.** The clerk shall transmit the notice of appeal, the motion for leave to appeal and any answer thereto to the clerk of the district court or the clerk of the bankruptcy appellate panel as soon as all parties have filed answers or the time for filing an answer has expired. The motion and answer shall be submitted without oral argument unless otherwise ordered.

**(c) Appeal Improperly Taken Regarded as a Motion for Leave To Appeal.** If a required motion for leave to appeal is not filed, but a notice of appeal is timely filed, the district court or bankruptcy appellate panel may grant leave to appeal or direct that a motion for leave to appeal be filed. The district court or the bankruptcy appellate panel may also deny leave to appeal but in so doing shall consider the notice of appeal as a motion for leave to appeal. Unless an order directing that a motion for leave to appeal be filed provides otherwise, the motion shall be filed within 10 days of entry of the order.

***(d)*** *If leave to appeal is required by 28 U.S.C. § 158(a) and has not earlier been granted, the authorization of a direct appeal by a court of appeals under 28 U.S.C. § 158(d)(2) shall be deemed to satisfy the requirement for leave to appeal.*

## Rule 9006 [Interim]. Time.

**(a) Computation.** In computing any period of time prescribed or allowed by these rules or by the Federal Rules of Civil Procedure made applicable by these rules, by the local rules, by order of court, or by any applicable statute, the day of the act, event, or default from which the designated period of time begins to run shall not be included. The last day of the period so computed shall be included, unless it is a Saturday, a Sunday, or a legal holiday, or, when the act to be done is the filing of a paper in court, a day on which weather or other conditions have made the clerk's office inaccessible, in which event the period runs until the end of the next day which is not one of the aforementioned days. When the period of time prescribed or allowed is less than 8 days, intermediate Saturdays, Sundays, and legal holidays shall be excluded in the computation. As used in this rule and in Rule 5001(c), "legal holiday" includes New Year's Day, Birthday of Martin Luther King, Jr., Washington's Birthday, Memorial Day, Independence Day, Labor Day, Columbus Day, Veterans Day, Thanksgiving Day, Christmas Day, and any other day appointed as a holiday by the President or the Congress of the United States, or by the state in which the bankruptcy court is held.

**(b) Enlargement.**

(1) In General. Except as provided in paragraphs (2) and (3) of this subdivision, when an act is required or allowed to be done at or within a specified period by these rules or by a notice given thereunder or by order of court, the court for cause shown may at any time in its discretion (1) with or without motion or notice order the period enlarged if the request therefor is made before the expiration of the period originally prescribed or as extended by a previous order or (2) on motion made after the expiration of the specified period permit the act to be done where the failure to act was the result of excusable neglect.

(2) Enlargement Not Permitted. The court may not enlarge the time for taking action under Rules 1007(d), 2003(a) and (d), 7052, 9023, and 9024.

(3) Enlargement Limited. The court may enlarge the time for taking action under Rules 1006(b)(2), *1007(c) with respect to the time to file schedules and statements in a small business case,* 1017(e), 3002 (c), 4003(b), 4004(a), 4007(c), 8002, and 9033, only to the extent and under the conditions stated in those rules.

**(c) Reduction.**

(1) In General. Except as provided in paragraph (2) of this subdivision, when an act is required or allowed to be done at or within a specified time by these rules or by a notice given thereunder or by order of court, the court for cause shown may in its discretion with or without motion or notice order the period reduced.

(2) Reduction Not Permitted. The court may not reduce the time for taking action pursuant to Rules 2002(a)(7), 2003(a), 3002(c), 3014, 3015, 4001(b)(2), (c)(2), 4003(a), 4004(a), 4007(c), 8002, and 9033(b).

**(d) For Motions—Affidavits.** A written motion, other than one which may be heard ex parte, and notice of any hearing shall be served not later than five days before the time specified for such hearing, unless a different period is fixed by these rules or by order of the court. Such an order may for cause shown be made on ex parte application. When a motion is supported by affidavit, the affidavit shall be served with the motion; and, except as otherwise provided in Rule 9023, opposing affidavits may be served not later than one day before the hearing, unless the court permits them to be served at some other time.

**(e) Time of Service.** Service of process and service of any paper other than process or of notice by mail is complete on mailing.

**(f) Additional Time After Service by Mail or Under Rule 5(b)(2)(C) or (D) F. R. Civ. P.** When there is a right or requirement to do some act or undertake some proceedings within a prescribed period after service of a notice or other paper and the notice or paper other than process is served by mail or under Rule 5(b)(2)(C) or (D) F. R. Civ. P., three days shall be added to the prescribed period.

**(g) Grain Storage Facility Cases.** This rule shall not limit the court's authority under § 557 of the Code to enter orders governing procedures in cases in which the debtor is an owner or operator of a grain storage facility.

## Rule 9009 [Interim]. Forms.

The Official Forms prescribed by the Judicial Conference of the United States shall be observed and used with alterations as may be appropriate. Forms may be combined and their contents rearranged to permit economies in their use. The Director of the Administrative Office of the United States Courts may issue additional forms for use under the Code. The forms shall be construed to be consistent with these rules and the Code. *References in the Official Forms to these rules shall include the Interim Rules approved by the Committee on Rules of Practice and Procedure to implement Public Law No. 109-8.*

# Table of Laws and Rules

(*Cited in the Commentary*)

### Bankruptcy Abuse Prevention and Consumer Protection Act of 2005



### Employee Retirement Income Security Act of 1974



### Small Business Act



### Social Security Act

**Social Security Act—Continued**



**Internal Revenue Code of 1986**



**Internal Revenue Code**



**Uniform Commerical Code**



**UNITED STATES CODE ANNOTATED**

## UNITED STATES CODE ANNOTATED—Continued

## UNITED STATES CODE ANNOTATED—Continued

## UNITED STATES CODE ANNOTATED—Continued

**UNITED STATES CODE ANNOTATED—Continued**

## UNITED STATES CODE ANNOTATED—Continued



## Public Laws



## Federal Rules of Bankruptcy Procedure



## House Reports

## Senate Bills

| No. | Sec. |
|---|---|
| 256 | 8:11 |

## STATE STATUTES

| N.J. Ann. | Sec. |
|---|---|
| tit. 25:2-25 | 8:11 |

# Table of Cases

*(Cited in the Commentary)*

Levit v. Ingersoll Rand Financial Corp., 874 F.2d 1186, 19 Bankr. Ct. Dec. (CRR) 574, 22 Collier Bankr. Cas. 2d (MB) 36, 11 Employee Benefits Cas. (BNA) 1323, Bankr. L. Rep. (CCH) P 72910 (7th Cir. 1989)—7:50, 9:48

Little Lake Industries, Inc., In re, 146 B.R. 463, 27 Collier Bankr. Cas. 2d (MB) 1609, Bankr. L. Rep. (CCH) P 74978 (Bankr. N.D. Cal. 1992)—9:47

Lucre, Inc., In re, 333 B.R. 151, 45 Bankr. Ct. Dec. (CRR) 172, Bankr. L. Rep. (CCH) P 80412 (Bankr. W.D. Mich. 2005)—9:42

M

Matter of—see name of party

McNabb, In re, 326 B.R. 785, Bankr. L. Rep. (CCH) P 80333 (Bankr. D. Ariz. 2005)—8:4

O

Owings, In re, 140 F. 739 (E.D. N.C. 1905)—8:3

P

Patterson v. Shumate, 504 U.S. 753, 112 S. Ct. 2242, 119 L. Ed. 2d 519, 23 Bankr. Ct. Dec. (CRR) 89, 26 Collier Bankr. Cas. 2d (MB) 1119, 15 Employee Benefits Cas. (BNA) 1481, Bankr. L. Rep. (CCH) P 74621A (1992)—8:6

Pioneer Inv. Services Co. v. Brunswick Associates Ltd. Partnership, 507 U.S. 380, 113 S. Ct. 1489, 123 L. Ed. 2d 74, 24 Bankr. Ct. Dec. (CRR) 63, 28 Collier Bankr. Cas. 2d (MB) 267, Bankr. L. Rep. (CCH) P 75157A, 25 Fed. R. Serv. 3d 401 (1993)—9:7

R

Rousey v. Jacoway, 544 U.S. 320, 125 S. Ct. 1561, 161 L. Ed. 2d 563, 44 Bankr. Ct. Dec. (CRR) 144, 53 Collier Bankr. Cas. 2d (MB) 181, 34 Employee Benefits Cas. (BNA) 1929, Bankr. L. Rep. (CCH) P 80263, 2005-1 U.S. Tax Cas. (CCH) P 50258, 95 A.F.T.R.2d 2005-1716 (2005)—8:6

V

Van Huffel Tube Corp., Matter of, 71 B.R. 155, 15 Bankr. Ct. Dec. (CRR) 1038 (Bankr. N.D. Ohio 1987)—9:47

Virissimo, In re, 332 B.R. 201 (Bankr. D. Nev. 2005)—8:4

Virissimo, In re, 332 B.R. 208, Bankr. L. Rep. (CCH) P 80385 (Bankr. D. Nev. 2005)—7:2

W

Watson, In re, 332 B.R. 740, Bankr. L. Rep. (CCH) P 80395 (Bankr. E.D. Va. 2005)—7:22

Williams, In re, 234 B.R. 801, 34 Bankr. Ct. Dec. (CRR) 600 (Bankr. D. Or. 1999)—9:48

Y

Young v. U.S., 2002-1 C.B. 954, 535 U.S. 43, 122 S. Ct. 1036, 152 L. Ed. 2d 79, 39 Bankr. Ct. Dec. (CRR) 45, 47 Collier Bankr. Cas. 2d (MB) 211, Bankr. L. Rep. (CCH) P 78601, 2002-1 U.S. Tax Cas. (CCH) P 50257, 89 A.F.T.R.2d 2002-1258 (2002)—7:51

# Index